Martine Robbeets
Diachrony of Verb Morphology

Trends in Linguistics
Studies and Monographs

Editor
Volker Gast

Editorial Board
Walter Bisang
Jan Terje Faarlund
Hans Henrich Hock
Natalia Levshina
Heiko Narrog
Matthias Schlesewsky
Amir Zeldes
Niina Ning Zhang

Editor responsible for this volume
Walter Bisang and Heiko Narrog

Volume 291

Martine Robbeets
Diachrony of Verb Morphology

Japanese and the Transeurasian Languages

ISBN 978-3-11-055512-7
e-ISBN (PDF) 978-3-11-039994-3
e-ISBN (EPUB) 978-3-11-040011-3
ISSN 1861-4302

Library of Congress Cataloging-in-Publication Data
A CIP catalog record for this book has been applied for at the Library of Congress.

Bibliografische Information der Deutschen Nationalbibliothek
The Deutsche Nationalbibliothek lists this publication in the Deutschen Nationalbibliografie; detailed bibliographic data are available on the internet http://dnb.dnb.de.

© 2017 Walter de Gruyter GmbH, Berlin/Boston
This volume is text- and page-identical with the hardback published in 2015.
Typesetting: Frank Benno Junghanns, Berlin
Printing and binding: CPI books GmbH, Leck

♾ Printed on acid-free paper
Printed in Germany

www.degruyter.com

Für Lars

Preface

This book took me ten years, much longer than I had initially expected. I can still vividly remember the day that I decided to start writing. It was early November 2004, one of these enchanting days of Japanese fall. Deep-blue sky, a splendid view on mount Fuji, the Ginkgo trees on campus wearing autumn colors. Tooru Hayashi had organized a conference on "Diversity in Data and Description in Peripheral Eurasian Languages" at the University of Tokyo, where I was doing postdoctoral research at that time. At the pre-conference dinner in a *tempura* restaurant near *Akamon*, the red entrance gate of the university, I was introduced to Lars Johanson. It was stimulating to hear that Lars had read my doctoral dissertation dealing with lexical evidence relating Japanese to the Altaic languages. "Thought-provoking", he challenged me: "but shared verb morphology would convince me more." And so a new research topic was born.

In the following ten years, I have been trying to build a case for common Transeurasian verb morphology, discussing my ideas with Lars, who agrees on some issues, but disagrees on others. I felt privileged to base my research at the universities of Mainz and Leuven, where I was hosted by scholars, who inspired and supported me: Lars Johanson, Hubert Cuyckens and Walter Bisang. I wholeheartedly thank my hosts for their professional guidance. The realization of my research in Europe was financially supported by various grants and research fellowships. The Alexander von Humboldt Foundation first created the resources for a two-year research stay at the Seminar für Orientkunde at the Johannes Gutenberg University Mainz, hosted by Lars Johanson. Then a "Back to Belgium" return mandate from the Belgian Federal Government allowed me to continue my research between 2009 and 2011 at the University of Leuven, where I collaborated with Hubert Cuyckens. Finally, with the support of Walter Bisang, the Deutsche Forschungsgemeinschaft funded a three-year research project on the Transeurasian languages at the Johannes Gutenberg University Mainz. I am grateful to the Canon Europe Foundation, the Japan Foundation, the Av Humboldt Foundation, the Belgian Federal Government and the Deutsche Forschungsgemeinschaft for providing me with challenging research opportunities.

Due to their generous financial support, we were also able to organize four symposia dealing with central thematic issues such as the relevance of verb morphology in affiliation questions, the distinction between borrowing and inheritance in shared morphology, shared grammaticalization and the historical development of paradigms. These symposia resulted in the edition of four volumes: Transeurasian Verbal Morphology in a Comparative Perspective: Genealogy, Contact, Chance, edited with Lars Johanson in 2010 (Harrassowitz), Copies versus Cognates in Bound Morphology, edited with Lars Johanson in 2012 (Brill), Shared Grammaticalization, edited with Hubert Cuyckens in 2013 (Benjamins) and Paradigm Change. The Transeurasian Languages and Beyond, edited with Walter Bisang in 2014 (Benjamins). My gratitude goes to the collaborators who contributed their ideas to these projects, at the same time inspiring and supporting me in the process of writing this book: Alexandra Aikhenvald, Anton Antonov, Ad Backus, Dik Bakker, Peter Bakker, Walter Bisang, Hendrik Boeschoten, Bernard Comrie, Greville Corbett, Éva Csató, Stig Eliasson, Victor Friedman, Francesco Gardani, Volker Gast, Anthony Grant, Tom Güldeman, Salomé Gutiérrez-Morales, Tooru Hayasi, Bernd Heine, Juha Janhunen, Lars Johanson, Andrew Joseph, Brian Joseph, Judith Josephson, Folke Josephson, László Károly, Seongyeon Ko, Frederik Kortlandt, Andrej Malchukov, Heiko Narrog, Irina Nevskaya, Johanna Nichols, Motoki Nomachi, Hans Nugteren, Brigitte Pakendorf, Seongha Rhee, András Róna-Tas, Claudia Römer, Laurent Sagart, Frank Seifart, Nikki van de Pol, Johan van der Auwera, George van Driem, Jim Unger, Jean-Christophe Verstraete and Lindsay Whaley.

A heartfelt word of thanks also goes to Milan van Berlo at the University of Leiden and Kristin Blanpain at the University of Leuven for their dedicated assistance in formatting and English editing, respectively. I would also like to thank editor Volker Gast and co-editor Heiko Narrog of the Trends in Linguistics/Studies and Monographs series for their enthusiasm in including this work in the series. Finally, I wish to thank Acquisitions Editor Birgit Sievert at Mouton de Gruyter for her initial interest and for her help and encouragement in seeing this project through.

To my seven years old son Yasu I apologize for being such a bookish mom, who is not always at home when you need her. At the same time I thank my husband Marc for making up for that by being an amazingly cool dad. Love you, boys.

Maaseik
February 14, 2015

Contents

Preface —— vii

1	**Introduction** —— 1	
1.1	Goals of this study —— 1	
1.2	The Transeurasian languages —— 4	
1.2.1	From "Altaic" to "Transeurasian" —— 4	
1.2.2	Internal taxonomy of the individual branches —— 7	
1.2.2.1	Turkic —— 7	
1.2.2.2	Mongolic —— 12	
1.2.2.3	Tungusic —— 16	
1.2.2.4	Koreanic —— 20	
1.2.2.5	Japanic —— 22	
1.2.3	The Transeurasian hypothesis —— 30	
1.2.4	The languages underlying the reconstructions —— 33	
1.2.4.1	Languages included in this study —— 33	
1.2.4.2	Transliteration conventions —— 37	
1.3	Previous research —— 41	
2	**Methodology** —— 45	
2.1	Historical comparative morphology —— 45	
2.2	Procedures for establishing morphological correlations —— 47	
2.2.1	Collection and reconstruction of participant morphemes —— 47	
2.2.2	Comparison of individual proto-morphemes —— 48	
2.2.2.1	Formal correlations —— 48	
2.2.2.2	Functional correlations —— 49	
2.2.2.3	Combinational correlations —— 51	
2.2.2.4	Typological correlations —— 51	
2.2.2.5	Paradigmatic correlations —— 53	
2.2.3	Top-level reconstruction —— 55	
2.2.3.1	Reconstruction of proto-morphemes —— 55	
2.2.3.2	Reconstruction of family-inherent grammaticalization patterns —— 56	
2.2.3.3	Reconstruction of proto-systems —— 57	
2.3	Reducing the chance factor —— 58	
2.4	Eliminating code-copying —— 61	
2.4.1	Understanding copiability —— 61

2.4.2	Indications of code-copying —— 64	
2.4.2.1	Productivity restricted to shared roots —— 64	
2.4.2.2	Unilateral morphological complexity —— 66	
2.4.2.3	Mismatch of morpheme boundaries —— 67	
2.4.2.4	Multiple marking of a single inflectional category —— 68	
2.4.2.5	Functional mismatch —— 69	
2.4.2.6	Phonological mismatch —— 70	
2.4.2.7	Distribution limited to contact zones —— 70	
2.4.2.8	Specific morphosyntactic subsystems affected —— 71	
2.4.3	Indications of genealogical retention —— 72	
2.4.3.1	Globally shared grammaticalization —— 72	
2.4.3.2	Categorial opacity —— 76	
2.4.3.3	Shared cumulation —— 76	
2.4.3.4	Unreduced allomorphy —— 77	
2.4.3.5	Multiple comparative setting —— 78	
2.4.3.6	Missing intermediaries —— 79	
2.5	Methodological misunderstandings —— 80	
2.5.1	"The comparative method is not universally applicable" —— 80	
2.5.2	"One cannot demonstrate unrelatedness" —— 81	
2.5.3	"Absence of evidence is evidence of absence" —— 83	
2.5.4	"Proto-languages are unrealistic" —— 84	
2.5.5	"Multiple comparison increases chance probability" —— 86	
2.5.6	"Shared morphology is a *conditio sine qua non*" —— 87	
3	**Verb Roots** —— **89**	
3.1	The distinction between nouns and verbs —— 89	
3.2	Verbal adjectives within a mixed adjective typology —— 91	
3.2.1	Japanese —— 91	
3.2.2	Korean —— 94	
3.2.3	Tungusic —— 95	
3.2.4	Mongolic —— 97	
3.2.5	Turkic —— 99	
3.2.6	Scenario for the development of Transeurasian adjective typology —— 101	
3.2.7	Underlying data —— 106	
3.3	Verbs —— 118	
3.3.1	Relevant consonant correspondences —— 118	
3.3.2	Relevant vowel correspondences —— 124	
3.3.3	Suprasegmental correlation —— 132	
3.3.4	Underlying etymologies —— 134	

3.4	Copular verbs —— 153	
3.4.1	pTEA *a:- 'to be' —— 154	
3.4.2	pTEA *bɔ:l- 'to sit down, be sitting; become, be' —— 159	
3.5	Stability —— 163	
3.5.1	Notion —— 163	
3.5.2	Basic vocabulary —— 164	
3.5.3	A typology of verbal borrowing —— 166	
3.5.4	Copy-proof properties of the verbal comparisons —— 169	
4	**Negation —— 174**	
4.1	The development of negation and its genealogical relevance —— 174	
4.2	Previous comparative approaches —— 177	
4.3	pTEA *ana- negative verb —— 179	
4.3.1	pJ *ana- negative verb —— 179	
4.3.1.1	Negative suffix —— 179	
4.3.1.2	Negative auxiliary —— 180	
4.3.1.3	Independent negative verb —— 183	
4.3.1.4	The development of pJ *ana- —— 183	
4.3.2	pK *an- negative verb —— 185	
4.3.3	pTg *ana- auxiliary negative verb —— 186	
4.3.3.1	Manchu aku: —— 186	
4.3.3.2	Even ac, acca, a:n ~ a:ŋ —— 187	
4.3.3.3	Evenki a:cin —— 188	
4.3.3.4	Udehe anci, ata- —— 189	
4.3.3.5	Nanai ana ~ ana: —— 190	
4.3.3.6	The development of pTg *a:na- —— 191	
4.4	pA *ə- negative verb —— 192	
4.4.1	No evidence for pJ *e- —— 192	
4.4.2	Insufficient evidence for pK *e- —— 192	
4.4.3	pTg *e- negative verb —— 193	
4.4.3.1	Even e- —— 193	
4.4.3.2	Evenki e- —— 193	
4.4.3.3	Udehe e- —— 194	
4.4.3.4	Nanai negative —— 194	
4.4.3.5	Overview —— 196	
4.4.4	pMo *e- negative verb —— 198	
4.4.4.1	Negative particle —— 198	
4.4.4.2	Independent negative verb —— 198	
4.4.4.3	The development of pMo *e- —— 199	
4.4.5	pTk *e- auxiliary negative verb —— 200	

4.4.5.1	Karakhanide *aŋ / eŋ* 'no, not' —— 200	
4.4.5.2	Chuvash an prohibitive —— 200	
4.4.5.3	The development of pTk **e-* —— 202	
4.5	Insufficient evidence for pTEA **ma-* auxiliary negative verb —— 202	
4.6	The historical development of negation in Transeurasian —— 205	
5	**Verbalization and actionality** —— **209**	
5.1	The suffix class "actionality" and its diachronic relevance —— 209	
5.2	Previous research —— 211	
5.3	pTEA **-lA-* manipulative denominal verb suffix —— 213	
5.3.1	pJ **-ra-* (~ *-rə-*) —— 213	
5.3.1.1	Manipulative denominal verb suffix —— 213	
5.3.1.2	Loan verb marker —— 216	
5.3.2	pTg **-lA:-* —— 217	
5.3.2.1	Manipulative denominal verb suffix —— 217	
5.3.2.1.1	Manchu *-lA-* —— 217	
5.3.2.1.2	Even *-lA:-* —— 218	
5.3.2.1.3	Evenki *-lA-* —— 219	
5.3.2.1.4	Udehe *-lA-* —— 219	
5.3.2.1.5	Nanai *-lA-* —— 220	
5.3.2.2	Loan verb marker —— 220	
5.3.3	pMo **-lA-* —— 221	
5.3.3.1	Manipulative denominal verb suffix —— 221	
5.3.3.2	Loan verb marker —— 222	
5.3.4	pTk **-lA-* —— 222	
5.3.4.1	Manipulative denominal verb suffix —— 223	
5.3.4.2	Loan verb marker —— 224	
5.3.5	The nature of the historical connection —— 224	
5.4	pTEA **-nA-* processive —— 227	
5.4.1	pJ **-na-* (~ **-nə-*) —— 227	
5.4.2	pK **-nO-* —— 229	
5.4.3	pTg **-nA-* —— 230	
5.4.3.1	Manchu *-nA-* —— 231	
5.4.3.2	Even *-(A)n$_{(2)}$-* —— 232	
5.4.3.3	Evenki *-nA-* —— 233	
5.4.3.4	Udehe *-nA-* —— 233	
5.4.3.5	Nanai *-nA-* —— 234	
5.4.4	pMo **-nA-* —— 235	
5.4.5	pTk **-(X)n-* —— 237	
5.5	pTEA **-ki-* iconic —— 239	

5.5.1	pJ *-ka-	239
5.5.2	pK *-(k)i-	240
5.5.3	pTg *-ki:- (~ *-gi:-)	241
5.5.3.1	Manchu -ki- ~ -gi-	242
5.5.3.2	Even -k-, -kA- ~ -gA-	242
5.5.3.3	Evenki -ki(:)- ~ -gi(:)-	242
5.5.3.4	Nanai -ki- ~ -gi-	243
5.5.4	pMo *-ki- (~ *-gi-)	243
5.5.5	pTk *-kI-	244
5.6	pTEA *-mA- inclination	246
5.6.1	pJ *-ma- (~ *-mə-)	246
5.6.2	pK *-mO-	250
5.6.3	pTg *-mA:-	252
5.6.3.1	Manchu -mi-	252
5.6.3.2	Even -mA:-, -mi:-	252
5.6.3.3	Evenki -mA-, -mi-	252
5.6.3.4	Udehe -mA-	253
5.6.3.5	Nanai -mAsi-	253
5.6.4	pMo *-mA-	253
5.7	pTEA *-gA- inchoative	255
5.7.1	pJ *-ka-	255
5.7.2	pK *-kO-	256
5.7.3	pTg *-gA-	259
5.7.3.1	Manchu	259
5.7.3.2	Even	260
5.7.3.3	Evenki	262
5.7.3.4	Udehe	262
5.7.3.5	Nanai	263
5.7.4	pMo *-gA-	263
5.7.5	pTk *-(X)k- (~ -(X)g-)	264
5.8	The historical development of actionality in Transeurasian	266
6	**Valence and voice**	**271**
6.1	The suffix classes "valence" and "voice" and their diachronic relevance	271
6.2	Previous research	274
6.3	pTEA *-ti- causative	276
6.3.1	pJ -*ta-	276
6.3.2	pK *-ti-	277
6.3.3	pTg *-ti-	281

6.3.3.1	Manchu -tA-	282
6.3.3.2	Even -t- ~ -ci-	283
6.3.3.3	Evenki -t- ~ -ci-	285
6.3.3.4	Udehe -si-	286
6.3.3.5	Nanai -ci- ~ -si-	287
6.3.4	pMo *-ti-	288
6.3.5	pTk *-ti-	290
6.4	pTEA *-pU- reflexive-anticausative	292
6.4.1	pJ *-pa- (~ -pə-)	292
6.4.2	pK *-pO-	294
6.4.3	pTg *-p-	296
6.4.3.1	Ma. ∅	297
6.4.3.2	Even -(A)b-	297
6.4.3.3	Evenki -p-	298
6.4.3.4	Udehe -p-	298
6.4.3.5	Nanai -p-	298
6.4.4	pMo *-βU-	299
6.4.5	pTk *-U-	300
6.5	pTEA *-dA- fientive	301
6.5.1	pJ *-ya-	301
6.5.2	pTg *dA:-	303
6.5.2.1	Manchu -dA-	303
6.5.2.2	Even -dA:-	303
6.5.2.3	Evenki -dA-	304
6.5.2.4	Udehe -dA-	304
6.5.2.5	Nanai -dA-	304
6.5.3	pMo *-dA-	305
6.5.4	pTk *-(A)d-	306
6.6	pTEA *-rA- anticausative	309
6.6.1	pJ *-ra-	309
6.6.2	pK *-(u)l-	310
6.6.3	pTg *-rA-	311
6.6.3.1	Manchu -rA-	312
6.6.3.2	Even -r-	312
6.6.3.3	Evk. -rA-	313
6.6.4	pMo *-rA-	313
6.6.5	pTk *-rA-	314
6.7	pTEA *-gi- causative	315
6.7.1	pJ *-(C)i-	315
6.7.2	pK *-ki-	320

6.7.3	pTg *-gi:-	321
6.7.3.1	Manchu	322
6.7.3.2	Even	322
6.7.3.3	Evenki	323
6.7.3.4	Udehe	324
6.7.3.5	Nanai	324
6.8	The historical development of valence and voice in Transeurasian	324
7	**Nominalization and the development of finite temporal distinctions**	**330**
7.1	Direct insubordination and its diachronic relevance	330
7.2	Previous research	335
7.3	pTEA *-rA aspectually neutral (ad)nominalizer	339
7.3.1	pJ *-ra (~ *-rə)	339
7.3.1.1	Ryukyuan	341
7.3.1.2	Mainland Japanese	344
7.3.2	pK *-l	347
7.3.3	pTg *-rA	349
7.3.3.1	Manchu -rA	350
7.3.3.2	Even	351
7.3.3.3	Evenki	352
7.3.3.4	Udehe	353
7.3.3.5	Nanai	354
7.3.4	pMo *-r	355
7.3.5	pTk *-rV	357
7.3.5.1	Old Turkic	357
7.3.5.2	Chuvash	359
7.3.5.3	Yakut	360
7.4	pTEA *-mA	361
7.4.1	pJ *-m	361
7.4.1.1	Ryukyuan	363
7.4.1.2	Mainland Japanese	364
7.4.2	pK *-m	366
7.4.3	pTg *-mA	367
7.4.3.1	Manchu	368
7.4.3.2	Even	371
7.4.3.3	Evenki	372
7.4.3.4	Udehe	373
7.4.3.5	Nanai	373

7.4.4	pMo *-m(A)	374
7.4.5	pTk *-m(A)	376
7.4.5.1	Old Turkic	377
7.4.5.2	Chuvash	378
7.5	pTEA *-n aspectually neutral (ad)nominalizer	379
7.5.1	pJ *-n	379
7.5.1.1	Ryukyuan	380
7.5.1.2	Old Japanese	381
7.5.2	pK *-n	383
7.5.3	pTg *-n(A)	385
7.5.3.1	Manchu	386
7.5.3.2	Even	386
7.5.3.3	Evenki	388
7.5.3.3	Udehe	390
7.5.3.4	Nanai	390
7.5.4	pMo *-n	391
7.5.5	pTk *-n	393
7.5.5.1	Old Turkic	393
7.5.5.2	Chuvash	395
7.6	pTEA *-xA ~ *-kA	396
7.6.1	pJ *-ka	396
7.6.1.1	Ryukyuan	397
7.6.1.2	Mainland Japanese	398
7.6.2	pK *-kAi	400
7.6.3	pTg *-xA: ~ *-kA:	402
7.6.3.1	Manchu	403
7.6.3.2	Even	405
7.6.3.3	Evenki	406
7.6.3.4	Udehe	406
7.6.3.5	Nanai	407
7.6.4	pMo *-xA ~ *-kA	408
7.6.5	pTk *-xA ~ *-kA	411
7.6.5.1	Old Turkic	411
7.6.5.2	Chuvash	416
7.7	pTEA *-sA	417
7.7.1	pJ *-sa	417
7.7.1.1	Ryukyuan	417
7.7.1.2	Mainland Japanese	418
7.7.2	pK *-s	422
7.7.3	pTg *-sA	423

7.7.3.1	Manchu —— 424	
7.7.3.2	Even —— 424	
7.7.3.3	Evenki —— 427	
7.7.3.4	Udehe —— 427	
7.7.3.5	Nanai —— 429	
7.7.4	pMo *-sA —— 431	
7.7.5	pTk *-sA —— 432	
7.7.5.1	Old Turkic —— 432	
7.7.5.2	Chuvash —— 434	
7.8	The historical development of finite suffixes in Transeurasian —— 436	
8	**Converbs** —— 449	
8.1	Converbs and their diachronic relevance —— 449	
8.2	Previous research —— 453	
8.3	pTEA *-i ~ ø deverbal noun suffix —— 455	
8.3.1	pJ *-i ~ ø —— 455	
8.3.1.1	Mainland Japanese —— 455	
8.3.1.2	Ryukyuan —— 458	
8.3.2	pK *-i ~ ø —— 459	
8.3.3	pTg *-i: ~ ø —— 461	
8.3.3.1	Ma. -i ~ ø —— 461	
8.3.3.2	Even —— 461	
8.3.3.3	Evenki —— 462	
8.3.4	pMo *-i ~ ø —— 462	
8.3.5	pTk *-I ~ ø —— 464	
8.4	pTEA *-xU ~ *-kU deverbal noun suffix —— 466	
8.4.1	pJ *-ku —— 466	
8.4.1.1	Mainland Japanese —— 466	
8.4.1.2	Ryukyuan —— 468	
8.4.2	pK *-ku ~ *-k(ʌ) —— 469	
8.4.3	pTg *-xu: ~ *-ku: —— 471	
8.4.3.1	Manchu —— 472	
8.4.3.2	Even —— 473	
8.4.3.3	Udehe —— 473	
8.4.3.4	Nanai —— 475	
8.4.4	pMo *-gU ~ *-kU < ? *-xU ~ *-kU —— 476	
8.4.5	pTk *-xU ~ *-kU —— 478	
8.4.5.1	Old Turkic —— 478	
8.4.5.2	Chuvash —— 480	

8.5	The historical development of converb suffixes in Transeurasian —— 482
9	**Evaluation —— 485**
9.1	The correlations —— 485
9.1.1	Formal correlations —— 487
9.1.2	Functional correlations —— 488
9.1.3	Combinational correlations —— 488
9.1.4	Typological correlations —— 489
9.1.5	Paradigmatic correlations —— 490
9.1.5.1	Ordered sets —— 490
9.1.5.2	Quirks —— 491
9.1.5.3	Extended paradigmaticity —— 493
9.2	How likely is coincidence? —— 493
9.3	How likely is borrowing? —— 494
9.3.1	Guidelines —— 494
9.3.2	Indications against code-copying —— 494
9.3.3	Indications in support of inheritance —— 497
9.4	Why is the evidence not consistent with the Indo-European model? —— 501
9.4.1	Inconsistency —— 501
9.4.2	Typological differences —— 501
9.4.3	Chronological differences —— 503
9.5	Conclusion: a family picture through morphology —— 505

Abbreviations —— 507
References —— 511
Language index —— 542
Subject index —— 547

1 Introduction

1.1 Goals of this study

The question of whether the languages here referred to as Transeurasian, namely the Japanic languages, the Koreanic languages, the Tungusic languages, the Mongolic languages and the Turkic languages, constitute a genealogical grouping remains one of the most disputed issues in comparative historical linguistics. The controversial classification has been on the table for nearly two centuries, but in spite of recent claims from both supporters and critics that the controversy has been resolved (Starostin et al. 2003: 7, Vovin 2005a: 71), the debate is too complex to be easily settled. It is a sign of the healthy state of the Transeurasian debate that it continues to generate new evidence and counter-evidence. The present volume has no intention to close the debate on Transeurasian classification, but it will propose new evidence from verb morphology, in addition to putting old evidence in a new light. Using the traditional comparative method as a basic tool, the present volume examines whether the correspondences in verb morphology between the Transeurasian languages suggest a common ancestorship.

What are the objectives of this study? First, it aims to contribute to the debate about the genealogical relationship of Japanese and to the discussions on the affinity of the so-called "Altaic" languages. The present work starts from the proposition that both issues are so closely interrelated that it is virtually impossible to discuss them independently. This assumption challenges a commonly used starting point in the Altaic literature, i.e. the following observation by Georg (2007: 268): "The core of the "Altaic" debate is the question whether the three ("western", "continental") families Turkic, Mongolian and Tungusic, are genetically related to each other in the first place, and only secondarily, whether Korean ("peninsular Altaic") and/or Japanese ("insular Altaic") can or should be added to this grouping." I argue, however, that it is nearly impossible to demonstrate that Turkic, Mongolic and Tungusic are genealogically related without considering Korean and Japanese. This viewpoint is supported by another observation made by the same author (Georg 2003: 433): "...most critics of Altaic maintain that these languages *do* share a great deal ... of... historical identical lexical and morphological elements, but that these -at least their majority- is better accounted for by assuming large-scale mutual borrowing than common genetic descent." It appears that the question whether the Transeurasian languages are genealogically related essentially boils down to a clash between diffusionist and retentionist explanations. Thus, the primary controversy in the Transeurasian debate is not fuelled by a shortage of similarities, but by the difficulty of accounting for them. The key question is whether all shared forms are generated by code-copying or whether some are the residues of inheritance. In the past, each of the three western families and the two eastern families maintained high-contact relationships amongst themselves. If a shared morphology is found between low-contact languages, including, for instance, Japanese and Turkic, code-copying can be ruled out with high probabilty. Starting from a hypothesis that includes low-contact languages therefore offers the best chance of resolving the longstanding copy-cognate debate for the Transeurasian languages.

In addition to contributing to the distinction between borrowing and inheritance, the present volume will address other objections against the genealogical relatedness of the Transeurasian languages. Ramer et al. (1998: 79–88) identify the main issues as the lack of a common basic vocabulary, the establishment of phonological correspondences, the lack of attention to common morphology including the interpretation of the shared personal pronouns and the lack of consistency with the evidence in support of Indo-European. The recent confrontation of opinions in publications such as Starostin et al. (2003), Robbeets (2004, 2005) and reviews of these studies has advanced our understanding of matters relating to phonology and basic vocabulary. The obstacles largely unaffected by these discussions are first, the need to identify a common morphology, second, the problem of distinguishing between code-copying and inheritance without over-reliance on vocabulary and third, the challenge of explaining the un-Indo-European characteristics of the evidence. As these issues are interconnected, treating one issue will elucidate the others. Thus, the present demonstration that the Transeurasian languages share a common morphology will shed light on the distinction between code-copying and inheritance, while insight into the different nature of the shared properties will prevent us from setting Indo-European as a standard against which Transeurasian is to be assessed.

A third objective of the present study is to add to the reconstruction of the common ancestor of Japanese and Korean. Whereas the inclusion of Japanese and Korean will shed light upon the nature of the relationship between the other Transeurasian languages, the reverse is also true; the comparison with Turkic, Mongolic and Tungusic is expected to have implications for the reconstruction of proto-Japanese-Korean. Although the pitch of their arguments mainly rely on lexical evidence, Martin (1968, 1990, 1991a, 1995, 2002) and his student Whitman (1985) have proposed a common morphology in support of a Japanese-Korean unity. Janhunen (2010: 132), however, warns that "Since Japanese and Korean are spoken in adjacent areas, a large proportion of their shared features must, in any case, be due to contacts, and it is important to eliminate the illusion of similarity created by these contacts before progressing to the level of deeper genetic studies." In line with this caveat, Vovin (2010) indeed attempts to refute the Martin-Whitman etymologies, proposing that the forms were actually copied from Korean into Japanese in early historical times. Unger (2009) attempts to rehabilitate the Martin-Whitman corpus by using the semantics of lexical items as an indication of the copy-cognate distinction. The present study takes a different approach, using shared morphemes and their distribution as indications against code-copying. Based on the argumentation that it is difficult to account for common Japanese-Korean verb morphemes by language contact when they are also shared by the continental families, the present study aims to contribute to the reconstruction of proto-Japanese-Korean.

Fourth, by examining morphological evidence in support of the relatedness of the Transeurasian languages, the volume will complement previous studies focussing on lexical correspondences. Since the beginnings of the historical comparative study of Transeurasian languages, the emphasis has been on lexical research. Recent illustrations of this trend include the extensive collection of lexical comparisons published by Starostin, Dybo and Mudrak (2003) and my own previous work (Robbeets 2005), a collection and evaluation of existing etymological proposals relating Japanese to Korean and to the Altaic languages. It is precisely the abundance of lexical look-alikes that has led to two diametrically opposed points of view: either that every single item is to be accounted for by code-copying or, that part of the shared vocabulary can be traced back to a common ancestor. Given the relative difficulty of copying bound verb morphology, this study can help to distinguish between the effects of contact and inheritance. This research also starts from the expectation that if a number of languages using morphological marking to express syntactic relations in the sentence are genealogically related, common ancestorship will be reflected in grammatical as well as in lexical morphemes. Moreover, demonstrating that the vocabulary and the grammar derive from the same source will enable us to reject theories of language mixing and creolization. Supporters and critics of Transeurasian relatedness seem to agree on at least this one point, i.e. that patterned morphology could substantially help unravel the question. Vovin (2005: 73) begins his critique of Starostin et al. (2003) with the postulation that "The best way ... is to prove a suggested genetic relationship on the basis of *paradigmatic* morphology", whereas Dybo & Starostin (2008: 125) agree that "regular paradigmatic correspondences in morphology are necessarily indicative of genetic relationship." It is my goal to examine whether morphological evidence confirms previous findings based on lexical data.

Finally, the study is not only aimed at specialists in Northern, Central and Eastern Asian languages, but also seeks to contribute to the current literature on language classification in general. Although the search for new methods to reach beyond the limitations of the comparative method, such as Nichols' (1992,

2003) structural comparison and Greenberg's multilateral comparison (2000, 2002), may bring innovation and progress to the field, I aim to demonstrate that the Transeurasian languages can be shown to be related within the limits of the traditional method. Before turning to new methods, we should exhaust existing ones to the best of our abilities. It will be shown that the use of an adequate methodology allows us to move the Transeurasian family to the more established end of the classification continuuum proposed by Campbell (2003: 262; Campbell & Poser 2008: 162–163), namely from a questionable unit to a plausible and supportable family. Besides inviting historical linguistic scholarship to rethink the relatedness of the Transeurasian languages, the present study will raise a number of methodological points, especially with regard to shared grammaticalization and the distinction between code-copying and inheritance. These methodological guidelines are not without relevance for other cases of controversial classification.

The remaining sections of this introduction will define the term Transeurasian, provide internal taxonomies for the individual branches and review previous research on the topic of this book. Chapter 2 will elucidate the methods used in this work. Chapter 3 presents etymologies for verb roots including verbal adjectives and copular verbs. These are arranged according to specific phonological correspondences relevant to assessing the formal correspondences of the bound morphemes, as discussed in the following chapters. Chapters 4 to 8 propose cognate morphemes distributed over various verb categories such as negation, actionality, diathesis and tense, including nonfinite forms such as participles, verbal nouns and converbs. By way of conclusion, Chapter 9 summarizes and evaluates the correlations established in the previous chapters. It further assesses the likelihood of non-genealogical explanations and tries to find an explanation for the inconsistency of the evidence in comparison to that in support of Indo-European.

1.2 The Transeurasian languages

1.2.1 From "Altaic" to "Transeurasian"

Although Europe and Asia are physically one great landmass commonly called Eurasia, a geographical boundary between the two continents is drawn along the Ural Mountains to the Ural River and the Caspian Sea and the along the Caucasus Mountains to the Black Sea. Clearly, linguistic boundaries do not necessarily coincide with geographical boundaries. Stretching from the Pacific in the east to the Mediterranean and the Baltic in the west, the Transeurasian languages form a vast linguistic continuum that crosses the physical boundaries between Europe and Asia. Contrary to the tradition to refer to these languages as "Altaic languages," Johanson and Robbeets (2010: 1–2) coined the term "Transeurasian" to refer to this large group of geographically adjacent languages, which share a significant number of linguistic properties and include at most 5 linguistic families: Japanic, Koreanic, Tungusic, Mongolic, and Turkic. Figure 1 is a map of the Transeurasian languages, indicating a selection of the main languages discussed in this book.

Figure 1. Map of the Transeurasian languages (generated with WALS tool)

Why is it necessary to adopt a new name even though a long-standing alternative is available in the linguistic literature? First, the new name avoids confusion between the different uses of the term "Altaic". Some scholars, for instance Doerfer, Benzing, Sinor, Róna-Tas, and Erdal, use the term in the traditional sense, as the collective name for the languages belonging to the Turkic, Mongolic, and Tungusic language families and the peoples that speak them. For a number of other scholars, e.g. Ramstedt, Poppe, Tekin, Baskakov, and Aalto, "Altaic" includes Korean but excludes Japanese. The authors of the *Etymological dictionary of the Altaic languages*, Starostin, Dybo, Mudrak, and many other scholars, e.g. Lee Ki-Moon, Street, Miller, Menges, Murayama, Itabasi, Vovin, Manaster Ramer, and Robbeets use "Altaic" in its broadest sense, i.e. covering all five families. This expanded grouping also became known as "Macro-Altaic", leading by back-formation to the designation "Micro-Altaic" to refer to Turkic, Mongolic, and Tungusic. In the present study, the term "Transeurasian" will be used in the expanded, "Macro-Altaic" sense.

Second, the suffix -*ic* in "Altaic" implies affinity in the same way as it does in Germanic, Semitic, or Austro-Asiatic. Defining "Transeurasian" as a group of geographically adjacent languages that share a significant number of linguistic properties, does not presuppose a genealogical relationship and hence the term is also acceptable to linguists who do not subscribe to the hypothesis that the Transeurasian languages are genealogically related. In this respect, the term "Transeurasian" is a more neutral term than "Altaic".

Moreover, the new term could have a psychological side-effect, in that it may reduce the strong and counterproductive polarization between "Pro-Altaists" and "Anti-Altaists". Doerfer (1974: 107), for instance, draws the following scheme.

Proaltaisten	Poppe	Doerfer	Antialtaisten

This labelling of positions as either pro-Altaic or anti-Altaic not only leads to oversimplification, but also brings battle-field rhetoric to the debate, with expressions such as "anti-Altaic activity" (Ramer et al. 1998: 78), "anti-Altaic attacks" (a.o. Ramer et al. 1998: 89), "anti-Altaic camps", "Anti-Altaists contra Altaists" (Miller 1991a), "the virulent anti-Altaic polemic firestorm" (Miller 2008: 264), or "anti-Altaicists try to sink Altaic theory" (Vovin 1994: 22). This belligerent approach evokes strong loyalty as researchers take sides and identify with one camp or another. Georg (2005: 2), for instance, orates: "Altaic linguistics is, still, the hotbed of polemically led controversies in comparative linguistics and the designation of certain scholars as "Anti-Altaicists" was originally coined as derogatory, but I am not the only person who wears it, I must say, with pride." The genealogical relationship of the Transeurasian languages has generated discussions which are at times so emotional that they create more heat than light. Abandoning extreme designations such as "Pro-Altaicist" and "Anti-Altaicist" may attenuate the hostile tone that marks some of the debate.

Finally, the term "Altaic" is not only rejected because of the suffix -*ic*, but also because of its root. Both critics and supporters of a genealogical unity would agree that the term "Altaic" is historically incorrect because the reference to the Altai mountains as a homeland does not keep pace with developments in interdisciplinary research. In his monograph, *Manchuria. An ethnic history*, Janhunen situates the original speech communities of Turkic, Mongolic, Tungusic, Korean, and Japanese in a rather compact area comprising North Korea, southern Manchuria and present day southeastern Mongolia. Janhunen (1996a: 238) adds: "If it only could be proven to be correct, the Altaic Hypothesis would fundamentally deepen our understanding of the prehistorical ethnic situation in Manchuria".

1.2.2 Internal taxonomy of the individual branches

1.2.2.1 Turkic

The Turkic language family consists of about 40 closely related Turkic languages and dialects spoken over a wide area of the Eurasian continent, including some parts of Europe, Asia Minor, Central Asia and Siberia. The languages show clear similarities in phonology, morphology and syntax. As a group, they are thought to reflect a certain conservatism (Johanson 1998: 81, 2001); contemporary Turkish, for instance, has preserved many basic features of the language of Old Turkic inscriptions. Using the principle of shared innovations, it is possible to divide the Turkic languages from a genealogical perspective (Tekin 1990). The unity of Turkic was dissolved by an early split of "Oghuric" from the rest of the family, commonly called "Common Turkic." The Oghuric branch refers to the western branch, whereas the rest of Turkic constitutes the eastern branch. One traditional observation that supports this early split is the regular correspondence between Common Turkic z and š and Oghuric r and l in certain words, e.g. Chuvash śĕr vs. Turkish yüz 'hundred' and Chuvash xĕl 'winter' vs. Turkish kiš 'winter', although in this case Turkologists disagree on which branch represents the phonological innovation.

The region where Turkic was spoken before it split into the eastern and western branches is thought to be in present-day East Mongolia (Janhunen 1996a: 185–189). It is known that the Xiongnu, a collection of ethnic groups of which some have been identified as linguistic ancestors of the Turkic people, lived as nomads in that area between 209 BC and 155 AD. The available lexical and onomastic material, however, does not provide much information about the languages of the Xiongnu (Doerfer 1973). Oghuric speakers are likely to have entered southern Siberia by the first century BC. At that time, southern Siberia was the location of proto-Samoyedic, which contains a number of Oghuric loanwords, such as *yür 'hundred' and *kil 'winter'. At the end of the second century, the remaining Xiongnu were overrun by the Xianbei, linguistic ancestors of the Mongols, who dominated the steppes of North China for several centuries. From the first centuries BC until the beginning of the 4th century AD, several Oghuric tribes moved to the west, developing a number of dialects such as Ogur, Avar, Khazar and Bulghar, which are extinct and poorly recorded.

As early as the fifth century Ogurs tribes, such as the Saragurs 'White Ogurs', Onogurs 'Ten Ogurs' and the Uturgurs 'Thirty Ogurs' arrived in Eastern Europe. They were overthrown by the Sabirs in the Volga region in 506, who, in turn, were overthrown by the Avars in 555. The Avars are first mentioned as "Ruanruan" in the Chinese sources in 385, when they occupied a territory in present-day Mongolia. Under pressure of the Türk empire they fled west and conquered the Carpathian Basin, where their descendants lived until the Hungarian conquest in 895 (Róna-Tas & Berta 2011: 19–21).

Around the middle of the 4th century Bulghar tribes appeared in present-day Khazakhstan, where they remained until they were crushed by the Khazars around 670. After the dissolution of the Bulghar empire, Bulghar speakers were divided into at least a Danube Bulghar group and a Volga Bulghar group.

The Danube Bulghar group went as far as the lower Danube region and founded Bulgaria in the Balkans. Toward the end of the 9th century, they converted to orthodox Christianity and their language rapidly shifted to Slavic. Few records exist of the Danube Bulghar language: there are some lexical borrowings into Hungarian, Old Church Slavonic or Slavic Bulgarian, onomastic material, a few scattered words, names and titles in Greek and Slavic inscriptions and small fragments of texts in Greek, Cyrillic or Runiform script that were either distorted or remain undeciphered (Róna-Tas 1982: 126–154; 1999: 113). Given that morphology is hardly represented, these bits and pieces of Danube Bulghar cannot add much to the topic of the present volume.

The Volga Bulgars slowly moved to the north and reached the Volga-Kama region, where they founded the Volga Bulghar Empire and started to develop Islamic culture in the 9th century. Although Volga Bulghar has been well deciphered, sources are very limited, consisting of personal names, place names or river names, some early borrowings into Russian or into Finno-Ugric languages of the Volga-Kama region, such as Votyak and Mordvinian, later borrowings into the Volga Kipchak dialects or into Meadow Mari (Cheremis), and inscriptions on coins and tombstones (Róna-Tas 1982: 154–169). The earliest Volga Bulghar inscription is dated 1281. Although Chuvash developed as a member of the Volga Bulghar branch, its speakers were apparently not much affected by the Volga Bulghar Islamic culture, given that they converted to Christianity in the sixteenth century. Since Chuvash is the only surviving representative of the western Turkic languages, it plays a key role in the reconstruction of proto-Turkic. It is spoken by approximately two million speakers in the Chuvash Republic of the Russian federation and in other parts of Russia. The first written records are Strahlenberg's word list, some texts and a grammar, all of which date back to the 18th century.

As far as the eastern branch of Turkic is concerned, the earliest split occurred when the so-called "Arghu" branch separated from East Turkic proper. The sole modern descendant of Arghu is Khalaj, spoken in central Iran by approximately 42,000 speakers. Doerfer who rediscovered Khalaj, has demonstrated that the language was the first to branch off from East Turkic proper. The correspondence between Khalaj *h-* with an initial zero in the other East Turkic languages (e.g. Khalaj *ha:v* vs. Tk. *ev*, Kaz. *üy*, Uig. *öy*, Shor *em* 'house' and Khalaj *hat* vs. Tk. *at*,

Kaz. *at*, Uig. *at* and Shor *at* 'horse') reflects a shared innovation. Doerfer (1971: 163–165, 1987) explained Khalaj *h-* as an archaic feature, with the other East Turkic languages representing the innovation. But even if one regards Khalaj *h-* as a case of secondary prothesis, the correspondence can still be used to support the proposed subbranching.

East Old Turkic proper is the ancestor of all contemporary Turkic languages except Chuvash and Khalaj. It represents a historical variety of Turkic that had not yet split into the Oghuz Turkic, Kipchak Turkic, Uighur Turkic and Siberian Turkic branches. The earliest known records, which date back to the eighth century, are inscriptions in runiform script on stone steles found in present-day north-central Mongolia's Orkhon valley. These inscriptions celebrate the successful resistance to Chinese domination of the eastern Türk steppe empire (551–745), a confederation of Turkic tribes spread over the Central Eurasian Steppe. A linguistically similar variant is known from ninth-century Old Kirgiz inscriptions in the Yenisei basin.

Soon after the successful resistance described in the Orkhon steles, the Türk empire was conquered by another Turkic confederation, the Uighur (Johanson 2003). Their territory expanded to the Tarim Basin in the west and present-day Gansu in the east. From the 9th C onwards, Old Uighur is documented in an extensive religious literature, which developed in the Tarim basin in the period up to the thirteenth century. First, it was written in runiform script, later in Uighur, Manichean, Brāhmī and other scripts. The language is a southeastern dialect that had just split from East Old Turkic proper.

Karakhanid was the first Islamic Turkic literary language, written mainly in Arabic script. It developed between the eleventh and fourteenth century under the Karakhanid dynasty in Eastern Turkistan. It is known as the language of Mahmud al-Kašyari's 'Compendium of the Turkic languages', a Turkic-Arabic lexicon and encyclopedia with grammatical notes. The language is close to Old Uighur, but its vocabulary is influenced by Arabic and Persian. The present study uses "Old Turkic" as cover term in reference to Orkhon Turkic, Old Uighur and Karakhanid, thus spanning a period from the eighth to the fourteenth century. Treating Old Turkic as one linguistic stage is to leave six centuries of language change out of consideration. For historical comparative purposes, this is legitimate as long as we keep in mind that we are not dealing with a synchronic stage.

The Mongol conquests launched by Chingis Khan in the thirteenth century and completed by his grandsons brought virtually all the Turkic regions, as well as Inner Asia, Siberia, western Eurasia and the Near East under their control. The high mobility of the Turkic nomads led to the expansion of their languages over a vast geographical area. Between the thirteenth and sixteenth century, written varieties of the Middle Turkic period such as Early Chaghatay, Middle

Kipchak and Old Anatolian reflect the further differentiation into an eastern Uighur Turkic branch, a northwestern Kipchak Turkic branch and a southwestern Oghuz Turkic branch, respectively. In addition to the varieties reflected in the literary languages, Turkic also developed a Siberian Turkic branch. The ensuing centuries can be seen as a preparatory stage during which the contemporary languages developed.

The northeastern Siberian Turkic languages consist of Yakut with about 450,000 speakers and Dolgan with about 5,000 speakers in North Siberia. The languages spoken in South Siberia include Tuvan with about 264,000 speakers in Russia, Mongolia and China; Tofa, an almost extinct variety spoken in Russia's Irkutsk province by fewer than 30 people; Shor, spoken in Russia's Kemerovo province by about 10,000 people; Khakas, with about 80,000 speakers in the Russian Republic of Khakassia; and Altay Turkic with about 68,000 speakers in Russia's Altai Republic along with its dialects Tuba and Telengit in the Altai Republic and Teleut in Kemerovo Province. The treatment of the intervocalic consonant in the word for 'foot' distinguishes most Siberian Turkic languages from the other East Turkic languages, e.g. Yak. *ataχ*, Dolgan *atak*, Shor *azaq*, Khakas *azaχ* 'foot', Tuva *adaq* 'bottom' versus forms with a medial glide in the other East Turkic languages such as Tk. *ayak*, Kaz. *ayak*, Uig. *ayaq*.

In the West, the southwestern Oghuz Turkic languages comprise the following: Turkish, spoken by over 77 million people in Turkey and worldwide; Azerbaijani with approximately 30 million speakers in the Republic of Azerbaijan and Northwestern Iran; and Gagauz with approximately 330,000 speakers in Moldavia, Ukraine, Rumania and Bulgaria. In the east, Turkmen is spoken by ca. 7.7 million people in Turkmenistan, Iran, Afghanistan, Pakistan, Russia and Ukraine, while Khorasani Turkic is spoken by about 400,000 people in Iran. In the south, the dialects of Iran include Qashqay and Aynallu, with 1.5 million and 7,000 speakers respectively, and Afshar with over 6 million speakers in Afghanistan, Iran, Syria and Turkey. One innovation that separates the Oghuz languages from the Kipchak and Uighur languages is the voicing of initial *t-* and *k-*, as in the word for 'mountain', Tk. *day*, Az. *day*, Gag. *da:*, Tkm. *da:G* versus and Kaz. *taw* and Uig. *tay*, and in the verb 'to go', Tk. *git-*, Az. *get-*, Gag. *get-*, Tkm. *git-* versus Kaz. *ket-* and Uig. *kät-*.

The northwestern Kipchak Turkic languages include, in the west, Crimean Tatar, spoken by nearly 500,000 people in Ukraine, Turkey, Uzbekistan, Romania and Bulgaria; Kumyk with about 366,000 speakers in Dagestan; Karachay-Balkar with about 400,000 speakers in the Russian Caucasus and; Karaim, a nearly extinct language with fewer than 50 speakers in Crimea, Lithuania and Poland. In the North, Tatar is spoken by 6.7 million speakers in Tatarstan, Uzbekistan and other countries across the world, and Bashkir by over 2 million people in Bashkiria, Uzbekistan and Kazakhstan. In the south, we find Kazakh with about 8 million speakers in Kazakhstan, Xinjiang China, and other parts of Asia Minor and Central Asia; modern Kirgiz with about 4.5 million speakers in Kirgizstan, Pakistan, Afghanistan, Tajikistan and Xinjiang China; Karakal-

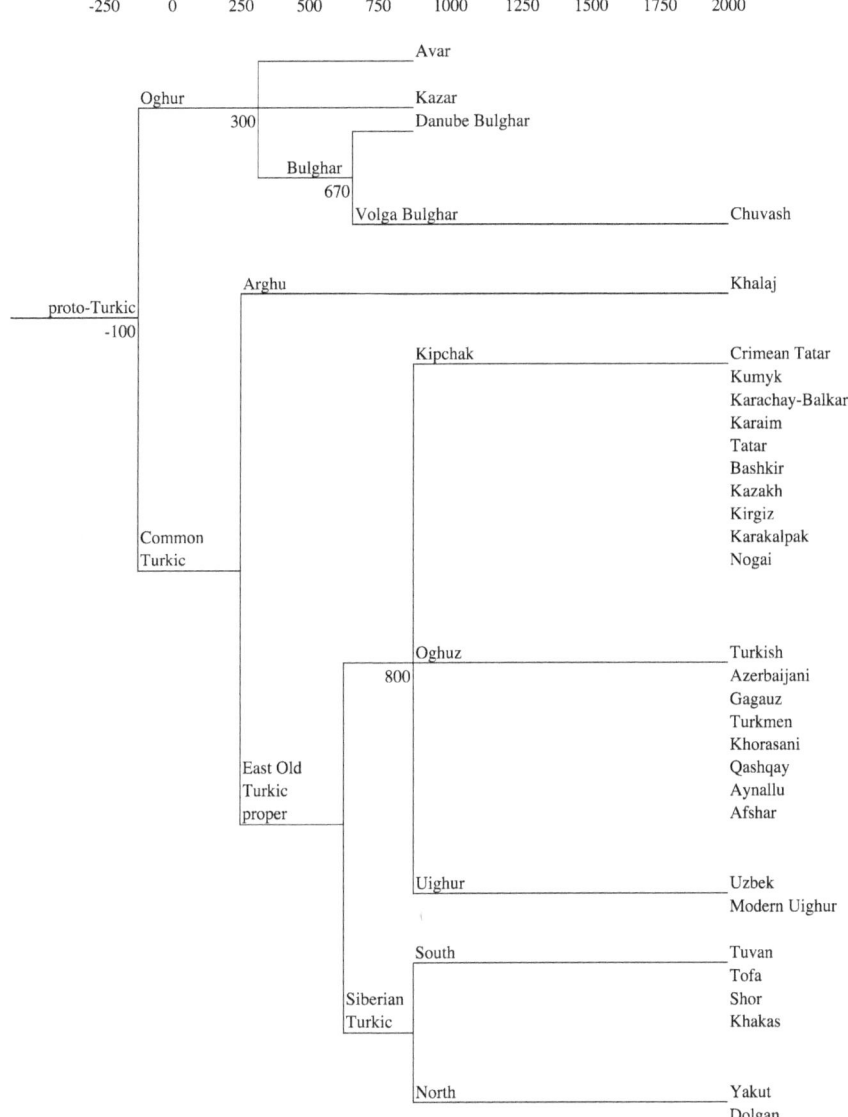

Figure 2. The Turkic family tree

pak with about 415,000 speakers in Uzbekistan, Kazakhstan, Afghanistan and Russia; and Nogai with ca. 90,000 speakers in the Russian Caucasus. A linguistic innovation that identifies the Kipchak languages as a distinct branch is the lenition of final -*y* in monosyllabic words, as in the previous example for 'mountain', Kumyk *taw*, Tat. *taw*, Bash. *tau*, Kaz. *taw*, Nog. *taw* versus Tk. *day*, Uig. *tay* and Shor *tay*.

Finally, the southeastern Uighur Turkic languages include, in the west, modern Uzbek and its various dialects, spoken by nearly 24 million people in Uzbekistan and elsewhere in Central Asia, and, in the east, modern Uighur, spoken by over 8 million people in Xinjiang China, Kazakhstan and elsewhere in central Asia along with different Eastern Turki dialects.

1.2.2.2 Mongolic

The Mongolic language family consists of about 12 closely related languages, extending over Central and Northeast Asia. All contemporary Mongolic languages can be traced back to the language spoken by Chinggis Khan, the founder of the Mongol empire (1206–1368). Originally, the designation "Mongol" was restricted to Chinggis Khan's tribe, but it was eventually extended to the entire population which came to speak the same language. Historical sources, such as the 'Secret History of the Mongols', mention other tribes coexisting with the Mongols, such as the Kereit, Ongniut and Naiman. It is safe to assume that these people spoke a dialect or a sister language of Mongol (Janhunen 2003b: 391–402).

The earliest populations whose languages are thought to have comprised Mongolic elements are the Donghu (ca. 300 BC-150 BC), traced back to the seventh century BC by the Chinese historical record *Shiji* ('Records of the Grand Historian' ca. 109–91 BC). The centralized power of the early Chinese Han dynasty (206 BC-220 AD) was matched by the nomadic power of the Xiongnu tribal state in the region of Mongolia, the Donghu tribes of Western Manchuria and the Sushen of Eastern Manchuria. While the Xiongnu and the Sushen contained elements of Turkic and Tungusic stock, respectively, the Donghu are seen as the ancestors of the historical Khitan and the Mongols (Janhunen 1996a: 183). The Donghu were conquered by the Xiongnu in 150 BC. By the end of the Western Han period (206 BC-8 AD) they split into the Wuhuan and the Xianbei confederations. Having conquered the Wuhuan, the Xianbei established the short-lived Xianbei empire (130–180 AD). From the Xianbei, two distinct populations emerged: the Shiwei people in the north, along the Amur, Argun' and Zeya rivers that form the border between present-day northeastern China and Russia, and the Tabgach people in the south, in the Liao basin in present-day China's

Liaoning province. The Tabgach ultimately contributed to the formation of the Northern Wei Dynasty (386–550) in Manchuria and northern China. On the basis of some fragmentary lexical and onomastic material, it is assumed that the Tabgach language was a Mongolic language, either an early form of Khitanic or perhaps even a language directly ancestral to Khitan (Ligeti 1970, Doerfer 1993). This ethnic division between Shiwei and Tabgach appears to be at the basis of the linguistic split between proto-Mongolic and proto-Khitanic, a branch to which Janhunen (2003b: 391) refers as "para-Mongolic." One phonological innovation that separates the Mongolic from the Khitanic languages seems to be the lenition of an original initial *p- preserved, for instance in Tabgach † *pörtögčin* 'post office clerk' and Khitan † *po* 'time' but lenited in WMo. *örtögeči(n)* 'driver of a mail coach, one on postal relay duty' and (SH) MMo *hon*, WMo. *on* 'year' (Doerfer 1993: 82).

The descendants of the Tabgach, i.e. the Khitan, began dominating the area to the northeast of China in the early T'ang period (618–907). After the collapse of the T'ang dynasty, they established the Liao dynasty (916–1125), which lasted for over two centuries until it was overthrown by the Tungusic Jurchen. After the fall of Liao, many Khitans moved further west and established the state of Kara-Khitai (1125–1218) in Central Asia, which was finally destroyed by the Mongol empire. Khitan sources include occasional words transcribed and glossed in Chinese sources and a corpus of preserved texts written in the Khitan language that has not yet been fully deciphered (Kara 1987, Janhunen 2003b, Kane 2009, Wu & Janhunen 2010). Indirect linguistic information comes from Khitan loanwords in contemporary Tungusic languages. The basic morphology and syntax of the language has to be inferred from imperfectly understood texts.

Proto-Mongolic is the technical term for the reconstructed ancestor of all living and historically well attested Mongolic languages. The actual language which it reflects was spoken at a time when the differentiation of the contemporary Mongolic languages hat not yet begun. The unification during the period of the Mongol empire extinguished the coexisting sister languages of Middle Mongolian and thus functioned as a linguistic bottleneck. It is therefore fair to say that the sources available for Middle Mongolian reflect a language that was very close to proto-Mongolic. The term "Middle Mongolian" refers to the Mongolic language recorded in the thirteenth to the early fifteenth centuries. The spoken variety corresponds to the relatively uniform speech of the Mongolians following the unification under Chinggis Khan. A large corpus is available for Middle Mongolian, comprising documents in various writing systems. The most extensively studied Middle Mongolian text is the 'Secret History of the Mongols', originally compiled in the mid thirteenth century, but only preserved in a somewhat modified seventeenth-century copy. Other sources include administrative and religious documents, belles-lettres, biographical inscriptions, Buddhist texts, translated Chinese non-Buddhist works and Chinese-Mongol or Arabic-Mongol lexicons.

Whereas the oral variety of Middle Mongolian dissolved into the contemporary Mongolic languages, the literary tradition was continued by Written Mongolian, a practice of writing Mongolic in the so-called "Old Script" which continues up to the present day. In comparison with the contemporary languages that have undergone innovation and diversification, Written Mongol is a conservative Mongolic language in its own right. The speakers of different present-day varieties use this distinct, archaic language when writing.

Due to different interpretations of the distinction between dialect and language, there is no general consensus on the number of contemporary Mongolic languages. Moreover, the close similarity of the Mongolic languages also leads to some disagreement about their internal classification (Poppe 1955: 14–23, Doerfer 1963, Binnick 1987, Nugteren 1997, Rybatzki 2003b). According to Nugteren, the earliest split occurred when a group of peripheral Mongolic languages branched off from Mongolian proper. Whereas word-medial palatal breaking is still in progress in Mongolian proper, it has been completed in the peripheral languages, for instance in the word for 'eye', a front vowel has been preserved in Dag. *nid* [ɲid], Khal. *nüd(en)*, Bur. *nyüde(n)*, Ordos *nüdün*, Kalm. *nüdn*, whereas it resulted in a back vowel in SYug. *nudun*, Mgr. *nudu*, Dong. *nuduŋ* and Moghol *nudun*.

As far as Mongolian proper is concerned, the central languages are generally agreed to form a single genealogical entity. Dagur is a clearly aberrant language, spoken by about 96,000 ethnic Dagur in China's provinces of Inner Mongolia, Heilongjiang and Xinjiang. In the seventeenth century, the Dagur inhabited the Middle Amur region from where they were moved to China. Due to its heavy borrowing from surrounding languages, such as Manchu, Evenki and Solon, Dagur was even mistakenly classified as a Tungusic language in the past (Grunzel 1894). Furthermore, it is not possible to exclude the possibility of a Khitan substratum underlying in Dagur (Doerfer 1993: 85). One common innovation shared by the central Mongolic languages, but not by Dagur, is the loss of the initial fricative, e.g. in the word for 'year', Dag. *xo:n* versus Khal. *on*, Bur. *on*, Kalm. *on* and Ordos *on*.

Apart from some minor peculiarities of pronunciation, vocabulary and syntax, the central Mongolic languages are largely mutually intelligible. They are divided into an eastern and a western branch. The best known member of the eastern branch is Khalkha, the official language of Mongolia, which is spoken by about 5.7 million people, including inhabitants of Inner Mongolia. Other eastern languages include Buriat, spoken by about 400,000 people along the Mongolian border in Russia, and Ordos, spoken in the southernmost part of Inner Mongolia, by fewer than 100,000 people. Kamnigan Mongol, which used to be spoken in Transbaikalia is classified as a dialect of Khalkha in Mongolia and as a dialect of Buriat in Russia. However, Janhunen (2005: 9) argues that it as a well-defined, distinct language. Apart from a few elderly speakers, the language is disappearing in Mongolia and Russia, but on the Chinese side there is still a speech community of about 1,500 people.

The western Mongolic languages are Oirat and Kalmuck. There are about 300,000 present-day speakers of Oirat. In the thirteenth century, the Oirat moved from the south of Lake Baikal to the Altai region, from where they dispersed over various regions, including Western Mongolia, Manchuria and the Xinjiang, Gansu and Qinghai provinces in China. Kalmuck, spoken by about 174,000 people in Russia's Kalmuck Republic represents an Oirat diaspora group. Under internal political pressure, the Kalmuck were forced to emigrate from their original homeland in northern Xingjiang to the Volga region in the seventeenth century. One linguistic innovation permitting us to classify the western languages as a separate branch is palatal umlaut, the fronting of back vowels under the influence of a following front vowel. The word for 'horse', for instance, is Khal. *mory*, Bur. *mori(n)*, Ordos *mori(n)* versus Kalm. *mörin*, Oirat *mörn*.

With regard to the peripheral languages, one can discern two geographical regions, i.e. Afghanistan and the Qinghai-Gansu region, which mirror the split between Moghol and the remaining languages. Moghol developed from a language spoken in the thirteenth and fourteenth centuries by a garrison that defended the western borders of the Mongolian empire. After its separation, this language never again came into contact with other Mongolic languages. Although the exact situation is unknown, the language is currently spoken by fewer than 200 speakers in different parts of Afghanistan and rapidly becoming extinct. An innovation similar to but independent from the loss of *h-* in Mongolian proper, is the loss of the initial fricative in Moghol, for instance in the word for 'red', Dong. *xulan*, Bao. *fulaŋ*, Mgr. *fulaan*, SYugh. *hlaan* versus Mogh. *uloon*.

The languages of the Qinghai-Gansu region can be classified into Shira-Yughur and the Shirongol languages. Shira-Yughur (Eastern Yughur) is spoken by fewer than 3,000 people in the central part of China's Gansu province. The Shirongol languages include Monguor, mainly spoken in Qinghai by fewer than 50,000 speakers; Dongxiang (Santa), spoken in Gansu and Xinjiang by about 250,000 people; and Bao'an spoken in Gansu and Qinghai by about 9,000 people. An innovation shared only by the Shirongol languages is the unrounding of the vowel *ö* as in the word for 'four', SYugh. *dörwen* versus Dong. *ʒieron*, Bao. *deraŋ*, Mgr. *de:ren*.

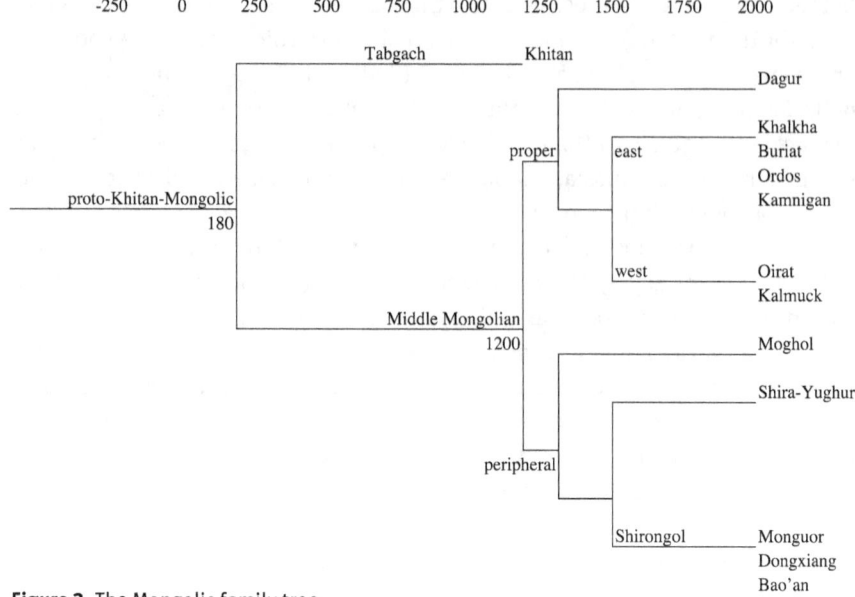

Figure 3. The Mongolic family tree

1.2.2.3 Tungusic

The Tungusic family comprises about 14 languages distributed over Manchuria and Siberia. The majority of these are currently facing extinction due to the impact of Chinese and Russian. Janhunen (1996a: 232, 2005: 39) situates the Tungusic homeland in a compact region comprising the eastern half of Southern Manchuria (Liaodong) and parts of North Korea. Before the Han period, around 300 BC, a population that probably contained Tungusic elements, the Sushen, lived to the east of the Donghu. The designation "Sushen" was replaced by the ethnonym "Yilou". By the beginning of the Eastern Han Dynasty (25–220), Manchuria consisted of three ethnic and political powers, i.e. the presumably Mongolic Xianbei in the west, the presumably Tungusic Yilou in the east, and the presumably Japanic Puyo (Fuyu) in the Sungari basin in between. The *Houhanshu* ('History of the Later Han' 5th. C.) and the *San-kuo chih* ('Records of the Three States' 284) mention that the Yilou spoke a language different from that of Puyo (HHS 85: 2812) and Koguryo (SKC 30: 847) (Kiyose 2002: 121, Beckwith 2004: 37–38). At the end of the Han period, the Yilou became known as the Wuji, later also as the Mohe. The Wuji were centered around the Sungari and Lower Amur basins. From this region Tungusic expanded to the Middle Amur region, leading to the differentiation between the Manchuric branch of Tungusic and Tungusic proper.

In Tungusic linguistic literature, the internal taxonomy of the family with respect to the early segregation of the Manchuric branch has been subject to two different interpretations. The first interpretation is one in which the separation of Manchuric (Jurchen, Manchu, Sibe) from the other Tungusic languages does not constitute the earliest split in the family. This idea is recurrent in earlier literature proposing a bipartite north-south classification such as Cincius (1949: 35) and Benzing (1955a), but it is also present in the recent bipartite classification proposed by Kormušin (1998: 11) and supported by Janhunen (2012a: 16) and Pevnov (2012: 19), be it under a different configuration. Whereas the north-south division of Tungusic put forth by Cincius and Benzing separates Evenki, Even, Negidal and Solon in the north from Manchu, Nanai, Olcha, Orok, Udehe and Oroch in the south, the division made by Kormušin, Janhunen and Pevnov adds Udehe and Oroch to the northern grouping. Some classifications reconstructing three taxonomic units such as Avrorin (1963: 404) and Menges (1968a: 26–28) also agree in regarding the separation of Manchuric as a later development: Avrorin distinguishes the northern Tungusic languages (Evenki, Negidal, Solon, Even) from the south-western (Jurchen, Manchu, Sibe) and south-central (Nanai, Olcha, Orok, Udehe, Oroch) languages, whereby he considers the southern languages to be closer to each other than to the northern ones. Menges proposes a transitional group (Negidal, Solon, Oroch, Udehe) between the southern (Jurchen, Manchu, Sibe, Nanai, Olcha, Orok) and the northern languages (Evenki, Negidal, Solon, Even).

The second interpretation of Tungusic internal taxonomy is one in which the separation of Manchuric from the other Tungusic languages is among the earliest splits in the family. A tripartition similar to Avrorin's, but different because the northern (Evenki, Negidal, Solon, Even) and southern (Nanai, Olcha, Orok, Udehe, Oroch) Tungusic languages are considered to be closer to each other than to the Manchuric languages is proposed by Sunik (1959: 333–335) and Vasilevič (1960: 44). Their classification is similar to Doerfer's (1978: 5) analysis, followed by Whaley et al. (1999: 291), except for the fact that Doerfer and Whaley regard the southern Tungusic languages as transitional between the northern and the Manchuric languages. Vovin (1993: 102) also proposes an early breakup between Manchuric and the rest of Tungusic, but in his view, the Tungusic branch is later separated into an Evenic (Even) and a non-Ewenic branch, which in its turn splits into Ewenki, Negidal and Solon in the west and Nanai, Olcha, Orok, Udehe and Oroch in the east. Finally, Ikegami (1974) proposed a four-partite classification, distinguishing between as much as four branches, i.e. Manchuric, Evenic (Evenki, Negidal, Solon, Even), Nanaic (Nanai, Olcha, Orok) and Udeheic (Oroch, Udehe). In Figure 4, I have represented the view adhered by most historical linguists today, agreeing that the Manchu branch of Tungusic is sufficiently distinct to warrant its early segregation from other groups.

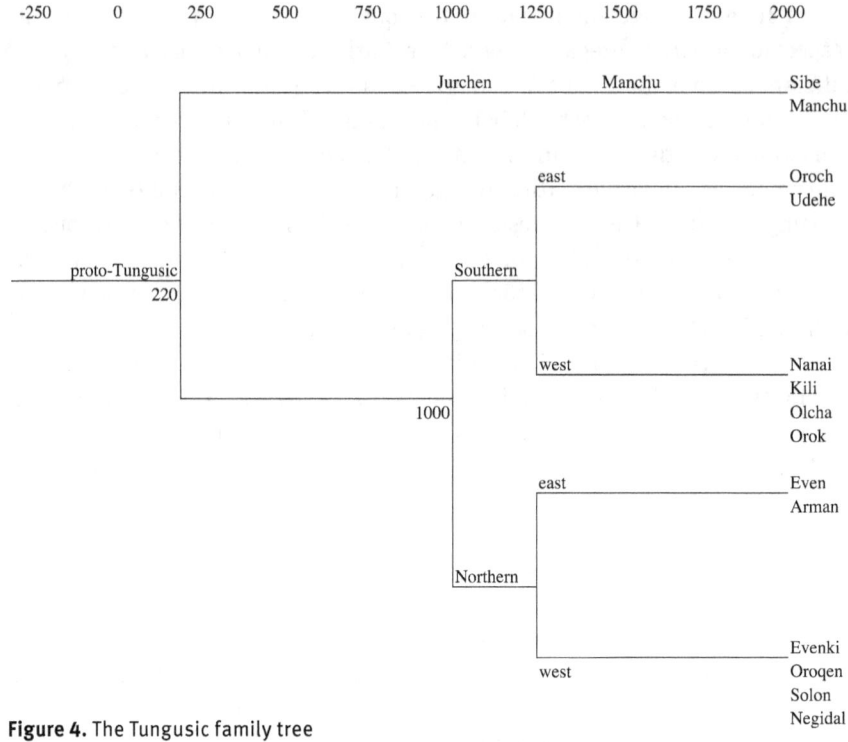

Figure 4. The Tungusic family tree

Jurchen was the official language of the Jin dynasty of Northern China and Manchuria (1115–1234). Written materials in Jurchen, preserved in a partially deciphered native script and dating from the 12th till the 16th centuries, imply that the language was the immediate ancestor of Manchu, the official language of the Qing dynasty (1644–1911). Among the ethnic Manchu in China today, there are fewer than 50 speakers left, living in the northern Heilongjiang province. However, a Manchu dialect, Sibe, has survived in the Xinjiang province, where it is still spoken by about 30,000 people. An innovation supporting the early separation of Tungusic proper from the Manchuric branch is the lenition of intervocalic *-b- in Tungusic proper, for instance in the verb 'put, place', e.g. Ma. *tebu-* versus Even *tew-*, Evk. *tew-*, Neg. *tew(u)-*, Oroch *tewu-/ teu-*, Ud. *teu-*, Na. *teu-*, Olch. *tew-či-*, Orok *tewe- / teu-*.

The modern distribution of Tungusic is largely the result of the split between the northern and the southern languages, which began about a millennium ago, when the northern languages spread from the Middle Amur region over the whole of Siberia, from the Okhotsk Sea in the east to the Yenisei basin in the west, and from Lake Baikal in the south to the Arctic Ocean in the north. An innovation reflecting the separation from the southern Tungusic languages is the deletion of final high vowels *-i, *-ï, *-u, *-ü in northern Tungusic, for instance in the word for 'head', e.g. Na. jïlï, Ud. dili, Olch. dïlï, Orok jïlï, Oroch dili versus Even dïl, Evk. dil, del, Neg. dïl, Solon dil(i). The innovation whereby word-initial pTg *p- lenited to h-, x- or ø in Northern Tungusic as opposed to its original retention in the Manchuric and in the southern Tungusic branch also indicates that northern Tungusic constitutes a separate branch. This can be illustrated by the reflexes in the word for 'lip': Evk. hemun, Even hemen, Neg. xemun, Solon emme vs. Ma. femen, Sibe femən, Na. pemü, Olch. pemu(n), Orok pemu(n), Oroch xemu(n) and Ud. xemu(n). Note, however, that the common retention of pTg *p- in Manchuric and southern Tungusic does not necessarily suggest that these branches once formed a single unit. The lenition of Old Jurchen p- to Jurchen and Manchu f- and the lenition of southern Tungusic p- in northeastern Tungusic (see below) in the course of the histories of these individual branches are to be considered as independent developments.

Northern Tungusic can further be divided into a northeastern group consisting of Even and Arman and a northwestern group consisting of Evenki, Oroqen, Solon and Negidal. Whereas the northeastern Tungusic languages preserve palatal fricatives c and j in word-final position, the northwestern languages have merged these fricatives into a dental stop -t, for instance in the word for 'girl' (e.g. Even huna:j and Arman ona:j versus Evk. huna:t, Neg. hona:t). Even, also known as Lamut, is spoken by fewer than 7,000 speakers, scattered over a vast area from Kamchatka and the Sea of Okhotsk in the east to the River Lena in the west, and from the Arctic coast in the north to the River Aldan in the south. In some classifications (Cincius 1949, Benzing 1955a, Doerfer 1978), Arman is regarded as a distinct language, but it is usually considered a dialect of Even. Evenki, in Russian terminology, corresponds to a population of fewer than 5000 Siberian Evenki speakers in the Krasnoyarsk region and on Sakhalin. Oroqen, spoken by roughly 2,000 people in Inner Mongolia, is usually treated as a dialect of Evenki, but Whaley (1999) treats it as a single language. Solon, called "Ewenke" in Chinese terminology, comprises about 20,000 speakers, spread over Inner Mongolia and northern Mongolia. Negidal is spoken by fewer than 150 aged speakers, living along the lower reaches of the Amur River.

The southern Tungusic languages in Russia's Far East can be divided in a western group comprising Nanai, Kili, Olcha and Orok and an eastern group with Oroch and Udehe. An innovation that reflects this separation is the lenition of the initial labial stop p- in northeastern Tungusic, for instance in the word for 'lip' (e.g. Na. pemü, Olch. pemu(n), Orok pemu(n) versus Oroch xemu(n) and Ud. xemu(n)). Nanai, also known as Goldi, is spoken by fewer than 4,000 speakers living near the confluence of the Amur and Ussuri rivers and in the Amur

Valley below Khabarovsk, and to a much smaller extent in China's Heilongjiang province, where it is known as Hezhe. Kili is usually regarded as a dialect of Nanai, but Doerfer (1978) suggests that it is a distinct language. Olcha is spoken by about 700 people along the Amur river and its tributaries. Orok has fewer than 70 adult speakers in the Poronaysk district of Sakhalin. Oroch has about 260 speakers on the estuary of some rivers that drain into the Strait of Tatary and near Kosmokolsk on the Amur. Udehe is spoken by 230 people in the south of the Khabarovsk Krai and in the Primorsky Krai.

1.2.2.4 Koreanic

It is a documented fact that two language families, Koreanic and Japanic, were once simultaneously present on the Korean peninsula. Their coexistence was discontinued when Japanic relocated to the Japanese Islands in the first millennium BC and when the Koreanic expansion unified the languages of the Korean Peninsula from the seventh century AD onwards. The cultural and linguistic homogeneity of the Korean Peninsula as we know it today is thus relatively recent.

Recent archaeobotanical studies show that Setaria and Panicum millet agriculture has spread from the Liaodong region to the north-western part Korean peninsula in the first half of fourth millennium BC (Crawford & Lee 2003, Miyamoto 2009). From there, millet agriculture gradually spread to the eastern and southern coasts of the peninsula. Miyamoto further proposes a second dispersion adding dry field rice cultivation to the millets; it spreads from Shandong through the Liaodong peninsula to the south of the Korean peninsula in the second half of the third millennium BCE. However, Ahn (2010) finds that the evidence for early dry-rice cultivation in the Korean peninsula is inconclusive. If the scenario of early millet dispersal is correct, Koreanic may represent an earlier, pre-rice cultivation dispersion from the Liaodong peninsula.

The transition from the Chulmun (6000–1300 BC) period to the Mumun (1300 BC-0) period, corresponding to the Bronze and Early Iron ages is marked by a change in subsistence and material culture. In the late second millennium BC rice was introduced to Korea via the Shandong and Liaodong peninsulas (Miyamoto 2009, Ahn 2010), along with other crops such as barley and wheat. New cultural elements, including agricultural tools such as reaping knives and stone adzes, bronze implements, and burials such as dolmen and stone cist, appear to have diffused from Liaodong along with the crops. Traces of Mumun occupations have been found as far south as the Nam River in present-day Jinju, Pusan and Ulsan. This agricultural dispersion may be associated with the entry of the Japanic language family into the Korean peninsula (see Section 1.2.2.5).

In the Proto-Three Kingdoms period (1–300), the northeastern Peninsula fell under the Han dynasty tributary system, whereas the south was divided into three regions known as the Samhan or 'Three Han': Mahan in the west, Pyonhan in the Nakdong River valley in the center, and Chinhan in the east. Of these, the largest and strongest region was Mahan with its 54 polities. Later, in the Three Kingdoms period (300–668), it was conquered by Puyo-Koguryoic peoples and became Paekche. The information we have about the language of Paekche is derived from the following sources: place names recorded in the *Samguk Sagi* ('Historical Records of the Three Kingdoms' 1145), one verse recorded in the *Samguk Yusa* ('Recollections of the Three Kingdoms' 1285) that has been attributed to a Paekche prince, and 42 Paekche words preserved in an Old Japanese source, the *Nihon Shoki* ('Chronicles of Japan' 720). Most reconstructed Paekche words have correspondences with Middle Korean vocabulary, suggesting that the Paekche language is closely related to the Silla language (Bentley 2000). A small number of words come in doublets consisting of one word from native Paekche and one that may be Puyo-Koguryoic in origin. This strengthens the claim made by Kōno (1987) that two languages were spoken in Paekche, i.e. one related to Koguryo, which was spoken by the ruling class, and one related to Silla Korean, which was spoken by their subjects. Chinese historical sources confirm that the ruling class and the common people called their king by different names.

The second Han was Pyonhan. This group, consisting of 12 small polities in the center of the southern peninsular coast, became known as Kaya in the Three Kingdoms period. The Pyonhan people spoke a language that was different from that of the Chinhan, according to the *Houhanshu* (HHS 85: 2820), although the *San-kuo chih* claims the opposite is true (SKC 30: 853). The *Houhanshu* further states that the Pyonhan people are close to Wa, the ethnonym for the inhabitants of the Japanese Islands. Besides, some Pyonhan toponyms are reminiscent of proto-Japonic (Bentley 1998). Apart from toponyms, metalinguistic remarks in Chinese historical sources and a small number of words in the Nihon Shoki that might be of Kaya origin (Kōno 1987), we have no direct information on the language of Kaya. While it seems likely that some languages of Kaya were related to the other Han languages, it cannot be excluded that pockets of Japanic speakers, who had moved to the southern tip of the Korean Peninsula in the first millennium BC, were still present.

The area of Chinhan that harboured twelve polities, became Silla in the Three Kingdoms period. The Silla language is believed to be the direct ancestor of Middle Korean and thus of the language spoken in Korea today. Since Silla was the kingdom where the political and the linguistic unification of the Korean Peninsula started in 668, its language is relatively better documented than the other Han languages. A few examples of Silla language were found in engraved inscriptions. The *Samguk Sagi* and the *Samguk Yusa* further contain toponyms, proper names and the names of government offices, which are also scattered in Japanese and Chinese historical sources. The *Samguk Yusa*, along with the appended biography of the priest Kyunyŏ, also contains 24 verses written by Silla poets between 600 and 879 AD.

When the Koryŏ dynasty (918–1392) was established, the ancient Silla capital was moved from Kyŏngju in the southeast to Kaesŏng, in the center of the peninsula, near to present-day Seoul. Thus, the central variety of the language became the standard language, which it still is today. Early Middle Korean (918–1446) represents the stage starting with the move to Kaesŏng and lasting until the promulgation of the Korean Hangŭl script. Although the new writing system had little effect on how the language developed, it drastically changed our linguistic knowledge of Middle Korean. The principal sources of Early Middle Korean, the *Kyerim Yusa* ('Recollections of the Cock Forest' 1103) and the *Hyangyak Kugŭppang* ('Collection of Local Medicine' 1250) were written in Chinese characters, whose interpretation remains somewhat unclear. A systematic and accurate transcription of the Korean language started with the Hangŭl texts of the Late Middle Korean period (1446–1592). Contemporary Korean, the standard language spoken by roughly 70 million speakers in both North and South Korea today, can be seen as the direct descendant of Middle Korean.

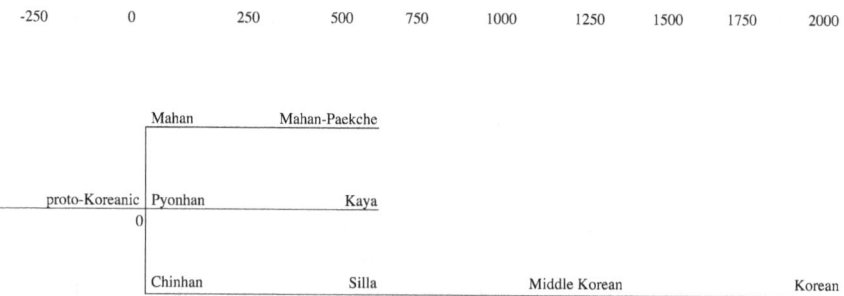

Figure 5. The Koreanic family tree

1.2.2.5 Japanic

In this volume, I distinguish between Japanic on the one hand and Japonic on the other. Following Janhunen (1996a: 77–78, 80–81, 1999: 2), I use the term "Japanic" in reference to a genealogical unity that comprises the historical continental varieties of the Japanese language as well as the varieties spoken on the Japanese Islands, including the Ryukyu Islands. The label "Japonic", coined by Serafim, is usually restricted to a branch of Japanic, namely the language family composed of Mainland Japanese and the Ryukyuan languages (Bentley 2008: 23, Vovin 2008a: 5).

Irrespective of one's stance on the Transeurasian hypothesis, the continental derivation of Japanic is well supported by both extra- and meta-linguisic evidence. Although some crops such as millet and soybean were introduced in Korea overland from northeastern China and Manchuria, the source of domesticated rice is south-central China (Crawford & Shen 1998). Recent archaeobotanical studies such as Crawford & Lee (2003: 92–93), Miyamoto (2009: 27–28), Ahn (2010: 92) show that the spread of wet rice agriculture to Korea and Japan begins in Shandong, crosses via the Liaodong peninsula, reaches the Korean peninsula around 1300 BC and the Japanese islands after 1000 BC. From a linguistic standpoint, it may be associated with the entry of the Japanic language family into the Korean peninsula, and subsequently with the advent of Japonic in the Japanese islands (Beckwith 2004: 35–36; Unger 2005, 2009; Whitman 2011: 149).

According to Sagart (2011: 127) it is not unlikely that wet rice agriculture was transmitted to the Japanic people by the Setaria- and rice-based pre-Austronesian Dawenkou culture (4100–2600 BC) in south Shandong. In his model, Dawenkou farmers spoke a language ancestral to proto-Austronesian, which would have had for 'rice ready to cook ' a cognate of proto-Austronesian *Semay. If one assumes that the sibilant at the beginning of this word changed to *h-*, a frequent change cross-linguistically, this word is a probable model for OJ $kome_2$ 'dehusked rice' < pJ *kəmai, given that proto-Japonic had no *h-* sound and treats foreign /h/ as k. Apart from rice agriculture, the practice of tooth evulsion, a puberty rite whereby the lateral incisors are extracted, may also have been part of the contact package. Having originated in Dawenkou in ca. 4000 BC (Han & Nakahashi 1996), the practice was introduced to Japan by Yayoi people (Brace & Nagai 1982: 405). Any Dawenkou or Japanic people left behind in the greater Shandong region after the spread of wet rice agriculture to Korea were absorbed by the expansion of Sinitic, without a trace of their languages remaining there. The absence of common rice vocabulary between Japanese and Korean puts the split of Japanic and Koreanic before 2600 BC, the end of Dawenkou culture. Such an early date is in line with the divergent nature of the Japano-Koreanic cognates.

Unger (2005) holds an alternative view, identifying the wet-rice agriculturists living on the Shandong peninsula before the spread of rice agriculture to the Korean peninsula and the Japanese islands as proto-Samhan-Wa, the ancestors of Koreanic and Japonic. Problems with this view are the absence of common rice vocabulary in Japanese and Korean, the linguistic divergence between both languages, and the time frame. If the proto-Samhan-Wa were responsible for spreading rice agriculture to the Korean peninsula, Koreanic and Japonic must have split on the Korean peninsula after 1300 BC. This is in contradiction with Unger's (2012) assumption that, in view of their linguistic divergence, Koreanic and Japanic separated no later than the first half of the second millennium BC. The present framework places the split of Koreanic and Japanic no later than the third millennium BC, which is more realistic given their divergence and the assumed Dawenkou-Japanic contact. Furthermore, Ungers view cannot account for the relative closeness of the Koguryo material to Japanese and for the Gilyak features in Koreanic.

Rejecting earlier views that wet rice cultivation was introduced into the Korean peninsula from the south, Ahn (2010: 92–93) suggests that it entered from Liaodong into the central west part of the Korean peninsula and gradually spread to southwest regions. In the northeast climatic and soil conditions were unsuitable for its cultivation and in the southeast the popularity of dry-field crops was higher than rice. From a linguistic standpoint, the settlements of rice cultivators can perhaps be associated with the pockets of Japanic speakers in Pyonhan, the center of the southern peninsular coast, discussed in Section 1.2.2.4.

Evidence for the presence of other Japanic languages on the Korean peninsula is provided by a small corpus of so-called Koguryo toponyms recorded in the *Samguk Sagi*, which refer to places on the former territory of Koguryo. The phonograms used in these toponyms transcribe words more closely relatable to Japonic than to Koreanic. Some scholars (Beckwith 2004, Blažek 2009, Lee & Ramsey 2011) take these toponyms to represent the Koguryo language, whereas others (Whitman 2002: 263, 2011: 153–154, Janhunen 2005b, Unger 2005 and Toh 2005) suggest that the toponyms transcribe indigenous names from different languages other than the own Koguryo language. Nevertheless, there is a relative consensus among linguistic scholarship to take the Samguk Sagi toponyms as a linguistic indication that a Japanic language was once spoken on the Korean peninsula.

Apart from these toponyms, there is an inscription on the Kwanggaet'o wang stele, a monument erected on the occasion of the death of the 19th king of Koguryo in 414 AD, but this has not entirely been deciphered yet nor does it reveal much information on the language spoken in Koguryo. As for textual evidence, unlike the 25 Old Korean poems written in the languages of Paekche or Silla, no Koguryo hyangga have been preserved. Based on the questionable assumption that Koguryo was the dominant language spoken in the Mohe Tungusic polity of Parhae (Reckel 1995, Hong 2010) after the Koguryo decline in 667 AD, Vovin (2005: 110–114) reconstructed Koguryo loanwords in Jurchen and Manchu, but these can be dismissed as evidence for the Koguryo language

(Robbeets 2007c: 119–120). In this earlier study, I characterized the Koguryo data as scarce, fragmentary and speculative. Nonetheless the data seem to reflect a unitary language that is genealogically closer to Japanese than to Korean, or to any other known Transeurasian language.

Occupying the southernmost fringe of Puyo territory, the Koguryo people were first attested in the western part of present-day Liaoning Province, west of the Liaodong Peninsula, roughly the area between the Liao river and present-day Tianjin. Byington (2004) identifies the ancient Puyo state (ca. 300 BC – 346 AD) with the modern city of Jilin as its capital, as the first state-level polity to emerge in the region to the northeast of Han China. The Koguryo people were in contact with the Chinese, the Xianbei and the Xiongnu, as can be inferred from an account dating to the time of the Han Dynasty usurper Wang Mang, ordering them to attack the Xiongnu in 12 AD.

Beckwith (2004: 35–36) further suggests that the ancestors of the Ye-Maek state of eastern Korea, may have moved to the Liaodong Peninsula and northern Korea by land, founding the polity known as Chosŏn under the leadership of Wiman in the second and first centuries BC. The Samguk Sagi and the Chinese sources mention that the Ye-Maek were located to the south of Okchŏ, east of Koguryo, and north of Silla in the Three Kingdoms Period. According to the *San-kuo chih* their language was similar to that of Koguryo and Puyo (SKC 30: 848). Other, presumably Japanic, people moved to the Sungari Basin to found the Puyo kingdom by the beginning of the Eastern Han, between the presumably Mongolic Xianbei in the west and the presumably Tungusic Yilou in the east. Later, the Koguryo and related people such as the Okchŏ moved into Liaodong, southern Manchuria and Korea by land. In the Three Kingdoms Period the Koguryo people were located east of the Liaodong Peninsula, north of the Han people and the Ye-Maek, and west of the Okchŏ, who lived on the northeast coast of the sea of Japan. According to the Chinese sources, the Okchŏ spoke a language related to that of Koguryo (SKC 30: 846; HHS 85: 2816). The latest to move were the Puyo-Paekche, who conquered the Mahan area in the mid-fourth century. As far as the languages of the Puyo, the Ye-Maek, the Okchŏ and the Puyo-Paekche are concerned we can only rely on metalinguistic information, mainly in Chinese historical sources.

Summarizing, the above extra- and metalinguistic considerations lead to the postulation of a proto-Japano-Koreanic unity, based in the Liaoning area, branching off no later than the third millennium BC into a Japanic and a Koreanic branch. The Koreanic people went northeastwards, towards the Manchurian coast of the Sea of Japan. The Japanic people, being the linguistic ancestors of the Puyo people remained in the area, except for one group that went southwards, to the north of the Shandong peninsula. In the second millennium BC the

Japanic people from Shandong entered the Korean peninsula with rice agriculture, whereas the descendants of the Puyo Japanic entered Korea only in the late first millennium BC.

Until the 1980s, the literature on the population history of the Japanese Islands was marked by controversy. However, with the advances of population genetics during the last decades, the continental migration theory is now supported by the majority of scholars. Among geneticists there is a relative agreement that Ainu and Ryukyuan people have a shared genetic ancestry reflecting indigenous Jomon genes, while mainland Japanese people are the result of admixture between indigenous Jomon (10000 BC – 1000 BC) and immigrating Yayoi (1000 BC – 300 AD) from the Korean peninsula (Hanihara 1991, Omoto & Saitou 1997, Jinam et al 2012: 793).[1] The indigenous Jomon evolved from hunter-gatherers crossing paleolithic land bridges and coming from Central Asia (Hammer et al. 2006), Northeast Asia (Omoto & Saitou 1997) and Southeast Asia (Hanihara 1991). Recent studies of autosomal DNA, such as Jinam et al 2012 find that Mainland Japanese is phylogenetically closest to Korean, followed by Tungusic and Mongolic populations in northeast Asia (i.e. Oroqen, Nanai, Dagur and Khalkha Mongolian) and then followed by the populations in southern China.

Population-based comparisons of mtDNA (Kivisild et al. 2002, Tanaka et al. 2004, Gokcumen et al 2008: 286, Dulik et al. 2012) find a maternal connection between Mainland Japanese and other Transeurasian populations, especially in the subhaplogroup D4 and D5c, the subhalogroups M8a, C, and Z and the Haplogroup M10. Tanaka and his team find that Mainland Japanese have the closest genetic affinity to Koreans, followed by Han from Shandong and Liaoning, then, Mongolian, Monguor (Qinghai/Gansu) and Han from Xinjiang and finally, Central Asian Turkic populations such as Uighur, Kazakh and Kirghiz.

Comparisons of Y-chromosonal DNA (Hammer et al. 2006, Rootsi et al 2007) find that the haplogroup N1 is particularly frequent in the Altai region and to a lesser extent in Manchuria and Korea and marginally in Mainland Japanese, while it is absent in Ainu and Ryukyan. This seems to be a haplogroup that connects the Transeurasian populations

The findings from genetics can be taken as evidence of the migration of a Northeast Asian population, which pushed the Jōmon-genes towards the peripheries in Japan, notably to Hokkaido in the North and the Ryukyus in the South. The modern Japanese are primarily derived from Yayoi immigrants with a regionally variable degree of Jōmon admixture. This dichotomy is further

---

[1] Traditionally the date of the Jōmon-Yayoi transition was set on 300 BC, but the revised date is ca. 1000 BC (Harunari & Imamura 2004; Habu 2004: 258).

confirmed by physical antrophology including osteological measurements and dental analyses.

The continental migration is also supported by archeological evidence. The Jōmon people formed a pre-agricultural society, hunting, fishing and collecting nuts and berries to survive. There was no broad-scale agriculture. Similar to the Chulmun-Mumun transition in Korea around 1500 BC, the Jōmon-Yayoi transition around 1000 BC is marked by drastic agricultural intensification, including the importation of wet-rice agriculture via the Korean peninsula. Apart from rice and other crops, Korean influences evidenced on Japanese archeological sites include pottery, stone and wooden agricultural tools, remains of domesticated pigs, ditched settlements and megalith burials. In line with studies such as Harunari (1990), Barnes (1993), Nelson (1993), Hudson (1999), Crawford & Shen (1998) and Crawford & Lee (2003), it is possible to posit an agricultural shift between Jōmon and Yayoi. Since the Jōmon-Yayoi transition represents the formative period for the Japanese people, genes and culture, language may have been involved as well. It seems plausibe to link the Jōmon-Yayoi revolution with the advent of Japonic speakers in Japan.

A reasonable estimate for the first arrival of rice in Japan is 1000 BC. Over the following 500 years, evidence of rice cultivation gradually accumulated, but this was mainly limited to north Kyushu. It is reasonable to assume that, during this period, Japonic diversified into a number of dialects. The following Yayoi period saw the development of full-scale agriculture along with a significant population expansion from Kyushu across western and eastern Japan. In the Initial Yayoi period (ca. 400 – 300 BC), Yayoi culture spread through much of western Japan, and in the Early Yayoi (ca. 300–100 BC) it reached parts of the eastern archipelago, as far as present-day Aomori prefecture. This time frame gives us an indication of the date when Mainland Japanese is likely to have branched off from the rest of Japonic.

Mainland Japanese separated into Central Japanese and Eastern Japanese before the seventh century. The large majority of the historically attested and contemporary varieties of Japanese derive from Central Japanese. Some sources dating to the late seventh and the eighth centuries, such as in *Man'yōshū* Book XIV and XX and in the *Hitachi Fudoki*, however, provide poems in Eastern Old Japanese. This was a dialect spoken in eastern Japan – the so-called 'Azuma' region – contemporaneously with the variety known as (Western) Old Japanese, which is the language of the bulk of the extant Old Japanese corpus. The area in which Eastern Old Japanese was spoken was centered on the Musashi Plain and extended at least from the provinces of modern Ibaraki in the northeast to modern Shizuoka in the southwest (Ikier 2006: 4–7). However, in the course of history, Central Japanese expanded considerably, pushing the descendants of the speakers of Eastern Old Japanese to the Hachijō Islands. In other words, the modern Northeastern dialects are not descendants of Eastern Old Japanese but of Central Japanese.

The ancestor of the languages now spoken in the Ryukyuan Islands is thought to have remained in northeastern Kyushu until around 900 AD, when full-scale agriculture was introduced in the Ryukyus. The crucial issue here is that the time of separation of proto-Ryukyuan from Mainland Japanese does not coincide with the spread of Ryukyuan speakers to the Ryukyu Islands. As for the break-up of proto-Ryukyuan many authors point to the early centuries AD (Hattori 1976: 43: between 0 and 500 AD, Heinrich 1994: 185: between 300 BC and 700 AD, Hudson 2002: 313: ca. 500 AD, Serafim 2008: 98: before 700 AD, Unger 2009: 104–105: later than 100 AD). These relatively late dates seem to reflect the spread of proto-Ryukyuan to the Ryukyuan Islands and its simultaneous break-up, rather than the separation of proto-Ryukyuan from Mainland Japanese. Frellesvig and Whitman's (2008) theory of mid-vowel raising in pre-Old Japanese implies that Ryukyuan must have split off considerably earlier than the first half of the sixth century. Words such as OJ *tera* 'Buddhist temple' and OJ *poto₂ke₂* 'Buddha', probably borrowed shortly after the introduction of Buddhism in Japan, indicate that the raising of *e* (pJ *$*e$ > OJ *i*) was completed by that time. Ryukyuan, however, preserves the original vowel (pJ *$*e$ = pR *$*e$) in a number of cases, for instance in the word for 'water', OJ *midu* versus pR *$*mezı$ (Serafim 2008: 85–86). While 500 AD constitutes an upper limit for the separation of Mainland Japanese, the archeological framework suggests that it is more likely to have occurred in the early centuries BC. This chronological estimation is in line with Lee and Hasegawa's (2011) Bayesian phylogenetic analysis, dating proto-Japonic at 182 BC. In sum, proto-Ryukyuan was spoken on Kyushu for some time until proto-Ryukyuan speakers moved southward to settle in the Ryukyu Islands.

The ancestor of the languages spoken in the Ryukyu Islands is thought to have spread from Kyushu sometime around 900 AD. Asato and Doi (1999) present evidence in favor of the hypothesis that the Ryukyuans and their language and culture came from Kyushu in what Asato has termed the proto-Gusuku period, starting around that time. The shift between the preceding Shell-Midden period and the proto-Gusuku period involved marked agricultural intensification and an influx of morphologically different people similar to the medieval Japanese mainlanders. This is reminiscent of the Jōmon-Yayoi transition discussed above. Serafim (2003: 471–473; 2008: 98–99), Bentley (2008: 27), de Boer (2005: 13) and Unger (2009: 101–105) find linguistic support for the assumption that Ryukyuan derived from a dialect once spoken in the northeastern part of Kyushu adjacent to the strait opposite from Yamaguchi Prefecture. Some innovations shared by

Ryukyuan and the northeastern Kyushu dialects suggest that Ryukyuan may have been derived from an early northeastern Kyushu dialect, separated from Mainland Japanese. Serafim points, for instance, to the assibilation of nominalizers and in the merger of the middle bigrade verb catgory. Whereas Old Japanese has preserved the original opposition between the root final vowel of verbs such as oki_2- 'arise' and uke_2- 'float (tr.)', proto-Ryukyuan verbs such as *oke- and *uke- have neutralized this distinction. A similar merger has occurred in the dialects of northeastern Kyushu, which have oke- and uke-, respectively.

De Boer finds evidence in the main accent types in Japan, which are distributed in a concentric pattern around Kyoto, suggesting that the dialects on the periphery may have preserved features that were lost in the center as a result of innovations. One such peripheral circle is represented by the Tokyo Gairin type accent, distributed over 4 widely separated blocks in the northeast of Honshū, in the centre of Honshū, in the west of Honshū, and in the northeast of Kyūshū. De Boer (2005: 164) argues that "The vast majority of the pitch shapes in the Ryūkyū Islands can be explained by a gradual spreading of pitch to the right, taking a Gairin Tōkyō type pitch as the starting point." This is consistent with the derivation of Ryukyuan from an early northeastern Kyushu dialect. Unger (2009: 105–106, 2011) does not exclude the possibility "that a proto-Ryūkyūan reconstruction may actually reflect an early convergence of two or more dialects brought by founder populations to different islands in the Ryūkyū chain at slightly different times", but there is little linguistic support for such a viewpoint.

If this model with Kyushu as the incubator for the development of Japonic is accurate, one would expect a much higher degree of linguistic variation in Kyushu than in the rest of Japan, similar to the internal diversity among the Formosan languages, which is greater than that in all the rest of Austronesian because the Austronesian expansion started from Taiwan. Since such diversity is obviously not the case, it must be assumed that heavy dialectal borrowing from Old and Middle Japanese resulted in the convergence of the varieties in Kyushu. The diffusion of the standard in the historical period must also have led to the obliteration of many of the features of the northeastern Kyushu dialects, that were initially shared with Ryukyuan.

Ryukyuan can be divided into a northern group, including the mutually intelligible Amami and Okinawa dialects, and a southern group called Sakishima, including the mutually unintelligible languages of Miyako, Yaeyama and Yonaguni (Pellard 2009, Shimoji 2010). The large expanse of open water between Okinawa and Miyako forms the geographical boundary between both groups. A phonological innovation that separates the Sakishima languages from the other Ryukyuan languages is the secondary voicing of the velar before *a and *u, for instance in the word for 'cave', e.g. Hirara *gama*, Ishigaki *gama*, Yonaguni *ga:ma* versus Shodon, Shuri *kama*. Northern Okinawa and Amami dialects share an innovation that separates them from the rest of the Okinawa dialects, namely secondary aspiration in relation to vowel height, for instance in the word for 'tree', e.g. Shuri *kii* versus Shodon *khii*. The literature disagrees on the exact position of Yonaguni within Ryukyuan taxonomy, but Bentley (2008: 237–242) classifies it as one of the three Sakishima branches. Although the southern languages were less affected by language contact than the northern ones, it is important to note that all Ryukyuan languages were and continue to be heavily influenced by Japanese.

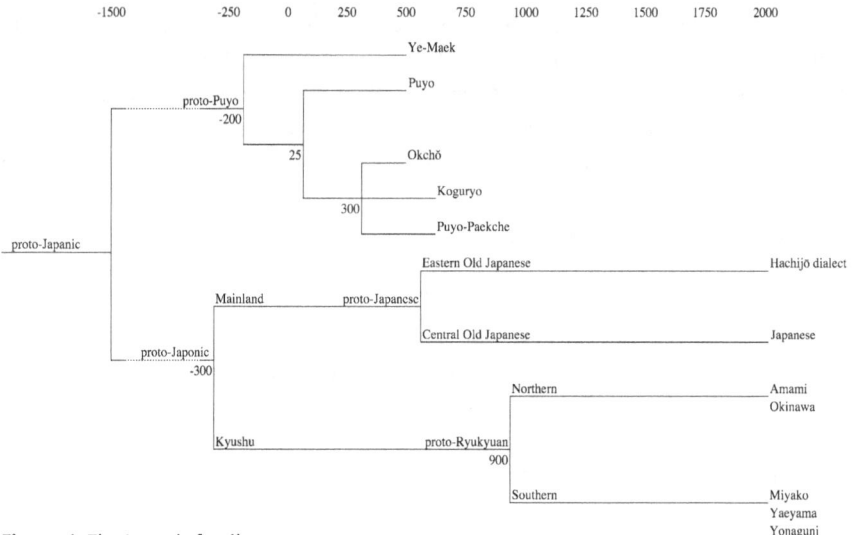

Figure 6. The Japanic family tree

1.2.3 The Transeurasian hypothesis

As such, the internal taxonomy yields ample ethnohistorical evidence for situating the five original speech communities of Turkic, Mongolic, Tungusic, Koreanic and Japanic in a rather compact area comprising North Korea, Southern Manchuria and present-day Southeastern Mongolia. The inevitable question is whether these families have always been genealogically distinct or whether they can ultimately be traced to one common ancestor. My previous research in comparative phonology and lexicon (Robbeets 2004a, 2004b, 2005, 2008, 2009b) has shown that the majority of etymologies proposed in support of a genealogical relationship between the Transeurasian languages are at least questionable. However, whereas similar observations have led to the wholesale rejection of the Transeurasian hypothesis, I have demonstrated that there is nonetheless a core of reliable etymologies that makes it possible to classify Transeurasian as a valid genealogical grouping. Shared innovations in phonology and (basic) vocabulary suggest the classification for the Transeurasian family, given in Figure 7.

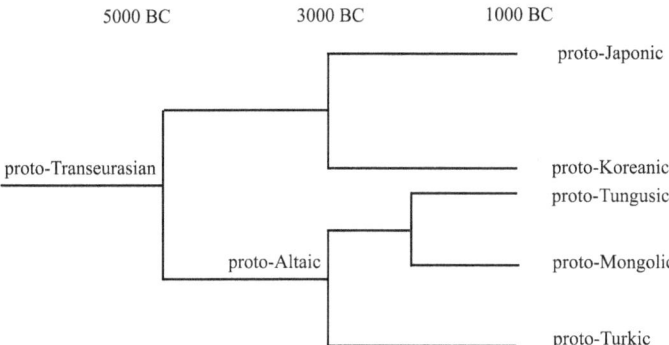

Figure 7. Hypothesized classification of the Transeurasian family

In the region of prehistoric Manchuria, where the original speech communities of Turkic, Mongolic, Tungusic, Koreanic and Japanic are situated, the predominant basis of life since the 7th millennium BC has been sedentary millet agriculture, supplemented by fishing, hunting and gathering in the surrounding woodlands (Barnes 1993: 92–107, Nelson 1995: 251–253, Janhunen 1996: 220). In the western part of this region, which is ecologically transitional towards Mongolia, nomadic pastoralism developed as an innovation after 2000 BC, probably as a response to increasing aridity. The Siberian expansion of the Tungusic speakers, which began only about a millennium ago may have led to a reversion to foraging along with reindeer breeding.

A plausible hypothesis about the homeland of the speakers of the ancestral language is correlating the Transeurasian homeland with the early Neolithic Xinglongwa culture (6200–5400 BC) that was situated on the border of Inner Mongolia and Manchuria. This assumption contradicts the hypothesis that locates the homeland in the Altai mountains and identifies the linguistic dispersal with nomadic expansions starting around 2000 BC, a theory which initially inspired the coining of the name "Altaic" and was later advocated by, among others, Menges (1977) and Miller (1990). It further challenges Starostin's (2008) proposal to associate the homeland with the Neolithic Yangshao (5000–2000 BC) culture along the central Yellow River.

Assuming a model in which Xinglongwa culture (6200–5400 BC) is linguistically associated with proto-Transeurasian, it is further conceivable to correlate Hongshan (4700–2900 BC) with Altaic, Lower Xiajiadian (2200–1600 BC) with

Mongolo-Tungusic and Upper Xiajiadian (1000–600 BC) with Tungusic. There are indications of a certain cultural continuity between the different Neolithic cultures of Neolithic Manchuria, whereas they clearly differ from the Peiligang (7000–5000 BC), Yangshao (5000–3000 BC) and Dawenkou (4100–2600 BC) assemblages of the Yellow River (Nelson 1995).

Given the ethnolinguistic picture, there are three extralinguistic indications of the hypothesis that the Transeurasian languages are related, i.e. (i) the late date of separation, (ii) Manchuria's high family density ratio, and (iii) the apparent unity of Neolithic culture in Manchuria.

First, consistent with the Farming/Language Dispersal Hypothesis, the formation and separation of the major language families of East Asia has been associated with the Neolithic revolution. This hypothesis, proposed by Bellwood & Renfrew (2002), Diamond & Bellwood (2003) and Bellwood (2005a, 2011), posits that many of the world's major language families owe their dispersal to the adoption of agriculture by their early speakers. Subsequent population growth steadily pushed the new farmers and their language into wider territories, displacing the languages of preexisting hunter gatherer populations. Since East Asia is home to one of the world's nine homelands of agriculture (Diamond & Bellwood 2003: 597), farming might seem an obvious explanation for this region's major language expansions. It has indeed been suggested that the Austroasiatic, Sino-Tibetan and Austronesian families spread and separate at different times between ca. 6000 and 4000 BC from agricultural homelands in China (e.g. Bellwood 2005b, Blench 2008, Sagart 2008, Sagart 2011, Fiskesjö & Hsing 2011, van Driem 2012, Heggarty & Beresford-Jones 2014).

The problem with the assumption of five distinct families in Manchuria is that the earliest linguistic differentiation started much later. As shown in the sections on the individual taxonomy, the first internal splits are assumed to have taken place in the first millennium BC or later. The hypothesis of a Transeurasian family separating around 5000 BC, consistent with the final stages of Xinglongwa culture, would conform to the Neolithic separation of language families in Eurasia and would account for the relatively short timespan of linguistic sub-differentiation in Manchuria.[2]

Second, we must explain why a compact area such as Manchuria attracted an exceptionally large number of distinct language families, compared to other regions in Eurasia, even though it offers no striking regional advantages. Janhunen (1996a: 219) suggests that "the rate of ethnic extinction has been lower

---

[2] Remark that this paleolinguistic dating is in line with the lexicostatistical dating proposed in Starostin et al. (2003: 234) and Blažek (2009: 24), estimating the first separation around 4750 BC.

in Manchuria than in those parts of Eurasia." Although a low extinction rate may have been the reason why the Caucasus region harbors so many different language families, leading to the designation "Mountain of Languages", the fluvial plains of Manchuria cannot be compared with the isolated mountain regions in the Caucasus. Therefore, it is difficult to understand how Manchuria was able to preserve more of its original diversity than, for instance, the flood plains of Central China.

Third, a serious challenge to the idea of five distinct speech communities is presented by the unity of Neolithic culture in prehistoric Manchuria. The first agricultural communities in the region showed a certain cultural continuity, whereas they clearly differed from the Peiligang, Yangshao and Dawenkou assemblages of the Yellow River (Nelson 1995). The Hongshan culture was contemporary to the Yangshao culture (ca. 5000–3000 BC) in the Central Plain of China, which has been associated with the homeland of Sino-Tibetan-Austronesian (Sagart 2008). Janhunen (1996a: 224) connects Hongshan culture with Mongolic elements, arguing that "[i]n view of the ethnic continuity postulated between Yangshao and the later Chinese of the same region, it is tempting to assume that the region of the Hongshan Culture was also ethnically stable until historical times." But if the Neolithic cultures of prehistoric Manchuria really represent a culturally unified continuum, how could the contemporary ancestors of the Turkic, Tungusic, Japanic and Koreanic speech communities each hold their own cultural complexes, without leaving any trace in the archaeological record?

The hypothesis of genealogical unity covering these five families and going back to the times of the Neolithic revolution would account for these three extralinguistic problems. Moreover it would be compatible with the internal and external taxonomies above. In this way, interdisciplinary research can help us to hypothesize that the Transeurasian languages are related. It is clear, however, that in testing such hypotheses, we should only rely on linguistic tools.

1.2.4 The languages underlying the reconstructions

1.2.4.1 Languages included in this study

The main part of this study, presented in the Chapters 4 to 8, is concerned with the comparison of formally and functionally congruent verb morphemes between the five proto-languages of the Transeurasian unity and with the subsequent reconstruction of the most plausible proto-Transeurasian form. The reconstruction of the individual morphemes for proto-Turkic, proto-Mongolic, proto-Tungusic, proto-Koreanic and proto-Japanic relies on material from their earliest unambiguously written stages – Old Japanese, Late Middle Korean, Middle Mongolian, Written Mongolian and Old Turkic – and is supplemented by the most relevant contemporary varieties. A contemporary variety is considered relatively relevant for reconstruction purposes if it derives from a major node in the family tree for which historical records are either lacking or do not provide satisfactory morphological information. Note that Chapter 3, which presents etymologies for verb roots, will take a wider range of contemporary varieties into account than the central chapters, which deal with suffixing morphology.

The reconstruction of proto-Turkic morphemes is based on the main sources of evidence of the earliest split into the western Oghuric branch and the eastern Common Turkic branch, namely Chuvash and Old Turkic. Old Turkic was spoken in the period from the eighth to the fourteenth century. The examples in this study consist of some old runic data, but mainly of Old Uighur and peripherally of Karakhanid. Since very few records exist of historical varieties of the Oghuric branch, and since verb morphology is only fragmentary represented in the extant material, contemporary Chuvash is used as the main representative of the western branch. When a certain verb morpheme is lacking in one branch or when the comparison of verb morphemes attested in these languages leads to an equivocal or incomplete proto-Turkic reconstruction, other contemporary varieties of Turkic, such as Khalaj or the descendants of Old Turkic are added in an attempt to fill the gaps in our knowledge.

The reconstruction of proto-Mongolic morphemes is based on Middle Mongolian and Written Mongolian. When supplementary information is needed, reference will be made to contemporary varieties. Due to the unification of the Mongolic languages in the thirteenth century, all contemporary varieties can be derived from Middle Mongolian, which means that reconstruction can only take us to the thirteenth century. Recently, however, Kane (2009: 144–158) found evidence of verbal morphology in Khitan texts. Where available, his findings will supplement the proto-Mongolic reconstructions. Since the split between proto-Mongolic and proto-Khitanic is situated around the beginning of our era, the Khitanic morphemes ultimately give greater time depth to the proto-Mongolic reconstructions.

For the historical study of Tungusic languages, records are unfortunately rather scarce for most of the languages. The oldest historical records are restricted to the Manchu branch of Tungusic, written in Jurchen, the official language of the Jin Dynasty (1115–1234), and in its immediate descendant, Manchu, the official language of the Qing Dynasty (1644–1911). Since Jurchen writing has not been completely deciphered yet and since the fragmentary attestations do not always preserve crucial parts of morphology, the present work will rely on an analysis of Manchu morpheme supplemented with Jurchen reconstructions where available. For Tungusic proper, there are no records dating back to the medieval period or before. Therefore, we will retrieve morphological information about this branch from contemporary varieties, on the one hand from Even and Evenki, as representatives of the eastern and western subbranches of Northern Tungusic, respectively, and, on the other hand, from Udehe and Nanai as representatives of the eastern and western subbranches of Southern Tungusic, respectively. When more clarity is needed, other contemporary varieties will take part in the proto-Tungusic reconstructions.

The reconstruction of proto-Koreanic morphemes is based on Middle Korean and contemporary Korean. As happened with Mongolic under Chingis Khan, the Silla unification erased all coexisting varieties of Koreanic. In this study, the label "Middle Korean" mainly refers to Late Middle Korean, the language written down after the invention of the Korean script in 1446. Early Middle Korean records are often poorly understood because the exact phonological value underlying the Chinese characters in which they are written is unclear. When available and relevant, reconstructions of Early Middle Korean morphology will nevertheless supplement the Late Middle Korean forms. Since the Old Silla and Old Paekche Korean material mainly consists of individual words and a few poems, it yields very little information about morphology. However, whenever Old Silla and Old Paekche forms can shed light on the reconstructions, they will be added to the analysis.

The reconstruction of proto-Japonic morphemes is based on representatives of its two branches, i.e. Mainland Japanese and Ryukyuan. The better attested earliest source of Mainland Japanese is (Western) Old Japanese, representing the language spoken in Central Japan in the Nara-period (710–794). It is the language of Japanese literary monuments: the poetry of the *Man'yōshu*, the cultural and geographical records of the *Fudoki*, and the dynastic chronicles of the *Nihonshoki*. Some of these texts offer evidence of Eastern Old Japanese language, but the material is very scarce and almost entirely consists of poetry. The roughly 400 surviving poems are expected to lack evidence for particular grammatical morphemes due to poor attestation and restriction to a single genre. However, where verbal morphology is attested, it will be added to the reconstructions. As far as the Ryukyuan languages are concerned, evidence will be added from Northern Ryukyuan languages such as Shodon or Shuri or from Southern Ryukyuan languages such as Hirara or Hateruma. The available Koguryo data consist of words, rather than sentences or texts. The lexical corpus includes mainly nouns, few adjectives and barely any verbs. Apart from five verb morphemes reconstructed by Beckwith (2004) on the basis of morphosyntactic features in the lexical corpus, there is no Koguryo morphology left. Adding some relevant Koguryo morphemes to the reconstructions, will occasionally help to project them back from the proto-Japonic to the proto-Japanic level.

Given the vast number of diachronic and synchronic language varieties underlying this study and given their distribution over many different written sources, it is practically impossible to rely on personal philological research and restrict this study to primary sources only. Long gone are the days when a single person could discover a genealogical connection between languages, by comparing a small number of historical texts in, say, Latin, Sanskrit and Greek. The establishment of a common verb morphology in the Transeurasian languages is an undertaking requiring the collective contributions of many specialists and sources over many years. The present enterprise relies on secondary sources, grammars and language descriptions written by field workers or by specialists of a particular historical stage. Recent decades have seen a considerable increase in the description and analysis of individual historical and contemporary varieties from the Transeurasian region. In part, this trend reflects the efforts undertaken in endangered-language projects aiming to support the study of individual minority languages, such as those of Turkic and Mongolic origin or of nearly extinct language families, such as Tungusic or Ryukyuan. The renewed interest in extinct historical varieties such as Khitan, Paekche and Koguryo may also be prompted by concern over China's territorial ambitions in the region. The Koguryo Research Foundation, for instance, was established in 2004 with the "mission of defending Korean history" against "historical distortion" by China.

Although integral analyses of Chuvash morphology, such as Andreev & Pavlov (1957) and Levickaja (1976), and partial approaches such as Benzing (1959), Krüger (1961) and Johanson (1975) are somewhat dated, they still provide reliable information. Fedotov (1996) is an up-to-date analysis of Chuvash morphology. The recent contributions to the analysis of Old Turkic verb morphology made by Erdal (1991, 2004) are comprehensive and relatively up-to-date. For Written Mongolian morphology reference is made to Poppe (1954) and Sárközi (2004), for Middle Mongolian to Street (1957), Weiers (1966) and Orlovskaya (1999), and for comparison of some contemporary Mongolic morphemes to Poppe (1955a) and Sanžeev (1964). For the reconstruction of Khitan verb morphology, I draw on Kane (2009).

Since the collapse of the Soviet Union, the number of English-language treatments of Tungusic languages has increased. The present study has benefited from the following recent sources: Gorelova (2002) for the description of Manchu, Nedjalkov (1997) for Evenki, Malchukov (1995) supplementing Benzing's (1955b) study for Even, and Nikolaeva (1999) and in joint authorship with Tolskaya (2001) for Udehe. Finally, I refer to the comprehensive grammar of Nanai compiled by Avrorin (1961).

An integral overview of Middle Korean morphology is provided by Ko's (1987) standard Middle Korean grammar and Martin's (1992) reference grammar of

Korean, the second part of which provides an access to Middle Korean grammar. The analysis of Korean verbs by Ramsey (1975, 1986, 1991) is particularly useful for the reconstruction of verb morphemes. Ramsey further shared an unpublished list of Middle Korean verbs that he compiled a number of years ago. For contemporary Korean, reference is made to Lewin (1970), Martin (1992) and Sohn (1994). A handful of verb morphemes reconstructed for Koguryo are taken from Beckwith (2004).

Bentley (2001) and Vovin (2009a) provide detailed access to Western Old Japanese verb morphology. Martin (1991b) and Kaiser et al. (2002) are reference grammars for contemporary Japanese. Aspects of the reconstruction of verb morphology are treated in Whitman (2008), Frellesvig (2008) and Wrona (2008). A comprehensive reconstruction of the proto-Japonic verbal system is advanced in Unger (1977), Martin (1987) and Russell (2006). Russell includes an exhaustive analysis of Eastern Old Japanese and Ryukyuan verb morphology. Additional reference is made to Thorpe (1983), Umemura (2003) and Serafim (2008) for Ryukyuan in general, to Bentley (2008) for Southern Ryukyuan, and to Martin (1970) and Serafim (1985) for Shodon, a northern Ryukyuan language.

1.2.4.2 Transliteration conventions

In transliterating Turkic forms, I follow Johanson & Csató (1998), whose system is based on the traditional 'Fudamenta' notation as used in Deny et al. (1959: xiv-xv). Exception is made for the probably reduced vowel type $\underline{o}$ for which the notation X is used. This represents a controversial Old Turkic vowel type that has not been explicitly written in runiform texts (Johanson 1998: 107–108; 2001: 1725). I do not reconstruct vowel length for the Old Turkic forms. Several modern languages such as Yakut, Turkmen, Khaladj reflect original vowel-length in proto-Turkic, but the evidence for Old Turkic is uncertain. The Chuvash vowel notation o and the consonant notations b, d, g, f, z, ž are restricted to copies from Russian only.

Table 1. Vowel notations for the Turkic languages

	Old Turkic	Chuvash
vowel notations	a, e, ė, ï, i, o, ö, u, ü	a, e, ă, ĕ, ï, i, o, u, ü
vowel harmony archphonemes	A = a / e, I = ï / i U = u / ü, X = ï /i /u /ü	Ă = ă / ĕ, A = a/ e, I = ï / i, U = u / ü

Table 2. Consonant notations for the Turkic languages

	Old Turkic	Chuvash
unvoiced	p, t, č, k, s, š	p, f, t, č, k, s, š, ś, ts, χ
voiced	v, d, y, g, z, l, r	b, v, d, y, g, z, ž, l, r
nasal	m, n, ń, ŋ	m, n

The transliteration of the Mongolic forms follows Poppe's (1954: 30–37) conventions for Written Mongolian (with the modification *j* for Poppe's notation *ǰ*) and, Rybatzki's (2003) conventions for Middle Mongolian (with the exception of č, š, γ for Rybatzki's notations *c, sh* and *gh*). The Written Mongolian consonant notation *v* is restricted to foreign copies.

Table 3. Vowel notations for the Mongolic languages

	Written Mongolian	Middle Mongolian
vowel notations	a, e, i, o, ö, u, ü	a, e, i, o, ö, u, ü
vowel harmony archphonemes	A = a / e	A = a / e
	U = u / ü	U = u / ü

Table 4. Consonant notations for the Mongolic languages

	Written Mongolian	Middle Mongolian
unvoiced	p, t, č, k, q, s, š, h	p, t, č, k, q, s, š, h
voiced	b, v, d, j, y, g, γ, l, r	b, d, j, y, g, γ, l, r
nasal	m, n, ng	m, n, ng

The transliteration rules for transcribing the individual Tungusic languages are as follows. For Manchu, the symbols used in this book follow the romanization proposed by Gorelova (2002: 55–70). For Evenki, they follow Nedjalkov (1997: xv-xvi) with the modifications e̊, ï, c, š, dy, j and ń for Nedjalkov's notations *je, y, ch, sh, d', ʒ* and *n'* respectively. The Even data are transliterated according to Benzing (1955b: 4) with the modifications ï, e, j, y, ń, ng, v for Benzing's notations *e, ə, ʒ, j, n̦, ŋ, w* respectively. The transliteration of Udehe follows Nikolaeva (1999: 19, 29) with the modifications c, j, y, ń, ng for Nikolaeva's notations č, z, j, ñ, ŋ respectively. The romanization of Nanai is based on Avrorin's (1961) and Onenko's (1980) Cyrillic transcription of Nanai. The logic underlying the modifications is a consistent use of c, j for the palatal fricatives, y for the palatal glide, ń for the palatal nasal and ng for the velar nasal.

Table 5. Vowel notations for the Tungusic languages

	Manchu	Evenki	Even	Udehe	Nanai
vowel notations	a, e, i, o, u	a, e, ė, ï, i, o, u	a, e, ï, i, o, u	a, ä, e, i, o, ö, u, ü	a, e, i, o, u
vowel harmony archphoneme	A = a / o / e	A = a / o / e	A = a / e	A = a / o / e	A = a / e U = u / o

Table 6. Consonant notations for the Tungusic languages

	Manchu	Evenki	Even	Udehe	Nanai
unvoiced	p, f, t, c, k, s, š, h	p, t, c, k, s, š, h	p, f, t, c, k, s, h	p, t, c, k, s, x, h	p, t, c, k, s, x
voiced	b, v, d, j, y, g, l, r	b, v, d, dy, j, g, y, l, r	b, v, d, j, g, y, z, l, r	b, d, j, g, w, y, l, r	b, d, j, g, w, y, l, r
nasal	m, n, ng	m, n, ń, ng	m, n, ń, ng	m, n, ń, ng	m, n, ń, ng

The transliteration conventions for transcribing Korean forms adopted in this work follow Martin (1992: 6–23). Yale romanization is used for cited linguistic forms such as verbs, verb suffixes and textual context whereas the classical McCune Reishauer system is employed for proper nouns, such as personal names, titles of books and articles, geographical names and historical periods. For Middle Korean the Yale romanization is modified to allow for the representation of unrounded vowels [ə] and [ɨ] by *o* and *u* and of rounded [o] and [u] by *wo* and *wu* respectively. The notation *ž* is used to represent the now obsolete Middle Korean triangle grapheme Δ. In earlier work (Robbeets 2005: 61–62), I have explained why the MK Δ grapheme is unlikely to represent a mere voiced /z/ and argued that an extra feature such as palatalization to /ž/ is probably involved. The capitals *W* and *G* are used for two other obsolete consonants for which the phonological interpretation is probably fricative [β] and [ɣ] respectively. Contrary to modern Hangŭl, the original Middle Korean alphabet used a special symbol to indicate non-automatic reinforcement following /l/, for instance in *hal kes* 'things to do' pronounced with reinforced [k] as opposed to [g] in Korean *phal-kwo* 'is selling and'. Reinforcement is represented by a special morphophonemic symbol *q*, e.g. *halq kes* 'things to do'. The dots in the Middle Korean words represent the distinctive pitch of the following syllable: one dot for high, two dots for rising, and unmarked syllables are treated as low.

Table 7. Vowel notations for Korean

	Middle Korean	Korean
simplex vowel notations	a, e, i, o, wo, u, wu	a, ay, e, ey, i, o, oy, u, wu
complex vowel notations	ay, ey, oy, uy, wa, we, wi, way, wey, woy, wuy, ya, yay, ye, yey	wa, way, we, wey, wi, ya, yay, ye, yey, yo, yu, uy
vowel harmony archphonemes	A = a / e U = u / o	A = a / e

Table 8. Consonant notations for Korean

	Middle Korean	Korean
lax	p, t, c, k, s	p, t, c, k, s
reinforced		pp, tt, kk, cc, ss
aspirate	ph, th, kh, ch, h	ph, th, kh, ch, h
fricative	W, ž, G	
nasal-liquid	m, n, ng, l	m, n, ng, l

The transliteration of Japanese expressions adopted in this work basically follows the Yale system according to Martin (1989) for cited linguistic forms such as glosses and text examples and the Hepburn system for proper nouns, such as personal names, titles of books and articles, geographical names and historical periods. The essential difference is that the syllables that are written as *tsu, shi, chi, fu* and *ji* in the Hepburn system appear as *tu, ti, hu, zi/ di* in the Yale system. Japanese verbs and verbal adjectives can be distinguished according to two prosodic classes, indicated as A and B. Type A corresponds to a high initial tone, type B to a low initial tone. Following nouns and nominal adjectives accent patterns are indicated by number combinations (1.1, 1.2, 2.1 to 2.5, etc.). In Old Japanese, the use of Chinese characters for phonetic value indicated two values for later *e, i, o* in certain syllables, the so-called *kōrui-otsurui* 'A type- B type' distinctions. Rather than using the Yale notation, which hints at preglided or postglided origins underlying these types, the vowel distinctions are indexed with more neutral subscripts, namely i_1 versus i_2, e_1 versus e_2 and o_1 versus o_2.

Table 9. Vowel notations for Japanese

	Old Japanese		Japanese
	Index	Yale	
neutral vowels	a, e, i, o, u	a, e, i, o, u	a, e, i, o, u
A-type	e_1, i_1, o_1	ye, yi, wo	
B-type	e_2, i_2, o_2	iy, ey, o̲	

Table 10. Consonant notations for Japanese

	Old Japanese	Japanese
unvoiced	p, t, k, s	p, t, k, s, h
voiced	b, d, g, z, w, y, r	b, d, g, z, w, y, r
nasal	m, n	m, n

For all languages, the capital letter V indicates any vowel, whereas C indicates any consonant. A colon (:) placed after a vowel is used to indicate length. A tilde (˜) placed on top of a vowel is used to indicate nasalisation. An asterisk (*) precedes reconstructed forms. The sign Ø is used for a zero element. A dash to the right of a word signifies a verb stem, e.g. J ik- 'go', whereas a dash to the left signifies a bound morpheme, e.g. J -te converb. Double arrows (>>) are used for borrowings, meaning 'has been borrowed into'. Single arrows (>) are used for inheritance, meaning 'has developed into'. The reconstruction of verb suffixes is supported by verb pairs consisting of a neutral base and its derived counterpart. Simple dashed arrows (→) are used to indicate a relation between base and derived verb. Capital letters in morpheme representations indicate phonemes that undergo morphophonological changes.

1.3 Previous research

Although it is legitimate to use extralinguistic evidence when constructing a linguistic hypothesis like the Transeurasian unity, only linguistic tools must be used when testing it. The application of linguistic methods to the Transeurasian languages represents a challenge which historical linguistic scholarship has met in the past, using a wide range of approaches and with varying rates of success. It is not within the scope of this work to present a complete history of the Altaic debate, thus reiterating state-of-the-art reviews such as Georg et al. (1998), Miller (1991a&b) or Robbeets (2005: 18–29).

These surveys reveal that, since the beginning of the debate in the nineteenth century, the research focus has been on lexical comparison. The overemphasis on words rather than affixes partly explains why comparative morphology has yielded poor results so far. This is not to claim that there have been no attempts to establish common morphological elements among the Transeurasian languages.

Research into this area may be said to have begun with Ramstedt (1903). Although the first part of this work treats the conjugation of Khalkha, the second part (59–119) is a historical comparative study including elements of Turkic or Tungusic verb morphology. It was followed by a closer investigation of the Mongolic-Turkic parallels in 1912. The posthumous publication of Ramstedt's *Formenlehre* in 1952 represents a milestone on the way to compiling a comprehensive comparative morphology of the Transeurasian languages. It gives an overview of nominal as well as verbal morphology, and of derivational as well as inflectional morphology. It adds Korean data to the Altaic comparisons, but although Ramstedt (1924a) had drawn the attention to common elements between Japanese and Altaic morphology, the *Formenlehre* did not deal with Japanese. This is particularly unfortunate given that branches such as Japanic, while occupying a geographically peripheral position in a family, linguistically play a central role in the reconstructions, because traces of conservative items are expected to have been preserved in remote areas. Furthermore, some of these proposals are now outdated in the light of more recent contributions to the description and reconstruction of the individual languages and language families. Other works dealing with aspects of comparative morphology include Baskakov (1974) on pronominal systems, Baskakov (1970, 1981) and Poppe (1977a) on nominal case and Poppe (1972a), Nasilov (1978) and Kormušin (1984) on verb morphology, but none of these contributions compare Japanese data.

Comparative studies of Transeurasian morphology including Japanese are rather limited, either by their actual number, their scope or by the number of branches they include. The Etymological Dictionary of the Altaic Languages published by Starostin, Dybo and Mudrak in 2003 includes Japanese, but being a dictionary rather than a comparative grammar, it does not investigate the morphological look-alikes listed in its Chapter 4 (173–229) in detail. More extensive treatments of aspects of Japanese morphology in relation to the Transeurasian languages can be found in the work of Murayama, Miller, Street, Menges, Finch, Itabashi, Vovin and Gruntov. However, nominal morphology is the area that has received most attention, mostly in studies on the comparison of case markers, such as Murayama (1957), Menges (1960, 1975: 111–121, 1984: 245–247), Street (1978), Finch (1985, 1999), Itabashi (1988, 1989, 1990, 1991), Miller (1993) and Gruntov (2002).

Verb morphology is covered relatively well in Miller's work with a study of deverbal verb suffixes (1981), denominal verb suffixes (1982a), negation (1971: 245–284, 1985) and gerunds (1971: 285–291). Menges treats transitivity pairs (1975: 32–35), negation (1975: 96–109, 1984: 262–63) and gerunds (1975: 110–111). Street deals with denominal verbs (1978: 44, 204, 219) actionality (1978: 74–75, 113, 115, 188, 178–179, 219–220, 247–249, 230–231), diatheses (1978: 53, 55, 71, 75, 179, 181–182, 185–188, 199–200, 208, 230, 239–242, 257–259) and converbs (1978: 200, 251–252). Finch (1987) reconstructs Altaic verb classes. Vovin (1998) provides a sketch of comparative Altaic verb morphology including Japanese, but in a later article (2001) he restricts the same evidence to a comparison of Japanese, Korean and the Tungusic languages. Overlooking the fact that positions close to the primary stem have a high diagnostic value for demonstrating remote genealogical continuity (cf. Section 5.1 and 6.1), Vovin's paper focuses on the markers in the outer ranks for aspect, mood, tense, final predication. These are exactly the categories in which replacement is expected to take place in the process of cyclic grammaticalization. It is thus not surprising that a considerable number of Vovin's etymologies can be dismissed on the suspicion of grammaticalization within Japanese (Robbeets 2005: 157–173). Discouraged by the weakness of the evidence, Vovin has recently (2005a) rejected the Altaic hypothesis, thus rejecting his own former position.

Martin's contributions are mostly restricted to the binary comparison of Japanese and Korean, with a predominant focus on the lexicon. In his seminal article on proto-Korean-Japanese lexical reconstruction, however, Martin (1966: 168) already hinted at complementary evidence from grammatical morphology: "Still, I believe it may be possible to find convincing proof in a few deep-seated grammatical devices shared by Korean and Japanese alone, as I will attempt to show in a later paper on grammatical evidence for the relationship of the two languages." The paper in question appeared in 1968 and included references to cognate morphemes in Tungusic, Mongolic and Turkic. The details of Martin's proposals were only elaborated much later, towards the end of his career. In 1991 (a), he published an updated and expanded version of the 1968 paper. In 1990, he dealt with nominal morphology such as cognate case suffixes and focus particles shared between Japanese and Korean, adding some final remarks on possible cognates in Tungusic, Mongolic and Turkic. In 1995 and 2002, he turned to the historical comparison of verb morphology between Japanese and Korean, concluding (1995: 148): "But this paper is too long, so I will save for another day…. the quest for possible cognates in Tungusic, Mongolian, and Turkic languages to match some of the structures discussed here." Martin died in 2009 before specifying what he meant by these possible Transeurasian cognates. Nevertheless, he has directed our attention to a challenging area of Transeurasian linguistics, still widely open to exploration and refinement, namely comparative verb morphology.

It is striking that linguists who extended Martin's historical comparative research, such as Ramsey, Whitman, Frellesvig and Unger never went beyond binary comparison of Japanese and Korean. Ramsey (1978, 1979, 1982, 1991) has compared accent patterns and has made some important contributions to the analysis of proto-Korean verb morphology mentioned above. Whitman's (1985) dissertation on the phonological comparison of Japanese and Korean includes valuable hints on morphological cognates, still waiting to be elaborated. Frellesvig (2001) explains a number of bound Korean and Japanese morphemes as derivations of a common copula. Although Vovin (2008a: 45–91) points to some weaknesses of the Koreo-Japanic morphological proposals, his remarks do not challenge the entire reconstruction, but rather – as Unger (2011) argues – suggest the need to probe more deeply into morphological cognates.

Even if historically documented varieties of Japanese are well studied by Japan-based scholars, few scholars have been active in the field of comparative morphological reconstruction. Most universities in Japan do not offer courses in historical comparative linguistics and those who do, tend to apply comparative reconstruction exclusively to Indo-European languages. The apparent lack of interest in the origins of the Japanese language may well be related to the deep-rooted belief that the Japanese people, their culture and language are unique. This myth of Japanese uniqueness figured prominently in the so-called *Nihonjinron* ('Japanese logic') discussions in the 1970s and 1980s. Although it has been pointed out that cultural, ethnic and linguistic diversity has always existed in Japan (Miller 1982b, Dale 1985, Denoon et al. 1996, Heinrich 2012), the image of a homogenous and unique society persists in Japan, as is evident from a statement by the former Prime Minister, Asō Tarō in Asahi Shimbun (15–11–2005): "*Itibunka, itibunmei, itiminzoku, itigengo no kuni wa nihon no hoka ni wa nai*. There is no other country in the world like Japan, with one culture, one civilization, one people and one language". Although efforts are being made to study linguistic diversity in contemporary Japan, the hypothesis that the Japanese language may have continental roots remains difficult to digest for most Japanese academics. Hence, historical linguists based in Japan focus their attention on internal developments attested in language varieties of the historical period. Although their research is extremely valuable, it is unfortunate that the search for prehistorical external connections receives hardly any attention.

2 Methodology

2.1 Historical comparative morphology

Historical comparative morphology is a subfield of historical comparative linguistics that is concerned with comparing morphological forms between languages in order to establish areal and/or genealogical relationships. The term "genealogical" is used here instead of "genetic" to distinguish linguistic inheritance from biological inheritance as studied in the discipline of genetics. Aspects of morphology open to comparison include the form and meaning of roots and affixes, the combinational possibilities of building up these elements, the phonological processes that apply when combining them, the general typological features reflected by these forms, the processes of grammaticalization by which they develop function and the organization of derivationally or inflectionally related forms in paradigms.

Two or more languages have morphology in common when their affixes share certain properties, either globally, including form and function, or selectively, restricted to certain – formal, functional, combinational, typological or paradigmatic – properties only. What holds for linguistic similarities in general, irrespective of whether these consist of lexical, phonological or grammatical correspondences, also holds for morphology shared between languages, namely that there are basically four different ways of accounting for correspondences: chance, universals, code-copying or inheritance. As pointed out in Section 2.3, the formal and functional resemblance between causatives in -*t* in a number of languages across the world as well as the coincidences between the proto-Eastern Miwok and Late Common Indo-European pronominal affixes were all caused by chance. Through certain universal principles in linguistic structuring, some shared properties may have developed "naturally" and thus in parallel but independently in each of the languages involved. Nichols (2012), for instance, partly attributes the specific clustering of pronominal paradigms with first person *m* and second person *t* or *s* in Eurasia to the impact of a universal *m-T* attractor state. Code-copying is the contact-induced replication of a bound morpheme from a model language into a basic language, a relatively uncommon phenomenon that is amply illustrated throughout the current literature (see Section 2.5). Inheritance refers to the residue of morphological similarities retained in the daughter languages after separation from their ancestral language, such as the global congruence of the present indicative paradigm of the copula among Indo-European languages (see Table 1 in Section 2.2.2.5).

The comparative method is the principal means available to historical linguists to test a hypothesis of linguistic relationship, by establishing correspondences between languages and weighing the different determinants that can account for them. Thus, to demonstrate that two or more languages are genealogically related we need to develop a positive argumentation followed by a negative one: first, we must establish a set of similarities between the languages compared, and then in a second step, we must rule out all but one of the four logically possible accounts for these correlations, so that only inheritance remains as an explanation.

Although the argumentation by elimination is stressed in recent scholarly work on methodology such as Aikhenvald & Dixon (2001: 1–4), Harrison (2003: 215), Campbell & Poser (2008: 194–223), it is sometimes not recognized as a basic requirement of the comparative method. Thomason and Kaufman (1988: 3), for instance, refer to "the Comparative Method's methodological requirement that the possibility of interference be ignored in its application". This chapter will describe the methodology used in this book by paying equal attention to both positive and negative argumentation: Section 2.2 will be concerned with procedures for establishing linguistic correlations, whereas the Sections 2.3 to 2.5 will deal with procedures for eliminating non-genealogical determinants of these correlations, focussing on the distinction between code-copying and inheritance in Section 2.5.

In stressing the requirement that all logically possible accounts of the similarities observed must be ruled out, so that the only remaining interpretation is inheritance, my present approach is based upon the same premises as my previous research on lexical comparison (Robbeets 2005: 41–51). As revealed by reviews of this research, not all specialists in the historical comparison of the Transeurasian languages agree with these basic methodological principles. Appreciations of the eliminative methodology used in Robbeets 2005 range from "a superb example of disciplined methodology," (Rozycki 2006: 114), "Well versed in historical comparative studies," (Kara 2007: 95), and "This methodology is, of course, legitimate" (Vovin 2009b: 106) to "Die Methoden sind jedoch recht zweifelhafter Natur" (Knüppel 2006: 363) and "entirely home-grown principles for the evaluation of claims of geneticity" (Georg 2007: 276). As there seems to be considerable disagreement and confusion in the Transeurasian field concerning the accurate application of historical comparative methods, I will examine a number of theoretical misunderstandings in Section 2.5.

2.2 Procedures for establishing morphological correlations

2.2.1 Collection and reconstruction of participant morphemes

The first step consists in an intuitive and impressionistic search, screening the Transeurasian languages for similar-looking bound morphemes. Taking a bottom-up approach, we first specify the participating morphological elements in detail at the level of the individual languages and are gradually piece them together to reconstruct proto-morphemes for the individual branches (i.e. proto-Turkic, proto-Mongolic, proto-Tungusic, proto-Koreanic and proto-Japonic) until this yields a top-level reconstruction of a common proto-Transeurasian morpheme.

It is important to expand our input from actually productive to petrified morphemes, resulting from so-called "demorphologization" and referred to as "morphological residue" by Hopper (1990: 154). Towards the end of one grammaticalization cycle, worn-out grammatical forms may be replaced by less grammaticalized forms, thereby giving rise to a new chain of development. The worn-out morpheme is either completely lost or becomes part of a host morpheme, which can be a lexeme or an affix. The Germanic present participle *-nd, for instance, is no longer productive in English but has lexicalized in certain lexemes such as *friend* and *fiend*, which derive from verbal roots meaning 'love' and 'hate' (Hopper & Traugott 1993: 165). An example of incorporation into another affix is the Latin inchoative suffix -sc-, which has fossilized in some inflectional forms of certain Romance verbs, such as in Italian *fini-sc-o* 'I finnish' and in French *nous fini-ss-ons* 'we finish' (Greenberg 1991: 311).

Since a morpheme may retain its phonological substance while it is gradually losing its grammatical contribution, we need to find several word-pairs with remnants of the same morphological residue in order to derive the original meaning of the morpheme through diagrammatic equivalence. A single derivational pair such as English *give* → *forgive* may not reveal much about the original function of *for-*, but on the basis of similar derivations such as *get* → *forget*, *go* → *forgo*, *swear* → *forswear* we can derive a common denominator 'off, away, past', which is confirmed by the use of the Old English prefix in *forshake* 'shake off', *forthrow* 'throw off' etc. In this way, we gain access to remnants of the earliest recoverable morphology. Since the present work is an attempt to reconstruct morphemes to relatively great time depths, a considerable amount of data will consist of word pairs reflecting morphological residue.

In internal reconstruction, alternations within a single synchronic stage of a language are "undone" as it were, and an earlier state is reconstructed. In this process, it must be ensured that a plausible developmental pathway can be traced from the earlier reconstructed form and function to the attested ones. In

Middle Korean, for instance, there is a causative-passive marker that has numerous allophones MK -*ki*-, -*Gi*-, -*hi*-, -*i*-, -(·)*y*-., and also has various functions: it either derives causatives from transitive and intransitive verbs or passives from transitive verbs. Combining phonological knowledge about velar lenition with insights into the general typology of the development from causatives into passives, allows us to undo the changes and reconstruct an original causative marker of the shape pK *-*ki*- (cf. Section 6.7.2).

2.2.2 Comparison of individual proto-morphemes

Each reconstructed morphological unit consists of a stretch of phonological substance (a form) associated with derivational or inflectional meaning (a function), characterized by certain combinational and typological properties and often systematically related to other morphemes in a set. It follows that potentially cognate proto-morphemes can be assessed with respect to regularity of sound correspondences, plausibility of assumed functional changes, correlation of combinational properties, typological similarity and paradigmatic coherence.

2.2.2.1 Formal correlations

The phonological assessment of morphological comparanda usually draws on regular correspondences established in previous research, a practice that has led to Anttila's oversimplification (1989: 351) that "comparative morphology is simply applied phonology". The sound correspondence in Indo-European markers with inchoative or present meaning such as Sanskrit -*ch*-, Iranian -*s*-, Hitite -*sk*-, Latin -*sc*-, Albanian -*h*-, Old Church Slavonic -*sk*- and Old High German -*sk*-, for instance, confirms a phonological correspondence established on the basis of the lexicon, e.g. in the words for 'shadow': Skt. *chāyā́*, Av. *saya*, Old Greek *skiā́*, Alb. *hie* and Gothic *skīnan* 'shine' (Lubotsky 2001; Joseph 2004: 1662)

Theoretically, it follows that morphological reconstruction should always be preceded by phonological reconstruction. This is especially true for the Transeurasian languages, which are agglutinative and thus tend to share fewer idiosyncrasies useful for the establishment of fusional families like Indo-European. Shared irregularities such as the suppletive *ego* / *me* pronominal stems can demonstrate the correspondence between morpheme shapes without reference to regular sound correspondences. With the exception of some shared residue of original allomorphy such as the velar fricative ~ stop *x ~ *k allomorphs for the inchoative and the perfective nominalizer (see Sections 5.7 and 7.6), shared formational irregularities are rare in Transeurasian morphology. Therefore, the formal evaluation of Transeurasian morphology must necessarily rely on the prior establishment of phonological changes on the basis of lexical cognates. Relevant sound correspondences will be illustrated in Chapter 2, which deals with verb roots and is based on prior phonological research of lexical items (Robbeets 2005).

It should be kept in mind that phonological regularity can be given up in favor of morphological regularity. This happens, for instance, in the case of analogical leveling, the reduction of morphophonemic alternation within a paradigm. As a result of Verner's law, which describes a regular sound change in Indo-European, whereby *s is voiced to *z in voiced environment if preceded by an unaccented syllable, proto-Germanic had two allomorphs for the verb root 'choose', namely pGerm. *keus- and pGerm. *kuz-, reflected in Old English in the first singular present *cēosu* as opposed to the past partciple *gecoren*. In the modern English and the modern German verb system, the regularity of Verner's law is eliminated by a process of analogy, e.g. *choose/ chosen* and *küren/ gekoren*, respectively.

A special instance of analogy is so-called "eidemic resonance" (Bickel & Nichols 2007: 209–210), whereby the forms of a paradigm tend to resonate with each other through alliteration or rhyme without entailing any consistent morpheme extractability. Resonance often tends to structure paradigms, as illustrated by the developments in the French singular object pronouns *me, te, le, se*, in which the vowel and the syllable structure have become uniform. Another example of this phenomenon is provided by the English deictic words *that, the, their, them, then*, which alliterate in a voiced fricative, although the expected outcome of an earlier English *þ* ("thorn"), originally a voiceless sound in initial position, is a voiceless fricative (e.g. *thank, think, three*). The unexpected low central vowel in the Japonic iconic suffix *-ka- and causative-anticausative suffix *-ta- (see Sections 5.5.1 and 6.3.1) will be explained by resonance, modelled on the majority of actional and diathetical suffixes in the suffix chain which have a final vowel *a.

Furthermore, function words or affixes often constitute prosodically weak environments, in which phonological regularity can be easily given up. The expected outcome of proto-Germanic *sk is ʃ in German (e.g. German *Schuld* 'debt'), but the future auxiliary verb *skal does not have the expected outcome in Old High German *sal*. Joseph (2006, 2013) attributes this phonologically irregularity to the position of low sentence or phrase-accent in which these function words occur.

2.2.2.2 Functional correlations

Whereas formal correspondences are assessed on the basis of regularities in phonological change, the evaluation of functional correspondences draws on regularities in grammatical change. Grammaticalization theory provides us with tools to test the plausibility of functional changes and to compare different grammatical functions to one another in a principled way. Grammaticalization is usually defined as a diachronic process leading from lexemes to grammatical markers, including the development of further grammaticalized functions by already grammaticalized markers (see Lehmann 1985; Heine, Claudi & Hünnemyer 1991; Hopper & Traugott 2003; Robbeets & Cuyckens 2013: 1–2). It is an operation by which content words lose some or all of their lexical properties and come to fulfill grammatical functions or, by which an existing mode of grammatical expression further increases its grammatical status. For example, an original verb of causation pTEA *ki-* still reflected in Turkic and Mongolic independent verbs meaning 'do, make' is assumed to have developed into a bound causative suffix in Japonic, Koreanic and Tungusic, further increasing its grammatical status to passive in Japonic and Koreanic (see Section 6.7).

Directional tendencies along specific grammaticalization pathways help us to compare functions and "undo" changes. A shift may take place between different properties in the same category, for instance from reflexive to reciprocal, anticausative to passive or continuous to habitual. Alternatively, the function may shift to one in a different category, such as third person agreement to passive voice, continuous aspect to present tense or potential mood to future tense. Finally, there may be an even more radical shift from derivational patterns to inflectional categories, such as desiderative derivation to future tense or from non-finite to finite marking.

Note that a certain degree of flexibility may be permitted in the functional comparison of morphemes, on condition that the correspondence is phonologically regular and that the morphological item under comparison shows up in various branches of the family. An example of less obvious functional parallelism is the above-mentioned comparison of the elements Sanskrit *-ch-*, Iranian *-s-*, Hitite *-sk-*, Latin *-sc-*, Albanian *-h-*, Old Church Slavonic *-sk-* and Old High German *-sk-* in some verbal forms, for example, in the verbs meaning 'to wish, search', e.g. Skt. *icháti*, Av. *isaite*, OHG *eiscōn*, OCS *iskati*, Arm. *hayc`em* 'I search'. In Sanskrit, the suffix is an unproductive formant in some ten odd presents; in Iranian, it represents a present with inchoative function; in Hittite it marks iterative action; in Latin, it marks inchoative action; in Albanian, it marks non-active voice in the present tense system, in Armenian, it functions as a present form; and in Germanic and Slavic, it is a petrified formant in a small number of verb stems. Although the meanings do not perfectly match the framework of grammaticalization theory, a common element of presentiality and inchoativity is usually considered sufficient grounds for arranging the morphemes in a tentative cognate set.

2.2.2.3 Combinational correlations

Combinational correlations are similarities in the combination of morphemes. These may involve morphotactic requirements concerning the ordering of the morpheme in the affix chain, the tendency of certain affixes to be reinforced by a particular morpheme, the inability to co-occur with a particular morpheme, restrictions on the part of speech of the derivational base, or the ability to combine with copied or onomatopoetic bases, etc. Although general combinational correlations need to be interpreted with caution because they may be contact-induced or due to universal principles in linguistic structuring, it is rewarding to compare the specific combinational properties of a morpheme in addition to its form and function. This approach has not been sufficiently taken in previous studies of comparative morphology across the Transeurasian languages.

Some general combinational properties such as the ordering of grammatical categories, may be subject to universal principles in linguistic structuring or to borrowing. Given a natural relation between the semantic relevance of an affix and its position with respect to the stem (Bybee 1985: 33–35), the order actionality-diathesis-negation-tense-mood-person-number, for instance, universally occurs more frequently than competing orders. Other broad positional properties, such as the final position of subject agreement in Altaic, may be caused by areal influence. This is because agreement suffixes have developed from unstressed postposed subject pronouns in Altaic, but the postposition of subject pronouns is a discourse strategy, which is prone to being borrowed due to its pragmatic nature.

Although such broad positional arguments cannot be used as evidence of genealogical relationship *per se*, more specific positional properties of a certain morpheme, such as its occurrence as a prefix or a suffix and its disposition or inability to co-occur with certain other morphemes can be taken into account. The shared aberrant original verb initial word order in negative constructions in Transeurasian (see Chapter 4), for example, adds a strong comparative dimension. The same is true for the exclusive use of a reflex of the verbalizer pTEA *-lA- for the accommodation of borrowed verb bases (see Section 5.3) and for the reinforcement of various nominalizers across the Transeurasian languages by attachment of a bound noun *i meaning 'fact, thing, this (one)' (see Chapter 7). Therefore, combinational correlations will be used to complement the evidence insofar as they are associated with correspondences of phonological substance and grammatical meaning.

2.2.2.4 Typological correlations

When it comes to grammatical evidence in support of genealogical relatedness, most historical linguists would favor morphological correspondences over structural similarities in the typology of the languages being compared. Structural similarities are matches between abstract features of the language system at different levels, such as phonology, morphology, or syntax. Since such features can be shared across genealogically unrelated languages and since it is often difficult to pinpoint the causes of similarity, most structural correlations are considered to be too indeterminate to be advanced as a genealogical arguments. A classical example of contact-induced structural similarity is the Balkan linguistic area. Although Greek, Albanian, Serbo-Croatian, Bulgarian, Macedonian and Romanian all belong to different branches of Indo-European, many of their structural parallels, for instance, the use of verb forms instead of infinitives, are due to areal influences. Next, it is easy to see how corresponding word order patterns such as SVO or SOV might arise by chance, given that there are about 6900 languages in the world, whereas the possibilities for arranging subject, object and verb in a sentence are limited to just six. Furthermore, some structural features tend to correlate naturally, such as the tendency for prepositions to correlate with verb-object order, and for postpositions to occur with object-verb order (Greenberg 1963, Dryer 1992, Plank 1998).

Nevertheless, it is possible to limit the probability that shared structural traits are coincidental, universally motivated or contact-induced. Factors such as coincidence and linguistic universals can be eliminated by focussing on phenomena that are relatively infrequent and randomly spread across the world's languages but frequent and geographically concentrated in a specific group of languages. Such phenomena are difficult to explain by chance or linguistic universals and, therefore, provide evidence of a historical connection – be it areal or genealogical – between the languages concerned (Croft 1990: 206–207). The strength of the argument increases when a number of features correlate in a particular part of the world, but not in the world as a whole. In Robbeets (forthcoming a), I have provided a typological profile of the Transeurasian languages in relation to that of selected languages immediately outside the region. The clear-cut delimitation of the language type in relation to its neighbours as well as the relatively low frequency of some shared features worldwide indicates that the shared properties are not due to a mere interplay of coincidence and universal principles in linguistic structuring. Moreover, a number of the structural similarities between the Transeurasian languages discussed in this article are further difficult to explain by areal diffusion on the basis of observations relating to geography, history, distribution and cyclicity of grammaticalization.[1]

---

[1] Distinguishing between stable, recessive, viable and consistent features, Nichols theory of stability (1992, 2003) provides an alternative means of accounting for the relative probability that shared structural features have been either inherited or copied.

The present study, however, will not deal with common structural features in the abstract; it will only be concerned with structural similarities insofar as the sharing of a typological feature or process coincides with the sharing of morphological form and function. This approach permits us to take into account diachronic typology in morphological reconstruction, a practice which is unseen in most previous comparative studies of verb morphology across the Transeurasian languages. As such, typology provides us with yet another angle from where to assess the similarity of morphemes, thus increasing the diagnostic value of the evidence. Indeed, when isostructuralism coincides with form-function isomorphism, the correlations are less likely to be motivated by non-genealogical factors. Typological assessment may involve either an abstract trait of a certain morpheme, or, alternatively, a process of grammaticalization according to which the morpheme developed. In Section 2.5.3.3 I will further investigate how grammaticalization theory can contribute to drawing inferences about remote linguistic relationship, particularly when it comes to distinguishing areal from genealogical influence.

2.2.2.5 Paradigmatic correlations

Robbeets and Bisang (2014: 6) characterize a paradigm as "an organized set of derivationally or inflectionally related items that derive a particular semantic or morphosyntactic category from a common base or root". As such, they favor the view that derivation, like inflection, is regulated by paradigmatic principles and that what really matters in both cases is a certain internal organization within a coherent whole. This characterization is in line with the definition of "paradigm" in morphological theory (see e.g., Bauer 1997, Booij 1997, Stump 2001, Baerman & Corbett 2010), but it is more general than the notion of "paradigmaticity" that has been advanced as diagnostic in historical comparison. I we define a paradigm as the full set of forms, inflectional and derivational, that a root enters into, it follows that it is not small and not inherently closed, since every root enters into a different array of derivations and not every root has the full set of inflections. However, "paradigmaticity" in the historical comparative context refers to a closed set of form slots with positions defined by intersections of category dimensions, or the like that can be defined independently of the forms that fill them (Robbeets 2014: 198–200). Since the set of forms is closed, it is not large, as illustrated, by the six forms filling the person-number paradigm of the copula in Indo-European in Table 1 below.

Table 1. The present indicative paradigm based on the Indo-European copula *h_1es- 'to be' (Beekes 1995: 13–14)

	Sanskrit	Homeric Greek	Latin	Gothic	PIE
root	as-	es-	es-	is-	*h_1es-
1 SG	as-mi	ei-mi	s-um	i-m	*h_1es-mi
2 SG	as-i	es-si	es	is	*h_1es-si
3 SG	as-ti	es-ti(n)	es-t	is-t	*h_1es-ti
1 PL	s-mas	ei-men	s-umus	s-ijum	*h_1s-més
2 PL	s-tha	es-te	es-tis	s-ijuþ	*h_1s-th_1é
3 PL	s-anti	ei-si(n)	s-unt	s-ind	*h_1s-énti

Lexical comparison has two dimensions: form and meaning. The Latin root *es-* 'to be', for instance, can be compared to the copula Sanskrit *as-*, Greek *es-* and Gothic *is-*, reflecting a common form *h_1es- and a common meaning 'to be'. Similarly, the Latin ending of the present indicative third singular *-t* in *es-t* 'he is' can be compared in form and function to Sanskrit *-ti*, Ancient Greek *-ti(n)* and Gothic *-t*, but here, as illustrated in Table 1, the patterning of person and number oppositions in the Latin present indicative paradigm can be compared to the oppositions in the other languages as well. In every language in the table, the copula fills a closed set of form slots with positions defined by intersections of the dimensions person and number agreement. The languages under comparison display correlations in grammatical patterning among ordered sets of disjunct forms, known as "multidimensional paradigmaticity" (Nichols 1996: 46), a correspondence which adds a third dimension to the comparison.

This dimension can further be expanded by a shared irregularity in the formation of the copula root in the plural paradigm. Indeed, all paradigms except Greek, show a full-grade form with a vowel in the singular in opposition to a zero-grade form with a vowel missing in the plural, e.g. Sanskrit *as-* vs. *s-*, Latin *es-* vs. *s-*, Gothic *is-* vs. *s-*. As such, it is not just the endings that match systematically, but there is also a systematic linkage between the roots that would be hard to explain without recourse to a common ancestor.

Moreover, we find similar paradigms for the athematic present indicative, for the imperfect indicative and for non-indicative moods such as subjunctive, optative and imperative. Joseph (2014: 97–98) introduces the notion of "extended paradigmaticity" to refer to external relationships of grammatical patterning among different paradigms, some of which may be the result of grammaticalization processes, such as the systematic linkage between personal pronouns and verb agreement markers. These external relationships of grammatical patterning among different systems make up the fifth dimension of paradigmatic evidence.

Hence, the strength of paradigmatic evidence as an indicator of genealogical relatedness lies in its combining of multiple dimensions of comparison. In addition to formal and functional criteria, the correspondences can be assessed in terms of paradigmatic behavior such as internal cohesion between the ordered slots of a set of forms, shared formational irregularity in specific parts of the system and external relationships of grammatical patterning among different systems.

2.2.3 Top-level reconstruction

2.2.3.1 Reconstruction of proto-morphemes

Positing a series of plausible processes of functional change which, in combination with phonological change, would transform the members of the etymology into one common form, enables us to reconstruct an appropriate proto-form. As in phonological reconstruction, the guidelines for devising the most realistic morphological reconstruction are directionality and economy. Directionality is the tendency of a certain morphological change to develop in one direction, giving preference to cross-linguistically more natural or common processes. The development from a causative to a passive marker, for example, is observed across the languages of the world, but the reverse change, i.e. from passive to causative, is unknown to occur. Another guiding principle is economy, also known as Occam's razor. When multiple alternatives are available, preference should be given to the the solution which involves the fewest changes between proto-language and descendant languages. One consequence of the economy principle is that the original form and function are likely to be the ones that show up in the greatest number of daughter languages.

A genealogical relationship can be demonstrated on the basis of regular correspondences in form and function. It should be kept in mind, however, that identifying correspondences does not require reconstruction. The reconstruction of proto-Transeurasian morphemes is a by-product, rather than the primary goal, of the comparative method. As Harrison (2003: 225) puts it: "One can use the comparative method to draw genetic conclusions without reconstructing a thing." Nevertheless, the present work will propose concrete reconstructions for ancestral morphemes because they make the posited set of changes between the daughter languages and the ancestral language more visible and because they serve as the basic units of the overall ancestral morphological system.

2.2.3.2 Reconstruction of family-inherent grammaticalization patterns

Cyclicity of grammaticalization refers to those repetitive waves of language renewal whereby more grammaticalized items are replaced by less grammaticalized items that again develop into more grammaticalized items. One example given by Hopper & Traugott (1993: 9–10, 42–44) is the replacement of the Latin future marker in *canta-bimus* 'we will sing', which has grammaticalized from a periphrastic construction in proto-Indo-European **kanta bhumos* 'we are singing', by a new periphrastic expression Lat. *cantare habemus* 'we have to sing'. This construction developed into the French future marker Fr. *chanterons* 'we will sing', which in turn is being replaced by *nous allons chanter*, literally 'we are going to sing'.

The mechanism behind this tendency of cyclic renewal is a matter of competing forces. Following Givón (1979: 208–209, 213, 220) it lies in the balance between the communicative gains and losses of grammaticalization, namely the balance between easy speech and clear speech.[2] Grammaticalization increases the speed and ease of transmitting messages by automatic processing. Renewal, by contrast, favors message transparency at the expense of fast morphologically coded processing. If the process speeds up, this results in lack of clarity. If clarity is restored, on the other hand, the process slows down,

Genealogically related languages show a disposition to repeat the 'same' grammaticalization processes over and over again. When cognate morphemes have a grammaticalization process in common, in addition to sharing form and function, this grammaticalization is likely to be genealogically motivated (see Section 2.5.3.1). The grammaticalization may either be inherited, in the sense that it was already completed in the proto-language and carried on as polysemy in the daughter languages, or, alternatively, it may have occurred independently in each of the daughter languages after separation from the common ancestor. The latter phenomenon, which is known as "parallel drift" or "Sapirian drift" seems to guide cognate morphemes over family-inherent pathways of grammaticalization. Even if there is evidence that a reconstructed morpheme underwent a specific process of grammaticalization after separation from the common ancestor, it may thus still be legitimate to reconstruct the grammaticalization process as such back to the common ancestor.

---

[2] Recently structural accounts have started to appear accounting for the cyclicity of grammaticalization. Van Gelderen (2008), for instance, refers to minimalist economy principles as mechanisms of cyclicity.

According to Joseph (2012: 163–164) "parallel drift" has a socio-linguistic explanation: "one should entertain the possibility that there was proto-language variation between X and X', where one is the fuller form and the other the apparently "grammaticalized" form, and posit further that each language inherited that variation and that the "grammaticalized" form bubbled up after being sociolinguistically suppressed." Sociolinguistically suppressed in this context seems to refer to the marginal presence of the grammaticalized form in the proto-language, either because it was used by a small group of speakers only, or because its productivity was restricted to the derivation of a limited set of forms only.

Although I believe that Joseph's account may be part of the explanation of parallel drift, in many cases it may not be necessary to posit submerged variation in the proto-language. The phenomenon may have a more obvious structural explanation. It is based on the expectation that languages try to maintain pre-existing categories in spite of formal renewal. Therefore, newly inserted items will be guided over family-specific pathways of grammaticalization to restore old categories. In this way, prior pathways of grammaticalization become decisive in shaping the new ones within a language family (Heath 1998, Aikenvald 2013).

The present study will attempt to reconstruct such family-inherent grammaticalization patterns for the Transeurasian languages, for instance for the development of negation in Chapter 4, the grammaticalization of deverbal actional suffixes from denominal verbalizers in Chapter 5, the development of passives from causatives in Chapter 6, direct insubordination and the development of temporal distinctions in Chapter 7 and converbialization of instrumental nominalizers in Chapter 8.

2.2.3.3 Reconstruction of proto-systems

It should be examined whether the reconstructed morphological units can be organized into internally structured sets and whether these sets build a grammatical system, displaying paradigmatic organization. In addition, we should identify shared irregularities in specific parts of the system and examine to what extent they can be derived from regularity in the ancestral paradigm. We should also try to establish external relationships of grammatical patterning among different subsystems. We should further test whether the different morphosyntactic subsystems are balanced in the sense that the cognate morphemes should be consistently spread over nominal and verbal morphology, inflectional and derivational morphology, and over the different grammatical categories that are part of these subsystems.

2.3 Reducing the chance factor

An important problem that reduces the diagnostic value of morphological comparisons is that morphological elements are typically very short, often mono- or bisegmental. As a result, similar forms tend to occur by coincidence even in unrelated languages. In Section 5.3, I will advance evidence from all branches of the Transeurasian family in support of the reconstruction of a causative-passive suffix pTEA *-ti-. However, it is easy to find reconstructions of causatives in *t in other language families across the world. Hyman (2014: 111) noted that a causative affix with a dental stop has been reconstructed for two macro groups and one family in Africa: proto-Niger-Congo *-ti, proto-Nilo-Saharan *-it̪' and proto-Chadic *-d. Outside Africa *t causatives appear in reconstructions such as the transitive-causative proto-Dravidian *-tt (Krishnamurti 2003: 283) and the denominal factitive and deverbal causative proto-Uralic *-tå- / -tä- (Janhunen 1982: 33). Some of these forms have even led to the reconstruction of a causative-reflexive in proto-Nostratic *t'V- by Kaiser and Shevoroshkin (1988: 313).

Nevertheless, even if the typical shortness of morphemes increases the probability of finding coincidental look-alikes across the languages of the world, this statistical effect is counterbalanced by a number of other characteristics inherent in the comparison of morphemes as pursued in this study. Factors reducing the probability that the proposed morphological correlations are coincidental include (1) the number of proposed etymologies, (2) the number of branches in which the morphological item has a match, (3) the relatively small size of the inventory of verb morphemes in an average language, (4) the verification of sound correspondences in matching morphemes against regular correspondences previously established on the basis of lexical data, (5) the number of matched segments in the morphological cognates, (6) shared polysemy, (7) shared irregularity and (8) the occurrence of systematic correlations.

First, apart from the supposedly coincidental matching of the *t causatives, there is only one other verb affix with a resemblance between the African macro-groups Niger-Congo, Afro-Asiatic and Nilo-Saharan (Hyman 2014: 111) and some so-called "Nostratic" groups such as Indo-European, Kartvelian and Dravidian (Kaiser & Shevoroshkin 1988: 313), notably a causative affix containing a common segment *s. These two instances may serve as an indication of the number of etymologies for verb affixes that can be expected to match by sheer chance when comparing a handful of random families. The present study proposes over twenty different etymologies for verb suffixes, well-represented in the five branches of the family. One intuitively feels that twenty etymologies with matching members in up to five branches is too striking a number to be attributed to coincidence.

Second, chance probability decreases with the number of branches in which the morphemes are matched. The only Transeurasian verb affix that displays a straightforward match in more than one other family is the causative-passive suffix pTEA *-ti. It is much easier, however, to find verb affixes that match in a binary setting, such as the resemblances between the Transeurasian and Uralic verb suffixes pTEA *-nA- processive and pUr *-n- denominal fientive (Section 5.4), pTEA *-pu- reflexive-anticausative and pUr *-w- reflexive-anticausative-passive (Section 6.4) and the deverbal noun suffixes pTEA *-mA and *-sA and pUr *-mə and *-śÄ (Sections 7.4 and 7.7). If not due to early contact or remote ancestorship, at least some of these similarities may be coincidental. It should not come as a surprise that it is difficult to add more coincidental look-alikes from the three African macro groups or from Dravidian to these matching pairs, for multiple comparison decreases chance probability, provided that the match is simultaneously present in each and every branch (See also Section 2.5.5).

Third, the probability that a certain correspondence is due to coincidence decreases with the number of elements that are open to comparison, i.e the number of trials made. My birthday being on October 24th, it is easier to find somebody who has their birthday on the same day in a group of 100 people than in a group of 20 people. The probability of finding somebody who is born on the same day therefore decreases with the number of people to select from. Whereas the average number of words in a language exceeds several tens of thousands, the average number of verb morphemes remains below one hundred. By consequence, the probability that a certain correspondence in verb morphology is due to coincidence will be lower than that for a similar correspondence within the lexicon, because the body of elements open to comparison is much smaller.

Fourth, comparing the causative-passive suffix pTEA *-ti- with the causatives proto-Niger-Congo *-ti, proto-Nilo-Saharan *-iṯ', proto-Chadic *-d, proto-Dravidian *-tt and proto-Uralic *-tå- / -tä-, we are unable to test the assumed consonant correspondences pNC t :: pNS ṯ' :: pC d :: pD tt :: pUr t – let alone the vowel correspondences – against regular sound correspondences established on the basis of lexical comparison. By contrast, the formal correspondences of morphological cognates across the Transeurasian languages can be confirmed on the basis of an independently established set of phonological rules. Obviously, the fact that the formal correspondences in matching morphemes can be verified against pre-existing rules decreases the likelihood of coincidental matches.

Fifth, as noted by Campbell (1988: 600), the greater the number of matched segments in a proposed cognate set, the less likely it is that accident accounts for the similarity. It is exponentially more difficult to find a match between a subsequent consonant and vowel than it is to find a match for a single segment. In many morphological similarities between Transeurasian and Uralic, such as pTEA *-ti causative-passive and pUr *-tå- / -tä- causative; pTEA *-nA- processive and pUr *-n- denominal fientive; pTEA *-pu- reflexive-anticausative and pUr *-w- reflexive-anticausative-passive; pTEA *-mA and pUr *-mə deverbal noun, only the consonant is matched, while the vowel remains un-matched. Chance probability decreases when we can account for the entire morpheme, not just for some arbitrarily segmented part of it.

Sixth, comparing forms with diffuse or general meanings such as the common denominator 'deverbal noun suffix' for pTEA *-mA and pUr *-mə or pTEA *-i and pUr *-i/ -y, may enhance coincidental matches. However, shared semantic specialization such as the distinctive use of pTEA *-mA in color nouns or shared polysemy such as the secondary use of pTEA *-i in converbs decreases chance probability. Note that such semantic specialization or polyfunctionality is not found in the parallels with Uralic.

Seventh, shared irregularity such as in the formation of the Indo-European copula root in Table 1 reduces the probability that the correlations are due to sheer chance. Shared irregularity in bound morphemes includes shared allomorphy conditioned by a specific phonological environment, such as the allomorphy in the reflexes of the deverbal noun suffix pTEA *-xA ~ -kA (see Section 6.6), depending on the fricativity of the preceding consonant. It may also consist in shared functional irregularity conditioned by a specific semantic environment, such as the aspectual and temporal distinctions of the reflexes of pTEA *-rA (see Section 6.3), which are conditioned by the telicity of the base verb.

Finally, the sharing of an ordered paradigm of individual morphemes is more difficult to attribute to chance than the sharing of a set of randomly amassed morphemes. Examples of coincidentally matching paradigms are extremely difficult to find across the languages of the world. As illustrated in Table 2, Campbell and Poser (2008: 188) refer to the coincidences between a set of verb agreement endings in Proto-Eastern Miwok (Central California) and in Indo-European, but in this case the matches only involve five cells of the paradigm and do not extend to the third person plural. Moreover, the Eastern Miwokan paradigm is not even found in Proto-Miwokan but formed secondarily.

Table 2. Coincidences between Proto-Eastern Miwokan and Indo-European (Campbell and Poser 2008: 188)

	Proto Eastern Miwokan declarative suffixes	Indo-European active suffixes
1SG	*-ma· ~ -m	*-m
2SG	*-sY ~ -ṣ	*-s
3SG	*-Ø	*-t < **-Ø
1PL	*-maṣ·i ~ *-maṣ	*-me(s)/-mo(s)
2PL	*-to-k	*-te

2.4 Eliminating code-copying

2.4.1 Understanding copiability

With respect to morphology, code-copying is the contact-induced replication of a morpheme from a model language into a basic language, whereas inheritance refers to the residue of morphological similarities retained in the daughter languages after separation from their ancestral language. Throughout this book, the term "copy" thus refers to a borrowed morpheme, whereas the term "cognate" designates a morpheme which is related to a morpheme in another language by virtue of inheritance. The terminology of "code-copying" is part of a descriptive model for contact-induced change, proposed by Lars Johanson. Terms such as "copy", "global copy", "selective copy", "model" language (or code), "basic" language (or code) are preferred to more traditional notions such as "borrowing", "direct transfer", "indirect transfer", "donor" language and "recipient" language, respectively. Metaphorically, the term "copy" is obviously more correct than the term "borrowing" because the model language does not give anything up, and the copying language does not give a borrowed item back. The main point, however, is that a copy is never identical with the model. Johanson's terminology highlights code-copying as an essentially creative act: under external influence, speakers shape their language in novel ways.

Stability refers to the likelihood of an item being inherited; it is the tendency to successfully resist both internally and externally motivated change. Copiability only concerns externally motivated change; it refers to the likelihood of an item being affected by copying. The assumption is that a word class, a category or a part of language structure is more likely to be copied if it is copied more frequently in cross-linguistic sampling. Empirically, it is observed that there is a difference in the copiability between nouns and verbs, between free and bound morphemes and between derivational and inflectional morphology. Substantial work on hierarchies of copiability has been carried out by e.g. Weinrich (1953: 35), Moravcsik (1978), Thomason & Kaufman (1988: 74–75), Wilkins (1996) and Matras (2009: 153–165). Their description of copiability as a relative tendency suggests that bound verb morphemes belong to the most stable parts of linguistic substance and provide fairly reliable evidence to demonstrate common ancestorship. Even though I believe that no single part of language structure is conclusive by itself, my decision to limit the scope of this book to bound verb morphology is based on this assumption.

The debate over the possibility of distinguishing inherited similarities from contact-induced similarities is known in the linguistic literature as "the Boas-Sapir controversy" (Jakobson 1944, Swadesh 1951, Darnell & Sherzer 1971). In their efforts to work out genealogical relationships among Native American Languages, Boas and Sapir took different positions about the question whether some core parts of linguistic structure, morphology in particular, were impervious to copying. Sapir (1921: 206) claimed that there were "no really convincing examples of morphological influence by diffusion", while Boas (1917: 4, 1938: 139) took the opposite view that for many languages it was impossible to tell whether shared forms resulted from common ancestorship or from external influence. It should be noted that the morphological similarity to which these authors referred did not consist of form-function matches, but of shared properties of morphological structure.

Sapir's constraint on morphological copying influenced a generation of scholars, such as Meillet and Swadesh, but there was a growing awareness that this constraint should be reformulated in terms of relative tendencies. Although Meillet (1921: 93) was confident that morphological paradigms were completely resistant to borrowing, he allowed for occasional borrowing of individual morphological elements: "En fait il est rare qu'on emprunte à une autre langue ... une forme grammaticale, quand pareil fait se produit, il ne modifie pas l'ensemble de chacun des systèmes et demeure un accident." (Meillet 1921: 84). Swadesh (1951: 17) stressed the relative character of stability: "It is understood that stability, whether of basic vocabulary or of formative elements, means relative and not absolute stability."

Even though scholars in the 1950s grew more aware of the ubiquity of borrowing, the received view remained that paradigms were stable and fully resistant to code-copying. Weinreich (1953: 43–44), for instance, found that inflectional morphology could be copied in some rare cases, but he ruled out the adoption of an entire inflectional paradigm: "The transfer of a full grammatical paradigm, with its formant morphemes, has apparently never been recorded."

However, with the increased interest in grammatical borrowing in the decades following Weinreich's study, such paradigmatic transfers have indeed been recorded, and in the 1980s Thomason and Kaufman (1988: 19–20) demonstrated that even the claim that paradigms resist code-copying needs revision. Nevertheless, Weinreich's constraint continues to circulate in the contemporary literature: Aikhenvald (2007b: 18), for instance, notes that "[t]here are no instances of one language borrowing a complete paradigm, say, of pronominal forms, or verbal inflection." Gardani (2008: 84) confirms that to his knowledge "no cases of genuine borrowing of entire inflectional paradigms have been attested." Moreover, Weinreich's constraint is echoed in the Transeurasian comparative literature, leading Vovin (2008: 45) to claim that "paradigmatic morphology is never borrowed (except in the case of language mixing)."

Nevertheless, there is counter-evidence even to this assumption of a minimal constraint on copying paradigmatic morphology, as shown by recent studies on morphological borrowing (Matras & Sakel 2007, Vanhove et al. 2012, Johanson & Robbeets 2012, Robbeets & Bisang 2014, Gardani et al. 2014). Furthermore, contributions such as those by Kossmann (2010) and Seifart (2012) even seem to support the view that languages tend to favor paradigmatic borrowing over the copying of individual morphemes. Seifart (2012: 477), for instance, predicts that: "cross-linguistically, sets of borrowed morphemes are more likely to be paradigmatically and syntagmatically related than not."

Taken at face value, the pervasiveness of contact-induced change constitutes a serious threat to the possibility of distinguishing inherited similarities from contact-induced similarities. If code-copying can result in shared bound morphology, including paradigms, is it still possible to subscribe to Nichols' (1996: 41) statement that "the evidence [for a genealogical relationship] is primarily grammatical and includes morphological material with complex paradigmatic and syntagmatic organization."? I believe that the answer to this question should be "yes" because, first, copiability is a relative tendency and, second, borrowed morphemes are expected to manifest themselves differently than inherited morphemes. Although copying bound verbal morphology is possible, it is not likely to occur. Hence, bound verb morphology is *relatively* impervious to foreign influence and, therefore, remains a safe diagnostic substance for classifying a language genealogically. In addition, the failure to define absolute criteria to rule out borrowing does not imply that there are no relative indications supporting such a distinction. By comparing copying patterns with genealogical patterns in a cross-linguistic sample of languages, I will propose several guidelines for identifying the effects of contact vs. inheritance in shared morphology in the Sections 2.4.2 and 2.4.3.

2.4.2 Indications of code-copying

Rather than pursuing constraints on copiability, we need to look at what does in fact get copied. This brings us to the question of how copies manifest themselves as opposed to cognates. In order to partially answer this question, I will compare cross-linguistic cases of historically identifiable borrowing with cases of well-established inheritance of morphology. Contrasting characteristics of contact-induced morphology with those of inherited morphology, I will infer possible ways to distinguish between the effects of copying and inheritance at more remote time-depths; see also Robbeets (2012). If the morphological comparanda meet one or more of the eight criteria below, the probability of inheritance decreases while the likelihood of code-copying increases.

2.4.2.1 Productivity restricted to shared roots

An indication of morphological borrowing is the restriction of shared morphemes to shared roots. This criterion is valid for derivational as well as for inflectional morphology. The borrowing of derivational morphology is a gradual process: first, the morphemes are borrowed along with lexical items; later, they become extracted and productive on other foreign bases and finally, on native bases. Matras (2009: 209) distinguishes between the term "forward diffusion" for the former case and "backwards diffusion" for the latter. The denominal verbalizers *-ize* and *-ify*, for instance, entered English in the 12th century through borrowings of Old French verbs ending in *-iser* and *-efier* /*-ifier* (e.g. *baptize, stupefy, sanctify*). From the 16th century onwards new verbs were derived, first, from Latinate (e.g. *equalize, objectify*), then from other foreign bases such as Greek (e.g. *chondrify* 'turn into cartilage (Greek *chóndros*)') and, finally, from some native bases (e.g. *womanize, ladify*), but even in contemporary English *-ize* and *-ify* combine more frequently with foreign than with native bases (Marchand 1960, 238–240, 255–259; Gottfurcht 2007: 84–85).

The borrowing of inflectional verb morphology can follow a similar pathway: first, the morphemes are borrowed along with loan verbs; later, they become applicable to other loan verbs and finally, to native verbs.[3] One example is the Sicilian Italian past participle ending, which has been copied into Maltese, an

---

[3] A second possible pathway is borrowing through analogy, based on perceived structural similarities, i.e. not hosted by loan verbs (Matras 2009: 215). Harris & Campbell (1995: 134) lists examples, such as the Finnish question marker *-ko* / *-kö*, which has been borrowed in various Lapp dialects in absense of a host verb. Similarly, Seifart (2012) shows that noun class markers in Resígaro were not primarily copied attached to a Bora free noun, but that they were copied in

originally Arabic dialect that developed in Malta (Gardani 2008: 38–39) The past participle morphemes are not only added to verb roots of Italian origin (e.g. *ittrattat* 'treated' from Italian *trattare*), but to English loans as well (e.g *koppja involuta* 'involved pair'). However, they have not been extended to native Semitic roots yet.

Another example is the Romani 3SG present agreement marker *-i*, which is copied from Greek (Matras 2009: 213). In many Romani dialects, it is limited to loan verbs from Greek, but in Arli Romani of Kosovo it also attaches to foreign Slavic verbal copies, e.g. *pomožin-i* 'he/she helps'. In Slovene Romani, it is generalized to all verbs, replacing the inherited Romani 3SG present agreement marker.[4]

Similarly, the contact with Spanish has substantially affected the morphology of three Amerindian languages, Quechua, Guarani and Otomi, but there are hardly any cases where the copied derivational and inflectional markers are found on native lexical entities; they are mainly restricted to nouns, verbs and adjectives copied from Spanish (Bakker and Hekking (2012: 199–202).

Moreover, Kossmann (2010) argues that the borrowing of entire morphological paradigms is a well-attested phenomenon in the languages of the world, but that in the majority of cases the borrowed paradigms are hosted by foreign lexicon. As illustrated in Table 3, Agia Varvara Romani, a Romani dialect spoken in a suburb of Athens, for instance, copied the Turkish nonfocal present paradigm, but all copied morphemes are hosted by verbs copied from Turkish (Igla 1996, 214–216; Friedman 2009, 112). Given the frequent borrowing of derivational and inflectional morphology along with foreign roots, an indication of a borrowing is the restriction of shared affixes to shared roots.

Table 3. Agia Varvara Romani copy of the present paradigm of Turkish *čalïš-* 'work'

	Turkish model (work-PRS-PERS)	Romani copy
1 SG	čalïš-ïr-ïm	*calusurum* 'I work'
2 SG	čalïš-ïr-sïn	*calusursun* 'you work'
3 SG	čalïš-ïr	*calusur* 'he works'
1 PL	čalïš-ïr-ïz	*calusurus* 'we work'
2 PL	čalïš-ïr-sïnïz	*calusursunus* 'you work'
3 PL	čalïš-ïr(-lar)	*calusur(lar)* 'they work'

isolation. These examples illustrate that a copied morpheme is not always hosted by a lexical item, but they do not challenge the diagnostic proposed here.

4 Greek also contributed its tense-aspect inflectional markers *-Vn-*, *-Vz-*, (present) and *-is-* (past) to Early Romani. First they were restricted to verbs copied from Greek, and subsequently they generalized to verbs from other contact languages.

2.4.2.2 Unilateral morphological complexity

Shared suffix strings that are morphologically segmentable in one language, but not in the other(s), are the result of copying. This is the case, for instance, for English *-ize* and German *-isieren*, which are borrowed from the Old French denominal verbalizer *-iser*. In contrast to the English and German suffixes, the Old French model can be compounded into a verbalizer *-is-*, which developed from Latin *-iz-*, and an infinitive suffix *-ier*, which marks a specific inflectional class of verbs going back to a subset of Latin verbs in *-a:re*. (Müller 1986: 75; Wilkinson 2000; Wohlgemuth 2009: 231–232). The correlations between the Romance and the Germanic verbalizers can easily be explained as borrowings because they go back to suffix strings in Romance, but not in Germanic.

An example from inflectional morphology is the borrowing of the evidential particle *-ka* in the Frasheriote Aromanian dialect of Gorna Belica from the Albanian third singular admirative present morpheme *-k-a* (Friedman 2003: 191, 196–197). Whereas the Albanian morpheme is morphologically complex, consisting of an admirative morpheme *-k-* and the third singular present ending *-a*, the Aromanian morpheme is an unsegmentable particle, used regardless of person and number.

Similarly, Wutun (Sinitic) has borrowed from Bao'an (Mongolic) the interrogative marker *-mu*, e.g. Wutun *qe-lio-mu* [eat-PFV-INTER] 'have (you) eaten?' (Janhunen 2012c: 25). The Wutun interrogative contains the Bao'an finite narrative marker *-m-* and the interrogative *-u*, e.g. Bao'an *ode-m-u* [go-FIN-INTER] 'do (you) go?'. However, Wutun reinterpreted the morpheme without taking into account the tense-aspect marking.

At the paradigmatic level, a similar observation goes for Table 3, where Agia Varvara Romani copies the Turkish present tense along with the entire paradigm of Turkish person marking. Other relevant examples are the copying of five cases of verbal paradigms from the Yakut into the North Tungusic dialects Uchur Evenki and Lamunkhin Even (Pakendorf 2009, 2014).[5] Table 4 illustrates the copying of the Yakut necessitative paradigm in Lamunkhin Even (Korkina 1982: 330; Pakendorf 2009: 97–102, 2014: 292–293). The copied strings consist of the Yakut future participle *-IAx* followed by the proprietive suffix *-LA:x-* along with the entire paradigm of Yakut person marking.[6] These suffixes do not occur as simplex morphemes in Even or elsewhere in Tungusic. The correlations can

---
[5] Whereas the assertive-presumptive paradigm has been copied into both dialects, the necessitative mood, the indicative present tense and the hypothetical mood are restricted to Lamunkhin Ėven only.
[6] It can be noted that the third person plural form of this paradigm takes the Even plural suffix *-(A)l* rather than Yakut plural marking. This is probably based on a structural analogy with

easily be shown to be copies because the suffix strings are morphologically complex in one language, but not in the other.

Table 4. Lamunkhin Even copy of the Yakut necessitative paradigm

	Yakut model (go-FUT.PCP-PROP-PERS)	Lamunkhin Even copy (know-NECC)
1 SG	bar-ïax-ta:x-pïn	ha:-jakta:kpịn
2 SG	bar-ïax-ta:x-xïn	ha:-jakta:kkịn
3 SG	bar-ïax-ta:x	ha:-jakta:k
1 PL	bar-ïax-ta:x-pït	ha:-jakta:kpịt
2 PL	bar-ïax-ta:x-xït	ha:-jakta:kkịt
3 PL	bar-ïax-ta:x-tar	ha:-jakta:k-al

2.4.2.3 Mismatch of morpheme boundaries

When the boundary of two corresponding morphemes does not coincide, the correspondences are probably contact-induced. One example is the borrowing of the Rumungro Romani verbalizer *-áz-* from Hungarian, which does not correspond to any allomorph of its Hungarian model. The extraction of the Hungarian verbalizer *-z-* involved a re-analysis of its boundary as *-áz-*, such as, for instance, in Rumungro *cigarett-áz-in-* (cigarette-VBL-LVM-) << Hungarian *cigarettá-z-* (cigarette-VBL-) 'to smoke cigarettes' (Elšík 2007: 278).

Another example is the borrowing of the nominalizers Sierra Populuca *-teeroj* and Pajapan Nahuatl *-tero* from the Spanish nominal agentive suffix *-ero*. The suffixes *-teeroj* and *-tero* have resulted from reanalysis of the boundary between the stem and the suffix, e.g. Spanish *carpint-ero* 'carpenter' is interpreted as *carpin-tero* (Gutiérrez-Morales 2012: 224–225).

A special case of mismatching boundaries is when a native verb in the recipient language needs an extra segment to accommodate for a copied suffix while attaching native suffixes as such. Table 5 illustrates the copying of the Yakut presumptive-assertive paradigm as a presumptive in Uchur Evenki and as an assertive in Lamunkhin Even (Mureeva 1964: 51; Malchukov 2003: 244, 2006: 126–127; Pakendorf 2009: 98–105, 109–110, 2014: 289–292; Comrie 2010: 26). The copied suffix strings require specific accommodation with a marker *-r-* in Evenki and with a connective glide *-j-* in Even, which is not needed for the affixation of native suffixes. In Lamunkhin Even, this glide has the function of integrating

---

the Yakut paradigm, whereby the third person plural indicative is derived with a plural marker from the unmarked third singular form.

copied Yakut verb morphology in general – not just the assertive-presumptive mood, but also the present tense and a converb (Pakendorf 2009: 97–100, 2014: 291). The overall mismatch of morpheme boundaries in general is therefore an indication of code-copying.

Table 5. Uchur Evenki and Lamunkhin Even copy of the Yakut assertive-presumptive paradigm

	Yakut model (go-PRES-PERS)	Uchur Evenki copy (kill-CONN-PRES)	Lamunkhin Even copy (spend the night-CONN-ASS)
1 SG	bar-day-ïm	wa:-r-dayim	a:ŋŋa-j-dagịm
2 SG	bar-day-ïŋ	wa:-r-dayiŋ	a:ŋŋa-j-dagịŋ
3 SG	bar-day-a	wa:-r-daya	a:ŋŋa-j-daga
1 PL	bar-dax-pït	wa:-r-dakput	a:ŋŋa-j-dakpịt
2 PL	bar-dax-xït	wa:-r-dakkit	a:ŋŋa-j-dakkịt
3 PL	bar-dax-tara	wa:-r-daktara	a:ŋŋa-j-daktara

2.4.2.4 Multiple marking of a single inflectional category

The repeated marking of an inflectional category that has already been expressed is an indication of code-copying. In Asia Minor Greece, for instance, the Greek dialects of Semenderé and Silli have copied the Turkish second plural possessive marker *-iniz* and added it to the native person endings of the first plural and the second plural (Dawkins 1916: 144; Thomason & Kaufman 1988: 219; Gardani 2008: 58–60; Matras 2009: 214). For example, the verb forms *kimumisti* 'we are sleeping' and *kimasti* 'you (PL) are sleeping' in other Greek dialects correspond to the Silli forms *kimumisti-niz* and *kimasti-niz*, in which *-iniz* is copied from Turkish as a general marker of plurality without regard to person. We can thus say that the forms are double-marked for plurality.

This additive effect is also found in the correlations for the first and second person indicative present between Bulgarian (South Slavic) and Megleno-Romanian (Balkan Romance), illustrated in Table 6. The endings of Megleno-Romanian are borrowed from the native Bulgarian person markers *-m* and *-š* for the first and second person singular. However, the morphemes involved seem to be added, not to the naked verb root, but to the corresponding inherited Romanian morphemes *-u* and *-i*, which are reflected in Daco-Romanian (Capidan 1925: 159–161, Weinreich 1953: 32–33, Thomason 2001: 77, 153, Gardani 2008: 67).[7]

---

[7] Friedman (2012: 325–326) objects that the phenomenon has potential language-internal explanations, i.e. analogy with the first person singular imperfect *-m* and the second singular of the fourth conjugation *-š* in Megleno-Romanian.

Table 6. Megleno-Romanian copies of Bulgarian person markers in comparison with Daco-Romanian forms

	Bulgarian model	Megleno-Romanian copy	Daco-Romanian sister
1 SG	namira-m	afl-u-m	afl-u
2 SG	namira-š	afl-i-ş	afl-i

An example of triple marking of the same category comes from Turkish and Greek contributions to Romani inflectional morphology (Matras 2009: 213). In the Balkan dialects of Romani, there are forms such as *anladi-s-ker-djom* 'I understood', where the form *anladi* is borrowed from the Turkish third person singular past tense *anla-dï* [understand-PST.3SG] 'he understood', *-(i)s-* is borrowed from the Greek aorist past marker, *-ker-* is the causative/transitive marker that integrates the loan verb and *-djom* the native first person singular past inflection. The fact that the form has three past markers is an indication of copying.

2.4.2.5 Functional mismatch

When the semantic correspondence is so divergent that it cannot be explained by referring to cross-linguistically attested pathways of grammaticalization or when it concerns a meaning that is demonstrably secondary to one of the participating morphemes, we are probably dealing with a copy. An example of the former case is the German suffix *-ieren*, which was already attested in Middle High German texts of the 12th and 13th century where it occurred with loan verbs from Old French and Latin. Gradually, the suffix became used as a denominal verbalizer following foreign (e.g. Old French *cimier* >> MHG *zimier* 'crest' → *zimieren* 'to decorate a helmet') and native bases (e.g. MHG *walke* 'plait' → *walkieren* 'to interlace tightly'). The Old French model *-ier*, however, is an infinitive suffix of one inflectional class going back to a subset of Latin verbs in *-a:re* whose stem ended in a palatal, like French *traitier* 'to treat' < Latin *tracta:re* (Müller 1986: 75; Wohlgemuth 2009: 230–231). The semantic mismatch between "infinitive" and "verbalizer", occuring in this example is a counter-argument against inheritance.

An example of a correlation restricted to secondary semantics is the case of the Yakut influence in Northern Tungusic, illustrated in Table 5 above. The Yakut suffix *-TAx* functions as a non-finite conditional-temporal marker in addition to marking the presumptive-assertive mood in the finite clause. It is safe to assume that the meaning of Yakut *-Tax* developed from temporal over conditional to presumptive and then to assertive. The Evenki and Even forms being restricted to finite use and the Even form in Pakendorf's corpus being restricted to finite assertive, the semantics shared with Yakut are secondary. This observation indicates that the similarities can be attributed to code-copying.

2.4.2.6 Phonological mismatch

If previous genealogical research has provided a system of sound correspondences on the basis of lexical comparison, it should be examined whether the affixes under comparison obey the same rules. When previously established sound correspondences are contradicted, and there is no clear conditioning factor explaining this mismatch, this can again be taken as an indication of borrowing. In the case of the borrowing of the English verbalizer *-ify*, for instance, the French model *-ifier* goes back to Latin *-ificare*, reflecting a fricative *-f-* in both Romance and Germanic. This goes against Grimm's law, according to which Germanic *-*f*- corresponds to Romance *-*p*- in cognates such as OE *nefa* vs. Latin *nepo:s* 'grandson', OE *häfer* vs. Latin *caper* 'buck', OE *re:ofan* vs. Latin *rumpere* 'break, tear', etc.

Another example comes from Acadian French spoken on Prince Edward Island in Canada. Here, the English loan *back* has replaced the French prefix *re-* in verbs such as *revenir* 'come back' as in *venir back, arriver back, mettre back* (King 1999, 116–125). In this case, Grimm's law can again prevent us from misinterpreting Acadian French *back* and English *back* as cognates. Lexical comparison shows that English word-initial *b-* corresponds regularly with French *f-*, as in *barley* and *farine* 'flour', *brother* and *frère* 'brother', *bottom* and *fond* 'bottom', *brass* and *ferre* 'iron'etc.

A final example is the borrowing of the Russian denominal verb suffix *-ova-* in some Lithuanian dialects as *-ova-*, a loan verbalizer, which ultimately became productive on native nouns (Wiemer 2009: 359). The corresponding cognate on the basis of regular correspondences is *-au(j)-* in Lithuanian (Arkadiev pc.).[8] Thus, contradiction of established sound correspondences is an indication of code-copying.

2.4.2.7 Distribution limited to contact zones

The limited distribution of morphemes within a particular contact zone is indicative of copying. The Yakut influence on Northern Tungusic verb morphology discussed above is restricted to the Yakut-Tungusic contact zone and does not occur in the Evenki and Even dialects to the East. The Albanian admirative present

---

8 The regular reflex *-au(j)-* results from a different (hetero- vs. tautosyllabic) treatment of *-non-front V + w + V- after the split of Baltic and Slavic.

-*ka* (Section 2.4.2.2) is copied into Romanian, but restricted to the Frasheriote Aromanian dialect of Gorna Belica, without spreading to other dialects spoken in that same village. The Lithuanian borrowing of the Russian denominal verbalizer -*ova*- (Section 2.4.2.6) is restricted to the extinct Lithuanian dialects of Zietela and Lazunai, which were once spoken in present-day Belarussia. It does not occur in those Lithuanian dialects, where the pressure of Slavic is less intensive. Therefore, the limitation of shared verbal morphology to contact zones is an indication of borrowing.

2.4.2.8 Specific morphosyntactic subsystems affected

The examples of copied verb morphology discussed above suggest that if morphemes are copied at all, it is often the case that more than one form is copied. As such, these examples seem to support Seifart's (2012: 475) hypothesis that "borrowing of paradigmatically and syntagmatically related grammatical morphemes is easier than borrowing of the same number of isolated grammatical morphemes." In some instances, such as in Table 3, 4 and 5 a form gets copied along with an entire paradigm, while in other cases, such as in Table 6, borrowing is restricted to a small subset of coherent functional pairings. Importantly, however, Seifart adds that paradigmatic copying is restricted to specific morphosyntactic subsystems. He points out that in Resígaro (Arawakan), for instance, certain morphological subsystems such as nominal classification and number marking have been copied entirely from Bora (Witotoan), while others have hardly been influenced at all. Similarly, the paradigms copied in Uchur Evenki and Lamunkhin Even, illustrated in Table 4 and 5, are clustered in a very specific morphosyntactic subsystem, notably mood (assertive-presumptive, necessative and hypothetical), while paradigms in other parts of the grammar are left unaffected. In most documented cases of paradigmatic borrowing, such as in Copper Island Aleut, Michif, Gurindji Kriol, Ma'a and the languages of Arnhem Land, we find a similar imbalance between copied and inherited morphosyntactic subsystems:[9]

---

[9] Copper Island Aleut, Michif, Gurindji Kriol and Ma'a can be regarded as "mixed" languages because different parts of grammar and lexicon come from different languages, to such an extent that it is impossible to assign them unequivocally to a single genealogical ancestor. The question arises whether in these cases 'mixed' refers to the nature of the languages having double ancestry or to the perception of the linguist, who may no longer be able to clearly distinguish the inherited from the copied subsystems. In my view, these "mixed" languages may represent instances of code-copying taken to an extreme.

Copper Island Aleut, spoken on the Commander Islands located to the east of Kamchatka, arose from a mixture of Aleut and Russian. As illustrated in Table 7 below, finite verb morphology is borrowed from Russian, whereas the majority of nouns (61%) and verbs (94%) along with nominal and verbal nonfinite morphology is of Aleut origin (Thomason & Kaufman 1988: 233–238, Sekerina 1994, Thomason 1997, Comrie 2008: 24–31, 2010: 28–30).

Michif, a language spoken in communities in North Dakota and nearby parts of Canada is a mixture derived from Cree (Algonquian) and French. In general, Michif verbs are of Cree origin and take Cree morphology, while nouns and most adjectives are contact-induced by French and take French morphology (Thomason & Kaufman 1988: 228–233, Bakker 1997: 97–102; Comrie 2008: 21–22).

Gurindji Kriol is a mixed language spoken in the Northern Territory of Australia derived from Kriol, an English-based creole and Gurindji, an Aboriginal language. Most of its verbs, nouns and nominal morphology are of Gurindji origin, while Kriol contributed specific verbal morphology such as tense-aspect-mood and transitivity marking (McConvell & Meakins 2005: 10–11).

Ma'a is a Cushitic language spoken in Tanzania that has massively copied from Pare, a Bantu language (Thomason 1983, Thomason & Kaufman 1988: 223–228). Much of the vocabulary and derivational morphology is of Cushitic origin, while the inflectional morphology, apart from some fossilized Cushitic features, has mainly been copied from Bantu.

The majority of copied morphemes in the Australian languages of Arnhem Land cluster in nominal paradigms such as case marking, plural marking, or noun class marking. Most derivational and inflectional verb morphology remains unaffected by borrowing (Heath 1978: 105).

These observations suggest that code-copying tends to be restricted to specific morphosyntactic subsystems, while inheritance will affect morphosyntactic subsystems in general. Therefore, shared paradigmaticity that is restricted to specific morphosyntactic subsystems is indicative of borrowing.

2.4.3 Indications of genealogical retention

If the morphological comparanda meet one or more of the six criteria below, the probability of borrowing decreases while the likelihood of inheritance increases.

2.4.3.1 Globally shared grammaticalization

Most cases of so-called contact grammaticalization referred to in the literature involve "selective semantic copying" (Johanson's 2002), also termed "replication" (Heine &Kuteva 2005: 7) or "pattern borrowing" Matras (2009). An example is the contact-induced grammaticalization of the verb 'to make, do', i.e. *ua* in Hmong, *làm* in Vietnamese and *tham* in Thai, to a causative auxiliary (Bisang 1996: 577).[10] As is typical in cases of contact grammaticalization, these Southeast Asian languages maintain their native form of the verb 'to make, do' and only borrow the causative meaning from each other. We can, therefore, conclude that shared grammaticalization due to contact is usually selective: it involves function, not form.

The linguistic literature offers few counterexamples of the tendency for contact-induced grammaticalization to be selective (Robbeets & Cuyckens 2013; Robbeets 2013). Two examples concern the development of a lexical verb 'to receive' into a passive marker. After globally copying the German verb *kriegen* 'to receive' as a lexical verb in the form *krynuś*, Sorbian speakers have grammaticalized it into a passive marker, perhaps under German influence (Nau 1995: 107; Heine & Kuteva 2006: 254). A similar example comes from the Old Chinese verb 得 *tˤək > tok > dé* 'to obtain', which was borrowed into Vietnamese as *được* 'to obtain, get'. Later the verb grammaticalized into a passive marker in Chinese, a development that is also attested in Vietnamese (Sagart p.c.).[11] Such examples global contact grammaticalization, i.e. displaying a full correspondence including form, are very rare cross-linguistically. Therefore, I have previously argued that globally shared grammaticalization is a strong indication of inheritance (Robbeets 2013).

The shared grammaticalization from denominal factitives 'to make the base' to deverbal causatives shared by several Uralic languages on corresponding forms of the shape *-tå-/ -tä-* (Janhunen 1982: 33), for instance, is probably genealogically motivated. It is unlikely that this example can be attributed to language contact because the shared grammaticalization involves formally corresponding morphemes.

Another example of genealogically motivated grammaticalization is the shared grammaticalization of the verbs 'to have' into future markers in the Romance languages. The verbs French *avoir*, Spanish *haber*, Portuguese *haver* and Italian *avere* are cognates and so are the grammaticalized future markers in

---

10 Even though it remains unclear which language served as the model, it seems likely that the grammaticalization is contact-induced.
11 Given the relative frequency of the grammaticalization of a verb 'to receive' into a passive worldwide (Heine & Kuteva 2002: 145–147), these examples may well represent a globally copied verb that later independently grammaticalized in the model and the recipient language, rather than undergoing contact-induced grammaticalization. Either way, the observable product of the historical process remains the same: globally shared grammaticalization.

French *chante-rons*, Spanish *canta-remos*, Portuguese *canta-remos* and Italian *cante-remo* 'we will sing' (Fleischman 1982: 15, Pinkster 1987: 203–214, Klausenburger 2000). This indicates that the process of grammaticalization was already well on its way in common Romance, which accounts for the same path being followed by so many Romance languages in the formation of a new future. This assumption is corroborated by 6th and 7th century attestations in Vulgar Latin of forms such as *daras* 'you will give' and *pussediravit* 'shall possess'.

Similarly, in Romance, the Latin verb *facere* 'to make' developed over a suffix *-facere* in the older stages of Latin into the Classical Latin suffix *-ificare* 'to make, convert into or bring into the state of the base'. Romance languages have inherited the source (French *faire*, Italian *fare*, Spanish *hacer*, etc.) as well as the target of this grammaticalization process (French *-éfier*, Italian *-ificare*, Spanish *-iguar*, etc.). However, the borrowing as English *-ify* involves only the target of grammaticalization.

Hence, I regard globally shared grammaticalization as a strong indication of inheritance. Nevertheless, the criterion in itself it is insufficient to "prove" that languages are related. A number of additional criteria are needed to reduce the likelihood of universal factors or contact and to sternghten the case for genealogical relatedness:

(i) The globally shared grammaticalization should involve a cross-linguistically infrequent and randomly spread development. As noted in Section 2.2.2.4, shared phenomena that are relatively uncommon and randomly spread across the world's languages are not likely to be accounted for by linguistic universals. It follows that instances of globally shared grammaticalization that reflect a cross-linguistically infrequent and randomly spread pathway are better accounted for by genealogical retention. For the shared grammaticalization of the verbs 'to have' into future markers in the Romance languages above, for instance, it is unlikely that the cognate verbs underwent the development independently in each language because, according to Heine & Kuteva (2002: 243), "while this grammaticalization is common in Romance languages, it does not appear to be a salient pathway for the development of future tense markers cross-linguistically."

(ii) The globally shared grammaticalization should concern two or more instances. A single case of globally shared grammaticalization could still be considered as a matter of language contact or parallel but independent developments occurring by chance on coincidentally similar forms. However, when a number of instances of globally shared grammaticalization cluster in a particular group of languages, this adds support to the genealogical argument.

(iii) The globally shared grammaticalization should involve the development of a less grammaticalized to a more grammaticalized bound morpheme. As noted in Section 2.2.2.2, grammaticalization is not restricted to lexical items, but also includes an increase in grammatical status by an already bound morpheme. The rare instances of globally shared grammaticalization that are not genealogically motivated, such as the development of 'to receive' into a passive marker above, concern the grammaticalization of a lexical item. It is generally known that bound morphemes are more resistant to code-copying than independent lexemes. Therefore, it is increasingly difficult to find instances of globally copied grammaticalization where the source is a bound morpheme. Consequently, such cases provide even stronger support for genealogical retention.

(iv) The globally shared grammaticalization should be spread over more than two (proto-) languages. The probability that a certain morphological copy will serve as a model for a new copy into another recipient language, repeatedly – say four times – is already small. The probability, however, that precisely this "Wandermorphem" will subsequently undergo the same grammaticalization process as in the model – again repeatedly in the 4 recipient languages – further decreases dramatically. I am unable to find examples of languages that are only distantly related, like German and Sorbian, or unrelated, like Vietnamese and Chinese, where two subsequent borrowing processes (a contact-induced grammaticalization on a copied source) have been repeated in yet another language. Neither Sorbian nor Vietnamese has globally transferred its verb 'to receive' and subsequently passed on the grammaticalization of 'to receive' into a passive marker to any third language. Extrapolating this observation to linguistic prehistory, it is unlikely that globally shared grammaticalization that is spread over more than two proto-languages is due to language contact.

(v) A specific pathway of grammaticalization should occur in more than one cognate set. Aikhenvald (2013) characterizes contact-induced grammaticalization as "change against the grain", whereas she regards genealogically motivated grammaticalization as "change that reinforces similarities". She finds that the former involves grammaticalization pathways atypical for a certain family, whereas the latter tends to maintain uniformity between genealogically related languages. Languages tend to renew their formal encodings in cyclic processes of grammaticalization, while maintaining their inherited grammatical categories. New encodings are thus expected to grammaticalize over shared conceptual pathways to restore old categories. Consequently, genealogically motivated grammaticalization is expected to recur on different formal encodings at various points in time, while contact-induced grammaticalization is expected to be restricted to a single formal encoding (or to a very limited number of encodings) during the period of contact. Therefore, I consider instances of globally shared grammaticalization where the specific pathway recurs in more than one set of formally related morphemes to be a strong indication of inheritance.

2.4.3.2 Categorial opacity

Categorial clarity refers to morphosemantic transparency whereby the grammatical function of a morpheme can be understood without considering the context of its broader morphosyntactic environment. Auxiliaries, for instance, are categorially more opaque than full-fledged verbs because they are governed by the main verb. Morphemes that are categorically opaque are firmly embedded in the sentence; at least one other morpheme must be simultaneously examined before they can be understood. As noted by Weinrich (1953: 34–35) morphemes with such "complex grammatical functions" tend to resist copying more successfully. Gardani (2008, 88) concludes that none of the copied morphemes involved in his research on inflectional borrowing can be viewed as categorially opaque. Heath (1978: 111–112) finds that in the Australian languages in the Arnhem Land area the verbal inflectional suffixes marking tense, aspect, mood and negativity are totally immune to copying. He attributes this to an interaction of impeding factors, one of them being opacity. In Nu, for instance, inflectional suffixes only make sense in the light of other morphemes such as prefixes and particles. The so-called 'past-2' in Nu can be past continuous, past negative, past potential, or past negative potential, dependent on which prefixes and negative particles are present in the verb complex. It appears that, if corresponding morphemes are categorially opaque, they are likely to be inherited.

2.4.3.3 Shared cumulation

Cumulative morphemes, i.e. morphemes with an unanalyzable form that simultaneously blend several distinct morphosyntactic features, are relatively impervious to copying.[12] Gardani (2008: 89) finds that 70 % of all cases of copied inflectional morphemes involved in his study are monofunctional. According to Heath (1978: 105–106) the Australian languages in Arnhem land show a propensity to copy noncumulative affixes rather than portmanteau ones. This tendency is reflected in the numerous examples of borrowed case suffixes provided by the Australian languages in Arnhem Land provide many examples of borrowing of case suffixes, whereas this is one of the rarest kinds of global copying in European languages. Indeed, the case markers in the languages in Arnhem Land are typi-

---

[12] Note that cumulative exponence differs from polyfunctionality; in the former case a morpheme simultaneously expresses distinct functions, whereas in the latter case a morpheme expresses a different function in a different context. In Arnhem Land, the ergative-instrumental case marker borrowed into Ngandi from Ritharngu (Heath 1978: 75–77), for instance, is polyfunctional but not cumulative because it is either ergative or instrumental but not both simultaneously.

cally noncumulative, while many Indo-European languages tend to mark case with portmanteau morphemes that simultaneously express gender and number. Similarly, the examples of copying verb agreement in Table 3, 4 and 5 all involve an agglutinative Turkic language as a model. In most Indo-European languages, however, verb agreement is blended in a single portmanteau morpheme, along with tense or mood, which makes inflection more resistant to code-copying.

Moreover, in cases where forms with cumulative exponence are copied, the cumulation tends to be reduced in the recipient language. When the Frasheriote Aromanian dialect copied the Albanian complex morpheme -*ka* expressing third singular admirative present, for instance, it reinterpreted the morpheme regardless of person and number. This is also the case for the borrowing of the Bao'an narrative interrogative -*mu* in Wutun, which was reinterpreted regardless of the narrartive marking (Section 2.4.2.2). This tendency also surfaces in the copying of the second plural possessive marker -*iniz* from Turkish into Semenderé and Silli as a general marker of plurality without regard to person (Section 2.4.2.4).

Another example is the copying of the inchoative -*ṭi*- denominal verb suffix from Ritharngu into Ngandi (Heath 1978: 92–93). In Ritharngu, as well as in other languages of the Yuulngu family, the suffix is cumulative in the sense that it derives intransitive verbs from nouns (including adjectival nouns) while adding an inchoative meaning, i.e. 'to become (the nominal base)', e.g. Ritharngu *ḍa:l* 'strong, firm' → *ḍa:l-ṭi-* 'to become/be strong, firm'. In Ngandi, which is not a Yuulngu language, the suffix is borrowed as a denominal verb suffix, but the inchoative meaning 'become' is lost, e.g. Ngandi *biṛ* 'many' → *biṛ-ṭi-* 'to be many'. Therefore, shared cumulation is regarded as an indication of inheritance.

2.4.3.4 Unreduced allomorphy

The recipient language tends to replace phonologically conditioned alternants by fewer allomorphs. In the example of the inchoative above (Section 2.4.3.3), the Ritharngu model displays a number of irregular allomorphs in which the suffix weakens to -*yi*- and contracts with the final vowel of the preceding stem, such as in *miḍiki-* 'become bad' from *miḍiku* 'bad'. Ngandi borrowed the default allomorph but left unusual allomorphic alternations unaffected.

Similarly, in the example given in Section 2.4.2.1, English reduces the allomorphy between Old French -*efier* and -*ifier* when borrowing the verbalizer from French. Except for a few verbs such as *liquefy* and *rubefy*, the majority of English loan verbs from Old French ended in -*ify*. For reasons of frequency, only the allomorph -*ify* was reanalyzed as a denominal verbalizer productive on native bases. With the exeption of *negrofy* and *argufy*, all denominal verbs only end in -*ify*, thus reducing the original allomorphy in the model language.

The Yakut presumptive-assertive mood in *-TAx-* in Table 5 above has a number of consonantal allomorphs that depend on the preceding stem-final consonant: the main allomorph *-tAx-* assimilates to *-lAx* after /l/, to *-dAx-* after /j/ and /r/ and to *-nAx-* after nasals. The introduction of the connectives *-j-* in Lamunkhin Even and *-r-* in Uchur Evenki seem to serve phonotactic purposes, namely to reduce the possible allomorphs to fewer variants, i.e. *-dAg-/-dAy-*.

Another example comes from Russian and Copper Island Aleut, which share a considerable amount of finite verb morphology, as illustrated in Table 7. Russian has two conjugational classes, differentiated by the inflectional person-number suffixes in the present tense. The most explicit difference is that the third person plural in the first conjugation is *-(j)ut*, whereas in the second conjugation it is *-(j)at*. Mednyi Aleut has reduced the allomorphy: it only has *-jut* in the third plural (Sekerina 1994, 25; Comrie 2008, 27; 2010, 29). Therefore, sharing complete allomorphy is regarded as an indication of inheritance.

Table 7. Shared finite verb paradigm in Copper Island Aleut and Russian

	Russian model		Aleut copy
	1. 'work'	2. 'speak'	'work'
1 SG	rabota-ju	govar-ju	aba-ju
2 SG	rabota-eš´	govar-iš´	aba-iš
3 SG	rabota-et	govar-it	aba-it
1 PL	rabota-em	govar-im	aba-im
2 PL	rabota-ete	govar-ite	aba-iti
3 PL	rabota-jut	govar-jat	aba-jut

2.4.3.5 Multiple comparative setting

Since morphological borrowing typically goes from a model language into a recipient language, most sets of borrowed verb morphemes discussed so far have a binary setting in common. Occasionally, however, the borrowing may proceed into a third or even a fourth language. Most commonly, such "Wandermorpheme" are found in the domain of nominal derivation, especially markers of agentivity (Matras 2009: 209–210). The Spanish agentive nominalizer *-ero*, for instance, was copied into Nahuatl and from there into Sierra Popoluca (Gutiérrez-Morales 2012). Similarly, the Turkic agentive *-ci* has been borrowed into a large number of languages, including Mongolic and Tungusic languages, Old Church Slavonic, New Persian, Rumanian, Modern Greek, Albanian, Iraqi Arabic etc.

Borrowing chains of verb morphemes are much less frequent. One example is the Classical Persian volitional prefix *be-*, which was copied into Kurdish and from there into Neo-Aramaic dialects (Josephson 2012).

Another example involves the borrowing chain of the Old French infinitive suffix *-ier* into the Finish verbalizer *-eera-*, via Middle Low German and Old Nordic. The Middle Low German denominal verbalizer *-êren*, which entered the language attached to verbs borrowed from Roman sources, served as a model for the Old Nordic loan verb marker *-era* (Simensen 2002: 955). This marker developed into Swedish *-era*, where it was ultimately borrowed as a loan verb marker *-eera-* by Finnish (Wohlgemuth 2009: 228–229). The loan verb markers were initially attached to foreign verb bases (e.g. LMG *spazêren* >> Old Nordic *spazera* 'to (take a) walk'; Swedish *citera* >> Finnish *sit-eera-ta* 'to quote'), but in Old Nordic, Swedish and Finnish they did not become productive in the verbalization of native nouns (Simensen pc., Petri Kallio pc., Lars Johanson pc.).[13] Hence, these morphemes are materially copied, but their semantics are only partially copied, since the function "denominal verbalizer" is restricted to Middle German.

It appears that instances of repetitive global copying of verb affixes are very rare. The greater the number of languages or language families involved in the comparison of a bound verb morpheme, the more likely it becomes that the similarity observed is due to inheritance.

2.4.3.6 Missing intermediaries

Code-copying is typically unidirectional and linear, progressing from one contact language into the other and then, perhaps, to the next. Genealogical divergence, by contrast, can be pictured as the concentric rings formed when a stone hits the water. Innovations start in the center and push the older forms towards the periphery. This may explain why some very conservative inherited items leave traces in remote areas, but are barely attested elsewhere in the linguistic continuum.

For example, only Sanskrit and Latin bear witness to the fact that Indo-European used a second imperative pIE *-to:d*, indicating that an action was supposed to take place in the near future. This element is reflected in forms such as Sanskrit *bhár-atá:t* and Latin *agi-to:* 'then you must carry', but has left no traces elsewhere in Indo-European (Beekes 1995: 248).

A similar observation goes for Samoyedic and Finno-Ugric. A large proportion of Samoyedic morphology, including both nominal declension (plural markers, case markers, possessive suffixes) and verbal conjugation (tense-aspect markers, participle markers, predicative personal endings) has parallels

---

13 Simensen informs me the verb suffix *-ere / -era* is not productive on native Norwegian bases, although there are two such verbs, i.e. *harpesere/harpesera* ‚to damage, destroy' and *harryfisere* ‚to give a vulgar impression. reveal bad taste', the latter being coined by a Norwegian scholar in the nineties.

in the western branches of the Finno-Ugric such as in Finnic, Saamic or Mordovic, but not elsewhere in Uralic (Janhunen 2014: 314).

The general explanation of these observations is that morphology is better preserved in the conservative peripheries of language families than in the more innovative centres. In this way gaps in the attestation of members of an etymology may be relevant. The absence of a morpheme in an intermediate contact language can be taken as an indication of genealogical relatedness.

2.5 Methodological misunderstandings

While it is generally agreed that successful demonstration of a genealogical relationship depends on adequate methods, there is considerable disagreement and confusion concerning what these methods are. In the Transeurasian field, this is largely due to diverging interpretations or applications of the historical comparative method. Given this state of affairs, it is useful to examine a number of theoretical presumptions and objections circulating in the Transeurasian linguistic literature and to determine the extent to which underlying methodological assumptions are justified.

2.5.1 "The comparative method is not universally applicable"

In his review of Robbeets (2005), Knüppel (2006: 358) objects to the application of the comparative method used for establishing Indo-European to the Altaic languages: "[es] scheint der Vf. in gar nicht erst der Einfall gekommen zu sein, daß sich die Methoden der Indogermanistik nicht ohne weiteres auf die altaischen Verhältnisse übertragen lassen." Bisang (1998: 220) makes a similar point, referring to "the "Altaic languages" for which the Indo-European concept of genetic relatedness may not be adequate." If such an objection were justified, it would imply that the historical comparative method is not universally applicable, for if its methodological principles do not apply to Altaic, its application would also be called into question elsewhere. The point of view that the comparative method is devised for the reconstruction of Indo-European only is incorrect for the following reasons.

First, the theoretical implication of this view would be that processes of language change such as grammaticalization and phonological change are not subject to universal tendencies, as is commonly assumed, which would undermine the validity of the comparative method *per se*, whether applied to Indo-European or to Altaic.

Second, the development of the comparative method was not restricted to the framework of Indo-European linguistics, as is implied by Knüppel's "Methoden der Indogermanistik". As Finno-Ugric was established well before Indo-European and as Gyarmathi's views on Uralic relationships are significantly more sophisticated than Jones' on Indo-European, comparative work in this field was highly influential in the development of comparative linguistics and had a major impact on scholars working on Indo-European (Campbell & Poser 2008: 49–50, 88–94).

Third, there are no empirical indications that the comparative method would be less operable in certain parts of the world than in others. In practice, a glance at the accepted language families of the world shows that the method has been successfully applied to many non-Indo-European languages, including a number of families in Asia such as Dravidian, Austronesian and Sino-Tibetan. The very fact that individual taxonomies can be established for Japanic, Koreanic, Tungusic, Mongolic and Turkic further supports the applicability of the comparative method to the Transeurasian languages.

2.5.2 "One cannot demonstrate unrelatedness"

Scholars working in the field of Transeurasian linguistic comparison often claim that hypotheses of linguistic relationships can be proved, but not disproved. Hamp's (1970: 189) principle that "[w]e can only demonstrate relationship, never non-relationship" is echoed by Vovin (2005a: 242): "First, it is only possible to prove genetic relationship, but it is impossible to prove a genetic non-relationship" and by Kempf (2008: 403): "only confirming the existence of something is possible, while proving the non-existence of something is methodologically impossible." These claims confuse existence or reality, i.e. what is actually the case, with demonstrability or relatability, i.e. what we can show to be the case on the basis of available evidence. They are true in the sense that one cannot prove absolute non-existence, in the same way as it is impossible to prove that God does not exist. Fortunately, we need not speculate on the philosophical and logical implications of "existing" or "non-existing", as the relevant question in historical comparative linguistics is whether languages are "relatable" or "unrelatable". If languages are relatable within the limits of the comparative method, the family "exists". If languages cannot be related to each other using the tools at our disposal, the language family may be either "non-existing" or "existing": either these languages did not descend from a common ancestor, or they did descend from a common ancestor, but there is insufficient evidence to demonstrate this.

How do we demonstrate that languages are unrelatable? Janhunen's answer (1996: 249) is straightforward: "it is sufficient to discredit a hypothesis by showing that the evidence brought in support of it must actually be explained in a different way." More specifically, if we reverse the criteria for relatability advanced in Anttila (1989: 302) and Harrison (2003: 215), we can consider the languages unrelatable if there are no similarities between them or if any observed similarities can best be explained as having (i) arisen independently in each of them by nature, or (ii) been diffused or copied amongst them, or (iii) arisen independently in each of them by chance. In sharp contrast to his recent claims about relatability, Vovin (1994: 242) previously argued that "it is considerably more difficult on the basis of the comparative method to disprove genetic relationship than to prove it. It is not impossible, however. One has just to demonstrate that there are no regular phonetic correspondences between two languages in question." It would appear that since the *credo* expressed in Vovin (1994: 241), i.e. "I believe there is an Altaic family, and that Japanese is one of the Altaic languages," not only has the author's "belief" in Altaic radically changed, but also his understanding of the comparative method.

Accounts aiming to demonstrate the unrelatability of the Transeurasian languages are riddled with logical fallacies, some of the most common being arguments from authority, observational selection and arguments from adverse consequences. Arguments from authority rely on an appeal to authority rather than on logic or on concrete counter-evidence to argue against relatedness. One example is the endorsement by Sinor (1988: 709) and Vovin (2009b: 105) of the view expressed by Sinor (1963: 144) on the validity of the Altaic hypothesis: "[i]f a scholar of Poppe's stature and knowledge fails to prove the theory of the genetic relationship of the Altaic languages, there must be something very wrong with that theory." Simply because an authority does not advance conclusive evidence in support of a hypothesis, however, does not necessarily mean that the theory is wrong.

Observational selection is the refutation of relatedness, on the basis of a small number of unfavorable etymologies, while ignoring favorable ones. On the basis of a critical item-by-item evaluation of more than 2,000 previous etymological proposals, Robbeets (2005) selects 359 lexical core etymologies supporting the relationship between Japanese and the Transeurasian languages. Of these, only a small proportion is refuted by the reviewers, whether or not legitimately. Vovin (2009b: 113–140) suggests eliminating 25 items, Georg (2007: 269–274) rejects 21 items and Kara (2007: 96–97) casts doubt on 18 items, a good number of which overlap. Although Kara does justice to the statistics of these small numbers, concluding that "As my remarks on the core evidence suggest, this "yes" [to relatedness] should rather be a 'maybe' or 'perhaps'," Georg (2007: 276) interprets these items as a justification to "cross out 'yes' and insert, in boldface, 'No'." Likewise, Vovin (2009: 141), in his ultimate assessment of Robbeets 2005, concludes that "scholarly-wise it is completely useless, but those who had the misfortune to purchase it should think twice before discarding it: it will hold your stacks of paper really well." The logical fallacy lurking behind observational selection is described as follows by Doerfer (1966: 111): "it would naturally be naïve to assert that in this way the Altaic hypothesis might be refuted. That would be the same as if, for example, one might wish to point to the numerous errors in the Indo-European dictionaries of Fick, Walde-Pokorny etc. and believe that the Indo-European hypothesis would thereby be refuted."

An argument from adverse consequences uses a certain negative circumstance as a ground for rejecting a hypothesis. The fact that accepting evolution theory may lead to eugenics, does not necessarily prove that evolution theory is false. In the same way, the occurrence of differences between the languages compared does not constitute proof that these languages are unrelated. The relationship of the Transeurasian languages is sometimes questioned because the languages display so many differences, in comparison with for instance the diversity between the Uralic languages. A similar kind of reasoning underlies Schönig's (2003: 415) remark that "Moreover, Turkic and Mongolic share many morphological elements, which earlier were often regarded as evidence of a genetic relationship. … However, the suffixes of several major morphological spheres, such as finite conjugation of verbs, show fundamental differences". The refutation of relatedness should be based on the elimination of proposed similarities rather than on the accumulation of differences.

2.5.3 "Absence of evidence is evidence of absence"

Within the present framework, evidence is considered to be missing if no cognates are found, i.e. if a linguistic form does not have a comparable form in one or more sister languages. Cognates may be lacking either because they never existed, or because existing cognates were lost, through the passage of time or through loss of attestations. In the course of time, languages branching off from a common ancestor tend to become more and more distant as they undergo changes independently of each other. Thus, linguistic forms that are actually "related" become "unrelatable" due to a cumulative effect of increasing divergence. This process of gradually decreasing evidence is called cognate attrition.

In the case of loss of attestations, a "relatable" form may have been present in a sister language, but due to the loss of the language in question, it is no longer recoverable. Khitan Mongolic and Paekche Old Korean, for instance, are attested in such a fragmentary way that many of the forms they share with Mongolian and Korean are no longer recoverable. A similar observation is true for Eastern Old Japanese: due to its limited attestation, some forms it may have shared with Western Old Japanese are simply not recoverable. Although cognates may have existed, they are no longer traceable. In these cases, absence of evidence does not mean evidence of absence. Or as Thomason & Kaufman (1988: 65) put it "as the old saying goes, you cannot prove that a platypus does not lay eggs by producing a videotape of a platypus not laying eggs."

Vovin (2010: 6) is only prepared to reconstruct a proto-Japanese form if a cognate is available in Eastern Old Japanese: "A word or morpheme is considered Proto-Japanese (PJN) if it is found: (1) in Western Old Japanese *and* Eastern Old Japanese (areas A and B); (2) in Middle Japanese *and* Eastern Old Japanese (areas A and B)" [emphasis added]. So, absence of evidence in Eastern Old Japanese is taken as evidence of absence in proto-Japanese. Based on the same logic, the absence of a form in Paekche Old Korean would make its reconstruction in proto-Koreanic impossible. Ignoring the possibility of cognate attrition, Vovin further considers any Western Old Japanese form that fails to occur in Ryukyuan dialects or in Eastern Old Japanese texts having possibly been copied from Korean after these languages separated. This is equivalent to claiming that any Germanic morpheme that lacks a cognate in Gothic must have been copied from a non-Germanic language after the separation of East Germanic. The reliability of this criterion in distinguishing copies from cognates will be discussed in more detail in Section 9.3. As shown by the examples above, it is a logical fallacy to appeal to negative evidence to demonstrate the non-existence of relatedness.

2.5.4 "Proto-languages are unrealistic"

Certain statements on the nature of proto-languages in the Transeurasian literature reflect confusion about what is being reconstructed. Thus, the near identity of proto-Mongolic and Middle Mongolian leads Kempf (2008: 406:) to claim erroneously that "Accordingly, Mongolian did not change during five millennia". This time span is supposed to cover the period between the fifth millennium BC, when proto-Mongolic branched off as a separate language family, and the thirteenth century, when Middle Mongolian was spoken. Kempf thus assumes that proto-Mongolic reflects the status of the language at the time when it separated from its nearest Transeurasian sister, which is not the case, however. Proto-Mongolic is the technical term for the common ancestor of all living and historically accessible Mongolic languages. The real language which it reflects was spoken at a time just before the differentiation of the contemporary Mongolic languages, rather than just after its presumed separation from Tungusic. This does not imply that Mongolic was a uniform entity in the five millennia leading up to the thirteenth century. Rather, it means that the currently available linguistic data do not provide access to earlier stages. However, future prospects are favorable. It is very likely that the texts preserved in Khitan writing, once fully deciphered, will enable us to reconstruct proto-Khitan-Mongolic at deeper time levels. Proto-Khitan-Mongolic is the language spoken just before the split between Khitanic and Mongolic around 200 AD, when Mongolic Shiwei and Khitanic Tabgach separated. Similarly, proto-Turkic reflects the ancestral language spoken just before the separation of Oghuric and Common Turkic around 100 BC; proto-Tungusic preceded the differentiation between the Manchu branch of Tungusic and Tungusic proper around 200 AD; proto-Koreanic refers to the language spoken just before the split of the Han languages, presumably around the beginning of our era, and proto-Japonic predates the separation of Mainland Japanese from the rest of Japonic around 100 BC.

Kempf's misunderstanding stems from the assumption that all proto-languages need to reflect a chronologically simultaneous stage in order to count as comparable entities. One of his criticisms of Starostin et al. (2003), for instance, is that "chronologically different data are compared to each other." The comparative method, however, does not require that the compared languages reflect simultaneous stages because it is based upon regular correspondences, i.e. relative similarity, rather than on absolute identity. If A is comparable to B and B is comparable to C it follows that A is comparable to C. Middle Mongolian regularly corresponds with its modern descendant Khalkha Mongolian. Hence, if there are regular correspondences between Middle Japanese and Middle Mongolian as spoken in the 14th century, Middle Japanese and modern Khalkha can also be assumed to exhibit regularity, even though these are not contemporaneous stages. Therefore, it is methodologically legitimate to compare proto-Turkic, proto-Mongolic, proto-Tungusic, proto-Koreanic and proto-Japonic to each other in spite of the chronological differences amongst them. Similarly, it is common place to reconstruct proto-Indo-European, comparing forms from Hittite (ca. 1700–1200 BC) Sanskrit (ca. 1000 B.C), Homeric Greek (ca. 800 BC), Latin (ca. 500 B.C), Gothic (ca. 400 AD) and Old Church Slavonic (ca. 800 AD), thus covering a time span of more than two millennia.

Proto-languages are both realistic and abstract at the same time, because the term 'proto-language' refers to two things. Following Campbell and Harris (2002: 600) it is "[1] the actual spoken ancestral language from which daughter languages descend" and "[2] the language reconstructed by the comparative method which attempts to replicate the once-existing ancestor language". The more [2] approximates [1], the more real and the less abstract the reconstruction becomes. Historical linguists draw the most plausible inferences from the available evidence and on the basis of their own insights into mechanisms of language change. While the results are often very good, they are never flawless. In this sense Whaley et al. (1999: 313) are correct in arguing that "Until the full complexity of synchronic variation is appreciated, our understanding of the diachronic relationships among these [Tungusic] languages is bound to be flawed." However, this applies to any language family in the world: since full understanding of synchronic variation cannot be attained, our reconstructions of diachronic relationships are bound to remain incomplete. Nevertheless, much more can be gained from applying the comparative method, than from discarding it.

2.5.5 "Multiple comparison increases chance probability"

The demonstration of genealogical relatedness is a probabilistic matter. Following Nichols (2010: 266) "relatedness is proved by showing that the number of resemblant elements between languages or language families significantly exceeds what would be expected by chance." Among other factors which have been discussed in Section 2.3, chance is relative to the number of branches involved in the reconstruction. Some scholars argue that multiple comparison increases chance probability, suggesting that the higher the number of branches being compared, the more likely elements are to be similar by sheer coincidence. Janhunen (1996a: 209), for instance, warns that "[t]he illusion of genetic relationship between the three groups of languages [Turkic, Mongolic and Tungusic] is largely due to the non-binary approach applied in conventional Altaic comparisons. It is this methodological error that has also allowed the Altaic hypothesis to be extended to comprise other languages, notably Korean and Japanese."

Let us first consider the probability of getting sixes when rolling dice. On a six-sided die, the odds of rolling a six are 1 in 6, or $p = .1667$. When rolling a pair of dice, the probability of getting two sixes decreases to $p = .1667 \times .1667 = .0278$. For five dice, the probability of getting five sixes is $p = .1667 \times .1667 \times .1667 \times .1667 \times .1667 = .00013$. In other words, the likelihood of success is much smaller with five dice than with two.

Let us now assume that a successful linguistic comparison is one in which a match is found across all branches of a language family. If we start from monophonemic consonantal morphemes with equivalent meanings, a successful match occurs when the consonants are comparable, for instance when all consonants are velars. By approximation, languages have inventories of 12 consonants, two of which (e.g. voiced velar and voiceless velar) are permissible matches; thus, the probability that a particular meaning is expressed by a velar is 2 in 12 or $p = .1667$. The probability that this meaning is simultaneously expressed by a velar in two branches is $p = .1667$ x $.1667 = .0278$. The probability that this meaning is simultaneously expressed by a velar in five branches is $p = .1667$ x $.1667$ x $.1667$ x $.1667$ x $.1667 = .00013$. In other words, the likelihood of success is much smaller when comparing five branches than when comparing two. Hence, a match found across five branches is more difficult to attribute to coincidence than one found between two branches.

However, there is also some truth in Janhunen's remark. Comparisons yielding a match over multiple branches e.g. between proto-Japonic, proto-Koreanic, proto-Tungusic, proto-Mongolic and proto-Turkic simultaneously, should be distinguished from comparisons over multiple branches that yield only pairwise matches, e.g. between Japonic and Tungusic for one morpheme and between Turkic and Tungusic for another. The first type of comparison can be described as AND-AND-AND-AND, whereas the second type consists of AND-OR-OR-OR. Janhunen's warning applies to this second type of comparison, i.e. pairwise multiple comparison, in which the likelihood of chance similarity is higher than in binary comparison.

The large majority of the morphemes compared in the present study, however, represent instances of AND-AND-AND-AND. In section 2.3, the probability of coincidental matches has been assessed in more detail, but it is a fact that matches found simultaneously over multiple branches are much more significant in excluding chance as an explanation than matches found during binary comparison.

2.5.6 "Shared morphology is a *conditio sine qua non*"

Although scholars seem to agree that shared morphology would greatly contribute to unraveling the genealogical question of the Transeurasian languages, there is some disagreement on the weight to be given to morphological evidence. Whereas some authors, such as Sinor (1963: 137) argue that "the question of the genetic relationship of Altaic languages thus stands or falls with the historical identity of their morphemes", considering shared morphology as a *conditio sine qua non*, others such as Doerfer (1981: 47) object that "the lack of common affixes does not exclude relationship", suggesting that a common morphology is not a prerequisite for showing that languages are related. Clearly, the former position is too strong. Southeast Asia is home to many analytic language families, including Tibeto-Burman, Tai-Kadai, Hmong-Mien and Mon-Khmer. For these languages, morphological comparison is impossible because they express syntactic relations through independent function words and thus lack comparable bound morphemes. Unger (2011: 412) recalls Aronoff's (1994: 165) remark: "Morphology is not necessary. There are languages that do without it, and those with morphology vary quite remarkably in their morphological structure and complexity." Nevertheless, for synthetic languages such as the Transeurasian languages, which express syntactic relations through morphological marking, it is reasonable to expect a common morphology in support of relatedness.

Another point of view, which is less excessive but still too strong, is the assertion that morphological evidence is conclusive in itself. Vovin's (2005a: 242:) claim that "[t]he best way to make it very tight is to prove a suggested genetic relationship on the basis of paradigmatic morphology (if it is present in languages included in a given proposal), and not on the basis of vocabulary, …" seems to suggest that morphology can be used as a sole criterion for establishing genealogical relationship instead of lexical evidence. This belief is inspired by Indo-European comparative linguistics, where a common morphology constitutes conclusive evidence of relatedness because of the fusional characteristics of the languages involved. The shared complexity of the Indo-European languages led to Meillet's (1921: 160) overreliance on morphology: "Et c'est par la morphologie à peu près uniquement qu'on peut faire la classification généalogique des langues". Since the Transeurasian languages are agglutinative, they lack shared formational irregularities of the Indo-European type. As discussed above, the formal evaluation of common morphemes can thus only rely on phonological correspondences already established on the basis of lexical cognates. It follows that morphology cannot be used by itself as a single subsystem for establishing a genealogical relationship. In this respect, the Transeurasian languages represent the standard case, whereas Indo-European is cross-linguistically rather exceptional. Or, as argued by Thomason and Kaufman (1988: 7): "Unfortunately neither the inflectional morphology nor the basic vocabulary is sufficiently stable internally and sufficiently impervious to restructuring or replacement through foreign influences to justify giving it status as a single definitive criterion for establishing genetic relationship." Rather than relying on morphological evidence alone, it is safer to start the present enterprise from the requirement that if synthetic languages display systematic correspondences in various linguistic subsystems, such as phonology, vocabulary, and syntax, these should be supported by morphological correspondences in order to demonstrate genealogical relatedness beyond reasonable doubt. The next chapter will deal with phonological and lexical correspondences, particularly among verbs and verbal adjectives, while Chapters 3 to 10 will provide complementary evidence from bound verb morphology.

3 Verb Roots

3.1 The distinction between nouns and verbs

In the Transeurasian literature, we find a misconception relating to the distinction between nouns and verbs. Miller (1980: 89) contends that: "the employment of such grammatical terms as "verb" and "noun" is simply a convention of scholarly convenience, and that it is not based on any rigorlously established descriptive categories". Later, he continues in this line that "Japanese does not invariably exhibit the same rigid distinction between nominal and verbal roots, stems and suffixes that is seen e.g., in Turkic and Mongolian. In this respect, then, Japanese of all historical periods is significantly closer to Tungusic... " (Miller 1982a: 391, 392). He argues that this feature is representative of an "extremely early inheritance of undifferentiated N/V [noun / verb] morphology." This viewpoint elaborates on Menges' (1978: 289) observation that in Tungusic "there is a relatively great number of stems which basically are neither exclusively verbal, nor exclusively nominal, so that they can function in either capacity".

However, the idea that some Transeurasian languages do not clearly distinguish between nouns and verbs is incorrect. It is based on the observation of a number of derivational pairs in Tungusic such as Even *halka* 'hammer' and *halka-* 'to hammer', Evk. *mu:* 'water' and *mu:-* 'to leak', Ud. *tigde* 'rain' and *tigde-* 'to rain', Ud. *lada* 'rain with snow' and *lada-* 'to rain with snow', Ud. *naŋda* 'debt' and *naŋda-* 'borrow', Neg. *mi:xi* 'snake' and *mi:xi-* 'to crawl', Ud. *tama-* 'to pay' and *tama* 'price', Ma. *bi-* 'to exist, to be' and *bi* non-verbal predicative copula. Synchronically, these pairs may suggest zero derivation, but diachronically they are probably the result of phonological erosion or merger. In the case of 'hammer,' for instance, comparison with Nanai *paloa* 'hammer' → *paloala-* 'to hammer' suggests erosion of an original denominal verb suffix *-lA:-* (see Section 5.3.2) through liquid loss. In the cases of 'water', 'rain' and 'debt,' it is clear that the nominal form is the base and that the verbal form is the derivation, because the noun is reflected in the majority of the Tungusic languages, whereas the corresponding verb is restricted to one or at most two languages, which again suggests erosion of *-lA:-*.[1] Many of the zero-derivations in Udehe have voiced dental stops

---

[1] The reflexes of 'water' in other Tungusic languages, for instance, Even *mö:*, Neg. *mu:*, Jur. *mo*, Olch. *mu:*, Orok *mu:*, Oroch *mu:*, Sol. *mu:* do not have a corresponding zero-derived verb. A verbal form 'to rain' is restricted to Sol. *tegde-*, whereas Evk. *tigde*, Even *ti:d*, Neg. *tigde*, Olch. *tugde*, Orok *tugde / tugje*, Na. *tugde* and Oroch *tigde* 'rain' are exclusively nominal. The reflexes for 'debt' are nominal, namely Even *nān*, Neg. *nāngna*, Olch. *nangda*, Orok *nangda*, Na. *nangda*, Oroch *nangna*, whereas zero-derived verbs are lacking.

preceding the stem final vowel, which could have triggered the liquid loss. The case of 'snake' and 'to crawl' can be explained as a merger of two originally distinct froms pTg *muyki 'snake' and pTg *mirku- 'to crawl,' because the reflexes in the other Tungusic languages are clearly distinct, with the exception of Ud. *miki* 'snake' and *miki-* 'to crawl', namely Ma. *meixe* and *micu-*, Olch. *mui* and *micu-*, Orok *mui* / *muyyi* and *mitu-*, Na. *muyki* and *miku-* and Oroch *mi:ki* and *mikki-* respectively. In the cases of 'to pay' and 'to exist,' the verbal form is the primary one, whereas the nominal from has been derived, because it is the verb rather than the noun that is widely attested across the Tungusic languages. The verb pTg *tama-* 'to pay' is reflected in Evk. *tama-*, Even *tam-*, Neg. *tama-*, Olch. *tama-*, Orok *tama-*, Sol. *tama-*, Oroch *tama-*, whereas only Nanai preserves another nominal form, namely Na. *tamã* 'price'. The nasal quality of the vowel in Nanai points to an original pTg *tama-n* 'price', which may preserve a relic of the original Tungusic nominalizer in *-n* (see Section 7.5.3), which was completely lost in Udehe. The non-verbal predicative copula Manchu *bi* can be derived as a contracted deverbal noun in *-i* (see Section 8.3.3.1) from the existential verb Ma. *bi-*.

The examples of so-called undifferentiated noun / verb morphology in Japanese are based on questionable morphological analysis. Miller (1982a: 392), for instance, refers to verb sets as OJ *nak-* A 'cry, weep' and OJ *nar-* A 'cry, make a sound'. Assuming cognacy with OJ *na* 'name' as well as with OJ *ne* 1.1 'sound; crying, weeping', which he treats as a deverbal noun on *-i* from pJ *na-* 'to sound', he deduces that the root is both nominal and verbal in origin. This assumption is problematic, however. First, it is unlikely that OJ *na* 'name' is related here because its original meaning is 'person' as in compounds such as OJ $womi_1na$ 'woman', OJ oki_1na 'old man', J *mina, minna* 'all, everybody, everything' and J *otona* 'adult', which reflect a common pathway of grammaticalization (Robbeets 2005: 232). Second, OJ *ne* 'sound' can be derived from an exclusively nominal form pJ *na-(C)i* in the same way as OJ te_2 'hand' comes from pJ *ta-(C)i* (e.g. OJ $tado_1r$- 'take by hand') or OJ me_2 'eye' and comes from pJ *ma-(C)i* (e.g. J *mabuta* 'eyelid'), including a suffix for deriving free morphemes from bound ones. The suffixes involved in OJ *nak-* 'to cry, weep' and OJ *nar-* 'to cry, make a sound' are original denominal verb suffixes (see Chapter 5).

The distinction between nouns and verbs is one of the few universal parts-of-speech distinctions. The Transeurasian languages are no exception to Schachter's (1985: 7) observation that "there are no languages that cannot be said to show a noun-verb distinction". Japanese, Korean and Tungusic reference grammars clearly distinguish nouns and verbs as distinct parts of speech, and there is no reason to suppose that the distinction was lacking in earlier periods. Nouns refer to entities such as animates, body parts, physical objects, and natural phenomena. They take specific inflectional morphology for number, case and possessive and they are characterized by typical derivational patterns. Syntactically, their most common function is as arguments or heads of arguments. Verbs indicate phenomena which take place during time, ie. activities, processes, states. They are morphologically marked by categories of voice, aspect, mood, tense and person. Syntactically, their characteristic function is predication. They are the center of the sentence because of valency.

3.2 Verbal adjectives within a mixed adjective typology

Nouns and verbs can be clearly distinguished in the Transeurasian languages, and within the present approach, this is also the case for adjectives. Although various studies on individual Transeurasian languages do not systematically describe adjectives as a discrete word class, the present approach follows the semantic, syntactic and morphological criteria described in Dixon (1977 [1982]), Schachter (1985) and Johanson (2006) to distinguish adjectives from nouns and verbs as a separate part-of-speech. Semantically, adjectives describe properties of entities, such as dimension, value, color. Syntactically, they occur in a modifier position or function as a predicate, which may or may not be accompanied by a copula and, they can also enter comparative constructions. Morphologically, adjectives make use of specific derivation patterns, such as intensifying and deintensifying elements or partial emphatic reduplication (cf. Fengxiang & Whaley 2000 on partial emphatic reduplication in the continental Transeurasian languages). Cross-linguistically adjectives have no prototypical encoding strategy of their own (Stassen 1997: 30): They will align themselves either with verbs or with nominals. Across the Transeurasian languages, the encoding of property words appears to be mixed, at least in the earlier stages: both the nominal and the verbal strategy is used. The mixed typology largely reflects split encoding in the sense that most property words have only a single encoding option, although all branches show cases of switching, whereby the same property word can have both nominal and verbal encoding.

3.2.1 Japanese

a) *Nominally encoded property words*

Japanese has a class of adjectives, such as OJ *awo* 'blue, green', OJ *ki₁yo₁ra* 'clear', OJ *yapara* 'soft', OJ *siduka* 'quiet', OJ *tasika* 'trustworthy', which are encoded exclusively nominally: they do not take inflectional morphology, show different negation patterns than the verbal adjectives and are used with a copula. In

Old Japanese they are followed by various forms of the copula *nar-* 'to be' (< *n-i ar-* be-CVB exist) or by *ni*, an adverbial form of the defective verb *n-* 'to be', e.g. OJ *tasika nar-u tukapi* (trustworthy be-PCP messenger) 'trustworthy messenger' (MYS 12: 2874). In Late Middle Japanese the participial form *nar-u* of the copula OJ/ MJ *nar-* 'to be' is abbreviated to LMJ *na*, with loss of final *-ru*, e.g. LMJ *katame na sika* (one-eyed be.PCP deer) 'one-eyed deer' (Frellesvig 2010: 342). This construction gives rise to the so-called *na*-adjectives of contemporary Japanese, e.g. *tasika na hito* 'trustworthy person', which maintain the adverbial form *ni* of the original copula, *e.g. tasika ni siru* 'know for sure'. These nominal adjectives are ambiguously defined by some Japanese linguists as *keiyoudousi* 'adjectival verbs', whereas western scholars refer to them as adjectival nouns (Martin 1991b: 179–81, Kaiser & al. 2001: 5, Vovin 2003: 93, Frellesvig 2010: 235) or simply as *na*-adjectives (Takeuchi 1999: 81, Backhouse 1984).

By origin, many nominal adjectives may be obsolete adnominal forms derived from verbs or verbal adjectives, e.g. OJ ki_1yo_1- 'be pure' → OJ ki_1yo_1ra 'clear', OJ *tura-* 'be though' → OJ $me_2duraka$ 'strange', OJ *par-* 'to open ground, clear land' → OJ *paruka* 'far, distant, remote' (see Section 7.6.1). Note that some of these deverbal adnominalizers have denominal counterparts of the same shape. Compare, for instance, OJ *-ka* in OJ *tuyu* 'dew' → *tuyuka* 'dewy' or OJ *-ra* in OJ *ata* 'empty, vain' → OJ *atara* 'regrettable'. The observation that verbal and nominal bases can be turned into a nominal adjective using one and the same morphological means suggests that "adjective" was originally perceived as a separate semantic category, distinct from nouns and verbs.

b) *Verbally encoded property words*

There is another class of adjectives in Japanese that are verbally encoded, such as J *aka-* '(be) red', OJ *aka-* '(be) clear, bright, red', J *taka-*, OJ *taka-* '(be) high', J *kata-*, OJ *kata-* '(be) hard, tough'. These verbal adjectives are sometimes called "quality verbs" (Vovin 2003: 187) because like verbs they attach endings to mark syntactic function. Although there are formal differences between verb and adjective suffixes, adjectives are essentially inflected in a similar way as verbs: Adjectives take a converbial form J / OJ *-ku* e.g. OJ *opo ki_1mi_1-ni kata-ku $tukape_2$-matur-am-u* (great lord-DAT strong-CVB serve-HUM-TENT-FIN) '[I] intend to serve faithfully to the emperor' (NK 78, Vovin 2009a: 446); they have an adnominal form J *-i* < OJ $-ki_2$, e.g. OJ $opo_2-ki_2 to_1$ (big-PCP door) 'big door' (NK 18, Vovin 2009a: 447) and a finite predicative form J *-i* < OJ *-si*, e.g. OJ $ko_2ko_2ro_2$ *sa mane-si* (thought so be.many-FIN) 'thoughts are so many' (MYS 1: 82, Vovin 2009a: 463). Used as predicates, they do not require a copula.

Vovin (2009a: 429) has argued that Old Japanese adjectives should be regarded as "a transitional class between nominals and verbs". In support of this assertion, he points out first, that the Old Japanese adjective can enter nominal compounds as an uninflected stem and, second, that the adnominal and finite predicative uses of the usually adnominal form OJ -ki_2 and the usually finite predicative form OJ -si have been confused. As will be shown in Chapter 6, this is due to the competition of two nonfinite adnominal forms OJ -ki_2 and OJ -si, which both grammaticalized into finite markers. Although this phenomenon reflects the development of inflectional markers, it does not support the idea that the verbal encoding of adjectives is a secondary development. A common view (Unger 1977: 55, Unger & Tomita 1983, Martin 1989: 802, 807) is that the Japanese adjective inflection is a relatively young phenomenon because markers such as OJ -ki_2 adnominal and OJ -si predicative may be derived from periphrastic constructions such as -ku ari (CVB exist) or -sa ari (NML exist). This supports the secondary nature of some endings of verbal adjectives, but not the secondary nature of verbal adjectives *per se*.

c) *Switched encoding*

According to Vovin's first argument, the alternative nominal nature of a closed class of verbal adjectives is an indication that their verbal nature is a secondary development. This closed class consists of about forty verbal adjectives, such as OJ *aka-* 'to be red', OJ *taka-* 'to be high', OJ to_2po- 'to be distant' and OJ *opo-* 'to be big' which can switch to nominal encoding, either as a bare adjective preceding the head noun e.g. *taka ki_2* 'high fortress' (KK 60, Vovin 2009a: 435), *opo $mono_2$* 'great things' (NK 15, Vovin 2009a: 436) or followed by a participial form of a defective copula OJ *n-* 'to be', e.g. OJ to_2po no_2 kuni (distant DV-PCP country) 'distant country' (MYS 15: 3688, Vovin 2009a: 433).[2] The use of uninflected verbal adjectives in Middle and Modern Japanese is no longer productive, but is restricted to a number of lexicalized compounds such as J *akatonbo* 'red dragonfly' (< *aka* 'red' + *tonbo* 'dragonfly') and J *takaboosi* 'high-crowned hat' (< *taka* 'high' + *boosi* 'hat'). However, all that these property words tell us is that Old Japanese adjectives have mixed encoding, i.e. either nominal or verbal, and that there are some cases of switching whereby the same property word can have both nominal and verbal encoding.

---

[2] In some cases of switching to nominal encoding, there is a difference in accent register (e.g. J *aka-* A 'be red' and *aka* 2.5. 'red, redness'). This has led to the reconstruction of an original denominal suffix *-m that became abraded, e.g. *aka* 2.5. < pJ *aka-m. (Polivanov 1924: 146, Vovin 1994: 250, 2001: 187). Such cases suggest that the nominal encoding is secondary and the verbal encoding is original.

In what follows, I will use the term "verbal adjectives" to refer to verbally encoded property words such as OJ *kata-* 'be hard' or OJ *taka-* 'be high' and the term "nominal adjectives" for nominal encodings such as OJ *tasika* 'trustworthy' or OJ *taka* 'high'.

3.2.2 Korean

a) *Nominally encoded property words*

Just like Japanese, Korean has a clearly mixed adjective typology. There is a subclass of adjectives such as K *kanan ha-* 'to be poor', *phikon ha-* 'to be tired', *ttattus-ha-* 'to be warm', *kkaykkus-ha-* 'to be clean', *kattuk-ha-* 'to be full', *kocak-i-* 'to be the most', *yelsim-i-* 'to be zealous,' that consist of a nominal root and the auxiliary *ha-* 'to be in the state of' or, more rarely, the copula *i-* 'to be'. Only by combining with the auxiliary or the copula can these adjectives be inflected. Their bases are called "adjectival nouns" (Martin 1992: 189, 190; Sohn 1994: 219–220; 1999: 206). A few bases, such as K *kanan* 'poor; poverty' or *phikon* 'tired; tiredness,' can also serve as free nouns that refer to an abstract concept and that can be separated from *ha-* by the particle *to* 'also', but in general no case suffix can be inserted between the base and the auxiliary.

By origin some nominal adjectives may be obsolete participial or nominal forms derived from verbs or verbal adjectives, e.g. K *cilki-* 'be tough, be durable, be lasting, be persisting' → *cilkis hata* 'be tough, stiff, stubborn', K *ku(s)-*, MK *kuzG-* / *kuzu-* 'draw a line (around), delimit' → K *kuuk*, MK *kuzuk* 'secluded, secret, private' and, K *ka:m-* 'be black' → *(k)kamak* 'black, dark, ignorant' (see Chapters 7 and 8).

b) *Verbally encoded property words*

Verbal adjectives are descriptive intransitive verbs such as K *pwulk-*, MK *pulk-* 'to be(come) red', K *kwut-*, MK *kwut-* 'to be(come) hard', K *noph-*, MK *nwoph-* 'to be high' (Martin 1992: 89, Sohn 1994: 95–96, 222–223). They are inflected in essentially the same way as verbs, and predication does not require a copula, but there are some formal differences between verb and adjective suffixes. The adnominal form manifests some differences, e.g. K *coh-un salam* (be.good-PCP person) 'good person' vs. *mek-n-un salam* (eat-PROC-PCP person) 'eating person' and unlike verbs adjectives lack the category of past in participial constructions. The nonpast indicative in plain speech is zero, e.g. K *salam-i coh-ta* (person-NOM be.good-FIN) 'the person is good' vs. *salam-i mek-nun-ta* (person-NOM eat-NPST-FIN) 'the person eats'. Some verbally encoded property words are original verbal adjectives. Others can be traced back to derived nominal roots (e.g. MK *.mul* 'water' → K *mwulk-*, MK *mulk-* 'to be watery, be thin'), to derived verbal roots (e.g.

MK *mit-* 'to believe' → MK *mit ·pu-* 'to be credible';) or, to descriptive extensions from originally processive intransitive verbs (e.g. K *cala-*, MK *·cola-* 'to reach, grow; be sufficient, be enough').

c) *Switched encoding*

Martin (1997: 12) notes that the Korean verbal adjective stem makes a few compound nouns by direct attachment to the noun. These lexicalized compounds retain traces of switching, whereby a verbal adjective can take nominal encoding, e.g. K *nulk-tali* 'old animal, old person' (< *nulk-* 'to be old' + *tali* 'leg'), K *mip-sang* 'disgusting appearance' (< *miw-* 'to be hateful' + *sang* 'appearance'), MK *polk-·cwuy* 'bat' (< *polk-* 'to be bright, red' + *·cwuy* 'rat'). Other traces of switching can be found in Middle Korean adjective doublets that switch between nominal and verbal encoding, such as MK *toso-* vs. MK *toso ho-* 'to be warm, mild, genial'; MK *·pha·la ho-* vs. MK *phwulwu-* 'to be blue', MK *·ha·ya ho-* vs. MK *·huy-/ ·huy-* 'to be white' etc.[3]

In what follows I will use the term "verbal adjectives" to refer to verbally encoded property words such as K *kwut-*, MK *kwut-* 'to be(come) hard' and the term "nominal adjectives" for nominal encodings such as K *kanan (ha-)* 'poor; poverty'.

3.2.3 Tungusic

a) *Nominally encoded property words*

The majority of property words in the Tungusic languages are nominally encoded: they generally show the same negation patterns as nouns, require a copula in predication, e.g. Ma. *bolgo oso* (honest be(IMP)) 'Be honest!' and, when used as abstract nouns, they can be followed by certain case markers.

A common conception is that adjectives cannot be distinguished from nouns in the Tungusic languages. As far as Manchu property words are concerned, Gorelova (2002: 145) finds that "Since their main function, which is the attributive one, is not manifested morphologically, the nouns of quality cannot be opposed to other nouns and be defined as adjectives as a part of speech". It is clear that there is a semantic distinction between nouns and adjectives in the sense that adjectives in Tungusic describe properties of entities, such as dimension, value, color. Confusion arises, however, because a number of adjectives in the Tungusic languages, such as Ma. *ajige* 'little, small, younger; the little one', Ma. *den* 'high, tall; heigth', Evk. *gugda* 'high, heigth', Evk. *aya* 'good, well; kindness; the good one', Udehe *zo:ngku* 'poor; the poor one' etc. have no distinctive morphological

---

[3] Note that Contemporary Korean preserves only the nominally encoded adjective K *ttasu ha-* 'id.'. For the vowel alternation in the colour terms, see Section 3.2.7 (2).

features. The nouns become adjectives by appearing in the syntactic adnominal position.[4] However, many adjectives use prototypical morphology to derive from nouns such as Ma. *-hon /-hun /-hu:n* in e.g. Ma. *oilo* 'surface' → *oilohon* 'superficial' (Goroleva 2002: 148–150), Evk. *-mA* in e.g. *altan* 'gold' → *altanma* 'golden', Evk. *-rA* in e.g. *taman* 'cost, price' → *tamu-ra* costly, expensive' (Nedjalkov 1997: 299), Ud. *-xi* in e.g. *amta* 'taste' → *amtaxi* 'tasty' (Nikolaeva 1999: 111) etc. Other morphological criteria to distinguish Tungusic adjectives from nouns are the use of specific adjectival markers, such as the plurality marker Ud. *-ngku* (Nikolaeva 1999: 98–99), which is not used for nouns, partial emphatic reduplication (e.g. Sibe *farxun* 'dark' → *fak-farxun* 'extremely dark') and other intensifying and deintensifying elements (e.g. Even *burna* 'grey' → *burna-mrin* 'greyish', Benzing 1955b: 25). Furthermore, syntactically, Tungusic adjectives can occur in modifier position (e.g. Ma. *amba alin* 'big mountain'), they can enter comparative constructions (e.g. Evk. *murin-duk hegdy-tmer* (horse-ABL big-COMP) 'bigger than a horse') and in some languages, for instance in in Evenki, it is claimed that "The negative element *a:chin* ... is employed after nouns which denote missing objects, and the negative form *eche* 'no' is positioned before adjectives and participles which denote missing qualities." (Nedjalkov 1997: 99).

By origin, many nominally encoded property words are obsolete adnominal forms derived from verbs or verbal adjectives, e.g. Ma. *gele-* 'to fear' → *gelecuke* 'dangerous, frightful', Ma. *wesi-* 'to ascend, raise, go up' → *wesihun* 'upward, eastward, honorable, respected', Evk. *chulbin-* 'to grow thin' → *chulbika* 'thin, meagre', Evk. *omngo-* 'to forget' → *omngomo* 'forgetful, absent-minded', Evk. *langa-* 'to break a tooth' → *langara* 'toothless', Even *gel-* 'to be cold' → *gelsi* 'cold' etc. (see Section 7.7.3). Note that some of these deverbal adnominalizers have denominal counterparts with the same form. Compare, for instance, Ma. *-hon /-hun /-hu:n* in Ma. *wesi-* 'go up' → *wesihun* 'upward' vs. Ma. *oilo* 'surface' → *oilohon* 'superficial', Evk. *-mA* in Evk. *omngo-* 'forget' → *omngomo* 'forgetful' vs. Evk. *altan* 'gold' → *altanma* 'golden' and, Evk. *-rA* in *langa-* 'to break a tooth' → *langara* 'toothless' vs. Evk. *taman* 'cost' → *tamura* costly'. The observation that verbal and nominal bases can be turned into a nominally encoded property word by one and the same morphological means, suggests that the concept "adjective" was originally perceived as a single category, distinct from nouns and verbs.

b) *Verbally encoded property words*

Although Japanese and Korean are usally described as having mixed adjective typology, it is commonly assumed that the Tungusic, Mongolic and Turkic adjec-

---

[4] Compare Evenki *gugda ure* (high mountain) 'a high mountain' and *ure gugda-n* (mountain high-POSS.3SG) 'the height of the mountain' in Nejalkov 1997: 299.

tives exclusively use nonverbal encoding (Stassen 1997: 383–390, 2005: 480–481). In standard terminology, the term "adjective" is only used in reference to nominally encoded property words. However, these languages also contain verbally encoded property words, which will be referred to as "verbal adjectives" for the present purpose.

The Tungusic languages use descriptive verbs to denote properties of entities, e.g. Ud. *dogbo ngengi-mi lä ngele-li-e:-ti.* (night go-INF very be.afraid-INC-PST-3PL) 'Walking in the night they were very much afraid' (Nikolaeva 1999: 511). There seems to be a tendency to apply the verbal strategy in the case of less permanent properties such as Ma *aka-* 'to be sad, grieve', Ma. *bere-* 'to be dumbfounded by fright or anger, to be lame', Ma. *ebi-* 'to be satiated', Evk. *ukti-* 'to be hungry', Evk. *uwi-* 'to be satiated', Evk. *buli:-* 'to be sad', Even *ad-* 'to be worn out, become thin, to become fragile', Even *hec-* 'to be tired', Even *urli-* 'to be jealous', Orok *sali-* 'to be angry', Olcha *peken-* 'to be embarrassed, to be troubled', Na. *irente-* 'to be ashamed', Ud. *omisi-* 'to be hungry', Ud. *agda-* 'to be happy', Ud. *su:le-* 'to be ill' etc.

c) *Switched encoding*

In the Tungusic languages, there are examples of switching whereby the same property word can have both nominal and verbal encoding, for instance in Manchu, Ma. *sakda-* 'to become old, to age' and Ma. *sakda* 'old (of people)', Ma. *jalu-* 'to be full, be fulfilled' and *jalu* 'full', Ma. *sula-* 'to be loose, be free; be idle; be left over' and *sula* 'loose, idle, unoccupied, free'; in Udehe, Ud. *bogo-* 'to become fat' and *bogo* 'fat', Ud. *kongo-* 'to become thin' and *kongo* 'thin', Ud. *mangga-* 'to be bad weather' and *mangga* 'strong' or; in Even, *hata* 'dark' ~ *hata-* 'to be dark', Even *bęlgu:r* 'greedy' ~ *bęlgu:r-* 'to be greedy', etc.

In what follows I will use the term "verbal adjectives" to refer to verbally encoded property words such as Evk. *buli:-* 'to be sad' and he term "nominal adjectives" for nominal encodings such as Evk. *aya* 'good, well; kindness; the good one'.

3.2.4 Mongolic

a) *Nominally encoded property words*

Most property words in the Mongolic languages are nominally encoded: they show the same negation patterns as nouns, require a copula in predication, e.g. WMo. *ene morin qurdun bui.* (this horse quick be(FIN)) 'This horse is big', and, when used as abstract nouns they can be followed by certain case markers.

With the exception of Moghol and Mangghuer, which clearly distinguish adjectives as a separate part of speech, probably due to the impact of foreign influence, it is generally assumed that adjectives cannot be regarded as a distinct word class in the majority of the Mongolic languages. In the Mongolic linguistic literature, adjectives are commonly described as a subgroup of nouns. This viewpoint is for instance found in Poppe (1954: 40): "There is no morphological difference between substantives and adjectives; all adjectives occur in only one constant form. All words expressing things can function as adjectives and all words expressing qualities can function as substantives, e.g. *modun* 'tree' and 'wooden', *mayu* 'bad' and 'evil'" and in Janhunen (2003a: 10): "There [in Proto-Mongolic] were two major parts of speech which may be identified as nouns (nominals) and verbs (verbals), combined with two separate sets of suffixes, respectively. [...] Adjectival words were also basically nominal, though their derivatives could function as verbs, [...]".

As is the case in the Tungusic literature, the assumption that adjectives do not constitute a separate word class stems from the fact that many adjectives in the Mongolic languages, such as e.g. WMo. *gün* 'deep; depth', WMo. *öndür* 'high, tall, heigth', WMo. *ulaɣan*, Khal. *ulaan* 'red; redness, the red one' have no distinctive morphological features of their own. However, there is a whole range of prototypical morphemes through which property words are derived from nouns (Poppe 1954: 40–44) such as WMo. *-dU* in e.g. *amin* 'life' → *amidu* 'live, living', WMo. *-KAi* in e.g. *qongqor* 'hole' → *qongqorqai* 'uneven', etc. Morphologically, certain derivational patterns are specific to adjectives: (de)intensifying suffixes, such as WMo *-msUy* , which designates exaggerated qualities, e.g. *yeke* 'big' → *yekemsüg* 'haughty, proud' (Poppe 1954: 43) while WMo. *-bUr* is used to form diminutives, e.g. *ulaɣan* 'red' → *ulaɣabur* 'reddish' (Poppe 1954: 40), nominalizers such as WMo. the suffix *-ngyui* which derives abstract nouns, e.g. *qara* 'black' → *qarangyui* 'darkness' (Poppe 1954: 43) or, partial emphatic reduplication (e.g. Khal. *ulaan* 'red' → *uv-ulaan* 'bright red').

Furthermore, adjectives can be distinguished syntactically since they occur in a modifier position (e.g. WMo. *öndür aɣula* 'high mountain') and they can enter comparative constructions, e.g. WMo. *nama-ača yeke* (I-ABL big-COMP) 'bigger than me'.

By origin, many nominally encoded property words are obsolete participial forms derived from verbs or verbal adjectives, e.g. WMo. *qata-* 'to become hard, dry (intr.)' → *qataɣu* 'hard, strong, severe, cruel', WMo. *qala-* 'to be(come)/ feel warm' → *qalaɣun* 'hot', WMo. *butara-* 'fall to pieces' → *butarqai* 'dismembered' (see Chapter 7). Note that some of these deverbal adnominalizers have denominal counterparts with the same form. Compare, for instance, WMo. *-KAi* in WMo. *butara-* 'fall to pieces' → *butarqai* 'dismembered' vs. WMo. *qongqor* 'hole'

→ *qongqorqai* 'uneven'. The observation that verbal and nominal bases can be turned into a nominally encoded property word using one and the same morphological means, suggests that the concept "adjective" was originally perceived as a single category, distinct from nouns and verbs.

b) *Verbally encoded property words*
Although the majority of property words are nominally encoded, Mongolic has a separate class of property words that grammatically behave like verbs, e.g. MMo. *ayu-n ba ayu-ba hiče-n ba hiče-ba bi* (be.afraid-NML INDEF.PT be.afraid-PST be.ashamed-NML INDEF.PT be.ashamed-PST 1SG) '[As for fear] I was afraid and [as for shame] I was ashamed' (SH 244). Again, there is a tendency to apply the verbal strategy in the case of less permanent properties such as WMo. / MMo. *ayu-* 'to be(come) afraid, fear (intr.)', WMo. *čad-/* MMo. *čat-* 'to be(come) saturated, be ripe', WMo. *iče-* / MMo. *hiče-* 'to be/ feel ashamed', WMo. *qata-* 'to become hard, dry (intr.)', WMo. *qala-* 'to be(come)/ feel warm', WMo. *soyta-* 'to be(come) drunk, intoxicated, be in rut', MMo. *sohta-* 'to be drunk' etc. Contemporary Mongolic languages maintain reflexes of these verbal property words, for instance 'be afraid', Khal. *ay-*, *ayu:-*, Bur. *ay-*, Kalm. *ä:-*, Ordos *ä:-*, Dong. *ayi-*, Bao. *ai-*, Dag. *ay-*, Mgr. *ayi-*, Mog. *ai:-*, or 'to become hard, dry (intr.)', Khal. *xat-*, Kalm. *xatə-*, Mgr. *xada:-*.

c) *Switched encoding*
Middle Mongolian and Written Mongolian retain traces of switching, whereby the same property word can have both nominal and verbal encoding, e.g. MMo. *bulqa* 'hostile; hostility' and MMo. *bulqa-* 'to be hostile', WMo. *boyus* 'pregnant (of animals); fetus' and WMo. *boyus-* 'to be(come) pregnant', WMo. *qarsi* 'contrary, opposed; obstacle' and WMo. *qarsi-* 'to be contrary, to be opposed' (Kara 1997: 158, 160), WMo. *tasi* 'slanting' (in *tasi zam* 'slanting, uphill road') and WMo. *tasi-* 'to deviate, slant, slope, incline (intr.)'.

In what follows, I will use the term "verbal adjectives" to refer to verbally encoded property words such as WMo. *qala-* 'to be(come) warm' and the term "nominal adjectives" for nominal encodings such as WMo. *öndür* 'high, tall, heigth'.

3.2.5 Turkic

a) *Nominally encoded property words*
The large majority of property words in the Turkic languages are nominally encoded: they show the same negation patterns as nouns, require a copula in predication, e.g. OTk. *ayguči-sï bilgä är-miš* (advisor-3SG wise be-EVI) 'his advi-

sors are said to be wise' (Tuń 20–21, Erdal 2004: 216) and when used as abstract nouns they can be followed by certain case markers.

As is the case in the analysis of the parts of speech in Tungusic and Mongolic, adjectives are often not clearly distinguished in the Turkic linguistic literature. Erdal (2004: 143) remarks: "The term [nominals] covers nouns (including proper nouns), adjectives, pronouns and numerals. We speak of 'adjectives' as a special sub-class because there is an (admittedly fuzzy) semantic distinction between the two classes: Adjectives tend to denote qualities and are used for referring less frequently than nouns." The distinction between noun and adjective is also rejected in Grönbech (1936: 24, 26–27). The borderline between the two word-classes, roughly distinguished by Gabain (1950: 64, 148), was more sharply defined by Johanson (2006). Supporting his description with examples from the contemporary Turkic varieties spoken in South Siberia, he uses semantic, syntactic and morphological characteristics to define the adjective as a distinct word class. Adjectives primarily describe properties of entities, they typically occupy the modifier position, e.g. OTk kïzïl kan-ïm (red blood-1SG) 'my red blood' and are marked for comparative degrees. Nevertheless, confusion may arise because some Turkic adjectives, such as OTk. kïzïl 'red', MTk. kïzïl 'red, intense; a kind of red bird', OTk täriŋ 'deep; depth', OTk bädük 'big, great; greatness' have no specific morphological features that distinguish them from nouns. The majority of Turkic adjectives, however, are derived from nouns by a range of distinct morphemes (Erdal 1991: 139) such as OTk -lXg in e.g. OTk ädgü 'goodness' → ädgülüg 'good', OTk. -gOk in e.g. OTk čam 'groundless objection' → čamgok 'slanderous', OTk -gAy in e.g. OTk küč 'strenghth' → küčgay 'violent' etc. Moreover, Turkic has specific adjectival morphology which includes (de)intensifying elements such as the intensifier OTk -rAk, e.g. OTk. yarp 'difficult' → yarprak 'quite difficult' and partial emphatic reduplication, e.g. OTk. kara 'black' → kap-kara 'quite black', none of which is possible with nouns (Erdal 2004: 150–151).

By origin, many nominal adjectives are obsolete deverbal derivations, e.g. OTk. kïzïl 'red' from OTk. kïz- 'be red', OTk bädük 'big, great; greatness' from OTk. bädü- 'be(come) big, great' and, OTk isig 'hot' from OTk. isi- 'to be hot'.

b) Verbally encoded property words

The Turkic languages use of smaller class of property words that align with verbs, e.g. OTk. ämtï karï-dï iglä-di (now become.old-PST become ill-PST) 'Now he has grown old and fallen ill' (Erdal 2004: 464). There seems to be a tendency to apply the verbal strategy in the case of time-unstable properties such as OTk. bädü- 'to be(come) big, great', OTk. isi- 'to be hot', OTk. kat- 'to be hard, firm, tough', OTk. kïz- 'to be red', OTk. tumlï- 'to be cold', OTk. tïnči- 'to be(come) putrid, smell foul', OTk. us- 'to be thirsty', OTk. yeni- 'to be(come) light', OTk. tïgra- 'to be tough',

OTk. *iglä-* 'to be(come) ill' etc. Contemporary Turkic languages maintain a few reflexes of these verbal property words, for instance for 'to be(come) big', Tk. *büyü-*, SUig. *pezi-*, Az. *böyü-*, Khalaj *bidi-*, Tuva *bedi-*, Gag. *bü:-*, Karaim *büyü-* and for 'to be(come) red, red-hot', Turkm. *Gïz-*, Tur. *kïz-*, Yak. *kï:s-*, but in the majority of cases, the earlier verbal property word has lexicalized its obsolete adnominal form and functions as a nominal adjective.

c) *Switched encoding*

Like the other Transeurasian languages, Turkic contains examples of switching, whereby the same property word can have both nominal and verbal encoding. Doerfer's (1982, 104–112) list of so-called 'Nomenverba' includes such pairs as OTk. *ač* 'hungry' and OTk. *ač-* 'to be hungry', OTk. *keč* 'late, slow' and OTk. *keč-* 'to be late, slow', OTk *köp* 'abundant' and OTk *köp-* 'to swell, boil over' and OTk. *karï* 'old' and *karï-* 'to become old'.

In what follows I will use the term "verbal adjectives" to refer to verbally encoded property words such as OTk. *kat-* 'to be hard, firm, tough' and I the term "nominal adjectives" for nominal encodings such as OTk. *täriŋ* 'deep; depth'.

3.2.6 Scenario for the development of Transeurasian adjective typology

The observations made in the previous section suggest that the Transeurasian languages, at least in their earlier stages, share mixed adjective typology with a single encoding option for most of the adjective stems and with relics of switching for a small number of adjectives. This is summarized in Table 1.

Table 1. Diachronic typology of adjective encoding in the Transeurasian languages

encoding	verbal	nominal	switching
Japanese	OJ *atu-* 'to be hot'	OJ *tasika nar-* 'to be trustworthy'	OJ *taka* 'high' OJ *taka-* 'to be high'
Korean	MK *kwut-* 'to be(come) hard'	K *kanan ha-* 'to be poor'	MK *toso ho-* 'to be warm' MK *toso-* 'to be warm'
Tungusic	Ud. *agda-* 'to be happy'	Ud. *zo:ŋku* 'poor; the poor one'	Ud. *bogo* 'fat' Ud. *bogo-* 'to become fat'
Mongolic	WMo. *qala-* 'to be(come)/ feel warm'	WMo. *qara* 'black'	MMo. *bulqa* 'hostile; hostility' MMo. *bulqa-* 'to be hostile'
Turkic	OTk. *kat-* 'to be hard, firm, tough'	OTk *isig* 'hot'	OTk. *ač* 'hungry' OTk. *ač-* 'to be hungry'

In a sample of 386 languages across the world, only 27 % (103) are found to have mixed adjective typology (Stassen 2005: 480). Logically, the proportion of languages sharing the same encoding option – single, switched or both – will be even lower, say about 10 % each. The fact that a group of geographically concentrated languages all share mixed adjective typology with single encoding and traces of switching can thus hardly be due to sheer chance. There must be a historical reason for this phenomenon: the adjective typology may have diffused areally; it may have been inherited from a common ancestor or, it may have resulted from an interplay of areal and genealogical factors. In this section, it will be shown that a considerable number of Transeurasian verbal adjective stems correspond not only in form and function, but also in encoding option. This suggests that at least the verbal adjective encoding was inherited from a common ancestor.

Table 2 and 3 list 17 adjectives with original verbal encoding in Japonic. The etymologies in Table 2 stretch over at least three branches of the Transeurasian family, whereas the etymologies in Table 3 are restricted to a comparison of Japonic and Koreanic only. All adjectives correlate in form and function, and the majority also share the verbal encoding option. A formal match means that all subsequent phonemes of the Japanese proto-form correspond regularly according to the sound correspondences proposed in Robbeets (2005: 373–376), with some exceptions for the stem-final vowel. Relevant sound correspondences are illustrated in Section 3.3. For an overview of references contributing to the proposed etymologies, I refer to the etymological index in Robbeets (2005: 453–975).[5]

Table 2. Etymologies relating Japanese verbal adjectives to adjectives in the Transeurasian languages

	TEA	Japonic	Koreanic	Tungusic	Mongolic	Turkic
(1)	'be clean'	OJ *ara-* 'be fresh' pJ **ara-*			WMo. *ari-l-* 'be(come) clear' pMo **ari-*	OTk. *arï-* 'be(come) clean' pTk **arï-*
(2)	'be hard'	OJ *kata-* 'be hard' pJ **kata-*	MK *kwut-* 'be hard' pK **kata-*		WMo. *qata-* 'become hard' pMo **kata-*	OTk. *kat-* 'be hard' pTk **kat-*
(3)	'be round'	MJ *maro-* 'be round' pJ **maru-*	MK *mulu-* 'turn around' pK **mili-l-*	Evk. *murume* 'round' pTg **muru-*	WMo *muru-* 'be curved' pMo **muru-*	OTk. *bür-* 'wind round' pTk **bur-*

---

[5] Brackets are used for consonants and vowels whose internal reconstruction (in part) depends on external comparison.

Table 2. (continued)

	TEA	Japonic	Koreanic	Tungusic	Mongolic	Turkic
(4)	'be languid'	J noro- 'be slow' pJ *n(i)r(i)-	MK nuluy- 'be languid' pK *niliy-	Ma. nurhu- 'do ceaselessly' pTg *nur	WMo. nöri- 'be lingering' pMo *nöri-	
(5)	'be early'	OJ paya- 'be early, fast' pJ *paya-	MK polo- 'be fast' pK *pʌlʌ-l-	Ud. baji 'early' pTg *badi(-)		OTk baya(-ki) 'recently' pTk *baya(-)
(6)	'be thick'	OJ puto₁- 'be thick' pJ *puto-	MK ˵pwuT- 'increase (intr.)' pK *pwuti-		WMo. büdügün 'large' pMo *büdü-	
(7)	'be white'	OJ siro₁- 'be white' pJ *siro-	MK ·huy- 'be white' pK *si(l)ʌ-	Ma. šara- 'become white' pTg *sia:ra- (<*si:ra-?)	[WMo sira 'yellow'] Copy?	OTk šarïg 'yellow' pTk *sia:rï- (< *si:ra-?)
(8)	'be(come) high'	OJ taka- 'be high' pJ *taka-	MK teu- 'increase (tr.)' pK *teki-	Even deg- 'go up' pTg *deg-	WMo. degere 'higher than' pMo *dege-	OTk. yeg 'better than' pTk *yeg
(9)	'be scarce'	OJ tomo-si- 'be scarce' pJ *t(i)m(i)-	MK ·tu·mul- 'be rare' pK *timili-		WMo. dömü- 'be scarce' pMo *dömü-	
(10)	'be(come) weak'	OJ yuru- 'loose' pJ *y(o)ru-		[Ma. duru- 'become worn out'] Copy?	WMo. doru(i) 'weak' pMo *doru(-)	Tk. yor- 'exhaust' pTk *yor-

Table 3. Etymologies relating Japanese verbal adjectives to Korean verbal adjectives and intransitive verbs

	pJK	Japonic	Koreanic
(11)	'be beautiful'	OJ kupasi- 'be beautiful' pJ *k(o)pa-	MK kwo·po- 'be beautiful' pK *kwopo-
(12)	'be painful'	OJ kurusi- 'be painful' pJ *k(o)ru-	MK kwolwuW- 'be painful' pK *kwolwu-
(13)	'be odorous'	OJ kusa- 'be smelly' pJ *kusa-	MK kwusu- 'be odorous' pK *kwusi-
(14)	'be(come) fragile'	OJ moro- 'be fragile' pJ *m(i)r(i)-	MK mulu- 'become soft' pK *milil-

Table 3. (continued)

	pJK	Japonic	Koreanic
(15)	'be(come) long'	OJ *naga-* 'be long' pJ **nanka-*	MK *nulk-* 'become old' pK *nilk-*
(16)	'be mild, warm'	Mod. J *nuku-* 'be warm' pJ **nuku-*	MK *nwuk-* 'become warm' pK **nwuk-*
(17)	'be foolish'	OJ *oroka* 'foolish' pJ **ərə-*	MK *·eleW-* 'be mad' pK **ele-*
(18)	'become clear'	OJ *sayaka* 'clear' pJ **saya-*	MK ¨*say-* 'dawn' pK **sa(l)i-*

Since mixed adjective typology with partially switched encoding is present in all branches of the Transeurasian languages, the hypothesis that it was a feature of the ancestral language makes the fewest new assumptions, and is therefore to be preferred according to Occam's razor. This hypothesis is corroborated by etymology (53), which suggests that an alternation can be reconstructed between verbally encoded pTEA **a:-* 'to be' and nominally encoded pTEA **a* 'being' in the ancestral language.

The etymologies presented in Table 2 and 3 yield a number of observations. First, there are 10 etymologies relating Japanese verbal adjectives with – generally descriptive – verbs in the other Transeurasian languages. This suggests that proto-Transeurasian made intensive use of verbally encoded property words.

Second, all proposed Korean cognates share the verbal encoding option with the Japanese adjective. Some continental Transeurasian cognates represent nonverbal encodings, but the large majority of these adjectives can be derived from verbal encodings, e.g. WMo. *ariɣ, ariɣun* 'pure, clear' in (1), WMo. *qataɣu* 'hard' and OTk. *katï y* 'hard' in (2), Evk. *murume* 'round' and WMo *murui* 'curved' in (3), WMo. *nöri(n)* 'lingering' in (4), WMo. *büdügün* 'large' in (6), OTk. *šarïg, sarïg* 'yellow' in (7) and WMo. *dorui* 'weak' in (9). This suggests that the closer one moves towards the West of the Transeurasian area, the stronger the tendency to shift to nominally encoded adjectives.

Third, about half of the etymologies proposed for verbal adjectives are restricted to a binary setting between Japanese and Korean. This suggests that verbally encoded adjectives are better preserved in the eastern part of the Transeurasian area.

The present analysis suggests that proto-Transeurasian displayed mixed adjective typology with partially switched encoding, but verbal adjective encoding was gradually replaced by nominal encoding in the west, whereas it survived more succesfully in the east of the area. The map depicted in Figure 1 (taken from The World Atlas of Language Structures) shows that all the languages of Europe display non-verbal encoding, whereas in East and South-East Asia verbal encoding is particularly strong. As could be expected, mixed adjective typology tends to appear in those areas where verbal and non-verbal encoding meet. The influence of the European languages probably pushed the western, continental Transeurasian languages towards predominantly nominal encodings, whereas the mixed typology was better maintained in the eastern, insular Transeurasian languages due to the areal influence of verbally encoding languages in East and South-East Asia.[6]

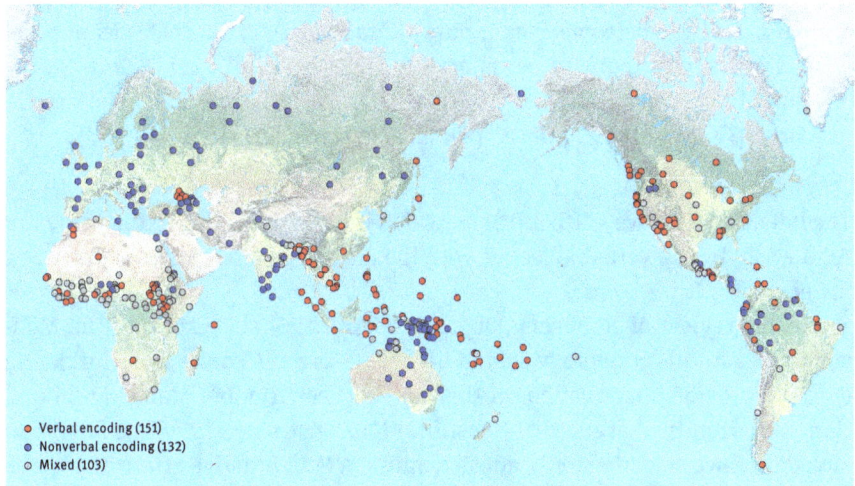

Figure 1. Cross-linguistic encoding of predicative adjectives (Stassen 2005: 480)

---

[6] According to Stassen (1997: 350–351), "the encoding of predicative adjectives is determined by the way in which a language expresses 'the location in time' (Comrie 1985: 9) of propositions...". Languages possessing a morphologically bound category of tense on the verb, which minimally involves a distinction between past and nonpast time reference, are expected to display nominal adjectives, while others will tend to use verbal adjectives. Hence, we can expect a correlation between the gradual increase of nominal adjectives in the Transeurasian languages, as proposed under the present scenario and the development from nonfinite aspectual markers into finite tense markers, discussed in Chapter 7.

3.2.7 Underlying data

(1) 'to be clean'

J *arai* A 'to be rough, natural, crude', OJ *ara-* 'to be rough, fresh, new', Yonaguni *ara-* 'to be new', J *ara* 'new, fresh', J *arau* A, OJ *arap-* 'to wash', pJ **ara-* 'to be clean, clear, pure'

WMo. *ariɣ* 'pure, clear', *ariɣun* '1 clean, pure, clear; purity' (WMo -*ɣun* / -*gün* deverbal noun deriving quality words (Poppe 1954: 46)), *arči-* '2 to wipe, clean, erase', MMo. *ariun* '1', *arči-* '2', *aril-* '3 to be(come) clear, clear up', *arilqa-* '2', Khal. *ariun* '1', *arči-* '2', *aril-* '3', Bur. *aŕūn* '1', *arša-* '2', Kalm. *ärü:n* '1', *arč-* '2', Ordos *aru:n* '1', *arci-* '2', Dong. *arun* '1', *ači-* '2', Bao. *aruŋ* '1', Dag. *aru:n* '1', *arči-* '2', Mgr. *arin* '1', Mgr. *arili-* '3', Mgr. *ariŋge* 'cleanly', *arire-* 'to become pure', Mogol *oru:n* '1', pMo **ari-* 'to be clean'

OTk. *arï-* '1 to be(come) clean, pure', Karakh. *arï-* '1', Tk. *arï* '2 clean, pure' , *art-* '3 to clean, purify', Osm. *arït-* 'to wipe', MTk. *arïɣ*, *arï* '2', *arït-* '3', Uz. (dial.) *ari-* '1', Az. (dial.) *arï* '2', *arït-* '3', Tkm. *arïg* '2', *art-* '3', Khalaj *arïɣ* '2', *arut-* '3', Tuva *arïɣ* '2', *arït-* '3', pTk **arï-* 'to be(come) clean'

The intensive-iterative suffix pJ **-pa-*, which is assumed to derive the verb *arau* A 'to wash' from a verbal adjective with the meaning 'to be clean,' is described in Section 5.4.1.

In his review of Robbeets 2005, Kara (2007: 96) suggests that the Mongolic forms in this etymology should be treated as early copies from Turkic. He does not provide a motivation for this copying scenario, but Marcel Erdal and Hans Nugteren (pc.) argue that the suffix -*l*- reconstructed in *aril-* is foreign to Mongolic since the commonly attested suffix WMo. -*l*- derives transitive verbs rather than intransitives as in this case. However, Poppe (1954: 61, 66 vs. 64) distinguishes two different homophonous suffixes WMo. -*l*-: one is a causative or transitive suffix (e.g. WMo. *uyu-* 'drink' → *uyul-* 'to give to drink'), while the other is an intensive-iterative suffix (e.g. WMo. *dusu-* 'fall (of drops)' → *dusul-* 'to drip') that can derive transitive as well as intransitive verbs. The latter suffix also lexicalized in a number of verb pairs granting an inchoative meaning to natural processes, e.g. WMo. *γasi-γun* 'bitter' → *γasal-* 'to lament, mourn', *öte-gü* 'grey'→ *ötel-* 'to become old' (Ramstedt 1912: 7–8). It is interesting to observe that, although the transitive suffix practically disappeared in Monguor (De Smedt & Mostaert 1964: 93–94 note), the intensive suffix still surfaces as Mgr. -*li*- (De Smedt & Mostaert 1964: 148) in e.g. Mgr. *γasen* 'bitter' → *γaseli-* 'to become bitter', *sači-* 'to sow' → *sačili-* 'to scatter, disperse' and *arin* 'clear, pure' → *arili-*

'to clear up (intr.)'. The Monguor forms Mgr. *ariŋge* 'cleanly' and *arire-* 'become pure' are relevant because they can be segmented in a root **ari-* 'to be clean' and native suffixes. The form Mgr. *arire-* 'become pure' represents the equipollent anticausative counterpart of the causative *arči-* 'wipe, clean ,' which is well represented elsewhere in Mongolic (cf. Section 5.6.4). Given the presence of the Japanese cognate and the native origin of the suffix *-l-* in MMo. *aril-*, these forms are more likely to have derived from inheritance than from code-copying.

(2) 'to be hard'

J *katai* A, OJ *kata-* 'to be hard, solid, tough, rigid', Shuri *kata-* A 'to be sturdy, sure, saturated', pJ **kata-* 'to be hard'

K *kwut-*, MK *kwut-* 'to be hard', K *kkatalop-*, MK *skatalwop-* 'to be hard, difficult, complicated; be harsh, severe' (adj. n. + MK *-lwop-* 'to be characterized by'; pK **s(u/o)-* intensive prefix), pK **kata-* 'to be hard, severe'

WMo. *qata-* '1 to become hard, dry (intr.)', *qata-ɣu* '2 hard' (WMo *-ɣu / -gü* deverbal noun deriving quality words (Poppe 1954: 46)), MMo. *qata'u* '2', Khal. *xat-*, *xatu:* '2', Mgr. *xada:-* '1', *xadoŋ* '2', pMo **kata-* 'to become hard'

OTk. *kat-* 'to be hard, firm, though', *katïɣ* '2 hard', Karakh. *kat-* '1', *katïɣ* '2', Tat. *katï* '2', Uz. *kɔtik* '2', Uig. *ketik* '2', Az. *gatï* '2', Tkm. *gat*, *gatï* '2', Khak. *xatïɣ* '2', Shor *kadïɣ* '2', Chu. *xïtă* '2', Yak. *kïta:nax* '2', Dolg. *kïta:nak* '2', Tuva *ka'dïɣ* '2', Kirg. *katū* '2', Kaz. *kattï* '2', Nog. *kat* '2', Bash. *katï* '2', KKalp. *kattï* '2' , pTk **kat-* 'to be hard'

In Korean, relatively retracted and non-retracted vowels alternate phonologically in certain color adjectives, mimetic and expressive adjectives, a phenomenon referred to as "ablaut" by Vovin (2008a: 6) and as "heavy and light isotopes" by Martin (1992: 343–344). The non-retracted vowels *e, ey, wu, wi* (< MK *wuy*) are typical of the heavy isotopes, while the retracted vowels *a, ay, o* (MK *wo*), *oy* (MK *woy*) are typical of the light isotopes. The non-retracted vowels are associated with weighty, bulky concepts, while the retracted vowels are used for small and unsubstantial things, e.g. K *ce:k-* 'to be small in number or quantity, few' vs. K *ca:k-* 'to be small in size, tiny' [7] It is not surprising that the adjective meaning 'to be large' has a more advanced vowel in its default form K *khu-*. A

---

[7] It can be noted that the interpretation of "heavy and light isotopes" in terms of a distinction between relatively high front versus relatively low back vowels (e.g. Martin (1992: 343–344) would suggest that lower vowels were used for smaller things. This runs counter the notions of "naturalness" of phonetic symbolism (a.o. Sapir 1929).

trace of a retracted alternant, however, can be found in the obsolete adjective K *ha-* (< MK ·*ho-*) 'to be large in number, much, many, be great', lexicalized, for instance, in K *hankul* 'hankul, lit. great script'. Similarly, the stem meaning 'to be hard' has developed an advanced vowel in its default form K *kwut-*, MK *kwut-* 'to be hard', while there is a trace of a retracted – and probably original – alternant in the adjective with metaphorical meaning K *kkatalop-*, MK *skatalwop-* 'to be hard, difficult, complicated; to be harsh, severe'. This form can be derived from **s-kata-lwop-* (INT-hard-be.characterized.by). The first element is the intensive prefix pK **s(u/o)-* > MK *s-* > K reduplication (Lee 1977: 145, Ramsey 1977: 64, Martin 1996: 24, 27, 91), e.g. MK *tih-* ~ *stih-* 'to pound'.[8] The last element is the verbal adjective formant pK **-lwop-* > MK *-lwop-* > K *-lop-* 'to be characterized by' (Martin 1992: 677), e.g. K *say* 'new' vs. *saylop-* 'to be new'. Apophony between the non-retracted vowel *wu* and the retracted vowel *a* can be found in other adjective pairs, such as in K *phalah-*, MK ·*pha·la ho-* ~ K *phwulu-*, MK *phwulwu-*, *phwulu* 'be blue', where it is used for its expressive effects only. A similar system of vowel gradation may have been present in an ancestral stage of Old Japanese, but this remains speculative. This hypothesis is based upon the observation that some expressive adjectives display pairs whereby relatively retracted vowels *a, *ə alternate with a relatively advanced vowel *u, e.g. pJ **nuru-* ~ **nərə-* 'to be slow' (cf. (4)), pJ **nuku-* ~ **nəkə-* 'to be warm' (cf. (16)), pJ **usu-* ~ **asa-* 'to be thin' (OJ *usu-* 'to be thin' vs. OJ *asa-* 'to be shallow').

(3) 'to be(come) round, turn around'

J *marui* A, EMJ (10th C) *maro-* 'to be round', J *maru*, OJ *maro₂* 'round thing', Shuri *marusaN*, pR **maro-* (Thorpe 1983: 321), pJ **maru-* ~ **maro-* 'to be round', OKog *mawr 'round, circle' (Beckwith 2004: 66, 114, 158)

K *mulu-* (*-ll-*) 'to turn around, retreat, go back (intr.); give back, return (tr.)', MK *mulu-* (*-ll-*) 'to retreat, withdraw', pK **mɨlɨ-l-* 'to turn around'

---

8 Whereas Martin reconstructs pK **s(u/o)-*, Ramsey and Lee refer to the s-clusters as reinforced pronunciations that do not necessarily go back to an original silibant prefix. The authors agree that the verbs with s-clusters represent intensive meaning. The intensification was apparently restricted to processive verbs in Middle Korean. Other examples of such verb pairs are MK *kužu-* ~ *skužu-* 'to pull', MK *pipuy-* ~ *spi·puy-* 'to rub', MK *twutuli-* ~ *stwu·tuli-* 'to beat', MK *sip-* ~ *ssip-* 'to chew', MK ·*sus-* ~ ·*ssus-* 'to wash', MK *kulh-* ~ *skulh-* 'to boil', MK *sa·hol-* ~ *ssa·hol-* 'to chop', MK *ku·cit-* ~ *skucit-* 'to scold'. Instances of a descriptive verb pairs reflecting the intensive prefix are MK *polo-* (*-ll-*) 'be straight, fast, act quickly' vs. MK ·*spol-* (*-ll-*) 'be fast; be sharp, pointed', MK ·*so-* 'be cheap' vs. MK ·*sso-* 'id.', MK *kel-* (~"*ke(l)-*) 'get stuck, obstructed' vs. MK ¨*skelW-* 'be difficult'.

Evk. *muru-* '1 to walk round, return', *murume* '2 round' (cf. pTg * *-mA* nominalizer; Section 7.4.3) , Even *merek-* 'to return', Even *mereldin-* 'to circulate, circle, orbit', *mere:ti* 'circle', Neg. *meyel* 2, Ma. *muri-* 'to twist, wring', *murigan* 'curved place on a road', *murcaku:* 'spiral, whorl, helix', Olch. *muru-muru* 2, Orok *morolime* 2, Na. *murgi* 2, pTg **muru-* 'to turn around'

WMo. *muri-* ~ *muru-* 'to go astray, act contrarily', WMo *muruyi-* 'to be bend, to be crooked, to turn, to meander (intr.)' (pMo **-yi-* anticausative), WMo *murui* 'awry, slanting, bending; bend, curve, crookedness (n. and adj.)' (cf. pMo **-i* deverbal noun suffix; Section 8.3.4), MMo. *muru, muri* '1 curve', Khal. *muruy* '1', Buriat *múŕu:* '1', Kalm. *múŕu:* '1', Ordos *mur^{w}i:* '1', Dag. *morčigui* '1', Mgr. *muri:* '1', pMo **muru-* 'to make a curve, turn round'

OTk. *bür-* 'to twist, wind round, screw (tr.)', MTk. *bur-*, Tk. *bur-*, Tat. *bor-*, Uz. *bur-, bura-*, Uig. *bur-*, Az. *bur-*, Tkm. *bur-, bürü-*, Khak. *pur-*, Shor *pur-*, Chu. *păr-* 'to turn, wind, bend, screw', Kirg. *bura-, bür-*, Kaz. *bura-, bür-*, Nog. *bur-, bura-, bür-*, Bash. *bor-*, Balkar *bur-*, Gag. *bur-*, Karaim *bur-*, KKalp. *bur-, bura-*, pTk **bür-* ~ *bur-* 'to bend, turn'

According to vowel correspondence 19 in Section 3.3.2, the regular medial vowel reflex of a high back vowel **-u-* is Japanese *-u-*. However, the reflex *-a-* in pJ **maru-* ~ **marə-* 'to be round' matches the particular phonological environment described in conditioning factor 19b, whereby the vowel is preceded by an initial labial consonant (**p-, *w-, *m-*) and followed by a medial resonant (**-r-, *-n-*). The phonological development probably involved the diphtongization of the high back vowel: **muru-* > **mauru-* > *maru-* > *marə-*. The final vowel alternation in pJ **maru-* ~ **marə-* reflects the change in medial vowel quality and the following assimilation of the final vowel. Note that MJ *waru-* ~ *waro-* 'to be bad' (< pJ **waru-* ~ **warə-* 'to be bad') reflects a similar development. Based on Beckwith's reconstruction of OKog **mawr* 'round, circle', the dissimilation may have already started in Japanic (Japanese-Koguryoic).

MK *mulu-* (*-ll-*) 'to retreat, withdraw' belongs to a small class of seven verbs that are marked by *-ll-* doubling infinitives.[9] Ramsey (1986: 186) derives these verbs from original verb roots that were closed by a final liquid *-l*. Given the intensive or iterative connotation of some of these verbs, it is inviting to set up a final intensive-iterative suffix pK **-l-* in some cases. The same suffix may also

---

[9] Among the other Korean class 8 verbs with -ll- doubling infinitives, we find MK *hulu-* 'to flow', MK *molo-* 'to dry up', MK *molo-* 'to cut out', MK *polo-* 'to apply to', MK *polo-* ~ *spolo-* 'to be fast', MK *pulu-* 'to sing, call'.

underlie the etymologies (5), (19), (20) and (52). It could be cognate with the Mongolic intensive-iterative suffix pMo *-l-*, discussed under etymology (1).

The deverbal anticausative suffix pMo *-yi-* can be reconstructed on the basis of verb pairs such as WMo. *sekü-* 'to raise, lift up (tr.)' → *seküyi-* 'to rise, stand out (intr.)', WMo. *čarda-* 'to starch (tr.)' → *čardayi-* 'to harden, become hard (intr.)' and WMo. *julbu-* 'to shed skin, to lose hair (intr.)' → *julbuyi-* 'for the hair to lie down (as when wet), to be short-wooled'. In view of WMo *muruyi-* 'to be bend', this suffix supports the reconstruction of a verb root pMo *muru-* meaning 'to make a curve, turn round'.

(4) 'to be languid'

   J *noroi* ?B, OJ *noro-* 'to be slow, dilatory, dull', J *nurui* B, OJ *nuru-* 'to be slow; to be tepid, lukewarm', pJ *niri-* ~ *nuru-* 'to be slow'

   K *nuli-*, MK *nuluy-* 'to be slow, languid', K *nul* 'always', pK *nuluy-* 'to be slow, ceaseless'

   Ma. *nurhu-* 'to do ceaselessly', Evk. *nur-nur* 'slightly', pTg *n(ö)r* 'ceaseless, slow'

   WMo. *nöri-* 'to be of long duration, to be annoying, to become a nuisance', WMo. *nöri(n)* 'of long duration, lingering', Khal. *nörö-* 'to be annoying, boring', *nör* 'boring', pMo *nöri-* 'to be boring, lingering'

The Tungusic attestations do not allow us to distinguish between the reconstruction of pTg *-u-* and *-ö-* because there is no conclusive evidence from Even or Udehe (cf. (49))

(5) 'to be early'

   J *hayai* B, OJ *paya-* 'to be quick, fast, early', Shuri *feesaN*, pR *paya-* (Thorpe 1983: 281), pJ *paya-* 'to be early, fast'

   K *pparu-* 'to be quick, fast; early', MK *polo-* (-ll-) 'to be straight, fast, act quickly' vs. MK *spolo-* (-ll-) 'to be fast; be sharp, pointed' (pK *s(u/o)-* intensive prefix; cf. Footnote 8), pK *pʌlʌ-l-* 'to be fast'

   Evk. *bajikir*, Even *baj*, Neg. *bajïɣ*, Oroč. *ba:jika*, Ud. *baji*, pTg *baji* < *badi* 'early'

   OTk. *baya* 'recently, in the immediate past', *bayakï* 'former, recent, earlier mentioned (n. / adv.)', Karakh. *baya*, Tk. *baya, bayak*, Tatar *baya*, MTk *baya*, Uz. *bɔya*, Uig. *baya*, SYug. *piya*, Az. *bayaG*, Tkm. *bayaq, baya-qi*, Khak.

paya, Shor *paya*, Oyrat *baya*, Khalaj *bayaq*, Chu. *pažăr*, Tuva *biye*, Tofalar *biyɛ*, Kirg. *baya*, Kaz. *baya-yi*, Nog. *baya-yi*, Bash. *baya*, Karaim *baya-yi*, *baya-qi*, Karakalpak *baya-yi*, Kumyk *baya-yi*, pTk **baya-*'earlier, recent'

As far as the Korean cognate is concerned, Vovin (2008a: 102–103) remarks that "we have no internal Korean evidence allowing us to segment the prefix *s-* in MK *spòlò-*". However, one might object that, along with MK *polo-* (*-ll-*) 'to be straight, fast, act quickly', MK *spolo-* (*-ll-*) 'to be fast; be sharp, pointed' belongs to a small class of seven verbs that are marked by *-ll-* doubling infinitives (see Footnote 9). Except for MK *spolo-* (*-ll-*) 'to be fast' and MK *hulu-* 'to flow', *-ll-* doubling is restricted to a specific phonological environment, namely low-low pitched disyllabic roots with an initial labial, a medial liquid and two minimal vowels. Even if Vovin would be correct in assuming that MK *polo-* (*-ll-*) 'to be straight' is not a related form, the expected initial labial suggests that the *s-* in MK *spolo-* (*-ll-*) 'to be fast' is a prefix. Moreover, it is possible to reconstruct pK **s(u/o)-* as an intensive prefix (see Footnote 8).

The expected medial consonant reflex in the Old Turkic cognate is *-d-*, according to the sound correspondence pJ **-y-*:: pK **-l-* :: pTg **-d-* :: pMo **-d-*:: pTk **-d-*. Intervocalic *-d-* in Old Turkic developed over a fricative *ď* in Kharakhanid to a glide *-y-* in Middle Turkic and in some contemporary varieties, e.g. OTk *adak* > Kharakh. *aďaq* > MTk *ayaq* 'foot'. In some cases, the lenition is already completed in Kharakhanid, e.g. OTk. *adaš* > Kharakh. *aďaš ~ ayaš* 'foot'. If the Turkic member pTk **baya-* 'earlier, recent' belongs here, we must assume that the lenition was already completed in Old Turkic, as was the case for the initial pTk **y-* < **d-*.

(6) 'to be thick'

J *hutoi* B 'to be thick, burly, fat', OJ *puto*₁*-* 'to be thick, fat' (< **puta-wo-ra* (thick-COP-PCP); cf. Section 7.3.1), Shuri *butasaN*, pR **buta-* 'stout, thick' (Thorpe 1983: 335), pJ **puta-* 'to be thick'

K *pu:s-* 'to swell (intr.)', MK ˮ*pwuT-* 'to swell, increase', pK **pwuti-* 'to become thick'

WMo. *büdügün, bidügün* 'large, huge, big' (WMo *-ɣun / -gün* deverbal noun deriving quality words (Poppe 1954: 46)), MMo. *bidun*, Khal. *büdü:n*, Kalm. *büdü:n, bödü:n*, Ordos *büdü:n, bidü:n*, Dong. *biedun*, Bao. *beidoŋ*, Dag. *budun, budu:n*, SYug. *büdü:n*, Mgr. *budin, bidun*, Mgr. *beidü:n, beidun*, pMo **büdü-* 'to be large'

The Old Japanese initial *p-* may require special notice because it has been suggested that its articulatory definition had already become a bilabial fricative *F* by the time of Old Japanese. Miyake (1999: 396–400) has argued against the spirantization of OJ *p*, demonstrating that *p* remained unchanged until Middle Japanese when it became a fricative *f*.

In Mongolic, two verbally encoded adjective stems alternate: pMo **büdü-* 'to be large' and pMo **bedü-* 'to be large'. The latter form may have arisen through convergence with a form ancestral to OTk. *bädü-* 'to be(come) big, great' (Doerfer 1963: 235; 1975: 275).

(7) 'to be white'

J *siroi* B, OJ $siro_1$- 'to be white', J *siro* (2.5), OJ $siro_1$ 'white' (< **sira-wo-m* (thick-COP-NML); cfr Section 7.3.1), J/ OJ *sira-* in e.g. J *sirakami*, OJ $sira-kami_1$ 'white hair', Shuri *sirusaN*, pR **siro-* 'white' (Thorpe 1983: 347), pJ **siro- ~ *sira* '(to be) white', OKog ☆*tśiar* 'silver' (Beckwith 2004: 100, 112), OKog **šilap* 'white' (Miller 1979: 7)

MK *hoy- ~* MK ·*huy-* 'to be white', MK *syey-* 'to become white (of hair, of face)', pK **si(l)ʌ- ~* pK **si(l)i- ~* pK **si(l)e-* 'to be white'

Ma. *šara-* 'to become white', Ma. *šari* 'light', Evk. *se:ru:-*, dial. *še:ru:-* 'to sparkle, glitter, flash', Evk. *se:ru:n*, dial. *še:ru:n* 'rainbow' (cf. pTg **-n* deverbal noun; Section 7.5.3), Evk. *sereme* 'yellow' (cf. pTg * *-mA* nominalizer; Section 7.4.3), Orok *se:rro, siro* 'rainbow', pTg **sia:ra-* 'to be light, white' (< **si:ra-?*)

WMo. *sira*, MMo. *šira, šira:*, Khal. *šar*, Bur. *šara*, Kalm. *šarə*, Ordos *šara*, Dong. *šəra, šira*, Bao. *šira*, Dag. *šara, šar, šari*, Mgr. *śira*, Mogh. *šira, sira:*, pMo **sira* 'yellow'

OTk. *šarïg, sarïg* '1 yellow', Karakh. *sarïɣ*, MTk. *sarïɣ*, Tk. *sari* 1, Tat. *sari* 1, Uz. *sariq* 1 Uig. *seriq* 1, SYug. *sarïɣ* 1, Az. *sarï* 1, Tkm. *sa:rï* 1, Khalaj *sa:ruɣ* 'orange', Chu. *šur, šură* 'white', *šur-* 'to become white', Tuva *sarïɣ*, Kirg. *sari* 1, Kaz. *sari* 1, Bash. *hari* 1, Sal. *sari* 1, pTk **sia:rï-* 'to be white, yellow' (< **si:ra-?*) (pTk **-(X)g* deverbal noun suffix; cf. Erdal 1991: 172–232)

The seven vowel system proposes a double origin for OJ *i*; the front vowel derives either from pJ **e* or from pJ **i*. In the case of OJ $siro_1$- 'be white', there is no internal or Ryukyan evidence, supporting the reconstruction of a mid front vowel. However, Frellesvig and Whitman (2008: 37) take the attestation of MK *syey-* 'become white (of hair, of face)' as external evidence for the reconstruction of pJ *sero* 'white'. This reconstruction seems implausible, however, in view of the attestation of two other, related stems MK *hoy-* 'be white' and MK *·huy-* 'be white'. I assume the following developments in Korean:

pK *si(l)ʌ-* >   *syo-* > *hyo-* (metathesis) > MK *hoy-* 'white'
pK *si(l)i-* >   *syu-* > *hyu-* (metathesis) > MK · *huy-* 'white'
pK *si(l)e-* > *si(l)ye-* > *syey-*   > MK *syey-* 'become white'

Proto-Korean had three apophonical alternants for the adjective root 'be(come) white'. The original final mid vowel in pK *si(l)e-* dipthongized. Dipthongization of mid front vowels by way of assimilation to a high front vowel also occurred in the derivation of MK *myey-* 'get stopped up' from MK *mek-* 'stop up' and a passive suffix MK *-i*.

After liquid loss, the vowels of the three alternants contracted. Initial pK *s-* developed into pre-MK *h-* whenever it was followed by a front vowel *-i-* or palatal glide *-y-*, but this development was blocked when a second glide was present in the syllable. This explains why MK *syey-* 'become white (of hair, of face)' maintained its silibant. The Koguryo cognate OKog ☆*tśiar* 'silver' proposed by Beckwith, while semantically rather distant, would support the high front vowel. Although Miller's Koguryo proposal would be a better fit, it may concern a ghost-word which has arisen via a modern scholar's handwritten copy of the character 刀 (Beckwith 2004: 72).

It is clear that Tungusic forms such as Ma. *sira* 'yellow', Even *hiraŋan* 'yellowish (of reindeer skin)' and Ud. *si:* 'yellow paint' are copies from Mongolic (Miller & Street 1975: 133, Doerfer 1985: 302, Rozycki 1994: 184). These are nominal forms with high front vowels meaning 'yellow'. However, the Tungusic stems proposed in the etymology can be derived from verbally encoded adjectives, reflect pre-glided low vowels and share the meaning 'to be light' or 'to be white'. The Mongolic forms may be borrowed from Turkic because they are restricted to the meaning 'yellow' and cannot be derived form verbally encoded adjectives. If the contact scenario is correct, the copies suggest that the Turkic model was an unbroken pTk *si:ra-*.[10] Some contemporary Mongolic forms have recently undergone "*i*-breaking" whereby the vowel *i* develops into *a* or *ia* before *a*. If the Koguryo, Tungusic and Turkic forms cited are indeed related, then they should

---

10 Contrary to Doerfer (1963: 220–221) who considers the parallel between the Mongolic and Turkic forms as a coincidence, Georg (2007: 274) explains it in terms of a loan connection. He finds that "adding Japanese to this does not lead to any serious objections on the semantic side, but the vowel does not fit the Turkic etymon (which is the source of Mongolian here)." But if Turkic indeed is the loan source of Mongolian, this indicates that the model was pTk *si:ra-* 'yellow' with a vowel that fits the Japanese etymon.

have undergone a similar development of "*i*-breaking". Although "*i*-breaking" must have occurred independently at different points in time in each of the languages, it may represent "Sapirian drift" (Sapir 1921: 126–127, Joseph 2012, 2013), a specific type of recurring changes in related languages at widely separated stages of their development.

Since the formant *-(X)g* is very frequent in deverbal nouns in Old Turkic, e.g. OTk. *isi-* 'to be hot' → *isi-g* 'hot; heat', the adjective pTk **siarï-* 'to be white, yellow' may originally have been verbally encoded. This is supported by the Chuvash descriptive verb *šur-* 'to become white'. The palatal sibilant in Chuvash, Khazar and in the Hungarian loanwords *šār* 'yellow' and *šārgå* 'yellow', as well as the palatalized variant Orkhon OTk. *šarïg* support the diphtong in the reconstruction.[11] Note that Róna-Tas et al. (2011: 691–695) propose that the West Old Turkic models underlying H *šār* 'yellow' and *šārgå* 'yellow' are WOT **šarï* and **šarug*, respectively, but they derive both forms from a single origin **siₐrï-g*. In my view, pTk **sia:rï-* 'to be white, yellow' represents the original proto-Turkic form, rather than deriving it from pTk **sa:rï-*, as is proposed by them. Róna-Tas et al. (2011: 693) further point out that the meaning 'yellow' is probably secondary because it denotes a light yellow colour, which probably evolved from the word for 'white'. The original meaning 'white' is preserved in Chuvash and in the Khazar place name.

(8) 'be high'

J *takai* B, OJ *taka-* 'to be high, elevated', Shuri *takasan*, pR **taka-* 'to be high, tall' (Thorpe 1983: 296), pJ **taka-* 'to be high'

MK *teu-* 'to increase (tr.)', MK *te* 'more, longer, further', K *tek*, *teki* 'plateau', pK **teki-* 'to increase, make high'

Ma. *deye-* 'to fly', *debsi-* 'to unfold one's wings', Sibe *dei-*, *dii-* 'to fly', Even *deg-* 'to rise, to ascend, to go up, to fly away', Evk. *deg-* 'to fly', Neg. *dey-*, Sol. *degelī-*, Olch. *degde-*, Oroch *deili-*, Ud. *dieli-*, Na. *degde-* 'to fly', Na. *depsi-* 'to see-saw, to pace around', pTg **deg-* 'to go up'

WMo. *degere* 'top, on top of, high; higher or better than (with the ablative) (n. / adj /postpos.)' (WMo *-ra* / *-re* adverbializer < *-r deverbal noun + *-a dative; cf. Section 7.3.4), WMo. *deyedü* 'higher, upper, best (adj.)' (WMo. *-du* / *-dü*

---

11 Old Turkic distinguished between two sibilants in native words: alveolar /s/ and palatal /š/ (Erdal 2004: 82–83). The distinction is found in most runiform inscriptions of Orkhon Old Turkic. Manichean writing uses two different characters, but other Old Uighur texts do not distinguish consistently, as is the case here for Orkhon OTk. *šarïg* vs. Uighur OTk. *sarïg*.

derives local nominal adjectives (Poppe 1954: 50)), WMo. *degegši* 'upward, above, higher than (adv.)' (WMo. *-yši / -gši* derives directional adverbs (Poppe 1954: 58)), WMo. *degde-* 'to rise, float, fly up (intr.)' (WMo. *-da- / -de-* fientive/passive suffix; cf. Section 6.5.3), WMo. *degüli-* 'to jump across, jump a distance, leap' (pMo **-li-* intensive; cf. (1)), MMo. *de'ere* 'top, on top of, high', Khal. *de:-* '1 above, up', *degde-* '2 'to rise, fly up (intr.)', *dü:lle-* '3 to jump, leap', Bur. *de:r(e)* 1, *degde-* 2, Kalm. *de:-* 1, *degdə-* 2, Ordos *de:-* 1, *degde-* 2, Dong. *ʒierə* 1, *ʒiedu* 'higher, upper, best (adj.)', Bao. *de-Goŋ* 1, Dag. *de:re* 1, *derede-*, *degede-* 2, Mgr. *dəre* 1, *dē-di*, *te-šə* 1, *digine:-* 'to jump on one leg', *dü:li-* 'to jump, dance, beat (heart)', Mogh. *de:rä* 'top, on top of, high', *dēkši* 'upward, better than', *dei-du* 'above', *dekšə-* 'to come up', pMo **dege-* 'to be high'

OTk. *yeg* 'better than (adv. with object of comparison in the ablative)', Karakh. *yeg*, Tk. *yeẏ*, *yey*, MTk. *yik*, Az. (dial.) *yeg* , Tkm. *yeg*, Chu. *śi*, *śiye* 'upper part, surface', pTk *yeg 'high part'

According to Martin (1996: 30) the MK verb *teu-* 'to increase (tr.)' and its adverb MK *te* 'more, longer, further' may have been derived from an original verb pK **teyi-* < **teki-*. The elision of the velar stop assumed here is reminiscent of the derivation of the MK verb *tao-* 'to get exhausted, come to an end' and its adverb ῭*ta* 'all' from **taɣʌ-* < **takʌ-* by Martin (1996: 79). The latter derivation is supported by the rising tone of the adverb and by the preservation of a velar in MK *takoy* 'all', which is probably a lexicalized deverbal noun. Even though in the case of MK *teu-* 'to increase (tr.)', the adverb *te* 'more, longer, further' lacks the rising tone, additional support for an original velar is provided by K *teki* 'plateau', which may be a lexicalized deverbal noun.

The common semantic feature in all branches is 'to be or become high'. As indicated by the Even meaning 'to rise, to ascend, to go up, to fly away' (Doerfer et al. 1980: 168), the Tungusic semantics 'to fly' derive from 'to go high'. See Section 7.7.3. for a discussion of the resultative nominalizer incorporated into Ma. *debsi-* 'to unfold one's wings' and Na. *depsi-* 'to see-saw, to pace around' and its connection to the *-sA* conjugation of the Even verb, i.e. *deg-se-n* 'it goes up'.

Since the suffix in WMo. *dege-re* 'top, high; higher or better than' is the adverbializer WMo *-ra / -re*, which derives from a deverbal noun suffix **-r* in the dative **-a*, it is clear that we are dealing with an original verbal base **dege-* 'be high'. The verbal origin is further supported by other lexicalizations, including various deverbal suffixes such as the fientive/passive suffix or the intensive suffix. OTk. *yeg* 'better than' has the same semantics as the Mongolic adverb and also puts its object of comparison in the ablative. In Chuvash *śi*, *śiye* 'upper part, surface' the meaning 'high place' is preserved.

(9) 'to be scarce'

> J *tomosii ~ tobosii* ?B 'to be scanty, meager, scarce', OJ *tomosi-* 'to be scarce', Shuri *tubus-* B, pJ **timi-* 'to be scarce',
>
> K *tumwul-*, MK *·tu·mul-* 'to be rare, uncommon', pK **timili-* 'to be rare',
>
> WMo. *dömü-*, Khal. *dömö-*, Kalm. *döm-*, pMo **dömü-* 'to be few, scarce, barely sufficient'

The adjective OJ *tomosi-* 'to be scarce' belongs to the adjectives of Class 2. Unlike Class 1 adjectives, which attach their suffixes directly to the adjective stem, Class 2 adjectives are extended with a suffix *-si-* between the stem and the adjective suffixes. It is therefore legitimate to reconstruct pJ **timi-* 'to be scarce'. The suffix *-si-* is also used for the derivation of adjectives from verb stems (Vovin 2009a: 491 "*-asi-*").

(10) 'be(come) weak'

> J *yurui* B'to be loose, lax, slow', OJ *yuru* 'loose, slack, lenient', OJ *yura-* 'to be loose, lenient, generous', OJ *yurum-*, J *yurumu* 'to loosen', Yonaguni *durankai* C 'loose', pJ **yoru- ~ *yora-* 'to be loose'
>
> [Ma. *duru-* 'to become worn out, old']
>
> WMo. *doru* 'weak, incompetent', *dorui* 'weak, feeble, emaciated' (cf. pMo **-i* deverbal noun suffix; Section 8.3.4), Khal. *dor, doroy*, Bur. *doroy*, Kalm. *doru:*, Mgr. *duri:*, pMo **doru-* 'to be weak, feeble'
>
> Tk. *yor-* '1 wear out, tire, exhaust', *yoryun* '2 tired', Gag. *yoryun* 2, Az. *yor-* 1, *joryun* 2, Tkm. *yor-* 1, *yoryun* 2, MTk. *yoryun* 2, Krm. *yoryun* 2, pTk **yor-* 'to exhaust'

The Manchu adjective is likely to have been copied from Mongolian, because the distribution in Tungusic is restricted to Manchu and the vowel correspondence is irregular (cf. Table 22). If this analysis is correct, the Manchu form, being a verbal property word, should have been copied from a verbally encoded model. This observation, together with the attestation of forms of the shape *dorui* in Mongolic, which are probably deverbal derivations with the suffix **-i*, indicates that the Mongolic proto-form is a verbal adjective. The corresponding Turkic form is an original transitive verb.

(11) 'to be beautiful'

J *kuwasii* B, OJ *kupasi-* 'to be beautiful, detailed, accurate' (OJ -*si*- Class 2 suffix; cf. (8)), pJ **kopa-* 'beautiful',

MK *kwo·po-* 'to be beautiful, attractive', pK **kwopo-* 'beautiful'

(12) 'to be painful'

J *kurusii* B, OJ *kurusi-* 'to be painful, difficult, hard' (OJ -*si*- Class 2 suffix; cf. (8)), pJ **koru-* 'be hard, painful',

MK *kwolwuW-* 'to be painful, troublesome, hard', (MK -*W-* < pK **-·po-* adjective suffix 'be characterized by'; cf. Martin 1992: 759), pK **kwolwu-* 'be hard, painful'

(13) 'to be odorous'

J *kusai* B, OJ *kusa-* 'to be ill-smelling', *kuso* (2.3), OJ *kuso*₁ 'dung' (< **kusa-wo-m* (stinky-COP-NML); cfr Section 7.4.1), pJ **kusa-* 'to be ill-smelling'

MK *kwusu-* 'to be (pleasantly) odorous', pK **kwusɨ-* 'to be odorous'

(14) 'to be fragile'

J *moroi* B, OJ *moro*₂-'to be brittle, fragile', pJ **miri-* 'to be fragile',

K *mwulu-*, MK *mulu-* 'to soften, become tender', K *mwulleng ~ mollang ha-* 'to be soft, tender', pK **milil-* 'to be(come) soft, mellow'

(15) 'to be long'

J *naga-* B, OJ *naga-* 'to be long', Shuri *nagasaN*, pR **naga-* 'long' (Thorpe 1983: 303), pJ **nanka-* 'to be long'

K *nul-* 'to increase, expand, lengthen', MK *nolk- ~ nulk-* 'to become old', pK **nʌlk- ~ nɨlk-* 'to become long'

(16) 'to be mild, warm'

J *nukui* B, Mod. J *nuku-* 'to be warm, mild, genial', dial. *noko-* 'to be warm', Shuri *nukusaN*, pR **nuku-* 'warm'(Thorpe 1983: 345), pJ **nuku-* 'to be mild, warm',

K *nwuk-*, MK *nwuk-* 'to be damp, moist, tender, soft, to become mild, become warm', MK *nwok-* 'to melt, dissolve, become warm', pK **nwuk- ~ *nwok-* 'to be(come) warm, mild, soft'

(17) 'to be foolish'

J *oroka*, OJ *oroka* 'to be foolish, stupid, dull' (pJ *-*ka* resultative nominalizer; cf. Section 7.6.1), J *oro oro* 'be flustered, nervous', pJ **oro-* 'to be stupid',

MK *e·li-* 'be foolish, stupid', MK ·*eleW-* 'be mad'(MK -*W-* < pK *-·*po-* adjective suffix 'be characterized by'; cf. Martin 1992: 759), pK **ele-* 'to be stupid, mad'

(18) 'to be bright'

J *sayaka*, OJ *sayaka* 'clear, bright' (pJ *-*ka* resultative nominalizer; cf. Section 7.6.1), pJ **saya-* 'to become clear, bright',

K *say-*, MK ¨*say-* 'to dawn, break', pK **saCi-* 'to dawn, become light'

3.3 Verbs

3.3.1 Relevant consonant correspondences

This section serves a double goal. Not only does it concentrate on the historical comparison of verb and verbal adjective roots across the Transeurasian languages, but it also establishes the formal requirements for the comparison of bound morphemes in the following chapters. The number of bound verbal morphemes in a language is low compared to the number of independent lexemes. Hence, formal correspondences in bound verb morphology will not be recurrent enough to establish phonological correspondences. It follows that a historical morphological study like the one undertaken here should ideally be preceded by the establishment of regular sound correspondences on the basis of lexical data. For this purpose, I refer to Robbeets (2005).

On the basis of etymologies for verb roots, this section illustrates the consonant correspondences that are significant for the formal evaluation of the bound morphemes in the following chapters. The sound rules are listed according to medial consonants, because the large majority of verb markers compared in this work are suffixes. It goes without saying, however, that the phonological correspondences between the verbs compared here are not restricted to the medial consonant, but encompass all subsequent phonemes of the Japanese proto-form, except for some instances of an occasional stem-final vowel. Table 4 gives an overview of the relevant medial consonant correspondences. Tables 5 to 15 each contain three etymologies for verb or verbal adjective roots in support of these correspondences.

Ōno (1953) demonstrated that – contrary to the classical syllabic verb paradigm analysis – the verbs of Old Japanese can be divided into two major classes from a synchronic perspective: consonant final stems (also called athematic stems or closed roots) and vowel final stems (also called thematic stems or open roots). From a diachronic perspective, Unger (1977) argued that the Old Japanese consonant final stems descend from original vowel final roots, a view also adopted in Martin (1987). However, in the context of Japanese-Korean comparison, Whitman (1985) reconstructed original consonant final roots underlying the Japanese athematic stems. Following the establishment of the basic shape of verb roots in earlier Korean as both consonant roots and vowel roots (Ramsey 1978, Martin 1996), Whitman (1999) and Unger (2000b) changed their view and now agree that – like proto-Korean – proto-Japanese had both consonant roots and vowel roots. However, their proposals have a different configuration and the criteria for reconstructing consonant roots and vowel roots are not completely overlapping.

In the present work, I reconstruct consonant final roots for all quadrigrade verbs, unless there is evidence from bigrade counterparts or covert stems for the final vowel of the root. In Section 6.7.1, external evidence will be advanced in support of the traditional analysis that the origin of the bigrade verb classes goes back to a formant with causative-anticausative connotation pJ *-Ci-. If a quadrigrade verb has a bigrade counterpart, this bigrade will be derived as a vowel root followed by this suffix. Quadrigrade OJ ki_1r- 'to cut', for instance, has a bigrade counterpart OJ ki_1re- 'to be sharp, get cut, run out', thus I reconstruct pJ *kira- 'cut'. Quadrigrade OJ ok- 'to put' has a counterpart OJ oki_2- 'arise', thus I reconstruct pJ *iki- 'to raise'. Other covert root forms in which various actional or diathetical suffixes (see Chapters 5 and 6) have lexicalized can help to reveal the underlying vowel. The doublet OJ oko_2r- 'to arise' and OJ oko_2s- 'to raise', for instance, reflects the root followed by the anticausative pJ *-ra- and the causative pJ *-sa-. The causative suffix also derives OJ ki_1ras- B 'to run/sell out of' from the reconstructed form.

Table 4. Medial consonant correspondences relevant for the formal comparison of bound morphemes

	pJ	pK	pTg	pMo	pTk	pTEA
1.	*-p-	*-p-	*-p-	*-y-	*-p-	*-p-
2.	*-p-	*-p-	*-b-	*-b- / *-y-	*-b-	*-b-
3.	*-t-	*-t-	*-t-	*-t-	*-t-	*-t-
4.	*-y-	*-l-	*-d- (-ji-)	*-d- (-ji-)	*-d-	*-d-
5.	*-k-	*-k-	*-k-	*-k-	*-k-	*-k-
6.	*-k-	*-k-	*-g-	*-g-	*-g-	*-g-

Table 4. (continued)

	pJ	pK	pTg	pMo	pTk	pTEA
7.	*-s-	*-s-	*-s-	*-s-	*-s-	*-s-
8.	*-m-	*-m-	*-m-	*-m-	*-m-	*-m-
9.	*-n-	*-n-	*-n-	*-n-	*-n-	*-n-
10.	*-r-	*-l-	*-l-	*-l-	*-l-	*-l-
11.	*-r-	*-l-	*-r-	*-r-	*-r-	*-r-

Table 5. Verbal etymologies reflecting pTEA *-p-

	TEA	Japonic	Koreanic	Tungusic	Mongolic	Turkic
	*-p-	*-p-	*-p-	*-p-	*-γ-	*-p-
(19)	'meet'	OJ *ap-* 'meet' pJ **apa-*	MK *awo(l)-* 'join' pK **apwo-l-*	Ma. *afa-* 'encounter' pTg **apa-*	WMo. *ayulja-* 'meet, join' pMo **ayu-*	
(20)	'swallow, inhale'	OJ *sup-* 'inhale' pJ **sup-*	MK ·*spo(l)-* 'inhale' pK **s(ʌ)p-ʌl-*			Tat. *sïpïr-* 'swallow' pTk **sïp-*
(21)	'prick'	OJ *nup-* 'sew' pJ **nup-*	MK *nwu(·)pi-* 'quilt' pK **nwupi-*	Evk. *lupa-* 'prick' pTg **nup-*		

Table 6. Verbal etymologies reflecting pTEA *-b-

	TEA	Japonic	Koreanic	Tungusic	Mongolic	Turkic
	*-b-	*-p-	*-p-	*-b-	*-b- / *-γ-	*-b-
(22)	'pursue'	OJ *ko₂p-* 'beg' pJ **kop-*		Evk. *goy-* 'hunt' pTg **gob-*		Karakh. *kov-* 'pursue' pTk **kob-*
(23)	'carry on back'	OJ *op-* 'carry on back' pJ **əpə-*	MK *ep-* 'carry on back' pK **ep-*	Evk. *ewe-* 'carry' pTg **ebe-*	WMo. *eyüre-* 'carry on back' pMo *eyüre-*	
(24)	'obstruct'	OJ *sape₂-* 'obstruct' pJ **sapa-*			WMo. *sayara-* 'be stopped' pMo **saya-*	Karakh. *savra-* 'be stopped' pTk **sab-*

Table 7. Verbal etymologies reflecting pTEA *-t-

	TEA	Japonic	Koreanic	Tungusic	Mongolic	Turkic
	*-t-	*-t-	*-t-	*-t-	*-t-	*-t-
(2)	'be hard'	OJ kata- 'be hard' pJ *kata-	MK kwut- 'be hard' pK *kata-		WMo. qata- 'become hard' pMo *kata-	OTk. kat- 'be hard' pTk *kat-
(25)	'go over/away'	J kati 'walking' pJ *kat-	MK ¨keT- 'walk' pK *keti-		MMo. ketül- 'cross, pass' pMo *ketü-	OTk. kät- 'go away' pTk *kät-
(26)	'shut'	OJ tat- 'cut off' pJ *tat-	MK tat- 'cut off' pK *tat-			

Table 8. Verbal etymologies reflecting pTEA *-d-

	TEA	Japonic	Koreanic	Tungusic	Mongolic	Turkic
	*-d-	*-y-	*-l-	*-d- (-ji-)	*-d- (-ji-)	*-d-
(27)	'be long-lasting'	EMJ oyos- 'get old' pJ *oya-	MK wo·la- 'be long(lasting)' pK *wola-			
(5)	'be early'	OJ paya- 'be early, fast' pJ *paya-	MK polo- 'be fast' pK *pʌlʌ-l-	Ud. baji 'early' pTg *badi(-)		OTk baya(-ki) 'recently' pTk *ba(d)a(-)

Table 9. Verbal etymologies reflecting pTEA *-k-

	TEA	Japonic	Koreanic	Tungusic	Mongolic	Turkic
	*-k-	*-k-	*-k-	*-k-	*-k-	*-k-
(28)	'break off'	OJ kake₂- 'break off' pJ *kaka-		Neg. kaki- 'cut off' pTg *xak-	MMo. qaqal- 'break' pMo *kaka-	Karakh. kak- 'strike' pTk *kak-
(29)	'insert'	OJ pak- 'slip on' pJ *paka-	MK pak- 'insert' pK *pak-	Evk. haku:- 'enclose' pTg *paku:-		
(30)	'burn'	OJ tak- 'burn (tr.)' pJ *tak-	MK tahi- 'set fire' pK *ta(k)ʌ-			OTk. yak- 'burn (tr.)' pTk *ya-k-

Table 10. Verbal etymologies reflecting pTEA *-g-

	TEA	Japonic	Koreanic	Tungusic	Mongolic	Turkic
	*-g-	*-k-	*-k-	*-g-	*-g-	*-g-
(8)	'be(come) high'	OJ taka- 'be high' pJ *taka-	MK teu- 'increase (tr.)' pK *teki-	Even deg- 'go up' pTg *deg-	WMo. degere 'higher than' pMo *dege-	OTk. yeg 'better than' pTk *yeg
(31)	'rise, raise'	OJ oko₂s- 'raise' pJ *(i)k(i)-		Evk. ug- 'mount' pTg *ug-		OTk. ük- 'heap up' pTk *üg-
(32)	'hit, beat'	OJ tuk- 'hit with force' pJ *tuk-	MK ·thi- 'hit, strike' pK *t(ʌ)ki-	Evk. dug- 'hit' pTg *dug-		

Table 11. Verbal etymologies reflecting pTEA *-s-

	TEA	Japonic	Koreanic	Tungusic	Mongolic	Turkic
	*-s-	*-s-	*-s-	*-s-	*-s-	*-s-
(33)	'catch'	OJ asar- 'catch (food)' pJ *asa(-)r-	MK ˗as- 'grab' pK *asʌ-			
(13)	'be odorous'	OJ kusa- 'be smelly' pJ *kusa-	MK kwusu- 'be odorous' pK *kwusi-			
(34)	'feel aversion'	OJ oso₂r- 'fear' pJ *(i)sə-		Ma. usa- 'be sad' pTg *usa-	MMo. ösül 'hate' pMo ösü-	

Table 12. Verbal etymologies reflecting pTEA *-m-

	TEA	Japonic	Koreanic	Tungusic	Mongolic	Turkic
	*-m-	*-m-	*-m-	*-m-	*-m-	*-m-
(35)	'make meet'	OJ kum- 'join' pJ *kum-	MK kom- 'join' pK *kʌm-	Evk. kumu- 'cover' pTg *kumu-	WMo. qumi- 'wrap up' pMo *kumi-	Yak. kumuy- 'wrap' pTk *kum-
(36)	'gather'	OJ tamar- 'gather' pJ *tama-	MK ˗tam- 'fill' pK *tamʌ-	Ma. tama- 'gather' pTg *tama-		
(9)	'be scarce'	OJ tomo-si- 'be scarce' pJ *t(i)m(i)-	MK ·tu·mul- 'be rare' pK *timili-		WMo. dömü- 'be scarce' pMo *dömü-	

Table 13. Verbal etymologies reflecting pTEA *-n- and *n-

	TEA	Japonic	Koreanic	Tungusic	Mongolic	Turkic
	*(-)n-	*(-)n-	*(-)n-	*(-)n-	*(-)n-	*(-)n-
(37)	'spring up'	OJ pane- 'spring up' pJ *pana-			WMo. unu- 'mount' pMo *punu-	
(4)	'be languid'	J noro- 'be slow' pJ *n(i)r(i)-	MK nuluy- 'be languid' pK *niliy-	Ma. nurhu- 'do ceaselessly' pTg *nör	WMo. nöri- 'be lingering' pMo *nöri-	
(46)	'be(come) wide'	OJ nobi₂- 'spread intr.' pJ *nənpa-	K nelp- 'be wide' pK *nelpʌ-	Evk. nepte- 'spread out' pTg *nepte-	WMo. nebsei- 'be broad/ long' pMo *nebse-	
(47)	'go out'	OJ in- 'go away' pJ *na-	MK na- 'go out' pK *na-	Evk. -na:- 'go out to' pTg *-na:-		

Table 14. Verbal etymologies reflecting pTEA *-l-

	TEA	Japonic	Koreanic	Tungusic	Mongolic	Turkic
	*-l-	*-r-	*-l-	*-l-	*-l-	*-l-
(38)	'move away'	OJ sar- 'depart' pJ *sara-	MK ·so(l)- 'make vanish' pK *sʌlʌ-	[Ma. sala-] ['hand out'] Copy?	WMo. sal(u)- 'part with' pMo *sala-	OTk. sal- 'move' pTk *sal-
(39)	'deceive'	J tarasu 'deceive' pJ *tara(-)s-	MK talay- 'wheedle' pK *tala(-)y-	[Ma. tala-] ['confiscate'] Copy?	WMo. tala- 'plunder' pMo *tala-	OTk. tala- 'damage' pTk *tala-
(40)	'be wet'	OJ urum- 'get wet' pJ *uru-	MK wuli- 'soak' pK *wuli-	Evk. ula- 'soak, wet' pTg *ula-		

Table 15. Verbal etymologies reflecting pTEA *-r-

	TEA	Japonic	Koreanic	Tungusic	Mongolic	Turkic
	*-r-	*-r-	*-l-	*-r-	*-r-	*-r-
(1)	'be clean'	OJ ara- 'be fresh' pJ *ara-			WMo. ari-l- 'be(come) clear' pMo *ari-	OTk. arï- 'be(come) clean' pTk *arï-

Table 15. (continued)

	TEA	Japonic	Koreanic	Tungusic	Mongolic	Turkic
(41)	'cut'	OJ ki_1r- 'cut' pJ *kira-		Evk. gir- 'cut out' pTg *giri-	[WMo. kira-] ['mince'] Copy?	Karakh. kïr- 'scrape' pTk *kïr-
(3)	'be round'	MJ maro- 'be round' pJ *maru-	MK mulu- 'turn around' pK *mïlï-l-	Evk. murume 'round' pTg *muru-	WMo muru- 'be curved' pMo *muru-	OTk. bür- 'wind round' pTk *bur-

3.3.2 Relevant vowel correspondences

Whereas a system containing at least seven vowels has been reconstructed for proto-Korean, proto-Mongolic and proto-Tungusic and an eight-vowel system has been reconstructed for proto-Turkic, it was common until recently to reconstruct only four vowels for proto-Japonic. Under the traditional reconstruction, we had to assume an involved system of mergers in Japonic to account for the reduction of the larger vowel inventories of the other Transeurasian languages. This led to a rather complex picture of vowel correspondences in Transeurasian.

Recently, however, Whitman and Frellesvig (2008) have proposed reconstructing the same number of vowels for proto-Japonic as for most of the other proto-languages. They challenge the widely accepted hypothesis, underlying the reconstructions in Robbeets 2005, that proto-Japonic consisted of only four vowels (*i, *a, *u, *ə). In contrast, they argue in favor of adding two mid vowels (*e, *o), a reconstruction that is supported by Ryukyuan (Thorpe 1983, Serafim 2008, Pellard 2008) and of reconstructing an additional high central vowel (*ï). The Old Japanese vowels i, o and u represent mergers of pJ *i and *e, pJ *ï and *ə and, pJ *u and *o, respectively. In the absence of internal, dialectal or comparative Ryukyuan support, it is sometimes difficult to trace the exact nature of the proto-Japonic vowel reflected in an Old Japanese vowel. Whenever reconstructions rely solely on external, comparative evidence, the proto-Japanese vowels are placed between brackets.

Whitman and Frellesvig's reconstruction of a seven-vowel system in proto-Japonic is also adopted in the present work, as it provides a more straightforward account of the vowel correspondences between Japanese and the Transeurasian languages than the previous literature (e.g. Starostin et al. 2003 and Robbeets 2005). Table 16 lists all nine medial vowel correspondences along with two conditioning factors reflected in the Transeurasian cognates.

Table 16. Medial vowel correspondences

	OJ < pJ	MK < pK	pTg	pMo	pTk	pTEA
12.	-a- < *-a-	-a- < *-a-	*-a-	*-a-	*-a-	*-a-
12b.	*CaCa	*CᴧCᴧ	*CaCa	*CaCa	*CaC	*CaCa
13.	-a- < *-a-	-e- < *-e- RTR *-ə-	*-e- RTR -ə-	*-e- RTR -ə-	*-e-	*-ə-
14.	-o- < *-ə-	-e- < *-e- RTR *-ə-	*-e- RTR -ə-	*-e- RTR -ə-	*-e-	*-ə-
15.	-o- <? *-o-	-wo- < *-o- RTR *-o-	*-o- RTR *-ɔ-	*-o- RTR *-ɔ-	*-o-	*-ɔ-
16.	-u- < *-o-	-wo- < *-o- RTR *-o-	*-o- RTR *-ɔ-	*-o- RTR *-ɔ-	*-o-	*-ɔ-
17.	-o- < *-i̇-	-u- < *-i̇- RTR *-i̇- < *o	*-ö- RTR *-o-	*-ö- RTR *-o-	*-ö-	*-o-
18.	-u- < *-u-	-wu- < *-u- RTR *-u-	*-u- (/ gü) RTR *-u- / -gʊ-	*-ü- RTR *-u-	*-ü-	*-u-
19.	-u- < *-u-	-o- < *-ᴧ- RTR *-ᴧ- < *ɔ	*-u- RTR *-ʊ-	*-u- RTR*-ʊ-	*-u- /-i̇-	*-ʊ-
19b.	PaRu- < *PauRu-	*PᴧRᴧ- / *PiRi-	*PuRu-	*PuRu-	*PuR-	*PʊRʊ-
20.	-i- < *-i-	-i- < *-i-	*-i-	*-i-	*-i-/-i̇-	*-i-

Vowel harmony is a characteristic feature of the Transeurasian languages, except Japanese. In Old Japanese, however, there is a restriction on the shape of root morphemes, whereby the vowel o_2 cannot occur in a root together with the vowels u, o_1 or a. This phenomenon, known as Arisaka's law has been taken as a kind of vowel harmony, but it has been rejected from comparisons with other Transeurasian languages because it applies to roots rather than to suffixes and because it does not reflect palatal harmony, the type of harmony which was attributed to the Transeurasian languages until recently (e.g. Frellesvig 2010: 44).

However, in petrified noun inflectional suffixes such as an archaic plural suffix and a genitive suffix, there are traces of $a \sim o_2$ vowel alternation according to the quality of the vowels in the preceding root, e.g. OJ no_2 genitive vs. OJ -na- petrified in compounds such as OJ mi_1-na-moto (< water-GEN-base) 'source, the headwaters' (Rickmeyer 1989: 316). A number of verb morphemes reconstructed in this volume leaves traces of a similar alternation, notably pJ *-ra- ~ -rə- manipulative verbalizer (Section 5.3.1), pJ *-na- ~ *-nə- processive (Section 5.4.1), pJ *-ma- ~ *-mə- inclination (Section 5.6.1); pJ *-pa- ~ -pə- reflexive-anticausative

(Section 6.4.1) and pJ *-ra ~ *-rə deverbal noun suffix (Section 7.3.1). Interestingly, especially "old" suffixes close to the verb root, which underwent a high degree of lexicalization leave traces of this harmony-like alternation. As such, there may be traces of vowel harmony applying to original suffixes in Japanese.

Moreover, it was recently demonstrated that the original vowel harmony in most Transeurasian languages was in fact based on the opposition between the advanced vs. retracted position of the tongue root, rather than on a palatal contrast. Ko (2012) argued that this is the case for original vowel harmony in Mongolic, Tungusic and Koreanic languages. He argued that the tongue root retraction system in Khalka (e.g. od-o:s (feather-ABL) vs. ɔd-ɔ:s (star-ABL)) represents retention rather than innovation. Furthermore, he supported the view that Tungusic vowel harmony is RTR based, as it is in Manchu and Evenki, and that the reduced vowel harmony in contemporary Korean derives from a tongue-root based system in Middle Korean. As far as the harmony-like opposition between o_2 and u, o_1 or a in Old Japanese is concerned, the recent reconstuction of a 7-vowel system in proto-Japonic by Frellesvig and Whitman (2008) implies an underlying opposition between pJ *i , *ə and *u, *o, *a, which does not exclude an original RTR based contrast.

The reinterpretation of the quality of the Koreanic, Tungusic and Mongolic vowels in Table 16 in the light of Ko's (2012) RTR interpretation, leads to the reconstruction of RTR harmony in the original Transeurasian vowel inventory. Under this scenario, it is plausible that Turkic shifted to a palatal harmony system and that the RTR system got distorted in Japanese, due to areal influences at the periphery of the Transeurasian family: contact with Uralic palatal harmony in the West and with non-harmonic Chinese in the east. Paleosiberian languages in the region such as Yukaghir, Chukchi and Nivkh have been described as having tongue root harmony (Janhunen 1981; Gruzdeva 1998: 10; Maslova 2003: 35; Ko et al. 2014). If the Transeurasian languages acquired RTR through influence of Paleosiberian languages, this must have happened at the proto-Transeurasian level. But, more likely, the Transeurasian family might have been the source of spreading RTR through the region, with the Tungusic languages as "vectors of diffusion".

Tables 17 to 27 each contain three etymologies for verb or verbal adjective roots in support of the correspondences listed in Table 16.

Table 17. Verbal etymologies reflecting 12. OJ -*a*- < pTEA *-*a*-

12.	TEA	Japonic	Koreanic	Tungusic	Mongolic	Turkic
	*-*a*-	-*a*- < *-*a*-	-*a*- < *-*a*-	*-*a*-	*-*a*-	*-*a*-
(28)	'break off'	OJ *kake₂*- 'break off' pJ **kaka*-		Neg. *kaki*- 'cut off' pTg **xak*-	MMo. *qaqal*- 'break' pMo **kaka*-	Karakh. *kak*- 'strike' pTk **kak*-
(2)	'be hard'	OJ *kata*- 'be hard' pJ **kata*-	MK *kwut*- 'be hard' pK **kata*-		WMo. *qata*- 'become hard' pMo **kata*-	OTk. *kat*- 'be hard' pTk **kat*-
(39)	'deceive'	J *tarasu* 'deceive' pJ **tara(-)s*-	MK *talay*- 'wheedle' pK **tala(-)y*-	[Ma. *tala*-] ['confiscate'] Copy?	WMo. *tala*- 'plunder' pMo **tala*-	OTk. *tala*- 'damage' pTk **tala*-

Table 18. Conditioning factor for Korean reflexes of 12b. pTEA **CaCa*

12b.	TEA	Japonic	Koreanic	Tungusic	Mongolic	Turkic
	*CaCa	*CaCa	*CʌCʌ	*CaCa	*CaCa	*CaC
(42)	'cut with an agricultural tool'	OJ *kar*- 'mow, shear' pJ **kar(a)*-	MK ·*kol*- 'whet, grind' pK **kʌlʌ*-			
(5)	'be early'	OJ *paya*- 'be early, fast' pJ **paya*-	MK *polo*- 'be fast' pK **pʌlʌ-l*-	Ud. *baji* 'early' pTg **badi(-)*		OTk *baya(-ki)* 'recently' pTk **baya(-)*
(38)	'move away'	OJ *sar*- 'depart' pJ **sara*-	MK ·*so(l)*- 'make vanish' pK **sʌlʌ*-	[Ma. *sala*-] ['hand out'] Copy?	WMo. *sal(u)*- 'part with' pMo **sala*-	OTk. *sal*- 'move' pTk **sal*-

There are some conditioned instances of the shape pTEA **CaCa* where *-*a*- is not reflected as such in Korean, but rather as a reduced vowel MK -*o*- < *-*ʌ*-. A form of the shape pJK **CaCa* is first weakened to pK **CaCʌ* if the vowel is word or root final. Then, the shape further weakens to pK **CʌCʌ* by assimilation to the second syllable vowel. The weakening process is blocked when a suffix -*i*- is added to the root. Internal indications that an ongoing weakening process has been blocked, can be found in the etymologies (30) 'to burn' and (39) 'to harm, deceive'.

Table 19. Verbal etymologies reflecting 13. OJ -a- < pTEA *-e-

13.	TEA	Japonic	Koreanic	Tungusic	Mongolic	Turkic
	*-e-	-a- < *-a-	-e- < *-e-	*-e-	*-e-	*-e-
(25)	'go over/away'	J kati 'walking' pJ *kat-	MK ⸚keT- 'walk' pK *keti-		MMo. ketül- 'cross, pass' pMo *ketü-	OTk. ket- 'go away' pTk *ke:t-
(43)	'bite'	OJ kam- 'bite' pJ *kam-			WMo. kemile- 'bite' pMo *keme-	OTk. kemür- 'gnaw' pTk *kem-
(44)	'burst'	OJ yabur- 'break' pJ *yanpu-		Solon delpe- 'burst' pTg *delpe-	WMo. delbere- 'split' pMo *delbe-	

Table 20. Verbal etymologies reflecting 14. OJ -o- < pTEA *-e-

14.	TEA	Japonic	Koreanic	Tungusic	Mongolic	Turkic
	*-e-	-o- < *-ə-	-e- < *-e-	*-e-	*-e-	*-e-
(45)	'fight'	OJ ko$_2$ro$_2$s- 'kill' pJ *kərə(-)s-			MMo. kere- 'fight' pMo *kere-	OTk. keriš- 'fight' pTk *keri-
(46)	'be(come) wide'	OJ nobi$_2$- 'spread intr.' pJ *nənpa-	K nelp- 'be wide' pK *nelpʌ-	Evk. nepte- 'spread out' pTg *nepte-	WMo. nebsei- 'be broad/long' pMo *nebse-	
(17)	'be foolish'	OJ oroka 'foolish' pJ *ərə-	MK ·eleW- 'be mad' pK *ele-			

Table 21. Verbal etymologies reflecting 15. OJ -o- < pTEA *-ɔ-

15.	TEA	Japonic	Koreanic	Tungusic	Mongolic	Turkic
	*-ɔ-	-o- <? *-o-	-wo- < *-o-	*-o-	*-o-	*-o-
(22)	'pursue'	OJ ko$_2$p- 'beg' pJ *kop-		Evk. goy- 'hunt' pTg *gob-		Karakh. kov- 'pursue' pTk *kob-
(48)	'put aside'	OJ noke- 'remove' pJ *noka-	MK nwoh- 'put aside' pK *nwo(k)-			
(54)	'sit, be(come)'	OJ wor- / wi- 'to sit, be' pJ *wo-	MK ·wᵘ/o- modulator pK *wo-		WMo. bol- 'become' *bol-	OTk. bol- 'be' *bo:l-

Table 22. Verbal etymologies reflecting 16. OJ -u- < pTEA *-ɔ-

16.	TEA	Japonic	Koreanic	Tungusic	Mongolic	Turkic
	*-ɔ-	-u- < *-o-	-wo- < *-o-	*-o-	*-o-	*-o-
(11)	'be beautiful'	OJ kupasi- 'be beautiful' pJ *k(o)pa-	MK kwo·po- 'be beautiful' pK *kwopo-			
(12)	'be painful'	OJ kurusi- 'be painful' pJ *k(o)ru-	MK kwolwuW- 'be painful' pK *kwolwu-			
(10)	'be(come) weak'	OJ yuru 'loose' pJ *y(o)ru-		[Ma. duru- 'become worn out'] Copy?	WMo. doru(i) 'weak' pMo *doru(-)	Tk. yor- 'exhaust' pTk *yor-

Table 23. Verbal etymologies reflecting 17. OJ -o- < pTEA *-o-

17.	TEA	Japonic	Koreanic	Tungusic	Mongolic	Turkic
	*-o-	-o- < *-i̯-	-u- < *-i̯-	*-ö- [ʌ]	*-ö-	*-ö-
(4)	'be languid'	J noro- 'be slow' pJ *n(i)r(i)-	MK nuluy- 'be languid' pK *niliy-	Ma. nurhu- 'do ceaselessly' pTg *n(ö)r	WMo. nöri- 'be lingering' pMo *nöri-	
(9)	'be scarce'	OJ tomo-si- 'be scarce' pJ *t(i)m(i)-	MK ·tu·mul- 'be rare' pK *timili-		WMo. dömü- 'be scarce' pMo *dömü-	
(49)	'hold'	OJ to₁r- ~ to₂r- 'hold' pJ *t(i)ra-	MK ˈtul- 'hold up' pK *tili-	Even toru- 'hold' pTg *töru-		

Table 24. Verbal etymologies reflecting 18. OJ -u- < pTEA *-u-

18.	TEA	Japonic	Koreanic	Tungusic	Mongolic	Turkic
	*-u-	-u- < *-u-	-wu- < *-u-	*-u-	*-ü-	*-ü-
(21)	'prick'	OJ nup- 'sew' pJ *nup-	MK nwu(·)pi- 'quilt' pK *nwupi-	Evk. lupa- 'prick' pTg *nup-		
(13)	'be odorous'	OJ kusa- 'be smelly' pJ *kusa-	MK kwusu- 'be odorous' pK *kwusi-			
(6)	'be thick'	OJ puto₁- 'be thick' pJ *puto-	MK ˈpwuT- 'increase' pK *pwuto-		WMo. büdügün 'large' pMo *büdü-	

Table 25. Verbal etymologies reflecting OJ -u- < pTEA *-ʊ-

19.	TEA	Japonic	Koreanic	Tungusic	Mongolic	Turkic
	*-ʊ-	-u- < *-u-	-o- < *-ʌ-	*-u-	*-u-	*-u- / -ï-
(35)	'make meet'	OJ kum- 'join' pJ *kum-	MK kom- 'join' pK *kʌm-	Evk. kumu- 'cover' pTg *kumu-	WMo. qumi- 'wrap up' pMo *kumi-	Yak. kumuy- 'wrap' pTk *kum- /*kïm-
(20)	'swallow, inhale'	OJ sup- 'inhale' pJ *sup-	MK ·spol- 'inhale' pK *s(ʌ)pol-			Tat. sïpïr- 'swallow' pTk *sïp-
(32)	'hit, beat'	OJ tuk- 'hit with force' pJ *tuk-	MK ·thi- 'hit, strike' pK *t(ʌ)ki-	Evk. duy- 'hit' pTg *dug-		

Table 26. Conditioning factor 19b for Japonic reflexes of pTEA *PʊRʊ-

19b.	TEA	Japonic	Koreanic	Tungusic	Mongolic	Turkic
	*PʊRʊ-	PaRu- < *PauR-	*PʌRʌ- / *PiRi-	*PuRu-	*PuRu-	*PuR-
(3)	'be round'	MJ maro- 'be round' pJ *maru- OKog *mawr	MK mulu- 'turn around' pK *mili-l-	Evk. murume 'round' pTg *muru-	WMo muru- 'be curved' pMo *muru-	OTk. bür- 'wind round' pTk *bur-
(50)	'remove'	OJ parap- 'remove' pJ *paru-	MK poli- 'throw away' pK *pʌl-	Ma. burubu- 'disappear' pTg *buru-		
(51)	'be bad'	MJ waru- 'be bad' pJ *waru			WMo. buruyu 'wrong, bad' pMo *buru-	

There are some conditioned instances of the shape pTEA *PʊRʊ- where *-ʊ- is reflected as -a- rather than as -u- in Japanese. These instances are restricted to a particular phonological environment, whereby the vowel is preceded by an initial labial consonant (pTEA *p-, *b-, *m-) and followed by a medial resonant (*-r- or *-n-). In most cases, the root final vowel is *-u-.[12] In his review of Robbeets

---

[12] The conditioning factor seems to be at work in two other etymologies, namely OJ pana 'nose' (Robbeets 2005: 400) and (37) OJ pane- 'jump, spring up, hop', but they lack internal evidence for a root-final *-u-.

(2005), Georg (2007: 271) objects "Here we see that Proto-Japanese *-a- may actually correspond to practically any vowel in Tungusic – even *-u- is (sometimes) among them. [...] ; there are all in all *five* examples in the whole material of this alleged development." As can be seen from Table 16, there are only two correspondences for pJ *-a-, namely to *-a- and to *-e- in proto-Tungusic and elsewhere. Thus "Practically any vowel" is clearly an overstatement. Georg further claims that five examples are too few to support the correspondence with *-ʊ-, but one may object that it concerns a conditioning factor, restricted to a very specific phonological environment.¹³ If Beckwith's reconstruction of OKog *mawr 'round, circle' is correct, dipthongization of high vowels in this environment may have started early in Japanic. This process seems compatible with mid-vowel raising as suggested by Whitman and Frellesvig (2008). Internal support comes from the observation that the Japanese cognates display doublets that reflect partial or full assimilation to the quality of the first vowel, namely pJ *maru- ~ *marə- 'to be round', pJ *waru- ~ *warə- 'to be bad', pJ *paru- ~ *para- 'to remove'. This suggest the development *PʊRʊ > *PauRu > *PaRu > *PaRə > *PaRa.

Table 27. Verbal etymologies reflecting 20. OJ -*i*- < pTEA *-*i*-

	TEA	Japonic	Koreanic	Tungusic	Mongolic	Turkic
	*-i-	-i- < *-i-	-i- < *-i-	*-i-	*-i-	*-i-/-ï-
(41)	'cut'	OJ ki₁r- 'cut' pJ *kira-		Evk. gir- 'cut out' pTg *giri-	[WMo. kira-] ['mince'] Copy?	Karakh. kïr- 'scrape' pTk *kïr-
(52)	'become dense'	OJ sik- 'grow dense' pJ *sik-	MK sko(l)- 'spread out' pK *s(i)kʌ-l-	[Evk. siyi:] ['thick growth'] Copy?	WMo. sigui 'thick growth' pMo *sigu-	
(7)	'be white'	OJ siro₁- 'be white' pJ *siro-	MK ·huy- 'be white' pK *si(l)ʌ-	Ma. šara- 'become white' pTg *sia:ra- (<*si:ra-?)	[WMo sira 'yellow'] Copy?	OTk šarïg 'yellow' pTk *sia:rï- (< *si:ra-?)

---

13 Furthermore, another manifestation of this conditioning factor will be discussed in the etymology for the reflexive pTEA *-pU- (see Section 6.4).

3.3.3 Suprasegmental correlation

Japanese verbs and predicative adjectives can be distinguished according to wordtone. Only two prosodic classes, called A and B, are needed to account for their accentual behavior. Type A corresponds to a high initial tone, type B to a low initial tone. Adequate information about these prosodic patterns is only available from the Middle Japanese stage onwards. Heian sources, such as the Ruiju Myōgishō (1081) reflecting the former dialect of Kyoto, use a system of dots to represent tones. In addition, most contemporary dialects reflect the distinction between the A and B register.

However, the assignment of a verb or adjective stem to type A or B is not always straightforward. In many cases, such as J *todomeru* ?A/B 'to stop, cease' or J *aseru* ?A/B 'to get shallow, fade' there is a discrepancy between modern dialects. In the contemporary Kyoto dialect, for instance, some longer verbs that were originally B have been absorbed into A. Tokyo speakers assume that few spoken verbs have B register, like the majority of familiar verbs. Even when the Ruiju Myōgishō register is known, it is sometimes assigned a different accent type than the proto-language. For example, B type is reconstructed for J *azukeru* B 'to put in trust' on the basis of its B register in the contemporary dialects Tokyo, Kyoto, Kagoshima, and Shuri, but the Heian sources indicate the A register for this verb. There are some instances in which etymologically related verbs have different registers: J *hiromaru* B 'to spread' and J *hirogaru* A 'to spread out'; J *tubomu* A 'narrow, close up (intr.)' but B when the closing up relates to flowers, namely in the meaning 'have a blossom about to open'; J *akasu* A 'to explain, prove' but B in the meaning 'to see the night through' although the derived noun *akasi* for both meanings 'proof, lantern' is assigned to A. Even transitivity alternants of the same verb may have conflicting type assignments. The intransitive meaning of MJ *hiroge-* 'to spread out' in the Ruiju Myōgishō, for instance, is assigned to A, while its transitive meaning is B. Furthermore, it will be pointed out in Chapter 8 that lexicalisation can cause anomalies in accent pattern, as is the case for the lexicalised deverbal noun suffix pJ *-i. When searching for external correlations for Japanese suprasegmental patterns, we should therefore keep in mind that the internal assignment of register is not always reliable.

Vovin (2008b) proposes a correlation between voicing and vowel length in pre-proto-Japanese, on the one hand and register in proto-Japanese, on the other. This correlation is represented in Table 28.

Table 28. Correlation between voice, vowel length and register in Japanese

pre-pJ	voiced initial	voiceless initial
short V (CVCV)	pJ low register (B)	pJ high register (A)
long V (CV:CV)	pJ low register (B)	pJ low register (B)

Vovin suggests that part of the distinction between low and high register goes back to an original voice distinction at the so-called "pre-proto-Japanese" level. However, with respect to the reconstruction of voice distinction in (pre-)proto-Japanese, Vovin (2008b: 154) must admit that "we simply have no evidence for that." The question thus remains why the register distinction is traced back to voice rather than to some other feature. If Vovin still supported the Transeurasian affinity, the answer would be simple: external comparison of the kind proposed by Vovin (1995). However, since Vovin (2005a) has rejected the so-called "Altaic debate" with a negative answer, voice distinction appears as a *deus ex machina* here. The correlation between proto-Japanese register and voicing distinction in the Transeurasian languages was earlier proposed by Kortlandt (1993). Among the above etymologies that reflect an original initial voiced stop, all but one, produce Japanese reflexes with B register, while voiceless initials are reflected as either A or B.[14] This observation, which is completely in line with the internal correlations proposed by Vovin, is illustrated in Table 29. For additional evidence, including bimoraic nouns and verbs, I refer to Robbeets (2009b: 148).

Table 29. Correspondence of proto-Japanese B register with an initial voiced stop in proto-Transeurasian

	TEA	Japonic	Koreanic	Tungusic	Mongolic	Turkic
(5)	'be early'	OJ *paya-* 'be early, fast' pJ **paya-*	MK *polo-* 'be fast' pK **pʌlʌ-l-*	Ud. *baji* 'early' pTg **badi(-)*		OTk *baya(-ki)* 'recently' pTk **baya(-)*
(6)	'be thick'	OJ *puto₁-* 'be thick' pJ **puto-*	MK ¨*pwuT-* 'increase (intr.)' pK **pwuto-*		WMo. *büdügün* 'large' pMo **büdü-*	

---

14 The sole exception is J *iru* A 'to be, exist', J *oru* A 'to be, exist' in etymology (54). But this exception may be due to the fact that these verbs go back to a monomoraic and thus automatically long root pJ **wo-*.

Table 29. (continued)

	TEA	Japonic	Koreanic	Tungusic	Mongolic	Turkic
(8)	'be(come) high'	OJ *taka-* 'be high' pJ **taka-*	MK *teu-* 'increase (tr.)' pK **teki-*	Evk. *deg-* 'go up' pTg **deg-*	WMo. *degere* 'higher than' pMo **dege-*	OTk. *yeg* 'better than' pTk *yeg
(9)	'be scarce'	OJ *tomo-si-* 'be scarce' pJ **t(i)m(i)-*	MK ·*tu·mul-* 'be rare' pK **timili-*		WMo. *dömü-* 'be scarce' pMo **dömü-*	
(10)	'be(come) weak'	OJ *yuru* 'loose' pJ **y(o)ru-*		[Ma. *duru-* 'become worn out'] Copy?	WMo. *doru(i)* 'weak' pMo **doru(-)*	Tk. *yor-* 'exhaust' pTk **yor-*
(22)	'pursue'	OJ *ko₂p-* 'beg' pJ **kop-*		Evk. *goy-* 'hunt' pTg **gob-*		Karakh. *kov-* 'pursue' pTk **kob-*
(32)	'hit, beat'	OJ *tuk-* 'hit with force' pJ **tuk-*	MK ·*thi-* 'hit, strike' pK **t(ʌ)ki-*	Evk. *dug-* 'hit' pTg **dug-*		
(41)	'cut'	OJ *ki₁r-* 'cut' pJ **kira-*		Evk. *gir-* 'cut out' pTg **giri-*	[WMo. *kira-*] ['mince'] Copy?	Karakh. *kïr-* 'scrape' pTk **kïr-*
(44)	'burst'	OJ *yabur-* 'break' pJ **yanpu-*		Solon *delpe-* 'burst' pTg **delpe-*	WMo. *delbere-* 'split' pMo **delbe-*	
(50)	'remove'	OJ *parap-* 'remove' pJ **paru-*	MK *poli-* 'throw away' pK **pʌl-*	Ma. *burubu-* 'disappear' pTg **buru-*		
(51)	'be bad'	MJ *waru-* 'be bad' pJ *waru			WMo. *buruyu* 'wrong, bad' pMo **buru-*	

3.3.4 Underlying etymologies

(19) 'to meet'

    J *au* B, OJ *ap-* 'to meet, encounter', OJ *ape₂-* 'to join', pJ **apa-* 'to meet'

    MK ·*awo(l)- /a·wolo-* 'to join together', Silla OK 阿火屋 [a] + [pwol ~ pwul] + 'house(s)' = 并屋 'side by side' + 屋 'house(s)' (SSK 34), pK **apwo-l-* 'to join' (pK **-l-* iterative)

Ma. *afa-* 'to encounter, run into', Ma. *afa-bu-* 'to hand over', Ma *afa-ndu-* 'to attack eachother' (Ma. *-ndu-* reciprocal), Na. *apa-*, *afa-* 'attack', Sol. *apaldi-* 'to attack eachother' (Sol. *-ldi-* reciprocal), pTg **apa-* 'to encounter',

WMo. *ayulja-* 'to meet, join', Khal. *u:lja-*, Kalm. *u:ljə-*, Dag. *aulji-*, pMo **aɣu-* 'to join' (pMo **-ljA-* suffix denoting multiple actants)

The two juxtaposed vowels in MK ·*awo(l)-* /a·wolo-/ 'to join together' indicate an earlier intervocalic *-G-* that probably goes back to a labial stop **-p-*. The reconstruction of **-p-* is supported by the Silla transcription from the Samguk Sagi (SSK 34) 比屋縣。本阿火屋縣。-云并屋。 The phonological representation of the Silla geographical name 阿火屋 consists of the phonograph 阿 [a] and the phonograph 火 [pwol ~ pwul] followed by the logograph 屋 'roof, house'. The semantic description of the place name 并屋 is represented by the logograph 并 'side by side' and the logograph 屋 'roof, house' and can therefore be interpreted as 'joined roofs'. This interpretation suggests that Silla OK **apwol* is the adnominal form of a verb 'to join together', which is supported by the attestation of MK ·*awo(l)-* /a·wolo-/. The final liquid may be the same original iterative suffix pK **-l-* that also underlies the etymologies (3), (5), (20) and (52).

Note that Poppe (1955a: 98) reconstructed a pre-Mongolian **β*, which converged with **ɣ* in proto-Mongolian and corresponds to **p* elsewhere in Altaic (e.g. OTk. *qap-* 'to close' vs. MMo. *qa'a-*, WMo. *qaɣa-* 'to hinder, close'). It is legitimate to posit a distributive formant pMo **-lja-/ -lje-* in reference to verbs expressing multiple actors such as MMo. *a'ulja-* 'pay one's respects to, meet', *bol-* 'become' vs. *bolja-* 'make an appointment', verbs expressing multiple objects such as MMo. *si'a* 'bone stone (n.)' (with a verbal derivate **si'ala-*?) vs. *si'alja-* 'play with bone stones', *unji-* 'rest, halt' vs. *unjilja-* 'hang down (e.g. of feet)', *alhun* 'be missing' vs. *alja-* 'be in distress', and verbs expressing multiple occurrences in rythmic motions such as MMo. *sicabalja-* 'crawl', *darbalja-* 'jiggle', *gilba-* 'gleam' vs. *gilbalja-* 'glimmer'.

(20) 'to inhale'

J *suu* A, OJ *sup-* 'to breathe in, inhale, absorb', pJ **sup-* 'to inhale'

MK ·*spo(l)-* / ·*spo*·*lo-* 'to sip, inhale', pK **s(ʌ)p-ʌl-* 'to inhale' (pK **-(ʌ)l-* iterative)

MTk. *sipqar-*, Tk. *sïp-*, Tat. *sïpïr-*, Bash. *hïpïr-*, Az. *sïfqar-*, pTk **sïp-* 'to swallow greedily' (pTk **-gAr* causative (Erdal 1991: 742–747); pTk **-(U)r* causative (Erdal 1991: 710–726))

Contrary to the distribution of clusters in the other Transeurasian languages, obstruent clusters do appear in initial position in Korean. Internal evidence, however, indicates that complex initials are secondary, internally generated through phonological or morphological developments. One phonological cause of complex initials is vowel syncope. In line with Ramsey (1993: 438; 1997), verb stems with complex initials that are tonic and monosyllabic and have minimal vowels (MK *o*, *u*, *i*) are thought to be created through the loss of a first-syllable vowel. This internal analysis justifies the reconstruction of the first vowel in pK **s(ʌ)p-ʌl-* 'inhale'. The final liquid probably concerns the iterative suffix pK **-(ʌ)l-*, discussed above (cf. (3)).

As far as the reconstruction of pTk **sïp-* 'swallow greedily' is concerned, the formant in MTk. *sipqar-* and Az. *sïfqar-* is probably the lexicalized causative pTk **-gAr*. The lack of voice is explained by the fact that the opposition /k/ : /g/ is very weak after consonants in Old Turkic. The causative underlying in the other Turkic forms may be pTk **-(U)r*.

(21) 'to pierce, prick'

J *nuu* B, OJ *nup-* 'to sew, stitch, embroider', pJ **nup-* 'to sew, stitch',

MK *nwu(·)pi-* 'to quilt', MK *nwu·pi* 'quilting', pK **nwupi-* 'to sew, quilt',

Neg. *lepu-* 'to pierce', Na. *lopqa-*, *loqpa-* 'to prick', Olch. *loqpa-* 'to prick', Orok *lüqqa-* 'to prick', Evk. *lupa-* 'to prick', *lupu:-* 'to pierce', Even *nu̧bas an-* 'to prick', pTg **nup-* 'to prick, pierce'

The Tungusic verb stem is probably a compound of pTg **nup-* 'to prick, pierce' with a suffix **-kA-*, perhaps the alternant of the inchoative suffix pTg **-xA-* in voiceless clusters (see Section 5.7.3). Poppe (1960, 74) finds that the initial *l-* in the Tungusic languages is a secondary development from an original **n-* : "Das anlautende *l* im Mandschu-Tungusischen ist sekundärer Herkunft und geht gewöhnlich auf ein anlautendes **n* (meistens vor einem folgenden **m*) zurück." This view is consistent with the general absence of initial liquid phonemes across the Transeurasian languages. The environment in which this development takes place needs further study, but it should probably be extended to the position before **-PK-* clusters, e.g. pTg **nabga:n-* 'to glue, stick' in Evk. *labgan-*, Even *nabgan-*, Neg. *labga:n-*, Orok *lamba-*, Ud. *lagbamu-*; pTg **nobgi* 'squirrel nest': Evk. *lopi* (dial. loki:); Neg. *lo:bi̧*, Ulcha *logbu̧*, Na. *lo:bi̧*, Ud. *loi*; pTg **napki* 'tiers, straps (for skis)': Ulcha: *la:xi̧*, Orok *la:pu̧*, Na. *la:pi̧*, Oroch *lappi*; pTg **napku-* 'to insert, hang: Evk. *lapku-*, Even *napkü-*. Note that Even consistently retains the initial nasal here.

(22) 'to pursue'

J *kou* B, OJ *ko₂p-* 'to ask, request, beg', pJ **kop-* 'beg'

Neg. *gobjo-*, Orok *gobdo-*, Evk. *goɣ-*, *govjo-*, Even *gobja-*, Oroč *gobjono-*, pTg **gob-* 'hunt',

Karakh. *kov-*, MTk. *kov-*, Tk. *kov-*, Gag. *qu:-*, Az. *Gov-*, Tkm. *qov-*, *qaw-*, Uz. *qaw-*, *quw-*, Tat. *quw-*, Kirg. *qu:-*, *qubala-*, Kaz. *quw-*, Chu. *xu-*, *xəv-*, pTk **kob-* 'follow, pursue, chase'

(23) 'to carry on the back'

J *ou* B, OJ *op-* 'to bear, carry on the back', EOJ *opuse-*, OJ *opose-*, J *ooseru* 'to charge with', J *obuu*, OJ *obup-* 'to carry on the back', pJ **əpə-* 'to carry on the back'

MK *ep-* 'to carry on the back', pK **ep-* 'to carry on the back'

Na. *iwarï-* 'to tunload', Evk. *ewe-* 'to carry', Oroč. *ewu-gi-* 'to bring', *iwa-dala-* 'to put a person on one's shoulder', pTg **ebe-* 'to carry'

WMo. *eyüre-*, *egür-*, *ügür-* 'to carry or load on one's back; to bear; to take a burden upon oneself (tr.)', (SH) MMo. *u'ur-* 'to lift on the shoulders, carry', Khal. *ü:re-* 'carry on one's back, bear', Kalm. *ü:r-*, pMo **eyüre-* 'to carry on the back'

The deep-velar consonant with velar origin WMo. *y* < **g* only occurs in stems with back vowels. In intervocalic position, it converged with the deep-velar consonant with bilabial origin WMo. *y* < **β* < **p/*b* (Poppe 1955: 98). In cases like WMo. *eyüre-*, where *y* occurs in stems with front vowels, a velar origin can be excluded.

(24) 'to obstruct'

J *sawaru* A, OJ *sapar-* 'to interfere with, affect, hinder (intr.)', J *saeru* A, OJ *sape₂-* 'to obstruct, bother', pJ **sapa-* 'to obstruct, hinder'

MMo. *sa'ara-* 'to hesitate, to hold off (intr.)' (SH), WMo. *saɣara-* 'to come apart, break up (intr.), *saɣata-* 'to be detained, delayed', WMo. *saɣad* 'obstacle, hindrance, delay' Khal. *sa:r-*, *sa:t-*, Bur. *ha:r-*, *ha:t-*, Ordos *sa:ta-*, Dag. *sa:ta-*, *sa:te-*, SYug. *sa:d* 'obstacle', *sa:du:l-*, pMo **saɣa-* 'to obstruct' (pMo **-dA- ~ *-tA-* passive: Section 6.5.3; pMo **-rA-* anticausative: Section 6.6.4)

Karakh. *savra-* 'to be stopped, hindered, discontinued', *savïl-* 'to decline', MTk. *sav-* 'to turn off (the road), get rid of', Tk. *sav-* 'to get rid of', *savuš-* 'to pass, pass away', Az. *sovul-* 'to stop, finish', Tkm. *sowul-* 'to stop, finish', Gag. *sauš-* 'to pass, pass away', Karaim *savuš-*'to pass, pass away', pTk **sab-* 'to stop, hinder'

(25) 'go over/away'

OJ *kati*, EOJ *kasi*, MJ *kati* 'walking' (deverbal noun on *-i* from unattested verb 'walk'), pJ **kat-* 'to walk'

K *keT-*, MK ¨*keT-* 'to walk', pK **keti-* 'to walk'

(SH) MMo. *ketü-gelje-*'to cross over, go across (intr.),' (pMo **-gA-ljA-* inchoative suffix denoting multiple actants; see Section 5.7.4), *ketü-s* 'crosswise, straight through (water)' (pMo **-s* adverbializer), *ketü-l-* 'to cross, pass (tr.)' (WMo. *-l-* intensive-iterative; cfr (1)), WMo. *ketül-* ~ *getül-* 'to traverse, cross, ford; be delivered', Khal. *getle-* '1 cross', Bur. *getel-* '1', Kalm. *getl̦-* '1', Ordos *getül-* '1', Dag. *hedele-* '1', *xedelgē-* '1', *xedle:-* '1', pMo **ketü-* 'to cross, traverse'

OTk. *ket-*, MTk. *ket-*, Tk. *git-*, Tat. *kit-*, Uz. *ket-*, Uig. *kät-*, Az. *gät-*, Tkm. *git-*, Kirg. *ket-*, Kaz. *ket-*, Nog. *ket-*, Bash. *kit-*, Gag. *get-*, Karaim *ket-*, KKalp. *ket-* pTk **ke:t-* 'to go, go away'

Vovin (2008: 150) rightly argues against Whitman's (1985: 225) suggestion that OJ *kati* is derived from a thematic verb pJ **kati-* because we would not expect palatalization to /si/ is Eastern Old Japanese if this were the case. However, his suggestion that "WOJ *kati* was borrowed from Korean as a set form, and then re-borrowed into Eastern Old Japanese as *kasi*" is difficult to support because the nominalized form in Korean would be pre-MK *keli* and pK **keti* 'walking'. The quality of the vowel and/or the liquid in the Korean model are difficult to reconcile with the Old Japanese form.

(26) 'to shut'

J *tatu* B, OJ *tat-* 'to cut off, shut off, interrupt', pJ **tat-* 'to shut off'

MK *tat-* 'to close, shut, cut off', pK **tat-* 'shut'

(27) 'to be longlasting'

J *oiru* ?B 'to grow old, age, get on in years', EMJ *oyos-* ?B 'to get old', OJ *oyo₂si* 'being old and esteemed', e.g. OJ *oyo₂si wo* 'old man', J *oya* 'parent', Shuri *uya* 'parent', pR **Uya* (Thorpe 1983: 315) , pJ **oyo-* < **oya-*

MK *wo·la-* 'to be long(lasting)', pK **wola-* 'to be longlasting'

(28) 'break off'

J *kaku*, MJ *kak-* A 'to break, lack', J *kakeru* A, OJ *kake₂-* 'to break off, be broken off', pJ **kaka-* 'to break off'

Neg. *aki-* / *kaki-* '1 cut off', Olč. *χaqpa-lu-* '2 tear off', Orok *χaqpa-* '2', Na. *χa:ga-* '1', *χaqpa:-* '2', Ud. *akpinda-* '1', *kakpaligi-* '2', pTg **xak-* 'cut off, tear off'

(SH) MMo. *qaqal-* '1 break, split, chip', *qaqaca-* '2 separate, break away from (tr./intr.)',WMo. *qayal-* 1 (WMo. *-l-* intensive-iterative; cfr (1)) , *qayala-* 1, *qayaca-* '2', Khal. *xaga-* '1', Bur. *xaxa-* '1', Kalm. *xayəl-* '1', Ordos *xagal-* '1', Mogh. *qakara-* '1', Dag. *xagala:-, hagere-, hagare-, hagela:-* '1', pMo **kaka-* 'break, split'

Karakh. *kak-* 'strike, knock, tap', Tk. *kak-*, Gag. *kak-*, Az. *gax-*, Tkm. *kak-*, *kakïl-*, MTk. *kak-*, Uzb. *kɔk-*, Uig. *kak-*, Krm. *kak-*, Tat. *kak-*, Bash. *kak-* Kirgh. *kak-*-, Kaz. *kak-*, KBalk. *kak-*, KKalp. *kak-*, Kum. *kak-*, Nog. *kak-*, Khak. *xax-*, Oyr. *kak-*, Tuva *kak-*, Tof. *ka'k-*, Dolg. *kakrïy-* 'break into small pieces', pTk **kak-* 'strike, knock, tap'

The Japanese, Tungusic and Mongolic forms have a close semantic fit, while the Turkic semantics deviate considerably. Given the form and the meaning of the Turkic participant, it cannot be excluded that the Turkic verb may have a sound symbolic origin and ultimately does not belong here.

(29) 'to insert'

J *haku* ?A, OJ *pak-* 'to slip on, put on (shoes, stockings, trousers)', Shuri *hak-* A, J *hakeru* ?A, OJ *pake₂-* 'to have/let someone put on', OJ *pakas-* 'to deign to put on', pJ **paka-* 'to slip on'

MK *pak-* 'to insert', pK **pak-* 'to insert'

Even *hak-* '1 to enclose, fence in, lock up', Evk. *haku:-* '1', Neg. *xaxụ-* '1', Sol. *axụ-* '1', pTg **paku:-* 'to enclose'

(30) 'to burn'

J *taku* A, OJ *tak-* 'to burn, boil, cook (tr.)', Shuri *tak-* 'to burn', pJ **tak-* 'to burn',

MK *·tho-* 'to burn, be on fire (intr.)', MK *ta·hi-*, K *ttay-* 'make (fire), heat (with fire) (tr.)' (MK *-i* causative-passive; Section 6.7.2), pK **tʌhʌ-* < pK **takʌ-* 'to burn'

Karakh. *yak-*, MTk. *yaq-*, Tk. *yaq-*, Tkm. *yaq-*, Gag. *yak-*, Az. *yax-*, Tat. *yaɣ-*, Krm. *yaq-*, Uz. *yɔq-*, Uig. *yaq-*,Yak. *saq-*, Kirg. *ʒaq-*, Kaz. *žaq-*, Bash. *yaq-*, Khalaj *ya:q-*, Chu. *śot-*, pTk *ya-k-* 'to ignite, burn (tr.)'

According to Ramsey's law (cf. (20)), the original root underlying MK ·*tho-* 'to burn, be on fire (intr.)' can be reconstructed as pK **tʌhʌ-* 'to burn'. In line with conditioning factor 12b, pK **tʌhʌ-* 'to burn' can be assumed to be an assimilation to the second syllable vowel from pK **tahʌ-*. The transitive verb MK *ta·hi-* 'make (fire)' can be derived from this root by adding a causative-passive suffix *-i-*. As expected, the addition of a final suffix *-i-* blocks the weakening process of the vowels. Velar lenition supports the reconstruction of pK **takʌ-* 'to burn'. The correspondence between Chinese donorwords and Korean loanwords (e.g. Ch. *cak* 'foot (measure)' is borrowed as MK ·*cah*), phonogram readings in the Kyelim Yusa (e.g. ¨*hwalq·huy* for MK *holk* 'earth'), elements in Paekche placenames (e.g. *tin·qak* for MK ¨*twolh* 'stone'), dialectal forms (e.g. dial. *tolk* for MK ¨*twolh* 'stone'), and internal doublets (e.g. MK *siphu-* versus MK *sikpu-* 'want') all suggest that velar lenition (*k > *h) took place at an early stage in Korean (Martin 1996: 36–37).

The correspondence with the Turkic verbs may of course be coincidental. Indeed, the proto-Turkic verb **yak-* 'to ignite (tr.)' may represent a complex form, while the inclusion of the Turkic form would lead us to expect register B rather than A in Japanese. The attestation of OTk *yal-* 'to blaze, burn, shine (intr.)' and OTk *yan-* 'to burn, blaze up (intr.)' suggests that these verbs are morphologically complex. The underlying verb being pTk **ya-* 'to burn (tr.)', OTk *yal-* 'to blaze, burn, shine (intr.)' would represent a derivation with a passive suffix pTk **-(X)l-* (Erdal 1991: 651–693), OTk *yan-* 'to burn, blaze up (intr.)' a derivation with an anticausative suffix pTk **-(X)n-* (Erdal 1991: 584–638) and, Karakh. *yak-* 'to ignite, burn (tr.)' with an inchoative suffix pTk **-(X)k-* (Erdal 1991: 645–650). This inchoative suffix can be traced back to proto-Transeurasian (see Section 5.7). Ultimately, Japanese and Korean may only have inherited the Transeurasian complex inchoative form.

(31) 'to rise, raise'

J *oku* A, OJ *ok-* 'to put', OJ *oki₂-* B 'arise', *okoru* B?, OJ *oko₂r-* 'to arise', *okosu* B, OJ *oko₂s-* 'to raise', Shuri *ukijuN* 'to rise', pR **oke-* (Thorpe 1983: 321), pJ **iki-* 'to raise'

Evk. *ug-* 'to mount, go up', Evk. *ugur-* 'to raise (head etc.), rise', *ugeski:* 'upwards', Even *uyi:* 'above, up', Even *u:-* 'to mount, go up', Neg. *okča-la:-*, Solon *ugu-*, Na. *o:-*, Olč. *u̯:-*, Orok *u̯:-*, Oroč *u:-*, Ud. *u:-na-* pTg **ög-* 'to mount'

OTk. *ük-*, Karakh. *ük-*, MTk. *ök-*, Tk *ögüš* 'many', Tat. *ǔy-*, Oir. *ü:-*, Uz. *uy-*, Khak. *üg-*, Kirg. *üy-*, Kaz. *üy-* Nog. *üy-*, Bash. *ǔy-*, KKalp. *üy-*, pTk **ög-* 'to heap up, accumulate'

In spite of the difference in register, J *oku*, OJ *ok-* A 'put' seems closely semantically and formally related to the other Japanese cognates. Section 3.3.4 contains more instances of internally related verb pairs with different register types. Moreover, the assignment of J *oku* to type A might not be completely reliable because the dialects of Shizuoka, Nagano and Yamanashi have B for this verb.

The sporadic attestation of the Tungusic vowel reflex *o* where *u* would be expected, may lead to the reconstruction of pTg **ög-* rather than **üg-* 'to mount'.

The historical stages of Turkic have a voiceless velar, but the modern forms lead to the reconstruction of pTk **ög-* 'to heap up' with a voiced velar stop.[15]

(32) 'to hit with force'

J *tuku* B, OJ *tuk-* 'to pound, husk, beat, hit with force', Shuri *cicun*, pJ **tuk-* 'to pound, hit with force'

MK *·thi-* 'to hit, strike', pK **t(ʌ)hi-* < **t(ʌ)ki-* 'to hit, strike'

Evk. *dug-* '1 to hit, beat, hammer', Even *duɣ-* '1', *dųɣ-* '2 to batter, hit repeatedly', Neg. *dųw- ~ dųɣ-* '2', *dukte-* '1', Ma. *du- ~ du:-* '1, thresh', Jur. *du-ŋu-mij* '1', Olč. *dų:či-* '2', Orok *du:* 1, *dų:či-* '2', Na. *du:-* 1, *do:či-* '2', Oroč. *du:-* '1, 2', Ud. *du:-* '2', *dukte-* '1', pTg **dug-* 'to hit with force'

According to Ramsey's law (cf. (20)), the reconstruction of a minimal vowel in pK **tʌhi-* is legitimate. Velar lenition (cf. (30)) supports the reconstruction of pK **tʌki-*. Although the semantic and formal correspondences among the Japanese, Korean and Tungusic participants are very close, we cannot exclude the possibility that we are ultimately dealing with a sound symbolic formation.

---

15 Note that WMo. *ögede* 'upward', (SH) MMo *o'e-de*, Khal. *ö:d*, Bur. *ö:de*, Kalm. *ö:də*, Ordos *ö:dö*, Dong. *ojie*, Bao. *odə*, Mogh. *öädä* and WMo. *ögse-* 'to go up', Khal. *ögsö-*, Bur. *ügse-*, Kalm. *öksə-* lead to the reconstruction pMo *öge* 'upper, above', followed by the adverbial marker *-dA*, which derives from nominally encoded adjectives (e.g. WMo. *batu* 'firm' → *batu-da* 'firmly' or, by the denominal verb suffix *-sA-* (e.g. WMo. *ayajim* 'slow, slowly (adv. / adj)' → *ayajimsa-* 'to slow down, become slow'). Although the form and meaning represent a good fit, it is not included here because there is no category correlation for this originally nominal adjective.

(33) 'to catch, grab'

J *asaru* B, OJ *asar-* 'to fish, forage, browse, hunt for, catch (food) (tr.)', Shuri *qasar-*, pJ **asa(-)r-* 'search (food), catch'

K *as-*, MK ¨*as-* (~ *ažo-*) 'to take away, grab', pK **asʌ-* 'grab'

(34) 'to feel aversion'

J *osoru* B, OJ *oso₂r-* 'to fear, dread, to be apprehensive', Shuri *qusuri*, J *osorosii* B, OJ *osorosi-* 'be horrible', Shuri *quturusyan*, pJ **oso-* 'to fear'

Neg. *osa* 'bad', Ma. *usa-* 'become sad', Sibe *usa-* 'be sad, grieve', Jur. *usu-ya-buren* 'hate', Evk. *usa* 'bad', Even *us* 'bad, guilt, crime', pTg **usa-* 'to grieve, be sad; to hate, be hateful' MMo. *ösül* '1 hatred, revenge' (WMo. *-l* deverbal noun suffix deriving abstract concepts (Poppe 1954: 47) , WMo. *ös* '1', *ösi-* 'to hate, bear extreme ill-will, feel vengeful; to spite', Bur. *ühö:(n)* '1', Khal. *ös* '1', Kalm. *ös* '1', pMo **ösü-* 'to hate, feel vengeful'

The common semantic denominator in this etymology is 'to feel aversion deriving from fear, anger or sorrow'. Since WMo. *-l* is a deverbal noun suffix deriving abstract concepts such as WMo. *ükü-* 'to die' → *ükül* 'death', MMo. *ösül* 'hatred, revenge' can probably be derived from an unattested verb base pMo **ösü-* 'to hate, feel vengeful'.

(35) 'to make meet'

J *kumu* A, OJ *kum-* 'to intertwine, assemble, join, unite', Shuri *kum-* B, pJ **kum-* 'to join, intertwine'

K *kam-* 'to shut, close (eyes)', MK *kom-* 'to shut, close (eyes), join, make meet', pK **kʌm-* 'to make meet'

Neg. *kumul-* '1 to cover', *komno:-* '2 to embrace', Na. *kumuligu-* '1', Olch. *kumul-* '1', Orok *kumele-* '1', Evk. *kumu-* '1', *kumle:-* '2', Even *kumle-* '1', Oroch *kumul-* '1', Solon *xumeli:-* '2', pTg **kum-* 'to cover, embrace'

WMo. *qumi-*, Khal. *xumi-*, Kalm. *xümə-*, *xömə-*, *xuṁə-*, pMo **kumi-* 'to wrap up, roll up, collect'

Uz. *qimti-*, Tat. *qịmti-*, Bash. *qịmti-*, Kirh. *qịmti-*, Kaz. *qịmti-*, *qịmta*, Nog. *qịmti-*, Alt. *qịm-*, Tuva *qumza*, Yak. *kumuy-*, pTk **kum-/ *küm-* 'to wrap, tuck'

The Korean forms K *kam-*, MK *kom-* have become specialized in the meaning of 'to close (eyes)', but the Yong Pi echen ka (1447 4: 118) contains an example of the meaning 'to make meet': MK *hotaka spolli kom-key ho-myen* (then quickly meet-ADV do-COND)'if then you quickly make them meet' (Whitman 1985: 222).

(36) 'to gather'

J *tamaru* A, OJ *tamar-* 'to gather, accumulate, collect (intr.)', Shuri *tamar-*, J *tameru*, OJ *tame-* 'to let accumulate, amass (tr.)', Shuri *tamir-*, pJ **tama-* 'to gather'

MK *tam- ~ ̈tam-* 'to put in, fill, pack, comprise', pK **tamʌ-* 'to fill'

Ma. *tama-*, Na. *tama-*, pTg **tama-* 'to gather, collect'

(37) 'spring up'

J *haneru* ?B, OJ *pane-* 'to jump, spring up, hop (intr.)', pJ **pana-* 'to jump'

WMo. *unu-* 'ride, mount', Khal. *un-*, Kalm. *un-*, Dong. *hun-tra-*, *unu-*, Bao. *fune-*, Dag. *ono-*, Mgr. *funi-*, Mogh. *uni-*, pMo **punu-* 'to ride, mount'

There are very few verb etymologies reflecting medial **-n-*. In order to support the nasal correspondence, I refer to a substantial number of etymologies reflecting intial **n-* (Robbeets 2005: 316–317).

(38) 'to move away, remove'

J *saru* A? 'to leave, move away, quit', OJ *sar-* 'to move forward, depart', J *sarasu* A 'to bleach, blanch, expose', J *sarau* A, OJ *sarap-* 'to clean, dredge, drag' (pJ **-pa-* intensive-iterative; cf. Section 6.4.1), pJ **sara-* 'to move away'

MK *·so(l)- / ·so·l(o)-* 'to make vanish (tr.)', MK *·su(l)- / ·su·l(u)-* 'to vanish (intr.)' pK **sʌlʌ- ~ *sɨlɨ-* 'to vanish'

[Copy: Ma. *sala-* 'to distribute, hand out']

WMo. *sal(u)-* '1 to separate, branch off, part with, take leave from; 2. to be detached, be parted from', MMo. *salqaxda-* 'to be separated', Khal. *sala-* '1', Buriat *hala-* '1', Kalm. *sal-* '1', Ordos *sal-* '1, Dag. *sala-* '1', Mgr. *sal-* '1', pMo **salu- ~ *sala-* 'to move away from, remove'

OTk. *sal-* 'move, put in motion', Karakh. *sal-* '1 to put in motion, throw, 2 to let fall, lower', Tk. *sal-* 'to let go, let free, send, throw oneself, ignore', Tat. *sal-* '1', MTk. *sal-* '1', Uz. *sɔl-* '1', Uig. *sal-* 'insert, put away, remove; let fall, hang', Az. *sal-* '2', Tkm. *sal-* '1', Khak. *sal-* '1', Shor *sal-* '1', Khalaj *sal-* '1', Chu. *sol-* '1', Tuva *sal-* '1', Kirg. *sal-* '1', Kaz. *sal-* '1', Nog. *sal-* '1', Bash. *hal-* '1', Gag. *sal-* '1', Karaim *sal-* '1', KKalp. *sal-* '1' pTk **sal-* 'to move away, put in motion'

The root Ma. *sala-* 'to distribute, hand out' is attested only in Manchu (Cincius 1977: 57). It is absent elsewhere in Tungusic. The poor distribution and the specialized semantics suggest that it is a copy from Mongolian.

(39) 'to harm, deceive'

MJ *taras-* A 'to deceive a person by telling him sweet things; deceive, cheat, trick', J *tarasu* 'to wheedle, cajole, deceive', pJ **tara(-)s-* 'to deceive'

MK *talay-* 'to wheedle, cajole; soothe, calm down,', pK **talay-* 'to deceive'

[Copy: Ma. *tala-* 'to confiscate, seize property as a legal punishment', Evk./Even *tala:-* 'to rob, plunder, take away']

WMo. *tala-* 'to take away, confiscate, plunder, ruin', (SH) MMo. *tala-* '1 to rob, plunder', Khal. *tala-* 'to rob, confiscate', Kalm. *talə-* '1', Ordos *tala-* '1', Dag. *tale-* '1', pMo **tala-* 'to plunder, harm'

OTk. *tala-* 'to damage, pillage', Karakh. *tala-* '1 to pillage, plunder', Tk. *tala-* '1', Tat. *tala-* '1', MTk. *tala-* '1', Uz. *tala-* '1', Uig. *tala-* '1', Az. *tala-* '1', Tkm. *ta:la-* '1', Khak. *tala-* '1', Chu. *tula-* 'harm, slander', Yakut *tala:-* '1', Kirg. *tala-* '1', Kaz. *tala-* '1', Nog. *tala-* '1', Bash. *tala-* '1', Karaim *tala-* '1', KKalp. *tala-* '1', pTk **tala-* 'to plunder, harm'

The verb MJ *taras-* 'to deceive' is attested only from the Middle Japanese period onwards. However, lack of evidence in Old Japanese does not equal evidence of lack. The Korean verb MK *talay-* is not subject to conditioning factor 12b because the weakening of the vowels is probably blocked by the incorporation of a causative-passive suffix **-i*.

The verb MMo. *tala-* occurs in the *Secret History* with the meaning 'rob, plunder'. Only later, within the context of Mongolian customary law, it developed the meaning 'confiscate', which is reflected in Khal. *tala-* 'rob, confiscate'. The Manchu verb *tala-* 'confiscate, seize property as a legal punishment' is restricted to this secondary, culturally specific meaning (Doerfer 1965: 543). This observation indicates that *tala-* is a copy from Mongolian into Manchu. The restricted distribution of the verb root in Tungusic further confirms the borrowing scenario. Apart from Ma. *tala-* 'confiscate, seize property as a legal punishment', Evenki and Even have *tala:-* 'rob, plunder, take away' (Cincius 1977: 156). The North-Tungusic verbs are thought to have been copied from Yakut *tala:-* 'rob, pillage, plunder' (Malchukov 2003: 246).

(40) 'to be wet'

OJ *urup-* ?B 'to get muddy, be wet', OJ *urum-* ?B 'to get wet, moist', pJ **uru-* 'to be wet'

K *wuli-*, MK *wuli-* 'to steep, soak, bleach', pK **wuli-* 'to soak'

Evk. *ula-* '1 to soak, wet', Evk. *ulap-* '2 to become wet', Even *ul-* '1', Even *ulab-* '2 to become wet' , Ma. *ulga-* ~ *ulha-* 'to wet, dampen, dip in a liquid', Orok *u̧la-* '1', Na. *u̧larïko:* (dial.) 'wet', Ud. *ula-* '1', Sol. *u̧lakku:* 'wet', pTg **ula-* 'to soak, wet' (pTg **-p-* anticausative, see Section 6.4.3).

(41) 'to cut'

J *kiru* B, OJ *ki₁r-* 'to cut', OJ *ki₁ras-* B 'to run/ sell out of', J *kireru* B, OJ *ki₁re-* 'to be sharp, get cut, run out', Shuri *cijuN* (Thorpe 1983: 276), pR **kiri-*, pJ **kira-* 'to cut'

Evk. *gir-*, Even *gïr-*, Neg. *gi:-*, *gïj-*, Ma. *giri-*, Olč. *gïrï-*, Orok *gïrï-*, Na. *gïrï-*, Oroč. *gi:-*, *giji-*, Ud. *gi:-*, pTg **giri-* 'to cut out'

[Copy: WMo. *kira-*, *kiru-*, Khal. *x'ar-*, Kalm. *kur-*, pMo **kira-* 'to cut into small pieces, mince']

Karakh. *kïr-* 'to scrape, strip (hair), pluck out (hair)', Tk. *kïr-* '1 break, demolish', Tat. *kïr-* '2 scrape, shave', MTk. *kïr-* '1, 2, cut off', Uz. *kir-* '2', Uig. *ki(r)-* '2', Az. *gïr-* '1', Tkm. *gïr-* '1, 2', Khak. *xïr-* '2, cut', Khalaj *kïr-* '1', Chu. *xər-* '1', Yak. *kïrïj-* 'to shear, cut', Dolgan *kïrïj-* 'shear, cut', Tuva *kïr-* '2', Kirg. *kïr-* '2', Kaz. *kïr-* '2', Nog. *kïr-* '2', Bash. *kïr-* '1, 2', Gag. *kïr-* '1', Karaim *kïr-* '1, 2', Kkalp. *kïr-* '2', pTk **kïr-* 'to cut, scrape'

The Mongolic forms that support the reconstruction of pMo **kira-* 'to cut into small pieces, mince' have been omitted since they can be assumed to have been copied from Turkic. If they were cognates, we would expect an initial voiced velar (**g-*) in Mongolic (Robbeets 2004b: 170–172).

(42) 'to cut with an agricultural tool'

J *karu* A, OJ *kar-* 'to cut, mow, shear, reap, clip', pJ **kara-* 'to cut using an agricultural tool'

K *kal-*, MK *·kol-* 'to whet, grind', MK *·koli-* 'to whack, cut', Mk *kolk-* 'to scratch (tr.)', pK **kʌlʌ-* 'to cut or reduce using an agricultural tool'

Since the Japanese cognate refers to cutting with a sickle or scythe and the Korean cognate refers to reducing something to small fragments using a whetstone or a chopping knife, the common denominator appears to be 'to cut with an agricultural tool'. The agricultural context distinguishes this root from the one in the previous etymology.

(43) 'to bite, chew'

J *kamu* B, OJ *kam-* 'to bite, gnaw, chew, masticate, eat', pJ **kam-* 'to bite, chew'

MMo. (Muq) *kemile-* 'to gnaw', WMo. *kemeli-*, *kemele-* '1 to gnaw, nibble, crack with one's teeth (tr.)', *kemki-* '2 to bite, snap with the teeth (tr.)', Khal. *ximle-*, *xemle-* '1', Bur. *ximel-* '1', Bur. (Bargu dial) *ximil-*, Kalm. *keml̦-* '1', Ordos *kemele-* '1', *kemχel-* '2', Bao. *kamel-*, Baoan (Dahejia dial.) *kamǝl-* 'bite', Dag. *keme-* '1', Eastern Yugur *kemle-*, *kelme-*, Kangjia *kemle-*, pMo **keme-* 'to bite' (pMo **-lA-/ *-li-* intensive-iterative suffix)

Karakh. *kemür-* 'to gnaw, chew (tr.)', MTk. *kömür-*, Tk. *gemir-*, *kemir-*, Az. *gämir-*, Tkm. *gemir-*, Gag. *kemir-*, Uz. *kemir-*, Uig. *kemi(r)-*, Tat. *kimer-*, Khak. *kimǝr-*, Krm. *kemir-*, Kirg. *kemir-*, Tuva *xemir-*, Tof. *xemir-*, Kazakh *kemir-*, Nogh. *kemir-*, Bash. *kimer-*, pTk **kem-* 'to bite, chew (intr.)' (pTk **-(U)r-* causative)

In his review of Robbeets (2005), Georg (2007: 273) objects: "Had they used more scientifically oriented sources [...] or any Mongolistic expertise for a change, they would have found the *meaning* of this verb to be 'to crack open a bone with one's teeth and to suck the marrow', which makes clear that it is derived from *kemi* 'marrow of bones' and has to be eliminated from this "etymology"." However, these Mongolic forms can be analysed in two different ways: whereas Georg derives them from pMo **kemi(n)* 'marrow of the bones', I derive them from pMo **keme-* 'to bite'. Thus, I take the general meaning 'to bite' as the primary one and assume that the peripheral attestation of MMo. *kemi-le-* is a case of metathesis. Both *-lA-* and *-li-* are attested as deverbal iterative-intensive suffixes in Mongolic. The intensive-iterative pMo **-lA-* is frequently lexicalized in verb pairs such as WMo. *alqu-* 'to step, walk (intr.)' → *alqula-* 'to march, walk with quick steps (intr.)', WMo. *seji-* 'to butt with the horns' → *sejile-* 'to butt repeatedly with the horns', WMo. *ili-* 'to caress, stroke'→ *ilile-* 'to touch or stroke repeatedly'. However, the suffix **-lA-* in Georg's analysis may also be the denominal verb suffix, e.g. WMo. *šibaɣun* 'bird' → *šibaɣu-la-* 'hunt birds' (see Section 5.3.3). The suffix **-ki-* in WMo. *kemki-* 'to bite, snap with the teeth (tr.)' can be explained either as a deverbal transitivizer or as a denominal verb formant; the second explanation based on Georg's analysis, is more problematic, however, since *-ki- is a grammaticalized form of MMo. ki- 'to make' with the meaning 'to make the verb base', e.g. WMo. *sayad* 'hindrance' → *sayadki-* 'to hinder'. The expected meaning of the derived verb would thus be 'to make marrow' rather than 'to bite'. In the present analysis, WMo. *kemki-* 'to bite, snap with the teeth (tr.)' reflects a deverbal transitivizer pMo *-ki-, lexicalized in verb pairs such as WMo. *kel-* 'to be strung (as pearls) (intr.)' → *kelki-* 'to string pearls (tr.)'. Furthermore, the final vowel in all contemporary attestations reflects -e- rather than -i-, which suggests that *keme- is the primary form.[16]

According to Clauson (1972: 723), the Turkic transitive verbs meaning 'to gnaw, chew' can be derived as a causative of pTk *kem-. The causative suffix *-(U)r- is lexicalized in Turkic verb pairs such as OTk. *ač-* 'to be hungry' → *ačur-* 'to starve (tr.)', OTk. *keč-* 'to be late (intr.)' → *kečür-* 'to delay (tr.)' (Erdal 1991: 710–726).

(44) 'to split, burst'

J *yaburu* ?B', OJ *yabur-* 'to tear, rip, break', J *yabureru* ?B', OJ *yabure-* 'to get torn, get burst, be worn out', Shuri *yanzun / yand-* 'to tear', Shuri *yandi/yaburi* 'to get torn', pJ *yanpu-* 'to split, break, burst'

Ma. *delhe-* 'to divide, separate', Neg. *detpejkin-* 'to split', Evk. *delperge-*, *delpem-* '1 to crack, burst, split', Even *depčerge-* '1', Solon *delpe-* '1', pTg *delpe-* 'to split, burst' (pTg *-rgA- decausative inchoative, see Section 5.7.3).

WMo. *delbele-* '1 to break, crack (tr.)', WMo. *delbere-* '2 to burst, go to pieces (intr.)', Khal. *delbele-* '1', *delbere-* '2', Bur. *delbel-* '1', *delber-* '2', Kalm. *delwḷ-* '1', Ordos *delbel-* '1', pMo *delbe-* 'to burst, break' (pMo *-lA intensive-iterative, cf. (43); pMo *-rA anticausative, cf. Section 6.6.4).

Robbeets (2005: 375; 2008) argues that the voiced series in Japanese, which are internally derived from original nasal clusters, can be traced back to clusters in the Transeurasian languages (see also etymology (15), (46), (49)). The original clusters can be divided into homoganic and heteroganic clusters (Sagart pc.) Homoganic clusters are composed of a sonorant and a stop (pTEA *-Rp-, *-Rt-, *-Rk-) and merge in a nasal cluster (pJ *-np- > OJ -b-, pJ *-nt- > OJ -d-, pJ *-nk- >

---

[16] Dagur has a verb *kəmʸ-* 'to ruminate, chew the cud', which reflects a final high front vowel. However, in view of the meaning of this form, it is probably a reflex of pMo *kebi- 'to chew, to ruminate' (Nugteren 2011: 407).

OJ *-g-) in Japanese. The sound correspondence reflected here, namely OJ -b- < pJ *-np- with pTg *-lp- and pMo *-lb- is regular from this perspective. Another illustration of a homoganic cluster correspondence is provided by etymology (15). In heteroganic clusters, on the other hand, the nasal and the stop have a different place of articulation, which results in the insertion of a parasitic stop (pTEA *-$m^{(P)}T$-, *-$n^{(T)}K$-, *-$ŋ^{(K)}T$-). The nasal is lost in the continental Transeurasian languages (*-PT-, *-TK-, *-KT-), whereas Korean and Japanese lose the final stop (pJ *-mp- > OJ -b-, pJ *-nt- > OJ -d-, pJ *-ŋk- > OJ *-g-.) Etymologies (46) and (49) illustrate this heteroganic cluster correspondence.

(45) 'to fight'

J *korosu* A, OJ *ko$_2$ro$_2$s*- 'to kill, murder', Shuri *kurus*-, pJ **koro(-)s*- 'to kill',

MMo. *kere*- (SH), *kiräldu*- '1 to quarrel, fight', WMo. *kere*-, *kereldü*- '1' (WMo. -*ldU* mutual interaction (Poppe 1954: 62)), WMo. *kereče*- '2 be angry', Khal. *xerelde*- '1', Ordos *kerelde*- '1', Kalm. *keṛldə*- '1', Dag. *xerəldə*- '1', Mgr. *kəre:di*- '1', Mogh. *kerälda*- '1', pMo **kere*- 'to quarrel, to fight'

OTk. *keriš*- (OTk -(X)š multiple participation (Erdal 2004: 552–583)), Karakh. *keriš*-, *küreš*-, MTk. *küreš*-, Tk. *güreš*-, Az. *güläš*-, Gag. *güreš*-, Tkm. *göreš*-, Kaz. *keris*-, *küres*-, Tat. *köräš*-, Kirg. *keriš*-, Uz. *kuraš*-, Uig. *küräš*-, Shor *küreš*-, Tuva *xüres*-, Yak. *küres* 'wrestling', Tof. *xireš*-, *xüreš*-, *xire*- 'to start a fight', Chu. *kəreš*-, pTk **keri*- ~ **kerö*- 'to quarrel, fight'

Given that both WMo. *kere*- and *kereldü*- are attested with the meaning of 'to fight', it is clear that the latter variant is a derivation with the suffix that expresses mutual interaction WMo. -*ldU*, e.g. WMo. *ala*- 'to kill' → *alaldu*- 'to kill each other'. In Turkic, only Tofalar preserves evidence of an underived base *xire*- 'to start a fight'. The suffix expressing multiple participation in Turkic is -(X)š, e.g. OTk *kun*- 'to rob' → *kunuš*- 'to rob eachother. Therefore, it is possible to reconstruct pTk **keri*- 'to quarrel, fight'. The variation between Karakhanide *keriš*- and *küreš*- may alow us to reconstuct pTk **kerö*-.

(46) 'to be(come) wide'

J *noberu* B, OJ *nobe$_2$*- 'to stretch, spread, lengthen (tr.)', J *nobiru* B, OJ *nobi$_2$*- 'to extend, lengthen, stretch, spread, grow; be postponed (intr.)', J *nobasu* B, OJ *nobas*- 'to extend, lengthen, stretch, spread (tr.)', pJ **nənpa*- > **nənpi*- 'to become long and wide'

K *nelp*- 'to be wide', MK *nep*- 'to be wide', MK *nelu*- 'to be wide', pK **nelp(i)*- 'to be wide'

Neg. *nepte-nepte* 'even', Na. *nepte-nepte* 'even', Olch. *nepte-nepte* 'even', Orok *nette-* 'spread out', Even *nebde-* 'to pull off the skin in one piece', *nebde* 'open(ness); wide(ness)', *nebden-* 'to unfold widely; open up (of cloth, wings); straighten out; open up (of leaves) (intr.)' (Even *-(A)n$_{(2)}$-* processive), *nebdeńe:* 'flat, wide' (Even *-ńA* deverbal adjectivizer), *nebder-* 'to open, come out (of flowers) (intr.)', *nebdeku* 'opened up; wide', Evk. *nepte-* 'to unfold, smooth out, spread out', pTg **nepte-* 'to become flat and wide'

WMo. *nebseger* 'wide and long' (WMo. *-GAr* deverbal quality noun (Poppe 1954: 46)), WMo. *nebseyi-* 'to be wide and long (of clothes), to be tattered, in rags (intr.)' (pMo **-yi-* anticausative, cf. (3)), WMo. *nebsegene-* 'to move (of something wide and long)' (WMo. *-GA-* factitive: Poppe 1954: 61; pMo **-nA-* processive: cf. Section 5.4.4), Khal. *nevsiy-*, Bur. *nebši-*, pMo **nebse-* 'to be(come) wide and long'

See etymology (44) for the explanation of the heteroganic cluster correspondence.

(47) 'to go'

OJ *in-* 'to go away, leave, depart' A, OJ *-in-* perfective auxiliary, J *nar-* B, OJ *nar-* 'to become, come into being', J *nas-* B, OJ *nas-* 'to make, do, give birth to', pJ **na-* 'to go out, become',

K *na-*, MK ·*na-* 'to go out, emerge, leave, become, come into being, come out', MK ¨*nay-* 'take out, produce' (**-i-* causative; see Section 6.7.2), MK *nat-* 'to appear' (**-t(i)-* passive; see Section 6.3.2), MK ··*na-* resultative, pK **na-* 'to go out',

Ma. *-na-* ~ *-ne-* ~ *-no-*, Na. *-nda-*, Olch. *-ŋda-*, Oroch, Ud. *-na-*, Sol. *-na:-*, Neg. *-na-*, Evk., Even. *-na:-*, pTg **-na:-* 'to go out'

OJ *in-* 'to go, leave, depart' belongs to the n-irregular verb paradigm (*na-hen*) along with only two other verbs: OJ *sin-* 'to die' and the perfect auxiliary OJ *-in-*, which are probably reflexes of the same etymon (Robbeets 2005: 123, 162). The n-irregular verb paradigm is an exception to the athematic paradigm (*yodan*) because it has 'long' adnominals (*rentaikei*) *-uru* and subjunctives (*meireikei*) *-ure* in contrast to the 'short' adnominals *-u* and subjunctives *-e* of the athematic paradigm.

Whitman (1985) has argued that at some proto-Japanese stage **-r-* was deleted after short vowels but retained after long vowels. The loss of the intervocalic *-r-* in the adnominals and subjunctives of the athematic paradigm is commonly attributed to this rule, so in the case of the n-irregular verb paradigm a preceding long original vowel must have blocked the application of the rule. Since the root vowel in monosyllabic morphemes was automatically long at the proto-Japanese stage, it is inviting to reconstruct monosyllabic pJ *na- 'to go'.

The prefix in OJ *in-* 'to go, leave, depart' is a lexicalized instance of the Old Japanese verb prefix *i-*. Various semantic and syntactic analyses of this prefix circulate in the literature[17], but, arguing that Old Japanese has active allignment in nominalized clauses, Yanagida and Whitman (2009: 117–119) demonstrate that the *i*-prefix is exclusively attached to active verbs, i.e. to transitive verbs and to intransitives verbs with an agentive subject. The separate accentuation of *i-* is high atonic 1.1. (Martin 1998: 668), which explains the B register in a number of lexicalisations such as J *imasu* B 'deign to be/stay/go/come' (< OJ *mas-* A 'to deign to be/stay/go/come'), OJ *ino₂r-* B 'to pray' (< OJ *no₂r-* A 'to declare') and OJ *ituk-* B 'to purify' (< OJ *tuk-* B 'to soak'). Lexicalized stems showing a reduced form of *i-* such as OJ *ik-* / *yuk-* 'to go', OJ *yokos-* 'to send here' and OJ *yusug-*'to wash out, rinse' have A register. OJ *in-* 'to go, leave, depart' and OJ *sin-* 'to die' have A register. However, in reference to Kindaichi, Martin (1998: 201) points out that the original accent type may be B because "these verbs originally had a fall (instead of just low) on the ending of the predicative [...] and that of the infinitive [...] like verbs of Type B." From this perspective, pJ *na-* 'to go' may underly derivations such as OJ *nar-* 'to become, come into being' and OJ *nas-* 'to make, do, give birth to' which have B register. The grammaticalization of 'to go' into a change-of-state verb is cross-linguistically well attested (Heine and Kuteva 2002: 156–157).

A similar pathway of grammaticalization probably underlies in MK ·*na-* 'to go out, emerge, leave, become, come into being, come out'. In addition to the most common meaning 'to become', the Korean verb is used in the sense of K *na-ka-* 'to go out, leave', e.g. in *nwun-ey nata* 'go out of a person's favor'. Rhee (1996: 215–216) shows that the basic denotation of MK ·*na-* was the motion of getting out of a bounded space. Derivations such as MK ¨*nay-* 'to take out, produce' with the causative suffix *-*i*- and MK *nat-* 'to appear' with the passive *-*t(i)- support this sematic analysis. Martin (1992: 263, 702, 933) further considers the so-called "effective suffix" MK ··*na-*, that can only apply to the verb MK ·*wo-* 'to come' yielding MK ·*wo·na-* 'to end up by coming, ultimately come', to be a grammaticalization from the auxiliary MK ·*na-* 'to go out, emerge'.

The Tungusic languages share a suffix that denotes departure from a place to other places or towards the object of an action (Benzing 1955a: 1068, Gorelova 2002: 239–240), such as Ma. *feku-* 'to jump' → *fekune-* 'to jump away from the

---

[17] Martin 1987: 94, 668: independent adverb; Hino 1997: 2–5: agentive marker; Unger 2000a: 676: reanalysis of a preceding -*i* converb Russell 2006: 141–142: goal focus marker; Vovin 2009a: 561: directive-locative focus marker

speaker, to jump to the other side', *guri-* 'to move' → *gurine-* 'to move to another place' and Ma. *omi-* 'to drink' → *omina-* 'to go to drink'. In Manchu, this construction can be replaced by a periphrastic converb construction with the verb *gene-* 'to go'. From the viewpoint of cyclic grammaticalization, the synthetic construction may also go back to an original verb pTg **na-* 'to go out'. Its origin as an independent verb is further supported by the observation that there is no development of vowel harmony for the suffix, except in Manchu.

(48) 'to put aside'

OJ *no₂k-* 'to get out of the way (intr.); leave (tr.)', J *nokeru* A, OJ *noke-* 'to remove, put out of the way; exclude', Shuri *nukir-*, pJ **noka-* 'to remove'

K *nwoh-*, MK *nwoh-* 'to put aside, let go', pK **nwoh-* < **nwok-* 'to put aside'

Although the reconstruction of **o* rather than **ə* in pJ **noka-* 'to remove' is mainly motivated by external comparison, it is also internally supported because pJ **nəka-* would represent a violation of Arisaka's law.

(49) J *toru* B, OJ *to₁r-* ~ *to₂r-* 'to hold, take, get, have', J *torasu* B, OJ *toras-* 'to give, let one have', *toraeru* ?B', OJ *to₂rape₂-* 'to capture', pJ **t(i)ra-* 'to take, hold'

K *tul-*, MK˜ *tul-* 'to hold up, lift, raise', pK **tili-* 'to hold up, lift, raise'

Evk. *tu:ri:n-* '1 to hold, retain, keep, support', Even *toru-* ~ *turu-* '1', Olcha: *turuwen-* '1', Orok *toroŋolo-* '1', Na. *turin-*, *turu:-* '1', Oroch *turi-* '1', pTg **töru-* 'to hold, retain' (Cincius 1977: 220)

The vowel alternation in the verb OJ *to₁r-* ~ *to₂r-* 'to hold, take, get, have' is reminiscent of a small number of verb doublets in Old Japanese such as OJ *to₁p-* ~ *to₂p-* 'to inquire', OJ *to₁k-* ~ *to₂k-* 'to untie' and OJ *so₁p-* ~ *so₂p-* 'to follow' (Martin 1989: 59). Since other verb stems all begin with *o₂* and since these verbs have dental initials, the variant with *o₂* can be assumed to represent the original form. This leads to the reconstruction of pJ **t(i)ra-* 'to take, hold'.

In many cases such as etymology (4), it is difficult to distinguish between the reconstruction of pTg **-u-* and **-ö-*.[18] However, in this case, the *-o-* in Even *toru-* and Orok *toroŋolo-* supports the reconstruction of pTg **töru-* 'to hold, retain'.

---

18 According to the correspondences in Benzing 1955a:

pTg	Ma.	Jur	Evk	Even	Sol	Neg	Oroch	Ud.	Olch.	Orok	Na
*ö [ʌ]	u		u	o	u	u	o/u	o	o/u	o/u	u
*u	u		u/ï-	u/ï-	u/ï-	u/ï-	u	u	u	u	u

(50) 'to remove, clear'

> J *harau* B', OJ *parap-* 'to remove, sweep away, purify, clear', J *hareru* B, OJ *pare-* B 'to disappear, be refreshed, get clear', J *haru* B, OJ *par-* 'open ground, clear land (for cultivation)', OJ *paruk-* ?B 'to clear up, open up, get bright, dispel', J *haruka*, OJ *paruka* (3.7b) 'far, distant, remote' (pJ *-ka* resultative nominalizer; cf. Section 7.6.1), OJ *para* (2.3) 'field, prairie, plain' (pJ *-a* nominalizer; cf. Section 3.4.1), pJ **paru-* 'to remove, clear, disappear'
>
> K *poli-*, MK *po·li-* 'to throw away, clear away, discard' (pK *-i-* causative-passive, cf. Section 6.7.2), MK *polk-* 'be bright' (pK *-kO-* inchoative, cf. Section 5.7.2), pK **pʌl-* 'to discard, clear'
>
> Ma. *burubu-* 'to disappear' (Ma. *-bu-* causative-passive (Gorelova 2002: 246–250)), Evk. *buri:-* 'let slip', pTg **buru-* 'to remove, disappear'

(51) 'to be bad'

> MJ *waru- ~ waro-*, J *waru-* B 'to be bad, inferior', pJ **waru- ~ *warə-* 'to be bad, inferior'
>
> WMo. *buruɣu* (WMo *-ɣu / -gü* deverbal noun suffix deriving quality words (Poppe 1954: 46)), Khal. *burə*, Kalm. *burə*, pMo **buru-* 'to be wrong, bad'

This word is not attested in Old Japanese; texts from that period use OJ *asi-* 'to be bad'.

(52) 'to become dense'

> OJ *sik-* A 'to pile up, continue without a break; proliferate, grow dense', OJ *sik-* A 'to spread out (tr.), control, rule', pJ **sik-* 'to become dense, spread out'
>
> K *kki-*, MK *·ski-* 'cloud up, gather, be filled with (smoke)', K *kkal-*, MK *·sko(l)- / sko·lo-* 'spread out, lay out, pave with (tr.)', pK **sikʌ-l-*
>
> [Copy: Evk. *hiyi:*, Even *hïyï*, Neg. *siwu:*, Olch. *sê:u*, Orok *si:yï*, Na. *sïo* 'thicket, brush']
>
> WMo. *siɣui*, MMo. *šikui*, Khal. *šuguy*, Bur. *šugi*, Kalm. *šuyu:*, Ordos *šux^wi:*, Dag. *šige:*, pMo **sigui* 'thick growth' (cf. pMo **-i* deverbal noun suffix; Section 8.3.4) < pMo **sigu-* 'to grow thick'

In view of the accentual and formal identity, the semantic proximity and the attestation of a similar doublet in Korean, OJ *sik-* A 'to pile up, continue without a break; proliferate, grow dense' and OJ *sik-* A 'to spread out (tr.), control, rule' can be derived from a single root pJ **sik-* 'to become dense, spread out'. In Korean, both meanings, i.e. 'to become dense' and 'to spread out,' are also attested. The first meaning is represented by monosyllabic, open and high pitched MK ·*ski-* 'to cloud up, gather, be filled with (smoke),' which is used when dust, dirt, smoke, fog, clouds etc. become dense. Following Ramsey's law (cf. (20)), we can derive this verb from a disyllabic root reflecting the loss of **i* or a minimal vowel, such as pK **sikʌ-*. The second meaning, 'to spread out,' is attested in MK ·*skol-* 'to spread out, lay out, pave with (tr.)', which probably contains the iterative suffix **-l-* (cf. (3)) and may derive from the same root. Note that the final high front vowel -*i* in Mongolic, may be the deverbal noun suffix -*i*. If that is the case, we might reconstruct the descriptive verb **sigu-* 'grow thick' in Mongolic. As argued by Doerfer (1985: 47), the Tungusic forms 'thicket, brush' seem to have been borrowed at a later stage from a Mongolic model in which the contraction of the final vowels was already under way.

3.4 Copular verbs

In contrast to main verbs, copular verbs have a mainly grammatical function in that they serve to link subject and predicate. On the border between lexicon and grammar, they are considered to be particularly telling when it comes to establishing a genealogical relationship. In the Indo-European family, the correspondences between the copula 'to be' are so systematic and paradigmatic that they suffice to prove that the languages involved are related (Beekes 1995: 15). Table 30 compares the conjugation of the copula 'to be' in Sanskrit, Homeric Greek, Latin and Gothic. The roots Sanskrit *as-*, Greek *es-*, Latin *es-* and Gothic *is-* correspond in form and function. All paradigms except Greek show a variant root with *s-*, which alternates between singular and plural in the paradigms. And finally, the present indicative endings correspond closely.

Table 30. Copula correspondence in Indo-European

	Sanskrit	Homeric Greek	Latin	Gothic
root	as-	es-	es-	is-
1 SG	as-mi	ei-mi	s-um	i-m
2 SG	as-i	es-si	es	is
3 SG	as-ti	es-ti(n)	es-t	is-t
1 PL	s-mas	ei-men	s-umus	s-ijum
2 PL	s-tha	es-te	es-tis	s-ijuþ
3 PL	s-anti	ei-si(n)	s-unt	s-ind

Although etymologies can be advanced for two copula roots pTEA *a:-* 'to be' and pTEA *bol-* 'to sit, be(come)' across the Transeurasian languages, they are not as convincing as in the case of Indo-European. Table 31 suggests that the copula roots correspond, but there is no shared formational irregularity or paradigmatic congruence involved. In Section 9.4, it will be argued that this inconsistency with the Indo-European evidence does not indicate unrelatedness, but follows from the chronological and structural differences between both language families.

Table 31. Copular verb correspondences in Transeurasian

	TEA	Japanic	Koreanic	Tungusic	Mongolic	Turkic
(53)	'to be'	OJ *ar-* 'exist' pJ **a-*	MK ·*e/a* converb pK **a-*		MMo. *a-* 'stay, be' pMo **a-*	OTk -*A*- denominal verb pTk **a-*
(54)	'to sit, be(come)'	OJ *wor-* / *wi-* 'to sit, be' pJ **wo-*	MK ··*wᵘ/o-* modulator pK **wo-*		WMo. *bol-* 'become' **bol-*	OTk. *bol-* 'be' **bo:l-*

3.4.1 pTEA *a:-* 'to be'

(53) 'to be'

> J *aru* B, OJ *ar-* 'to exist' (< **a-* + **-ra-* fientive; Section 5.3.1), Shuri *qan* B 'to exist'; OJ -*aku* bound noun (< **a-* + **-ku* nominalizer; Section 8.4.1); OJ -*am* tentative (< **a-* + **-ma-* inclination; Section 5.6.1); J *eru*, OJ *e-* 'to get, obtain' (< **a-* + **-Ci* causative-passive; Section 6.7.1), Shuri *yiiyuN-* B, pR **ye-* 'to get' (Thorpe 1983: 290), Ryukyuan perfect participles e.g. Shodon -*an*, -*ar*, -*am* (< **a-* + pJ **-n*, **-ra*, **-m* nominalizer; Sections 7.3.1, 7.4.1 and 7.5.1), pJ **a-* 'to be'.

> K -*e/a*, MK··*e/a* converb, MK ¨*et-* 'to get, receive' (< **a-* + **-ti-* causative; Section 6.3.2), pK **a-* 'to be'

> (SH) MMo. *a-* 'to stay, live, be', WMo. *a-* 'to be', Khal. *a-* 'to be', Dag. *a:-* 'to be', Mog. ʌ- 'to be', pMo **a-* 'to stay, live, be', Khitan **a-* 'to be' (Kane 2009: 158)

> OTk -*A*- denominal verb (Erdal 1991: 418–429), Caucasus Turkic, Karakalpak -*AgAn*, Chuvash -*AkAn*, Khalaj -*AgAN* durative participle, (< pTk **-A* converb + **a-* 'to be' + -*gAn* habitual participle), OTk -*(A)r* deverbal nominalizer, OTk -*A* converb, OTk. -*(A)r-* denominal intransitive

In Japanese and Korean, copulae and existential verbs occupy an ambivalent position between verb and verbal adjective. Sharing some properties with verbal adjectives, copulae and exisistential verbs enter double nominative constructions, e.g. J *Yasu-ga kokoro-ga ii* (Yasu-NOM heart-NOM be.good) 'It is Yasu who is goodhearted' and *Yasu-ga hon-ga aru* (Yasu-NOM book-NOM exist) 'It is Yasu who has a book'.) They can also occur with static locative particles, e.g. J *Tōkyō-ni atsui* (Tokyo-LOC be.hot) 'It is hot in Tokyo' and *Tōkyō-ni aru* (Tokyo-LOC exist) 'It exists in Tokyo'. Furthermore, the Korean copulae and exisistential verbs can even take adjectival morphology, such as the zero ending of the finite nonpast indicative suffix at the plain speech level, e.g. K *cwuk-nun-ta* 'it dies', K *yeyppu-ta* 'it is pretty', K *i-ta* 'it is' and K *iss-ta* 'it exists', but K *iss-nun-ta* 'it stays' (Sohn 1994: 95, 222–223).

I suggest to derive OJ *ar-* 'to exist' from a copula pJ **a-* 'to be' followed by the (deadjectival) anticausative **-ra-*. The anticausative suffix can also derive intransitive descriptive verbs expressing properties 'be a property' into verbs expressing the spontaneous development of that property, i.e. 'become a property', e.g. in OJ *aka- A* 'to be clear, bright, red' → OJ *akar- A* 'to brighten, redden (intr.)' (see Section 5.6.1). The meaning 'become' can be treated linguistically as a spontaneously occuring intransitive process, which is here derived as an anticausative of the state verb 'to be'. As such, the reconstructed development is following: pJ **a-* 'to be' → pJ **a-ra-* 'to become, come into being, be formed' > OJ *ar-* 'to exist'. The development of a change of state verb 'to become' into a state verb 'to be, exist' is commonly observed across the languages of the world (Heine and Kuteva 2002: 64). The complex origin of the verb OJ *ar-* 'to exist' is supported by Martin (1987: 677). The derivation is reminiscent of the derivation of MK ˇ*il-* 'to become' from the copula MK *i-* 'to be' by way of the anticausative suffix **-l-* (see Section 6.6.2).

The OJ tentative suffix *-am-* may go back to the copula **a-* 'to be' and the inclinational suffix pJ **-ma-*, as discussed in Section 5.6.1.

The verb OJ *e-* 'to get, obtain' is likely to have been derived from the same copula root pJ **a-* 'to be' followed by the causative-anticausative suffix pJ **-Ci-* (see Section 6.7.1). in the sense of 'to cause to be one's own' > 'to get, obtain'. The morphological complexity of OJ *e-* 'to get, obtain' is supported by the observation that its converb form is OJ *e* rather than ***i*. Unger (2000a) finds that monosyllabic morphemes are automatically long in proto-Japonic. It follows that if pJ **e-* can be reconstructed as a monosyllabic root, it is expected to have a long vowel. The same goes for the converb suffix pJ **-i*. Still in line with Unger (2000a: 663) we expect the first vowel to drop in sequences where two long vowels meet. The converb of the verb 'to get, obtain', pJ **e-* + pJ **-i*, is thus expected to yield ***i*. The fact that OJ *e* is yielded instead can be explained by the assumption of a disyllabic complex verb pJ *aCi- 'to get, obtain,' to which the converb pJ *-i is suffixed before monophthongization occurs: pJ *aCi- + pJ *-i > *aCi > OJ e. The complex origin of the verb OJ e- 'to exist' is supported by Martin (1987: 681).

A case in which the copula pJ *a- 'to be' appears to take adjectival morphology is that of the nominalizer OJ -aku. Since the nominalizer OJ -aku follows the adnominal form of verbs (e.g. OJ mi_1-r-aku 'seeing') and verbal adjectives (e.g. OJ tura-ke₁ku 'what is trying' < *turaki aku) it is likely to go back to a bound noun. While the deverbal noun suffix OJ -i only nominalizes the preceding verb, OJ -aku nominalizes the whole clause. This suggests that OJ -i is more archaic, while OJ -aku may go back to a more recent formation. From this perspective, Martin's (1987: 805) proposal to derive OJ -aku from the copula pJ *a- 'to be' and the nominalizer *-ku seems to be convincing. The nominalizer -ku derives nouns from verbal adjectives, as illustrated in Section 8.4.1. However, in the light of the adjectival properties assigned to the copula, the deadjectival nature of the nominalizer -ku cannot serve as an objection.

Finally, the Ryukyuan perfect participles preserve evidence of the reconstruction of the copula pJ *a- 'to be'. In Shodon, for instance, we find three participles of the shape -an, -ar, -am that attach to the perfect infinitive base of the verb. This supports their derivation from the existential auxiliary *a- 'exist' followed by an adnominalizer pJ *-n, *-ra or pJ *-m, e.g. Shodon yud-án '(the person) who called' < *yonp- 'call' + *-i CONV + *-ta- PERF + *-i CONV + *a- 'to be' + *-n ADN. This derivation will be discussed in more detail in Section 7.5.1.

Given that Japanese copulae occupy an ambivalent position between verb and verbal adjective and that switched adjective encoding occurs in Japanese (cf. Section 3.2.1.2), we can reconstruct an alternation between verbally encoded pJ *a- 'to be' and nominally encoded pJ *a 'being', the latter of which grammaticalized into the nominalizing suffix pJ *-a hypothesized by Sakakura (1966: 286–303). This ending is preserved in such noun-verb pairs as OJ par- (B) 'open ground, clear land (for cultivation)' → OJ para (2.3) 'field, plain, prairie', OJ tuk- (A) 'build' → OJ tuka (2.2) 'mound, hillock, tumulus', OJ por- (B) 'to dig' → OJ pora (2.4?) 'cave, cavern', OJ nap- (B) 'twist, make rope' → OJ napa (2.3) 'rope, cord' and OJ tuk- (B) 'be attached, come in contact' → OJ tuka (2.3/2.4?) 'bundle'. This probably concerns the same suffix as the exceptional adnominal form on -a in Eastern Old Japanese, e.g. EOJ kayo₁p-a to₂ri (go.over-NML bird) 'birds that go over' (Vovin 2009a: 627).

Martin (1992: 70, 1996: 13, 2006: 222) has compared the Japanese copula to the Korean converb suffix K -e/a, MK -ˑe/a. Many of the Korean monosyllabic high-accent stems that end in a vowel lose the accent in common paradigmatic forms but retain it before the converb ˑe/a. This seems to indicate that the converb was originally a bound stem. Given that Korean copulae occupy an ambivalent position between verb and verbal adjective and that switched adjective encoding occurs in Korean (cf. Section 3.2.1.2), we can reconstruct an alternation between verbally encoded pK *a- 'to be' and nominally encoded pK *a 'being', the latter of which grammaticalized into the converb marker.

Indications that the vowel harmonic alternant ··e developed after the grammaticalization of the copula pK *a- into the converb suffix have been preserved in dialects and early texts. Some Kyengsang dialects use only -a, regardless of the preceding vowel. The earliest Hyangka indicate that this was also the case in Silla Old Korean: OK *kesk-a* 'breaking and' (Hyangka IV: 4), OK *tul-a* 'entering and...' (Hyangka V: 3), OK *el-a* 'marrying and...' (Hyangka VI: 2) instead of the expected **kesk-e, **tul-e and **el-e. In Middle Korean texts we find some instances of ··a in alternation with the expected forms on ··e: MK *ëp·sa* 'not exist', MK ¨*e·ta* 'get', MK *mwu·la* 'inquire', MK ·*tula* 'enter' etc. (Martin 1992: 415).

The verb MK ¨*et-* 'to get, receive' belongs to Class 5, a small class of monosyllabic rising verbs. The rising tone seems to result from the contraction of two syllables. For most of the verbs in Class 5 the second syllable can be traced back to a separate suffix. The front vowel of MK ¨*et-* 'get, receive' may have resulted from the contraction of the copula with a causative-passive suffix *-ti- with front vowel (see Section 6.3.2). The proposed derivation resembles that of the Japanese verb *e-* 'to get, obtain' in the monophthongization of the copula and the use of a causative-passive suffix.

There are no traces of the copula in Tungusic, but a number of contemporary Mongolic languages use a defective copula 'to be', reflecting pMo *a- (Poppe 1955: 74). The copula *a-* 'to be' is used as a productive form in Middle Mongolian and Dagur. In Written Mongolian, not all forms of this copula are used. According to Nugteren (2011: 263), the Dagur vowel length is expected in monosyllables ending in a vowel, but the long vowel in the derived noun Dag *a:dəl*, Mgr. *a:dal* 'life' may support an original long vowel in pMo *a:-. A number of Mongolic suffixes incorporate the copula *a-*. The Written Mongolian praesens imperfecti suffix *-nam*, for instance, is derived from the nominalizer *-n and *a-m, the extinct narrative present of the verb *a-* 'be'. This is reminiscent of the formation of participial forms in the Ryukyuan languages. A semantic problem is the fact that Middle Mongolian reflects the meanings 'to stay, live', next to 'to be' for this form. In line with grammaticalization theory, the primary meaning of pMo *a- should be reconstructed as 'to stay'. However, Kane's (2009: 158) reconstruction of Khitan *a- 'to be' suggests that proto-Khitan-Mongolic already had the polysemy 'to stay, be'. We cannot exclude the possibility that the Mongolic polysemy may have been inherited from the Transeurasian proto-language.

The suffix OTk -*A*- derives verbs from nouns (Erdal 1991: 418–429), e.g. OTk *kor* 'loss, damage' → *kora-* 'to suffer loss, to get destroyed'. Quite commonly, the bases are property nouns, e.g. OTk *kür* 'self-willed, uncontrollable' → *kürä-* 'to desert, make oneself independent' or deverbal nouns of participial origin. The deverbal noun suffix *-(X)n* , which includes adnominal use (see Section 7.5.5.1) is often expanded with the verbalizer *-A-*, e.g. OTk *es-* 'to blow (gently) (intr. / trans)' → *esin* 'a breeze' → *esn-e-* 'to blow (of a breeze) (intr.)'. Erdal (1991: 434) notes: "*-Xn +A-* verbs are also surprisingly numerous, whereas *-Xn+lA-* is exceedingly rare." The predicative nature of most bases, the unique association of *-A-* with *Xn* and the presumed (ad)nominal origin of *-Xn*, suggest that the origin of *-A-* may be a copula 'to be'. This hypothesis is supported by the parallel with incorporations of the copula in complex suffixes in Japanese and Ryukuan and a similar formation in Mongolic (WMo. *-nam* < *-n* nominalizer + *a-* copula).

It cannot be excluded that OTk. *-(A)r-* which derives intransitive verbs from nouns is derived from an original copula pTk **a-* (see Section 3.4.1) and the anticausative suffix pTk **-(I)r-* (see Section 6.6.5).

Kipchak languages, such as Karachay, Balkar, Kumyk and Nogay as well as Khalaj in Central Iran, exhibit a durative participle suffix of the shape *-AgAn*. Khakas spoken in Southern Siberia has *-igAn* and Chuvash in the Volga area has *-AkAn* for this suffix, refelecting a common form pTk **-AgAn*. According to Johanson (2000a: 236, 2005: 153) and Erdal (2004: 252), this durative participle has developed from a combination of a vowel-final converb suffix with the copula 'to be' followed by the habitual participle *-gAn*. Both authors suggest that the ancestor of OTk *er-* 'to be' is involved in this derivation. This would assume the existence of a *-gAn* participle from *er-* besides the petrified conjunction for temporal clauses OTk. *erken*. Erdal (1991: 383) and Johanson (1996: 91) suggest that OTk. *erken* should be derived from OTk. *er-* 'to be' and the habitual participle OTk. *-gAn*. The devoicing of the initial velar /g/ in the habitual participle may be conditioned by the preceding /r/ (cf. Section 7.6.5). The voiced velar in the durative suffix *-AgAn* supports a derivation from a suffix string consisting of converb, copula and durative, in which the copula is pTk **a-* rather than **er-* 'to be'.

The Turkic deverbal noun suffix pTk **-r(V)* can still be recovered in the so-called "aorist" (cf. Section 7.3.5). It is formed by adding *-Ir* to diathetic and some other consonants stems, *-Ar* to most underived consonant stems, *-Ur* to most derived consonant stems and *-yUr* or *-r* to vowel stems. The vowel in the *-Ir* aorist is the result of reanalysis of the original stem-final vowel (Ramstedt 1952: 86, Johanson 1975: 111–112, Erdal 1979b). The OTk *-Ur* aorist may derive from a vowel converb followed by a copular verb **u-* and the deverbal noun suffix **-r(V)*; *-yUr* may derive from *I*-converbs on vowel bases followed by the same copula. Note that OTk *u-* 'be able to' may well have grammaticalized from an original verb meaning 'to become'. In a similar way, the OTk *-Ar* aorist may derive from a vowel converb followed by a copula *a- 'to be' and the deverbal noun suffix *-r(V). This derivation may be taken as the third indication of the existence of pTk *a- 'to be'.

Given the observation made in Section 3.2.1.5, i.e. that Turkic has switched encoding for some property words such as OTk. *ač-* 'to be hungry' and OTk. *ač* 'hungry', it would be plausible to assume that switched encoding was also a feature of the copula. In addition to a verbal encoding *a- 'to be', the copula would have a nominal encoding *a 'being', similar to the situation in Japanese and Korean. The formant of proper names OTk. -A, which derives from nouns, adjectives and verbal imperatives (Erdal 2004: 144) may be a reflex of the nominal encoding 'being'. Assuming that it was further grammaticalized to a deverbal noun and to a converb suffix, the converb suffix OTk. -A may represent the same etymon. This is supported by the non-adverbal functions of the vowel converb in Old Turkic, such as the adnominal use in e.g. OTk. *tikä kulgak-ïn* 'with cocked ears' (Erdal 2004: 308, 312–313).

It follows that a verb pTEA *a:- 'to stay' can be reconstructed. This verb had already grammaticalized into a copula 'to be' in the ancestral language and leaves traces in the polysemy between 'to stay' and 'to be' in Mongolic. Since switched adjective encoding can be reconstructed for the proto-language (cf. Section 3.2.1.2) and since the original copula occupied an ambivalent position between verb and verbal adjective, we can reconstruct an alternation between verbally encoded pTEA *a:- 'to be' and nominally encoded TEA *a 'being' in the original language. This switched encoding for the copula left traces at the peripheries of the Transeurasian area, namely in Japanic, Koreanic and Turkic. Other studies reconstructing a common copula *a- / a:- 'to be' include Poppe 1976: 471, Miller 1981: 852, Martin 1996: 13, 83, 110, 2006: 222–223 and Kortlandt 1997.

3.4.2 pTEA *bɔ:l- 'to sit down, be sitting; become, be'

(54) 'to sit, be(come)'

J *iru* A, OJ *wi-* 'to sit, be' (< *wo + *-(C)i-), J *oru* A, OJ *wor-* 'to be, exist' (< *wo- + *-ra- anticausative), OJ *wos-* ?A 'deign to control/rule/eat/drink/ wear' (< *wo- + *-sa- causative), OJ *wo* focus marking in nominalized clauses of the type O-*wo* S-*ga* V, Shuri *un* 'to be, exist', Shuri *jijuN* 'to sit', Shuri *ir-* A 'to sit', pR *wir-* 'to sit', Ryukyuan imperfect (ad)nominals e.g. Shodon -*un*, -*ur*, -*um*, pJ *wo-* 'to sit, be'

MK -w^u/o- modulator, MK -w^u/o adverbializer, pK *wo- 'to be'

WMo. *bol-* 'become, take place, be, exist; be able, be possible', (SH/ HY/ Muq.) MMo. *bol-*, (IM) MMo. *bul-* 'to become, be; be possible', Khal. *bol-*, Bur. *bolo-*, Kalm. *bol-*, Ordos *bol-*, Dag. *bol-*, Shary-Yoghur *bol-*, Huzhu Mgr. *olə-, o:li-*, Minhe Mgr. *boř-* 'to become', *bər-* 'to be able', Bao. *ol-*, Dong. *bolu-, olu-* 'to be possible, be proper', Mog. *bol-*, pMo *bo(:)l-* 'to become', Khitan **po-* 'to become, promote' (Kane 2009: 112)

OTk. *bol-* 'to become', Karakh. *bol-* 'to become', *ol-* 'to be', MTk. *bol-* 'to become', *ol-* 'to be', Khalaj *ǫl-*, Tk. *ol-*, Az. *ol-*, Gag. *ol-* 'to become', Tkm. *bol-*, Tat. *bul-*, Uzb. *bųl-*, Uig. *bo(l)-*, Sary-Yughur *pol-*, Khak. *pol-*, Shor *pol-*, Oyr. *bol-*, Chu. *pol-*, Yak. *buol-*, Dol. *buol-*, Tuva *bol-*, Kirg. *bol-*, Kaz. *bol-*, Nog. *bol-*, Bash. *bul-*, Balk. *bol-*, Krm. *bol-*, KKalp. *bol-*, Sal. *vol-, vo:-, bo:-*, Kum. *bol-* 'to become', pTk **bo:l-* 'to become'

The Japanese verbs OJ *wi-* 'to sit, be', OJ *wor-* 'to be, exist' and OJ *wos-* 'to deign to control/rule/eat/drink/ wear' are usually derived from a common root followed by the suffixes **-(C)i-* causative-anticausative (see Section 6.7.1), **-ra-* anticausative (see Section 6.6.1), and **-sa-* causative respectively (Martin 1989: 698, 742, 743). The semantics of OJ *wos-* suggest a common semantic denominator 'take possession of', which can be interpreted as the causative of an existential auxiliary. Yanagida & Whitman (2009: 127–129, 134) find that the function of the object marker OJ *wo* in nominalized clauses of the type O-*wo* S-*ga* V is really a focus marker and that its relative position is such that it always precedes the subject. Therefore, they suggest that it has grammaticalized from an original copular verb. Given the switched encoding reconstructed for the copula, the Eastern Old Japanese (ad)nominalizer -o_1 (cf. Section 7.3.1) may be a reflex of the nominal encoding of the copula.

The Ryukyuan languages further support the reconstruction of the copula with independent auxiliaries such as Shuri *un* 'to be, exist' and petrified reflexes such as Ryukyuan imperfect (ad)nominals, e.g. Shodon *-un, -ur, -um* (see Sections 7.3.1, 7.4.1 and 7.5.1).

The original form of the copula is traditionally considered to involve an o_2 and is thus derived from pJ **wə-* according to Frellesvig & Whitman's (2008) analysis. However, it may also be derived from pJ **wo*, because OJ makes no distinction between o_1 (< **o*) and o_2 (< **ə*) after *w*. Moreover, Pellard (2011: 10) advances evidence from Ryukyuan that the original shape indeed was pJ **wo-*. The expected reflex of pJ **wə-(C)i-* 'to sit, be' in Ryukyuan is pR **wer-*. In reality, however, attestations such as Shuri *jijuN* reflect an original pR **wir-* 'to sit' (Thorpe 1983: 328–29), which derives from pJ **wo-(C)i-* 'to sit, be'.

Taking into account grammaticalization theory, the primary meaning of pJ **wo-* should be reconstructed as 'to sit'. We cannot exclude the possibility, however, that the polysemy 'to sit, to be' may already have been present in the proto-language ancestral to Ryukyuan and Japanese.

As proposed by Martin (1996: 13, 83; 2006: 222), the Korean cognate is the modulator MK -·wᵘ/o-. It is a bound stem that attaches itself to other verb stems and is more often than not followed by the (ad)nominalizers MK -(·u/o)m, MK -(·u/o)l and MK -(·u/o)n (Martin 1992: 269–273; Ramsey & Lee 2011: 205–207; see Sections 7.3.2, 7.4.2., 7.5.2). These suffixes may appear either in the modulated or unmodulated form, seemingly without semantic difference. MK ¨wul- 'to cry' and MK kich- 'to cough', for instance, form two alternating deverbal nouns MK wul·wu·m ~ wul·um 'crying' and MK ki·ch·wu·m ~ ki·ch·um 'coughing', respectively. However, some derivations such as MK yelum 'fruit' and MK yelwum 'the bearing (of fruit)' from MK yel- 'to bear (fruit) (tr.)' suggest that MK -·wᵘ/o- is added in sentential nominalizations (Ramsey and Lee 2011: 177). The modulated alternants may well go back to a periphrastic construction consisting of copula and (ad)nominalizer, reminiscent of the Ryukyuan (ad)nominal forms. Note that verb compounding in Middle Korean did not require a converbial form, as it does in Contemporary Korean, e.g. MK pilmek- 'to beg one's bread' from MK pil- 'to beg' and mek- 'to eat'.

Vowel harmonic violations in early texts such as MK te·wo·m 'becoming more so' (1481 Twusi 23: 23a) (< teu- 'become so' -·wo MOD -m NML) 'becoming more so' and MK ·tulwolq 'entering'(1462 Nung 2: 11a) (< ·tul- 'enter' -·wo MOD -lq PCP) suggest that the vowel harmonic alternant -·wu represents a secondary development.

Given the switched encoding reconstructed for the copula, the lexicalised deverbal noun suffix and adverbializer K -wu / -o may be a reflex of the nominal encoding of the copula. This suffix can be recovered in pairs such as K nalu- 'to transport' → nalwu 'ferry', palu- 'be straight, direct' → palwu / palo 'right, directly', ttalu- 'be different' → ttalwu / ttalo 'separately, apart' and tol- 'turn around, circle' → tolwu / tolo 'again, back'. The vowel harmonic alternation seems to have receded in favor of -wu.

Although Benzing (1955a: 120) and Doerfer (1965: 358) suggest a historical connection with pTg *o:- 'to become, make', reflected in Evk. o:-, Even o:-, Neg. o:-, Ma. o:-, Sibe o:-, Jur. o-fia, Olch. o-, Orok o-, Na. o-, Ud. o- / o:- and Solon o:-, we cannot include this form as a cognate because there is no evidence of an initial voiced labial stop and a root-final liquid in Tungusic. As far as the labial lenition is concerned, however, observing that Tungusic lacks words with initial *v- followed by a labial vowel, Doerfer suggests that it went over *v- to zero here. Benzing assumes that the root-final liquid was dropped because it was reanalyzed as the inchoative suffix *-l. Nevertheless, these suggestions remain speculative.

The historical and contemporary Mongolic languages support the reconstruction of pMo *bo(:)l- 'to become', which grammaticalized into a copula or into verbs of ability and possibility. The final vowel in Mangghuer and Dongxiang is epenthetic in nature (Nugteren 2011: 244–245). The Huzhu Monguor form *o:li-* may point to original vowel length in Mongolic. Note that there is no final liquid in the Khitan reconstruction *po- 'to become, promote'.

The historical and contemporary varieties of Turkic support the reconstruction of pTk *bo:l- 'to be(come)'. Vowel length is reflected in Yakut *buol-* 'to become'. There is sporadic elision of initial *b- in the forms with the meaning 'to be' in Old Turkic and Middle Turkic. The *b-* was also elided in the verbs meaning 'to become' in Khalaj, in the Oghuz Turkic languages in the West and in Salar, probably through an intermediate form with *v-*. Sporadic lenition of initial *b- is found in the same geographic distribution for other monosyllabic roots with non-high vowels and final liquids, such as pTk *be:r- 'to give' reflected as Khalaj *ver-*, Tk. *ver-* , Az. *ver-*, Gag. *ver-*, Sal. *be(r)-, ve(r)-, ve:(r)-*, pTk *ba:r 'existence' reflected as Khalaj *va:r*, Tk. *var* , Az. *var*, Gag. *var*, Sal. *ba:r, va:r* and pTk *bar- 'walk' reflected as Khalaj *var-*, Tk. *var-* , Az. *var-*, Gag. *var* , Sal. *ba:r-, var-*. In view of the sporadic lenition of initial *b-, the copular verb pTk *bo:l- 'to be(come)' may be internally related to pTk *olur- ~ *oltur- 'to sit down, be seated, settle down, reside', an etymology that has been proposed by Räsänen (1969: 79, 360). The original verb stems are reflected in the alternation between OTk. *olur-* and *oltur-* 'to sit down, be sitting' and in historical and contemporary varieties reflecting one stem or the other.[19] The underived root pTk *ol- 'to sit down, be sitting' may be reflected in Mongolic copies such as WMo. *olbuy* 'square cushion for sitting, mattress'. Clauson (1972: 150) has proposed to explain the Turkic reflexes of *oltur- as instances as resulting from dissimilation of -l- to -lT-, but it is more likely to regard pTk *ol-ur- ~ *ol-tur- as derivations with the suffixes -Ur and -tUr, which both derive causatives in Turkic (Erdal 1991: 710, 799). Section 6.3.5 shows that the lexicalization of causative suffixes, such as pTk *-t(i)- in Soy. *olït-* 'to sit, be sitting' is recurrent in posture verbs, suggesting the development of valence-neutral meaning such as intensive and progressive-resultative from original causative suffixes. If the posture verbs and copular verbs can indeed be related, grammaticalization theory would lead to the reconstruction of pTk *bo:l- 'to sit down, be sitting; become, be', with static and dynamic posture as the original

---

[19] Karakh. *oltur-*, Tk. *otur-*, Tat. *utïr-*, MTk. *oltur-*, Uzb. *ụtir-*, Uig. *oltur-*, Az. *otur-*, Tkm. *otur-*, Khak. *odïr-*, Oyr. *otur-*, Chu. *lar-*, Yak. *olor-*, Dol. *olor-*, Tuva *olur-*, Tof. *olir-*, Kirg. *otur-*, Kaz. *otïr-*, Nog. *oltïr-*, Bash. *ultïr-*, Balk. *oltur-*, Gag. *otur-*, Krm. *otur-*, KKalp. *otïr-*, Sal. *oht(ir)-* 'to sit down, be sitting'.

meaning and static and dynamic copula semantics 'to become, be' as the secondary meaning.

Given the polysemy of 'to sit, be' reconstructed for Japonic, it cannot be excluded that the grammaticalization from the posture verb 'to sit down, be sitting' into a copular verb 'to become, be' was already under way in proto-Transeurasian. The original polysemy seems to have left traces at the peripheries of the family, namely in Turkic and Japonic. The loss of the final liquid in proto-Japanese-Korean may be explained by the originally monosyllabic nature and long vowel of the verb pTEA *bɔ:l- 'to take a position, become, be'. The same explanation can account for the development of pTk *bo:- 'to become' into Sal. vo:-/ bo:-. Other studies reconstructing a common copular verb pJK *bo- 'to be' or pTEA *bo(:)l- 'to become' include Poppe 1960: 99, Menges 1968b: 145–146, Miller 1981: 851, Street 1985: 639, Kortlandt 1997, Starostin et al. 2003: 372–73 and Martin 2006: 222–223.

3.5 Stability

3.5.1 Notion

A comparative study of verb morphology should ideally include a discussion of both verb roots and verb affixes. This chapter has dealt with verb roots, whereas the following chapters will concentrate on affixes. Out of the 170 etymologies for verbs proposed in Robbeets (2005: 380–395), a selection of 54 etymologies, including verbal adjectives and copular verbs have been discussed here. The similarities among the verb roots encompass formal and semantic correspondences, a category correlation including adjective encoding and a shared structural property, namely mixed adjective typology with switched encoding.

Are these similarities likely to be the result of inheritance, or are they easier to account for by chance, universals or borrowing? Chance similarity can be ruled out on the basis of the regularity and systematic nature of the sound correspondences. The phonological correspondences are regular in the sense that they recur in more than three etymologies including a Japanese participant, within a non-binary setting. They also apply to all subsequent phonemes of the Japanese proto-root except for some instances of the stem-final vowel. Sound correspondences are systemic in the sense that their overall inventory reflects voiced-voiceless opposition, cluster correspondences, a two-fold liquid system, a natural vowel inventory etc.

As far as universal principles of linguistic structuring are concerned, none of the verbs in this chapter are suspected of being nursery terms and only three instances, namely (28) 'break off', (32) 'to hit with force', (3) 'to be(come) round, turn around', may raise suspicion of being sound symbolic. The shared structural property discussed here is unlikely to be determined by linguistic universals because mixed adjective typology with switched encoding is randomly distributed and rather infrequent cross-linguistically, whereas it is geographically concentrated and widespread in the Transeurasian area.

Since chance and universals can be ruled out with relative ease, most Transeurasian scholars – critics and supporters of its affiliation alike – would agree that the similarities must have some historical cause, i.e. borrowing or inheritance. Distinguishing between both determinants, however, is one of the main obstacles to consensus in the Transeurasian field. In this respect, shared verb roots are powerful data because they are particularly stable. Stability refers to the likelihood of an item to have been inherited; it is the tendency to successfully resist both internally and externally motivated change. Thus, stability occurs when there is both a low probability of attrition and a low probability of borrowing. In the following sections, different perspectives on the stability of the evidence are advanced, namely the concept of basic vocabulary, tendencies in the typology of verbal borrowings and specific copy-proof properties of the verbal comparisons under discussion.

3.5.2 Basic vocabulary

One way of testing the stability of the evidence is through the concept of basic vocabulary. Traditionally, the strength of this argument mainly lies in the fact that words with basic meanings tend to resist borrowing more successfully than random lexical items. The basic vocabulary list most commonly used in historical linguistics is the Swadesh 100 list (Swadesh 1955). A shortcoming of the Swadesh list is that it contains mostly nouns and too few verbs. For languages where verbs are basic to word formation and many nouns are derived from verbs, standard wordlists produce therefore too few useful comparanda (Nichols 2014). Such languages are numerous in the Americas and around the Pacific Rim but they also include Indo-European languages (Janhunen 2001: 209) as well as Transeurasian languages.

Recently, the Swadesh list has been updated by the Leipzig-Jakarta list (Tadmor et al. 2010), which partly remedies this imbalance in the vocabulary. Although 62 items on the lists overlap, it is remarkable that many adjectival and verbal meanings that are not part of the Swadesh list, appear on the Leipzig-Jakarta list. The differences between both lists are triggered by the inclusion of factors other than low borrowability such as the degree to which the meanings are universal, the degree to which the words are simplex and the probability of attrition.

If we restrict the evidence to etymologies for verbs and verbal adjectives that have members in at least three different branches of the Transeurasian unity, 13 items belong to the basic vocabulary Leipzig-Jakarta (LJ) or Swadesh (S) 100-list. This can serve as a good indication of the stability of the evidence. Table 32 provides an overview of the relevant etymologies.[20]

Table 32. Basic verbs and verbal adjectives shared across the Transeurasian languages

No	LJ/ S item	Japonic	Koreanic	Tungusic	Mongolic	Turkic
(47)	LJ 3 'go'	OJ in- 'go away' pJ *na-	MK na- 'go out' pK *na-	Evk. -na:- 'go out to' pTg *-na:-		
(M5)	LJ 25 'do/make'	pJ *-ka- iconic	pK *-ki- iconic	pTg *-ki- iconic	WMo. ki- pMo *ki- 'do, make'	OTk. kïl- pTk *kï(-)l- 'do, make'
(32)	LJ 36 'hit, beat'	OJ tuk- 'hit with force' pJ *tuk-	MK ·thi- 'hit, strike' pK *t(ʌ)ki-	Evk. dug- 'hit' pTg *dug-		
(43)	S 56/ LJ 46 'bite'	OJ kam- 'bite' pJ *kam-			WMo. kemeli- 'bite' pMo *keme-	OTk. kemür- 'gnaw' pTk *kem-
(30)	S 84/ LJ 53 'burn'	OJ tak- 'burn (tr.)' pJ *tak-	MK ·tho- / tahi- 'be on / set fire' pK *tʌkʌ-/*taki-			OTk. yak- 'burn (tr.)' pTk *ya-k-
(23)	LJ 70 'carry'	OJ op- 'carry on back' pJ *apa-	MK ep- 'carry on back' pK *ep-	Evk. ewe- 'carry' pTg *ebe-	WMo. eyüre- 'carry on back' pMo eyüre-	
(6)	LJ 76 'be thick'	OJ puto₁- 'be thick' pJ *puta-	MK ¨pwuT- 'increase intr.' pK *pwutʌ-		WMo. büdügün 'large' pMo *büdü-	
(46)	LJ 96 'be(come) wide'	OJ nobi₂- 'spread intr.' pJ *nənpa-	K nelp- 'be wide' pK *nelpʌ-	Evk. nepte- 'spread out' pTg *nepte-	WMo. nebsei- 'be broad/long' pMo *nebse-	
(2)	LJ 99 'be hard'	OJ kata- 'be hard' pJ *kata-	MK kwut- 'be hard' pK *kata-		WMo. qata- 'become hard' pMo *kata-	OTk. kat- 'be hard' pTk *kat-

---

[20] Etymology M5 is discussed in detail in Section 5.5.

Table 32. (continued)

No	LJ/S item	Japonic	Koreanic	Tungusic	Mongolic	Turkic
(25)	S 65 'walk'	J kati 'walking' pJ *kat-	MK ¨keT- 'walk' pK *ketʌ-		MMo. ketül- 'cross, pass' pMo *ketü-	OTk. ket- 'go away' pTk *ket-
(54)	S 68 'sit'	OJ wor- / wi- 'to sit, be' pJ *wo-	MK -wᵘ/o- modulator pK *wo-		WMo. bol- 'become' *bol-	OTk. bol- 'be' *bo:l-
(7)	S 90 'be white'	OJ siro$_1$- 'be white' pJ *sira-	MK ·huy-/ hoy- MK syey- 'be(come) white' pK *si(l)ʌ-	Ma. šara- 'become white' pTg *sia:ra- (<*si:ra-?)	[WMo sira 'yellow'] Copy?	OTk šarïg 'yellow' pTk *sia:rï- (< *si:ra-?)
(3)	S 99 'be round'	MJ maro- 'be round' pJ *maru-	MK mulu- 'turn around' pK *mɨlɨ(-)l-	Evk. murume 'round' pTg *muru-	WMo murui 'curve' pMo *muru-	OTk. bür- 'wind round' pTk *bur-

3.5.3 A typology of verbal borrowing

Basic vocabulary items, such as those discussed, indicate that the similarities in the verb roots are more likely to be due to inheritance than to borrowing. However, tendencies in the typology of verbal borrowing provide yet another indication. Only few descriptive studies, for instance Moravcsik (1975, 1978), Muysken (2000), Wichmann & Wohlgemuth (2008) and Wohlgemuth (2009), are devoted to verbal copies.

Starting from the assumption that a word class is more likely to be copied, if it is copied more frequently in cross-linguistic sampling, it is well known, however, that languages are more likely to copy nouns than verbs. This is not only due to the fact that languages simply have fewer verbs than nouns. In their collaborative study of loanwords in 41 languages, Tadmor & al. (2010: 231) find that "the verb-to-noun ratio is 1:2.5, but the corresponding ratio among the loanwords is 1:5.5. While almost a third of all nouns are loanwords, less than a sixth of the verbs are loanwords." Factors responsible for this phenomenon are discussed in detail in Wohlgemuth (2009: 246–264), but the implication for genealogical linguistics is that verbs are about twice as stable as nouns to begin with.

As far as the mechanisms of loan verb accomodation are concerned, Wohlgemuth (2009: 71, 87–117) distinguishes between three major strategies: direct insertion, indirect insertion and the light verb strategy. In the case of direct insertion, the verbal copy is inserted as such in the recipient language without any morphosyntactic adaptation, e.g. Western Yughur *tay-* << Eastern Yughur *tai-* 'to sacrifice' (Nugteren pc.), Tuvan *ele-* 'to wear out (intr.)' << pMo **ele-*: MMo. *el-*, WMo. *ele-*, Khal, Bur. *ele-* 'to wear out (tr.)' (Khabtagaeva 2009: 260); Tofa *hemne-* << Bur. *χemne-* 'measure' (Kincses Nagy 2006); Eastern Yughur *yayqal-* << Western Yughur *yayqal-* 'to shake (intr.)'; Ordos *dʉǐ-* << Mandarin *duì* 'to be adjusted, to behave properly' (Mostaert 1941–1944: 168b), Even *zvoni-* << Russian *zvoni-t'* 'to phone' (Malchukov 2003: 239); Evenki *vypolńaj-* << Russian *vypolnja-t'* 'to fulfill, carry out' (Malchukov 2003: 238); Manchu *amila-* 'anoint a Buddhist icon's eyes with blood and thereby impart life to it' << WMo. *amila-* 'give live, enliven, animate an image by making strokes on a sacred image, come to life' (Rozycki 1994: 5, 17–18).

Indirect insertion uses a verbalizer of some kind to allow the verbal copy to be inflected, e.g. Chuvash *mešet-le-* << Russian *meša-t'* 'to disturb, interfere' (Kincses Nagy 2006); Turkish *klik-le-* << English *click* (Wohlgemuth 2009: 221); Yakut *mehay-da:-* 'to interfere' << Russian *mešaj* IMP.SG of *meša-t'* 'to disturb, interfere' (Malchukov 2003: 239, 246); Kazakh *zvanit-ta-* << Russian *zvonit* 'to phone' (Kincses Nagy 2006); Uighur *yala-* << Mandarin *ya* 'to escort' (Kincses Nagy 2006); Eynu *χorla-* << Persian *χor-* 'to eat' (Lee-Smith 1996: 858); Western Yughur *darla-* < < Tibetan *dar-* 'to prosper' (Nugteren pc.); Buriat *zvoni:-l-* << Russian *zvoni-t'* 'to phone' (Khabtagaeva 2009: 137); Monguor *čiu:la-* << Mandarin *k'iou* 'to beg, request' (De Smedt & Mostaert 1964: 149); Dongxiang *qifu-la-* << Mandarin *qifu* 'to afflict' (Kim 2003: 353); Eastern Yughur *tugla-* < Tib *thug-* 'to meet'; Udehe *zawoni-la-* << Russian *zvoni-t'* 'to phone' (Nikolaeva 1999: 13, 171), Nanai *voprosa-la-* << Russian *voproša-t'* 'to inquire, question' (Malchukov 2003: 239); Japanese *demo-r-* << English 'to demonstrate' (Martin 1987: 673).

The light verb strategy integrates the verbal copy in a complex predicate, often joined by a native "light verb" such as for instance 'to do' , 'to make', 'to be' or 'to become', e.g. Turkish *klik et-* << English *click (*Wohlgemuth 2009: 221); Karaim *pazdravit' et'-* << Russian *pozdrávit'* 'to congratulate' (Csató 2002: 316); Western Yughur *tuq bol-* << Tib *thug-* 'to meet' (Nugteren pc.); Kazakh *nastroit' et-* 'to tune (the television)' << Russian *nastroit'* 'to set, tune'; Karakalpak *kontrolirovat' et-* << Russian *kontrolirovat'* 'control'; Tatar *mobilizovat' it-* << Russian *mobilizovat'* 'mobilize'; Uighur *fuyin qil-* << Mandarin *fuyin* 'to copy'; Uzbek *zanyat qil-* << Russian *zanjat'* 'to occupy, reserve'; Yakut *zvoni gïn-* 'to ring' << Russian *zvoni* IMP.SG of Russian *zvoni-t'* 'to phone'; Chuvash *organizovat' tu-* 'organize' << Russian *organizovat'* 'to organize' (all Kincses Nagy 2006); Dongxiang *gunzo gie-* << Mandarin *gunzo* 'to work' (Kim 2003: 352); Ñantoq Baoan *dargə-* << Tibetan *dar-* 'to prosper' (Nugteren pc.); K *coking ha-*, J *zyogingu suru* 'to jog' << English *jog*.

Although a few languages simultaneously use both strategies, most recipient languages can be categorized into two clearly distinct groups. As Wohlgemuth (2009: 292) puts it "In the slightly larger group, borrowed verbs arrive as verbs and need no verbalization whatsoever. They are accomodated by Direct Insertion[...] On the other hand there are many languages where borrowed verbs arrive as non-verbs or underspecified for their part-of-speech membership and need formal accommodation, either by verbalization (Indirect Insertion) or by integration into a complex predicate (Light Verb Strategy)."

The Transeurasian languages can be assigned to the second group because they display a clear preference for the non-verbal strategy. Investigating 2 Japanic, 1 Koreanic, 4 Tungusic, 4 Mongolic and 13 Turkic languages, Wohlgemuth (2009: 159, 161) finds the following absolute frequencies for direct insertion vs. indirect insertion vs. light verb strategy: Japonic (1:1:1), Koreanic (0:0:1), Tungusic (2:2:0), Mongolic (1:4:1) and Turkic (2:7:10). The Transeurasian preference for the non-verbal strategy is compatible with the orientation of affixation and basic word order. Wohlgemuth (2009: 205) formulates a statistical universal of loan verb accommodation: "Languages with a basic order orientation of "dependent before head" will, with overwhelmingly more than chance frequency, use the Light Verb Strategy to accommodate borrowed verbs." He also finds that "suffixing languages and languages with "strong" affixation actually show a statistically significant preference to avoid Direct Insertion in favor of Light Verb Strategy and Indirect Insertion" (2009: 202, 294).[21] It is safe to assume that, like their descendants, the ancestral languages of Japonic, Koreanic, Tungusic, Mongolic and Turkic used suffixing, had an SOV order and preferred non-verbal copying strategies.

In the borrowing scenario, the 54 correspondence sets for verb roots advanced above should be explained as direct insertions. This is unlikely because, first, it would go against the assumed correlation between the orientation of affixation and basic word order and the accommodation strategies for verbal copies. Second, it would run against the observable preference of the Transeurasian languages to apply the non-verbal strategy to verbal copies. And, third, assuming that the accommodation strategy of proto-Korean was restricted to the light verb strategy, as is the case in all attested stages of Korean, it would be even harder to explain the Korean members of the etymologies as direct insertions. Furthermore, given the cultural isolation of Japanese speakers, it is puzzling how so many verbs could have been directly borrowed into Japanese without a Korean intermediary.

---

21 Note that the Uralic languages are excepional in this respect because they show a strong preference for direct insertion (13:3:0) (Wohlgemuth 2009: 161).

Across the Transeurasian languages, the examples of direct insertion seem to be restricted to cases of intensive bilateral contact with a high degree of bilingualism such as Even and Evenki with Russian, Mangghuer and Ordos with Mandarin, Tofa with Buriat, Eastern and Western Yughur reciprocally and, Manchu, Yakut and Tuvan with various stages and varieties of Mongolic.[22] This is not surprising because formal accommodation of non-verbs requires more integrational effort than direct insertion of verbs. Wohlgemuth's (2009: 285; Wichmann & Wohlgemuth 2008: 108) assumption that "with an increasing degree of bilingualism, less integrational effort would be required to accommodate borrowed verbs" implies that direct insertions are indicative of intensive contact with a high degree of bilingualism. The borrowing scenario for the Transeurasian verbal etymologies outlined above is unlikely because it would require to set up an intensive multilateral contact situation with a high degree of multilingualism in Turkic, Mongolic, Tungusic, Koreanic and Japanic, for which no evidence has been preserved in the archeological records.

The co-occurence of the three accommodation strategies is only attested for 4 out of 352 verbs, which equals 1.1% of all cases (Wohlgemuth 2009: 148). A good number of Transeurasian languages such as Chuvash, Turkish, Kazakh, Uighur, Dongxiang and Japanese make use of both indirect insertion and the light verb strategy. According to the borrowing scenario for the verb roots above, yet a third strategy, namely direct insertion, should be added to their contact history. This is unlikely because it would assume exceptional behavior for a whole range of Transeurasian languages.

In sum, in a borrowing scenario the above etymologies for verb roots should be interpreted as direct insertion, an interpretation which is inconsistent with (1) the strong preference for a non-verbal copy strategy that can be observed in the Transeurasian languages, (2) the correlation between suffixing morphology along with SOV order and non-verbal copying strategies, (3) the lack of archeological evidence of a prehistorical intensive multilingual contact setting, (4) the probability of co-occurence of the three accommodation strategies for verbal copying.

3.5.4 Copy-proof properties of the verbal comparisons

Although the typology of verbal copies above indicates that it is unlikely for Transeurasian verbs to have been copied through direct insertion, it is possible that some verbs may have slipped the net. In such cases, however, there are still

---

22 The examples of Eastern and Western Yughur, Tuvan, Ordos and Manchu are not mentioned by Wohlgemuth.

a number of characteristics that would betray a set of copied verbs as such. If a set of look-alike verbs has one of the following characteristics, the similarity is not convincing as genealogical evidence.

1. Morphological complexity

When the similarity concerns a morphologically complex verb in one language that cannot be analyzed as such in the other language, it cannot serve as genealogical evidence. A clear example is the correspondence between Ma. *amila-* 'anoint a Buddhist icon's eyes with blood and thereby impart life to it' and WMo. *amila-* 'give live, enliven, animate an image by making strokes on a sacred image, come to life' mentioned above. The Mongolian verb is a denominal derivation from WMo. *ami(n)* 'life, breath' with the denominal verb suffix WMo. *-lA-* (see Section 5.3.3), but this does not hold for Manchu where the underived nominal form is not attested. Therefore, the similarity is indicative of borrowing. Except for etymology (30) 'to burn' there are no cases of shared morphological complexity among the etymologies advanced for verbs above.

2. Secondary semantics

The borrowing scenario is confirmed by the observation that the meaning of Ma. *amila-* is restricted to a Buddhist cultural context, whereas the Mongolian verb has a more general meaning 'to give live, enliven' from which the religious meaning can be derived. When the shared meaning is restricted to secondary semantics, we are probably dealing with a copy. This is the reason why, for instance, the Manchu verb *tala-* 'confiscate, seize property as a legal punishment' has been eliminated from etymology (39) 'to harm, deceive'. All cases of exclusively shared secondary semantics have been left out of the etymologies.

3. Poor distribution

In addition to Manchu, the Tungusic verb *tala-* only occurs in Even en Evenki. When a verb is poorly distributed within an individual branch, it is likely to be a copy. Since the Manchu roots Ma. *duru-* 'to become worn out' and Ma. *sala-* 'to distribute, hand out' and are absent elsewhere in Tungusic, they have been left out from etymologies (10) and (38), respectively.[23] All poorly distributed verbs have been eliminated from the comparisons above.

---

[23] Interestingly, indications for borrowing of verb roots into Tungusic are limited to the Manchu and northern branch. This is not surprising given the preference of these languages for direct insertion (see Section 5.3.2.2). The southern Tungusic languages, however, show a preference for indirect insertion. By consequence, bare verb roots shared by the southern lan-

4. Irregular sound correspondence
Irregular phonological correspondences can also help to unmask verbal borrowings. The Mongolic forms that allow us to reconstruct pMo *kira- 'cut into small pieces, mince' in etymology (41) 'to cut', for instance, are omitted, as they are assumed to have been copied from Turkic. In the case of inheritance, we would expect an initial voiced velar (*g-) in Mongolic. All verbal cognates advanced above correspond regularly for every subsequent phoneme of the Japanese proto-form, with an occasional exception for the root-final vowel.

Extensive contact can nevertheless result in strata of loanwords that exhibit systematic sound correspondences. The strata of loanwords from Middle Chinese that entered both Japanese and Korean during the Tang period (618–906 AD) are known as Sino-Japanese and Sino-Korean, and these strata display regular sound correspondences with Middle Chinese (Miyake 1997: 180). Nevertheless, phonological correspondences in strata of loanwords are the result of model sounds being imitated as accurately as possible within the limits of the recipient's phonology. In contrast, the phonological correspondences between cognates are expected to reflect divergence.

The cognates in etymology (3) 'be round', for instance, reflect a regular sound correspondence between an initial voiced labial stop *b- in Turkic and a labial nasal initial *m- elsewhere in Transeurasian. Words with initial b- in Turkic are usually imitated with initial b- in Mongolian. Old Turkic basa 'also, in addition, once more', which is probably a gerund on -A- from OTk. bas- 'press, crush, oppress', is borrowed into Mongolian as (SH) MMo. basa 'also, then, thereafter' (Haenisch 1939: 13, Clauson 1972: 370, 371, Clark 1980: 39). Only if a nasal follows the first syllable boundary, will there be nasal assimilation in Mongolian. This happens in (SH) MMo. minga(n) ~ minVan 'thousand, military unit of thousand men' which is borrowed from OTk. bïN > biN > miN 'thousand' with the addition of a native suffix (Haenisch 1939: 109, Clauson 1972: 346–347, Doerfer 1975: 33, 1985: 77, Schönig 2003: 405). Since etymology (3) reflects a non-imitative sound correspondence, it is a good indication of inheritance.

The following two characteristics further indicate that the verbal comparisons are relatively copy-proof.

1. Broken contact chain
Code-copying is typically unidirectional and linear, progressing from one contact language into the other and then, perhaps, into the next. Genealogical

---

guages are an indication against borrowing into Tungusic. This observation is relevant for the etymologies (19), (28), (31), (32), (36), (40), (41), (46), (47) and (49).

divergence, by contrast, can be pictured as the rings formed when a stone is thrown into the water: innovations start in the center and push the older forms towards the periphery. This observation explains why some very conservative inherited items leave traces in remote areas, but are barely attested elsewhere in the linguistic continuum. Thus, gaps in the attestation of members of an etymology may be relevant. When the contact chain is broken, a genealogical explanation presents itself. The absence of a corresponding verb in one or more intermediate contact languages can be observed in 21 out of 54 etymologies, namely in (1), (2), (6), (9), (10), (20), (22), (24), (25), (28), (30), (31), (34), (37), (41), (43), (44), (45), (51), (53) and (54).

2. Multiple setting

Most examples of borrowed verbs have a binary setting in common: they typically go from a model language into a recipient language. Examples of the same verb progressing into a third or fourth language are relatively rare, except in prestige settings where one language serves as a lingua franca or dominates many others. The English verb *to film*, for instance, has been exported to many other languages such as German / Dutch *filmen*, French *filmer*, Polish *filmować*, Greek *filmaro*, Hungarian *filmez*, Finnish *filmata* etc. However, even in such settings it is hard to find directly inserted verbs shared over multiple linguistic families. In their database of Old Chinese reconstruction, which is accessible online, Baxter and Sagart (n.d.) find 38 words borrowed simultaneously from Chinese into Tai-Kadai, Hmong-Mien and Austroasiatic. Among these only 3 words are verbs, namely the verbs borrowed from Old Chinese 報 *pˤuk-s 'to repay, to report', 攪 *kˤruʔ 'to disturb' and 白 *bˤrak '(to be) white'. Although these languages represent only 4 families, use direct insertion as the default strategy for verb accommodation, and bear evidence of strong Chinese dominance, which is clearly visible from the archeological records, they have as few as 3 naked verb roots in common. In contrast, the Transeurasian languages represent five families, prefer non-verbal accommodation and, based on the archeological records, do not reflect a unilateral prestige relationship. Hence, it is unlikely that the above 54 verb roots shared across the Transeurasian families should be accounted for by borrowing.

It should be kept in mind that determining the stability of the evidence is a probabilistic matter, depending of the likelihood of borrowing versus inheritance on the one hand, and, of attrition versus preservation, on the other. Even though admittedly it is not possible to unequivocally decide whether the 54 etymologies for verbs above are due to inheritance or borrowing, it is nevertheless clear that various diagnostics of stability, including basic vocabulary, typology of verbal copies and copy-proof properties of shared verbs reinforce eachother. Linguistically, it is far more plausible to attribute the verb roots shared across the Transeurasian languages to inheritance rather than to borrowing. In the following chapters, it will be investigated whether this viewpoint is supported by evidence from bound verb morphology.

4. Negation

4.1 The development of negation and its genealogical relevance

The basic definition of negation in propositional logic is an operator that asserts the falsity of a given proposition. Negation is one of the few truly universal grammatical categories since every language possesses at least one means to express clausal negation, that is a construction that serves to reverse the truth value of an ordinary declarative sentence. Yet the expression of this category varies significantly both from language to language and historically within the same language, the main division being between morphological ('synthetic') and syntactical ('analytic') ways of expressing negation (Dahl 1979). Among syntactic constructions, there are negative particles, negative verbs and negative nouns, whereas morphological negation makes use of prefixes, suffixes or circumfixes (Payne 1985). Miestamo (2005) proposed an alternative distinction between symmetric and asymmetric negation, according to whether or not negative constructions differ structurally from affirmatives in addition to the presence of negative markers.

As far as the historical development of clausal negators is concerned, it is possible to distinguish basically between two grammaticalization pathways, one involving non-verbal sources and the other verbal sources. The phenomenon coined "Jespersen's cycle" by Dahl (1979) – even if the notion of cyclicity in language change may not be entirely representative of Jespersen's thinking – is often representative of the first type.[1] Jespersen (1917: 4) observed a development whereby elements that serve to reinforce negation are reanalyzed as negative markers. A single negative construction such as French *ne*, for instance, is replaced by a reinforced construction with a minimizer *pas* 'step', and subsequently the *ne* is falling into disuse, thus yielding a pattern with just *pas*. This process represents a repetition of an earlier pattern observed in the development from early Latin through to French, in which the original negator *ne* was reinforced by a generalizer *oenum* 'one (thing)', the two elements merging as Latin *non* and phonologically reducing to *ne*. Nominal minimizers and generalizers

---

[1] Note that Jespersen (1922: 424–425) rejected the notion of cyclicity in language change: "Now, it is often said that the history of language shows a sort of gyration or movement in spirals, in which synthesis is followed by analysis, this by new synthesis, and this again by analysis, and so forth... But this pretended law of rotation is only arrived at by considering a comparatively small number of phenomena, and not by viewing the successive stages of the same language as wholes and drawing general inferences as to their typically distinctive characteristics."

are frequent sources for the grammaticalization of negators in the Indo-European languages of western Europe (van der Auwera 2009, 2010; Larrivée 2011; Willis, Lucas & Breibarth 2013).

While Jespersen' s cycle may be the best-known historical pathway for the development of sentential negators, it is not the only grammaticalization process to be found. There is a second type of development, which is less common cross-linguistically, whereby the negators arise from verbal auxiliaries; for a functional perspective, see Payne (1985: 221) and for a formal perspective, see van Gelderen (2008). Among the ultimate sources of these auxiliaries we find independent negative verbs such as negated forms of the copula 'to be', negated existential verbs – a strategy known as Croft's (1991) cycle – or verbs with a negative connotation such as 'to refuse', 'to deny', 'to reject', 'to avoid', 'to fail', 'to leave' or 'to lack' (Givón 2001: 267–8; Heine & Kuteva 2002: 188, 192).

One of the characteristics of the Uralic languages, for instance, is the expression of negation by means of a construction, comprising an inflected negative auxiliary and a non-finite form of the lexical verb. This construction gradually develops in ways, which result in a redistribution of inflectional categories between the negative and the lexical verb until the negative auxiliary becomes totally denuded and turns into an invariant negative particle. According to Comrie (1981: 354), the behavior of negative constructions in the Uralic languages suggests the following universal hierarchy of verb categories: imperative > person / number > tense > mood > aspect > voice. The hierarchy predicts that categories to the right will be the first to transfer to the lexical verb, while categories to the left such as imperative tend to remain as long as possible on the auxiliary.

In Uralic, the inherited pattern of richly inflected auxiliaries is best retained in the eastern Finno-Permic and in the Samoyedic languages. Example (1) from Livonian can be regarded as close to its proto-Uralic source construction because the negative auxiliary is inflected for the categories tense, person and number, while the lexical verb is free from inflections (Honti 1997). The western Finno-Permic languages have limited the extent of inflection such as, for instance, in example (2) from Finnish, in which tense marking is transferred to the lexical base, but person number marking is still present on the auxiliary. Unlike the majority of Uralic languages, Estonian in example (3) has ultimately moved towards an invariant negative particle *ei*. Although Estonian marks tense on the lexical verb, it completely lacks the category person/ number in its negative paradigm. Instead it regularly uses subject pronouns to indicate person and number.

(1) Livonian

> *Lug-iz.*   *I-z*   *lu'G*
> read-PST.1SG   NEG-PST.1SG   read.PCP
> 'I read'   'I did not read' (Comrie 1981: 351)

(2) Finnish

> *Lu-in.*   *E-n*   *luke-nut*
> read-PST.1SG   NEG-1SG   read.PCP-PST
> 'I read'   'I did not read' (Dahl 1979: 84)

(3) Estonian

> *Luge-sin.*   *Ei*   *luge-nud*
> read-PST.1SG   NEG   read-PCP.PST
> 'I read'   'I (you, he/she) didn't read' (Payne 1985: 219, 221)

More common than the failure of a verb category to show in either the negative auxiliary or lexical verb, as in Estonian, is the redundancy whereby a particular category is added to both auxiliary and lexical verb. This phenomenon is especially widespread with the imperative, as in the Votic example in (4), where the second person plural imperative suffix is attached to both auxiliary and lexical verb.

(4) Votic

> *El-ka:*   *lukə-ga:*
> NEG-IMP.2PL   read-IMP.2PL
> 'Don't all read!' (Comrie 1981: 351)

Similarly to Estonian, the Ugric languages express negation with the help of a negative particle. Whereas the negative particles in Ob-Ugric, Khanty *antə* and Mansi *at*, can be derived as invariant forms of an original negative auxiliary, Hungarian represents an atypical development because the source of the negative particle *nem* is an indefinite pronoun 'something' that initially served to reinforce the original negation (Gugán 2012). As such, Hungarian displays an instance of Jespersen's cycle, a development which has been triggered through contact with Indo-European languages and which can be considered as a "change against the grain" in Aikhenvald's (2013) terms. The repetition of similar negative grammaticalization processes on various formally related negative auxiliaries across the Uralic languages, by contrast, indicates that we are dealing with an inherited pattern, which tries to maintain uniformity between the daughter languages.

From this perspective, the diachronic study of negation is a promising topic because the repetition of similar negative grammaticalization processes, both horizontally, across the Transeurasian languages and, vertically, within the same language may be taken as an taken indication of inheritance. Moreover, the observation that a shared diachronic pattern of negation combines with a formal correspondence of the negative markers reflecting the pattern is a powerful diagnostic of genealogical relatedness (see Section 2.5.3.1). In this respect, verbal strategies of negator development are more telling than nominal strategies because of their relative rarity cross-linguistically. The expression of negation via negative auxiliaries is worldwide a minor type to begin with, found in only 40 (17%) out of 240 languages in Dahl's (1979) sample, which is areally biased towards Uralic and Altaic languages, in 45 (4%) out of 1011 languages in Dryer's (2005) sample, and in 16 (5%) out of the 297 languages in Miestamo's (2005) sample. By consequence, the particular development of negative auxiliaries to invariant particles is logically even rarer. If this specific grammaticalization process is found geographically concentrated in a particular region, it is, therefore, unlikely to be the result of universal principles in linguistic structuring or mere coincidence.

4.2 Previous comparative approaches

Three negative forms recur in Transeurasian comparison: *ana-, *e- and *ma-. As far as *ana- is concerned, Ramstedt (1939: 10) already proposed relating the Korean negative adverb *ani* to the Nanai negative noun *ana*, suggesting some connection to the Manchu negative noun *aku:*.[2] Although Miller (1971: 255–285) regarded the negative suffix OJ *-ana-* as a compound of a thematic vowel *-a- and *-na-, he added it to this comparison but rejected the Korean cognate proposed by Ramstedt. The binary comparison of Japanese and Korean cognates, however, is commonplace in the linguistic literature, for instance in Whitman 1985: 244, Martin 1991: 288, Unger 2000a, 664 and Frellesvig 2010: 121. Reviewing Miller's proposal, Menges (1975: 96–110) suggested that it is the so-called thematic *-a- in Japanese that carries negative meaning, which led him to compare

---

[2] According to Vovin 2001: 186: "In the Japanese-Korean comparison suggested by Martin 1966, Manchu and other Tungusic parallels were proposed for the first time." However, Martin does not suggest this Japanese-Korean comparison in his 1966 article, and the Manchu and other Tungusic parallels were suggested almost two decades earlier by Ramstedt.

it with the initial vowel in some Tungusic negative nouns such a Ma. *aku:*, Evk. *a:cin* and Jurchen *a-ĉwi*. This analysis did not prevent him from restoring the Korean negative *ani* as a cognate, deriving it from pK **a-* and an unexplained segment, a suggestion that was accepted by Miller (1985: 38, 49–50). Starostin (1991: 253, 267, 277; et al. 2003: 228, 300) compared the same cognates, starting from a different internal analysis with the reconstruction of the original negatives as pJ **na-*, pK **an-* and pTg **a(n)-*, and further adding the Chuvash prohibitive *an*. This comparison was supported by Robbeets (2005: 414), reconstructing the Japanese member as pJ **an-*. Choi (2005: 42–43) supported a binary comparison between the Chuvash prohibitive and Karakhanide *aŋ / äŋ* 'no, not', on the one hand, and Korean *ani*, on the other. Leaving out the Chuvash cognate, Vovin (2001: 186–87) followed Starostin's (1991) proposal, be it without reference to this study. Recently, Vovin (2008a: 77–78; 2009a: 793) has rejected his former proposal, adding that the negative marker "[...] invites various wild long-range comparisons, for the unrealistic 'Altaic' comparisons, e.g., Starostin et al. 2003: 228, and Robbeets 2005: 414" (Vovin 2009a: 664).

As far as the negative auxiliary **e-* is concerned, Ramstedt (1924b, 1935: 128, 1952: 106) was the first to reconstruct it on the basis of Tungusic and Mongolic negatives. He found a further cognate in the Turkic negative suffix *-mA-*, which he regarded as a compound of a nominalizer **-m* and a negative auxiliary **e-*, an internal and external analysis that has been supported by Menges (1975: 96–110). Ramstedt (1952: 83) further argued that the Chuvash prohibitive particle *an* should be derived from pTk **eŋ*, consisting of a negative auxiliary **e-* and an imperative **-ŋ*. The Tungusic-Mongolic part of his proposal was followed by Starostin (1991: 44, 291; Starostin et al. 2003: 488) and by Poppe (1960: 65, 1972: 122), who later added the possibility of including the Chuvash prohibitive (Poppe 1974: 146). According to Poppe (1977b: 222), the negative verb **e-* 'not to be' is an important feature common to all Uralic and Altaic languages, which can not have been borrowed. Even opponents of the Transeurasian hypothesis, like Janhunen (1996b: 215, 216) seem to agree on this point, arguing that the comparison of the negative auxiliary **e-* between Tungusic and Mongolic is so convincing that "the likelihood of a binary relationship between Mongolic and Tungusic appears greater than within any other pair of adjacent entities." In contrast, Miller's (1971: 280–84, 1985, 37–46) attempt to add a Japanese cognate, i.e. a so-called negative potential pJ **e-*, will be shown to lack plausibility. The same is true for Menges (1975: 100–101) and Martin's (1997: 27) suggestion that the comparison should include a negative prefix pK **e-*, which left a trace in the Korean negative existential verb *eps-* 'not to be'.

Finally, the reconstruction of a negative **ma-* is proposed under different configurations by Ramstedt (1939: 138–139), Miller (1971: 147, 275; 1985: 61),

Menges (1984: 277), Martin (1991: 288, 1996: 77) and Starostin et al. (2003: 228), but their proposals remain speculative, mainly because the suggested morphological segmentation is obscure.

Whereas previous studies have mainly compared the form and function of isolated negative markers, the present approach will integrate diachronic typological considerations into the argumentation. As I will not only attempt to establish the internal progress of a single negative cycle, but I will also try to reconstruct successive cycles of grammaticalization, grammaticalization theory is – as opposed to earlier work – of central importance in the reconstructions. Moreover, I will contrast the areal preference for verbal patterns of marking negation in the Transeurasian region with the relatively uniform Jespersen negation patterns found in western Europe and distinguish it from similar behavior in the Uralic languages.

4.3 pTEA *ana- negative verb

4.3.1 pJ *ana- negative verb

4.3.1.1 Negative suffix

The default negative marker in Old Japanese is the suffix *-(a)n-*, illustrated in example (5). The allomorph *-an-* is used after consonant verbs and after *r-* and *n-*irregular verbs, while the allomorph *-n-* is used after vowel verbs, including irregular verbs. This form is reflected in Eastern Old Japanese and in Ryukyuan as well (Vovin 2009a: 779–792). According to Frellesvig (2010: 154) the Eastern Old Japanese negative suffix has the shape *-(a)nap-*, but example (6a) suggests that the basic shape is EOJ *-(a)n-*, which is occasionally marked with the iterative suffix *-pa-*, as in example (6b). The observation that the negative suffix follows the iterative in Western Old Japanese, while it precedes it in Eastern Old Japanese, indicates that the affixation of the iterative auxiliary **apa-* (reflected in OJ *ap-* 'to meet') and the negative auxiliary **ana-* 'not to exist' took place around the same time in their common ancestor, resulting in two competing forms pJ **ana-pa-* (not.exist-ITER) and **apa-na-* (meet-NEG).

(5) The use of the Western Old Japanese negative suffix *-(a)n-*

ki_1mi_1-ga k-i_1-*mas-an-u*
lord-GEN   come-CONV-deign-NEG-ADN
'You did not come, [my] lord' (MYS XX: 4497; Vovin 2009a: 788)

(6) The use of the Eastern Old Japanese negative suffix -(a)n-

    a. *ak-an-u-wo*
        satisfy-NEG-ADN-ACC
        'since it is not satisfying' (MYS XIV: 3404; Vovin 2009a: 789)

    b. *ap-ana-pa-ba*
        meet-NEG-ITER-COND
        'If [we] continue not to meet' (MYS XIV: 3426; Vovin 2009a: 790)

The negative suffix OJ *-(a)n-* has the allomorphs *-(a)z-* and *-en-*. The negative allomorph OJ *-(a)z-*, illustrated in example (7), is reflected in Eastern Old Japanese as well as in Ryukyuan (Vovin 2009a: 789–792). The allomorphs OJ *-az-* and *-z-* are distributed in the same way as the allomorphs OJ *-an-* and *-n-*. The choice between the allomorphs *-(a)n-* and the allomorphs *-(a)z-* depends on the following morpheme: OJ *-(a)z-* appears only before the nominalizer *-u*, the converb *-u* and the finite *-u*, which is derived from a single form in proto-Japanese (see Section 5.6.1). As suggested by uncontracted examples such as (8), the negative suffix *-(a)z-* probably represents a contraction of a nominalized negative suffix *-an-i* and the verb OJ *se-* 'to do'.

(7) The use of the Western Old Japanese negative suffix *-(a)z-*

    ko₂no₂ mi₁-ki₁ pa   *wa-ga mi₁-ki₁*   *nar-az-u*
    this HON-rice.wine TOP I-GEN HON-rice.wine be-NEG-FIN
    'This rice wine is not my rice wine.' (KK 39; Vovin 2009a: 781)

(8) The use of the Western Old Japanese negative construction *-ani se-*

    ak-an-i   *se-m-u*
    be.satisfied-NEG-NML do-TENT-FIN
    '[you] would not be satisfied' (MYS XVII: 3901; Vovin 2009a: 779)

4.3.1.2 Negative auxiliary

As illustrated in (9) and (10), Old Japanese uses two negative imperative markers with a similar functional range, i.e. one adverb OJ *na* and one suffix OJ *-una* (Vovin 2009a: 569–573, 660–664).[3] Given that the imperative was originally formed on the basis of the bare verb stem, the adverb OJ *na* can be derived as an

---

[3] Note that Vovin (2009a: 569–573) analyzes the preposed negative marker *na* as a prefix rather than an adverb.

imperative form of the existential auxilary pJ *(a)na- 'not to exist'.[4] This analysis implies that in proto-Japanese, the negative auxiliary was preposed to the lexical verb and that it inflected for the category imperative. Note that contrary to Vovin's (2009a: 570–571) gloss of na-ne-sime$_2$ as NEG-sleep-CAUS(INF), the negative imperative probably does not precede the infinitive, but rather the imperative form of the verb. This can be deduced from negative constructions in na ... -so$_2$, encircling the infinitive form of the verb, e.g. na tir-i-so$_2$ (NEG fall-INF-do.IMP) 'Do not fall!' (MYS V: 849). In line with Martin (1988: 967) and Vovin (2009: 569), I analyze -so$_2$ in this construction as a form of the verb OJ s(e)- 'to do', but in my opinion the form is in the imperative, rather than being the verb root. The replacement of negative constructions, by constructions consisting of a converbial form of the earlier negative verb plus a verb 'to do, make' is a productive process in Japanese, Korean (see Section 4.3.2) and Tungusic (see Section 4.4.3.4). While the forms of imperative and converb (so-called "infinitive") coincide for regular vowel verbs, the verb OJ s(e)- 'to do' distinguishes between an imperative so$_2$ and an infinitive si.

Given that na ... -so$_2$ constructions go back to a negative auxiliary in the imperative followed by a the verb 'to do' in the imperative , the negative imperative construction with na can be explained as a negative auxiliary in the imperative followed by a lexical verb in the imperative. This recalls the tendency of the imperative to be redundantly marked, illustrated by the Votic negative imperative construction in (4).

(9) The use of the Western Old Japanese negative imperative adverb na

yasu   i   na   ne-sime$_2$
easy   sleep   NEG.IMP   sleep-CAUS.IMP
'Do not let [my beloved] sleep an easy sleep'
(MYS XIX: 4179; Vovin 2009a: 570–571)

In spite of the problematic high back vowel in OJ -una, the negative imperative suffix illustrated in (10) seems to be formally and functionally related to the adverb OJ na. The marker OJ -una (< pJ *-ona) cannot be a mere phonological

---

[4] In contrast to Middle Japanese, where vowel and vowel irregular verbs take the imperative suffix -yo$_2$, there are examples in Western Old Japanese in which these verbs form an imperative on the basis of the bare verb stem, e.g. OJ ko$_2$ 'come!'. The suffix -yo$_2$ e.g., in OJ ne-yo$_2$ 'sleep!' is an extension of the zero-imperative, which goes back to an exclamation particle. Consonant verbs including -r and -n irregular verbs, form an imperative in -e$_1$, e.g. OJ katare$_1$ 'speak!', which probably derives from the nominalizer in *-i and the bare root imperative of the copula *a- 'to be'.

variant of OJ *na-* or OJ *-ana* because the vowel remains intact after vowel stems, while the initial vowel of OJ *-ana* is dropped in the same environment. This retention indicates that the vowel may have a separate morphological origin, perhaps as a copula pJ **wo-* 'to be', thus OJ *-una* < pJ **-ona* < pJ **wo ana* (be.IMP NEG.IMP) or *wo-na* (be.NEG.IMP); see Sections 3.4.1, 7.3.1, 7.4.1 and 7.7.1.2.

(10) The use of the Western Old Japanese negative imperative suffix *-una*

    a-wo   *wasur-as-una*
    I-ACC   forget-HON-NEG.IMP
    'Do not forget me!' (MYS XII: 3013; Vovin 2009a: 662)

As such, the negative imperative suffix OJ *-una* would reflect either postposed auxiliary or suffix use of the negative. Another indication of the use of pJ **ana-* as a postposed negative auxiliary comes from adjectival negative nominalizations in *-ke₁naku*, illustrated in (11). Since these constructions are retained in only two verbal adjectives, OJ *na-* 'to be non-existent' and OJ *yasu-* 'to be easy', it is clear that we are dealing with archaic formations, even if the formation has left no traces in Eastern Old Japanese or Ryukyuan attestations.[5]

The construction in OJ *-ke₁naku* goes back to the adjectival adnominal form pJ **-ki* (> OJ *-ki₁*) plus the postposed negative auxiliary **ana-* (> OJ *-an-*) and the bound noun **-aku* (> OJ *-aku*), thus OJ *yasu-ke₁naku* 'what is not easy' in (11) derives from **yasu-ki an(a)-aku* (be.easy-ADN NEG-NML). Since the adnominalizer OJ *-ki₁* is a word-final suffix, **ana-* must have had an auxiliary status at the time before the word boundary disappeared through the contraction of **i* and **a* to OJ *e₁*.

(11) The use of the Western Old Japanese negative construction *-ke₁naku*

    nage₂k-u   *so₁ra*   *yasu-k-e₁n-aku*   *n-i*
    lament-ADN   PT   be.easy-ADN-NEG-NML   DV-CONV
    'although even to lament is not easy...' (MYS XVII: 3969, Vovin 2009a: 786)

Note that Japanese verbal adjectives tend to take an analytical negative, except for some lexicalized instances of verbal adjective stems marked by the negative suffix **-(a)na-*.[6] The morphological negative in **-(a)na-* was probably replaced

---

[5] Note that like other existential auxiliaries, *na-* 'to be non-existent, not to exist' tends to preserve traces of archaic morphology; the contemporary Japanese forms *na-ki* and *na-si* 'non-existent', for instance, preserve relics of Old Japanese adjective inflection.

[6] Martin (1987: 817, 1988: 387) lists a number of verbal adjective stems, such as OJ *abuna-* 'dangerous', OJ *wozina-* 'inept, ignorant, feeble', OJ *sepasina-* 'busy' etc., that include an etymological negative suffix **-na-*.

by the periphrastic construction *-ki an(a)-aku, which grammaticalized to OJ -ke₁naku and, in its turn, was replaced by a newer periphrastic construction in OJ -ku arazu. The latter construction consists of a converb form of the adjective, followed by a negative form of the copula ar- 'to be', e.g. OJ puto₁-ku ar-az-u (thick-CONV be-NEG-FIN) '[it] is not thick'.

4.3.1.3 Independent negative verb

Old Japanese uses an independent negative existential adjective na- B 'to be non-existent, not to exist', illustrated in example (12), which is also reflected in Eastern Old Japanese and Ryukyuan. If we assume that initial vowel loss occurred due to prosodic factors, the negative existential OJ na- may be internally related to the suffix OJ -an- and reflect an original independent negative existential verb pJ *ana- 'not to exist'. The internal relationship between the negative adjective and the negative suffix is in agreement with Martin's (1987: 821) analysis that the adjective pJ *na- derives from a defective negative verb, which is also reflected in constructions with the negative suffix. Indications that the original negative verb may have occupied an ambivalent position between verb and verbal adjective come from the observation that OJ na- takes atypical adjective morphology such as final OJ -si rather than adnominal OJ -ki₁ before the locative marker OJ -ni in example (12); that na- is the suppletive negative form of the existential verb ar- in Middle Japanese and; that Japanese existential expressions in general tend to occupy an ambivalent position between verb and verbal adjective (see Section 3.4).

(12) OJ yo₂-k-e₁ku pa   na-si-ni

good-ADN-NML TOP   not.exist-NML-LOC

'As there was no improvement' (MYS V: 904; Vovin 2009a: 464)

4.3.1.4 The development of pJ *ana-

The development of the negative verb pJ *ana- basically passes over three stages. Similar to the development of negation described for the Uralic languages in Section 4.1, Japanese reflects a pathway, whereby an independent negative verb (pJ *(a)na-) grammaticalized into a construction consisting of an inflected auxiliary (pJ *ana-) plus an invariant form of the lexical verb. In spite of SOV morphology, the finite auxiliary originally was preposed to the lexical verb. Gradually, all categories, except imperative marking, became transferred to the lexical verb. Probably for pragmatic reasons, the negative auxiliary was moved to postposed position, where it ultimately fused with the preceding lexical verb to become a suffix (pJ *-*ana*-). Since the synchronic coexistence of preposed negative adverbs and negative suffixes is not unusual from this perspective, Vovin's (2009: 660) assumption of a "restructuring of the language, where the original SVO type morphology is gradually fazed [phazed] out under the influence of the neighboring SOV languages" seems too far-fetched.

In the history of Japanese, negative markers on verbs have been replaced by reinforced periphrastic constructions such as negative imperative OJ *na* ...-*so$_2$* or negative OJ -*ani se*-, consisting of the negative plus a verb 'to do'. Following adjectives, the morphological negative has been replaced by reinforced periphrastic constructions such as pJ *-*ki an(a)-aku*, in its turn, was replaced by OJ -*ku arazu*.

Table 1. Reflexes of the negative verb pJ *ana*- in the Japonic languages

proto-Japonic	WOJ	EOJ	Ryukyuan
pJ *(a)na- independent	*na*- 'not to exist'	*na*- 'not to exist'	*nee* 'not to exist'
pJ *ana- auxiliary	-*ke$_1$naku* NEG NML *na* NEG IMP	— *na* NEG IMP	— —
pJ *-ana- suffix	-*an*- NEG -*una* NEG IMP	-*an*- NEG -*una* NEG IMP	-*an*- NEG -*una* NEG IMP

Table 1 shows reflexes of the negative verb pJ *ana*- in the Japonic languages. As far as the formal reconstruction pJ *ana*- is concerned, it can be argued that the initial vowel in OJ -*ana*- belonged to the negative suffix rather than being part of the preceding verb stem or being a separate morpheme. Current linguistic scholarship (Whitman 1985: 244; Takeuchi 1999: 91, Unger 2000a: 664; Vovin 2003: 168; Robbeets 2005: 158–159; Frellesvig 2010: 112) would mostly agree with Ōno (1953) that the *a*- stem of consonant verbs – the so-called *mizenkei* – is nothing but a surface stem that diachronically reflects resegmentation of suffixes in initial *a*-. For prosodic reasons, this vowel was lost in the negative adjective and in the negative imperative, but it was preserved in -*ke$_1$naku* constructions. The final vowel in pJ *ana*- surfaces in the suffix OJ -*(a)n*- when consonant-initial suffixes are added, such as in the negative-iterative EOJ -*(a)nap*- in example (6b). It is further reflected in the negative auxiliary OJ *na*- B 'not to exist' and in the negative imperatives OJ *na*- and OJ -*una*.

4.3.2 pK *an- negative verb

In Middle Korean, the verbal negator *a·ni* functions as a pre-copular noun, as in example (13a), or as an adverb, as in example (13b). This polysemy is consistent with its derivation from an auxiliary negative verb pK *an- and pK *-i, a suffix that derives both nouns and adverbs from verbs (see Section 8.3.2). As such, the negator derives from a non-finite verb form. It is an invariant particle, lacking traces of original finite inflection.

(13) The use of the Middle Korean negative particle *a·ni*

    a. ¨ma·l-i   a·ni   '·la
        saying-NOM NEG COP.FIN
        'it is not to say that...' (1447 Sek 6: 36a; Martin 1992: 423)

    b. ¨es·tyey a·ni ·wo-no-··n-ywo
        why   NEG come-PROC-ADN-Q
        'Why [the disciple of your master] is not coming?'
        (1447 Sek 6: 29b; Martin 1992: 420)

Gradually, however, the particle *ani* is being renewed by an inflected negative auxiliary MK/K *anh-* 'not to be/ do'. The auxiliary derives from a reinforced negative construction consisting of *ani* plus MK *ho-*, K *ha-* 'to do, be', which parallels the replacement of Japanese negation by OJ *-ani se-* > *-(a)z-* constructions. As illustrated in (11), the negative auxiliary takes full finite inflection and follows the lexical verb *ka-* 'to go', which is in an invariant nominal form.

(14) Korean

    apenim un   ka-ci   anh-usy-e
    father   TOP   go-NML NEG-HON-FIN
    'Father is not going'

Vovin (2008a: 77–78; 2009a: 793) objected to the comparison of the Japanese and Korean negative because "MK infinitives are *-e/-a* not *-i*" and because "the OJ negative suffix *-an-* [...] follow[s] verbal roots, while MK *ani* [...] precedes verbs." However, pK *-i can be assumed to be parallel to pJ *-i as a nominalizer and converbializer (see Section 8.3.2). The second objection can be nuanced by the reconstruction of an originally preposed position for the Japanese negative auxiliary and by parallel formations such as OJ *-ani se-*. Contrary to Vovin's suggestion, Japanese and Korean show a remarkable correlation, including form (pJ *ana-* ~ pK **an-*), function (sentential negator), combinational properties (OJ *-ani se-* ~ MK *a·ni ho-*), source of grammaticalization (independent negative verb) and replacement pattern (by a reinforced periphrastic auxiliary construction).

4.3.3 pTg **ana-* auxiliary negative verb

4.3.3.1 Manchu *aku:*

Manchu makes use of the negative noun *aku:* 'there is no, does not exist, is not here,' illustrated in (15). The examples (15a) and (15b), in which the negative noun is either used predicatively or adnominally and takes a nominal argument, indicate that *aku:* can be derived from an original independent negative verb. The examples (15c) and (15d) reflect the use of *aku:* as an auxiliary, which fused with the *-rA* adnominal form of the lexical verb, e.g., Ma. *bai-ra-ku:* 'I didn't seek' < **bai-ra a-ku:* (seek-ADN NEG-FIN). In (15c) *aku:* reflects finite use of the auxiliary, whereas (15d) reflects adverbial use.

(15) The use of the Manchu negative noun *aku:*

    a.   *ubaci   goro   aku:*
         from.here far   NEG
         'It is not far from here.' (Pashkov 1950 (2): 22; QW; Gorelova 2002: 273)

    b.   *gu:nin aku: niyalma*
         brains   NEG   person
         'a person who has no brains; stupid person' (Gorelova 2002: 273)

    c.   *erge-re-be   bai-ra-ku:*
         rest-ADN-ACC   seek-ADN-NEG
         '[I] didn't seek rest' (Pashkov 1950 (2): 328; Gorelova 2002: 262)

    d.   *muke   inengdari   lakca-ra-ku: eye-mbi*
         water   every.day break.off-ADN-NEG flow-FIN
         'Water will flow uninterruptedly every day.' (SK; Gorelova 2002: 263)

The Manchu negative *aku:* can be derived from an auxiliary negative verb pTg **a:na-* 'not to exist' and the resultative deverbal noun suffix pTg **-xU ~ kU*, reconstructed in Section 8.4.3. Following continuants such as pTg **n*, the allomorph pTg **-kU* was used, yielding Manchu *-ku:* with regular loss of the nasal in Manchu nasal-velar clusters, thus pTg **ana-xu* (not.exist-NML) > **anku* > Ma. *aku:*. Insubordination (cf. Chapter 7) and adverbial use of the deverbal noun suffix (cf.

Section 8.4.3) can account for the adnominal, adverbial and finite function of Ma. *aku:*. The observation that *aku:* is the suppletive negative of the existential predication Ma. *bi* 'there is, there are', which is derived from existential *bi-* 'to exist' plus nominalizer *-i* (see Section 8.3.3.1) supports a parallel derivation for the negative noun, i.e. from an existential verb and a nominalizer.

4.3.3.2 Even *ac, acca, a:n ~ a:ŋ*

In Even, the negative proprietive is formed periphrastically by a prepositional negative particle *ac* and an accusative indefinite suffix *-a/ -e* attached to nouns ending in *-n* or *-la/-le* attached to other nouns. This is illustrated in example (16). The indefinite accusative, also called "partitive accusative" (Benzing 1955b: 56–58, Menges 1968: 63), is nearly obsolete in Even, but it is still commonly used with certain verbal categories such as future imperative and verb negation in Evenki. This indicates that the particle *ac* was originally a derived verb, probably a reflex of the negative verb pTg **a:na-* and the obsolete perfect suffix *-c*, which has left traces in some negative and other verb forms (Benzing 1955b: 94–95), such as in Even *e-c* in (24b). Note that the nasal is sporadically lost in Even and Evenki reflexes of pTg **-nc-* clusters, such as in **xü:nce:n* 'elbow', e.g. Even *iecen*, Evk. *i:ce:n*, Olch. *unce(n)*, Sol. *i:ncẽ:*.

(16) Even   Iwan   ac   nod-la
               Iwan NEG beauty-ACC.INDEF
               'Iwan is not handsome' (Benzing 1955b: 30)

Even also uses of a negative noun *acca* 'there is no, does not exist, is not here,' which is used in (ad)nominal and postposed predicative function, as illustrated in examples (17a) and (17b). Although the doubling of *c* remains unaccounted for, *acca* may be derived from the negative verb pTg **a:na-* and the resultative adnominal suffix pTg **-cA* (Benzing 1955b: 95), the finitization of which can account for the various functions of the negative.[7] Cincius (1975: 41, 60) further mentions negative nouns of the shape Even *a:n ~ a:ŋ* , which probably derive from pTg **a:n(a)-kA* (NEG-RES.NML).

---

[7] Compare Even *ma-ca hulican* (hunt.down-PERF.NML fox) 'a dead fox' and *hulica-m ma-ca* (fox-ACC hunt.down-PERF.NML) '[He] has killed a fox'.

(17) The use of the Even negative noun *acca*

    a.   min   acca-du-w
           my   NEG-DAT-POSS.1SG
           'in my absence' (Benzing 1955b: 63)

    b.   klub-le: kulak-al   acca
           club-LOC big.farmer-PL NEG
           'There are no big farmers in the club' (Benzing 1955b: 63)

4.3.3.3 Evenki *a:cin*

Evenki uses a postposed negative noun *a:cin* 'there is no, does not exist, is not here', in alternation with a plural form *a:ci-r* 'there are no'. As illustrated in example (18), the negative is used in nominal, adnominal and finite functions. Similar to the preposed negative particle *ac* in Even, the non-finite form calls for an indefinite accusative. The indefinite accusative *-(y)A* can be used for indefinite or non-specific objects, or in the designative function, marking that the object is understood as destined for a certain person, to which the possessive marker refers. It shows also other designative functions, such as marking the subject under negation, or an object complement (Nedjalkov 1997: 147; Bulatova & Grenoble 1999: 8–9; Malchukov & Nedjalkov 2010: 12; Kazama 2012: 145). The use of the indefinite accusative in (18a/b) therefore signals a deverbal origin of the negative noun.[8] The negative *a:cin* is likely to have been derived from a verb base reflecting the negative verb pTg **a:na-* followed by the resultative suffix Evk. *-t- ~ -ci-* (cf. Section 6.3.3.2 and the deverbal noun suffix Evk. *-n* with suppletive plural *-r* (cf. Section 7.5.3.3). A morphologically and functionally similar form is Evk. *ece* 'there is no,' which is derived from the negative verb *e-* and the resultative suffix Evk. *-cA*.

---

8 By way of illustration, consider the following examples of the use of the Evenki indefinite accusative (Nedjalkov 1997: 193, 147; Malchukov & Nedjalkov 2011: 12).

(19) a.   *Oron-mo/ Oron-o*   *d'ava-kal!*
         reindeer-ACC/reindeer-ACC.IND catch-IMP.2SG
         'Catch the/a reindeer!'

      b.   *D'av-ja-v*   *oo-kal!*
         boat-ACC.IND-1SG.POS make-IMP.2SG
         'Make a boat for me!'

(18) The use of the Evenki negative noun *a:cin*

    a. *girki-ye*   *a:cin-di*
        friend-ACC.INDEF   NEG-INST
        'without a friend' (Nedjalkov 1997: 100)

    b. *oron-o*   *a:cin*   *beye*
        reindeer-ACC.INDEF   NEG   man
        'a man without reindeer' (Nedjalkov 1997: 99)

    c. *min-du*   *jeptile-l*   *a:ci-r*
        I-DAT   food-PL   NEG-PL
        'I have no food' (Nedjalkov 1997: 97)

4.3.3.4 Udehe *anci, ata-*

Udehe uses a postposed negative noun *anci* 'there is no, does not exist, is not here', which is used in nominal, adnominal and finite functions, as illustrated in the examples in (20). The non-finite form calls for an accusative indefinite, which signals a deverbal origin. Like Evk. *a:cin*, the form can be derived from an original compound pTg *a:n(a)cin* consisting of the negative verb pTg *a:na-*, the resultative suffix pTg *-t- ~ -ci-* and the deverbal noun suffix pTg *-n*. According to the sound correspondences in Benzing (1955a: 983), the expected reflex of pTg *-c-* is Ud. *-s-*, which explains why the Udehe resultative is expressed by *-si*, e.g. Ud. *jawa-* 'take (tr.)' → *jawasi-* 'hold (tr.)'. However, Ud. *anci* may reflect an earlier, lexicalized instance of a resultative suffix. Note that in Nanai the resultative suffix *-ci-* alternates with *-si-*, e.g. Na. *anaci- ~ anosi-* 'push', representing two different stages of palatalization. Word-final *-n* is regularly dropped in Udehe, such as in pTg *palgan* 'foot' reflected in Evk. *halgan* 'foot' and Ud. *xaga* 'paw; bear's trace' or in pTg *pa:kin* 'liver' reflected in Evk. *ha:kin* and Ud. *xa`i*.

(20) The use of the Udehe negative noun *anči*

    a. *exe-ni*   *anči-du-ni*
        elder.sister-3SG   NEG-DAT-3SG
        'while her older sister is absent' (Nikolaeva 1999: 477)

    b. *ńukte-le*   *anči*   *ni:*
        hair-ACC.INDEF   NEG   man
        'a bald person' (Nikolaeva 1999: 477)

    c. *o-du*   *tue*   *ima:*   *anči*
        this-DAT   winter   snow   NEG
        'There is no snow here in winter.' (Nikolaeva 1999: 469)

Udehe further uses *ata-*, an irregular stem of the negative verb in the permissive and the subjunctive (Nikolaeva 1999: 123), as illustrated in example (21b). In other Tungusic languages the non-indicative negative form is derived from the auxiliary negative verb pTg **e-* and the subjunctive-permissive marker pTg **-tA*, e.g. Neg. *o-to-*, Evk. *e-te:-*, Even *e-te:-*. This derivation pattern strongly suggests that *ata-* represents an earlier formation, consisting of similar elements, i.e. the earlier auxiliary negative verb pTg **a:na-* and the same subjunctive-permissive marker.

(21) The use of the Udehe negative subjunctive *ata-*

    a.   *diga-ta-mi*
          eat-SUBJ-1SG
          'I will perhaps eat'

    b.   *ata-mi*   *diga*
          NEG-1SG   eat.ADN
          'I will perhaps not eat'

4.3.3.5 Nanai *ana* ~ ana:

Nanai uses a postposed negative noun *ana ~ ana:* 'there is no, does not exist, is not here', which is used in nominal, adnominal and finite functions, as illustrated in the examples in (22). The negative does not require an accusative indefinite. Given the Orok cognate *ana ~ anaga*, the Nanai alternant with length on the final vowel may indicate contraction of the negative verb pTg **a:na-* with a resultative deverbal noun suffix pTg **-xA* (see Section 7.6.3). The eventual finitization of pTg **-xA* may account for the various functions of the negative noun.

(22) The use of the Nanai negative noun *ana*

    a.   *miocan   ana-ji*
          gun   NEG-INST
          'without a gun' (Avrorin 1959: 245)

    b.   *simata   ana   tue*
          snow   NEG   winter
          'a winter without snow' (Avrorin1961: 260)

    c.   *si   sasango   ana-si-nu?*
          you   firewood   NEG-POSS.2SG-Q
          'Don't you have firewood?' (Avrorin 1959: 245)

4.3.3.6 The development of pTg *a:na-

The Tungusic languages have preserved evidence supporting the reconstruction of an auxiliary negative verb pTg *a:na-. In many languages, the negative noun calls for an accusative indefinite, which signals a deverbal origin. This view is consistent with the analysis summarized in Table 2, which derives the various negative nouns from a single negative auxiliary followed by formally distinct resultative noun suffixes and the negative subjunctive auxiliary in Udehe from a negative verb plus subjunctive suffix. It is further supported by parallel formations on the basis of the negative auxiliary *e-. The nominal, adnominal and finite uses of the negative nouns can be understood in the light of the finitization process associated with deverbal nominalizers.

Table 2. Reflexes of the auxiliary negative verb pTg *a:na- in the Tungusic languages

pTg *a:na-	Manchu	Even	Evenki	Udehe	Nanai
+ *-xU RES.NML	aku: negative noun				
+ *-xA RES.NML		a:n ~ a:ŋ negative noun			ana ~ ana: negative noun
+ *-c PERF.NML		ac negative noun			
+ *-ca RES.NML		acca negative noun			
+ *-ci-n RES-NML			a:cin negative noun	anci negative noun	
+ *-ta- SUBJ/PERM				ata- SUBJ/PERM negative	

As far as the formal reconstruction pTg *a:na- is concerned, the nasal loss in Manchu, Even and Evenki represents the expected outcome. Other Tungusic reflexes of a nasal in the negative noun are Oroch *ana*, Olcha *ana*, Orok *ana* ~ *anaya*, Nanai *anaa*. The negative nouns Evenki *a:cin* and Negidal *a:cin* preserve original vowel length.

The preposed use of Even *ac* and Ud. *ata-* indicates the gradual movement of the Tungusic negative auxiliary from a preposed to postposed position, paralleled by the development of the negative auxiliary pTg *e-, discussed in Section 4.4.3 below.

4.4 pA *ə- negative verb

4.4.1 No evidence for pJ *e-

Miller (1971: 280–84, 1985: 37–46) proposes reconstructing a negative verb pJ *e- on the basis of the occurrence of the potential prefix OJ e- in negative constructions, as illustrated in (23). However, the internal evidence he offers for considering this prefix as a redundant negative is rather weak: the prefix only expresses negative meaning in combination with a negative suffix; it is used as a positive potential as well; and it can be diachronically derived from a converb form of the verb OJ u 'to get, obtain'.

(23) OJ mi_1-ato_2-sura-wo   ware pa   e-mi_1-z-u-te
     HON-footprint-PT-ACC   I TOP   POT-see-NEG-NML-CONV
     'I was not able to see even the footprint of the Buddha and'
     (BS 3; Vovin 2009a: 594)

4.4.2 Insufficient evidence for pK *e-

The only evidence for the reconstruction of a negative prefix pK *e- comes from the existential verb pair K iss- 'to be, exist' and eps- 'not to be, be nonexistent, lack'. The Middle Korean reflex of the existential verb is MK is- ~ is(i)- 'to be, exist, stay' with a contractile dissyllabic vowel stem that is still present in nominalized stems such as MK isi-lq, isi-m and isi-n, which enables us to reconstruct pK *isi- 'to be, exist' with a disyllabic root. Ramstedt (1939: 56), Menges (1975: 100–101) and Martin (1997: 27) have proposed deriving the negative existential from its affirmative counterpart prefixed by a negative marker. This leads Martin to reconstruct the negative pK *e- and the existential pK *pisi- 'to exist' on the basis of its negative counterpart MK ¨eps- < *e-pisi-. Even if pK *pisi- 'to exist' would provide a clear parallel with the Tungusic copula pTg *bi-si- (be-ADN; cf. Section 7.7.3), this would not explain the disappearance of the initial *p- in pK *isi- 'to be, exist'. Although copular verbs are expected to preserve traces of obsolete morphology, it remains speculative to reconstruct a negative prefix pK *e- on the basis of a single verb pair.

4.4.3 pTg *e- negative verb

4.4.3.1 Even e-
The Even negative verb *e*- acts as a finite auxiliary to the lexical verb, which assumes an invariant participial – adnominal or so-called "aorist" – form, for example in (24). The negative auxiliary is marked with most of the basic categories (non-finite/ finite, mood, tense, person-number), except for actionality and diathesis, which is marked on the lexical verb, as illustrated in (24c). The negative auxiliary precedes the lexical verb but may also be separated from the latter by objects or adverbials as in (24a).

(24) The use of the Even negative auxiliary *e*-

    a.   oro-r   e-s-ten   tiwsen   ongka-r
        reindeer-PL NEG-FIN-POSS.3PL quietly   graze-ADN
        'The reindeers don't graze quietly' (Benzing 1955b: 86)

    b.   tarakam   sowet engi-n   e-c   bi-s
        back.then   soviet force-POSS.3SG NEG-PERF.FIN be-ADN
        'Back then the Soviet regime did not exist' (Benzing 1955b: 94)

    c.   e-se-m   ma-p-ta
        NEG-FIN-1SG   kill-REFL-ADN
        'I did not kill myself' (Benzing 1955b: 86)

4.4.3.2 Evenki e-
The Evenki negative verb *e*- acts as a finite auxiliary to the lexical verb, which assumes an invariant participial – adnominal or so-called "aorist"– form (Nedjalkov 1994: 8–27; Nedjalkov 1997: 96–99). The auxiliary negative verb is marked with most of the inflectional categories (non-finite/ finite, mood, tense, person-number), but the lexical verb may take derivational markers such as actionality, diathesis, modality and evaluation, as illustrated by the causative marking on the verb 'to go away' in (25b). The negative auxiliary precedes the lexical verb, and may also be separated from the latter by objects or adverbials. In emotive sentences, however, it may follow the lexical verb, as is the case in (25c). There are some examples of independent use of the negative verb, i.e. without a lexical verb, in the meaning of 'not to be, not to exist, not to live' as in (25a).

(25) The use of the Evenki negative verb *e-*

    a. *esile e-dyeli-m   tadu-gla*
         now   NEG-FUT-1SG there-ENCL
         'Now I will not be (live) there' (Nedjalkov 1994: 27)

    b. *nungan nekun-mi   e-ce-n   suru-v-re.*
         he   younger.brother-POSS.REFL NEG-PST-3SG go.away-CAUS-ADN
         'He did not lead his younger brother away.' (Nedjalkov 1994: 11)

    c. *nungan songo-ro e-ce-n*
         he   cry-ADN   NEG-PST-3SG
         'He did not cry [— what's the use of crying?]' (Nedjalkov 1994: 8)

4.4.3.3 Udehe *e-*

The Udehe negative auxiliary *e-* acts as a finite auxiliary to the lexical verb, which assumes an invariant form. The invariant form of the lexical verb is synchronically analysed as "the bare verbal stem" by Nikolaeva (1999: 124–125), but diachronically it is derivable from the adnominal Tungusic "*-rA aorist" (see Section 7.3.3). As illustrated in (26), the auxiliary negative verb is marked with most of the basic categories (temporal, aspectual, modal) and precedes the lexical verb.

(26) The use of the Udehe negative auxiliary *e-*

    sin-tigi   e-zenge-i   dian-a
    you-LAT   NEG-FUT-1SG say-ADN
    'I won't tell you' (Nikolaeva 1999: 125)

4.4.3.4 Nanai negative

In Nanai, the auxiliary negative verb is commonly reduced to a suffix on the lexical verb, as illustrated in (27). The lengthened form Na. *xola:-* in (27b) can be derived from **xola-ra-e-* (read-ADN-NEG-), a contraction of the adnominal "aorist" form and the negative marker. The suffix is used in both predicative constructions such as in (27b) as in adnominal constructions such as in (27c).

(27) The use of the Nanai negative suffix

    a. *xola-xa-si*
         read-PST-2SG
         'You read'

b. xola:-ci-si
    read.NEG-PST-2SG
    *xola-ra   e-ci-si
    read-ADN   not.exist-PST-2SG
    'You didn't read'

c. xola:-cin   naoṅjokan
    read.NEG-PFV.ADN   boy
    *xola-ra   e-ci-n   *naoṅjokan
    read-ADN   not.exist-PFV-ADN   boy
    'a boy who did not read' (Menges 1968: 236)

An alternative way of expressing sentential negation in Nanai consists in the use of preposed negative particles, but these expressions are restricted to adnominal constructions such as in (28) or to predicative future constructions such as in (29). There are two negative particles, one is the imperfective *em*, illustrated in (29), the other the perfective *ecie* in (28). The perfective negative particle *ecie* derives from the negative auxiliary **e-* plus the resultative-perfective pTg **-ci-* and the adnominal **-rA*. The original auxiliary has thus petrified as an invariant past particle maintaining its original perfective and adnominal inflection, whereas the lexical verb remains in an invariant adnominal form. The imperfective negative particle *em*, which derives from the negative auxiliary **e-* and the converb suffix **-mi* (Section 7.4.3.5) is restricted to reinforced periphrastic constructions in combination with the verb *ta-* 'to do, make'. As such, *em* goes back to an inflected auxiliary in a converbial form, governing a postposed lexical verb in an invariant form. Note that the replacement by the *em ta-* periphrastic construction is remarkably parallel to the replacement by OJ *na ... -so₂, -ani se-* and MK *a·ni ho-* constructions.

(28) The use of the Nanai perfective negative particle *ecie*

   ecie   xola: naoṅjokan
   PST.NEG   read.ADN   boy
   *e-ci-re   *xola-ra   *naoṅjokan
   not.exist-PFV-ADN   read-ADN   boy
   'a boy who didn't read' (Menges 1968: 238)

(29) The use of the Nanai negative particle *em*

   si   em   xola: ta-ja:-si
   you   NEG   read.ADN   do-FUT-2SG

*si   *e-mi   *xola-ra   *ta-ja:-si
you   not.exist-CONV   read-ADN   do-FUT-2SG
'You will not read' (Menges 1968: 239)

Traces of the original preposed auxiliary negative verb can further be found in the negative imperative *eji*, which derives from the negative auxiliary **e-* plus the imperative second singular suffix *-ji*. As illustrated in (30a), the lexical verb is in an invariant form, derived by the uncontracted adnominalizer *-rA*. In the plural imperative, illustrated in (30b), the adnominalizer contracts with the lexical base and takes second plural possessive marking.

(30) The use of the Nanai negative imperative *eji*

    a.   *eji*   *xola-ra*
         NEG.IMP   read-ADN
         *e-ji   **xola-ra*
         'Don't read!' (Menges 1968: 239)

    b.   *eji*   *xola:-su*
         NEG.IMP   read.ADN-POSS.2PL
         *e-ji   **xola-ra-su*
         not.exist-IMP.2SG   read-ADN-POSS.2PL
         'Don't all read!' (Menges 1968: 239)

4.4.3.5 Overview

The Tungusic languages have preserved evidence supporting the reconstruction of an negative verb pTg **e-* 'not to be, not to exist, to lack'. As an auxiliary, the form is widely distributed in the northern Tungusic languages, e.g. Evk. *e-*, Even *e-*, Neg. *e-*, Sol. *e-*, as well as in the southern, e.g. Na. *e-*, Olcha *e-*, Orok *e-*, Ud. *e-* and Oroch *e-*, but is absent in Manchu. However, its predecessor Jurchen preserves traces in the negative nouns *ei-xe* and *esi(n)* (Starostin et al. 2003: 488). Since some languages such as Evenki preserve evidence for independent use of the negative existential verb in the sense of 'to live, to exist', it can be assumed that the independent negative verb, taking nominal arguments was the ultimate source of grammaticalization for the negative auxiliary, taking verbal arguments.

    The basic Tungusic pattern of sentential negation, reflected in Even, Evenki and Udehe, consists of an negative auxiliary followed by a lexical verb in an invariant adnominal form. Inflectional categories such as tense, mood, person and number markings are carried by the negative auxiliary, whereas derivational categories such as actionality and diathesis are indicated by the lexical verb. When undergoing grammaticalization in preposed position, the auxiliary gradually transferred its inflections to the lexical base, starting with categories to the left of Comrie's hierarchy, discussed in Section 4.1. In Orok, for instance, the negative auxiliary can optionally transfer its function as person-number carrier to the lexical verb; see example (31). Moreover, in line with Comrie's hierarchy, imperative was retained as long as possible on the auxiliary, for instance in the Nanai negative imperative. Since prefixing is very rare in the Tungusic languages, preposition of auxiliaries inhibited affixation and the ultimate target of this grammaticalization process, therefore, was preposed invariant negative particles, such as Nanai *ecie* and *em*.

(31) Optional transfer of inflections in Orok

    a.   *si*   *e-ci-si*   *bu:-ra*
         you NEG-PST-2SG give-ADN

    b.   *si*   *e-cil*   *bu:-ra-si*
         you NEG-PST give-ADN-2SG
         'You didn't give' (Payne 1985: 214)

Alternatively, the mobility of the negative auxiliary within the sentence, as in emotive sentences in Evenki, could make room for postposed use of the auxiliary. In contrast to preposed auxiliaries, postposed auxiliaries were free to fuse with the lexical verb and ultimately they became a suffix on the verb stem, as in the Nanai negative suffix. It has been pointed out that in Nanai, where morphologically compact processing by way of lengthening has weakened the visibility of negation, new reinforced periphrastic negative constuction are replacing the earlier synthetic ones.

A similar grammaticalization process similar to the one described here may have occurred earlier, leading to the development of the negative pTg **ana-* from an independent verb to an auxiliary and, eventually to a suffix. Since strongly grammaticalized units tend to be replaced by new lexemes, it is likely that the morphological negative expressed with **-ana-* was replaced by a new periphrastic negative construction with **e-*. The worn-out negative on **-ana-* completely disappeared as a verbal category, but it petrified in some composite forms, such as the negative nouns discussed above. In this way, we can reconstruct an evolutionary cycle of grammaticalization and replacement, known as "cyclic grammaticalization".

4.4.4 pMo *e- negative verb

4.4.4.1 Negative particle

Written Mongolian and Middle Mongolian use a preposed negative adverb *ese* (Poppe 1954: 175, 1955: 287), which may go back to a resultative nominalization of an original negative auxiliary **e-* (Sanžeev 1962: 280; Bese 1974: 7). For the reconstruction of the resultative nominalizer pMo **-sa*, **-si*, see Section 7.7.4. The examples in (32) illustrate the negative auxiliary in its invariant form, while all inflection is attached to the lexical verb.

(32) The use of the Written Mongolian negative particle *ese*

    a.   ese   ire-gsen   kümün
         NEG   come-PERF.ADN   person
         'a person who did not come' (Poppe 1954: 175)

    b.   manu   bayši   ese   ire-be
         our   teacher   NEG   come-PST
         'Our teacher did not come' (Poppe 1954: 175)

4.4.4.2 Independent negative verb

The negative adverb *ese* goes back to a verb stem *ese-*, which has lexicalized into a few conjugated forms, such as *esekü* 'not being like that' with the imperfective nominalizer *-KÜ*, *esegsen* 'that has not been like that' with the perfective nominalizer *-GsEn*, *esebe* 'was not like that' with the past tense *-bA*, *esebesü* 'if it is not like that, if not' with the conditional converb *-bAsU* and *esebečü* 'although it is like that, nevertheless' with the concessive converb *-bAčU*. Examples (33a/b) show that, contrary to the examples (32a/b) above, the verb stem *ese-* has the same clause status as the lexical verb that it accompanies. Not taking any verbal argument, it is used as an independent lexical verb with the meaning 'not to be (in the state resulting from the preceding verb)'. The original resultative suffix **-se* may be used to express the semantic component 'in the state resulting from the preceding verb'.

(33) The use of the Written Mongolian negative verb *ese-*

    a.   WMo.   ire-gsen   ese-gsen-i   ülü   mede-müi
                  come-PERF.ADN   NEG-PERF.ADN-ACC   NEG   know-PRES
                  '[We] do not know whether he came or not' (Poppe 1954: 175)

b. WMo. *ükü-be-üü ese-be-üü*
   die-PST-Q   NEG-PST-Q
   'Did [he] die or did [he] not?' (Poppe 1954: 175)

The negative verb **e-* 'not to be(come), be(come) non-existent, come to lack' may have lexicalized in the verbs WMo. *eče-* 'to become lean, thin, gaunt; become exhausted or tired (intr.)' and WMo. *ele-* 'to wear out (as by attrition) (tr.)', if these are regarded as derivations with the progressive *-čA-* and the intensive-iterative *-lA-*, respectively.[9] The verb WMo. *ečül-* 'to end, cease, stop, cease to exist, come to an end, be destroyed, die (intr.)' seems to be related to the same negative root **e-*, but the identity of **-čül-* remains unclear.

4.4.4.3 The development of pMo **e-*

The Mongolic languages have preserved evidence for reconstructing an auxiliary negative verb pMo **e-* 'not to exist'. Lexicalizations of derived verbs and of a few conjugated negative forms show that pMo **e-* was used as an independent negative verb, taking nominal arguments as well as derivational and inflectional morphology. The original Mongolic pattern for verbal negation may well have consisted in a fully inflecting negative auxiliary followed by a lexical verb in an invariant adnominal form. By the time of Middle Mongolian, however, all inflections were transferred to the lexical verb, leaving the adverb *ese* as a denuded, invariant form, a development which recalls example (3) from Estonian.

In the process of cyclic grammaticalization, the strongly grammaticalized *ese* construction may have been gradually replaced by a new periphrastic negative construction with the negative auxiliary pMo **ü-*. Traces of this form can be found in negative nouns such as MMo./ WMo. *ügei* and MMo./ WMo. *ülü* (Poppe 1954: 174), which can be derived from a negative auxiliary followed by a persistent perfect nominalizer and a perfect respectively (Ramstedt 1903: 81, Bese 1974: 4). The negative existential *iú-* 'not to exist, to die' reconstructed for Khitan by Kane (2009: 157) may be related here.

---

9 The progressive suffix *-čA-* is used to derive continuous action, e.g. WMo. *ergi-* 'to turn or move around' → *ergiče-* 'to keep going or coming back, make rounds', WMo. *selgü-* 'to change, alternate, shift, take turns' → *selgüče-* 'to go from place to place, replace each other by turns, crisscross (of tracks or footprints)', WMo. *orki-* 'to throw, cast away (tr.)' → *orkiča-* 'to bandy, toss to and from (as a ball) (tr.)' etc. The intensive-iterative suffix *-lA-* is used for intense or repeated actions, e.g. WMo. *büle-* 'to stick, stab' (tr.)' → *bülele-* 'stab repeatedly, churn (tr.)', WMo. *ili-* 'to caress, stroke with one's hand (tr.)' → *ilile-* 'to pet, stroke repeatedly', WMo. *orki-* 'to throw out, cast away (tr.)' → *orkila-* 'to scatter, throw about without order, litter (tr.)' etc.

4.4.5 pTk *e- auxiliary negative verb

4.4.5.1 Karakhanide *aŋ / eŋ* 'no, not'
Mahmud al-Kašγari's 'Compendium of the Turkic languages' mentions a negative interjection and particle *eŋ* in alternation with *aŋ* meaning 'no, not'. According to Kašγari's lexicon, this interjection was used in Oghuz Turkic: when a man is given an order he says *eŋ eŋ* or *aŋ aŋ* 'no, no' (DLT (1): 40; Clauson 1972: 165; Choi 2005: 42–43).

4.4.5.2 Chuvash *an* prohibitive
Chuvash uses a negative particle *an* in the second and third persons of the prohibitive mood, as illustrated in Table 3. In reality, the second person forms in this paradigm are imperatives, whereas the first persons can be regarded as optatives and the third persons as voluntatives (Johanson pc.). Unlike optatives and voluntatives, imperatives give direct commands, so their subject is always the addressee, i.e. the second person. This may explain why the bare stem *vula* is used in the second person singular imperative.[10] Since the imperative plural *vulăr* 'read!' includes the second plural possessive suffix *-ăr* (e.g. *ača* 'child' → *ač-ăr* 'your (PL) child'), it probably derives from an optative nominalization **vula-a-ăr* (read-OPT.NML-POSS.2PL); for the optative in *-A* see Section 7.6.5.2. Note that this derivation of the imperative plural recalls a similar formation in Nanai in (30b). The voluntatives carry a marker *-tĂr* or *-ččĂr* that has no connection with third person endings, but may be related to the Chuvash causative suffixes *-tAr-* and *-ttAr-* (Benzing 1959: 721). If this morphological analysis is correct, the voluntatives would go back to imperative causative constructions, e.g. *vulatăr* 'let [somebody] read!', *vulaččăr* 'let [somebody] read!' and *an* would be the negative imperative marker. This would explain why the second and third persons of the so-called "prohibitive" share a single negative marker *an* ('Do not have the reading!' = 'Don't read!'; 'Do not have the causation of the reading!' = 'Let him not read!'), while the first person uses the finite form *mar* of the negative verb ('My optative reading does not exist' = 'I will not read'). Note that the redundant marking of the imperative on the auxiliary and on the lexical is a recurrent phenomenon, see example (4) from Votic and (9) from Old Japanese.

Johanson (2002a: 76) suggested that the Chuvash negative particle *an* may have been copied from Finno-Ugric, the first high-contact language that comes to mind being Mari (Cheremis). However, the closest match would be *ana* the

---

10 Note that athematic stems such as Chu. *pïtan-* 'to hide oneself' form an athematic imperative *pïtan* 'Hide yourself!', which shows that the imperative is the bare stem.

first person plural of the negative auxiliary of the present indicative in Western Mari.[11] Since Chuvash *an* is absent in the first person and since it is used in the imperative rather than the indicative, Mari *ana* is unlikely to have served as a model for Chuvash *an*. Johanson (pc. 12.03.2010) now agrees that the internal analysis suggested here is much more promising.

Table 3, The prohibitive mood in Chuvash (Krüger 1961: 158–159) and its possible derivation

		vula- 'to read'		
1SG	*vulam mar* 'I will not read'		1PL	*vular mar* 'we will not read'
2SG	*an vula* *a-n *vula NEG-IMP read.IMP 'do not read!'		2PL	*an vulăr* *a-n *vula-a-ăr NEG-IMP read-OPT.NML-2PL.POSS 'do not all read!'
3SG	*an vulatăr* *a-n *vula-tar NEG-IMP read-CAUS.IMP 'let him not read'		3PL	*an vulaččăr* *a-n *vula-ttar NEG-IMP read-CAUS.IMP 'let them not read'

As noted in Section 4.2, previous studies have tried to derive Chuvash *an* from a proto-Turkic negative *an, but this is very unlikely given the fact that Chuvash *a* corresponds to OTk *e* and derives from pTk *e rather than *a, e.g. OTk *sev-*, Chu. *sav-* < pTk **seb-* 'to love', OTk *ber-*, Chuv *par-* < pTk **be:r-* 'to give', and OTk *ev*, Chu. *av-la-n-* 'to marry' < pTk *eb 'house'. Furthermore, Chuvash *-n* corresponds to OTk -*ŋ*, for instance in OTk *teriŋ*, Chu. *tarăn* < pTk *teriŋ 'deep' and MTk *seŋ*, Chu. *san* < pTk *seŋ 'frazil'. Therefore, the expected regular correspondence for Chuvash *an* in Old Turkic is *eŋ*, reflecting pTk *eŋ.

Given the attestation of an imperative suffix -*ŋ* in Old Turkic, illustrated in (34), it is tempting to analyze the negative imperative pTk *eŋ as a compound of a negative auxiliary **e-* and this imperative suffix, a suggestion made earlier by Ramstedt (1952: 83) and Poppe (1974: 146).

(34) The use of the Old Turkic imperative suffix -*ŋ*

kod-ma-ŋ-lar
put-NEG-IMP-PL
'don't put!' (DLT fol.289; Erdal 2004: 235)

---

11 The conjugation of the negative auxiliary of the present tense in Western Mari is *am* 1SG, *at* 2SG, *ak* 3SG, *ana* 1PL, *ada* 2PL and *ak* 3PL.

4.4.5.3 The development of pTk *e-

Although the evidence is only weakly preserved in Karakhanide and Chuvash, there are indications for the reconstruction of an negative verb pTk *e- 'not to be, not to exist, to lack'. The Karakhanide negative *eŋ* 'no, not' and the Chuvash negative imperative *an* correspond regularly in such a way that pTk *eŋ can be reconstructed as the negative imperative. Given the imperative suffix OTk -ŋ, it is plausible to derive pTk *e- as an auxiliary negative verb. According to Croft (1991: 8), a negative interjection is cross-linguistically frequently derived from an independent negative existential verb, for instance in Amharic, where the negative interjection *yälläm* 'no' is the 3rd singular masculine form of the negative existential verb. Note that the Russian negative interjection *net* 'no' has also developed from a negative existential predicate *net*, which derives from *ne je tu (not is here) 'there is not'.

This analysis seems to conform to the basic pattern of negation in the other Transeurasian languages, whereby inflectional categories, such as imperative (*-ŋ), are carried by a preposed negative auxiliary, whereas derivational categories such causative (Chu. *-tĂr* or *-ččĂr*) are indicated by the invariant lexical verb. In the process of cyclic grammaticalization, the lexicalized and almost obsolete negative construction reflecting *e- may have been replaced by a new periphrastic negative construction with the negative auxiliary pTk *ma-, discussed below.

4.5 Insufficient evidence for pTEA *ma- auxiliary negative verb

Although, as mentioned in Section 4.2, the Old Turkic verbal negative suffix -mA- in (35), has been the subject of numerous etymological proposals, none of them is convincing enough to enable us to reconstruct a third negative verb pTEA *ma-.

(35) The use of the Old Turkic negative suffix -mA

    yek   ičgek-ig   kėrtgün-me-z   er-ti-ler
    demon ghost-ACC believe-NEG-ADN be-PLUPERF-3PL
    'They did not believe in demons' (TT VI: 131; Erdal 2004: 246)

Like Old Turkic, Chuvash reflects the verbal negative as a suffix -m(A)- (Krüger 1961: 142–143), which is clearly internal to the verb morphology; it precedes inflectional affixes such as those of tense, mood, person and number, while it follows all of the valence and voice suffixes such as those indicating reflexives, reciprocals, causatives and passives. The internal position of negation in Turkic can be explained on the grounds that the original negative was a negative verb, inflected for tense, mood, person and number, which fused with an invariant, though possibly derivationally complex, lexical verb.

In Chuvash, we also find some instances, such as the optatives in Table 3 and the debitive in example (36), where the negative marker is expressed analytically. Whereas the optatives in Table 3 reflect auxiliary use of *mar* (< pTk **ma-r* (not.exist-FIN)), the debitive construction in (36) reflects independent use of the negative verb. The debitive *-mAllA* is formed from the verbal noun in *-mA* by the addition of an old directive *-llA*. The negative postposition *mar* represents the adnominal – or so-called "aorist" – form of an original negative auxiliary **ma-*. Its counterpart in Old Turkic is the adnominal negative suffix *-mA-z*, for example in (35), word-final **-r* having changed to *-z* in Eastern Turkic, but being retained in Western Turkic, of which Chuvash is a contemporary representative (see Section 7.3.5.1). The negative particle *mar* may have originated as an independent negative verb pTk **ma-* 'not to exist', an assumption supported by its lack of boundedness, the possible finite function of its component **-r* and the observation that it takes a nominal argument. Literary the debitive example in (36) can thus be understood as "the coming direction does not exist for me". The reduction of the negative to the status of a suffix on the lexical verb across the Turkic languages probably represents the final stage of its development.

(36) The use of the Chuvash debtitive

    epĕ kil-melle   mar
    I   come-DEB   NEG
    'I don't have to come' (Krüger 1961: 159)

Given the originally independent nature of pTk **ma-* 'not exist', lexical comparisons are more convincing than morphological ones. The comparison with the Japanese negative tentative- hortative OJ *-amasizi-* > MJ *-amazi-* > J *-(a)mai* 'probably not / let's not' proposed by Miller (1971: 147, 275; 1985: 61), Martin (1996: 77); Starostin et al. (2003: 228) has been rejected by Robbeets (2005: 159) because OJ *-amasizi-* can be explained as the subjunctive marker OJ *-amasi* followed by a negation marker *-zi-*, which indicates that the negation is not expressed by the element *-(a)ma-*.

Martin's (1991: 288) alternative suggestion that MJ *mana* 'don't!' in nominalized expressions of the type *verb koto mana* 'refrain from verb!' should be compared, is more convincing because the *-na* element may be the desiderative suffix, which in Old Japanese can express the speaker's desire that the addressee should perform an action (Vovin 2009a: 665). From this viewpoint, pJ **ma-* may be a negative auxiliary meaning 'not to do, to refrain from'. However, the proposal remains speculative because, being a Kanbun reading aid that only occurs in the literature from the mid Heian period onwards, *mana* is not attested in Old Japanese.

Martin (1991: 288, 1996: 77) further proposed including MK ¨*ma(l)*-, K *ma:(l)*- 'to desist, refrain from (tr.)' used as an auxiliary in nominalized expressions of the type MK verb-*ti* ¨*mal.la* 'refrain from verb!'. However, the original root of the verb, pK *malʌ-, probably had a final liquid, which is reflected neither in Turkic nor in Japanese. Starostin et al. (2003: 228) suggest including the negative adverb MK :*mwot* 'not possibly, not at all' in the etymology, but this goes against Martin's (1991: 288)) internal analysis, deriving it form the adverb MK *mwo·ta* 'all, alltogether', which in its turn goes back to the verb MK *mwot*- 'gather, come together, cluster'. Martin's proposal is plausible in the light of Jespersen's cycle, whereby elements that strengthen negation such as Latin *rem* 'thing' or OTk *näŋ* 'thing,' may develop into negation markers such as French *rien* 'nothing' or OTk *näŋ* '(not) at all'.

Martin's (1996: 77) comparison with the verb pMo *margu- 'to quarrel, resist, contest', which is reflected in WMo *marɣu*- 'to argue, refuse, decline, resist (tr. / intr.)', Khal. *marga*-, Bur. *marga*-, Kalm. *maryə*-, Ord. *marGuči*-, Shary Yoghur *marGāda* 'quarrel' and Mgr. *marGāndo* 'quarrel' is problematic because the identity of the final -*ryu*- remains unexplained. His Manchu cognate *mara*- 'to decline, refuse' is also proposed by Ramstedt (1939: 138–139) and Menges (1984: 277), but given the poor distribution of the verb in Tungusic, Doerfer (1985: 144) and Rozycki (1994: 155) are probably right in treating it as a copy from Mongolian.[12] Even if it were a native Tungusic root, the morphological segmentation would remain unclear. This is probably also true for the Even verb *man*- 'to annihilate, ruin, eat up, abolish'.

Another possible cognate in Mongolic is WMo *maɣu ~ maɣui*, (SH) MMo. *ma'u(n)* 'bad, evil, unfavorable, poor, below standard', if this form is a compound of pMo *ma- 'not to become, be unbecoming' and the deverbal noun suffixes WMo. -*ɣU* / -*ɣUi* / -*ɣUn* (Poppe 1954: 46).

---

[12] Further attestations with a slightly different meaning in Tungusic are Na. *maria*-, Oroch *mari*-, Ud. *malea*- 'to quarrel'. Note that another relevant verb root may be pTg *maya- 'to fail, be unsuccessful, be spoiled', reflected in Evk. *maya*-, Even *may*-, Neg. *maya*-, Ma. *maya*- 'disappear', Orok *maya*-, Na. *may*-, *maña*-, Oroch *may-maki*- 'to lack, be absent', Ud. *maya*-, *mayasi*-, but here the final element -*ya*- remains unaccounted for.

4.6 The historical development of negation in Transeurasian

The Transeurasian languages have preserved evidence supporting the reconstruction of at least two auxiliary negative verbs: an older proto-Transeurasian form *ana- 'not to be, not to exist' and a newer proto-Altaic form *ə- with the same meaning. Although there are no clear traces left of pTEA *ana- in Mongolic or Turkic, a word that comes to mind is OTk. *anïg ~ anïg ~ ayïg* 'evil, sin, bad; badly, extremely'. If the word is indeed a derivation with the deverbal noun suffix OTk. *-(X)g* as suggested by Erdal (1991: 181), the base may be a negative verb pTk *an- 'not to be(come), be unbecoming', which would be an acceptable match. Whereas pTEA *ana- was preserved in the eastern Transeurasian languages, it was replaced by an innovative negative auxiliary *ə- in Altaic. Only the Tungusic languages show a clear trace of the cyclic replacement of *ana- by *e-.

Table 4. Reflexes of the negative verbs pTEA *ana- and pA *ə- in the Transeurasian languages

pTEA	pJ	pK	pTg	pMo	pTk
pTEA *ana- independent	*ana- independent auxiliary suffix	*an- independent	*ana- independent auxiliary suffix		[*an- independent]
pA *ə- independent auxiliary			*e- independent auxiliary suffix	*e-se- independent auxiliary	*e- independent auxiliary

The basic pattern of sentential negation shared by the Transeurasian languages is a construction consisting of a preposed inflected negative auxiliary and an invariant lexical verb, whereby inflectional categories are carried by the negative auxiliary and derivational categories by the lexical verb. This pattern is cross-linguistically relatively rare as it occurs in less than 10 % of the languages of the world.

The historical development of negation in the Transeurasian languages seems to involve the pathways schematized in Figure 1.

negative verb → preposed negative auxiliary ↗ negative particle
↘ postposed negative auxiliary → negative suffix

Figure 1. Pathways of negative grammaticalization shared by the Transeurasian languages

The source is independent negative verbs, either negative existentials such as *e- and *ana- or verbs with implied negative properties such as 'refrain from'. These verbs grammaticalized into fully inflecting auxiliaries which take an invariant form of the lexical verb as their argument. In spite of the SOV morphology of the Transeurasian languages, the finite auxiliaries tend to be preposed to the lexical verb. In preposed position, the auxiliaries gradually transferred their inflection to the lexical verb to become totally denuded. Since prefixing is rare among the Transeurasian languages, affixation was inhibited and the final stage of grammaticalization is an invariant preposed particle. Alternatively, the auxiliaries could move to a postposed position, where they were ultimately free to assume a suffix status. The negatives OJ -ana-, OTk -mA-, Chu. -m(A)- and the Nanai suffixed vowel length all have an internal position to the verb morphology in common, preceding inflectional suffixes, but following derivational ones. This can be explained on the grounds that their source used to be a negative auxiliary, inflected for tense, mood, person and number, which fused with an invariant, though possibly derivationally complex, lexical verb.

The observation that these processes of grammaticalization are shared across the Transeurasian languages does not necessarily imply that they were already completed in proto-Transeurasian and inherited as polysemy in the daughter languages. The reflexes of pTEA *ana-, for instance, all share the source "independent negative verb", but not the target "auxiliary", which suggests that the grammaticalization of negation took place independently in some of the daughter branches. As discussed in Section 2.2.3.2, the phenomenon whereby cognate morphemes undergo parallel processes of grammaticalization long after separating from the ancestral language is known as "parallelism in drift" or "Sapirian drift". Under the present scenario, the pathway of development discussed here was a specific, language-internal force in proto-Transeurasian, which remained decisive in shaping new grammaticalization pathways of negation in the daughter languages.

Morphologically compact processing by way of particles and suffixes increases the speed and ease of transmitting messages at the expense of transparency. As one gains speed, one loses clarity. When the notional importance of negation was outbalanced by its formal weakness, time had come for replacement. Replacement by a fully inflecting auxiliary construction marks a new cycle of grammaticalization. The evidence indicates successive waves of grammaticalization for the Transeurasian negative markers. In Japanese and Korean, the reflexes of pTEA *ana- have been replaced by reinforcement of a converbial form of the earlier negative verb plus a verb 'to do, make'. Similar reinforced constructions have replaced the reflex of pTg *e- in Nanai. The replacement may also involve an entirely new negative verb, as is the case for the renewal of pTEA *ana-* by **ə-* in the Altaic branch of Transeurasian. Subsequently, Mongolic and Turkic have replaced their reflexes of pA **ə-* by yet newer negative auxiliaries such as pMo **ü-* and pTk **ma-*. It must be noted that the sequencing of the grammaticalization processes is not absolute: one process does not necessarily have to be completed before the next one begins (Croft 1991: 22).

Although the formal correspondences of the etymologies above are completely regular according to correspondences 9, 13 and 14 (see Section 3.3), a phonological objection to the etymology of pTEA **ana-* made by Robbeets (2005: 414) is that, cross-linguistically, nasals tend to be frequently incorporated in negative markers, perhaps because they are relatively unmarked. A similar criticism is made by Vovin (2009a: 793): "I must also add that negatives in **-n-* are so widespread in Eurasia that it makes this comparison non-specific. Thus, it should be rejected." Many language families such as Uralic, Semitic, Indo-European, Kartvelian and Eskimo indeed share negative markers in (-)*n-*. Nevertheless, the integration of diachronic typology argues against the explanation of the Transeurasian negatives of the shape **an(a)-* as the result of natural phonological convergence. Since the basic pattern of negation using an auxiliary is cross-linguistically uncommon to begin with, applying to only 5 % of languages in Miestamo's (2005) or 4 % in Dryer' s sample, the development of negative auxiliaries to preposed particles and suffixes is logically even rarer. Therefore, the geographical concentration of this particular negative cycle in the Transeurasian languages deserves a historical motivation: it has either areally diffused or it is inherited from a common ancestor.

Arguably, the indications of inheritance are stronger than those of diffusion. As has been pointed out in Section 2.5.3.1, the observation that the shared grammaticalization pattern of negation combines with a formal correspondence of the negative markers reflecting the pattern is highly indicative of inheritance. Besides, contact-induced grammaticalization has been characterized as "change against the grain" or atypical grammaticalization as in the case of Hungarian *nem* whereas genealogically motivated grammaticalization has been regarded as "change that reinforces similarities" because it tends to maintain uniformity between related languages. The repetition of similar grammaticalization processes on various formally related negative verbs at different points in time across the Transeurasian languages indicates that we are dealing with an inherited pattern.

We see clear areal preferences for certain patterns of marking negation: Indo-European languages in western Europe make use of non-verbal Jespersen cycles, whereas Uralic and Transeurasian make use of verbal strategies. It is further possible to draw a boundary between Uralic and Transeurasian based on the tendency for the Transeurasian languages to develop negative auxiliaries to suffixes, which is unseen in Uralic. It can be noted that the negative auxiliary reconstructed for proto-Uralic is *e-* (Janhunen 1982: 37). This marker has a similar form as the Altaic negative *ə-*, in addition to sharing the same basic pattern for negation and some grammaticalization patterns. Although it concerns only a single, monophonemic marker, this is suggestive of a historical connection – perhaps even a genealogical connection – between the two language families concerned.

5 Verbalization and actionality

5.1 The suffix class "actionality" and its diachronic relevance

The term "actionality" is used as an equivalent for the more common German term "Aktionsart" to refer to aspectual distinctions, such as telic/atelic, semelfactive/iterative, stative/active, intensive, inchoative etc., that are expressed either lexically or by derivational morphology. The inchoative distinction, for example, is expressed lexically in English *know* vs. *realize*, but derivationally in Latin *amo:* 'I love' → *ama-sco:* 'I begin to love'. According to Bybee (1985: 100) the semelfactive in Russian *kašljanut'* 'to cough' and *blesnut'* 'to flash' is situated halfway between lexical and derivational expression because these stems do not occur without the element *-nu-*, which prevents us from identifying *-nu-* as a suffix. Since the present study is mainly concerned with the historical comparison of verb affixes, it will only deal with actionality in the sense of "derivational aspect".

Actional affixes derive verbs from lexical stems and modify the basic meaning of these stems. German, for instance, is particularly rich in such markers as verbal diminutive (e.g. *lächeln* 'to laugh a little' from *lachen* 'to laugh'), intensive (e.g. *verspüren* 'to feel consciously' from *spüren* 'to feel, sense'), inchoative (e.g. *abfahren* 'to depart, start to drive' from *fahren* 'to drive'), resultative (e.g. *aufessen* 'to eat up, to finish (food)' from *essen* 'eat'), iterative (e.g. *Heulerei* 'constant bawling' from *heulen* 'to bawl, howl'), momentaneous (e.g. *aufschreien* 'to cry out, cry loudly and shortly' from *schreien* 'to cry') or durative (e.g. *fliegen* 'to fly' vs. *durchfliegen* 'to fly nonstop'). On the basis of semantic criteria, we can distinguish between three types of actionality, according to (1) the intensity of the event (e.g. low in *lächeln* vs. high in *verspüren*), (2) the frequency of the event (e.g. once in *abfahren* vs. repeatedly in *Heulerei*) and (3) the development of the event over time (e.g. limited in *aufschreien* vs. delimited in *durchfliegen*).

Actionality can be distinguished from (inflectional) aspect, which provides a temporal viewpoint on the preceding action described by the verb, such as perfective/imperfective, habitual, continuous etc. Semantically, aspect – unlike actionality –, leaves the basic meaning of the verb unaffected; it only indicates how the action described by the verb should be viewed in the context of the discourse. Aspect refers to the internal temporal structure of the sentence, while actional markers may contain other components of meaning, such as the intensity or the frequency of an event.

Combinationally, actional affixes can derive verbs from any lexical stem, whereas aspect operates exclusively on verbs. Given their high semantic relevance, actional affixes logically precede markers of voice and negation, whereas aspect markers follow them. They are often restricted by their meaning to a certain semantic class of verbs; for example, inchoatives tend to be restricted to stative verbs and iteratives to semelfactive and activity verbs, whereas aspect applies to all verbs.

Morphosyntactically, actionality is usually expressed by affixes, i.e. by morphological means, as opposed to aspect, which is expressed by verb forms, i.e. lexical means. Hence, actionality is lexicalization in progress: it gradually converts separate morphemes into lexical distinctions in verbal meaning. Aspect, on the other hand, is grammaticalization in progress: it systematically develops a grammatical status for formerly independent lexemes.

Even though actional affixes are prototypically derivational, often subject to lexicalization, not generally applicable, restricted to certain semantic classes and thus infrequently attested and rather difficult to reconstruct, they are usually thought to provide reliable genealogical evidence. Johanson (1992, 1999, 2002a) includes actionality in a restricted core of verbal affixes that are highly telling in matters of genealogical relatedness, arguing that "[i]n the verbal flection, suffixes closest to the primary stem, markers of actionality and diatheses, seem relatively little susceptible to copying. It would be a strong clue to a common origin if this 'intimate' part of verbal morphology exhibited systematic correspondences of materially and semantically similar morphemes with congruent combinational patterns" (Johanson 1999: 8). In his foreword to Johanson 2002a (xi), Comrie agrees that "[...] in particular the extreme resistance to copying of the positions closest to the verbal stem might provide a more reliable tool than many of those used in the past to whether there are indeed shared elements that testify to genetic relatedness, [...], among the groups of languages that constitute Altaic."

Since the positions closest to the verb stem, such as actionality, valence and voice, are situated towards the derivational end of the morphological continuum (see Section 6.1), it would seem that, contrary to the expected hierarchy, some types of derivational morphology are more resistant to code-copying than inflectional morphology. A possible way out of this paradox could be that stability obtains when low probability of attrition coincides with low probability of copying. Although the copiability of actionality may be higher than that of inflectional categories, it is more resistant to loss. This follows from the expectation that derivational categories with high semantic content and relevance will lexicalize more easily than inflectional markers that do not affect the meaning of the stem (Bybee 1985). With sufficient lapse of time, replacement will lead to the entire loss of inflectional markers, but it will leave lexicalized evidence from derivational morphology unaffected. In this sense, derivation is less resistant to copying but more resistant to replacement and loss, which might explain why actionality is genealogically more stable.

5.2 Previous research

In this chapter, five actional suffixes will be reconstructed: a denominal verb suffix pTEA *-lA- expressing achievement or use of the nominal base, a processive pTEA *-nA-, an iconic pTEA *-ki-, an inclinational pTEA *-mA- and an inchoative pTEA *-gA-.

As far as the denominal verb suffix pTEA *-lA- is concerned, Ramstedt (1912: 80, 1952: 195–196) and Baskakov (1981: 68) proposed the comparison below for Tungusic, Mongolic and Turkic, but they did not include a Japanese cognate. The Japanese cognate proposed here was compared by Miller (1981: 853) to a different set of Altaic forms, which he derived from a factitive pA *-l-. Starostin et al. (2003: 186–190) reconstructed a morpheme pA *-l- but left the semantics open and did not include the Japanese suffix treated here. Opponents of the Transeurasian affinity hypothesis, such as recently Schönig (2003: 416) and Vovin (2011: 18–19), explain the parallel between the Altaic suffixes as a case of morphological borrowing. The present approach differs from previous ones in that it proposes a Japanese cognate, includes shared processes of grammaticalization into a loan verb marker in the comparison and assesses the borrowing hypothesis in more detail.

As far as the processive suffix pTEA *-nA- is concerned, Ramstedt (1912: 62–64) considered the Turkic suffix below as a "reflexive" and compared it to a Mongolic element -ni-, which will not be included here due to semantic problems and the phonological mismatch of the vowel. Later (1952: 168–169), he added a Tungusic form -ni-, which he believed to be a composite element in two suffixes, but this internal analysis is too speculative. Poppe (1972a: 140–41) followed Ramstedt's analysis for Mongolic -ni-, but updated it by proposing another Tungusic cognate pTg -*nA-, which he labeled "reiterative", following Benzing's (1955a: 1064) terminology. The examples below, however, show that the designation "processive" is more appropriate for the Tungusic suffix. I further propose a different Mongolic cognate, pMo *-nA-, a form that Poppe and Ramstedt briefly mention without providing concrete illustrations of its occurrence. I am unaware of any contributions advancing the Japanese and Korean reflexes that are included here.

As far as the iconic suffix pTEA *-ki- is concerned, Ramstedt (1912: 36–37, 1951) restricted his comparison to the Mongolic and Turkic iconic suffixes discussed below. Tekin (1982) updated this proposal with Tungusic cognates. Erdal (1991: 468) argued in favor of the connection proposed by Ramstedt. Miller (1982a: 401) advanced the Japanese cognate discussed below, but he proposed a different Korean reflex from the one proposed here.

I am unaware of previous reconstructions of the inclinational suffix pTEA *-mA-. Ramstedt (1952: 182) refrained from etymologizing the Tungusic suffixes because he considered them as grammaticalizations from independent verbal forms. Although there are no etymologies available for the Japanese inclinational suffix pJ *-ma- in section 5.6.1, Martin (1991a: 285, 1992: 248), Unger (2000a: 664), Vovin (2001: 194) proposed various Korean cognates for the modal suffix OJ -(a)ma-, which is probably internally related to pJ *-ma-. Among other things, they compared it with the Korean modal suffix K/ MK -ma 'will, be willing to, intend to, promise', which is probably morphologically complex (see Section 7.4.2). Vovin further added the Evenki desiderative suffix -mu-, but this will be disregarded due to its problematic phonology and semantics. Miller (1985: 68–69) compared a derived complex suffix OJ -maku (< *-ma- + *-ku- nominalization) with Turkic infinitives in -mAk. Miller (1985: 61) and Vovin (2001: 194–195) compared another derived suffix, the subjunctive and desiderative marker -amasi (< *-ma- + *(po)si- 'be desired') with various Tungusic suffixes. Vovin (2001: 191–192, 198) further suggested that the converbial element OJ -mi₁ is cognate with the Korean coordinative converb -(u/o)mye and the Manchu converb -me, Tungusic -mi. Recently (Vovin 2010: 84), he altered his view, suggesting instead that the Japanese form represents a borrowing from Old Korean, but his new explanation is at odds with the complex nature of the Japanese (and probably also the Korean) suffix.[1] Thus, I do not support the majority of previous proposals, because they compare forms that are morphologically complex in Japanese with forms that coincidentally look similar in the other languages.

Finally, as far as the reconstruction of the inchoative suffix pTEA *-gA- is concerned, Ramstedt (1912: 54–59) was the first to compare the denominal and deverbal inchoatives in Mongolic and Turkic. Later (1952: 200–201) he added the Korean denominal inchoative to the etymology. Although he labeled them 'intensives', Miller (1981: 867–868) compared the Japanese with the Turkic deverbal suffixes and included Korean, Tungusic and Mongolic cognates in a subsequent publication (1982a).

In short, the approach taken here intends to complement the previous proposals for actional suffixes by supplementing Altaic etymologies with material from Japanese and Korean, proposing new cognates, assessing the borrowing hypothesis in more detail and including shared grammaticalization in the argumentation. This chapter consists of a revision of Robbeets (2007a), my earlier treatment of cognate actional suffixes in the Transeurasian languages.

---

[1] Martin (1992: 892) derived the Korean coordinative converb -(u/o)mye from the nominalizer -(u/o)m and the copula converb i-e.

5.3 pTEA *-lA- manipulative denominal verb suffix

5.3.1 pJ *-ra- (~ -rə-)

While many Japanese verbs appear to be simplex at first glance, internal analysis reveals that they are covert complex verbs resulting from the addition of one or more suffixes, such as -ra-, -na-, -ma-, -ka- etc. to the lexical root. Due to processes of lexicalization, the meaning that an individual suffix adds to the neutral base is often obscured, which is why Martin (1987: 665–800) reconstructs the suffixes formally, but leaves the semantics open. Unger (1977: 127–142), however, adds a broad semantic tag, i.e. -ra- spontaneous action, -na- 'be the same as', -ma- seemingness or attempt to achieve, -ka- punctual or iterative action. The reconstruction of Japanese actional suffixes in this chapter basically confirms Martin's and Unger's internal analysis, but it elaborates on a number of semantic and combinational properties in greater detail.

5.3.1.1 Manipulative denominal verb suffix

The suffix pJ *-ra- has lexicalized in at least 13 Old Japanese verb stems, illustrated below. Apart from its function as a denominal verb suffix, it modifies the meaning of the base in two different ways: 1. 'to achieve, overcome or execute a difficult action with success on the base noun', whereby the base noun is often a spatial concept or a weather condition and 2. 'to make use of the base noun'. The suffix is also used to derive verbs from onomatopoetic expressions.

The denominal verbalizer is reconstructed as pJ *-ra-, with a final vowel that surfaces in further derivations such as the iterative *-pa- in OJ wata-ra-p- 'to cross over, maintain oneself' and OJ wa-ra-p- 'to laugh' or the inchoative *-ka- in OJ pipi-ra-k- 'to smart with pain' and OJ we-ra-k- 'to laugh with joy'. In some cases such as OJ susu-ro-p- 'slurp' and OJ no_2-ro_2-p- 'curse', however, the suffix vowel agrees with the quality of the vowel in the root and the reconstruction should be pJ *-rə-, a behavior that resembles vowel harmony.

Although Vovin (2011: 18) objects that "this denominal -r- is limited to one word, which is found only in Central Japanese", the list below contains at least 13 Old Japanese noun-verb pairs with matching vowels and congruent register, not counting the pairs between square brackets with problematic vowels or register. Vovin further objects to the irregular voicing of the obstruents in J modor- 'return, revert', OJ $kagi_1$r- 'set limits' and OJ sagar- 'to descend, but in spite of its sporadic occurrence, this may be due to the suffix-initial liquid; see the voicing phenomenon described in Miller (1981: 853). Secondary voicing under influence of the following liquid suffix is supported by the observation that OJ $tagi_1$r- 'to seethe, boil, foam' has preserved a voiceless alternant OJ $taki_1$r-.

Contrary to Vovin's claim, these denominal verbs are well attested outside Central Japanese: the suffix has lexicalized in cognate Ryukyuan verb stems, such as Shuri *kumur-* B 'to get cloudy, cloud (intr.)', *mudur-* A 'to return, revert', *simari* B 'doorstop', *sagar-* B 'to descend, go down, sink, hang down (intr.)', *watar-* A 'to cross over, span, get transferred (tr./ intr.)' and *nar-* A 'to sound, ring'. The period in which this suffix was productive must thus predate the split of Mainland Japanese and Ryukyuan, i.e. in proto-Japonic.

Reflexes of pJ *-ra- in Old Japanese

a) *denominal*

1. 'to achieve a position expressed by the base, to accumulate the base noun, to overcome or execute a difficult action with success on the base noun'

    pJ *$k\partial i$ 'fog' (Thorpe 1983: 288–89) in Miyako dialect, i.e. Sarahama *cïï*; Uechi / Nakasuji *kïï* 'fog' → OJ ki_2r- A 'to fog up, get foggy (intr.)'

    OJ ki_1pa 2.3. 'limit, brink' → OJ ki_1par- B 'to come to an end, wear out (intr.)'

    OJ $kubi_1$ 2.1. 'neck' → OJ $kubi_1r$- A 'to strangle (tr.)'

    OJ $kumo_1$ 2.3. 'cloud' → OJ $kumo_1r$- B 'to get cloudy, cloud (intr.)'

    OJ mo_2to_2 2.3. 'root, origin, base' → J *modor-* B 'to return, revert'

    OJ *saka(-)* 2.1. 'backward, opposite direction' → J *sakar-* ?A 'turn ones back on'

    OJ *saka* 2.3. 'incline, slope' → OJ *sagar-* B' 'to descend, go down, sink, hang down (intr.)'

    OJ *sima* 2.3. 'piece of marked-off land, territory, quarters, island' → J *simar-* B 'to bind, restrict, shut tight; be shut, be tight (tr. / intr.)'

    OJ $take_2$ 2.3. 'height, stature' → J *taker-* ? A/B 'to get excited, show spirit/ courage'

    OJ *wata* 'sea' ?2.1 → OJ *watar-* A 'to cross over, span, get transferred (tr./ intr.)'

    [OJ *se* 1.1 'narrow place, valley, narrows/rapids (in a river)' → J *ser-* B 'to narrow the gap, press for quick action']

    [OJ $kaki_1$ 2.2. 'fence, hedge' → OJ $kagi_1$-*r*- B 'to set limits']

2. 'to make use of the base noun'

   OJ *ipo* 2.3 'hut' → OJ *ipor-* B 'to lodge in a hut'

   pJ **na-* in OJ *ne* 1.1. 'sound, crying, weeping' → OJ *nar-* A 'to sound, ring'

   OJ *taki*$_1$ 2.1. 'waterfall, rapids' → OJ *taki*$_1$*r-* ~ *tagi*$_1$*r-* A 'to seethe, boil, foam'

   [OJ *ko*$_2$*to*$_2$ 2.3. 'word, speech, statement' → OJ *katar-* A 'to tell']

   [OJ *te*$_2$ ~ *ta-* 1.3. 'hand' → OJ *to*$_1$*r-* ~ *to*$_2$*r-* B 'to take, hold in hand' (Unger 1977: 111)]

b) *onomatopoetic*

   pJ **kisi* (mimetic for high-pitched, unpleasant sounds) → J *kisir-* 'to creak, rasp'

   pJ **nə* (mimetic for scolding, cursing) → OJ *nor-* 'to scold', OJ *no*$_2$*ro*$_2$*p-* 'to curse'

   pJ **pika* in J *pika-pika* 'sparkling, glittering, shining (mimetic)' → OJ *pi*$_1$*kar-* 'to shine'

   pJ **pipi* (mimetic for quick, light up and down movement) → OJ *pipir-* 'to flutter up'

   pJ **pipi* (mimetic for tingling sensation) → OJ *pipirak-* 'to smart with pain, produce a sharp stinging pain'

   pJ **səsə* (mimetic for nervous motion) in OJ *soso-mek-* 'to fidget, move nervously, rush'[2], OJ *sosog-* 'to ruffle, move back and forth' → J *sosor-* 'to excite, incite, stimulate, stir up'

   pJ **susu* (mimetic for slurping sound) → OJ *susurop-* 'to slurp'

   pJ **we* ~ **wa* (emotional exclamation) in OJ *we* (lamenting interjection), OJ *we-warap-* 'to laugh out loud', J *wa-meku* 'to scream, shriek' → OJ *werak-* 'to laugh with joy', OJ *warap-* 'to laugh'

---

[2] J *-mek-* is an auxiliary that derives verbs from iconic expression, such as J *hatamek-* 'flutter, flap', J *kiramek-*'glitter, sparkle', J *ugomek-* 'wriggle, squirm', OJ *sosomek-* 'fidget, rush; whisper', OJ *sabame*$_1$*k-* 'murmur, buzz, clamor', J *sasamek-*'whisper, murmur', J *sazamek-* 'make an uproar', OJ *sosomek-* 'fidget, move nervously, rush', J *sosomek-* 'whisper', J *tutumek-*'murmur', J *wamek-* 'scream, shriek', J *zawamek-* 'be noisy, rustle', etc. The auxiliary indicates that the preceding segment is a mimetic expression.

On the basis of the following observations, the deverbal noun suffix pJ *-$ra_{(1)}$- can be distinguished from the anticausative suffix pJ *-$ra_{(2)}$- (e.g. in OJ *kak-* 'hang (tr.)' → OJ *kakar-* 'hang (intr.)'), which will be discussed in Section 6.6.1.[3] First, the meaning is different in that pJ *-$ra_{(1)}$- modifies the lexical base adding the semantics described above, whereas pJ *-$ra_{(2)}$- marks a verb base as anticausative and thus affects the valency of the preceding verb. Whereas pJ *-$ra_{(1)}$- has neutral transitivity, deriving transitive verbs (e.g. J *kubir-* 'strangle (tr.)') as well as intransitives (e.g. OJ ki_2r- 'to fog up, get foggy (intr.)', pJ *-$ra_{(2)}$- only derives transitive verbs and it commonly alternates with an intransitive verb derived with the suffix pJ *-*sa*- (e.g. OJ *nokor-* 'remain, be left' vs. OJ no_2ko_2s- 'leave')

Second, the combinational properties differ in that pJ *-$ra_{(1)}$- derives verbs from nouns and onomatopoea, while pJ *-$ra_{(2)}$- derives verbs from verbs. Third, the morphotactic behavior differs in that pJ *-$ra_{(1)}$- occupies the first position in the suffix chain, closest to the lexical stem, while pJ *-$ra_{(2)}$- occurs in more remote positions. Whereas pJ *-$ra_{(1)}$- can be followed by other actional suffixes such as the inchoative *-*ka*- in e.g. OJ *werak-* 'to laugh with joy', pJ *-$ra_{(2)}$- is always preceded by them, e.g. OJ *tir-* 'to scatter, get scattered' → MJ *tirakas-* 'to scatter (tr.)' vs. MJ *tirakar-* 'to get scattered (intr.)'. The actional suffix pJ *-$ra_{(1)}$- can be followed by the causative pJ *-*sa*-, e.g. OJ *nar-* 'make a sound, ring' vs. OJ *naras-* 'sound, ring (tr.)' and OJ ki_2r- 'fog up, get foggy' vs. OJ ki_2ras- 'cause to fog, make cloudy', whereas the anticausative pJ *-$ra_{(2)}$- is logically exclusive with it.

5.3.1.2 Loan verb marker

Contemporary Japanese uses a loan verb marker -*r*-, corresponding to the form of the denominal verbalizer. There do not seem to be any unambiguous examples of direct insertion into Japanese, whereby simplex verbs were copied from Chinese or other non-Transeurasian foreign languages without any morphosyntactic adaptation. If the need for borrowing a verb does arise, for instance English *to jog*, there is a clear preference for the light verb strategy, which copies a a nominalized form of the verb such as *zyogingu* 'jogging' and joins it by the native "light verb" *suru* 'to do'. However, there is a small number of examples of indirect insertion, whereby foreign loan verbs supply a nominal base and the verbalizer -*r*- is used to accommodate for the copy. The loan verbs J *demor-* 'to demonstrate', J *sabor-* 'to cut class' and J *azir-* 'to agitate' can be derived as denominal verbs from Eng *demonstrate,* Fr. *saboter* and Eng. *agitate* over the abbreviated nominal copies J *demo* 'demonstration', J *sabo* '(industrial) slow down' and J

---

[3] The subscripts (1) and (2) are used to indicate that we are dealing with two different morphemes.

azi 'agitation' respectively. More examples can be found in Martin (1987: 673). A number of verbs have also been recently derived from copied nouns that lack a verbal counterpart in the foreign language, e.g. J *gebar-* 'to engage in strong-arm tactics', derived from J *gebaruto* 'strong-arm tactics', a copy from German *Gewalt* and J *gyuuzir-* 'to boss, manipulate at will' derived from J *gyuuzi* 'ears of an ox', a copy from Mandarin. However, the suffix is not productive on native Japanese words. It is likely that loanverbs like *demor-* or *sabor-* are simply formed in analogy with the most frequent verb ending *-r-* in Contemporary Japanese. This final *-r-* has different origins; only in a small proportion of verbs it goes back to the original denominal verbalizer. Nevertheless, the outcome is the same: the original denominal verbalizer appears to be reanalysed as a loan verb marker.

5.3.2 pTg *-lA:-

The suffix pTg *-lA:-* has lexicalized in all contemporary Tungusic languages as a denominal verb suffix, deriving both transitive and intransitive verbs (Benzing 1955a: 1064). It modifies the meaning of the base in two different ways: 1. 'to achieve, accumulate, overcome or execute a difficult action with success on the base noun', a meaning that is commonly extended to successful engagement in a relationship, and 2. 'to make use of the base noun', a meaning that is extended to 'to act in the way of the base' following nominal adjectives. In the southern Tungusic languages, the denominal verb suffix has grammaticalized from a verbalizer into a productive loan verb marker.

5.3.2.1 Manipulative denominal verb suffix

5.3.2.1.1 Manchu *-lA-*

Manchu *-la-* ~ *-le-* ~ *-lo-*, illustrated below, is still highly productive in Manchu (Gorelova 2002, 235).

1. 'to achieve, accumulate or overcome the base noun, to execute a difficult action with success on the base noun'

    Ma. *bata* 'enemy; hostility' → *batala-* 'to be an enemy, oppose'
    Ma. *gucu* 'friend' → *gucule-* 'to be friends with, make friends'
    Ma. *oron* 'vacant post, vacancy' → *orolo-* 'to fill in, fill a vacancy'
    Ma. *sadun* 'relative by marriage' → *sadula-* 'to form an in-law relationship'
    Ma. *songko* 'trace, track, footprint' → *songkolo-* 'to follow in the tracks of, imitate'

2. 'to make use of the base noun'

> Ma. *akdun* 'firm, strong' → *akdula-* 'to protect, defend'
> Ma. *ejen* 'ruler, master; rulership' → *ejele-* 'to rule, master, occupy by force, establish control over'
> Ma. *erun* 'torture, punishment' → *erule-* 'to torture, punish'
> Ma. *hahi* 'urgent, hurried' → *hahila-* 'to act quickly or urgently, hurry'
> Ma. *kobto(n)* 'respect, reverence' → *kobtolo-* 'to treat respectfully'
> Ma. *suhe* 'ax' → *suhele-* 'to split with an ax'

5.3.2.1.2 Even -*lA:*-

The examples of Even -*la-* ~ -*le-* are restricted to just a few lexicalized verb pairs, illustrated below (Benzing 1955b: 35). However, the suffix has also petrified in a suffix string with the perfect suffix pTg *-c- (see Section 4.4.3.2), yielding -*lA:c-* 'to have (achieved), to possess the base noun', e.g. *asi:* 'wife' → *asi:la:c-* 'to have as wife', *ha:rak* 'friend' → *ha:raklac-* 'to be friends', *ju:* 'yurt, house' → *ju:la:c-* 'to have a yurt'.

1. 'to achieve, accumulate or overcome the base noun, to execute a difficult action with success on the base noun'

> Even *mo:* 'tree, wood' → *mo:la:-* 'to gather wood, go to get wood'
> Even *mu:* 'water' → *mu:le:-* 'to gather water, go to get water'
> Even *tew* 'berry' → *tewle:-* 'to gather berries, go to get berries'
> Even *jur* 'two' → *jurle:-* 'to hunt two animals / two fishes'

2. 'to make use of the base noun'

> Even *usi:* 'cord, rope, strap' → *usi:-le:-* 'to control (a reindeer) with a rope, to encircle the reindeers'
> Even *jewle:n* 'armour' → *jewle:le:-* 'to apply one's armour'
> Even *gïd* 'lance, spear' → *gïdla:-* 'to pierce with a lance'

5.3.2.1.3 Evenki -lA-

The examples of Evenki -la- ~ -le- ~ -lo- are restricted to just a few lexicalized verb pairs, illustrated below (Nedjalkov 1997: 301).

1. 'to achieve, accumulate or overcome the base noun, to execute a difficult action with success on the base noun'

    Evk. *dikte* 'berries' → *diktele-* 'to gather berries, go to get berries'
    Evk. *mo:-* 'firewood' → *mo:la-* 'to gather firewood, go to get firewood'
    Evk. *mu:-* 'water' → *mu:le-* 'gather water, go to get water'

2. 'to make use of the base noun'
    Evk. *auun* 'hat' → *aula-* 'to put on a hat'

5.3.2.1.4 Udehe -lA-

Udehe -la- ~ -le- ~ -lo-, illustrated below, is a very frequent suffix in Udehe (Nikolaeva 1999: 170–71).

1. 'to achieve, accumulate or overcome the base noun, to execute a difficult action with success on the base noun'

    Ud. *anda* 'friend' → *andala-* 'to make friends'
    Ud. *anga* 'night shelter' → *angala-* 'to make a night shelter'
    Ud. *ingme* 'needle' → *ingmele-* 'to put a thread in a needle'
    Ud. *mamasa* 'wife' → *mamasala-* 'to marry, take a wife'
    Ud. *sita* 'child' → *sitala-* 'to adopt'

2. 'to make use of the base noun'

    Ud. *aisi* 'gold' → *aisile-* 'to gild'
    Ud. *cob'o* 'handful' → *cob'olo-* 'to scoop with one's hand'
    Ud. *kusige* 'knife' → *kusigele-* 'to stab with a knife'
    Ud. *mäusa* 'gun' → *mäusala-* 'to shoot'
    Ud. *santu-* 'fist' → *santule-* 'to hit with one's fist'
    Ud. *uninga* 'spoon' → *uningala-* 'to scoop with a spoon'

5.3.2.1.5 Nanai -*lA*-

Nanai -*la*- ~ -*le*- , illustrated below, is a frequent suffix in Nanai (Avrorin 1961: 16, 44–45, Menges 1968a: 201).

1. 'to achieve, accumulate or overcome the base noun, to execute a difficult action with success on the base noun'

    Na. *amin* 'father' → *amila*- 'to be like a father to somebody, behave like a father'
    Na. *anda* 'friend' → *andala*- 'to make friends'
    Na. *asi* 'wife' → *asila*- 'to marry, take a wife'
    Na. *mue* 'water' → *muele*- 'to get water'
    Na. *usin* 'garden, field' → *usile*- 'to grow vegetables, work in the garden'
    Na. *xopan* 'group, artel' → *xopanla*- 'to form a group, join an artel'

2. 'to make use of the base noun'

    Na. *apun* 'hat' → *apola*- 'to put on a hat'
    Na. *dedu* 'dear, beloved' → *dedule*- 'to love, be fond of, care for (tr.)'
    Na. *epu* 'torture, torment' → *epule*- 'to torment, harass'
    Na. *ilga* 'ornament' → *ilgala*- 'to decorate'
    Na. *oma* 'footwear, shoes' > *omala*- 'to put on one's shoes'
    Na. *paloa* 'hammer' → *paloala*- 'to hit once with a hammer'
    Na. *pao* 'cannon, gun' → *paola*- 'to fire a gun'

5.3.2.2 Loan verb marker

Whereas the Manchuric branch and the northern Tungusic branch prefer to borrow verbs through direct insertion (see Section 3.5.3), e.g. Ma. *tala*- 'confiscate, seize property as a legal punishment', Evk./ Even *tala:*- 'to rob, plunder, take away' from Yakut *tala:*-, Even *zvoni*- from Russian *zvoni-t'* 'to phone', Evk. *vypolńaj*- from Russian *vypolnja-t'* 'to fulfill, carry out'; Ma. *amila*- 'anoint a Buddhist icon's eyes with blood and thereby impart life to it' from WMo. *amila*- 'give live, enliven, animate an image by making strokes on a sacred image, come to life', the southern Tungusic languages have grammaticalized the deverbal noun suffix pTg *-*lA*- into a loan verb marker. Nikolaeva (1999: 13, 171) finds that the suffix Ud. -*lA*- regularly attaches to verbal stems borrowed from Russian in order to adjust the Russian verb to the Udihe derivational system. Examples are Ud. *zawonila*- from Russian *zvoni*- 'to phone', Ud. *tancewala*- from Russian *tancewa*- 'to dance', Ud. *snimala*- from Russian *snima*- 'to shoot (a film)' etc. Malchukov (2003: 239) observes a similar tendency in Nanai, e.g. Na. *voprosa-la*- from Russian *voproša-t'* 'to inquire, question'.

5.3.3 pMo *-lA-

The suffix pMo *-lA- has lexicalized in Mongolic as a denominal verb suffix, deriving both transitive and intransitive verbs. It modifies the meaning of the base in two different ways: 1. 'to achieve, accumulate or overcome the base noun, to successfully execute a difficult action on the base noun' and 2. 'to make use of the base noun', a meaning that is extended to the specific use of time and, when added to nominal adjectives, to acting in the way of the base. It can also derive from onomatopoetic bases. In most contemporary Mongolic languages, the denominal verb suffix has grammaticalized from a verbalizer into a productive loan verb marker.

5.3.3.1 Manipulative denominal verb suffix

The suffix pMo *-lA- is reflected as a denominal verb suffix in MMo. -lA- (Street 1957: 63, 65, 66, Rybatzki 2003a: 65) and in WMo. -lA-, where it alternates with -nA- after stem final -m- and -ng- (Poppe 1954: 65). A number of onomatopoetic expressions have been derived with -lA-, but some verbs such as WMo. *joila-* 'to moan, groan' and WMo. *orila-* 'to cry out, shout, scream,' lack a clear mimetic base. Since only very few words can be reconstructed for Khitan (354 in Kane 2009: 84–130), it is unlikely that many derivational pairs will be found. However, the pair Khitan *ku.u* 'man' (Kane 2009: 105) → Khitan *ku.û.ul-* 'to grow up, become a man' (Kane 2009: 148) may leave a trace of the suffix. If so, the denominal verb suffix *-lA- goes back to proto-Khitan-Mongolic.

a) *denominal*

1. 'to achieve, accumulate or overcome the base noun, to execute a difficult action with success on the base noun'

    WMo. *ang* 'game' → *angla-* ~ *angna-* 'to hunt, trap or catch (game) (tr.)'
    WMo. *arsi* 'hermit' → *arsila-* 'to live as a hermite (intr.)'
    WMo. *čegeji(n)* 'breast, memory' → *čegejile-* 'to learn by hart, memorize (tr.)'
    WMo. *ger* 'yurt, house' → *gerle-* 'to marry, found a house of his own (intr.)'
    SH MMo. *hoi* 'forest' → *hoila-* 'to go/ flee into the forest (intr.)'
    WMo. *šibaγun* 'bird' → *šibaγula-* 'to hunt (birds) (tr.)'

2. 'to make use of the base noun'

    WMo. *altan* 'gold, golden' → *altala-* 'to gild, decorate with gold (tr.)'
    SH MMo. *aqa* 'elder brother; older' → *aqala-* 'to behave like an elder brother, dominate (intr.)'

SH MMo. *aqta* 'a riding horse' → *aqtala-* 'to ride horseback (intr.)'
SH MMo. *čag* 'time' → *čagla-* 'to spend time, deliberate (intr.)'
WMo. *emegel* 'saddle' → *emegelle-* 'to saddle (tr.)'
WMo. *em* 'medicine' → *emle-* ~ *emne-* 'to medicate, treat, cure (tr.)'
SH MMo. *kelen* 'tongue, word, speech, statement' → *kelele-* 'to utter words, say, narrate (tr. / intr.)'
SH MMo *morin* 'horse' → *morila-* 'to depart'
SH MMo. *öter* 'quick' > *öterle-* 'to hasten, do quickly (intr.)'
WMo. *usun* 'water' → WMo. *usula-* 'to water (animals/plants), irrigate (tr.)'

b) *onomatopoetic*

WMo. *qai* (grieving interjection) → *qaila-* 'to weep, cry, shed tears'
WMo. *γoγuu* 'cry of a rooster' → *γoγuyla-* 'to cackle'

5.3.3.2 Loan verb marker

In most contemporary Mongolic languages, the denominal verb suffix has grammaticalized from a verbalizer into a productive loan verb marker. Examples include Buriat *zvoni:l-, dežuril-* and *arestoval-* from Russian *zvoni-t'* 'to phone', *dežuri-t'* 'to be on duty' and *arestova-t'* 'to arrest' (Khabtagaeva 2009: 137); in Eastern Yughur *tugla-* and *darla-* from Tibetan *thug-* 'to meet' and *dar-* 'to prosper' and in Eastern Yughur *tuolaji kai-la-* 'to drive a tractor' from Mandarin *kai tuolaji* 'to drive a tractor' (Nugteren 2003: 269); in Monguor *čiu:la-* from Mandarin *k'iou* 'to beg, request' (De Smedt & Mostaert 1964: 149); in Dongxiang *qifu-la-* from Mandarin *qifu* 'to afflict'; and in Mangghuer *shangliangla-* 'to discuss' and *dayingla-* 'to promise' from Mandarin *sha:ngliang* 'to consult, talk over, discuss' and *da:ying* 'to agree, promise' (Slater 2003: 323).

5.3.4 pTk *-lA-

The suffix pTk *-lA-* is reflected as a frequent denominal verb suffix in Old Turkic and in most subsequent varieties of Turkic, deriving both transitive and intransitive verbs. It modifies the meaning of the base in two different ways: 1. 'to achieve, overcome or successfully execute a difficult action on the base noun', a meaning that is commonly reflected in verbs of 'hunting' and 'giving birth to', and, 2. 'to make use of the base noun' with a semantic extension to the specific use of time and, when added to nominal adjectives, to the meaning 'to consider as the base'. It can also be used to derive onomatopoetic verbs. In many contemporary Turkic languages, the denominal verb suffix has grammaticalized from a verbalizer into a productive loan verb marker.

5.3.4.1 Manipulative denominal verb suffix

According to Erdal (1991: 429–455), OTk. *-la- ~ -le-*, illustrated below, is the most common denominal suffix in Old Turkic. Attached to onomatopoea and sound-producing nouns it can also derive onomatopoetic verbs, for some of which, e.g. OTk. *tigilä-* 'to make a certain sound, perhaps a droning one', *kakïla-* 'to produce cackling sounds (of birds)', *bozla-* 'to bellow (of camels)' etc., the base is not attested in isolation.

1. 'to achieve, accumulate or overcome the base noun, to execute a difficult action with success on the base noun'

    OTk. *av* 'wild game' → *avla-* 'to hunt (wild game) (tr.)'
    OTk. *boguz* 'throat' → *boguzla-* 'to cut (somebody's/ an animal's) throat (tr.)'
    OTk. *buzagu* 'calf' > *buzagula-* 'to calve (intr.)'
    OTk. *ev* 'house' → *evle-* 'to furnish (sb.) with dwellings, marry (sb.) off (tr.)'
    OTk. *yagï* 'enemy, hostile' → *yagïla-* 'to engage in hostilities (with sb.) (tr.)'
    OTk. *yėr* 'place, land' → *yėrle-* 'to travel through, to settle in a place (tr.)'

2. 'to make use of the base noun'

    OTk. *adut* 'palm of one's hand' → *adutla-* 'to scoop up with the palm of one's hand (tr.)'
    OTk. *agïr* 'heavy, important, burdensome' > *agïrla-* 'to honour, respect (tr.)'
    OTk. *at* 'horse' → *atla-* 'to ride a horse (tr. / intr.)'
    OTk. *kïš* 'winter' → *kïšla-* 'to spend the winter somewhere, go into winter quarters (intr.)'
    OTk. *söz* 'word, speech, statement' → *sözle-* 'to speak, say, talk with somebody (tr.)'
    OTk. *so* 'chain' → *sola-* 'to chain, fasten with chains (tr.)'
    OTk. *yavïz* 'bad' > *yavïzla-* 'to think badly of something'
    OTk. *yïl* 'year' → *yïlla-* 'to spend a year (intr.)'

b) *onomatopoetic*

    OTk. *kaŋ* (mimetic for honking of geese) → *kaŋsïla-* 'to cackle (of birds)'
    OTk. *orï:* 'shout, outcry' → *orïla-* 'to shout'
    OTk. *yïgï* 'lament, yammering' → *ïgla- ~ yïgla-* 'to weep'

As far as Western Turkic is concerned, the denominal verb suffix -*lA*- can still be found in Chuvash today (Levickaja 1976: 165–166). Although it has broadened its semantic scope, the semantic axes 1. 'to achieve the base noun' and 2. 'to make use of the base noun' are still clearly present, for instance in 1. Chu. *puś* 'head, beginning' → *puśla*- 'to begin', Chu. *av* 'house, dwelling' → *avlan*- 'to marry, found one's house', Chu. *yĕrke* 'order, row' → *yĕrkele*- 'to line up' and in 2. Chu. *xĕl* 'winter' → *xĕlle*- 'to spend the winter', Chu. *suχa* 'wooden plow' → *suχala*- 'to plow with a wooden plow', Chu. *ut* 'horse' → *utlan*- 'to mount a horse' etc. The suffix also occurs in onomatopoetic verbs such as Chu. *kăšla*- 'to nibble, to murmur (of a forest)', Chu. *kĕrle*- 'to murmur, rustle, roar (of airplaines)', Chu. *yanăravla*- 'to sound, make noise' etc. The occurrence of the suffix in Chuvash, the only contemporary representative of Western Turkic, indicates that the suffix predates the split of Eastern and Western Turkic; it can thus be reconstructed for proto-Turkic.

5.3.4.2 Loan verb marker

Although some Turkic languages use borrowing strategies such as direct insertion or the addition of a light verb (see Section 3.5.3), others accommodate for a verbal copy through indirect insertion, in most cases by suffixation of the deverbal noun suffix -*lA*-. Among other examples, Eynu *nigala-* and *χorla-* are copied from Persian *niga(r)-* 'to look' and *χor-* 'to eat'; Uighur *yala-* from Mandarin *ya* 'to escort'; Turkish *egavla-* 'to get' from Armenian *egav*, the third singular past of *gal* 'to come' or Turkish *klikle-* from English *click*; Kazakh *zvanitta-* from Russian *zvoni-t'* 'to phone'; Western Yughur *darla-* from Tibetan *dar-* 'to prosper'; Yakut *mehayda:-* 'to interfere' from the Russian singular imperative form *mešaj* from *meša-t'* 'to disturb, interfere'; and Chuvash *mešetle-* from Russian *meša-t'* 'to disturb, interfere'. Erdal (1991: 454) further notes that in Old Turkic the deverbal noun suffix -*lA*- is the only marker which is added freely to foreign bases. The verb OTk. *lala-* 'to cut something up', for instance, has an unattested base, which must be foreign since *l-* does not appear word-initially in native Turkic words. The base of OTk. *öṭiKle-* 'to record, mention, remember one by one' is believed to be Chinese *ötiK* 'register, memorandum, memoir' (Erdal 1991: 444).

5.3.5 The nature of the historical connection

Even opponents of the Transeurasian affinity hypothesis such as Schönig (2003: 416) and Vovin (2011: 18–19) would agree that the similarity of the deverbal noun suffix across the Altaic languages is not the result of chance or universal principles in linguistic structuring but requires a historical explanation. However, they attribute the historical connection to borrowing, whereas in line with other proponents of the Transeurasian hypothesis, I would suggest it is due to inheritance.

According to Vovin's scenario, Turkic has the original suffix. As verbs are borrowed from Turkic, including those derived with *-lA-, such as MMo. *bo'orla-* from OTk. *boguz-la-* 'to cut (somebody's/ an animal's) throat (tr.),' this suffix becomes productive in Mongolic. Note that the majority of borrowed verbs lack a native base: there is no *bo'or* 'throat' from which MMo. *bo'orla-* could have been derived. Subsequently, Tungusic borrows verbs from Mongolic, including verbs derived with a borrowed *-lA-, such as Ma. *šejile-* 'repeat by heart' from WMo. *čegejile-* 'to learn by hart, memorize' and, finally, the suffix becomes productive in Tungusic. The Japonic correlations, then, are coincidental. This scenario is unlikely, however, because it fails to explain the chronological framework, the divergence of meaning in some pairs, the unrestricted distribution of some pairs, the occurrence of the suffix in Japonic and the scope of the shared properties.

First, as far as chronology is concerned, 500 years can serve as a reasonable indication of the minimal time it will take borrowed morphology to become productive on native items. This estimation is based on cross-linguistic studies such as Bakker and Hekking 2012. These authors find that, while over 500 years of contact with Spanish has substantially affected the morphology of the three Amerindian languages, Quechua, Guarani and Otomi, examples of copied morphology being applied to native bases are extremely rare. While none are found in Guarani, they are extremely restricted in Quechua and Otomi, suggesting that the productive application of borrowed morphology is still at an early stage. Otomi, for instance, applies only a single borrowed marker, i.e. *-a* for female gender, to only a single lexical base, i.e. ‚*be:ta* 'granddaughter' derived from ‚*be:t'o* 'grandchild', originally a gender neutral form.

The Turkic model *bogur-la-* 'to cut the throat' yielding MMo. *bo'orla-* had *-r- rather than *-z- and – at least according to Vovin and Schönig – the *-r- variant only developed in Eastern Turkic. Therefore, the earliest identifiable layer of borrowings of -lA- derived verbs from Turkic into Mongolic seems to postdate the split of Eastern and Western Old Turkic, which took place around 100 BC, when Oghur loanwords, such as *yür* 'hundred' entered Samoyedic (see Section 1.2.2.1). If we apply Bakker and Hekking's estimation of 500 years to Vovin's contact scenario, it is fair to estimate that *-lA- may not have become productive in Mongolic before 400 AD. From 400 AD onwards, Tungusic may have started to borrow *-lA- derived verbs from Mongolic, to become productive by 900 AD at the earliest. These estimated dates for productivity, summarized in Table 1, conflict with the real dates of productivity proto-Khitan-Mongolic (see Section 1.2.2.2) and proto-Tungusic (see Section 1.2.2.3). Since Khitan preserves reflexes of *-lA-, the suffix can be traced back to the common ancestor of Khitan and Mongolic, i.e. before 180 AD. This argument is even stronger for Tungusic: as all contemporary Tungusic languages reflect *-lA- it must have been productive in proto-Tungusic, i.e. at least before 220 AD.

Table 1. Chronological conflict in Vovin's borrowing scenario of the deverbal noun suffix *-lA-

Stage in borrowing process	Example	Estimated date
proto-Turkic original	OTk. *boguz* 'throat' → *boguzla-* 'to cut the throat (tr.)'	before 100 BC
Mongolic borrows Turkic verbs	No base → MMo. *bo'orla-* 'to cut the throat (tr.)'	after 100 BC
productivity pMo *-lA-	WMo. *čegeji(n)* 'memory' → *čegejile-* 'to memorize (tr.)'	after 400 AD
Tungusic borrows Mongolic verbs	No base → Ma. *šejile-* 'repeat by heart'	after 400 AD
productivity pTg *-lA:-	Ma. *gucu* 'friend'- > *gucule-* 'to make friends' Even *tew* 'berry' → *tewle:-* 'to gather berries' Ud. *anda* 'friend' > *andala-* 'to make friends'	after 900 AD

A second reason why Vovin's scenario is contradicted is the divergence of meaning in some derivational pairs. In the contact scenario, the baseless borrowings are assumed to be older than the productive *-lA- derivational pairs. If the borrowings are older, their semantics have developed during a longer period of time than the meanings of productive derivations. In reality, the opposite can be observed. Whereas productive derivations have developed secondary semantics, such as WMo. *gerle-* 'to marry' from *'to build a house', SH MMo. *morila-* 'to depart' from *'to use a horse', Ud. *sita* 'child' > *sitala-* 'to adopt' from *'to get a child', Even *usi:le:-* 'to control (a reindeer) with a rope, to encircle the reindeers' from *'to use a rope' and Ma. *songkolo-* 'to imitate' from 'to follow the tracks', this is not the case for baseless borrowings: MMo. *bo'orla-*, MMo. *ögütle-*, WMo. *orila-* have exactly the same meanings as their Turkic models, reflected in OTk *boguzla-* 'to cut the throat (tr.)', OTk. *ögüt-le-* 'to advice' and OTk. *orïla-* 'to shout,' respectively. The same is true for Ma. *jaila-* and Ma. *šejile-* copied from a model reflected in WMo. *čegejile-* 'to learn by hart' and WMo. *jayi-la-* 'to avoid', respectively. This observation suggests that, contrary to Vovin's claim, the productive derivations are older than the baseless borrowings.

Third, the unrestricted distribution of derivational pairs as opposed to the restriction of baseless borrowings to specific contact zones suggests that – unlike the borrowings – the derivation goes back to the ancestral languages. This observation is particularly relevant for Tungusic, where most examples of baseless borrowings are from Mongolic into Manchu, whereas the productive derivations are spread equally across the Tungusic languages.

Fourth, the borrowing scenario cannot account for how the *-lA- suffix made its way into Japonic, without a Korean intermediary. This highlights the importance of low-contact languages like Japanese in solving the genealogical question for the Transeurasian languages.

Finally, the wide scope of the shared properties strongly argues against borrowing. In addition to sharing form and function, the similarities include shared cumulation of the deverbal nominalizer function and specific actional meaning, shared allomorphy between vowel harmonic alternants in Altaic (and some traces of vowel alternation in Japanese) and a shared process of grammaticalization from deverbal noun suffix to loan verb marker (see Section 2.5).

5.4 pTEA *-nA- processive

5.4.1 pJ *-na- (~ *-nə-)

The suffix pJ *-na- has lexicalized in at least 19 Old Japanese verb stems, illustrated below. It derives transitive and intransitive verbs from nominal, adjectival and verbal bases. The adjective bases can be either nominal or verbal. Apart from its function as a verbalizer, pJ *-na- modifies the meaning of the base in the sense of 'to develop or form the concept denoted by the base'. Some transitive derivations of nominal bases extend their meaning to 'processing or evaluating the base noun'. The suffix pJ *-na- thus denotes dynamic processes, some of which cannot be caused by an agent, while others can.

The suffix is reconstructed as pJ *-na-, with the final vowel surfacing in further derivations with the anticausative *-ra- (e.g. OJ tura-na-r- 'to form a line (intr.)'), the causative *-sa- (e.g. MJ kata-na-s- A 'to summarize (tr.)'), the causative-anticausative *-(C)i- (e.g. OJ katane- 'to summarize (tr.)') and derived with the iterative *-pa- in numerous examples below. The derived verb OJ udunap- alternates with udunop- 'to prize, value (tr.)', suggesting an allomorph pJ *-nə-, a behavior that resembles vowel harmony.

All the verb pairs below, except for the bracketed derivation of OJ tatane- ?A'to fold up, pile up (tr.)' reflect congruent register. The derivation from verbal bases remains speculative because it involves few examples, one of which has incongruent register, and somewhat diverging semantics.

Although strings consisting of two or more lexicalized actional suffixes are rare, there are some contemporary Japanese verbs that indicate that pJ *-na- is followed by all other actional suffixes, except for the deverbal noun suffix pJ *-ra-.[4]

At least two verbs among the examples below have counterparts in Ryukyuan, i.e. 'to deal in, sell, trade (tr.)' in Shuri *qacinee* B and 'to compare' in Shuri *kurabir-* / *kunabir-* A, which suggests that pJ *-na-* was productive as a non-spontaneous processive in Japonic.

denominal

1. 'to develop/form the concept denoted by the base noun'

   OJ *aki*₁ ?*2.3 'barter, trade, peddling' → *aki*₁*nap-* ?B 'to deal in, sell, trade (tr.)'

   OJ *ata* 2.2a 'enemy, hostility' → OJ *atanap-* A 'to harm, injure (tr.)'

   J *kasa* 2.2b' bulk' → J *kasanar-* A 'to grow in bulk (intr.)', OJ *kasane-* A 'to pile up, layer (tr.)'

   OJ *mapi*₁ ? 2.3 'gift, offering' → OJ *mapi*₁*nap-* ?B 'to bribe (tr.)'

   OJ *oto*₂ 2.2a 'sound' → OJ *oto*₂*nap-* ?A 'to make a noise (intr.)'

   OJ *pusa* 2.3 'bunch' → OJ *pusanar-* B 'form a bunch, bunch out (intr.)', OJ *pusane*₂- B 'bunch together, make into a bunch (tr.)'

   OJ *to*₂*mo*₂ 2.1. 'companion' → OJ *to*₂*monap-* A 'accompany, go (with) (intr.)', OJ *tomonape*₂- 'let accompany, take along (tr.)'

   J *tuka* ?2.4 ?2.3 'bundle' → OJ *tukane-* B 'bundle (into one) (tr.)'

   OJ *tura* ?2.1 ?2.2a 'row, line' → OJ *turanar-* A 'to form a line, stand in a row (intr.)', OJ *turane-* ?A 'to put in a row, line up, link (tr.)'

   OJ *ura* 2.4 'divination, foretelling' → OJ *uranap-* B 'to divine, foretell (tr.)'

2. 'to evaluate/process the concept denoted by the base noun'

   OJ *kura* 'position established on a higher level', OJ *kurawi* 3.1 'level, rank' → OJ *kurabe-* A 'to compare (tr.)' (< *kura-n(a)-pa-*)

   J *ni* 1.3b 'burden' → OJ *ninap-* ?B 'to shoulder, bear, carry on one's shoulder (tr.)'

---

[4] See Robbeets (2007a: 11–12) for 24 instances of *-n(a)-ka*₍₂₎-, 2 of *-na-ma-* and 3 of *-n(a)-ka*₍₁₎- sequences in contemporary Japanese verbs.

OJ *tumi₁* 2.4. 'crime, sin' → OJ *tuminap-, tuminape₂-* B 'to punish (tr.)'

OJ *udu* 2.x. 'treasure, precious (thing)' → OJ *udunap- ~ udunop-* ? 'to prize, value (tr.)'

deadjectival: 'to develop the property denoted by the base adjective'

OJ *maro₂* 2.1 ' round (thing), circle' → OJ *maro₂b-* A 'to tumble (intr.)' (< **maro-n(a)-pa-*)

OJ *ama-* A 'sweet' → OJ *amanap-* ?A 'to cooperate, be nice/friendly to (intr.)'

OJ *kata-* A 'hard' → OJ *katane-* A 'to lump/bunch together, summarize (tr.)', MJ *katanas-* A 'to summarize (tr.)'

deverbal: 'to develop the state or action denoted by the base verb'

OJ *ok-* A 'to put (tr.)', [OJ *oko₂r-* B 'to arise, happen' ~ *oko ₂s-* B 'to raise'] → OJ *oko₂nap-* A 'to handle, act, do, perform, carry out (tr.)'⁵

[OJ *tat-* B 'to stand, be built' → OJ *tatanapar-* A 'to get piled up', OJ *tatanaduk-* ?A 'to pile up (tr.)', OJ *tatane-* ?A 'to fold up, pile up (tr.)']

OJ *uk-* A 'to float' > OJ *ukab-* A 'to float (intr.)', OJ *ukabe₂-* A 'to let float, let rise to the surface (tr.)' (< **uka-n(a)-pa-(C)i-*)

5.4.2 pK *-nO-*

The processive suffix MK *-no-* is incorporated in the contemporary Korean progressive adnominal *-nun* and in the progressive indicative *-nunta*, but in Middle Korean grammar it still behaves as a productive suffix. MK *-no-* derives processive intransitive verbs from verbal adjectives, as in the examples (1) and (2), and progressive transitive or intransitive verbs from verbs, as in the examples (3) to (5). Martin (1992: 722) uses the term 'processive' in both cases, but I reserve the term 'processive' for dynamic events that are not caused by an agent and develop spontaneously, such as 'to petrify', 'to bloom', 'to grow', whereas I use 'progressive' for actions and events that develop over a longer period of time. Note that all de-adjectival examples involve adjective bases that can function both as a descriptive intransitive verb ('to be the property') and as processive intransitive verb ('to develop the property spontaneously'), e.g. MK *kwut-* 'to be(come) hard', MK *hoy-* 'to be(come) white, light', MK *·ha-* 'to be(come) big, plentiful' etc.

---

5 For the problematic assignment of register in this derivation, see Section 3.3.4.

Early attestations, such as (3), indicate that MK ··*no*- alternated with MK ··*nu*- according to the rules of vowel harmony, but due to a merger MK ··*nu*- completely disappeared in the 16th century.

Martin (1992: 261) places the suffix in the leftmost positions of the verbal suffix chain. Only occasionally can it be preceded by suffixes expressing status, while other markers of actionality, politeness, aspect or mood follow the suffix. The processive MK ··*no*- is mutually exclusive with the resultative MK ··*kA*- and with the retrospective MK ··*tA*-.

deadjectival 'to spontaneously develop the property denoted by the base adjective'

(1) MK *wuh-·kwa a·lay   nung·hi selu   kwut-no-·n-i   i-·ta*
    top-COOR bottom fairly   reciprocally be.hard-PROC-ADN-fact be-FIN
    'The top and the bottom, they both become fairly solid'
    (1586 Sohak 4: 53b; Martin 1992: 716)

(2) MK *e·tuw-u·l-ak   twolwo   ·hoy-no-·n-i*
    be.dark-ADN-one.of.two   again   be.light-PROC-ADN-fact
    'It gets dark and then again it gets light.'
    (1481 Twusi 7: 14b; Martin 1992: 716)

deverbal 'to develop the action denoted by the base verb over a longer period of time'

(3) MK ¨*wu-·nu-n   swo·li*
    cry-PROC-ADN   sound
    'the sound of crying' (1447 Sek 19: 14b; Martin 1992: 723)

(4) K *atok ho-n   kono-n   pi   wo-no-s-ta*
    dim be-ADN   be.fine-ADN   rain   come.down-PROC-EMO-FIN
    'A dim fine rain sets in.' (1632 Twusi-cwung 12: 25b; Martin 1992: 721)

(5) MK ¨*manh-i   tut-·tolwok* ¨*etwuk ·sin-thi   a·ni   ·ho-no-·n-i*
    be.many-ADV hear-extent   more   believe-NML NEG do-PROC-ADN-fact
    'The more I hear, the less I believe' (1482 Nam 1: 36 b; ; Martin 1992: 719)

5.4.3 pTg *-nA-

The processive suffix pTg *-nA- is well reflected in all contemporary Tungusic languages (Benzing 1955a: 1064, 1068; Poppe 1972: 140–141). It generally derives intransitive processive verbs from nouns, from nominal adjectives and from (in) transitive verbs. Denoting dynamic events that are not caused by an agent and develop spontaneously, pTg *-nA- is often used for natural phenomena or bodily activities. The deverbal processive occasionally grammaticalizes into a reflexive, denoting that the verb base is carried out on oneself or, into a processive-distributive, denoting that the action spontaneously takes place on the whole surface of the subject. The processive is situated in the leftmost positions of the verbal suffix chain; in Udehe it can be preceded by the inchoative suffix, while other markers of actionality usually follow.

5.4.3.1 Manchu -nA-

Manchu -na- ~ -ne- ~ -no-, illustrated below, productively derives processive verbs from nouns (Gorelova 2002: 236). It is also incorporated as a deverbal suffix in a few irregular imperfective vs. resultative (ad)nominal forms in Ma. -ndArA vs. -ngkA (see Section 7.6.3.1), which can be analyzed as *-nA-dA-rA (PROC-da-IPFV.NML) and *-na-xA (PROC-RES.NML) respectively. There are 14 verbs taking the irregular resultative nominalizer -ngkA and semantically they all share a semantic component open for 'spontaneous development'. Some of these verbs have preserved an alternating stem in -nA-, e.g. Ma. ba- ~ bana- 'to be(come) lazy', Ma. fu- ~ fune- 'to become numb', Ma. we- ~ wene- 'to melt', etc.

denominal 'to spontaneously develop the concept denoted by the base noun'

Ma. *abdaha* 'leaf' → *abdahana-* 'to leaf, produce leaves'
Ma. *asha-* 'wing' → *ashana-* 'to get wings'
Ma. *edun* 'wind' → *eduna-* 'to become windy'
Ma. *eifun* 'pimple, swelling' → *eifune-* 'to develop a swelling'
Ma. *talin* 'lightning' → *talino-* 'to flash (of lightning)'
Ma. *umiyaha* 'worm' → *umiyahana-* 'to get worms (of fruit)'

deverbal 'to spontaneously develop the action denoted by the base verb'

Ma. *ba-* 'to be lazy, tired, gnaw a hole' → *bana-* 'to be(come) lazy'; *ba-ndara* (be.lazy-IPV.NML) ~ *ba-ngka* (be.lazy-RES.NML)

Ma. *fu-* 'to become numb' → *fune-*'to become numb'; *fu-ngke* (become.numb-RES.NML)

Ma. *jo-* 'to bring to mind, recall, mention' → *jono-* 'to recall'; *jo-ndoro* (mention-IPV.NML) ~ *jongko* (mention-RES.NML)

Ma. *ša-* 'to dry (tr.)' → *ša-ngka* (dry-RES.NML)

Ma. *sa-* 'to stretch' → *sa-ngka* (stretch-RES.NML)

Ma. *su-* 'to cover with frost' → *su-ngke* (cover.with ·frost-RES.NML)

Ma. *we-* 'to melt' → *wene-* 'to melt'; *we-ndere* (melt-IPV.NML) ~ *we-ngke* (melt-RES.NML)

5.4.3.2 Even -(A)n$_{(2)}$-

Even verbs with stem-final -*n* fall into two distinct conjugational classes: the first class forms its adnominal or "aorist" on -*nA*- (e.g. Even *gö:n*$_{(1)}$- 'to say' → *gö:-ne-m* 'I say'), while the second class forms it on -*rA*- (e.g. Even *ŋen*$_{(2)}$- 'to go' → *ŋen-re-m* 'I go'). The first class of verbs, which goes back to verb stems with an original stem-final nasal in Tungusic (< pTg **gu:n-* 'to say'), drops the nasal before the majority of actional suffixes and suffixes of valence and voice. The stem-final -*n*$_{(1)}$- will therefore be traced back to an original adnominal form **-n* in Section 7.5.3.2. The second class of verbs, which goes back to verb stems with an original stem-final vowel in Tungusic (< pTg **ŋene-* 'to go'), maintains its nasal as a part of the verb stem before other derivational markers. The word pairs below suggest that at least a part of these stem-final -*n*$_{(2)}$- nasals originate from a processive suffix. As illustrated below, the suffix derives verbs from nouns, nominal adjectives and (in)transitive verbs. Note that some verbs such as *udan*$_{(1)}$- ~ *udan*$_{(2)}$- 'to drizzle (intr.)' or *batan*$_{(1)}$- 'to freeze, get covered with ice' ~ *batan*$_{(2)}$- 'to freeze, ice over (of ground) (intr.)' can fall into both categories; the latter verb may represent a processive derivation of the first. The verb *hagdi:n*$_{(1)}$- 'to grow old (intr.)' has -*n*$_{(1)}$, but seems to belong in this category on semantic grounds. Furthermore, some verbs for natural phenomena or bodily activities, such as *be:wen*$_{(2)}$- 'to appear (of the moon)', *hapkan*$_{(2)}$- 'to bite (of cold)', *jelgen*$_{(2)}$- 'to grow wild, imbrute' and *kogun*$_{(2)}$- ~ *kugan*$_{(2)}$- 'to cast off the skin of the antlers', are probably derivations with the processive suffix, even if they lack a clear base.

denominal 'to spontaneously develop the concept denoted by the base noun'

> Even *ewgi:* 'here in the vicinity' → *ewgen*$_{(2)}$- 'to cast/shoot too short (intr.)'
> pTg **xima* 'snow' → Even *ïman*$_{(2)}$- ' to snow (intr.)'
> Even *udan* 'rain', *udal-* 'to begin to rain' → *udan*$_{(2)}$- ~ *udan*$_{(1)}$- 'to drizzle (intr.)'

de-adjectival 'to spontaneously develop the property denoted by the base adjective'

> Even *gu:d* 'high' → *gudan*$_{(2)}$- 'to rise to one's feet (intr.)'
> Even *hagdi:* 'old, grey' → *hagdi:n*$_{(1)}$- 'to grow old (intr.)'

deverbal 'spontaneously develop the action denoted by the base verb, to carry out the verb base by oneself'

> Even *ge:w-* 'to repeat (tr.)' → *ge:wan*$_{(2)}$- 'to dawn (intr.)'
> Even *hor-* 'to fall into a trap (intr.); to catch, capture (tr.)' → *horan*$_{(2)}$- 'to fall into a trap (intr.)'

Even *me:yi:-* 'to swing, cradle (tr.)' → *me:yi:n*₍₂₎- 'to swing oneself (intr.)'

Even *nebde-* 'to pull of the hide as a whole (tr.)', Even *nebde-ńe* 'flat, wide' → *nebden-* 'to unfold widely; open up (of cloth, wings); straighten out; open up (of leaves) (intr.)'

5.4.3.3 Evenki -nA-

Evenki *-na-* ~ *-ne-* ~ *-no-*, illustrated below, has lexicalized in processive verbs deriving from nouns or verbs.

denominal 'to spontaneously develop the concept denoted by the base noun'

    Evk. *juseren* 'lightning' → *jusene-* 'to flash (of lightning)'
    Evk. *sugi:* 'breath' → *sugina-* 'to breathe'
    pTg **xima* 'snow' in Evk. *imana* 'snow' → *imana-* 'to fall (of snow)'

deverbal 'spontaneously develop the action denoted by the base verb, to carry out the verb base by oneself'

    Evk. *belge-* 'to quiver, shudder, startle'→ *belgene-* 'to be agitated, fret oneself about something'

    Evk. *dukte-* 'to hit, pond, beat (tr.)' → *duktīne-* 'to beat (of the heart) (intr.)'

    Evk. *kiki:-* 'to whistle, pipe (intr.)' → *kikine-* 'to howl (of wind) (intr.)'

    *nasa- 'to stretch, wave (tr.)' in Evk. *nasas o:-* 'to wave', *nasaka-* 'to stretch one's arms sideways' → *nasana-* 'to wave one's arms, flap its wings'

5.4.3.4 Udehe -nA-

Udehe *-na-* ~ *-ne-* ~ *-no-*, illustrated below, productively derives processive verbs from nouns, nominal adjectives and verbs (Nikolaeva 1999: 172, 173, 183). The denominal suffix often derives subjectless verbs that denote the appearance of a particular natural phenomenon. The deverbal suffix only applies to intransitive bases, frequently with inchoative meanings. It denotes that the action spontaneously takes place on the whole surface of the subject.

denominal 'to spontaneously develop the concept denoted by the base noun'

    Ud. *b'ata* 'boy, fellow' → *b'atana-* 'to become grown up (of a boy) (intr.)'
    Ud. *edi* 'wind' > *edine-* 'to blow (of wind) (intr.)'
    Ud. *ima:* 'snow' > *ima:na-* 'to snow (intr.)'
    Ud. *lusa* 'Russian' → *lusana-* 'to become russified (intr.)'

Ud. *mo:* 'tree' → *mo:no-* 'to become a tree (intr.)'
Ud. *sogdo* 'steam' > *sogdono-* 'to appear (of steam) (intr.)'
Ud. *ute* 'rotten wood' → *utene-* 'to molder away, become old (intr.)'

de-adjectival 'to spontaneously develop the property denoted by the base adjective'

Ud. *ede* 'weak' → *edene-* 'to become weak'
Ud. *mangga* 'strong' → *manggana-* 'to become strong'
Ud. *ńangma* 'cold' > *ńangmana-* 'to freeze'
Ud. *xoligi* 'yellow' > *xoligine-* 'to become yellow'

deverbal 'spontaneously develop the action denoted by the base verb over the whole surface of the subject'

Ud. *tingme-* 'to fall down (intr.)' → *tingmene-* 'to collapse over the whole surface, fall into pieces (intr.)'

Ud. *bukta-ga-* 'to break (inchoative)' > *buktagana-* 'to break all over / in several places (intr.)'

Ud. *kakta-ga-* 'to crack (inchoative)' > *kaktagana-* 'to crack all over / in several places (intr.)'

5.4.3.5 Nanai -nA-

Nanai *-na- ~ -ne-*, illustrated below, productively derives processive verbs from nouns and nominal adjectives (Avrorin 1961: 18, 49–50). Benzing (1955 a: 1064, 1068) and Poppe (1972a: 140) treat the deverbal reiterative suffix Na. *-nAsi-* as a compound of *-nA-* and *-si-*. They relate the former element to the deverbal suffixes discussed above. Na. *-si-* is attested as an actional suffix deriving continuous, multiple or occasional actions (Avrorin 1961: 46). The semantic parallel with the Udehe verbs above, in the sense of spontaneous development of the action denoted by the base verb over the whole surface of the subject or at multiple times, supports this derivation.

denominal 'to spontaneously develop the concept denoted by the base noun'

Na. *xuren* 'mountain, hill' → *xurene-* 'to become mountainous (intr.)'
Na. *jolo* 'stone' → *jolona-* 'to turn to stone, petrify (intr.)'
Na. *juke* 'ice' → *jukene-* 'to ice over, become covered with ice (intr.)'
Na. *saksa* 'frost pattern' → *saksana-* 'to develop frost patterns (intr.)'
Na. *sugbin* 'steam' → *sugbine-* 'to vaporize, appear of steam (intr.)'

de-adjectival 'to spontaneously develop the property denoted by the base adjective'

 Na. *dai* 'big' → *daina-* 'to be(come) big (intr.)'
 Na. *egji* 'many' → *egjina-* 'to be(come) many (intr.)'
 Na. *masi* 'strong, firm' → *masina-* 'to become strong (intr.)'
 Na. *sagji* 'old' → *sagjina-* 'to become old (intr.)'
 Na. *segjen* 'red' → *segjene-* 'to be(come) red (intr.)'

deverbal 'spontaneously develop the action denoted by the base verb over the whole surface of the subject or at multiple times'

 Na. *gele-* 'ask, request, want' > *gelenesi-* 'to beg, cadge (intr.)'
 Na. *kalma-* 'to crack, burst' > *kalmanasi-* 'to crack all over, chap (intr.)'
 Na. *omi-* 'to drink, smoke' → *ominasi-* 'to take to the bottle, smoke from time to time (intr.)'

5.4.4 pMo *-nA-

The processive suffix pMo *-nA- is lexicalized as -nA- in Written Mongolian. It generally derives intransitive processive verbs from nouns, from nominal adjectives and from (in)transitive verbs. Denoting dynamic events that are usually not caused by an agent and develop spontaneously, pMo *-nA- is often used for natural phenomena or bodily activities. The suffix can also derive sound-producing and onomatopoetic verbs that are caused by an agent, in so far as the basic sounds are produced with the speech organs. Considering alternations such as *qubina-* ~ *qubigina-* 'to whisper', the analysis proposed by Poppe (1972a: 141) and Tekin (1982: 507) of the onomatopoetic suffix WMo. -*ginA*-, as a coumpound of iconic pMo *-Ki- (see Section 5.3.4) and processive pMo *-nA- is probably correct. The deverbal processive occasionally grammaticalizes into a reflexive, denoting that the verb base is carried out on oneself.

 The examples of de-adjectival derivation are restricted to nominal adjectives on -*GAr*, regularly losing the final liquid before a nasal suffix. However, it is more likely that these are actually instances of deverbal derivation following the causative suffix -*GA*- (Poppe 1954: 61) or the inchoative suffix -*GA*- (see Section 5.7.4). The base *degdege-* 'to raise, startle up, stir up (tr.)' below, for instance, is in its turn a causative derivation from *degde-* 'to rise, float; jump, hop; fly up; happen, occur (intr.)'. Since all adjectival bases have verbal counterparts derived with the resultative suffix -*yi*- and lacking the segment -*GA*-, such as *arjayi-* 'to show one's teeth, grin; to stand on end (of hair), to be rough or uneven (intr.)', *irjayi-*

'for a row of small objects to move or appear, for teeth to show, to grin, sneer (intr.)' and *bülteyi-* 'to be pop-eyed, to bulge (of eyes), to open one's eyes wide, to stare (intr.)', they are likely to be verbal in origin.

denominal 'to spontaneously develop the concept denoted by the base noun'

> WMo. *alčaɣa* 'crotch of legs, scissors etc.' → *alčaɣana-* 'to walk with legs apart, straddle (intr.)'
>
> WMo. *čang* 'hoarfrost' → *čangna-* 'to be(come) covered with hoarfrost (intr.)'
>
> WMo. *küür* 'conversation, discourse, word' → *küüne-* 'to talk, converse (intr.)'
>
> WMo. *toɣusu(n)* 'dust' → *toɣusuna-* 'to rise (of dust), to be filled with dust (of the air) (intr.)'

de-adjectival 'to spontaneously develop the bodily property denoted by the base adjective'

> WMo. *arjaɣar* 'showing teeth, grinning, uneven, rough' → *arjaɣana-* 'to show one's teeth, grin; to stand on end (of hair), to be rough or uneven (intr.)'
>
> WMo. *irjaɣar* 'showing teeth, gaping, having protrudung teeth' → *irjaɣana-* 'to move or appear (of a row of small objects), to show (of teeth), to consist of many small pieces'
>
> WMo. *bülteger* 'bulging (of eyes); pop-eyed person' → *bültegene-* 'to open one's eyes wide, to stare (intr.)'

deverbal

> WMo. *degdege-* 'to raise, startle up, stir up (tr.)' → *degdegene-* 'to be agile, lively, quick; to hop, move by short brisk leaps; to be flippant, light-minded or flighty (intr.)'
>
> WMo. *dorba-yi-* 'to stick out, bulge out, swell (intr.)' → *dorbaɣana-* 'to protrude, bulge out (of lips) (intr.)'
>
> WMo. *jigi-* 'to stretch, extend, prolong (tr.)' → *jigine-* 'to extend or stretch by itself, to attain peace of mind, calm down (intr.)'
>
> WMo. *jagatu-lča-* 'to rub against eachother (reciprocal) (intr.)' > *jagatuna-* 'to itch (intr.)'

onomatopoetic

> WMo. *qubi* onomatopoetic expression for whispering → *qubina-* ~ *qubigina-* 'to whisper (intr.)'

WMo. *yangyur* onomatopoetic expression for honking → *yangyuna-* 'to honk as geese (intr.)'

WMo. *günggür* onomatopoetic expression for murmering, distant voices → *günggüne-* 'to hum (of a bumble bee), to speak with a nasal twang, to mumble (intr.)'

WMo. *siber šabir* 'whispering, in a whisper' → *sibene-, sibana-, sibine-* 'to whisper (intr.)'

5.4.5 pTk *-(X)n-

The suffix pTk *-(X)n- has lexicalized as -(X)n- in Old Turkic and as -(Ă)n- in Chuvash. OTk. -(X)n- derives intransitive or transitive verbs from verbal adjectives and (in)transitive verbs, adding processive, reflexive or benefactive meaning, denoting, respectively, spontaneous development of the verb base, accomplishment of the verb base on oneself, or, accomplishment of the verb base for one's own benefit (Erdal 1992: 584–639). Although the majority of -(X)n- derived verbs do not refer to a direct object, some verbs, such as OTk. *basïn-* 'to come under stress (intr.), impose restraint on oneself (intr.), oppress, repress (metaphorically) (tr.),' can become transitive when used in a metaphorical, benefactive sense. This semantic modification without impact on the valency of the verb can serve as an indication that we are dealing with an original actional suffix instead of a diathetical marker.

The processive suffix occupies a position to the left of the verbal suffix chain. It is often preceded by the denominal verb marker -lA-, such as in the derivation from OTk. *bašla-* 'begin, lead (tr.)' below and, similarly to Mongolic, it can be preceded by the causative marker *-t(I)-, such as in the derivation from OTk. *agït-* 'to raise, make climb (intr.)' below, in its turn a causative from OTk *ag-* 'to rise, to climb (intr.)'. Other suffixes, such as the reciprocal -(X)š-, always follow the processive.

In contrast with the Japonic, Tungusic and Mongolic languages and Chuvash, the Old Turkic processive does not derive from nouns or nominal adjectives. Although only nominal bases such as OTk. *ogür* 'herd', OTk. *ag(ï)z* 'mouth' and OTk. *uvuš* 'a way of rubbing with the hands', seem to be attested for verbs such as OTk. *ögren-* 'to be domesticated, tame (of an animal)', OTk. *ag(ï)zan-* 'to utter, recite' and OTk. *uvšan-* 'to be crushed, crumbled', respectively, these verbs may have involved unattested derivations with the denominal verb suffix -A.

deadjectival 'to spontaneously develop the property denoted by the verbal adjective base'

> OTk. *a:r-* 'to be tired, exhausted, weak' → *arïn-* 'to tire (intr.)'
> OTk. *arï-* 'to be(come) clean, pure' → *arïn-* 'to purify oneself, be pure (intr.)'
> OTk. *isi-* 'to be hot' → *isin-* 'to have warm feelings towards someone (intr.)'
> OTk. *kat-* 'to be(come) hard' → *katïn-* 'to become hard, though (intr.)'

deverbal

1. 'to spontaneously develop the action denoted by the base verb'

    > OTk. *bar-* 'to go (intr.)' → *barïn-* 'to flow off from a person's body (intr.)'
    > OTk. *bašla-* 'to begin, lead (tr.)' → *bašlan-* 'to begin (intr.)'
    > OTk. *to-* 'to close, block (tr.)' → *ton-* 'to be closed, be blocked (intr.)'

2. 'to carry out the action denoted by the base verb on oneself'

    > OTk. *ač-* 'to open (tr.)' > *ačïn-* 'to open one's clothes, baring the bosom; disclose one's sins (intr.)'
    > OTk. *alk-* 'to destroy, use up, finish (tr.)' → *alkïn-* 'to consume or exhaust oneself (intr.)'
    > OTk. *yu-* 'wash (tr.)' > *yun-* 'wash, wash oneself (intr.)'

3. 'to carry out the action denoted by the base verb for ones own benefit'

    > OTk. *agït-* 'to raise, make climb (intr.)' → *agtïn-* 'to rise, climb, get to, go up to the capital (intr.)'
    > OTk. *bak-* 'to look at' > *bakïn-* 'look for one's own benefit, look around'
    > OTk. *bas-* 'to press, impress, crush, attack (tr.)' → *basïn-* 'come under stress (intr.), impose restraint on oneself (intr.), oppress, repress (metaphorically) (tr.)'

As far as Western Turkic is concerned, the processive suffix is reflected as Chuvash *-(Ă)n-* (Levickaja 1976: 166–167, Krüger 1961: 180). Contrary to Old Turkic, the suffix can derive from nominal bases, such as Chu. *as* 'memory, mind, understanding' → *asăn-* 'to remember, pray, implore, ask (tr.)', Chu. *pur* 'presence, existence' → *purăn-* 'to live, to exist (intr.)' and Chu. *puś* 'head, beginning' → *puśăn-* 'to begin (intr.)' and from nominal adjectives, such as Chu. *ăšă* 'warm' → *ăšăn-* 'to warm oneself, get warm, melt (intr.)', Chu. *pušă* 'empty, vacant' → *pušăn-* 'to empty oneself, unload oneself (intr.)', Chu. *yĕpe* 'wet' → *yĕpen-* 'to become wet (intr.)'. It further derives verbs from transitive or intransitive bases, such as Chu. *śit-* 'to arrive, get to, succeed; reach, attain (intr.)' → *śitĕn-* 'to grow up (intr.)', Chu. *šăv-* 'to wash (tr.)' → *šăvăn-* 'to wash oneself (intr.)', Chu. *kur-* 'to see (tr.)' → *kurăn-* 'to be seen, seem, be visible, look like (intr.)'. The meaning of Chuvash *-(Ă)n-* is processive, extending to reflexive or benefactive semantics. The majority of the derived verbs are intransitives but some, such as Chu. *asăn-* 'to remember (tr.)', may take a direct object. The preservation of denominal and de-adjectival derivation in Chuvash indicates that these features were present in proto-Turkic but were lost in Eastern Old Turkic.

The restriction to deverbal derivation in Turkic makes it difficult to account for the similarities between Turkic and Mongolic by language contact, because it projects the borrowing of processive verbs back to the time before the split of Eastern and Western Old Turkic or restricts the borrowing to Mongolic and Western Turkic. A scenario whereby speakers of Eastern Turkic copied deverbal derivations from Mongolic, but left the denominal derivations unaffected is unlikely. It goes against common sense to presuppose awareness of diachronic derivational processes in the Mongolic model language by Turkic speakers because this attributes historical linguistic meta-knowledge to the speakers. If the verbs, historically deriving denominal processives, were not massively borrowed from Mongolic into Eastern Turkic, or *vice versa*, the same expectation would exist for verbs in general, which, in reality, is not the case.

5.5 pTEA *-ki- iconic

5.5.1 pJ *-ka-

The iconic suffix OJ *-k(a)-* derives verbs from onomatopoetic interjections and nouns meaning 'sound', adding the meaning 'to produce a sound or a sensation like the base onomatopoea'. Contrary to Martin's (1987: 665–800) analysis, I distinguish between an iconic pJ *-$ka_{(1)}$-* and an inchoative pJ *-$ka_{(2)}$-* because, in spite of their homophony, these suffixes have a different meaning (iconic vs. inchoative), attach to different bases (onomatopoea vs. nouns/adjectives/verbs) and occupy a different position in the suffix chain. Whereas pJ *-$ka_{(1)}$-* occupies the leftmost position in the verbal suffix chain, pJ *-$ka_{(2)}$-* can be preceded by other actional suffixes such as the inclinational suffix pJ *-ma-* in the derivation of OJ *okumake-* 'to anticipate' from OJ *ok-* 'to put' (compare also OJ *okumape-* 'to anticipate').

The original vowel in the iconic suffix pJ *-ka-* can be reconstructed on the basis of further derivations, such as with the lexicalized causative pJ *-sa-* in OJ *pararakas-* 'make flutter' and OJ *ugokas-* 'move (tr.)'.

At least three verbs among the examples below have counterparts in Ryukyuan, i.e. Shuri *nak-* A 'to cry', Shuri *sawag-* A 'to cause commotion', Shuri *qnzuk-* B , *qwiik-* B 'to move'. Other sound symbolic verbs in Ryukyuan such as Shuri *çiçik-* B 'to peck, nudge, poke, incite' seem to be derived with the same velar suffix. This observation indicates that the iconic suffix was productive in proto-Japonic.

onomatopoetic 'to produce a sound or a sensation like the base onomatopoea'

*kororo (mimetic for animal sounds) → OJ *ko₂ro₂ro₂k-* A 'to bark (in a hoarse voice), neigh, chirp'

OJ *ne* 1.1 'sound, crying, weeping'> OJ *nak-* A 'to cry'

*parara (mimetic for quick up and down motion) → OJ *pararakas-* 'to make flutter'

*pipi (mimetic for tingling sensation) → OJ *pi₁pi₁k-* ?A 'to smart, be pungent, give a tingling sensation'

OJ *sawa-sawa ni* 'noisily, turbulently (mimetic)' → OJ *sawak-* ?A?B 'to cause commotion, disturbance, create a fuss'

*soso (mimetic for a gurgling sound) → OJ *so₂so₂k-* A 'to poor a liquid with a gurgling sound'

OJ *to₂do₂* (mimetic expression for knocking on a door or for the trampling of horse hoofs) → OJ *to₂do₂ro₂k-* B 'to roar, rumble, throb'

*toyo (mimetic for reverberation) → OJ *toyok-* ?B 'to clamor, resound, say loudly'

J *ugo-meku* ? A/B 'to wriggle' (*-meku* iconic auxiliary; cf. footnote 2) → OJ *ugok-* B 'to move (intr.)', OJ *ugokas-* B 'to move (tr.)'

*uta (mimetic for a loud sound) → OJ *utak-* ?A 'roar'

5.5.2 pK *-(k)i-*

Korean derives sound symbolic verbs from onomatopoea (= O) using the constructions *O-ha-* 'to do O', *O-keli-* 'to do O repeatedly or continuously, sound like O' and, less frequently, *O-i-* 'to do O repeatedly or continuously, sound like O'. Since the large majority of the onomatopoea followed by K *-i-* 'to do repeatedly, sound like' end in a velar stop *-k* (except for a few cases where K *-i-* 'to do repeatedly, sound like' occurs after a final liquid *-l* or velar nasal *-ng*), it is not unlikely that K *-i-* resulted from the reanalysis of pK *-ki-*. This is supported by some word alternations: in Korean, **wumcik keli-/ ha-* is not attested, we find *wumcil keli-/*

ha- 'moving timidly' from *wumcil*, *wumccil* 'moving timidly' instead, which may serve as an indication that the velar in K *wumcik-i-* originally belonged to the suffix (? < pK **wumci(l)-ki-*). The alternation between K *(s)swukteki-* and K *(s)swuktel-keli-* 'to whisper' points in the same direction.

Ramstedt (1939: 140) reports to have found K *-ki-* following onomatopoetic expressions, but I am unable to trace these forms. Martin (1992: 588) regards K *-i-* as a reduction from K *(kel)i-*, but given the relative infrequency of the former vis-à-vis the latter, I tend to consider K *-i-* (< pK *-ki*) as a more conservative element.

onomatopoetic 'to produce a sound or a sensation like the base onomatopoea'

> K *kkancak kkancak* 'being persistent' → *kkancaki-*/ *kkancak-keli-* 'to stick to, adhere to, cling to, be persistent'
>
> K *kutek, kkutek, kkuttek* 'nodding, bobbing, making a slight movement' → K *kuteki- / kutek-keli-* 'to nod', MK *kuteki-* 'to nod (one's head)'
>
> K *tulmek* 'shaking' → K *tulmeki- / tulmek-keli-* 'to shake'
>
> K *(s)swuktek (s)swuktek* 'in whispers, under one's breath' → K *(s)swukteki- / K (s)swuktek-keli-* 'to whisper'
>
> K *(s)swuktel (s)swuktel* 'in whispers, under one's breath' → K *(s)swukteli- / K (s)swuktel-keli-* 'to whisper'
>
> K *tallang tallang* 'frivolously, restlessly' → *tallangi- / tallang-keli-* 'to act frivolously, be restless, be always on the move'
>
> K *wumcik wumcik* 'budging, stirring, moving' → *wumciki-* 'to move, stir, put in motion'

5.5.3 pTg *-ki:- (~ *-gi:-)

The iconic suffix pTg *-ki:-* 'to produce a sound or a sensation like the base onomatopoea' has lexicalized in onomatopoetic verbs ending in Ma. *-ki- ~ -gi-*, Evk. *-ki:- ~ -gi:-*, Even *-k- ~ -g-*, *-kA- ~ -gA-* and Na. *-ki- ~ -gi-*. The voiced velar alternant is the result of lenition under the influence of a preceding liquid *r*. Since most onomatopoetic verbs have cognates in the other Tungusic languages and lack an independently attested base in the individual language, it is likely that they were formed in the proto-Tungusic stage and inherited as a lexicalizations in the daughter languages.

5.5.3.1 Manchu -*ki*- ~ -*gi*-

With the surface exception of Ma. *carki*- 'to rattle together (as belt pendants), create a dissonance, tinkle,' which is borrowed from WMo. *čargi*- 'rattle, make a harsh sound, speak harshly' (Rozycki 1994: 45), the iconic suffix Ma. -*ki*- voices to -*gi*- following *r*. Among the Manchu sound symbolic verbs that lack an independently attested base are Ma. *dabki*- 'to whip on a horse', *teŋki*- 'to flutter, shake, wave', *čoŋki*- 'to peck' etc.

onomatopoetic 'to produce a sound or a sensation like the base onomatopoea'

Ma. *jor* 'sound of many humans or of screaming animals' → *jorgi*- 'to chirp, twitter, hum'

Ma. *tur* (mimetic for the sound of a horse clearing its nose) → Ma. *turgi*- 'clear the nose (of horses), snort'

Ma. *holor* (mimetic for the sound of the sound of a bell) → Ma. *ho:rgi*- 'to ring'

5.5.3.2 Even -*k*-, -*kA*- ~ -*gA*-

In non-initial syllables in Even, there is a tendency to drop *-*i*- after simple consonants and to reduce it to -*a*- ~ -*e*- after consonant clusters, in accordance with vowel harmony (Benzing 1955a: 969–970). This phonological behavior explains why the reflex of the iconic suffix in Even is -*k*- following vowels and -*kA*- (~ -*gA*-) following consonants, e.g. Even *pasak*- 'to slash, to whip, to clap hands', *pisak*- 'to whistle (of marmots)', *hi:mke*- 'to cough' (< pTg **sim-ki:*-) , *congka*- 'to peck' (< pTg **cong-ki:*-), *harga*- 'to snort, gasp, pant, puff' (< pTg **sar-gi:*-), *borga*- 'to crush, demolish' (< pTg **bur-gi:*-), *cụrga*- 'to flow, drip' (< pTg **cur-gi:*-) etc. Other reflexes of pTg **sim-ki:*- 'to cough' are found in Evk. *simki*-, Neg. *simki*-, Olcha *siŋbi*-, Orok *sipki*-, Na. *siŋbi*-, *simki*-, Oroch *simpi*-, Ud. *simpi*- and Solon *simki*-; pTg **cong-ki:*- 'to peck' in Evk. *coŋki:*-, Neg. *coŋki*-, Ma. *coŋki*- and Na. *coŋkị*-; pTg **sar-gi:*- 'to splatter' in Evk. *sargi*- and Na. *sargị*-; pTg **bur-gi:*- 'to crush, demolish' in Evk. *burgi:*- and pTg **cur-gi:*- 'to flow, drip' in Evk *curgi:*- and Na. *corgi*-.

5.5.3.3 Evenki -*ki(:)*- ~ -*gi(:)*-

The iconic suffix Evk. -*ki*- surfaces in Evk. *simki*- 'to cough', *ungki*- 'to cry, weep', *ńeki*- 'to gnaw, crunch', *he:lki*- 'to flash (of lightning)' etc., voicing to -*gi(:)*- following *r* in *burgi:*- 'to crush, demolish', *cirgi*- 'to chirp, twitter', *kergi*- 'to snort', *sirgi*- 'to make a clattering noise, creak, screak', *dergi*- 'to shiver, tremble', *sargi*- 'to splatter (of water, rain)' etc. In written Evenki, vowel length is often not distinguished, especially after high vowels. This can explain why vowel length only sporadically appears on the iconic suffix.

5.5.3.4 Nanai -ki- ~ -gi-

The iconic suffix Na. -ki- surfaces in Na. *coŋki̭-* 'to peck', *siŋbi-* ~ *simki-* 'to cough', *tatki-* 'to hit the target' etc., voicing to -gi- following *r* in *nirgi-* 'to thunder', *xurgi-* 'make noise', *dergi-* 'shiver, tremble', Na. *corgi-* 'to flow, drip', Na. *sargi-* 'to splatter'. Again, iconic stems borrowed from Mongolic do not respect the conditioning of the allomorphy: Na. *fulgi-* 'to blow' is probably borrowed from WMo. *üliye-*, MMo. *hüliye-* 'to blow, to inflate, to play a wind instrument, to boast', perhaps by intermediary of the Manchu copy *fulgiye-* 'to blow' (Rozycki 1994: 81).

5.5.4 pMo *-ki- (~ *-gi-)

The iconic suffix WMo. -ki- derives verbs from onomatopoetic interjections and nouns meaning 'sound', adding the meaning 'to produce a sound or a sensation like the base onomatopoea'. The voiced velar allomorph WMo. -gi- is the result of lenition in a vocalic environment and following the liquid *r* and the velar nasal *ng* (Poppe 1954: 67).

onomatopoetic 'to produce a sound or a sensation like the base onomatopoea'

> **čis* (mimetic for *chirping*) → WMo. *čiski-* 'to chirrup, chirp, twitter, tweet'
>
> WMo. *kürd* (mimetic for sudden explosive noise) → *kürdki-* 'to make noise, shout, talk nonsense'
>
> WMo. *tüs* (mimetic for sudden blow or banging noise) → *tüski-* 'to make a crashing sound'
>
> WMo. *čar* (mimetic for harsh voice, cry, clamour) → *čargi-* 'make a harsh sound, rattle, speak harshly'
>
> WMo. *čuu* 'sound, noise, echo, rumor' → *čuugi-* 'to make noise, shout (of many people), quarrel'
>
> WMo. *ša* (mimetic for downpour) → *šagi-* 'to pour, rain heavily'

Mongolic makes use of other iconic markers, such as WMo. -kirA- ~ WMo. -girA-, WMo. -ginA-, WMo. -gilja- (Poppe 1954: 67), e.g. *qaškira-* 'to shout, scream, yell, howl', *qanggira-* 'to rattle', *yanggina-* 'to emit a sharp, high-pitched sound, ache' and *činggilja-* 'to ring, resound, reverberate (intr.)'. Tekin (1982: 507) analyzes WMo. -ginA- as a coumpound of iconic pMo *-gi- and the processive pMo *-nA-, but all these suffixes are likely to be derived from the same iconic suffix *-ki- ~ -gi- because (i) -rA-, -nA- and -lja- are attested as separate morphemes with anticausative (see Section 6.6.4), processive (see Section 5.4.4) and distributive function (see Section 3.3.4. (19)), all of which are semantically compatible with the iconic suffix; (ii) the complex iconic markers generally alternate between voiced and voiceless allomorphs under the same phonological conditions as the simplex ones; and (iii) most iconic verbs cluster in sets, based on the same interjection, but derived with various simplex or complex suffixes, e.g. WMo. *burgi-* ~ *burgira-* 'to whirl (of water, dust, smoke), to fume with anger (intr.)'; *dargi-* ~ *dargira-* 'to roar or rush noisily (of water)'; *šuugi-* ~ *šuugina-* 'to whistle, rustle, sing, howl (of wind/waves)'; WMo. *qubina-* ~ *qubigina-* 'to whisper (intr.)'; *čanggilja-* ~ *čanggina-* 'to ring, resound, reverberate (intr.)'; *qanggir* 'rattling or ringing sound', *qanggina-* 'to sound, ring, resound, whine, creak', *qanggira-* 'to rattle', *qanggilja-* 'to resound, ring' etc.

A number of iconic verbs, such as WMo. *barkira-* 'to roar, bellow, cry, yell', WMo. *arkira-* 'to growl, snarl', WMo. *kürki-* 'talk nonsense, chatter indiscretely' and WMo. *kürkire-* 'to grow, grunt, snarl, roar (as a waterfall)' seem to contradict the velar voicing following a liquid. In the case of WMo. *kürki-* and WMo. *kürkire-*, this is probably due to erosion of an original base-final *-d*, reflected in WMo. *kürdki-* 'to make noise, shout, talk nonsense'. The other verbs may represent borrowings from Turkic on the model of OTk. *bakïr-* 'to bellow' and OTk. *aykïr-* 'to shout out loud'.

The source of the iconic suffix may be an independent verbal root for 'to do, make', i.e. pMo **ki-*, which is attested in the Secret History as MMo. *ki-*, in the literary language as WMo. *ki-*. The verb preserves reflexes across all contemporary Mongolic languages: Khal. *xij-*, Bur. *xe-*, Kalm. *ke-*, Ordos *kī-*, Dong. *kie-*, Bao. *ke-*, *giə-*, Dag. *kī-*, *xī-*, *šī-*, Mgr. *gi-*, *gə-*, Mogh. *ki-*.

5.5.5 pTk *-kI-*

In Old Turkic, we find a trace of a lexicalized iconic marker *-kI-* in a small number of onomatopoetic verbs (Erdal 1991: 468, Tekin 1982: 508), illustrated below.

onomatopoetic 'to produce a sound or a sensation like the base onomatopoea'

> pTk **bir* (mimetic for snorting) → pTk **bir-kï-* in OTk. *bïrkïg* 'snort (of a horse)', OTk. *bïrkïr-* 'to snort' [6]
>
> pTk **o* (mimetic for calling) in OTk. *o:* (particle in response to a caller) → OTk. *okï-* 'call, call out loud, recite'

---

6 OTk *-g* derives deverbal nouns, as e.g. in OTk. *bilig* 'mental process' from *bil-* 'know' and in OTk. *bag* 'bale, bundle' from OTk. *ba-* 'bind, tie, fasten' (Erdal 1991: 182).

pTk *o(k) (mimetic for vomiting) → OTk. *okï-* 'to vomit'
pTk *su (mimetic for snapping) → OTk. *sukï-* 'snap (one's fingers)'[7]
OTk. tok tok (mimetic for knocking) → OTk *tokï-* 'to hit, knock, beat, weave'

More frequent in the derivation of sound symbolic verbs is the Turkic suffix OTk. *-kIr-* (Erdal 1991: 466–467; Tekin 1982: 509–510), deriving, for instance, OTk. *ay* 'oh, hi (interjection)' → *aykïr-* 'shout out loud', pTk *bar* in Tk. *bar bar* (mimetic for bellowing) → OTk. *ba-kïr-* 'to bellow', OTk. *kï:* 'hi (interjection)' → *kï:kïr-* 'to shout'. Since both pTk *-kI- and *-(I)r- are separately reflected in Turkic, respectively, as an iconic and anti-causative suffix (see Chapter 5) and since we find derivational pairs such as OTk. *bïrkïg* 'snort (of a horse)' vs. OTk. *bïrkïr-* 'to snort', it is likely that OTk. *-kIr-* represents a complex suffix. Previously, this has been proposed by Ramstedt (1912: 36–37), Tekin (1982: 508) and Erdal (1991: 468), suggesting that the compounding may have taken place in the common ancestor of Turkic and Mongolic.[8]

As is the case in Mongolic, the source of the iconic suffix may be an independent verbal root for 'to do, make', i.e. pTk (or earlier pTEA) *ki-. An independent root pTk *kïl- 'do, make' is reconstructable in Turkic. In the Orkhon inscriptions and Old Uighur we find OTk. *kïl-*, Karakhanide has *kïl-* and Middle Turkic *qïl-*. In the contemporary Turkic languages we find Tk. *kïl-*, Tat. *qïl-*, Uzb. *qil-*, Uigh. *qil-*, Az. *gïl-*, Tkm. *qïl-*, Khak. *xïl-*, Shor *qïl-*, Chu. *əś-xəl* 'deed', Tuva *qïl-*, Kirg. *qïl-*, Kazakh *qïl-*, Nog. *qïl-*, Bash. *qïl-*, Karaim *qïl-*, Karakalpak *qïl-*, Kumyk *qïl-* (Clauson 1972: 616). Interestingly Yakut and Dolgan have Yak. *kïn-* and Dolg. *gïn-* with a different root-final consonant. This could suggest that the original root is *kï- and that *-l-* and *-n-* are petrified suffixes. The problem with this explanation, however, is that the suffix *-(X)l-* derives passives and that *-(X)n-* derives medial verbs in Turkic. The verb *kïl-*, however, is typically causative.

It is undisputed that some iconic verbs have been borrowed between Turkic and Mongolic but it can be argued that the iconic suffixes were native to both language families. If OTk. *-kIr-* had been copied from the predecessor of WMo. *-ki-rA-* ~ WMo. *-gi-rA-*, we would have to explain why the Mongolic predecessors of the verbs derived with WMo. *-gi-nA-* and WMo. *-gi-lja-* remained totally immune to borrowing, although they were at least as frequent in Mongolic. Fur-

---

[7] According to Erdal (1991: 468) the base looks so similar to OTk. *suk erngek* 'index finger' that the verb may alternatively be derived from pTk *suk 'index'.
[8] Erdal (1991: 465, 468) contends that "they [OTk -kI- and -kIr-] must have been related in proto-Turkic or in proto-Altaic (if such a language ever existed)." and that "This analysis [OTk -kIr- as a composite] is not in contradiction with a connection with Mo. +kirA-, as that could also be a composite suffix."

thermore, since the voiceless allomorphs in Mongolic are much less frequent than the voiced ones, it is difficult to understand why Turkic would have selected the voiceless suffix as a model.

The Chuvash cognate of OTk. -kIr- is the iconic suffix Chu. -xĂr- / -kĂr- in e.g. Chu. čaškăr- 'to hiss (of a snake)', kaškăr- 'to cry out', makăr- 'to cry, weep, bewail' and tălxăr- 'to neigh, snort' (Benzing 1943: 95, 1959: 719).

5.6 pTEA *-mA- inclination

5.6.1 pJ *-ma- (~ *-mə-)

As illustrated below, the inclinational suffix pJ *-ma- has lexicalized in numerous Old Japanese verb stems. It derives transitive and intransitive verbs from nouns, nominal and verbal adjectives and (in)transitive verbs, modifying the meaning of the base in the sense of 1. 'to consider as the base', 2. 'to reach the base', 3. 'to achieve the dimensions of the base', whereby the base commonly denotes a position or a dimensional property. The suffix is also used to derive verbs from onomatopoetic adverbs, which are situational rather than sound-symbolic. With the exception of those marked between square brackets, all the derivations below have congruent register.

The inclinational suffix is reconstructed as pJ *-ma-, with a final vowel that surfaces in further derivations such as with the anti-causative *-ra- in OJ se-ma-r- 'to get narrow, draw near', the causative-anticausative *-Ci- in OJ puka-me$_2$- 'make deep (tr.)' and the inchoative *-ka- (followed by *-Ci-) in OJ okuma-ke- 'to anticipate (tr.)'. In some cases, such as OJ ugu-mo-t- 'to bulge up (of earth)' and OJ to$_2$yo$_2$-mo-s- B 'to make resound', however, the suffix vowel agrees with the quality of the vowel in the root and, reminiscent of vowel harmony, the reconstruction should be pJ *-mə-.

The suffix is well attested outside Central Japanese, having lexicalized in cognate Ryukyuan verb stems, such as Shuri tugami B 'fault', ciwamir- B 'to carry to the extreme', ciwamar- B 'to reach an extreme', yudumir- B 'to let it stagnate', karamacun B 'to tangle, get entwined', karamir- B 'to twine round', kurusim- B 'to suffer', nikum- B 'to hate', qaratamar- B 'to get renewed', qaratamir- B 'to renew', katami A 'oath of love', shizumir- B 'to tidy up', yaşim- B 'to become cheap(er)', qagamir- B 'to respect, worship', qayamar- B 'to err, make a mistake, apologize', nuzum- A 'to hope or' and mutumir- B 'seek, pursue, desire' etc. Therefore, the period in which it was productive must predate the split of Mainland Japanese and Ryukyuan, i.e. in proto-Japonic.

denominal

1. 'to consider as the base'

    OJ *ata* 2.2 'enemy, hostility' → OJ *atam-* A 'to regard as an enemy, hate (tr.)'

    OJ *to₂ga* 2.5 'blame, offence' → OJ *to₂game₂-* B 'to censure, find fault with (tr.)'

2. 'to reach the base'

    OJ *api₁da* 3.2b 'interval' → OJ *api₁dam-* ?A 'to take a break, rest'

    OJ *ki₁pa* 2.3 'limit, brink' → OJ *ki₁pam-* B 'to reach the limit, reach an extreme'

3. 'to acquire the dimensions of the base'

    OJ *kubo* 2.1 'hollow (place), depression' → OJ *kubom-* A 'to become hollow, cave in, be dented, have a hollow area'

    OJ *para* 2.3 'belly' → OJ *param-* B 'to get pregnant, get filled, get swollen'[9]

    OJ *siwa* 2.1 'wrinkle' → OJ *siwam-* A 'to get wrinkled'

    [OJ *se* 1.1 'narrow place, valley, rapids (in a river)' → OJ *semar-* ?B 'to get narrow, draw near']

    OJ *yo₂do₂* 2.4 'stagnant place (in a river)' → OJ *yo₂do₂m-* ?B 'to stagnate, be stagnant'.

onomatopoetic

J *koro-koro* 'rolling, over and over', J *kuru-kuru* 'round and round, twirling' → OJ *karame-* B 'to twine round, entwine, entangle', J *karam-* ?B 'to tangle, get entwined', ?A/B J *kurum-* 'to wrap in, lap in'

J *suu suu* 'smoothly (mimetic)' → J *susum-* A 'to advance, go forward'

*toyo ~ **doyo* (mimetic for reverberation) in *doyomeku* ? A/B 'to resound, reverberate → OJ *to₂yo₂m-* ~ MJ *doyom-* B 'to resound', OJ *to₂yo₂mos-* B 'to make resound'

J *ugo-mek-* ? A/B 'to wriggle, squirm' → OJ *ugumot-* B, J *ugomor-* B, J *uguro-mot-* B 'to bulge up (of earth) (intr.)'

---

[9] A semantically similar derivation is present in Tamambo *bange* 'stomach' → *bange-bange* 'to be pregnant' (Aikhenvald 2011a: 233).

de-adjectival

1. 'to consider as the base'

    OJ *kurusi-* B 'painful, bitter' → OJ *kurusime$_2$-* B 'to suffer (intr.)'

    OJ *niku-* B 'hateful' > OJ *nikum-* B 'to hate, dislike, reprove (tr.)'

    OJ *wosi-* B 'regrettable; lovable, cute' → OJ *wosim-* B 'to grudge, regret; prize, value (tr.)'

2. 'to become like the base'

    OJ *arata* 3.4 'new' → OJ *aratame$_2$-* B 'to renew, improve (tr.)'

    OJ *kata-* A 'hard' → OJ *katame$_2$-* A 'to make hard, lump together, mass together (tr.)'

    OJ *niko$_1$-* 'gentle, soft' → *niko$_1$m-* 'to soften, get gentle, calm down (intr.)'

    OJ *sidu* ? 2.5 'poor, miserable; quiet' → OJ *sidum-* B 'to get quiet (intr.)'

    OJ *yasu-* B 'easy' → OJ *yasum-* B 'to rest, sleep (intr.)'

3. 'to acquire the dimensions of the base'

    OJ *naga-* B 'long' → OJ *nagame$_2$-* B 'to prolong voice, recite, drone (tr.)'

    OJ *pi$_1$ro$_2$-* B 'broad' → OJ *pi$_1$ro$_2$me$_2$-* B 'to spread (tr.)'

    OJ *puka-* B 'deep' > OJ *pukame$_2$-* B 'make deep (tr.)'

deverbal

1. 'to (metaphorically) consider as the base'

    [OJ *agar-* A 'to rise (intr.)' → OJ *agame$_2$-* ?B 'to respect, honor, worship (tr.)']

    OJ *nade-* B 'to pat, stroke' → OJ *nadame$_2$-* B 'to soothe, placate, pacify (tr.)'

2. 'to attempt to reach the base verb'

    OJ *kakus-* B' 'to hide, conceal (tr.)', OJ *kakur-* B' 'hide (intr.)' → OJ *kakumap-* B 'to shelter, give refuge to (tr.)', [OJ *kakum-* A 'to surround (tr.)']

    OJ *kitap-* ?A 'to drill, train, forge (tr.)' → OJ *ki$_1$tam-* ?A 'to punish, chastise (tr.)'

    OJ *mo$_2$t-* B 'to hold, have (tr.)' → OJ *moto$_2$me$_2$-* B 'to seek, pursue, desire, request'

    *nənsə- 'to see' in OJ *nozok-* A 'to peek, peer' → OJ *nozom-* A 'hope for, wish for, look for, look over, view (tr.)'

    OJ *ok-* A 'to put (tr.)' → OJ *okumake-* 'to anticipate (tr.)'

The inclinational suffix pJ *-ma- may be incorporated in the element OJ -mi_1 in the construction N-wo ADJ-mi_1 'because N is ADJ', which Vovin (2009a: 485) defines as a "consecutive gerund"; see the examples (6) and (7).

(6) OJ *yama-wo   taka-mi_1*
     mountain-ACC be.high-CONV
     'because the mountain is high' (MYS I: 44; Vovin 2009a: 486)

(7) OJ *$tabi_1$-wo   kurusi-mi_1*
     travel-ACC be.painful-CONV
     'because travel is painful' (M XV: 3674)

Mainly on the basis of these N-*wo* ADJ-mi_1 constructions, Vovin (1997) suggests that OJ *wo* is an absolute case marker, because it seems to mark not only the objects of transitive verbs but also the subjects of non-active intransitives, primarily adjectives. This assumption leads Vovin to the hypothesis that Old Japanese is an active language. However, analyzing OJ -mi_1 as an ACC-ing gerund such as 'travel being painful' in English, Whitman and Yanagida (2009: 131) show that it is unnecessary to jump to such conclusions. They suggest that the transitivity of the element -mi_1 "may have a diachronic motivation, as one etymology for -mi_1 derives it from the infinitive of the transitive verb *mi-* 'see'." In Robbeets (2005: 165–166), I followed this etymological analysis, but I would now suggest analyzing OJ -mi_1 as the -*i* converb (see Chapter 7) of inclinational verbs on *-m-*. Against this internal analysis, Martin (1987: 805) argues that "... most of the ..*mu* verbs are intransitive and the transitive counterparts (..*mey-* <*-ma-Ci-*) have an extra counterpart: ..." However, as illustrated above, most derived verbs with the meaning 'to consider as the base' are transitive and can thus account for the presence of the accusative case marker *wo* in the Japanese construction.[10] For semantic reasons, the derivations are more often de-adjectival 'to consider as a property' than not, which could explain why the OJ -mi_1 converb is restricted to adjective bases.

The inclinational suffix pJ *-ma-* may further be incorporated in the tentative OJ -(*a*)*m*-, that was productively used in Old and Middle Japanese for a wide range of meanings, such as intention, volition, inclination, suggestion and presumption. (Martin 1991b: 605–615; Vovin 2003: 273–282, 2009: 793–803). In Section 3.4, the tentative has been derived from the copula **a*- 'to be' followed by pJ *-ma-*. The tentative construction in OJ -ke_1*m-u* in example (8) derives from

---

10 OJ $kurusime_2$- 'suffer (intr.)' derives from an original transitive **kurusim-* 'to regard as painful, suffer (tr.)' and a so-called "transitivity-flipper" *-(*C*)*i*- (see Chapter 5).

a word-final past suffix OJ -ki_1 followed by a nominalized form of the tentative OJ -(a)m-, which suggests an independent copular origin, i.e. pJ *a-ma-.

(8) OJ simo$_1$-no$_2$ pur-i-k-e$_1$m-u
      frost-GEN fall-CONV-PST/FIN-TENT-NML
      'the fact that the frost would have fallen' (MYS V: 804; Vovin 2009a: 805)

5.6.2 pK *-mO-

The inclinational suffix pK *-mi- ~ mʌ- has lexicalized in a number of transitive and intransitive verb stems derived from nouns, adjectives and (in)transitive verbs, as illustrated below. It modifies the meaning of the base in the sense of 1. 'to achieve the dimension or position denoted by the base', 2. 'to use the base' and 3. 'to become like the base'. One derivational pair suggests that the suffix is also used to derive verbs from situational onomatopoetic adverbs.

The suffix pK *-mi- ~ mʌ- has left a segmental trace in -m- following bases ending in liquids and vowels, but bases ending in nasals (-n/-m) undergo zero derivation. Compare, for instance, the -m- in K pa:l-m- 'to measure in arm spans' to the zero derivation in K pye:m-'to measure in hand spans'. Since most derived verbs have a rising tone in Middle Korean or length in Korean, they can be traced back to a disyllabic origin with loss of a suffix-final minimal vowel. Although the verbal derivation of nouns ending in -n, -m is zero segmentally, the suffix thus leaves a suprasegmental trace. Martin (1996: 5) asks: "Why are there so few ..n-stems to begin with? Were they derived from nouns?," because there are only three simple verb stems ending on -n in Middle Korean (i.e. MK ˙˙sin- 'to wear (shoes)', MK ˙˙an- 'to embrace' and MK ˙˙ten- 'to wager, bet'), two of which can be derived from noun bases, as in the examples below.

denominal

1. 'to achieve the dimension or position denoted by the base noun'

    K an, MK ·anh 'interior, inside' (-h place suffix) → K a:n-, MK ˙˙an-'to hold in one's arms, embrace (tr.)'

    K kwul 'hole, cave, cavity, empty', K kwulh- = kolh-, MK kwolh- 'to be empty' → K kwulm- 'to starve, skip a meal, go hungry', MK ˙˙kwulm- 'to hunger, go without food, become empty (intr.)'

    K pa:l 'the span of two arms, unit of length equal to the span of two arms, 2 yards' → K pa:lm-, MK palm- 'measure off the length in double-arm spans (tr.)'

K *phum*, MK ·*phum* 'width of a coat, bosom, space between the chest and clothes' → K *phum-*, MK ·*phum-* 'to carry in the bosom, embrace, harbor (tr.)'

K *pye:m* 'span, span of a hand' → K *pye:m-* 'to measure by the span, span off with one's hand (tr.)'

2. 'to make use of the base noun'

K *sal* 'frame, spoke, teeth (of a comb etc.), fish spear' → K *sa:lm-* 'to harrow (the soil), rake (the soil) (tr.)'

K *sin*, MK ·*sin* 'footgear, (Korean style)shoes' → MK ¨*sin-*'to wear (shoes), use as footgear (tr.)'

onomatopoetic

K *tetum keli-* 'to be groping (for), be feeling for, fumble (for) (tr.)' (see Section 5.5.2 for *keli-*) → K *tetum-* 'to grope (for), feel (after), fumble (for) (tr.)'

de-adjectival 'to become like the base'

pK **kwol-* 'to be purulent, be rotten' in K *kolum* 'pus, purulent matter' (pK *-*m* deverbal noun suffix; see Section 7.4.2), K *kolh-* 'to go bad, rot, spoil, get stale', MK ¨*kwolq-* 'to fester (intr.)' → K *kolm-*, MK *kwolm-* 'to form pus, fester (intr.)'

pK **tele-* 'to be dirty' in K *telep-* ~ *talap-*, MK ¨*telep-* ~ ¨*talap-*, ¨*teleW-* ~ ¨*talaW-* 'to be muddy, dirty' (MK *-W-* ~ *-p-* < pK *- ·*pO-* anticausative suffix; see Section 6.4.2) → MK ¨*telm-* 'to become dirty, get stained, get dyed (intr.)'

pK **cye-* 'to be small' in MK ¨*cyek-* 'to be small, few' (pK *-·*kO-* inchoative, see Section 5.7.2) → K *ce:lm-*, MK ¨*cyem-* 'to be young (intr.)'

deverbal 'to attempt to reach the base verb'

MK ·*soy-* 'to leak (intr.)', K *saym*, MK ¨*soym* 'source, well, spring' (pK *-*m* deverbal noun suffix; see Section 7.4.2) → MK ¨*soym-* 'to spring up, spurt up, spout, spray (intr.)'

K *mek-*, MK *mek-* 'to eat; harbor (a feeling) (tr.)' → K *mekum-*, MK *me*·*kwum-* 'to hold in the mouth; to swallow, gulp down; harbor (a feeling/idea) (tr.)'

5.6.3 pTg *-mA:-

The inclinational suffix pTg *-mA:- has lexicalized in Tungusic verbs ending in Evk. -mA-, Even -mA:-, Ud. -mA- and Na. -masi-. It derives transitive and intransitive verbs from nouns and nominal adjectives, modifying the meaning of the base in the sense of 'to achieve the base noun', whereby the base often concerns a product of nature or a position (Benzing 1955a: 1064). The suffix is incorporated in pTg *-mi:- 'to make sb./sth. achieve the base noun', frequently used in the sense of 'hunting' or 'attaching' and derived from pTg *-mA:- and the causative suffix pTg *-gi- (see Chapter 5; Benzing 1955a: 1065). In some languages, such as Even, the causative meaning has completely bleached.

5.6.3.1 Manchu -mi-
denominal 'to make sb./sth. achieve the base noun' (Gorelova 2002: 236)

    Ma. *doko* 'lining of a garment' → *dokomi-* 'to line (a garment) (tr.)'
    Ma. *tohon* 'button' → *tohomi-* 'to button (up) (tr.)'
    Ma. *ture* 'leg of a boot' > *turemi-* 'to attach the leg of a boot (tr.)'

de-adjectival 'to achieve the property denoted by the base' (Gorelova 2002: 236)

    Ma. *bolgo* 'clean, clear' → *bolgomi-* 'to abstain, fast'
    Ma. *goro* 'far' → *goromi-* 'to do from afar, go a long distance'

5.6.3.2 Even -mA:-, -mi:-
denominal 'to achieve the base noun' (Benzing 1955b: 35)

    Even *caj* 'thee' → *cajma-* 'to go and get tea'
    Even *digen* 'four' → *digenme-* 'to catch four (animals)'
    Even *ńoka* 'a Yakut person' → *ńokama-* 'to go to a Yakut, visit a Yakut'
    Even *olra* 'fish' > *olrama-* 'to go fishing'
    Even *olra* 'fish' → *olrami:-* 'to fish, catch fish'
    Even *niki* 'duck' → *nikimi-* 'to catch ducks'

5.6.3.3 Evenki -mA-, -mi-
denominal -mA- 'to achieve the base noun' (Nedjalkov 1997: 300)

    Evk. *ollo* 'fish' > *ollomo-* 'to fish'
    Evk. *taman* 'cost, price' → *tamanma-* 'to pay'
    Evk. *uluki* 'squirrel' > *ulume-* 'to hunt squirrels'

denominal -mi- 'to (make) achieve the base noun' (Nedjalkov 1997: 300)

    Evk. *bejun* 'wild reindeer' > *bejumi-* 'to hunt wild reindeer'
    Evk. *here* 'lower part, bottom, sole' → *hermi-* 'to sole, attach a sole'
    Evk. *ollo* 'fish' → *ollomi-* 'to fish'
    Evk. *sen* 'eye of a needle' → *senmi-* 'to thread a needle'

5.6.3.4 Udehe *-mA-*

denominal -mA- 'to achieve the base noun' (Nikolaeva 1999: 169–170)

    Ud. *a:da* 'mountain pass' → *a:damasi-* 'to cross the mountain'
    Ud. *xoton* 'city' → *xotomo-* 'to go to the city'
    Ud. *zege* 'reference point' > *zegeme-* 'to orientate oneself'
    Ud. *olondo* 'ginseng' > *olondomo-* 'to collect ginseng'
    Ud. *oloxi* 'squirrel' > *oloxime-* 'to hunt for squirrels'

5.6.3.5 Nanai *-mAsi-*

Benzing (1955a: 1065) and Avrorin (1961: 21) treat the denominal suffix Na *-mAsi-* 'to hunt for the base noun' as a compound of *-mA- and *-si-. Avrorin (1961: 46) suggests that the second element is the Nanai suffix for continuous, multiple or occasional actions, which also underlies in the reiterative suffix Na. *-nAsi-* in Section 5.4.3.5.

denominal 'to hunt for the base noun'

    Na. *gasa* 'goose' > *gasamasi-* 'to hunt geese'
    Na. *moksa* 'hare' > *moksamasi-* 'to hunt for hares'
    Na. *sogda* 'fish' > *sogdamasi-* 'to fish, catch fish'

5.6.4 pMo *-mA-

The inclinational suffix pMo *-mA- is reflected in a few Written Mongolian verbs with the meaning 'to reach a state resulting from the base verb'. The suffix derives transitive and intransitive verbs from verbs and verbal adjectives. The suffix is incorporated in a number of complex suffixes, extending its meaning to 'to be inclined to carry out the verb base' and 'to be able to carry out the verb base', i.e. WMo. *-mAG* deverbal noun suffix denoting inclination (< pMo *-mA- + *-G deverbal noun suffix), WMo. *-mAGAi* deverbal noun suffix denoting inclination or ability to act (< pMo *-mA- + -GAi deverbal noun suffix), WMo. *-mAl* deverbal noun suffix denoting the result of craftsmanship (< pMo *-mA- + -l deverbal noun suffix), WMo. *-mAr* deverbal noun suffix denoting suitableness or fitness (Poppe 1954: 45–49).

de-adjectival

'to make achieve the property denoted by the base'

WMo. *ayu-* 'to be frightened' → (**ayu-ma-* 'to make frightened' →) *ayumar* 'horrible, frightening'

WMo. *γaiqa-* 'to be astonished, surprised' → (**γaiqa-ma-* 'to make astonished' →) *γaiqamar* 'astonishing, surprising'

deverbal

1. 'to reach a state resulting from the base verb'

    WMo. *kele-* 'to speak, say (tr.)' → (**kele-me-* →) *keme-* 'to say, be named, intend (tr./intr.)'[11]

    WMo. *üyi-* 'to mix (tr.)' → *üyime-* 'to become disturbed, bustle (intr.)'

    WMo. *delge-* 'to spread, expand (tr./intr.)', *delge-r* 'vast, flourishing' → (**delge-me-* 'to become spread' →) *delgemel, delgemer* 'spread, developed'

    WMo. *üje-* 'to see, behold, look at, glance at (tr.)' → (**üje-me-* 'to become seen' →) *üjemer* 'scene, sight, exhibition'

    WMo. *neke-* 'knit, weave (tr.)' → (**neke-me-* 'to become woven' →) *nekemel* 'woven, knitted, textile'

2. 'to be inclined to carry out the verb base'

    WMo. *ide-* 'to eat, consume (tr.)' → (**ide-me-* 'to be inclined to eat' →) *idemeg* 'having a good appetite, greedy', *idemegei* 'voracious, venal', *idemer* 'edible, consumed, eaten, having a keen appetite'

    WMo. *jori-* 'to move in the direction of, strive, be resolved (intr.)' → (**jorima-* 'to be inclined to move in a certain direction' →) *jorimay* 'willful, intentional, having a purpose, courageous', *jorimagai* 'enterprising, decided, resolute'

    WMo. *umta-* 'to sleep (intr.)' → (**umta-ma-* 'to be inclined to sleep') → *umtamqai* 'sleepy'

3. 'to be able to carry out the verb base'

    WMo. *sur-* 'to learn, study, ask, inquire (tr.)' → (**sur-ma-* 'to be able to learn' →) *surmaγai* 'be gifted, be trained, be experienced'

---

[11] The derivation of WMo. *keme-* 'say, be named, intend' suggests the same liquid syllable loss as is observed in the alternation of WMo. *kele-* 'speak, say' with WMo. *kelele-* 'say, speak', derived from from *kelen* 'word, speech, tongue'.

WMo. *ide-* 'to eat, consume (tr.)' → (**ide-me-* 'to be possible to eat' →) *idemer* 'edible, consumed, eaten, having a keen appetite'

5.7 pTEA *-gA- inchoative

5.7.1 pJ *-ka-

As illustrated below, the inchoative suffix pJ *-ka-* has lexicalized in numerous Old Japanese verb stems. The suffix derives transitive and intransitive verbs from nouns, nominal and verbal adjectives and (in)transitive verbs, modifying the meaning of the base in the sense of 1. 'to enter a state or to begin an action denoted by the base' and 2. 'to use (as) the base noun'. All derivations below have congruent register.

The inchoative suffix is reconstructed as pJ *-ka-*, with a final vowel that surfaces in further derivations, such as with the anti-causative *-ra-* in OJ *maro$_2$kar-* 'to form a lump (intr.)', the causative *-sa-* in *maro$_2$kas-* 'to make round (tr.)', and the causative-passive *-Ci-* in *sirake$_2$-* 'to whiten, get white (intr.)'.

The suffix has lexicalized in a few cognate Ryukyuan verb stems, such as Shuri *hwirak-* B, *hwirakir-* B 'get opened' and *cirakas-* A 'to scatter (tr.)'. This allows us to trace the suffix back to the proto-Japonic stage.

denominal

1. 'to enter a state denoted by the base'

    OJ *ata* 2.2a 'enemy, hostility' → MJ *atake-* 'to violate, start a tumult'

    OJ *mi$_1$du* ?2.1a 'water' → *mi$_1$duk-* ?A 'to get soaked (in water) (intr.)'

    OJ *se* (~ *so-*) 1.2 'back' → *so$_2$k-* ? 'to get distant, recede (intr.)'

    J *susu* 2.5 'soot' → J *susuke-* ?B 'to become sooty, soiled (intr.)'

2. 'to use (as) the base'

    OJ *kadura* 3.7a 'crown, hair ornament' → *kadurak-* B 'to use as a crown, as a decoration or ornament in the hair (tr.)'

    OJ *makura* 'pillow' 3.5a/b → *makurak-* B 'to use as a pillow (tr.)'

    OJ *obi$_1$* 2.4 'belt, girdle' → J *obik-* B' 'to gird, inveigle (tr.)'

    OJ *te$_2$* ~ *ta-* 1.3 'hand' → ? *tak-* 'to do (something) with the hands, use ones hands (e.g. in order to dress hair, row a boat, pull a net, guide a horse) (tr.)'

    OJ *ude* 1.3a 'arm' → *udak-* 'to embrace (tr.)'

    OJ *wana* 2.4 'trap, snare, lasso' → *wanak-* B 'throttle, strangle, choke off (tr.)'

de-adjectival 'to (make) acquire the property denoted by the base'

OJ *maro₂* 2.1 'round (thing)' → *maro₂kas-* A 'to make round, make into a lump (tr.)', *maro₂kar-* A 'to form a lump (intr.)'

OJ *sira(-)* ?2.3 'white (bound)' → *sirake₂-* ?B 'to whiten, get white (intr.)'

OJ *utu(-)* ?2.x 'empty (bound)' → *utuke₂-* ?A 'to get empty'

OJ *pi₁ro₂-* B 'wide, broad, vast' → *ta-pi₁ro₂kas-* 'to open the hand and wave', *pi₁rak-* B 'to open (tr.)', *pi₁rake₂-* B 'to open (intr.)'

OJ *tapasi-* A 'reckless, profligate' → *tapake₂-* ?A/B 'to fool around, misbehave, engage in adultery'

deverbal 'to enter a state or to begin an action denoted by the base'

**kuta-* 'to detoriate' in MJ *kudat-*, OJ *kutat-* ?A/B 'to detoriate' → OJ *kudak-* B 'to shatter, break (tr.)', *kudake₂-* B 'to be shattered, get broken (intr.)'

**nənsə-* 'to see' in OJ *nozom-* A 'hope for, wish for, look for, look over, view (tr.)' → *nozok-* A 'to peek, peer'

**paru-* 'to clear' in OJ *par-* B 'to open (ground), clear (land) (tr.)' → *paruk-* ?B 'to clear up, open up, get bright, dispel (intr.)', *parukas-* ?B 'to make clear'

OJ *pasir-* B 'to run, rush (intr.)' → *pasirakas-* B 'to make run, bring in gallop (tr.)'

OJ *tir-* A 'scatter, get scattered, disperse (intr.)' → MJ *tirakas-* A 'to scatter (tr.)', MJ *tirakar-* A 'to get scattered (intr.)'

5.7.2 pK *-*kO*-

As illustrated below, the inchoative suffix pK *-·*ki-* ~ -·*kʌ-* has lexicalized in a number of transitive and intransitive verb stems derived from nouns, adjectives and (in)transitive verbs. The suffix modifies the meaning of the base in the sense of 1. 'to enter a state denoted by the base' and 2. 'to use the base'. In some cases, such as MK ¨*cyek-* 'to be small, few', MK *kisk-* 'to rejoice' and K *kyekk-* 'to experience' below, the meaning has completely bleached.

The majority of derived verbs consist of one low-pitched syllable and are closed with a consonant cluster, thus belonging to Ramsey's (1991: 223–228) Class 1. Ramsey's proposal that Class 1 verbs should be derived from original verb stems ending in a minimal vowel leads to the reconstruction of a final vowel in pK *-·*ki-* ~ -·*kʌ-*.[12] Note that proto-Korean was characterized by a non-distinc-

---

[12] Instead of Ramsey's suggestion of original voicing distinction (*in casu* *-*g-* > -*ɣ-*), I follow Martin's (1996) lenition theory whereby following a vowel, a plain obstruent lenites to a frica-

tive prosodic system in which the last (or only) syllable of a morpheme was automatically given high pitch (Ramsey 1991: 219). Morphologically complex morphemes consisting of a high-pitched base followed by a high-pitched suffix yield low pitch in contracted stems, for instance, MK ·*pso*- 'to wrap' and -·*i*- causative-passive yield MK *psoy*- 'to be wrapped'. The suprasegmental pattern of derivations such as MK *mulk*- 'to be watery', MK *pulk*- 'to be red', MK *naksk*- 'to fish' etc. thus indicate incorporation of pK *-··*ki̇*- ~ -··*kʌ*- and an originally high pitched final syllable.

The rising tone in Class 5 verbs, such as MK ¨*cyek*- 'to be small, few' below, usually results from the contraction of two syllables. This provides further support for a suffix-final minimal vowel in the suffix. Note that derivations from Class 4 stems (monosyllabic with *ye* vocalism) with high-pitched suffixes yield a rising tone, e.g. MK *sye*- 'to stand (intr.)' + -·*i*- causative-passive → ¨*sye*- 'to stand (something) up (tr.)'. Another Class 5 verb that may be derived with the inchoative suffix is MK ¨*kulk*- 'be thick, big'. Although we do not find evidence for a base pK *kul* 'thick(ness)', there are external parallels for such a word in Mongolic and Turkic.[13]

The capital *G* in MK *kužG*- 'to draw a line, delimit' and MK *wulG*- 'to howl' represents a lenited velar /ɣ/ and reflects the preliminary weakening of a /k/ on its way to erosion. For MK *wulG*- 'to howl' the environment for obstruent lenition is met (*CV ·*ki̇*/ʌ- > *CV ·ɣi̇/ʌ-), while we must reconstruct an original vowel-final pK *kisi̇ underlying MK *kus* 'line, limit'. In MK *tao*- 'to come to an end' the velar has completely eroded, although it may be preserved in a lexicalized deverbal noun MK *takoy* 'all'.

---

tive (*in casu* *-*k*- > -ɣ-) before a minimal vowel, i.e in the environment *CV ·Ci̇/ʌ- (Robbeets 2005: 63). If we restrict the reconstruction of a stem-final minimal vowel to Class 1 verbs ending in a consonant cluster, Martin's (1996) expectation that pK *-*k*- will undergo lenition to -ɣ- in a minimal vowel environment is not violated.

13 A possible external parallel is found in pMo *kur* ~ *kür* 'abundant, thick, fat' reflected in WMo. *kür*, *kür-tei* 'abundant', *qur-tai* 'having accumulated fat', *qur-la*- 'accumulate fat, grow thick' (Lessing 1960: 503, 507, 991) and in pTk *kür* 'abundant, thick, dense' in Tk. *gür*, Az. *gür*, Tkm. *gür*, Gag. *gür*, Karaim *kür* 'abundant, thick, dense'; Tuva *xür* 'healthy, well fed'; Karakhanide *kür* 'stout-hearted, courageous'; Chuv. *kəʷrəʷ* 'abundant, courageous'; Bash. *kör* 'well fed, courageous' and Tat. *kör* 'well fed, courageous'. Although attested earlier, the meaning 'courageous' appears to be a metaphorical extension of 'abundant' in Turkic. Whether this word is considered a borrowing or a cognate does not influence the argumentation.

denominal

1. 'to (make) enter a state denoted by the base'

    K *mwul*, MK ·*mul* 'water' → K *mwulk-*, MK *mulk-*, *mwulk-* 'to be watery, be thin (intr.)' (< pK **mil·ki-*)

    K *pwul*, MK ·*pul* 'fire' → K *pwulk-*, MK *pulk-* 'to be red, be crimson (intr.)' (< pK **pil·ki-*)

    MK *mwus* 'sheaf, bundle' → K *mwukk-*, MK *mwusk-* 'to tie up into a bundle (tr.)' (< pK **mus·ki-*)

    MK *kul* 'writing' → MK *kulk-* 'to scratch (intr.)' (< pK **kɨl·ki-*)

2. 'to use the base'

    MK *kus* 'line, limit' → MK *kužG-* 'to draw a line, delimit' (< pK **kɨsi·ki-*)

    K *o:l*, MK ¨*ol* 'strand, ply, warp' → K *olk-* 'to tie up, bind, weave' (< pK **ol·kʌ-*)

    MK ·*naks* 'fishhook' → MK *naksk-* 'to fish' (< pK **naks·kʌ-*)

de-adjectival 'to acquire the property denoted by the base'

pK **cye-* 'be small' (see Section 5.6.2) in MK ¨*cyem-* 'be young' → MK ¨*cyek-* 'to be small, few (intr.)' (< pK **cyekɨ-*)

pK **kis-* 'to be happy' in MK *kispu-* 'to be happy' (pK *-·*pO-* anticausative; see Chapter 5) → MK *kisk-* 'to rejoice (intr.)' (< pK **kis·ki-*)

pK **pʌl-* 'to be clear' in K *poli-* 'to clear away, make clear (tr.)' (pK *-·*i-* causative; see Chapter 5) → MK *polk-* 'to be(come) bright (intr.)' (< pK **pʌl·kʌ-*)

MK *nul-* 'to increase, be(come) longer, be better' → MK *nulk-* 'to be old, grow old (intr.)' (< pK **nɨl·ki-*)

deverbal 'to enter a state or to begin an action denoted by the base'

MK *kyes-* 'to experience' → K *kyekk-* 'to experience' (< **kyes·ki-*)

MK *pužu-* 'to break (tr.)' → MK ·*psku-* 'to shell, peel (tr.); hatch (intr.) (< **pɨsi·ki-*)

MK *tah-* 'to touch, reach, arrive' → MK *tao-* 'to get exhausted, come to an end'(< pK **ta·yʌ-* < **ta·kʌ-*)

pK **u·li-* 'to cry' in MK ¨*wul-* 'to cry (intr.)' → MK *wulG-* 'to howl, roar, shout loudly (intr.)' (< pK *uli·yi-* < **uli·ki-*)

5.7.3 pTg *-gA-

The inchoative suffix pTg *-gA- is reflected as Ma. -hA-, Evk. -gA-, and Even -g- ~ -gA- in a few transitive and intransitive verbs derived from nouns, adjectives or (in)transitive verbs. Since voiced velars tend to undergo lenition to -w-, -y- and Ø in Southern Tungusic, the suffix does not leave visible traces in Nanai and Udehe.[14] The suffix pTg *-gA- modifies the meaning of the base in the sense of 1. 'to enter a state denoted by the base' and 2. 'to use the base'. It is also incorporated in the decausative inchoative suffix pTg *-rgA- (Benzing 1955a: 1070: "Medium, Intensiv?"), reflected in Ma. -ja-, Even -rgA-, Evk. -rgA-, Ud. -gA-, Na. -A-, which derives intransitive inchoatives from transitive or intransitive verbs.[15] Unlike the inchoative suffix pTg *-lu- reflected in Evk. -l-, Even -l-, Ud. -li- and Na. -lo- (e.g. Ud. galu- 'to hate (tr.)' → galu-li- 'to start hating (tr.)'), pTg *-rgA- cannot derive transitive inchoatives. Given the polysemy "decausative" and "inchoative", the suffix pTg *-rgA- can probably be derived from the anticausative pTg *-rA- (see Section 6.6.3) and the inchoative *-gA-. This is supported by instances whereby a single root appears in an anticausative as well as in a decausative inchoative derivation, e.g. pTg *kongdo- 'to break in two (tr.)' in Oroch kondo 'half', Evk. kongdor 'crosswise' → pTg *kongdo-ro- in Even kongdor- 'to break in pieces (intr.)' → pTg *kongdo-r(o)-go- in Evk. kongdorgo- 'to break, snap, be broken (intr.)'.

5.7.3.1 Manchu

The simplex inchoative pTg *-gA- has left traces in Manchu -ha- ~ -he- ~ -ho-, which appears in denominal verbs with the meaning 'to use the base' and in deadjectival and deverbal derivations with inchoative meaning, even if the semantic opposition between the base and the inchoative verb has often bleached. It is not inconceivable that the deverbal noun suffix Manchu -han~ -hen ~ -hon (Gorelova 2002: 196) is a complex suffix consisting of the inchoative followed by the deverbal noun suffix pTg *-n (see Section 7.5.3). Note, for instance, the alternation between Ma. olgo- 'to become dry' and olhon 'dry'.

The suffix pTg *-rgA- is reflected in Manchu -ja- ~ -je- ~ -jo-, which has lexicalized in inchoative decausatives derived from transitive or intransitive verbs

---

14 The regular reflex of pTg *-g- is Ma. -g- ~ -h-, Evk. -g-, Even -g-, Ud. -g- and Na. -g-, with frequent lenition to -w-, -y- and Ø in vocalic environment, especially in Manchu and in the southern Tungusic languages, e.g. pTg *toga 'fire' in Evk. togo, Even tog, Ma. tuwa, Na. tao, Ud. to: 'fire'.

15 Decausative derivation reduces the valency pattern of the base verb by detransitivizing it: intransitives remain intransitive, transitives become intransitive. The regular reflex of pTg *-rg- is Ma. -j-, Even -rg-, Evk. -rg-, Ud. -g- and Na. -G-, e.g. pTg *xirga 'gad-fly' > Ma. ija, Evk. irga-kta, Even i̇rga-t, Ud. iga, Na. si̇Ga-qta.

(Gorelova 2002: 251), such as Ma. *fondo-* 'to penetrate, go through (tr.)' → *fondojo-* 'to be broken or torn through (intr.)' and Ma. *fulara-* 'to be red, to blush'→ *fularja-* 'to get a red appearance'.

Denominal 'to use the base'

> Orok *quwaį* 'plough' → Ma. *quwafiha-* 'to scrape off'
>
> pTg **siantu* 'fist' in Olcha *sê:ntu̧*, Oroch *sä:antu*, *säntu*, Na. *sįantu*, Ud. *santu* 'fist' → Ma. *sindaha-* 'to clench fists'
>
> Russian *tiski* 'vice, grip' >> Evenki *kiski*, Na. *kiskiẽ* 'tongs, vice' → Ma. *xisha-* 'to sharpen (a knife)'

Deadjectival 'to acquire the property denoted by the base'

> pTg **a:ma-* 'to be sleepy' in Evk. *a:me-*, Even *a:mol-*, Neg. *a:ma-*, Orok *a:ma-*, Na. *a:malo-*, *a:masį-* → Ma. *amha-* 'to sleep'
>
> pTg **olo-* 'to be afraid, startled' in Evk. *olo-*, Even *ol-*, Orok *olo-*, Na. *olo-*, Solon *olo-* → Ma. *oliho-* 'to be afraid, startled'

Deverbal inchoative

> pTg **xol-* 'to dry (tr.)' in Evk. *olgo-*, Even *olga-*, *olgi:-* 'to become dry', Orok *xoldoxo* 'dry', Olcha *xoljo(n)* 'dry' → Ma. *olgo-* 'to become dry (intr.)'→ *olhon* 'dry'
>
> Ma. *neme-* 'to add, increase (tr.)' → (**neme-he-* 'to become increased' →) Ma. *nemehen* 'addition, increment'
>
> pTg **soŋo-* 'to weep (intr.)' in Evk. *soŋo-*, Even *hoŋ-*, Neg. *soŋo-*, Ud. *soŋo-*, Solon *soŋo-* → Ma. *soŋho-* 'to weep (intr.)'

5.7.3.2 Even

Even preserves some traces of an inchoative suffix *-g-* following vowels and *-gA-* following consonants, which derives verbs from nouns, adding the meaning 'to use the base' or 'to enter a state resulting from the base' and inchoatives from verbs.[16]

---

[16] There are some deverbal derivations in which the semantic connotation seems to be "to completely accomplish the action expressed by the base" rather than "to begin the action expressed by the base", e.g. Even *cu:-* 'to lick sth. (tr.)' → *cug-* 'to lick sth. up/clean (tr.)'; Even **ha:ma-* 'to mark (tr.)' in *ha:mab-* 'to become marked' → *ha:mag-* 'to mark, to dignify, to bring out, to accentuate'; Even *hęl-* 'to put on a spit, put fish on a spit' → *hęlga-* 'to pierce, drill through

The suffix pTg *-rgA- is reflected in Even -(A)rg(A)-, which derives inchoative decausatives (Benzing 1955b: 36), e.g. Even *hine- 'to be pale' in hineñe 'to be pale, greyish' → hinerge- 'to turn pale'; pTg *pula- 'to be red' in Evk. hulama, hularin 'red', Even hulal- 'become red', hulaña- 'red', Ud. xulaligi, Solon ulā: 'red'→ Even hularga- 'to become red'[17]; Even *hunda- 'to be wide' in hundaña 'wide' → hundarga- 'to widen, become wide', pTg *huta- 'to be gleaming' in Evk. hutal-, Even hutal- 'to sparkle, blaze', hutaña 'light red', hutati: 'red, gleaming' → Even hutarga- 'to become red'; pTg *delpe- 'to split' in Evk. delperge-, delpem-, Solon delpe- 'to split' → Even depčerge- 'to split'.

Denominal

1. 'to use the base'

   pTg *kiri in Olcha kiri 'front tooth'→ Even kirga- 'to gnaw'

2. 'to enter the state denoted by the base'

   Even her 'ground, base, bottom' → herge- 'to go down'

Deverbal inchoative

Even bori:- 'to divide (tr.)' → borga- 'to disperse, scatter (intr.)'

pTg *nime- 'to be a guest' in Even nime:k 'neighbor', Evk. ñime-, Neg. ñimey-, Na. nimeri-, Ud. ñimeli-, Solon nimau- 'to visit, be a guest' → Even nime:g- 'to go to the neighbors'

Even *tal- 'to shine' in talal- 'to shine in the sun (of water) (intr.)', talaña 'bright, shiny' → talga- 'to be shiny, calm (of weather) (intr.)'

pTg *xol- 'to dry (tr.)' in Even ola:- 'to wither, dry up (intr.)', Even olgi:- 'to dry (tr.)', Orok xoldoxo 'dry', Olcha xoljo(n) 'dry' → Even olga- 'to become dry (intr.)'

---

sth. (tr.), to edge one's way through (intr,)' and Even *uci- 'to turn' in ucil- 'to begin to turn' → ucilga- 'to unwind, unscrew (tr.)'.

[17] Even -ñA derives deverbal adjectives, e.g. kot- 'to bend (intr.)' → kotaña 'bent', kapta- 'to flatten (tr.)' → kaptaña 'flat' (Benzing 1955b: 41).

5.7.3.3 Evenki

Evenki preserves some faint traces of an inchoative suffix *-ga- ~ -ge- ~ -go-*, which derives the meaning 'to use the base' from nouns (Konstantinova 1964: 200, Nedjalkov 1997: 301) or inchoative transitive meaning from verbs (Konstantinova 1964: 161, Nedjalkov 1997: 231), as illustrated below.

The suffix pTg *-rgA- is reflected in Evk. *-rg(A)-*, which derives inchoative decausatives (Nedjalkov 1997: 228, 302), e.g. Evk. *teke-* 'to tear (tr.)' → *tekerge-* 'to tear (intr.)', Evk. *jangu-* 'to break (tr.)' → *jangurga-* 'to break (intr.)'; Evk. *kasi-* 'to tear, wear out (tr.) → *kasirga-* 'to tear, become worn out (intr.)'; pTg *koŋno-* 'to be black' in Evk. *kongnomo, kongnorin* 'black', Even *ko:ŋa-* 'be black', Solon *xoŋnorī*, Neg. *koŋnoji:n* 'black' → Evk. *kongnorgo-* 'to turn black' and pTg *pula-* 'to be red' in Even *hulama, hularin* 'red' → Evk. *hularga-* 'to redden, turn red'.

Denominal 'to use the base'

> Evk. *kolto* 'fist' → *koltogo-* 'to hit with the fist'
>
> Evk. *asaki:* 'wing' > *asaga-* 'to flap the wings'
>
> pTg *kiri* in Olcha *kiri* 'front tooth' > Evk. *kirge-* 'to gnaw'

Deverbal inchoative

> Evk. *ada-* 'to fly past (intr.)' → *adaga-* 'to try to escape (intr.)'
>
> Evk. *iti-* 'to come into being (intr.)' → *itiga-* 'to set things going, organize, plan to do (tr.)'
>
> Evk. *kapu-* 'to break (tr.)' → *kapuga-* 'to break (tr.)'
>
> Evk. *kamñi:-* 'to defend oneself (intr.)' → *kamñiga-* 'to attack, tackle (tr.)'
>
> Evk. *tati-* 'to be used to (intr.)' → *tatiga-* 'to get (sb) used to, accustom (sb) to, train, learn (tr.)'

5.7.3.4 Udehe

Since the voiced velar pTg *-g-* frequently undergoes lenition to *-w-, -y-* and Ø in the southern Tungusic languages, we do not find clear traces of the inchoative pTg *-gA- in Udehe and Nanai. However, the complex suffix pTg *-rgA- is preserved in the inchoative decausative Ud. *-ga- ~ -ge- ~ -go-* (Nikolaeva 1999: 178). As illustrated below, the suffix derives the decausative counterpart of transitive verbs with the inchoative suffix *-li-*.

Ud. *guza-li-* 'to tear' → *guzaga-* 'to get torn'

Ud. *bukta-li-* 'to break in two' > *buktaga-* 'to get broken in two'

Ud. *xudu-li-* 'to dislocate' > *xuduge-* 'to get dislocated'

5.7.3.5 Nanai

Given that the reflex of pTg *-rg- clusters further lenits to -G- or Ø in Nanai, the decausative inchoative suffix pTg *-rgA- is reflected as Na. -a- ~ -e- (Menges 1964: 399–400: "Intransitiv Suffix"). As illustrated below, the suffix derives the decausative counterpart of transitive verbs with the inchoative suffix -li-.

Na. *lopto-li-* 'to detach, disconnect (tr.)' → *loptoa-* 'to detach, disconnect (intr.)'

Na. *moqto-li-* 'to break (tr.)' → *moqtoa-* 'to break (intr.)'

Na. *xetu-li-* 'to break off, dismantle, tear off (tr.)' → *xetue-* 'to fall down, be dismantled, be torn (intr.)'

5.7.4 pMo *-gA-

In Mongolic, the causative suffix -gA- is generalized to such an extent that it may have superseded the original deverbal inchoative *-gA-. Under pressure of the causative, inchoative verbs on -gA- got lost, but their stems survived in various derivations such as nominalizations on -i (see Section 8.3.4), (ad)nominal forms on -r (see Section 7.3.4), processives on -nA- (see Section 5.6.4) and distributives on -ljA- (see Section 3.3.4 (19)). The observation that derivations with -gA-I tend to be adjectives and that all verb bases derived with -gA-i are only attested in a form derived with the anticausative -yi- rather than in their bare root form (Poppe 1954: 45), suggests that the meanings of -gA- and -yi- are overlapping and distinguishes the suffix -gA-i from the resultative nominalizer -gA (see Section 7.6.4), for which bare basic roots are widely attested and which derives nouns as well as adjectives.

de-adjectival / deverbal 'to enter a state denoted by or resulting from the base'

pMo *kabta-* 'to be flat' in *qabtaγa* 'flat, even; flatness; plane surface' (pM *-gA resultative nominalizer; see Section 7.6.4), WMo. *qabtayi-* 'to become flat' → pMo *kabtaga-* 'to become flat' in WMo. *qabtaγai* 'flat, even; flatness; plane surface', *qabtaγar* 'flat, level'

pMo *kaja-* 'to bend (tr.)' in WMo. *qajayi-* 'to bend, to incline, to become crooked (intr.)' → pMo *kajaga-* 'to be(come) bent' in *qajaγai* 'curved, oblique, crooked (adj)', *qajaɣar* askew, bent; crippled (adj and adv)', *qajaɣalja-* 'to limp, hobble, sway from side to side (intr.)', *qajaɣana-* 'to limp, hobble, sway from side to side (intr.)'

pMo **serte-* 'to be upright, erect' in WMo. *serteng* 'upright or erect (of ears)', *serteb* 'upright (of nostrils)', *serteyi-* 'to stick out or up, bulge out, stand on end (of hair)' → pMo **sertege-* 'to become erect' in WMo. *serteger* 'protruding, erect, standing upright'

pMo **kelte-* 'to be inclined' in WMo. *kelteyi-* 'to incline, lean, be crooked (intr.)', *kelteng* 'inclined to one side, awry, lopsided' → pMo **keltege-* 'to become inclined' in WMo. *keltegei* 'slanting, askew, divergent, unfair', *kelteger* 'slanting, askew, inclined (adj.)'

Note that there are indications that pMo **-gA-* devoices in a sonorant environment, more particularly following /r, m/. When the Written Mongolian suffix *-ɣai ~ -gei* (< pMo **-gA-i* INCH-NML), for instance, is added to verb stems longer than two syllables ending in *-rV-* or *-mV-*, the stem-final vowel tends to drop to reduce the length of the sequence and in the resulting sonorant cluster, the initial /g/ of the suffix will devoice to /k/, e.g. WMo. *ide-* 'to eat, consume (tr.)', **ide-me-* 'to be inclined to eat' → *idemegei* 'voracious, venal' ~ *idemkei* 'voracious'; WMo. *butara-* 'break to pieces, smash, disperse, scatter (intr.)' → *butarqai* 'dispersed, scattered, crumbled, crushed (adj./ n.)'; WMo. *tasura-* 'to be torn away from, cut off, be interrupted, stopped (intr.)' → *tasurqai* 'torn off, cut off, decisive; piece torn off, fragment (adj. /n.)'; WMo. *todura-* 'to be(come) clear, obvious; appear, be reborn (intr.)' → *todurqai* 'clear(ly), obvious(ly) (adj. /adv.)', etc.

5.7.5 pTk *-(X)k-* (~ *-(X)g-*)

The inchoative suffix pTk **-(X)k-* has lexicalized as *-(X)k-* in Old Turkic (Gabain 1950: 82, Erdal 1991: 492–499, 524, 645–649) and as *-(Ă)x-* in Chuvash (Benzing 1959: 719, Levickaja 1974: 173–175). It derives intransitive verbs from nouns, nominal and verbal adjectives and (in)transitive verbs, modifying the meaning of the base in the sense of 'to enter a state resulting from the base'. Although, some semantics have bleached – particularly in deverbal derivation – the inchoative meaning is still clear from the examples below.

denominal 'to enter a state denoted by the base'
    OTk. *ada* 'danger' → *adak-* 'to be or come into distress'
    OTk. *šï ~ čï* 'moist' → *čïk-* 'to get moist'

OTk. *tag* 'mountain' → *tagïk-* 'to go to the mountains'

OTk. *yėr* 'place, land' → *yėrik-* 'to settle'

OTk. *küz* 'autumn' → *küzük-* 'to turn to autumn, become autumnal'

deadjectival 'to acquire the property denoted by the base'

alï- 'to be bad' in OTk. *alïg* 'bad' → *alïk-* 'to turn septic, fester, detoriate'

amrï- 'to be peaceful' in OTk. *amrïl-* 'to be at peace, be at ease' → *amrïk-* 'to acquire peace, become peaceful'

OTk. *us-* 'to be thirsty' → *usuk-* 'to be thirsty, be overcome with thirst'

OTk. *ač-* 'to be hungry' → *ačuk-* 'to be famished, be overcome with hunger'

deverbal 'to enter the state resulting from the base'

OTk. *čom-* 'to sink (intr.)' → *čomuk-* 'to drown (intr.)'

OTk. *oŋ-* 'to turn pale, fade, wilt (intr.)' → *oŋuk-* 'to become pale, become lean because of illness, wilt (intr.)'

OTk. *sor-* 'to ask, inquire about (tr.)' → *soruk-* 'to be inquired about (intr.)'

OTk. *tar-* 'to disperse, scatter, do away with (tr.)' → *tarïk-* 'to disperse, be driven away, go away (intr.)'

The converb and "aorist" vowel of OTk. *-(X)k-* verbs is usually /A/. If this vowel can be taken to reflect the original stem-final vowel – as it does with the causative-passive pTk *-ti* (see Section 6.3.5) –, then this may indicate original *A*-vocalism of the suffix. Since the standard causative counterpart of OTk. *-(X)k-* is OTk. *-gAr-* (e.g. *ičik-* 'to submit, capitulate (intr.)' vs. *ičger-* 'to subdue, conquer (tr.)'), Erdal (2004: 79, 747) suggests that *-gAr-* verbs should be treated as expansions with the causative suffix *-Ar* from inchoative verbs.[18] The initial vowel loss can be explained because in complex suffixes this vowel is expected to elide. The voicing of the suffix, however, is more problematic. Erdal explains it as a secondary development, but he also notes that in other suffixes, the change goes in the opposite direction, i.e. devoicing; in the causative suffix OTk. *-Xz-*, for instance, /z/ devoices to /s/ after /r, l, n/ (Erdal 2004: 704, 757–760) and a similar environment will be suggested for the devoicing of the adnominal resultative pTk *-gA* (see Section 7.6.5). Note that the exceptionally unvoiced causative counterparts OTk. *tarkar-* 'to restrain, restrict' of *tarïk-* 'to be constricted' and OTk. *muŋkar-* 'to cause distress' of *muŋuk-* 'to be distressed' indeed seem to suggest devoicing in a sonorant environment.

---

18 Note that the opposition /k/ vs. /g/ appears to be very weak after consonants in Old Turkic.

The cognate Chuvash inchoative suffix -(Ă)x-, however, suggests that the original shape of the suffix was a voiceless pTk *-(X)k-, because it reflects a regular sound correspondence whereby pTk *-k- yields OTk -k- and Chuvash -k- or -x- (Benzing 1959: 713; Starostin et al. 2003: 143–144).[19] The suffix derives verbs from nouns (e.g. Chu. *tut* 'rust' → *tutăx-* 'to become rusty', *věcě* 'furry, rage' → *věcěx-* 'to be(come) angry'), from adjectives (e.g. Chu. *šură* 'white' → *šurăx-* 'to become pale', *vĭšă* 'to be hungry' → *vĭšăx-* 'to famish, go hungry') and from other verbs (e.g. Chu. *păš-* 'to be sad, be miserable' → *păšăx-* 'to worry about, be anxious', *kuš-* 'to get dry' → *kušăx-* 'to get dry, dry out', *yăš-* 'to exhaust oneself' → *yăšăx-* 'to ache') (Levickaya 1974: 172–175, Fedotov 1996: 351–352).

5.8 The historical development of actionality in Transeurasian

The Transeurasian languages preserve evidence supporting the reconstruction of five actional suffixes: a denominal verbalizer pTEA *-lA-, an iconic pTEA *-ki-, a processive pTEA *-nA-, an inclinational pTEA *-mA- and an inchoative pTEA *-gA-. This is illustrated in Table 2.

Table 2. Reflexes of actional suffixes in the Transeurasian languages

pTEA	pJ	pK	pTg	pMo	pTk
*-lA-	*-ra-		*-lA:-	*-lA-	*-lA-
manipulative	manipulative		manipulative	manipulative	manipulative
denominal VBL	loan verb marker		loan verb marker	loan verb marker	loan verb marker
	denominal		denominal	denominal	denominal
*-nA-	*-na-	*-nO-	*-nA-	*-nA-	*-(X)n-
processive	processive	processive	processive	processive	processive
	denominal		denominal	denominal	
	de-adjectival	de-adjectival	de-adjectival	de-adjectival	de-adjectival
	deverbal	deverbal	deverbal	deverbal	deverbal
*(-)ki-	*-ka-	*-ki-	*-ki-	*(-)ki-	*ki(-)l- /-kl-
'do, make'				'do, make'	'do make'
iconic	iconic	iconic	iconic	iconic	iconic

---

[19] The sound correspondence is reflected in, for instance, Karakh. *bïrak-* 'to abandon' and Chu. *părax-* 'to throw' from pTk *bïrak- 'to dispose of'.

pTEA	pJ	pK	pTg	pMo	pTk
*-mA- inclination	*-ma- inclination denominal de-adjectival deverbal	*-mO- inclination denominal de-adjectival deverbal	*-mA- inclination denominal de-adjectival deverbal	*-mA- inclination de-adjectival deverbal	
*-gA- inchoative	*-ka- inchoative denominal de-adjectival deverbal	*-k(O)- inchoative denominal de-adjectival deverbal	*-gA- inchoative denominal de-adjectival deverbal	*-gA- inchoative de-adjectival deverbal	*-(X)k- (-(X)g-) inchoative denominal de-adjectival deverbal

The etymologies have members in all five branches, except for the lacking Korean reflex of the denominal verbalizer pTEA *-lA- and the Turkic reflex of the inclinational pTEA *-mA-. The absence of the latter suffix in Turkic can perhaps be explained by the presence of the Turkic negative suffix -mA- (see Section 4.5), which may have superseded an original tentative in *-mA-. Note that the absence of cognates may be relevant for the distinction between inheritance and language contact. It is difficult to explain, for instance, how Tungusic and Japanese could borrow verb suffixes from each other, without a Korean intermediary. Moreover, verb morphology is usually borrowed over loan verbs hosting the particular morpheme. Within a borrowing scenario, we would thus need to explain why certain derived verbs like inchoatives and processives would have been so extensively borrowed between Turkic and Mongolic (and the other Transeurasian languages), whereas verbs derived with other actional suffixes like inclinationals would have been totally immune for borrowing.

a) *Formal assessment*
With the exception of the voiceless velar in the Turkic inchoative *-(X)k, the consonants correspond regularly according to the correspondences 10. (*-l-), 9. (*(-)n-), 5. (*-k-), 8. (*-m-) and 6. (*-g-) in Section 3.3.1. If the velar in the Turkic inchoative indeed originally was a voiceless velar as suggested by one complex suffix, then the correspondence would be regular and the devoicing of the suffix in sonorant environment would be shared by Turkic and Mongolic.

According to the correspondences 12. (*-a-), 13. (*-ə-) in Section 3.3.2, the vowel harmony between pTEA *-a- and *-ə- regularly merges into pJ *-a-. Due to this merger, the large majority of Japanese suffixes display *a*-vocalism. Resonance with the wide-spread *a*-vocalism in the actional paradigm has probably triggered the replacement of *-*ki*- by *-*ka*- (see Section 3.2.2.1). This is reminiscent of the developments in the French singular object pronouns *me, te, le, se*, in which the vowel and the syllable structure have become uniform.

The consistently reduced vowel reflexes (*-*i̯*- / -*ʌ*-) in the Korean suffixes are probably due to vowel reduction in final position, similar to the weakening of the final vowel involved in conditioning factor 12b.

b) *Functional assessment*
The functional correspondences go beyond general tags such as manipulative, iconic, processive, inclinational and inchoative, since there are correlations of the concrete submeanings that make up the functional tag. The denominal verbalizer is considered under the category "actionality" because, apart from the derivation of verbs from nouns, it adds manipulative meaning to the base, i.e. 'to achieve, accumulate or overcome the base noun, to execute a difficult action with success on the base noun', 'to make use of the base noun' and 'to sound or feel like the base onomatopoea'. It is telling that these submeanings correlate across the Transeurasian languages in addition to the common function as verbalizer and loan verb marker. For the processive pTEA *-*nA*- the common denominator is spontaneous development, often of natural phenomena, except for Japanese where pJ *-*na*- denotes dynamic processes which could but need not be caused by an agent.[20]

c) *Combinational assessment*
As far as combinational correlations are concerned, the ordering of a particular morpheme in the actional suffix chain displays a general overlap. Logically, the denominal verbalizer pTEA *-*lA*- occupies the first position in all languages. It is followed by the processive pTEA *-*nA*-, which occurs in leftmost position in Japanese, Korean, Tungusic and Turkic, but more to the right (following iconic and inchoative) in Mongolic. The inclinational pTEA *-*mA*- and inchoative pTEA *-*gA*- tend towards the rightmost positions of the actionality chain in most languages, but they always precede markers of valence and voice. These correlations do not necessarily indicate common ancestorship, because the relative position of a morpheme in the suffix chain may be guided by universal principles in linguistic structuring: morphemes of comparable semantic relevance

---

[20] Note that Collinder (1965: 117) reconstructs a denominal fientive proto-Uralic *-*n*- 'to become like the base' attested in derivations such as 'old' → 'to grow old, older'. The marker has the same form and a similar function, although it is not used in deverbal derivations.

and content are logically expected to be arranged at a similar distance from the verb root (Bybee 1985). Nevertheless, the correlating position in the suffix chain supports the observation that the suffixes are of comparable semantic relevance and content, which thus supports the functional comparison. Note also that I have argued in favour of the genealogical stability of categories in a position close to the verb root.

d) *Typological assessment*
From a typological perspective, it seems characteristic for the Transeurasian languages that a single derivational suffix can simultaneously apply to nominal, adjectival and verbal bases. This is the case for all actional suffixes in Table 2, except for the manipulative denominal verbalizer and the iconic suffix, which, by their very nature, derive from nouns and from onomatopoetic adverbs, respectively. Although the co-occurence of suffixes on nominal, adjectival and verbal bases is particularly common in the Transeurasian area, it is by no means restricted to these languages. Old English *ge-*, for instance, derives adjectives that code a quality associated with the state of the base from nouns and adjectives, e.g. OE *swāt* 'sweat' → *geswāt* 'sweaty' and OE *friðsum* 'peaceful' → *gefriðsum* 'safe', and it is found in the past participle as in OE *helpen* 'to help' → *geholpen* 'helpt'. Indo-European uses a suffix pIE *-ie-* in order to derive verbs from nouns, reflected in e.g. Skt. *námas-* 'honor' → *námasyáti* 'to honor', Lat. *cu:ra:* 'care' → *cu:ra:io:* > *cu:ro:* 'to care' and the same suffix is used to form intensives from verbs, reflected in e.g. Skt. *dédiṣ-ṭe* → *dediśyá-te* 'to display' (Beekes 1995: 230).

The synchronic co-occurence of verb suffixes on nominal, adjectival and verbal bases in the Transeurasian languages may be the result of a diachronic process whereby the suffixes were transferred from nouns to adjectives to verbs. Arguably, this development represents a process of grammaticalization, because it involves an increase in grammatical status (verb suffixes that derive from nominal or adjectival bases are category changing, whereas deverbal verb derivation is category-constant) and a loss of semantic content (denominal verb suffixes express more concrete meanings than deverbal verb suffixes).

The direction of grammaticalization can be illustrated by the development of the Old Turkic desiderative suffix -*sA*- (Erdal 1991: 527–529). Whether or not the suffix developed from a lexical verb pTk **sa:-* 'reckon (as), count (on), desire' reflected in Karakhanide *sa-* 'count, reckon (as)' and still present in a number of contemporary Turkic languages (Clauson 1972: 782–783), it is clear that its basic meaning is 'to want some kind of alimentation' since the large majority of denominal derivations involve this desire, e.g. OTk. *suv* 'water' → *suvsa-* 'to be thirsty', OTk. *balïk* 'fish' → *balïksa-* 'to want fish' etc. There are only few nominal derivates expressing a metaphorical hunger, such as OTk. *ev* 'house' → *evse-* 'to long for one's home' and OTk. *kök* 'sky' → *kökse-* 'want (to rise to) the sky'. As its lexical content further decreases, the suffix is transferred to the deverbal realm to derive desiderative verbs such as OTk. *yese-* 'wish to eat' from *ye-* 'eat' and OTk. *körse-* 'wish to see' from *kör-* 'see'.

The common transfer of verbalizers from nominal to verbal bases in the Transeurasian languages is probably enhanced by the originally mixed adjective typology (see Section 3.2.1). Denominal suffixes are applied to nouns and by extension to "nominal adjectives", property words that syntactically behave like nouns. Since we find instances of "switching," whereby the same property word can have both nominal and verbal encoding across the Transeurasian languages, it is easy to see how the suffixes could become applied to "verbal adjectives", property words that syntactically behave like verbs. This opens the way for the ultimate transfer to verbal bases. Consequently, we can consider the recurrent development of verbalizers to deverbal actional suffixes as instances of globally shared grammaticalization, which, as proposed in Section 2.5.3.1, can be best be accounted for by common ancestorship. The grammaticalization from verbalizer to loan verb marker shared by the reflexes of the denominal verbalizer pTEA *-*lA*- or from a lexical verb 'to do, make' to an iconic suffix in Turkic and Mongolic may also represent such a case.

6 Valence and voice

6.1 The suffix classes "valence" and "voice" and their diachronic relevance

Valence markers are affixes that can be applied to the verb to change the number or the role of arguments required by the verb. They derive intransitive verbs that are univalent or, transitive and causative verbs that can take two (bivalent) or three (trivalent) arguments. Voice markers change the relation that the surface subject has to the verb. In the active, the subject is the agent or doer of the action; in the passive the subject is the undergoer or patient, affected by the action; in the reflexive, reciprocal and anticausative, the subject both performs the action and is affected by the action. Valence and voice markers share a common logical base, namely the modification of the syntactic environment of the verb in placing certain requirements on the surrounding constituents. Since this leads to historical correlations between both suffix classes cross-linguistically, they will be dealt with in one chapter.

Reflexive means that the agent of the action performs the action on himself, whereas reciprocal means that plural agents perform the action on each other. Resultatives derive states resulting from the preceding action. I use the term anticausative to denote a spontaneous process without an implied agent. In my use of the term, the basic verb does not necessarily denote a transitive action. A deadjectival anticausative, for instance, derives a spontaneous process without an implied agent from an intransitive property verb. Potential passive denotes that the subject is capable of undergoing the action. Fientives derive a process of becoming from property words, i.e. from nominal or verbal adjectives.

The suffix classes "valence" and "voice" are situated on the interface between derivation and inflection. Theoretical morphologists conceptualize the distinction between derivation and inflection in two major ways: the split morphology approach regards derivation and inflection as two distinct classes (a.o. Anderson 1992), whereas the continuum approach regards them as opposite poles on a morphological scale (a.o. Bybee 1985, Dressler 1989, Plank 1994, Aikhenvald 2007 [1985]). Basically, derivational morphology results in the creation of a new word with a new meaning, whereas inflectional morphology involves an obligatory syntactic function characteristic of a particular word class. There are a number of criteria that can help us to distinguish between derivation and inflection (Bybee 1985: 81–87, Haspelmath 2002: 70–77; Aikhenvald 2007 [1985]: 36; Gardani 2008: 33–35). Some of these involve discrete divisions such as change of base semantics (yes vs. no), change of word-class (possible vs. impossible), obligatoriness (no vs. yes), applicability (limited vs. unlimited), recursivity (possible vs. impossible), cumulative expression (impossible vs. possible) etc., but others involve relative properties such as semantic content (from concrete to abstract), semantic relevance to base meaning (from high to low), semantic transparency (from low to high), syntactic relevance (from low to high), paradigmatic organisation (from loose to tight), morpheme distance from root (from close to far) etc. Since these non-discrete criteria allow for a continuum of possible properties, the continuum approach of derivation and inflection is almost inevitable.

It is not surprising that across the languages of the world valence is found to be frequently mentioned as a derivational category for verbs (Bybee 1985: 83). Indeed, valence-changing categories produce large meaning changes in verbs (e.g. *die* vs. *kill*), they have a high semantic relevance and add concrete meanings. Moreover, valence distinctions tend to lexicalize easily and often lack semantic transparency. Cross-linguistically, it is rare to find a case where valence could be considered obligatory in the sense that every finite clause contains a morphological indicator of the number and the role of the arguments. Since there exist certain events that are inherently transitive, and not divisible into an intransitive event plus a transitivizer, the applicability of valence markers is naturally limited. Recursivity of valence markers is possible, such as for instance in the double causative constructions that will be mentioned below. Finally, valence markers are in a position close to the verb root, usually following actionality and preceding voice in the suffix chain. Although the category of voice is more inflectional than valence, it still reflects a number of derivational properties, such as its substantial modification of the meaning of the base and its position close to the verb root.

The situation of valence and voice markers on the interface between derivation and inflection affects the expectations with regard to the genealogical stability of these categories. Using the designation "diatheses" in reference to the suffix classes voice and valence[1], Johanson (1992, 1999, 2002a) finds that these markers provide particularly strong genealogical evidence, arguing that (2002a: 152) "Certain parts of the Turkic verbal system are apparently more stable than others, specifically the inflectional categories close to the primary stem, e.g. the markers forming secondary verbal stems and used to denote actionality and diatheses. Among their characteristics are an internal position, a high degree of cohesion, firm incorporation into the complex lexico-syntactic combinational

---

[1] Voice markers only change the communicative organization of the message and leave the situational content intact. Whereas the passive, for instance, denotes a single situation ('Y is loved by X' = Y is V-ed by X), the causative denotes two situations in a causal relation ('Y makes X love [someone]' = Y did do sth. and X does V because of that). This addition of situational meaning has led to the exclusion of causatives from the category of diathesis (Mel'čuk 1993: 11).

system, and an often central role which also concerns sentence-hierarchy. It appears that these features are most resistant to the kinds of restructuring processes that occur in every verbal system."

It is clear that markers of valence and voice are relatively resistant to copying in comparison to lexemes or to nominal derivational morphology. This is interrelated with a number of factors such as a high degree of semantic abstraction, boundness, variant allomorphy, an occasional monophonemic shape, a low number of applicable units which increases the frequency of use an an incorporation in larger paradigms. However, since these features are also shared by more inflectional verb morphology, they do not explain the relative stability of the suffix classes valence and voice vis à vis more inflectional classes, such as mood, tense and person-number agreement. Just like in the case of actional suffixes discussed in Section 5.1, the relative stability here obtains because of a lower probability of attrition – and not so much because of lower copiability – in comparison with inflectional suffixes. Since markers of valence and voice will lexicalize more easily, they are expected to leave a trace in the language, even after all inflectional morphology has been replaced by new formal encodings.

As a consequence of their relative conservativism, many valence and voice markers are no longer productive: they have lexicalized into verb stems. Proto-Germanic, for instance, had a *-j- causative, that was added to the ablaut stem (e.g. *lag-, *sat-, *trank-) of strong verbs (e.g. *lig- 'lie', *sit- 'sit', *trink- 'drink'). Although the suffix lost its productivity and was replaced by periphrastic causative constructions in the Germanic languages, it is traceable in lexicalized verb pairs such as in the German verbs *führen*, *fällen*, *senken*, *setzen*, *stellen*, *tränken* and *wecken* which are derived from neutral bases *fahren*, *fallen*, *sinken*, *sitzen*, *stehen*, *trinken*, *wachen*. The additional formal element -y-, which leaves a trace in the umlaut of the derived verb stem, correlates with an additional function, namely causativity. Although the causative suffix is no longer productive in German, it can be reconstructed for proto-Germanic on the basis of the diagrammatic equivalence between the form -y- and its causative function. Note that this element can be reconstructed back all the way to the Indo-European causative in *-éy-. In a similar way, lexicalized suffixes of valence and voice in the Transeurasian languages are reconstructable as productive markers through diagrammatic equivalence. The comparison of these reconstructed suffixes between the Transeurasian languages is expected to yield evidence that is relatively resistant to the passage of time.

In his review of Johanson 2002a, Schönig (2008: 198) objects to the use of abstract typological features relating to voice and valence in support of genealogical relationship because these might be attributed to code-copying or to universal implicational tendencies: "Hier führt Johanson die Diathesen innerhalb der sogenannten altaischen Sprachen an, ... Doch wäre hier zum einen zu fragen, ob nicht auch diese Parallelen nicht letztlich auf Entlehnung zurückgehen, zum anderen, ob es nicht vielleicht der Gemeinsame Sprachtyp ist, der solche Parallelen unabhängig voneinander entstehen läßt." In the present approach, however, I compare concrete forms rather than abstract features and I consider these forms to be more stable than inflectional forms because of their particular resistance to attrition. Hence, I argue that voice and valence-changing forms resist the passage of time more successfully, not that they are less susceptible to code-copying than inflectional forms.

6.2 Previous research

In this chapter, five suffixes of valence and voice will be reconstructed: a causative pTEA *-ti-, a reflexive-anticausative pTEA *-pU-, a fientive pTEA *-dA-, an anticausative pTEA *-rA- and a causative pTEA *-gi-.

As far as the causative pTEA *-ti- is concerned, Ramstedt (1912: 21–23) first mentioned a parallel between the causative suffixes in Mongolic and Turkic. In his Korean grammar (1939: 136), he adds a Korean cognate *-thi- and a Tungusic cognate -ti-, či, but clear evidence of the Tungusic suffix is missing, also from Ramstedt's (1952: 175–176) study. Miller (1981: 855) marginally referred to a dental suffix in Altaic: "pA *-t- was used in both denominal and deverbal formations, deriving transitive verbs, indicating that an action relating to the original noun or verb was performed in a sudden, jolting or otherwise particularly conclusive fashion." However, it remains unclear whether he is referring to the same causative marker as the one mentioned by Ramstedt. Whereas Ramstedt's comparisons do not include Japanese data, Miller (1981: 857) described four of the Japanese verbs analyzed below (i.e. OJ *panat-* 'separate, alienate (tr.)', OJ *sakat-* 'butcher, kill (tr.)', OJ *wakat-* 'break apart, rip open, split, share (tr.)' and OJ *pagat-* 'destroy, tear out, peel off (tr.)') as inherited secondary derivates in pA *-t-, but he did not define the meaning of the Japanese suffix.

As far as the reflexive-anticausative pTEA *-pU- is concerned, Ramstedt (1912: 67–73) compared the Mongolic anticausative -bu- with a vague Turkic element -p-, which will not be regarded here. In his 1952 study (157–160), however, he added the anticausative suffix OTk -U- along with a Tungusic causative-passive suffix pTg *-bu- and Korean suffix -bu- ~ -pu- with "passive or intransitive" meaning. The Tungusic cognate proposed by Ramstedt is also compared to the Mongolic anticausative by Poppe (1972a: 128–134), Street (1978: 185–186, 239–242) and Miller (1981: 858–59), but should probably be eliminated from the etymology because it seems to have grammaticalized from the Tungusic verb pTg *bu:- 'to give'. However, Ramstedt's (1952) proposal for Turkic and Korean will be considered. There seems to be insufficient internal evidence for reconstruction of a Japanese cognate *-p(a)- in the function of "causative", as suggested by Miller (1981: 858–59), but a different Japanese cognate will be proposed here.

As far as the fientive pTEA *-dA- is concerned, Ramstedt (1912: 40–43, 1952: 196–197) proposed the comparison discussed below for the Mongolic and Turkic cognates, but contrary to the present approach, he treated the denominal and deverbal formatives as distinct suffixes. Poppe (1972a: 136–137) followed Ramstedt in his comparison of the deverbal suffixes. Miller (1981: 869–870) added a Japanese formant -ya- to the comparison, but did not take into account denominal derivations with this suffix. In the present account, the Japanese cognate will be reconstructed in greater detail and a Tungusic cognate will be proposed.

As far as the anticausative pTEA *-rA- is concerned, Ramstedt (1912: 33–36, 1952: 199–200) proposed to compare the Mongolic and Turkic anticausatives, adding the Tungusic decausative inchoative *-rgA- as a complex suffix incorporating this marker in his 1952 study. His proposal was followed by Poppe (1972a: 139–140), who added a simplex anticausative cognate from Evenki. Street (1978: 187, 259–260) added the Japanese anticausative *-ra- to this comparison, but Miller (1971: 131–140) suggested a different etymology for this suffix, relating it instead to the Turkic equipollent anticausative marker -l- in verb pairs such as OTk. tol- 'to be full (intr.)' / OTk. toš- 'to fill (tr.)'. In the present account, a Korean cognate will be suggested.

As far as the causative pTEA *-gi- is concerned, the Japanese causative-anticausative suffix *-(C)i- has been frequently compared with the Korean causative-passive marker *-ki- (Martin 1987: 64, Takeuchi 1999: 93, Unger 2000a: 667, Vovin 2001: 187–189). Vovin added Evk. -gii- to the etymology, which he labeled "transitivity switcher". In Robbeets 2005a (54, 161, 960–961), I rejected this etymology because in Japanese, internal evidence for the precise reconstruction of the initial consonant is missing. However, for reasons explained below, I now think that it is legitimate to reconcile internal and external evidence in this case.

This chapter consists of a revision of Robbeets (2007b, 2010), my earlier treatment of cognate suffixes of valence and voice in the Transeurasian languages. The approach taken here intends to complement the previous approaches by reviewing Altaic etymologies and supplementing them with material from Japanese and Korean. The individual suffixes underlying this study will be defined more accurately in terms of form, function and combinational properties and their comparison will lead to a paradigmatic reconstruction of the suffix class valence and voice. Whereas previous studies have mainly compared form and function, the present approach will integrate combinational properties and diachronic typology, including grammaticalization theory, into the argumentation.

6.3 pTEA *-ti- causative

6.3.1 pJ -*ta-

Formally, the lexicalized verb suffix OJ -t- < pJ -*ta- is reconstructed by Unger (1977: 140), Miller (1981: 857) and Martin (1987: 794–795). Whereas Miller and Martin leave the semantics open, Unger describes pJ *-ta- as a causative, adding the meaning 'cause (obj.) to attain the state of (the preceding root)'. Given the unidirectionality in the grammaticalization from causatives into passives (Haspelmath 1990: 49), the verb pairs below suggest that the causative suffix extended its meaning to passive. The instances where the formal element OJ -t- derives transitive verbs from transitive bases seem to involve a semantic nuance of intensity of the action and/ or multiplicity of the object. This can be explained from the viewpoint that cross-linguistically causative morphology applied to transitive verbs can have non-valence-increasing effects relating to the intensity of the action and the size or distribution of the objects (Kulikov 1993: 127–136, Aikhenvald 2011b: 163–166, 170–178). The verb pairs further suggest that the passive development went over resultative meaning.

In some of the derivations below a neutral base is missing, but it is attested in verb stems derived with various other suffixes such the equipollent anticausative/causatives *-ra-/ -sa- (see Section 6.6.1) and the causative-anticausative *-(C)i- (See Section 6.7.1). The suffix *-ta- seems to occupy the first position in the chain of valence and voice markers, since it is never preceded by these markers.

Since the causative suffix has lexicalized as stem-final s- in cognate Ryukyuan verbs such as Shuri hanas- B 'separate, alienate (tr.)', kuus- B 'take apart, tear down', qakas- B 'to disperse, divide (tr.)', hagas- B 'to destroy, tear out, peel off', the period in which this suffix was productive as a causative must predate the split of Mainland Japanese and Ryukyuan and thus belongs to the proto-Japonic stage. The reconstructed verb roots may be ambitransitive and polarized for transitivity by way of suffixes.

Causatives from intransitive verbs

>OJ ke_2- A 'to get extinguished (intr.)' → OJ ke_2t- A 'to make vanish, extinguish (tr.)'

>pJ *kata- 'to be one-sided' in OJ kate- B 'to join, unite, blend', OJ katap- 'to become intimate', OJ kata(-) 2.3. 'one side of two, one of a pair, inclined toward (bound)' → J katat- ?B 'to honor, favor (tr.)'

>*kəpə- 'to break' in OJ kopore- B 'to fall, drop, be scattered; be shattered, broken (intr.)', OJ kopare- B 'to break, get broken, get ruined (intr.)', OJ kopas- B 'to break, ruin (tr.)' → MJ kofot- 'to shatter (tr.)'

pana- 'to be distant, separated' in (Eastern) OJ *panar-* ?B 'to get distant, be expelled (intr.)', OJ *pane-* ?B 'to exclude (tr.)' → OJ *panat-* B 'to separate, alienate (tr.)'

ta- 'to reach (an end)' in [OJ *itar-* A 'to arrive, reach, attain', OJ *itas-* A 'to do, cause, bring about'], OJ *taye-* B 'to come to an end (intr.)', OJ *tayas-* B 'to end, put an end to, let come to an end (tr.)' → OJ *tat-* B 'cut off, abstain from, exterminate (tr.)'

uka- 'to be opened, bored' in OJ *uke$_2$-* ?B 'to open up, be bored (of a hole) (intr.)' → OJ *ukat-* B 'dig, bore (tr.)'

Intensives from transitive verbs

OJ *pag-* ?B 'to peel, strip (tr.)' → OJ *pagat-* B 'to destroy, tear out, peel off (tr.)'

OJ *sak-* ?B 'to rip, split (tr.)' → OJ *sakat-* B 'to butcher, kill (tr.)'

OJ *wak-* B 'to divide (tr.)' → OJ *wakat-* B 'to break apart, rip open, split, share (tr.)', OJ *akat-* B 'to disperse, divide, separate, wean (tr.)'

Resultatives

ina- 'to go away' in OJ *in-* A 'to go away (intr.)' → *ina-ta-* 'to be gone' in OJ *id-* B 'to emerge (intr.)' and *ina-ta-sa-* in OJ *idas-* B 'put out (tr.)' (Martin 1995: 147)[2]

sənpə- 'to rain, to wet' in J *sober-* 'to sprawl, spread, (dial.) fall down (intr.)', J *sobo-hur-*, OJ *sopo-pur-* 'drizzle, rain (intr.)' → OJ *so$_2$pot-* 'to get drenched (intr.)'

Passives from transitive verbs

ayama- 'to mistake' in OJ *ayamar-* B 'to err, make a mistake, apologize (intr.)' → OJ *ayamat-* B 'to err, make a mistake (intr.)'

ku(n)ta- 'to lower' in OJ *kudas-* A 'to take down, put down, lower, defeat (tr.)', OJ *kudar-* A 'to go down, descend (intr.)' → MJ *kudat-*, OJ *kutat-* ?A/B 'to come down, end, deteriorate (intr.)'

6.3.2 pK *-ti-*

The causative-passive suffix pK *-t(i)-* surfaces in only a small number of alternating verb pairs in Middle Korean. The pairs below leave traces of causative and passive derivation of intransitive verbs. Note that the passive derivation of MK

---

[2] See Section 3.3.4 (47) for an explanation of why the original accent of OJ *in-* 'to go away (intr.)' may be B.

nat- 'to appear (intr.)' is parallel to the one suggested for OJ *id-* 'to emerge (intr.)' in Section 6.3.1 above and that the verb roots are cognate as well (see Section 3.3.4 (47)). Therefore, we cannot exclude that the passive derivation of the root goes back to the stage of proto-Koreo-Japonic. While the high front vowel has been elided in stem-final position in the three monosyllabic and low verbs on stem final *-t* which belong to class 1, it leaves a trace in the contracted verb MK ¨*et-* 'get, receive'. which belongs to class 5. Class 5 represents a small class of mono-syllabic rising verbs. The rising tone seems to result from the contraction of two syllables. For most of the verbs in class 5 the second syllable can be traced back to a separate suffix. The front vowel of MK ¨*et-* 'get, receive' may be the result of the contraction of the existential stem with a causative suffix **-ti-* with front vowel. The proposed derivation is reminiscent of how the Japanese verb *e-* 'to get, obtain' may have resulted from the monophthongization of the copula and causative-passive suffix. The reconstruction of the copular verb pK **a-* 'to be, exist' is discussed in Section 3.4.

Causatives

    **a-* 'to be, exist (intr.)' → MK ¨*et-* 'to get, receive (tr.)'
    MK *ti-* 'to become, form (intr.)' → MK *tit-* 'to light (a fire) (tr.)'

Passives

    **mwo-* 'to gather' in MK ¨*mwoy-* 'to accompany, escort (someone respected) (tr.)' (incorporates *-i-* causative), ¨*mwosi-* 'to accompany (tr.)', *mwoy·ho-* 'to gather, bring together (tr.)' → MK *mwot-* 'to come together (intr.)'
    MK ·*na-* 'to go out, emerge, become (intr.)' → MK *nat-* 'to appear (intr.)'

The original causative suffix pK **-ti-* is further incorporated in the causative-passive and intensive suffix K *-chi-*, MK ··*chi-* (Martin 1992: 450, 623) and in the causative and intensive suffix K *-chwu-*, MK ··*chwu-* (Martin 1992: 452). Next to the intensive use of these suffixes, there are also examples of other non-valence increasing effects such as the marking of iterative action, complete affected-

---

3 The assumption that the causative MK ··*chi-* and the intensive MK ··*chi-* reflect different uses of a single suffix is in contradiction with Martin's (1992: 224) contention that: "The voice-deriving bound postverbs should not be confused with the intensive bound postverb *-chi-*, which is morphemically related to the auxiliary verb *chi-* that is used after the infinitive as an intensifier." The auxiliary verb to which Martin refers is K *chi-* 'to do, do hard' (e.g. *mek-* 'eat' → *mek-e chi-* 'devour') grammaticalized from the independent verb K *chi-*, MK ·*thi-* 'to make, do, create, construct, reproduce, perform'. It is different from the intensive suffix because the auxiliary has recently grammaticalized and combines with the converb form (*-e-/-a-*) of the verb, while the intensive suffix is added immediately after the stem, already in Middle Korean.

ness of the object, and multiple distribution of the object.³ The suffix K -*chi*-, MK -·*chi*- can also derive a passive from a transitive verb.⁴

Causative

    K *cop*- 'be narrow, be limited (intr.)' → K *(c)copchi*- 'to make too narrow, close (tr.)'

    K *kulu*-, MK *kulu*- ~ *kulh*- 'to be wrong (intr.)' → K *kuluchi*-, MK *kulu·ch(wu)*- 'to ruin (tr.)'

    K *sos*-, MK *swos*- 'to tower up, spring up, rise (intr.)' → K *soschi*- 'to raise, lift up (tr.)'

    K *kot*- 'to be straight (intr.)' → K *kotchwu*- 'to straighten (out) (tr.)'

    K *yath*- 'to be shallow, low, light (intr.)' → K *yathchwu*- 'to make shallow (tr.)'

Non-valence increasing effects

    K *cina*- 'to pass (by), go past/by (tr. / intr.)' → *cinachi*- 'to exceed, go beyond, overdo (tr. / intr.)'

    K *nem*- 'to exceed, pass beyond (intr.)' → *nemchi*- 'to overflow, flood, brim over (intr.)'

    K *soskwu*- 'to make rise (tr.)' → *soskwuchi*- 'to raise quickly, make a quick rise (tr.)'

    K *ppet*- 'to spread, stretch (tr. / intr.)' → *ppetchi*- 'to open out (intr.); give a good stretch to (tr.)'

    K *tul*- 'to raise, hold (tr)' → *tulchwu*- 'to reveal, expose (tr.)'

Passive

    K *kam*- 'to wind, roll, coil (tr.)' → *kamchi*- 'to hem, put a hem in, sew up (tr.); linger in one's mind (intr.)'

    K *kel*- 'to hang, put on, apply (tr.)' → *kelchi*- 'to hang, put on (tr.); extend, spread (intr.)',

    K *kunh*-, MK *kunh*-'to cut, break, stop, give up (tr.)' → K *kuchi*-, MK *kunchi*- 'to stop, discontinue, put an end to (tr.); stop, end, come to an end (intr.)'

    K *coch*-, MK *cwos*- 'to follow, go after, pursue (tr.)' → K *ccochki*-, MK *cwoschi*- 'to be pursued, be driven away (intr.)'

    K *ttel*- 'display, show (tr.)' → *ttelchi*- 'to be widely felt, be wielded (of power, influence) (intr.)'

---

4 This observation goes against Ramstedt's (1957: 176) remark that: "Diese Annahme würde auch gut erklären, warum die Endung -t- (kor. -thi-) immer nur transitiv-kausativ ist, während die oben besprochenen -bu-, -gu-, -gi-, -l- eigentlich nur reversiv, d.h. bald kausativ, bald passiv, sind."

The suffixes MK -·chi- and MK -·chwu- can be derived as double causatives from pK *-ti- followed by the causative-passive K -ki-, MK -·ki- /-·Gi-, -·hi-, -·i- (see Section 6.7.2) or the causative K -kwu-, MK -·kwu-/ -·Gwu-(Martin 1992: 513, 669) respectively.[5] This derivation which involves loss of the high front vowel of the first causative suffix *-ti- leaving a trace in the palatalization of the dental initial and, velar lenition of the second causative suffix, is illustrated in Table 1 below.

Table 1. The complex nature of the causative suffixes MK -·chi- and MK -·chwu-

MK -·chi- 1. causative-passive 2. intensive	< *-ti- causative	+ MK -·ki- causative-passive
MK -·chwu- 1. causative 2. intensive		+ MK -·kwu- causative

From a phonological point of view, the palatalization is supported by Ramstedt's (1939: 133) observation that some North Korean dialects preserve -thi- for the suffix reflected as MK -·chi-. Some standard Korean verbs like kelchi- 'to put a thing over another (tr.), extend, spread (intr.)', a derivation from K kel- 'to put on (tr.)' implying multiple distribution, preserve the unpalatalized form of the suffix in lexicalized compounds such as K kelthe anc- 'to sit astraddle' or K kelthe tha- 'to ride astride'. Velar lenition (*k > *h) and the loss of *-i- leading to the contraction of two syllables into one tonic cluster initial syllable took place at an early stage in Korean (Martin 1996: 36–37, Ramsey 1993: 438; 1997; see Section 3.3.4 (20), (30)).

From a semantic point of view, the derivation is supported by Kulikov's (1993: 127–136) and Aikhenvald's (2011b: 157–158, 173–174) study of double causative constructions. Next to double causation as in Tk. öl-dür-t- (die-caus.-caus.) 'to have somebody killed', the most frequent meaning is an intensive and/or iterative to the first causative, but complete affectedness or multiple distribution of the object is wide-spread as well. The fact that the suffixes MK -·chi- and MK -·chwu- have non-valence-increasing effects next to marking causatives indicates that they may derive from double causation. This is corroborated by the observation that the suffixes alternate with, respectively, MK -·ki- and MK -·kwu-, suffixes that derive only causatives but no intensives or other non-valence-increasing functions.

---

[5] Verb pairs that reflect the causative suffix K -kwu-, MK -·kwu- are, for instance, K tot-, MK twot- 'to rise (intr.)' → K totkwu- 'raise (tr.)', MK ·sul- 'to vanish (intr.)' → MK sul ·Gwu- 'to cause to vanish (tr.)', MK ¨mey- 'to shoulder (tr.)' → MK ¨mey ·Gwu- 'to cause to shoulder (tr.)'.

6.3.3 pTg *-ti-

The causative suffix pTg *-t- ~ -ti- is reflected in the Tungusic languages as Ma. -tA- ~ -cA-, Evk. -t- ~ -ci- , Even -c-/ -t- ~ -ci-, Neg. -c-/ -t- ~ -ci-, Ud. -si- and Na. -ci- ~ -si-.[6] However, only Even, Evenki and Manchu preserve the valence-increasing function of the causative proper next to secondary non-valence changing uses; the other Tungusic languages have all lost the primary causative function but maintained non-valence changing meanings relating to the object such as distributive and complete affectedness of the object, or, to the action such as intensive, iterative and progressive. All languages further preserve resultative function and Even displays valence-decreasing function, namely passive.

The development of non-valence changing meanings on causative markers is wide-spread across the languages of the world (Aikhenvald 2011b: 163–166, 170–178, 184–188; Kiessling 2004; Hyman 2007: 161, 2014). The semantic mechanism is well understood: Causatives which basically derive from intransitives come to be attached to transititive verbs, implying volitionality or manipulative effort from the causer. The semantic modification of force is then transferred to mark intensive action, which subsequently grammaticalizes to repetitive to progressive action, a process that may be triggered through the intensification of punctual action with verbs where repetition is possible (e.g. jump intensively > jump repeatedly > be jumping). Since causative markers add a causee to the verb, which is completely involved in the action, they can also develop into a valence preserving marker for the complete affectedness of the object.

The progressive marker has further developed into a resultative in most Tungusic languages, signaling that a state exists as a result of past action. This function is particularly frequent following verbs of position and location such as 'to sit', 'to stand' etc, which are mostly lexicalized as punctual change of state verbs ("achievement verbs") in Tungusic as well as in other Transeurasian languages. Examining languages such as Japanese, Korean, Mandarin Chinese and English that show a pattern of convergence between progressive and resultative in a single grammatical form, Shirai (1998) found that the development of resultative meaning on progressive markers is dependent on the inherent aspectual value of the base verb: on punctual change of state verbs the progressive marker is found to express resultative meaning. This observation is consistent with the frequent occurrence of the Tungusic suffix with verbs of position and location. Note that some derived verbs such as Even ïlat- 'to be standing, keep standing (intr.)' or

---

6 Since Benzing (1955a: 1067) finds uses of the suffix that go beyond the intensive, he adds a question mark in his description "intensiver Aspekt?". Closer inspection of the application of the suffix pTg *-ti- suggests that we are dealing with an original causative.

Evk. *ilit-* 'to stand for a while, be standing' can have progressive or resultative meaning depending on the context. The coreferentiality of agent and patient in these verbs (the agent is sitting himself down) implies reflexivity and is probably triggering the final development from resultative to the passive meaning.

This passive meaning is present in some Even verb pairs. The resultative is often similar to the passive in that it makes the patient the subject of the clause when it applies to a transitive verb (as in *The door is closed*), but differs in that only the resultative signals that the state persists at reference time. When the semantics of persistence bleach the resultative derived from transitive verbs may develop into a passive with some contextual indication of an agent (e.g. *The door is closed by the doorman*). The development of resultative into passive markers has been observed by Nedjalkov & Jaxontov (1988: 61), Bybee et al. (1994: 67), Haspelmath (1990: 54).

6.3.3.1 Manchu -*tA*-

The following verb pairs derived with the suffix Ma. -*ta*- ~ -*te*- ~ -*to*- are taken from Gorelova (2002: 243) and arranged according to the assumed grammaticalization cline. Note that some derivations such as Ma. *jafata-* 'grasp or grip repeatedly; keep in rein, restrain (tr.)' are on the interface between iterative, progressive and resultative. The vocalism of this suffix is problematic, since the reflexes in the other Tungusic languages call for a high front vowel.

Intensive

Ma. *uša-* 'to pull (tr.)' → *ušata-* 'to pull with force (tr.)'

Iterative

Ma. *ana-* 'to push (tr.)' → *anata-* 'to push repeatedly (tr.)'

Ma. *fehu-* 'to step on (tr.)' → *fehute-* 'to trample repeatedly (tr.)'

Ma. *jafa-* 'to take in the hand, grasp, grip (tr.)' → *jafata-* 'to grasp or grip repeatedly; keep in rein, restrain (tr.)'

Progressive

Ma. *niyece-* 'to mend, fill in (a post), supplement, nourish (tr.)' → *niyecete-* 'to mend continually, fill in regularly (tr.)'

Ma. *debsi-* 'to fan, flap, flutter (intr.)' → *debsite-* 'to fan or flutter continually (intr.)'

Ma. *tuksi-* 'to pound, throb (of the heart) (intr.)' → *tuksite-* 'to throb (of the heart) continually, be greatly anxious (intr.)'

The suffix Ma. -cA- (Gorelova 2002: 243) is used to derive progressives such as Ma. *hira-* 'to look askance at, spy on' → *hiraca-* 'to keep looking askance, spy on intently' and intensives such as Ma. *feku-* 'jump, leap' → *fekuce-* 'leap up, hop over', *jolho-* 'to gush up, well up' → *jolhoco-* 'to stampede, rush off in a fury, press forward in rage'. It is a reflex of the so-called "intensive" pTg *-ca-* (Benzing 1955a: 1067), which can be derived from the causative pTg *-ti-* and the imperfect pTg *-ja-* (Benzing 1955a: 1066).

Lebedeva & Gorelova (1994: 41) and Gorelova (2002: 151) reconstruct an obsolete Manchu causative suffix *-cu-* which precedes the participle in -kA (see Section 7.6.3.1) in the composite suffix -cukA in e.g. Ma *gele-* 'to fear' → *gele-cu-ke* 'dangerous, frightful', *jobo-* 'to worry, be distressed' → *jobo-cu-ka* 'causing concern, worrisome, distressing', *ulhi-* 'understand, comprehend' → *ulhi-cu-ke* 'understandable'. Although the vocalism of this suffix is problematic, it could be internally related to and preserve the original causative function of pTg *-ti-*.

6.3.3.2 Even -t- ~ -ci-

The Even suffix -*t-* ~ -*ci-* plays a central role in the reconstruction of the proto-Tungusic causative, because it preserves the causative function as such. Whereas Benzing (1955b : 44) describes it as a suffix for "unvollendete intensive Handlung", Menges (1968: 116) labels it as "aspectus status, des eingetretenen Zustandes". Both observations are correct, but the verb pairs below suggest that the suffix primarily had a causative function from which the other functions can be logically derived.

The causative suffix appears as -*t-* after vowels and as -*ci-* after consonants. The vowel allomorph -*t-* alternates with -*c-*. At first sight the alternation seems to be random, but it probably has a historical explanation related to the "intensive" pTg *-ca-* discussed above, which is the result from an assimilation process between the causative pTg *-ti-* and the imperfective pTg *-ja-*. The Even reflex of the imperfective is -*j-*. The absence of a final vowel has led to the merger of the reflexes of the causative-imperfect *ti-ja-* and the causative *ti* as -*ci-* after consonants in Even. However, after vowels the distinction is still present: pTg *-ti-ja-* yields Even -*c-*, whereas pTg *-ti-* yields Even -*t-*. In the following verb pairs derivations with -*t-* are given along those with -*c-* because both relate to the same original suffix.

Causative from intransitive

Even *gele:-* 'to crave, be longing (intr.)' → *gele:t-* 'to search (tr.)'
Even *huk-* 'to be hot (intr.)' → *hukci-* 'to warm, heat up (tr.)'
Even *hong-* 'to cry (intr.)' → *hongit-* 'to make cry (tr.)'

Even *turu:-* 'to open up (intr.)' → *turu:c-* 'to open up (intr.), open (mouth, trap) (tr.)'

Even *ïlu:-* 'to stand up (intr.)' → *ïlu:c-* 'to put (tr.)'

Causative from transitive

Even *ole:-* 'to boil (tr.)' → *ole:t-* 'to bring to boil (tr.)'

Even *kol-* 'to drink, smoke (tr.)' → *kolu :c-* 'to let drink (tr.)'

Complete affectedness of the object

Even *hï:wi-* 'to enkindle (tr.)' → *hï:wic-* 'to set on fire, light up (tr.)'

Even *ko:ye:-* 'to see, have a look at, catch a glimpse of (tr.)' → *ko:ye:c-* 'to oversee, observe, examine (tr.)'

Even *yaru-* 'to observe (tr.)' → *yarut-* 'to see over, get granular on (tr.)'

Intensive

Even *manru-* 'to take some trouble (intr.)' → *manruc-* 'to exert oneself, make every effort (intr.)'

Even *ño:n-* 'to run' → *ño:ngci-* 'to run fast, sprint, gallop'

Even *tan-* 'to pull (tr.)' → *tanci-* 'to drag, haul (tr.)'

Resultative

Even *a:nga:-* 'to open (tr.) → *a:nga:c-* 'to be open, open oneself (intr.)'

Even *bori:-* 'to divide (tr.)' → *bori:c-* ~ *bori:t-* 'to be divided (intr.)'

Even *do:-* 'to sit down (of birds) (intr.)' → *do:c-* 'to be sitting (of birds) (intr.)'

Even *ïl-* 'to stand up (intr.)' → *ïlat-* ~ *ïlac-* 'to be standing, keep standing (intr.)'

Even *kïm-* 'to prepare oneself on (intr.)' → *kïmu:c-* 'to be prepared on (intr.)'

Even *teg-* 'sit down (intr.)' → *teget-* ~ *tegec-* 'to sit, be sitting (intr.)'

Passive from transitive

Even *hor-* 'to fall into a trap (intr.), catch, capture (tr.)' → *horci-* 'to be caught, be captured'

Even *kad-* 'to press together (tr.)' → *kadac-* 'to be pressed together (intr.)'

6.3.3.3 Evenki -t- ~ -ci-

Konstantinova (1964: 164–165) labels the suffix as progressive aspect, Nedjalkov (1997: 247, 303) describes it as an aspectual suffix that refers to the process or result of an action. In the majority of the derivations the suffix appears as -t-. Before certain suffixes such as the ingressive -l- and the habitual -ngnA- it surfaces as -ci-. The verb Evk. *luptu-* 'to pull out (tr.)', for instance, is derived as *luptut-* 'to pull out, pluck (tr.)', but a front vowel appears before the ingressive suffix in *luptu-ci-l-* 'to start to pluck'. Note that the negative noun *a:cin* has been derived from the negative verb pTg **a:na-* followed by the resultative suffix Evk. -ci- (see Section 4.2.3.3) and the deverbal noun suffix Evk. -n.

Causative from intransitive

> Evk. *koyi-* 'to be confused (intr.)' → *koyici-* 'to deceive'

Complete affectedness of the object

> Evk. *ice-* 'to see, catch a glimpse of (tr.)' → *icet-* 'to be looking at, gaze at, examine, watch, (tr.)'
>
> Evk. *loko-* 'to hang up (tr.)' → *lokot-* 'to weigh out; spread, stretch out, hang (tr.)'

Distributive

> Evk. *bu:-* 'to give (tr.)' → *bu:t-* 'to distribute, give out, hand out (tr.)'
>
> Evk. *luptu-* 'to pull out (e.g. a tooth) (tr.)' → *luptut-* 'pull out, pluck (e.g. a fowl) (tr.)'

Intensive

> Evk. *ungku-* 'to fill with, pour out (tr.)' → *ungkut-* 'to spill, pour out (tr.)'
>
> Evk. *wa:-* 'kill (tr.)' → *wa:t-* 'massacre, slay (tr.)'

Progressive

> Evk. *do:ldï-* 'to hear (tr.)' → *do:ldït-* 'to listen (for a while) (tr.)'
>
> Evk. *togo-* 'to lie down (intr.)' → *togot-* 'to lie for a while'
>
> Evk. *ollomo-* 'to fish' → *ollomot-* 'to be fishing for some time'

Resultative

> Evk. *il-* 'to stand up (intr.)' → *ilit-* 'to stand for a while, be standing (intr.)'
>
> Evk. *tege-* 'to sit down (intr.)' → *teget-* 'to sit for a while, be sitting (intr.)'

Konstantinova (1964: 164) notes that the imperfective marker Evk. -*ja*- assimilates to -*ca*- following the progressive -*t*- (e.g. *ilit-ca*- be.standing-IPFV-). A similar assimilation process may have been at work earlier in proto-Tungusic between pTg *-*t(i)*- and the imperfect pTg *-*ja*-, yielding the "intensive" suffix pTg *-*ca*- (Benzing 1955a: 1067). This suffix is reflected in Ma. -*cA*- and Evenki -*c*- above. According to Konstantinova (1964: 166–167) the suffix characterizes conditions with a nuance of continuity. Nedjalkov (1997: 303) describes it as a resultative-stative suffix. It derives progressive-resultatives in e.g. Evk. *loko*- 'to hang (tr.)' → *loku-ca*- 'to hang (for a while), be suspended (intr.)', *anga:*- 'to open (tr.)' → *anga:ce*- 'to stay open (intr.)', *xaku*- 'to close (tr.)' → *xakuca*- 'to stay closed (intr.), Evk. *java*- 'to take (tr.)' → *javuca*- 'to hold, keep (tr.)', Evk. *do:ldï*- 'hear (tr.)' → *do:lca*- 'listen (tr.), remain attentive for a while (intr.)'. The derivation of this suffix as a compound marker incorporating pTg *-*t(i)*- is supported by the fact that the verbal bases of -*ca*- and -*t*- ~ -*ci*- derivates overlap.

6.3.3.4 Udehe -*si*-

According to the sound correspondences in Benzing (1955a: 983), Ud. -*s*- reflects a regular correspondence to the palato-alveolar affricate -*c*- in most of the other Tungusic languages.[7]

The following verb pairs are taken from Nikolaeva (1999: 184–85).

Complete affectedness of the object

    Ud. *ise*- 'to see (tr.)' → *isesi*- 'to look (tr.)'

Distributive

    Ud. *camna*- 'to break (intr.)' → *camnasi*- 'to break (of several things) (intr.)'
    Ud. *tingme*- 'to fall (intr.)' → *tingmesi*- 'to fall (of several people) (intr.)'
    Ud. *bukta*- 'to break (tr.)' → *buktasi*- 'to break (several objects) (tr.)'
    Ud. *buge*- 'to bury (tr.)' → *bugesi*- 'to bury (several people) (tr.)'

Iterative

    Ud. *digan*- 'to say' → *digasi*- 'to talk'
    Ud. *nagda*- 'to guess, hit (tr.)' → *nagdasi*- 'to hit several times (tr.)'
    Ud. *teti*- 'to dress (tr.)' → *tetisi*- 'to dress many children, dress one child many times (tr.)'
    Ud. *xuine*- 'to dive (intr.)' → *xuinesi*- 'to dive several times (intr.)'

---

[7] The correspondence established by Benzing is:
Ma. -č-:: Na. -c-:: Olč. -č-:: Orok -č-:: Oroč. -č-:: Ud. -s- :: Sol. -s- :: Neg. -č-:: Evk. -c-:: Even -c-

Progressive

    Ud. *olokto-* 'to cook (tr.)' → *oloktosi-* 'to be cooking (tr.)'
    Ud. *songo-* 'to cry (intr.)' → *songosi-* 'to be crying (intr.)'
    Ud. *oño-* 'to write, decorate (tr.)' → *oñosi-* 'to be making ornaments'

Resultative

    Ud. *jawa-* 'to take (tr.)' → *jawasi-* 'to hold (tr.)'
    Ud. *ngelewen-* 'to frighten (tr.)' → *ngelewensi-* 'to be frightening (intr.)'

6.3.3.5 Nanai *-ci-* ~ *-si-*

According to the sound correspondences in Benzing (1955a: 983), the regular correspondence expected for the Nanai suffix is *-ci-*. However, we also find the suffix *-si-* with similar functions in Nanai. The internal *c~s* alternation in verb pairs such as Na. *anaci-* ~ *anosi-* 'to push (continually)' suggests that we are dealing with a sporadic phonological development. Therefore, Nanai *-ci-* and *-si-* probably represent two different stages of palatalization of the same suffix pTg *-ti-*. The following examples are taken from Avrorin (1961: 45–46) and Menges (1968: 199–200).

Iterative

    Na. *garpa-* 'to shoot, beam, rise (of sun)' → *garpaci-* 'to shoot many times, shine constantly'

Progressive

    Na. *ana-* 'to push' → *anaci-* ~ *anosi-* 'to push (continually)'
    Na. *ango-* 'to make, create' → *angosi-* 'to make (continually)'
    Na. *xisango-* 'to speak' → *xisangosi-* 'to speak (continually)'
    Na. *songo-* 'to cry' → *songoci-* 'to cry continually'
    Na. *pu-* 'to blow' → *puci-* 'to blow (continually)'

Resultative

    Na. *apola-* 'to put on a hat (intr.)' → *apolaci-* 'to wear a hat'
    Na. *te:-* 'to sit down (intr.)' → *te:si-* 'to sit, be sitting (intr.)'
    Na. *ili-* 'stand up (intr.)' → *ilisi-* 'stand, be standing (intr.)'
    Na. *tagda-* 'to get angry (intr.)' → *tagdasi-* 'to bear malice (intr.)'

6.3.4 pMo *-ti-

As far as the deverbal suffix WMo. -či- is concerned, Ramstedt (1952: 176) observes "..., dass im Mongolischen die Verba auf -či- grösstenteils solche sind, die die Bedeuting 'schlagen' einschliessen können" and Poppe (1954: 66) describes WMo -či- as an intensive suffix that derives transitive verbs from adverbs and functions to "express actions performed energetically or with strength".

The observed intensive connotation of -či-, however, is a consequence of the natural force that is involved in verbs expressing a spontaneous development. It is clear that some -či- derived verbs such as WMo. *arci-* 'to wipe, clean, weed (tr.); *iǰaci-* 'to thicken, condense, coagulate, curdle (tr.)'; *jadaci-* 'untie, unroll, undo (tr.)' lack intensive meaning. More importantly, the naked verb base and the anticausative counterpart on -rA- reflect exactly the same (commonly intensive) meaning, although they are not derived with -či-. The underived verb WMo. *ebde-* 'to destroy, break, ruin (tr.)' and the anticausative *ebdere-* 'to break down, fall to pieces, be wrecked (intr.)', for instance, express the same degree of intensity as the derivate *ebdeci-* 'break, destroy, ruin (tr.)'.

Poppe (1954: 66) further characterizes WMo -či- as a deadverbial suffix because some of the -či- derivations such as WMo. *suyuči-* 'pull out' and WMo. *tasuči-* 'tear to pieces' correlate to a naked adverbial base, WMo. *suyu* 'off' and WMo. *tasu* 'asunder' respectively. However, derivations with deverbal suffixes such as *suyul-* 'pull out' and *tasul-*'tear to pieces' with the iterative or factitive -l- or *suyura-* 'fall out' and *tasura-* 'be pulled off' with the anticausative -rA- indicate that we are dealing with original verb roots, from which the adverbs are derived. Further support comes from the fact that some of the bases like WMo. *ebde-* 'destroy, break, ruin (tr.)' are attested as a naked root and that some -či- derivates lack a corresponding adverbial form.

Contrary to the description proposed by Poppe and Ramstedt, I suggest that -či- is an equipollent causative suffix that polarizes the causativity of the base. In equipollent anti-causative verb pairs, such as for instance Hindi-Urdu *šuruu honaa* 'to begin (intr.)' vs. *šuruu karnaa* 'to begin (tr.)' or OJ *okor-* 'to rise (intr.)' vs. *okos-* 'to raise (tr.)', both the anticausative and the causative are derived from a neutral base by means of different markers (Haspelmath 1993).[8] From the verb pairs below it can be understood that WMo -či- derivates occur as the causative counterpart of verbs derived with the anticausative suffix WMo. -rA-, discussed in Section 6.6.4. Given the fact that it can only occur with punctual change-of-

---

[8] Haspelmath (1993) uses the term 'inchoative' in reference to a verb meaning that excludes a causing agent and presents the situation as occuring spontaneously, but in order to avoid confusion between actional and diathetical suffixes this term is here replaced by 'anticausative'

state verbs that can be conceived as occurring spontaneously, without an agent, the equipollent causative *-či-* puts more restrictions on the semantics of the preceding verb than the general causative suffix *-l-* (Poppe 1957: 61). An action like 'drink' (e.g. WMo. *uVu-* 'to drink' → *uVul-* 'to give to drink') that does not express a change of state and has agent-oriented meaning can therefore not be derived with *-či-*. The fact that WMo. *-či-* has not further grammaticalized to non-valence changing meanings or to passive meaning may be due to the maintenance of polarity between the causative *-či-* and the anticausative *-rA-*.

The form of the suffix *-či-* can be derived from an original pMo *-ti-*. Just like in Korean and Tungusic, the palatalization of a dental stop before a high front vowel is a common development in Mongolic. Other indications of the dental stop come from early copies of Mongolic verbs into Tungusic or into Turkic. In reference to WMo. *öble-* 'to divide into parts (tr.)', for instance, the verb WMo. *öbci-* 'to flay, skin (tr.)' is analysable as a *-či-* derivate from a root **(p)öb-* 'to separate'. The morphological complex form **(p)öb-či-* 'to flay, skin (tr.)' was copied in Tungusic as pTg **pupte-* 'to disembowel, operate', reflected in Evk. *hupte- ~ hupti-*, Neg. *hupte-*, Oroč. *hukte-*, Ud. *hukte-*, Olč. *pukte-*, Orok *pukte-*, Na. *pukte-* 'to rip open, disembowel, operate'.[9] The indication that we are dealing with an early copy comes from the preservation of the Mongolic **p-*. Interestingly, pMo *-t-* is preserved as well. The word was imitated with relatively back vowels (*u* and *e*) which blocked the palatalization process and preserved the Mongolic dental stop.

Equipollent causative

WMo. *balbal-* 'to break into pieces, shatter, smash (tr.)', *balbara-* 'to break or smash to pieces (intr.)' → *balbaci-* 'to break or smash to pieces (tr.)'

WMo. *ebde-* 'to destroy, break, ruin (tr.)', *ebdere-* 'to break down, fall to pieces, be wrecked (intr.) → *ebdeci-* 'to break, destroy, ruin (tr.)'

WMo. *jadal-* 'to unwrap, unroll, undo (tr.)', *jadara-* 'to unfold, unwrap, loosen (intr.)' → *jadaci-* 'to untie, unroll, undo (tr.)'

WMo. *ijara-* 'to thicken, condense, coagulate, curdle, burst, break open (intr.)' → *ijaci-* 'to thicken, condense, coagulate, curdle, burst, break open (tr.)'

WMo. *nuγul-* 'to fold, bend, curve (tr.)', *nuγura-* 'to be folded, bend, stoop (intr.)' → *nuγuci-* 'to fold, crumple, separate bones at joints (tr.)'

---

[9] Indications that these verbs are copied rather than cognates come from the observation that, unlike the Tungusic verbs, the Mongolic form is morphologically complex and, that the Tungusic meaning 'to operate' represents a culturally more specific meaning.

WMo. *suɣul-* 'to pull out, pluck out (tr.)', *suɣura-* 'to come off, slip out (intr.)'→ *suɣuci-* 'to pull out, pluck out (tr.)'

WMo. *tasul-*'to break apart, tear asunder, discontinue (tr.)', *tasura-* 'to be torn away from, be interrupted (intr.)' → *tasuci-* 'to break apart, tear apart (tr.)'

MMo. *ququl-* 'to break (off) (tr.)', *ququra-* 'to break, break off (intr.)' → *ququci-* 'to break, break through (tr.)'

6.3.5 pTk *-ti-*

The causative-passive in the Turkic languages is a well-studied topic. Among others, Röhborn (1972), Johanson (1974, 1975), Kormušin (1976) and Erdal (1991: 760–799) have contributed to the clarification of the phenomenon. Given its first position in the valence chain, the suffix OTk *-(X)t-*, illustrated below, probably reflects the most archaic causative-passive suffix in Turkic. It can be extended with other causative suffixes or with markers of voice such as cooperative *-Xš-*, anticausative *-Xn-* and passive *-Xl-*, but it never follows these suffixes. In the large majority of the cases, OTk. *-Xt-* is valence-increasing: it derives a causative from either an intransitive or a transitive verb. Its valence-decreasing function as a passive is limited to a few verb pairs. Only some Turkic languages have verbs on final *-t-* that preserve traces of non-valence changing functions such as Yak. *käpsät-* 'to talk' (iterative? cf. Ud. *digasi-* 'id.'), Yak. *ïarït-* 'to be ill' (resultative?), Yak. *ihit-* 'to hear' and MTk. *yorït-* 'to ride quickly, to trot' (Johanson 1975: 129), which seems to be an intensive extension of the Old Turkic causative derivation *yorït-* 'to make march' from OTk. *yorï-* 'to walk, march, go'. It is further interesting to note that, similar to the Tungusic languages, static posture verbs such as Soy. *olït-* 'to sit, be sitting' and Chu. *vïrt-* 'to lie, be lying' appear to incorporate the suffix (Johanson 1974: 127). These data suggest that causatives from intransitives became attached to transitive verbs, developed to non-valence changing meanings such as intensive (Aikhenvald 2011b) and progressive-resultative (Shirai 1998) and finally took up a valence-decreasing function as a passive (Nedjalkov & Jaxontov 1988: 61, Bybee et al. 1994: 67, Haspelmath 1990: 54).

On the basis of internal reconstruction it is legitimate to reconstruct a front vowel in the original causative-passive suffix pTk *-ti-*. Erdal (1979a: 152–155) shows that the converb and aorist of *-(X)t-* changed from *I* to *U* in the course of the use of Old Turkic. Older texts reflect *-I(r)* aorists, such as for instance the Old Turkish aorist *tetir* 'it is said, it is called by a particular name' that appears as a frozen form also in later texts much more frequently than *tetür*. The viewpoint that deleted stem or suffix final vowels, such as the original front vowel of the causative-passive suffix, are recoverable in converbs and aorists is supported by

Ramstedt (1952: 86), Johanson (1975: 111–112), Erdal (1979b).[10] Following Johanson (1975: 112–115) the loss of the front vowel in *-ti- led to an asyllabic realization of the suffix. When the original short stem final vowels were reduced and finally lost, the stem final vowel was retained by the causative-passive suffix in order to avoid problematic consonant clusters (pTk *CVCV̆-ti > OTk. CVC-Xt-). Processes of vowel loss and assimilation reduced the phonological distinctiveness of -Xt-, especially following Old Turkic consonant stems. This explains why the replacement -Xt- by the syllabic causative -tUr- is especially widespread after consonants. As suggested in Ramstedt (1912: 28), Johanson (1975: 126–128) and Erdal (1991: 830), I analyze OTk. -tUr- as a morphologically complex form, consisting of two juxtaposed causative suffixes OTk. -(X)t- and -Ur-.[11] The semantic difference between both suffixes lies in the occasional passive nuance of the former suffix. It becomes clear from pairs such as OTk. basït- 'to be overwhelmed, be oppressed' (intr.)' and OTk. basur- 'to press sth. onto sth. else, weigh down (tr.)' derived from OTk bas- 'press, oppress (tr.)'. The complex semantics of the double causative are preserved in OTk. tetür- 'to arrange for something to be said (tr.)' in comparison to the simplex causative-passive OTk. tet- 'to be called so and so, to be so and so (intr.)' from OTk. te- 'say (tr.)'.

Causative from intransitive

    OTk. arï- 'to be(come) clean, pure (intr.)' → arït- 'to clean, purify (tr.)'

    OTk. bädü- 'to be(come) big, great (intr.)' → OTk. bädüt- 'to make grow, increase, rear (tr.)'

    OTk. bayu- 'to be(come) rich (intr.)' → OTk bayut- 'to enrich, make rich (tr.)'

    OTk. bak- 'to look at (intr.) → OTk. bakït- 'to make someone look at something (tr.)'

Causative from transitive

    OTk. sözlä- 'to speak, say, talk (tr.)' → sözlät- 'to make (somebody) speak or talk (tr.)'

---

10 Johanson 1975: 111–112: "Die Tatsache, daß -[ǝ]t- unter den Aorist- und Konverbsuffixen die jeweilige I-Variante bevorzugt (yaɣutïr, tükäti etc.), spricht natürlich zugunsten der Auffassung Ramstedts (1912, 22), daß es "dem mongolischen verbum auf -či- < *-ti-" entspreche, und zuungunsten der übrigen (oben kurz angedeuteten) Herleitungsversuche."
11 I refer to Erdal (1991: 710–734) for an extensive list of OTk. -Ur- causatives e.g. OTk bas- 'press, oppress (tr.)' → basur- 'press sth onto sth else, weigh down (tr.)', OTk ič- 'drink (tr.)'→ ičür- 'give someone sth to drink', OTk. käl- 'come (intr.)' → kälür- 'bring (tr.)'.

OTk *tokï-* 'to hit, knock, beat, weave (tr.)' → OTk. *tokït-* 'to have something beaten, knocked (tr.)'

OTk. *uk-* 'to understand (tr.)' → *ukït-* 'to explain (tr.)'

Passive from transitive

OTk *bas-* 'to press, oppress, make a surprise attack on (tr.)' → *basït-* 'be overwhelmed, be oppressed, be taken by surprise, be overcome, fall victim to (intr.)'

OTk *kov-* 'to follow, pursue, chase' → *kovït-* 'to get chased'

OTk. *kavza-* 'to surround' → *kavzat-* 'to be surrounded, surround oneself with (intr.)'

OTk. *säv-* 'to love, like' → OTk *sävit-* 'to be loved, make oneself loved (intr.)'

OTk *te-* 'to say (tr.)' → OTk *tet-* 'to be said to be, be called, be considered (intr.)'

OTk. *yay-* 'to shake (tr.)' → OTk *yayït-* 'to be shaken, be moved (intr.)'

The causative suffix OTk. *-(X)t-* corresponds to *-(Ă)t-* in Chuvash (Andreev et al. 1957: 175, Benzing 1959: 720, Fedotov 1996: 387) where it derives causatives from intransitive verbs such as Chu. *tip-* 'to dry (intr.)' → *tipĕt-* 'to dry, make dry (tr.)', *lar-* 'to sit, seat oneself' → *lart-* 'to set, place' and, from transitive verbs such as Chu. *vĕren-* 'to learn' → *vĕrent-* 'to teach', *yurla-* 'to sing' → *yurlat-* 'to let sing'. Non-valence increasing effects are reflected in verb pairs such as Chu. *kür-* 'to bring, produce, yield (tr.)' → *kürt-* 'to bring in, let in, lead into (tr.), *anla-* 'to widen, broaden, enlarge (tr.)' → *anlat-* 'to drag out, stretch out in width (tr.)' (complete affectedness of the object?) and *al-* 'to plow (tr.)' → *alt-* 'to dig' (intensive?). Resultative meaning may be reflected in Chu. *xĕr-* 'to become glowing' → *xĕrt-* 'to glow' and probably also in Chu. *vïrt-* 'to lie', discussed above. These polysemies support a grammaticalization pathway from causative to intensive to progressive-resultative to passive.

6.4 pTEA *-*pU*- reflexive-anticausative

6.4.1 pJ *-*pa*- (~ -*pə*-)

Formally, the lexicalized verb suffix OJ *-p-* < pJ *-*pa*- is reconstructed by Unger (1977: 138), Miller (1971: 265, 1981: 857–859) and Martin (1987: 794–795), but whereas Martin does not specify the function of the suffix, Unger restricts his description to "intensive" and Miller mentions "durative for repeated continuous action" and "causative". Whereas I do not find evidence for Miller's description "causative", I propose to reconstruct a homophonous suffix *-pa- with reflexive-anticausative meaning distinct from Miller and Unger's intensive-iterative suffix. The examples below indicate that following, verbal adjectives, the suffix expresses reflexive-anticausative meaning in the sense of 'to develop the property spontaneously on oneself' and, following verbs it expresses reflexive meaning in the sense of 'to execute the action on oneself'.

Note that in some derivations such as OJ *urupop-* 'get damp, get moist, receive profits, get enriched' and OJ *kurufosi-* B 'to be mad', the suffix vowel agrees with the quality of the vowel in the root and the reconstruction should be pJ *-pə-, a behavior that is reminiscent of vowel harmony.

As far as the Ryukyuan languages are concerned, I find only one Shuri cognate where the suffix has lexicalized, i.e. Shuri *maziwar-* B 'to socialize'. However since the form of this verb differs from the root reflected in Shuri *mancun* (*mank-*) B 'to get mixed', I do not exclude that it is a borrowing from Mainland Japanese.

Deadjectival 'to develop the property spontaneously on oneself'

OJ *ita-* B 'to be painful' → OJ *itapar-* ?A/B 'to fall ill, strain oneself, go to trouble (intr.)'

kana- 'to be one' in OJ *kane₁-* B 'to make one, combine, unite' → OJ *kanap-* ?B 'to be a match (for), be suitable / be appropriate (for), be possible for, be realized', OJ *kanape₂-* B 'to make suitable, possible, make fit, grant (a request)'[12]

kata- 'to be one-sided' in OJ *kata*(-) 2.3. 'one side of two, one of a pair, inclined toward (bound)', J *katat-* ?B 'to honor, favor', OJ *kate-* B 'to join, unite, blend' → OJ *katap-* 'to become intimate'

OJ *yuru-* B 'to be slack' > OJ *yurup-* B 'to relax'

nipə- 'to be red' in OJ *nipoye-* B 'to become red, beautiful, fragrant' (pJ *-ya- fientive, see Section 6.5.1) → OJ *nipop-* B 'to get red, shine beautifully, be fragrant'

uru- 'to be wet' in OJ *urum-* ?B 'to get wet, moist' → OJ *urup-* ?B 'to get muddy, be wet', OJ *urupop-* 'get damp, get moist, receive profits, get enriched'

---

[12] Note that the verbs OJ *kanap-* ?B 'to be a match (for), be suitable / be appropriate (for), be possible for, be realized' and OJ *atap-* A 'to be suitable, be possible' can be traced back to anticausative meaning in the sense of 'to become a hit / a fit/ a match' in the context of the grammaticalization of double affirmative necessitive contructions of the type 'only if V, it becomes' to deontic modality in Japanese (Unger 2013).

Deverbal reflexive

>OJ *atar-* A 'to hit, touch, face, be equal to, apply to', *ate-* A 'to apply, hit, succeed' → OJ *atap-* A 'to be suitable, be possible'
>
>OJ *kur-* B 'to wind, reel', OJ *kurusi-* B 'to be painful' → OJ *kurup-* B 'to go mad', EMJ *kurufasi-* ~ *kurufosi-* B 'to be mad'
>
>OJ *maze-* B 'to mix (tr.)', OJ *mazir-* B 'to get mixed' → OJ *mazipe-* 'to mix, cross, exchange (tr.)', OJ *mazipar-* B 'to mingle (intr.)', Shuri *maziwar-* B 'to socialize'
>
>OJ *ter-* B 'to shine' → OJ *terap-* ?B' 'to show off, pretend, affect (intr.)', OJ *terapas-* ?B 'to sell by showing (tr.)'
>
>OJ *tute-* A 'to transmit (tr.)' → OJ *tutap-* A 'to go along, to follow along'

There is a homophoneous suffix pJ *-pa-* that is much more frequent and can be distinguished from the reflexive-causative marker on the basis of its intensive-iterative semantics and its position more to the right in the suffix chain (Unger 1977: 138; Miller 1972: 265, 1981: 857–859; Vovin 2009a: 820–821: OJ -*ap*- ~ -*o₂p*-). The intensive-iterative follows valence and voice suffixes such as the causative marker *-sa-* (e.g. OJ *teras-* 'to shine on, illuminate' → *terasap-* 'to show clearly') and the anticausative marker *-ra-* (e.g. OJ *mo₂to₂po₂s-* 'to turn (tr.)' ~ *mo₂to₂po₂r-* 'to turn round, to go around (intr.) ' → *mo₂to₂po₂ro₂p-* 'to constantly go around'), while the reflexive-anticausative pJ *-pa-* precedes these markers (e.g. OJ *terapas-* 'to sell by showing', OJ *itapar-* 'to fall ill', OJ *mazipar-* B 'to mingle').[13] Moreover, there are instances where the reflexive-anticausative is followed by the intensive such as OJ *urupop-* 'to get damp, get moist, receive profits, get enriched'.

6.4.2 pK *-pO-*

In Korean the suffix K -*pu-*, MK -(·)*pu-* ~ -(·)*pu-* can derive verbal adjectives from verbs, adding potential-passive ('to be such that the activity or state expressed by the base becomes possible') or resultative ('to be the result of the past activity or state expressed by the base') meaning. After vowels the suffix has an allomorph K, MK -*p-* (Ramstedt 1952: 157–160, 1939: 128, Ramsey 1978: 218–221, Martin 1992: 759, 760–761).

---

[13] Note that the observation that *-pa-* can be followed by causative and anticausative suffixes suggests that it originally was a reflexive suffix, which subsequently grammaticalized to anticausative use.

There are also some petrified instances of deadjectival use, where the suffix originally added anticausative meaning in the sense 'to spontaneously develop the property expressed by the base'. Martin (1992: 217) lists MK *e·twup-* 'to get dark, be dark' and MK *ˉtelep-* 'to get dirty, be dirty' among at least fourteen Korean verb stems that underlie complete paradigms as both processive and descriptive verbs. In consideration of the unidirectional grammaticalization of change of state into copula (Heine and Kuteva 2002: 64) this polysemy between 'to become the property' and 'to be the property' indicates a development from processive to descriptive meaning. The observation that the deadjectival adjectives below are restricted to natural phenomena such as the weather or express feelings resulting from a natural process (e.g. 'the inside becomes empty' = 'one feels hungry') implies sponteaneous development that lacks an external agent.

Therefore, it seems justified to reconstruct pK **-pO-* as an original anticausative suffix. The development from anticausative to potential-passive is well attested cross-linguistically (Haspelmath 1990: 36, 42–46, 54). The development from anticausative to resultative verbal meaning should be seen in the context of the development from processive to descriptive meaning on verbs.

Deadjectival 'to spontaneously develop the property expressed by the base'

*chi- 'to be cold' ~ MK *·cho-* 'to be cold' → MK *·chip-* 'to feel cold (of weather)'[14]

*etwu- 'to be dark' in MK *e·twuGi-* 'to make dark', K *etwuk ha-* 'to be dark', K *etwun ha-* 'to be stupid' → K *etwup-*, MK *e·twup-* 'to get dark, be dark'

MK *kwuc-* 'to be bad' → K (*so:k i*) *kwuppu-*, MK *kwucpu-* 'to be hungry'

*tele- 'to be dirty' in MK *ˉtele·Gi-*, K *te:ley-* 'to soil, stain, make dirty', K *te:lem tha-* 'to be easily dirty, soiled' → MK *ˉtelep-*, K *te:lep-* 'to get dirty, be dirty'

MK *toso-* 'to be warm, mild' → K (*t*)*tasup-* ~ (*t*)*tusup-* 'to be nice and warm'

Deverbal potential passive

MK *kwoy-* 'to love (tr.)' → MK *ˉkwop-* 'to be pretty, lovely'

MK *mit-* 'to believe (tr.)' → MK *mit·pu-* 'to be credible, trustworthy (intr.)'

MK *muy-* 'to hate (tr.)' > MK *muyp-* 'to be hateful (intr.)'[15]

MK *wuž-* 'to laugh (intr.)' → MK *ˉwuzpu-* 'to be funny (intr.)'

MK *ˉsuy-* 'to rest (intr.)' → MK *ˉsuyp-* 'to be easy'

---

14 The adjective root pK **chi-* is probably a vowel expressive variant of MK *·cho-* 'to be cold' (see Section 3.2.3 (2). Note that contemporary K *chup-* 'feel cold (of weather)' has yet another vocalism.

15 Note that OJ *kirap-* 'to be hateful' may reflect a similar derivation and include a cognate formant, but the underived base in Japanese is lacking.

Deverbal resultative

MK *alh-* 'to ail (intr.)' → K *aphu-*, MK *alpho-* 'to be painful'

MK ·*ay tol-* 'to fret, to become vexed (intr.)' → K *aytalphu-*, MK *ay·tolp-* 'to be anguishing'

MK *ich-* 'to tire, make tired (tr.)' → MK *ispu-* 'to be tired'

MK ·*ku·li-* 'to yearn after (tr.)' → K *kulip-*, MK ·*ku·lip-* 'to be yearned after'

MK *kisk-* 'to rejoice (intr.)' → K *kippu-*, MK *kispu-* ~ *kiskpu-* 'to be joyful'

MK *pach-* 'to rush (intr.)' → K *pappu-*, MK *pachpo-* ~ *paspo-* 'to be busy'

MK *sulh-* 'to grieve (intr.)' → K *sulphu-*, MK *sulphu-* 'to be sad'

6.4.3 pTg *-p-

On the basis of reflexes such as Ma. ø, Na. -*p*-, Olč -*p*-, Ud. -*p*-, Evk. -*p*- and Even -*b*-, Benzing (1955a: 1070) reconstructs a suffix pTg *-p- which he tentatively labels 'reflexiv?'.

Although the derived verbs are anticausative in the majority of the Tungusic languages, because they lack an agent role rather than marking coreferentiality of agent and patient, the reflexive use of this suffix is indeed preserved in Even.

Formally, it is possible to distinguish the reflexive-anticausative pTg *-p- from the causative-passive pTg *-bu-, with reflexes Ma. -*bu*-, Na. / Olč. -*o*- / -*u*-, Ud. -*u*-, Sol. -*u*- ~ -*gu*-, Neg. -*v*-, Evk. -*v*-, Even -*v*-, Oroqen -*v(u)*- (Benzing 1955a: 1070–1071).[16] Miller (1981: 858–59) tries to relate the latter form to a Japanese formant *-p(a)- which he labels "causative". Besides the analysis of the Japanese form, this suggestion is doubtful because pTg *-bu- is a good candidate for grammaticalization from the Tungusic verb pTg *bu:- 'give' with reflexes in Evk. *bu:-*, Even *bö:-*, Neg. *bu:-*, Solon *bu:-*, Sibe *bu-*, Ma. *bu-*, Olč. *bu:wu-*, Orok *bu:-*, Na. *bu:-*, Oroč *bu:-*, Ud. *bu:-* (Gabelentz 1861: 518, Haspelmath 1990: 48–49, Nedjalkov 1993, Li & Whaley 2011).

---

[16] The following sound correspondences reflecting pTg *-p- and *-b- according to Benzing (1955a: 981–982) enable us to distinguish between the reconstruction of pTg *-p- anticausative and *-bu- causative-passive.

pTg	Ma.	Na.	Olč.	Orok	Oroč.	Ud.	Sol.	Neg.	Evk.	Even
*-p-	f~ø	p~ø	p~ø	p~ø	p~ø	f~ø	g~v	p~v	p~v	b~v
*-b-	b	ø	ø	ø	v~ø	u~ø	v~γ	v	v	v

6.4.3.1 Ma. Ø

Since the Manchu reflex of this suffix is zero, it is difficult to trace it in verb pairs. However, some etymologies for Tungusic verbs indicate that the suffix has completely eroded in Manchu. The verb pTg *jalu-p-* 'to fill up, become filled (intr.)', which can be understood as an anticausative of *jalu-* 'to fill (tr.), for instance, is reflected in the Tungusic verbs meaning 'to fill up (intr.)': Ma. *jalu-*, Na. *jalop-*, Olcha *jalpu-*, Orok *dalup-*, Solon *jalu:-*, Neg. *jalup(i)-*, Evk. *dyalup-* and Even *jalu:-* 'to satiate oneself' (Cincius 1975: 304). The stem-final *-p-* is not reflected in Manchu, but it leaves a trace in the irregular perfective adnominal form Ma. *jaluka*, appearing instead of the regular allomorph on Ma. *-hA*.

In Manchu all verb stems invariably end in a vowel; original consonant-final stems have lost their final consonant. However, an original stem-final *..p-* can leave a trace in the irregular allomorph Ma. *-kA* of the perfective adnominal *-hA* (< pTg *-xA*, see Section 7.6.3), e.g. pTg *jep-* 'to eat' is reflected as Ma. *je-* 'to eat', but the verb has an irregular perfective adnominal *jeke*. In Manchu there are 185 verbs ending in the irregular allomorph *-kA* (Zakharov 1879, Vovin 1997: 271–273, Gorelova 2002: 256). Interestingly, the large majority of these verbs have anticausative meaning: *akša-* 'to become spoiled', *arsu-* 'to sprout', *badara-* 'to become wide, expand', *bilte-* 'to overflow', *cilci-* 'to swell (of waves)', *ede-* 'to go bad', *elde-* 'to shine, glow', *gere-* 'to become bright, to dawn', *guru-* 'to redden, to become inflamed', *mukde-* 'to rise', *nioro-* 'to turn green', *sengse-* 'to dry (intr.)', etc. This observation may be due to the incorporation of an original anticausative suffix *-p-* that has been lost in Manchu, but leaves a trace in the irregular *-kA* perfective adnominal.

6.4.3.2 Even *-(A)b-*

Benzing (1955b: 48) refers to the Even suffix *-(A)b-* as "Reflexivum oder Medium". It occurs in the verb pairs below.

Reflexive

    Even *duk-* 'to write' → *dukub-* 'to register oneself'
    Even *ma:-* 'to kill, hunt, fish (tr.)' → *ma:b-* 'to harm oneself, kill oneself (intr.)'
    Even *dür-* 'to burn, to be on fire (intr.)' → *düreb-* 'to burn oneself (intr.)'

Anticausative

    Even *hepken-* 'to grab, hold (tr.)' → *hepkeb-* 'to stick to, adhere to (intr.)'
    Even *iri:-* 'to boil (tr.)' → *iri:b-* 'to boil (intr.)'
    Even *beri:-* 'to lose (tr.)' → *beri:b-* 'to get lost, disappear, die (tr.)'
    Even *ugur-* 'to lift, to raise (tr.)' → *ugureb-* 'to rise (intr.)'

6.4.3.3 Evenki -*p*-

Nedjalkov (1997: 228) refers to anticausative forms in -*p*- /-*v*- / -*mu*-. However, the allomorphs on -*v*- / -*mu*- should be kept separate here because they reflect the causative-passive pTg *-*bu*-. The anticausative verbs *manap*- and *solip*- below, for instance, alternate with verbs of similar meaning lexicalizing an original causative-passive, i.e. *soliv*- 'to become mixed up' and *manav*- 'to become finished' (Nedjalkov 1997: 217–222, 230). The passive has an allomorph -*mu*- following stem-final nasals, e.g. *edïn*- 'to blow (of wind)' → *edïnmu*- 'to be caught by the wind'.

Anticausative

> Evk. *mana*- 'to finish (tr.)' → *manap*- 'to finish (intr.)'
> Evk. *sula*- 'to leave behind (tr.)' → *sulap*- 'to stay behind'
> Evk. *soli*- 'to mix up (tr.)' → *solip*- 'to become mixed up, confused'
> Evk. *ula*- 'to soak (tr.)' → *ulap*- 'to soak (intr.)'

6.4.3.4 Udehe -*p*-

Although Nikolaeva (1999) does not describe this suffix for Udehe, Menges (1968: 155) refers to an anticausative -*p*- in e.g. Ud. *nodo*- 'to lose' → *nodop*- 'to lose oneself, get lost'. I am unable to find more verb pairs reflecting this suffix. However, Nikolaeva (1999: 177) refers to the decausative suffix -*pta*-, which detransitivizes transitive bases. According to Schneider (1936: 141) the element -*ta*- in this suffix -*pta*- is originally a present tense suffix and it is not present in other temporal forms. Even if this account is valid historically, Nikolaeva finds that in contemporary Udehe the suffix -*pta*- cannot be further segmented and appears in all tenses.

6.4.3.5 Nanai -*p*-

The anticausative suffix -*p*- has lexicalized in Nanai verb pairs, whereby the final consonant of athematic verb stems drops before the suffix (Avrorin 1961: 4, Menges 1968: 198).

Anticausative

> Na. *gulde*- 'to stretch, unroll, unwind, unfold, display (tr.)' → *guldep*- 'to stretch, unroll, come unwrapped, unfold, display oneself (intr.)'
> Na. *kala*- 'to change (tr.)' → *kalap*- 'to change, undergo a change (intr.)'
> Na. *xoji*- 'to complete, end (tr.)' → *xojip*- 'to end, come to an end (intr.)'
> Na. *xuede*- 'to lose (tr.)' → *xuedep*- 'to get lost, disappear (intr.)'
> Na. *xumie*- 'to cover, overwhelm, drag out (tr.)' → *xumiep*- 'to grow all over, overwhelm, be dragged out (intr.)'

6.4.4 pMo *-βU-

The anticausative suffix *-βU- has lexicalized in a small number of verb pairs in Mongolian (Ramstedt 1912: 67–73, 1952: 157–160, Poppe 1972: 128–134). Poppe (1955a: 98) reconstructed a pre-Mongolian *β , which has converged with *y in proto-Mongolian and corresponds to *p elsewhere in Altaic (e.g. OTk. *qap-* 'to close' vs. MMo. *qaʻa-*, WMo. *qaɣa-* 'to hinder, close'). However, in consonant clusters the lenition has been blocked and the bilabial stop is preserved as a voiced labial stop (e.g. WMo. *qabqay* 'lid' < *qaβa- 'to close'). Athematic verb stems as well as thematic verbs that have lost their stem-final vowel before certain suffixes, reflect the anticausative suffix as *-bu-* / *-bü-*, as illustrated below.

Note that there are some verb pairs such as WMo. *cib-/ jib-* 'to sink, become submerged (intr.)' → *cibbü-/ jibbü-* 'to sink, become submerged (intr.)' and WMo. *köb-* 'to rise to the surface, float, drift (intr.)' → WMo. *köbbü-* 'rise to the surface, float, drift (intr.)' in which the base verb seems to have lost its transitivity distinction. Since the suffix *-bu-* / *-bü-*can be followed by the anticausative suffix *-rA-* (e.g. *jilbura- ~ jilyura-* 'to fall out (of hair) (intr.)'), it may reflect an original reflexive suffix, which subsequently grammaticalized to anticausative use. This is also supported by the observation that some derived meanings specialize in the sense of bodily activities (e.g. 'shed skin, lose hair' or 'spit, excrete body fluids').

There are a few thematic verb stems that have preserved their stem-final vowel and where the suffix is reflected as *-yu-/ -gü-*, such as in WMo. *ayduyulja-* 'to move by contracting and stretching alternately (as a caterpillar) (intr.)' and in WMo. *küyigü-* 'to gather, assemble reunite (intr.)' below.

Ramstedt (1912: 16) and Poppe (1972a: 131–132) regarded the Mongolian causative suffix WMo. *-yul-/ -gül-* as a compound suffix, incorporating the anticausative *-βU-*. The element *-l-* may then be the antecedent of the causative WMo *-l-* (Poppe 1954: 61). This is supported by the observation that *-l-* causatives indeed seem to derive from *-yu-* anticausatives, e.g. in WMo. *nayiyu-* 'to flutter in the wind, to shake, sway (intr.)' → *nayiyul-* 'to let flutter, shake (tr.)'. Note also that some *-yul-/ -gül-* derivations from transitive verbs reflect causativized anticausative meaning rather than factitive meaning, e.g. WMo. *toyuyul-* 'to impose, to assign, charge with (tr.)' derived from WMo. *toyu-* 'to put on or over (tr.)' does not mean 'to make put on', but rather 'to cause to be charged'.

Anticausative

> *aydu-* 'to make short' in *ayduyi-* 'to shorten, shrink, contract (intr.)' (pMo *-yi-* anticausative, see Section 3.2.3 (3)) → *ayduyu-* 'to shorten, contract' in WMo. *ayduyyulja-* 'to move by contracting and stretching alternately (as a caterpillar) (intr.)' (pMo *-lja-* iterative in rythmic motion, see Section 3.2.3 (20))

WMo. *dele-* 'to wave, flap (as wings), fan (tr. / intr.)' → MMo. *dilbu-* 'to fan (intr.)', WMo. *delbegene-* 'to move, sway (of flat, protruding objects) (intr.)'

WMo. *jilu- ~ julu-* 'to flee, go away, avoid (intr.)' → *julbu-* 'to shed skin, lose hair, escape (intr.)', *jilbura- ~ jilɣura-* 'to fall out (of hair) (intr.)', *julburang* 'short-haired fur coat' (*-ng* deverbal suffix designating result of actions, Poppe 1954: 49; pMo *-rA-* anticausative, see Section 6.6.4)

*küyi- 'to gather (tr.)' in WMo. *küyis* 'bouquet, bunch of flowers' → *küyigü-* 'to gather, assemble reunite (intr.)'

WMo. *nila-* 'to smear, rub (tr.)' → *nilbu-* 'to spit, excrete body fluids (tr. /intr.)'

MMo. *neme-*, WMo. *neme-* 'to add, supplement, increase (tr.)' → MMo. *nembe-* 'to cover (intr.)', MMo. *nembule* 'hut'

WMo. *ol-* 'to find (tr.)' → **olbu-* 'to be found (intr.)' in *olburi* 'thing found, find, acquisition, gain, profit', *olbuya* 'track in the grass, downtrodden grass'

6.4.5 pTk *-U-

The Old Turkic anticausative suffix *-U-* is attested in 11 verbs (Erdal 1991: 474–479). In the majority of cases the suffix derives verbs from adjectival bases, with the meaning 'to spontaneously develop the property of the base'. There are 3 instances where the suffix attaches to verb bases, adding anticausative meaning. The expected reflex of the anticausative in Chuvash would be ***-(b)ă- / -(b)ĕ-*, but I am unable to find a trace of such a suffix. Since the suffix *-U-* can be followed by the anticausative suffix *-(I)r-*, as is the case for OTk. *alaŋur-* 'to become weak (intr.)' from *alŋu-* 'to wane (intr.)', it may reflect an original reflexive suffix, which subsequently grammaticalized to anticausative use.

Deadjectival 'to spontaneously develop the property of the base'

OTk. *agïr* 'heavy (in physical sense); burdensome, painful' → *agru-* 'to be(come) heavy, to become serious or severe (of an illness)'

OTk. *boš* 'free; empty' → *bošu-* 'to free oneself, become empty'

OTk. *kalïn* 'thick, dense' → *kalnu-* 'to become thick'

OTk. *keŋ* 'wide, broad' → *keŋü-* 'to become wide, broad'

OTk. *kïz* 'expensive' → *kïzu-* 'to rise in price (of merchandise)'

Deverbal anticausative

   OTk. *säš-* 'to loosen, untie, unfasten (tr.)' → *säšü-* 'to loosen oneself, come loose'

   OTk. *adïr-* 'to separate (tr.)' → *adru-* 'to be superior to, excel (intr.)'

   OTk. *alkïn-* 'to bring to an end, wipe out (tr.)' → *alŋu-* 'to wane (intr.)'

6.5 pTEA *-dA- fientive

6.5.1 pJ *-ya-

Following Haspelmath's (1990: 34) terminology, fientive markers derive a process of becoming from stative expressions, especially adjectives. The fientive suffix pJ *-ya-* has lexicalized in some verbs derived from nouns and from nominal and verbal adjectives with the meaning 'to become like the base'. The verbs derived from OJ *me$_2$* 1.3 'sprout, bud' and OJ *pi$_1$* 1.3 'ice, hail' seem to specialize semantically in the sense of 'to cover with elements from nature'. Note that bases that possess a nominal as well as a verbal encoding such as OJ *su* 1.3 'vinegar, sour' and OJ *su-* B 'to be sour' probably enhanced the transfer of the suffix from nominal to verbal bases. The fientive has further grammaticalized into a deverbal passive marker and lexicalized as such in some Old Japanese verb pairs, that often denote mental activity or motion (Unger 1977: 130). It is also incorporated in the passive suffix *-(a)ye-*, which is still productive in Old Japanese (Vovin 2009a: 829, Frellesvig 2010: 63). Similar to the derivation of the tentative OJ *-(a)ma-* (see Section 5.6.1) and the Ryukyuan perfect participles reflected in Shodon *-an, -ar, -am* (see Sections 7.3.1.1, 7.4.1.1 and 7.5.1.1), the productive passive OJ *-(a)ye-* may have been derived from the copula *a-* 'to be' followed by the original passive *-ya-* and *-(C)i-*.

   Since the fientive suffix has lexicalized in cognate Ryukyuan verb stems, such as Shuri *miir-* B 'to sprout (intr.)', *şiir-* B 'to turn sour, spoil (intr.)', *cikwiir-* A 'to be heard, be audible', *qubir-* B 'to remember, learn, know', *kweer-* B 'to grow fertile, get fat', *sakeer-* A 'to flourish, prosper' and *teer-* B 'to come to an end (intr.)' the period in which this suffix was productive must predate the split of Mainland Japanese and Ryukyuan and thus belongs to the proto-Japonic stage.

Denominal 'to become like the base'

   OJ *me$_2$* 1.3 'sprout, bud' → OJ *moye-?* (A/) B 'to sprout (intr.)', OJ *moyas-* ? A/B 'to make it sprout'

   OJ *pi$_1$* 1.3 'ice, hail' → OJ *piye-* B 'to get cold (intr.)', OJ *piyas-* B 'to cool, make cold (tr.)'

[OJ *tupi₁* 2.5 (M 4508) '(at the) end' → OJ *tupiye-* A 'to be spent, wasted, routed', OJ *tupiyas-* A 'to spend, waste']

Deadjectival 'to become like the base'

OJ *su* 1.3 'vinegar, sour' / OJ *su-* B 'to be sour, acid, tart' → OJ *suye-* B 'to turn sour, spoil (intr.)'

OJ *wo(-)* ?1.1 'little (bound nominal)' → OJ *woyas-* ? 'weaken (tr.)', OJ *woye-* ? 'get weakened, be enfeebled (intr.)'

*nipə 'red' in OJ *nipop-* B 'to get red, shine beautifully, be fragrant' → OJ *nipoye-* B 'to become red, beautiful, fragrant'

OJ *waka-* B 'to be young' → OJ *wakaye-* B 'to get younger, be rejuvenated (intr.)', OJ *wakayag-* B 'to feel renewed, rejuvenated'

OJ *ko₁-* ? 'to be saturated' → OJ *ko₁ye-* B 'to grow fertile, get fat', J *koyas-* B 'to fertilize, fatten, enrich'

OJ *ama-* A 'to be sweet' → OJ *amaye-* A 'to seek favor, fawn', OJ *amayakas-* 'to indulge, pamper'

Deverbal passive

OJ *i-* ?A 'to shoot' → OJ *iy-*, *iye-* ?A 'to get shot'

OJ *ki₁k-* A 'to hear' → OJ *ki₁ko₂ye-* A 'to be heard, be audible'

OJ *mi₁-* B 'to see' → OJ *mi₁yar-* 'to view the distance, overlook, survey', OJ *mi₁ye-* B 'to be seen, seem, be visible'

OJ *omop-* B 'to think, feel' → OJ *omopoye-* B 'to remember, come to mind'

OJ *sak-* ?A 'to bloom (intr.)' → OJ *sakaye-* ?A 'to flourish, prosper'

OJ *sin-* A 'to die' → OJ *sinaye-* ?B 'to wither, droop'[17]

*ka- in OJ *ik-* A 'to go', OJ *kayo₁p-* A 'to go back and forth, commute, go regularly', OJ *kare₂-* A 'to get apart, cease, go away' → OJ *kaye-* ?A 'to be parted, get apart'

*ta- 'to reach (an end)' in OJ *tat-* B 'cut off, abstain from, exterminate (tr.)', [OJ *itar-* A 'to arrive, reach, attain', OJ *itas-* A 'to do, cause, bring about'] → OJ *taye-* B 'to come to an end (intr.)', OJ *tayas-* B 'to end, put an end to, let come to an end (tr.)' [18]

---

[17] The verb OJ *sin-* 'to die' has accent type A in modern dialects, but the accentuation of the conclusive and converb ending indicates that it originally belonged to accent type B (Martin 1987: 201).

[18] The reconstruction of the motion verb roots pJ **ka-* 'to go' and pJ **ta-* 'to reach' is externally supported by the Korean cognates pK **ka-* 'to go', reflected in MK ·*ka-* 'to go', and pK **ta-* 'to

6.5.2 pTg *-dA:-

The fientive suffix pTg *-dA:- has lexicalized in Tungusic in some contemporary verbs ending in Manchu -dA-, Evk. -dA-, Even -dA:-, Ud. -dA-, Na. -dA- (Benzing 1955a: 1064). It derives verbs from nouns and nominal adjectives with the meaning 'to become like the base', 'to cover with the base' or 'to make use of the base to perform an action'. Although the denominal and deadjectival meaning 'to become like the base' is frequently attested in Manchu, it only sporadically occurs in Udehe and Nanai and it has not been preserved in the Northern Tungusic languages. In the Tungusic languages the fientive has not grammaticalized into a deverbal passive.

6.5.2.1 Manchu -dA-
denominal (Benzing 1955a: 1064, Gorelova 2002: 236–37)

1. 'to become like the base'

    Ma. *jili* 'anger, temper' → *jilida-* 'to get angry, become mad'
    Ma. *yobo* 'fun' → *yobodo-* 'to have fun, joke'

2. 'to make use of the base to perform an action'

    Ma. *ceku* 'swing' → *cekude-* 'to swing in a swing'
    Ma. *eruwe* 'drill, auger' → *eruwede-* 'to drill, make a hole with an auger'
    Ma. *faka* 'wooden stick with a fork at one end' > *fakada-* 'to hit a ball with a wooden stick (play a type of game)'

deadjectival 'to become like the base' (Benzing 1955a: 1064, Gorelova 2002: 236–37)

   Ma. *goho* 'elegant, dandy' → *gohodo-* 'to adorn oneself'
   Ma. *hu:lhi* 'confused' → *hu:lhida-* 'to act in a confused manner, be in a daze'
   Ma. *bayan* 'rich' → *bayanda-* 'to become rich'

6.5.2.2 Even -dA:-
denominal (Benzing 1955b: 35)

1. 'to cover with the base'

    Even *hel* 'iron' → *helde-* 'to stud with iron sheet'

---

reach', reflected in MK *tatoT-* 'to reach' (< *ta-* 'reach' and *toT-* 'run') and K *tah-* 'to reach' (Robbeets 2005: 382).

2. 'to make use of the base to perform an action'
   Even *momi* 'boat' → *momida-* 'to use a boat'
   Even *tangńa* 'reindeer antlers' → *tangńada-* 'to use reindeer antlers for something'
   Even *ya:* 'what' → *ya:da-* 'drive what, use what, make from what'

6.5.2.3 Evenki *-dA-*
denominal (Benzing 1955a: 1064, Nedjalkov 1997: 301)

1. 'to cover with the base'
   Evk. *sekte* 'branches' → *sektede-* 'to cover with branches'
   Evk. *turuke* 'salt' → *turukede-* 'to salt'
2. 'to make use of the base to perform an action'
   Evk. *suke* 'axe' → *sukede-* 'to hew, hack'
   Evk. *dyal* 'thought' → *dyalda-* 'to think'

6.5.2.4 Udehe *-dA-*
denominal (Nikolaeva 1999: 170–71)

1. 'to cover with the base'
   Ud. *ńongo* 'glue' → *ńongodo-* 'to cover with glue'
2. 'to make use of the base to perform an action'
   Ud. *tiu* 'stick' → *tiude-* 'to lean against a stick'
   Ud. *suala* 'ski' → *sualada-* 'to ski'
   Ud. *ungtu* 'tambourine' → *ungtude-* 'to play the tambourine'

deadjectival 'to become like the base' (Nikolaeva 1999: 174)
   Ud. *ge:-* 'bad' → *ge:de-* 'to feel bad'

6.5.2.5 Nanai *-dA-*
denominal (Benzing 1955a: 1064; Avrorin 1961: 17–18, 45; Menges 1968a: 201)

1. 'to cover with the base'
   Na. *alman* 'tin, zinc' → *almada-* 'to fill cracks with tin'
   Na. *nute* 'tar' → *nutede-* 'to cover with tar'
2. 'to make use of the base to perform an action'
   Na. *merxe* 'comb with close teeth' → *merxede-* 'to comb with a close comb'
   Na. *cokor* 'chisel' → *cokorda-* 'to work with a chisel'
   Na. *ciun* 'flint' → *ciunde-* 'to strike fire'

deadjectival 'to become like the base'

    Na. *bayan* 'rich' → *bayanda-* 'to become rich'

    Na. *xele* 'dumb, mute; stammerer' → *xelede-* 'to mutter, mumble, stammer'

6.5.3 pMo *-dA-

The fientive suffix pMo * -dA- has lexicalized in Mongolic, deriving verbs from nouns and nominal adjectives with the meaning 'to become like the base', 'to cover with the base' or 'to make use of the base to perform an action'. It has grammaticalized into a deverbal passive marker -dA-, still productive in Middle Mongolian and Written Mongolian. The passive suffix devoices to -tA- when added to consonant final stems ending in *b, s, d, g, r*.

The suffix WMo. / MMo. -dA- in its denominal and deadjectival use alternates with WMo. /SH MMo. -d- (Poppe 1954: 64, Street 1957: 63, 64, Rybatzki 2003a: 65). We find examples where both suffixes attach to the same nominal base, such as SH MMo. *yodoli-d-* ~ WMo. *yoduli-da-* 'to shoot a horn-tipped arrow (intr.)'. Therefore, it is not unlikely that WMo. /SH MMo. -d- represents a phonologically eroded allomorph of pMo *-dA- with epenthesis of the final vowel.

Note that Kane (2009: 112) reconstructs the Khitan verb *kė̂-* 'to bury' with an unspecified element *-d- in passive-like interpretations such as Khitan *kė̂-d-er* (bury-PASS-PST) 'buried' and *kė̂-d-ha-ai* (bury-PASS-CAUS-CONV) 'having been buried'. If this concerns a reflex of the pMo *-dA- passive, the suffix can be traced back goes back to proto-Khitan-Mongolic.

denominal (Poppe 1954: 64, Street 1957: 63, Rybatzki 2003a: 65)

1. 'to become like the base'

    WMo. *aya* 'fitness, aptness' → *ayada-* 'to adapt oneself, adjust oneself (intr.)'

    WMo. *idermeg* 'fray, chip, score' → *idermegde-* 'to become frayed, chipped or scored (intr.)'

    WMo. *nere* 'name' → *nerede-* 'be known as, give a name (tr. / intr.)'

2. 'to cover with the base'

    WMo. / SH MMo. *cisun* 'blood' → *cisuda-* 'to become bloody, be bloodstained, smear with blood (tr./intr.)'

    WMo. *alta(n)* 'gold' → *altada-* 'to gild, decorate with gold (tr.)'

3. 'to make use of the base to perform an action'

    WMo./ SH MMo. *arya* 'trick, craft, plan' → *aryada-* 'to deceive, outwit, cajole (tr.)'

WMo. *buu* 'gun, firearm' → *buuda-* 'to shoot with a firearm (intr.)'

WMo. *ig* 'spindle' → *igde-* 'to turn the spindle, spin (tr.)'

deadjectival 'to become like the base'
(Poppe 1954: 64, Street 1957: 63, Rybatzki 2003: 65)

WMo. *bačiyu* 'narrow, tight, pressing, too short (of time); narrowness' → *bačiyuda-* 'to be pressed, stiffled, to be in agony, to be too short (of time) (intr.)'

WMo. *keyi* 'air, wind; empty, idle, in vain; hysterical, insane' → *keyide-* 'to be blown away by the wind; become empty; become hysterical or insane (intr.)'

WMo. *yasiyun* 'bitter(ness), sour' → *yasiyuda-* 'to grow bitter or rancid, sorrow, mourn (intr.)'

deverbal passive (Street 1957: 65; Poppe 1954: 62, 1955: 253)

WMo. *ab-* 'to take' → *abta-* 'to be taken'

WMo. *dugul-* 'to hear' → *dugulda-* 'to be heard, be audible'

WMo. *ol-* 'to find' → *olda-* 'to be found'

6.5.4 pTk *-(A)d-

The fientive suffix pTk *-(A)d- has lexicalized in Old Turkic, deriving verbs from nouns and nominal adjectives with the meaning 'to become like the base', often of human subjects. The meanings 'to cover with the base' and 'to make use of the base to perform an action' are only marginally attested. Although there seems to be an internal connection between the nouns OTk. *buz* 'ice', *sig* 'urine' and the verbs OTk. *bud-* 'to be very cold, freeze to death', *sid-* 'to urinate', the final consonant of the nominal root remains to be explained, perhaps as an original collective suffix in the first case and as a contraction of *-g(V)d- in the latter.[19]

Old Turkic has further lexicalized a deverbal anticausative marker OTk. -(X)d-, that was already obsolete by the time of Old Turkic. It occurs in a small number of verb pairs denoting states and activities of the body and the mind. In spite of the vowel harmonic difference in the suffix, the anticausative may have grammaticalized from the fientive. This is supported by the shared frequency of human subjects and by the observation that the anticausative verbs OTk. *tod-* 'to be(come) full, satiated' and *uyad-* 'to be ashamed' have /U/ in the aorist and

---

19 Note that the derivation of OTk. *bud-* 'to be very cold, freeze to death' from OTk. *buz* 'ice' is reminiscent of the derivation of OJ *piye-* B 'to get cold (intr.)' from OJ *pi*$_1$ 1.3 'ice, hail'.

converb, just like most denominal and deadjectival fientives.[20] Note also that in the Chuvash cognate, the denominal fientive and the deverbal anticausative have the same vocalism.

denominal (Erdal 1991: 485–492)
1. 'to become like the base'
    OTk. *baš* 'head' → *bašad-* 'to be or become a leader'
    OTk. *buŋ* (OUigh. *muŋ*) 'sorrow, grief, distress' → *buŋad-* (OUigh. *muŋad-*) 'to get in trouble, to be worried'
    OTk. *kut* 'favour of heaven, good fortune' → *kutad-* 'to become a blessing, enjoy divine favour and good fortune'
2. 'to cover with the base'
    OTk. *buz* 'ice' → *bud-* 'to be very cold, freeze to death'
    OTk. *sig* 'urine' → *sid-* 'to urinate'
3. 'to make use of the base to perform an action'
    OTk. *og* 'pause, free time' > *ogad-* 'to tarry, fall behind'

deadjectival (Erdal 1991: 485–492) 'to become like the base'
    OTk. *kïrgïl* 'grey haired' → *kïrgïlad-* 'to turn grey haired'
    OTk. *yagï* 'enemy, hostile' → *yagïd-* 'to be(come) hostile'
    OTk. *yogun* 'thick' → *yogunad-* 'to become thicker'

deverbal anticausative (Erdal 1991: 642–644, Gabain 1950: 80)
    OTk. *sök-* 'to kneel down (intr.)' → *söküd-* 'to kneel in somebody's presence'
    OTk. *to-* 'to close, block (tr.)' → *tod-* 'to be(come) full, satiated'
    OTk. *uya-* 'to put to shame (tr.)' → *uyad-* 'to be ashamed'

The regular correspondence of Old Turkic -*d*- being -*r*- in Chuvash, the fientive suffix OTk. -*(A)d*- corresponds to -*(A)r*- in Chuvash.[21] The suffix -*(A)r* derives tran-

---

20 OTk. *tod-* 'to be(come) full, satiated' has a parallel formation with /A/ converb and aorist. OTk *bud-* 'to be very cold, freeze to death', *sid-* 'to urinate' and *söküd-* 'to kneel in somebody's presence' have /A/ as aorist and converb vowel.
21 The correspondence between OTk -*d*- and Chu. -*r* is reflected in cognates such as OTk. *tïd-* 'to hinder, obstruct' vs. Chu. *čar-* 'id.', OTk. *ïd-* 'to send' vs. Chu. *yar-* 'id.', OTk. *qod-* 'to put, leave, abandon' vs. Chu. *xor-* 'id.', OTk. *qïdïɣ* 'edge, border, seashore, frontier' vs. Chu. *xĕrĕ* 'id.', OTk. *küdegü* 'son-in-law' vs. Chu. *kĕrü* 'id.' etc.

sitive and intransitive verbs from nouns and adjectives (Andreev et al. 1957: 162–163, Levickaya 1974: 177–178, Fedotov 1996: 352–353). The denominal meaning of the suffix is 'to become like the base' (e.g. Chu. *pală* 'sign, indication characteristic' → *palăr-* 'to be revealed, to be noticeable (intr.)', Chuv. *xuyxă* 'care, sorrow, grief' → 'to weep, bemoan (intr.)'); 'to cover with the base' (e.g. Chu. *pas* 'hoarfrost, rime' → *pasar-* 'to become covered / cover oneself with hoar frost (intr.)') and 'to make use of the base to perform an action' (e.g. **kăk* 'rope, lace'→ *kăkar-* 'to tie, bind, fasten (tr.)', **tĕlĕ* in Chu. *tĕlĕk* 'dream' → *tĕlĕr-* 'to sleep, doze, drowse (intr.)') [22] The suffix further derives verbs meaning 'to become like the base' from adjectives, e.g. Chu. *čal* 'grey, grey haired' → *čalar-* 'to grow grey haired' and Chu. *śĭvăx* 'near' → *śĭvxar-* 'to become near'. Finally, Fedotov (1996: 369) finds traces of a deverbal anticausative suffix which he relates to the denominal marker, for instance in Chu. *xăp-* 'to increase, grow, advance, swell (intr.)' → *xăpar-* 'to rise, ascend, go up (intr.)', Chu. *pos-/pus-* 'to press, step (tr.)' → *posar- /pusar-* 'to weigh (upon), to suppress (intr.)'.

However, Fedetov proposes to relate the Chuvash suffix *-(A)r-* to the Old Turkic causative suffix *-gAr*. Although some transitive derivations with *-(A)r-* in Chuvash seem indeed to go back to a causativizer pTk **-gAr-*, the intransitive derivations can be traced to the fientive pTk *-(A)d-*.[23] The correspondence between the fientive suffixes OTk. *-(A)d-* and Chuvash *-(A)r* is supported by the observation that some Old Turkic verbs with stem-final *d-*, such as OTk. *sid-* 'to urinate', OTk. *öŋed-* 'to recuperate' and OTk. *sud-~ sod-* 'to spit out' are identified as obsolete compounds by Erdal (1991: 642–644), while they have cognates reflecting stem-final *r-* in Chuvash, such as Chu. *šăr-* 'to urinate', Chu. *ĕner-* 'to tune a musical instrument' and Chu. *sor-* 'to spit out'. Since the isolated base is not attested in Chuvash, the derivation was probably made at a time before the split of the Eastern and Western Turkic branches, i.e. in proto-Turkic.

---

[22] The bases **kăk* and **tĕlĕ* are unattested in Chuvash, but reflected in Tkm. *kök* 'rope made from raw silk' and OTk. *tül* 'dream' respectively.

[23] Transitive derivations such as Chu. *šĭv* 'water' → *šĭvar-* 'to give to drink, to pour (tr.)' and Chu. *xăt* 'favour of heaven, good fortune' → *xătar-* 'to save (tr.)' have counterparts derived with OTk. *-gAr*, such as OTk. *suvgar-* 'to pour (tr.)', OTk. *kurtgar ~ kurtkar ~ kutkar* 'to save (tr.)'. Unlike OTk. *bašad-* 'to be or become a leader', Chuvash *puśar-* 'to begin (tr.)' is a transitive verb derived from Chu. *puś* 'head, beginning', which probably reflects pTk **-gAr*.

6.6 pTEA *-rA- anticausative

6.6.1 pJ *-ra-

The suffix pJ *-ra- derives verbal meaning that excludes a causing agent and presents the situation as occuring spontaneously. Unger (1977: 140) refers to it as a marker of "spontaneous action, endo-activity", Martin (1987: 672) calls it "endoactive (intransitive or passive)". The suffix functions as an anticausative polarizer in equipollent anticausative-causative pairs, in which the anticausative and the causative are derived from a neutral base by means of the suffixes *-ra- and *-sa- respectively (Haspelmath 1993). It further derives anticausatives from verbal adjectives in the sense of 'to become the property of the base', some of which also appear in equipollent pairs. In Section 5.3.1.1. it has been explained why the anticausative pJ *-ra$_{(2)}$- can be kept distinct from the homophonous denominal verb suffix pJ *-ra$_{(1)}$-. Since the anticausative suffix pJ *-ra- has lexicalized in cognate Ryukyuan verb stems, such as Shuri *kusarir-* B 'to spoil, rot (intr.)', *qukur-* B 'to arise, happen' (~ *qukus-* B 'to raise, arouse, wake'), *sugurir-* 'excel' etc., its productivity must predate the split of Mainland Japanese and Ryukyuan.

Deadjectival equipollent anticausative

OJ *aka-* A 'to be clear, bright, red' → OJ *akar-* A 'to brighten, redden (intr.)' ~ *akas-* A 'to spend (the night), to reveal, explain, enlighten'

OJ *kusa-* B 'to be stinky' → OJ *kusar-* B 'to spoil, rot (intr.)' ~ *kusas-* ?A/B 'disparage, spoil, let rot (intr.)'

OJ *omo-* A 'to be heavy' → MJ *omor-* A 'to become heavy, serious'

OJ *pi$_1$ro$_2$-* B 'to be wide, broad, vast' → OJ *pi$_1$ro$_2$r-* ?B 'to be widespread (intr.)'

OJ *usu-* A 'to be thin' → OJ *usure-* A 'to get thin, pale, abate (intr.)', OJ *usurag-* A 'get thin, pale, abate (intr.)'

Deverbal equipollent anticausative

OJ *kap-* A 'to transfer, exchange, buy' → OJ *kapar-* A 'to change, be substituted for (intr.)' ~ *kapas-* ?A 'to exchange, shift (tr.)'

OJ *ok-* A 'to put'[24] → OJ *oko$_2$r-* B 'to arise, happen' ~ OJ *oko$_2$s-* B 'to raise, arouse, wake'

---

[24] The dialects of Shizuoka, Nagano and Yamanashi have B for this verb.

OJ *oti-* B 'to fall' (<**ətə-Ci-*) → OJ *otor-* ?B 'to be inferior, fall behind (intr.)' ~ *otos-* B 'to drop (tr.)'

OJ *sugi₂-* B 'to pass by, exceed; elapse' (< **sunku-Ci-*) → OJ *sugur-* B 'to pass by, exceed (intr.)' ~ *sugus-* ?A/B 'to pass, spend (time), get through, overdo (tr.)'

6.6.2 pK *-(u)l-

Korean has a number of defective converbs, recognizable by the converb ending *-e/ -a* and preceded by an element *-(u)l-* (Ramstedt 1939: 137–138; Martin 1992: 219). They occur with the auxiliary verbs *ci-* 'to become', that polarizes their intransitivity and *ttuli-* 'to make', that makes them into transitives. These converbs derive from verbal adjectives as well as from verbal bases. The transitive analytic construction in *-(u)l-e-ttuli-* replaces an older and almost obsolete suffix in *-(u)li-* that likewise adds transitive meaning and goes back to a synthetic form *-l-i-*, whereby *-i-* represents the causative (see Section 6.7.2). Among the verb pairs below, derivations on *-(u)li-* are *(k)kwupuli-* 'to bend, curve (tr.)' and *wukuli-* 'to crouch, crush (tr.)' [25]. The element pK * *-(u)l-* can be identified as an original anticausative because it requires a causative suffix to derive its causative counterpart. This is further supported by the observation that the common denominator of the deadjectival verbs is spontaneous development and that some deverbal meanings are specific in that the agent spontaneously develops the base verb on himself (e.g. 'to be frightened' and 'to frighten' from 'to rise').

The anticausative formant is also incorporated in the extended copula MK ¨*il-* 'to become, come into being, be formed, get accomplished' found defectively in a modulated stem MK *i·l-·wo* and in a converbial form *i·l-e*, as illustrated in (1). This formation is reminiscent of the derivation of OJ *ar-* 'to exist' from a copula pJ **a-* 'to be' and the anticausative *-*ra-*. (See Section 3.4). The anticausative also occurs in MK *nwu·lul-* 'to become yellow' and it attaches to the deictic to make the defective adjectival verbs MK ·*il-* 'to become this way', MK *kul-* 'to become that way' an MK ·*tyel-* 'to become that way', which are preserved in the derived adverbs MK ·*il-·i, kul-·i, ·tyel-·i* and in the converbs and adjectival nouns MK ·*il-·e, kul-·e, ·tyel-·e* (Martin 2002: 375).

---

[25] Note that Ramstedt (1939: 137–138) also mentions K *nwukuli-* 'to soften (tr.)' and *nelpuli-* 'to spread out widely (tr.)' as causative derivations on *-(u)li-* for K *nwuk-* 'be soft, be loose' and K *nelp-* 'be wide, broad, spacious', but I am unable to find these forms in standard dictionaries of contemporary Korean.

(1) MK ˝nay·h-i   i·l-e
     stream-NOM   be.formed-CONV
     'it becomes a stream and [goes into the sea]' (1445 Yong 2; Martin 1992: 567)

Deadjectival anticausative

K *kwup-* 'to be crooked, bent' → *(k)kwupule ci-* 'to be bowed or bent, to bend oneself', *(k)kwupule-ttuli-* 'to bend forward, to curve (tr.)', *(k)kwupuli-* 'to bend, curve (tr.)'

MK *nwu·lu-* 'to be yellow' → MK *nwu·lul-* 'to become yellow'

K *nwuk-* 'to be soft, be loose' → *nwukule ci-* 'to calm down, loosen up, get milder, become soft (intr.)' ~ *nwukule-ttuli-* 'to soften (tr.)'

K *nelp-* 'to be wide, broad, spacious' → *nelpule ci-* 'to spread/scatter out widely, become wide' ~ *nelpule ttuli-* 'to spread out widely, scatter out widely (tr.)'

Deverbal anticausative

MK *i-* 'to be, to equal' → MK ˝*il-* 'to become, come into being, be formed, get accomplished'

K *pes-* 'to take off, remove, slip off (tr.)' → *pesule ci-* 'to have skin come of, to get skinned, peel off, come off (of hair, skin) (intr.)'

K *sak-* 'to decay, turn bad' → *sakule ci-* 'to collapse, whither, decompose (intr.)'~ *sakule-ttuli-* 'to collapse, wither (tr.)'

K *sos-* 'to rise, tower; gush out; flame up' → *sosule ci-* 'to be frightened, take fright, be startled' ~ *sosule-ttuli-* 'to frighten, startle (tr.)'

K *wuk-* 'to get bent, turn' → *wukule ci-* 'to curl up, warp, be crushed out of shape', *wukule ci-* 'to be dented, curled, be crushed out of shape', *wukule-ttuli-* 'to make a dent in, crush out of shape (tr.)', *wukuli-* 'to crouch, crush (tr.)'

6.6.3 pTg *-rA-

Poppe (1972a: 139–140) reconstructs an anticausative suffix *-rA:-* in Tungusic, but his examples are restricted to Evenki *-ra:-* ~ *-re:-*. I find a cognate anticausative suffix *-r-*, which has lexicalized in Even as well as a deadjectival formant meaning 'to become like or to act according to the property expressed by the base', which may be cognate, in Manchu. The suffix seems to be absent in the southern Tungusic languages. However, it is probably incorporated in the decausative inchoative suffix pTg *-rgA-*, reflected in Ma. *-ja-*, Even *-rgA-*, Evk. *-rgA-*, Ud. *-gA*, Na. *-A-*, which can be derived from the anticausative pTg *-rA-* and the inchoative *-gA-* (see Section 5.7.3).

6.6.3.1 Manchu -rA-

Manchu uses a denominal and deadjectival suffix Ma. *-ra- ~ -re- ~ -ro-* meaning 'to become like or to act according to the property expressed by the base' (Gorelova 2002: 235). This may be a reflex of the original anticausative.

Deadjectival 'to become like the property expressed by the base'

Ma. *ehe* 'bad, evil' → *ehere-* 'to become evil or fierce, be on bad terms with someone'

Ma *hehe* 'woman, female' → *hehere-* 'to act in a feminine way'

Ma. *monggo* 'Mongolia, mongolian' → *mongoro-* 'to speak Mongolian, act in a Mongolian manner'

Ma *nitan* 'weak, diluted, light' → *nitara-* 'to become weak, diluted'

Ma. **saha* 'black, dark' in *sahalan* 'dark', *sahahūn* 'blackish, rather black', *sahaliyan* 'black', *sahaltu* 'having a black face' → *sahara-* 'to turn black'

6.6.3.2 Even -r-

The suffix *-r-* has lexicalized in Even verbs, where it derives from verbs and verbal adjectives, expressing anticausative meaning.

Deadjectival

Even *hata-* 'to be dark' → *ha:tar-* 'to become dark'

Even **cuta-* 'to be wet' in *cutańa:* 'wet, sodden', *cutal-* 'to suck up, absorb (tr.)' → *cutar-* 'to enter, penetrate (of liquid)'[26]

Anticausative

Even *but-* 'to break (down), destroy (tr.)' → *butar-* 'to collapse, decay (intr.)'

Even **cobda-* 'to pierce through (tr.)' in *cobdas* 'through, throughgoing', *cobdal-* 'to bore through, pierce (tr.)', *cobdak-* 'to insert, stick into (tr.)' → *cobdar-* 'to become perforated, get holes, be full of holes (intr.)'

Even *delke-* 'to divide, split, separate (tr.)' → *delker-* 'to separate, dissociate, detach oneself (intr.)'

Even **debge-* 'to move (tr.)' in *debgek-* 'to move, turn, dislocate (tr.)', *debgel-* 'to move, turn, dislocate (tr.)', *debgem-* 'to move, get out of place (intr.)' → *debger-* 'to get out of place, relocate, change a position (intr.)'

Even *hinda-* 'to overthrow, knock over (tr.)' → *hindar-* to collapse, cave in (intr.)'

---

[26] Even *-ńA* derives deverbal adjectives, e.g. *kot-* 'to bend (intr.)' → *kotańa* 'bent' (Benzing 1955b: 41)

6.6.3.3 Evk. -rA-

Vasilevič (1958: 13) refers to Evenki -ra:- ~ -re:- as a suffix that derives verbs with middle meaning.

Deverbal anticausative

Evk. *awga-* 'to cure, heal (tr.)' → *awgara:* 'to recover (intr.)'
Evk. *barca-* 'to dry (fish) (tr.)' → *barcara:-* 'to wrinkle up (of nose, brow) (intr.)'
Evk. *koti-* 'to constrict, to tighten (tr.)' → *kotira:-* 'to dry up (intr.)'
Evk. *ńekce-le:-* 'to bend, curve (tr.)' → Evk. *ńekcere:-* 'to bend, bow (intr.)'
Evk. *teke:-* 'to tear off (tr.)' → Evk. *tekere:-* 'to be turned up, agitated (intr.)'

6.6.4 pMo *-rA-

The anticausative suffix WMo. -ra- ~ -re- is described by Poppe (1954: 64) as adding middle meaning to verbs and denoting the acquirement of a property following adjectives (Poppe 1954: 65). When added to stems containing the liquid r, the suffix dissimilates to -la- ~ -le-. Note that the deverbal anticausative appears in equipollent pairs with the causative WMo -či-, discussed in Section 6.3.4. More examples can be found there.

Deadjectival 'to become like the property expressed by the base'

WMo. *köke* 'blue' → *kökere-* 'to become blue'
WMo. *šira* 'yellow' → *širala-* 'to become yellow'
WMo. *kögšin* 'old' → *kögšire-* 'to become old'
WMo. *ügei* 'poor' → *ügeyire-* 'to become poor'

Deverbal equipollent anticausative

WMo. *asqa-* 'to pour out, scatter, splash out, spill (tr./intr.)' → *asqara-* 'to gush out, poor out, be spilled (intr.)'
WMo. *ebde-* 'to destroy, break, ruin (tr.)' → *ebdere-* 'to break down, fall to pieces, be wrecked (intr.)' ~ *ebdeci-* 'to break, destroy, ruin (tr.)'
MMo. *ququl-* 'to break (off) (tr.)' → *ququra-* 'to break, break off (intr.)' ~ *ququci-* 'to break, break through (tr.)'
MMo. *mültül-* 'take off (tr.)' → *mültüre-* 'to become loose, come off'

6.6.5 pTk *-rA-

In Old Turkic a formative -(I)r- derives the meaning 'to become like the property expressed by the base' from verbal adjectives and anticausative meaning from verbs (Erdal 1991: 535–538). In some derivates below, such as OTk. *aðïr-* 'to separate ((from) things), part from (people) (tr./intr.)', OTk *alaŋur-* 'to become weak (intr.)', *ägir- ~ äŋir-* 'to surround, encircle, besiege, twist, spin (tr.)' the polarization of transitivity seems to have bleached. Erdal (1991: 505) lists a number of verbs, such as OTk. *alvir-* 'to rave', *ögir-* 'to rejoice', *tälmir-* 'to throw expectant, longing or intense glances', *yakar-* 'to beg and pray' that seem to incorporate this suffix, but lack the attestation of a plausible base.

Deadjectival 'to become like the property expressed by the base'

OTk. *süči:-* 'to be sweet' → OTk. *süčir-* 'to become sweet'

OTk. *yïlï:-* 'to be or become hot' → OTk. *yïlïr-* 'to become hot'

OTk. *yunčï:-* 'to be or become weak, emaciated (intr.)' → OTk. *yunčïr-* 'to be put in a bad way, to begin to worsen (intr.)'

*ad- 'to be different' in OTk *aðïn* 'other, another', OTk. *aðna-* 'to become different, change' → OTk. *aðïr-* 'to separate ((from) things), part from (people) (tr./intr.)'

*ürpe:- 'to be shaggy, be disheveled' in OTk. *ürpet-* 'to make (hair) disheveled (tr.)', *ürpek* 'shaggy, disheveled' → *ürper-* 'to bristle, stand on an end (of hair) (intr.)'

Deverbal anticausative

OTk. *alŋu- ~ algu-* 'to wane (intr.)' → OTk. *alaŋur-* 'to become weak (intr.)'

OTk *äg- ~ äŋ-* 'to bend (tr.)' → OTk *ägir- ~ äŋir-* 'to surround, encircle, twist, spin (tr.)'

*köpi- 'to make froth/ foam (tr.)' in OTk. *köpik* 'foam, froth' → *köpir-* 'to foam or froth (intr.)'

*talpï- 'to make flutter (tr.)' in *talpïn- / talpïš-* 'to flutter (intr.)' (OTk. -*n*- processive, -*š*- reciprocal) → *talpïr-* 'to flutter (intr.)'

It cannot be excluded that OTk. -(A)r- which derives numerous intransitive verbs from nouns (Erdal 1991: 499–507), e.g. OTk *ak* 'white' → *akar-* 'to become white', OTk. *bu* 'stem' → OTk *bur-* 'to turn into steam, steam, give odor', OTk. *kök* 'sky, blue, green' → *kökär-* 'to be(come) blue, green' etc., is derived from an original copula pTk **a-* (see Section 3.4) and the anticausative suffix pTk *-(I)r-*.

Borrowings from anticausative verbs into Mongolian seem to suggest that OTk. *-(I)r-*originally had a final vowel, which got lost and recompensed by a binding vowel (*-I-*) after consonant-final stems (< pTk **-rA-*). Clauson (1972: 66) suggests that OTk. *aðïr-* 'to separate ((from) things), part from (people) (tr./intr.)' has been borrowed into Mongolic as the verb reflected in MMo. *ajira-* 'to part from (people), return home (intr.)'. The direction of the borrowing must be from Mongolic into Turkic because in Mongolic the meaning is more specialized and there is no simplex transitive base ***aji-* attested. If this assumption is correct the Turkic model must have had a final vowel.

Further support for the final vowel comes from the observation that some anticausative lexicalizations in verb pairs in later stages of Turkic, e.g. MTk. *sač-* 'to disperse (tr.)' → *sačra-* 'to squirt (intr.)', Kaz. *jay-* 'to spread (tr.)' → *jayra-* 'to scatter (intr.)', Tat. *köy-* 'to be on fire, burn' → *köyra-* 'to catch fire, burn' etc. (Räsänen 1957: 163, Poppe 1972: 139–140).

Moreover, Chuvash preserves a final vowel in some faint traces of a suffix *-ra / -re* that derives anticausatives from adjectives, such as Chu. *yĕpe* 'wet, moist' → Chu *yĕpre-* 'to get wet, soak (intr.)' and verbs, such as Chu *tü-* (conjugated as *tĕv-*) 'to break up, crush, crumble' → Chu **tĕpre-* 'to crumble, crush, go to pieces' in *tĕpreke* 'crumbly, friable', *tĕpren-* 'to crumble (intr.)', *tĕpret-* 'to crumble (tr.)' (Levickaya 1974: 170–171, Fedotov 1996: 356–357).

6.7 pTEA *-*gi*- causative

6.7.1 pJ *-*(C)i*-

The formative element *-(C)i-* that derives bigrade verbs from quadrigrade counterparts is referred to by Unger (1977: 68, 131) as a formant *-gi-* that "changes endo-active verbs into exo-active and vice versa", by Martin (1987: 672) as a "formant making transitive/ intransitive forms" and by Vovin (2001: 187–189) as a "transitivity flipper". However, I will use the term causative-anticausative suffix because the suffix does not necessarily reverses the transitivity of the base: it can also derive causatives from transitive bases or, anticausatives from intransitive bases such as from the copular verb or from verbal adjectives.

As illustrated below, the suffix *-(C)i-* derives verbs from nouns, adding the meaning 'to create/become the concept expressed by the base', from adjectives, adding the meaning 'to create/become the property expressed by the base' and, from other verbs, adding causative or anticausative meaning. Whitman (2008: 170) notes that all derivations from adjectives or stative substantives are inchoative (intransitive) verbs, but this is contradicted by some of the examples below.

With the exception of OJ *aye-* 'to be similar', the denominal derivations are transitive as well as some deadjectival derivations such as OJ *kane₁-* B 'to make one, combine, unite (tr.)', OJ *kate-* B 'to join, unite, blend (tr.)' and *nage₂-* B 'to throw (away), abandon (tr.)'.[27]

The transitivity of most denominal and some deadjectival derivations may indicate that the suffix developed from a verb 'to do, make' at an early time in the prehistory of Japanese. The grammaticalization of causative suffixes from independent transitive verb meaning 'to make' is well attested cross-linguistically (Moreno 1993). The development from causative to anticausative, then, is a common stage on the unidirectional pathway leading to passive meaning (Haspelmath 1990: 46–49, 54).

Denominal 'to create/become the concept expressed by the base'

OJ *ata* 2.2a 'enemy, hostility' → *ate-* A 'to hit, strike, guess, succeed (tr.)'

OJ *sima* 2.3. 'piece of marked-off land, quarters, territory, island' → *sime₂-* ?B 'to delimit, mark out as one's territory, occupy, take possesion of'

OJ *aya* 2.3. 'design, model' → *aye-* 'to be similar'

Deadjectival 'to create/become the property expressed by the base'

OJ *aka-* A 'to be red, bright' → *ake₂-* A 'to get bright, dawn (intr.)'

OJ *ara-* A 'to be rough' → *are-* A 'to rage, run wild, get devastated (intr.)'

*kana- 'to be one' in OJ *kanap-* ?B 'to be a match (for), be suitable / be appropriate (for), be possible for, be realized' → OJ *kane₁-* B 'to make one, combine, unite (tr.)'

*kata- 'to be one-sided' in OJ *kata(-)* 2.3. 'one side of two, one of a pair, inclined toward (bound)', J *katat-* ?B 'to honor, favor', OJ *katap-* 'to become intimate' → OJ *kate-* B 'to join, unite, blend (tr.)'

OJ *kura-* A 'to be dark' → *kure-* A 'to get dark, come to an end (intr.)'

OJ *naga-* B 'to be long' → *nage₂-* B 'to throw (away), abandon (tr.)'

OJ *opo-* B 'to be great, big' → *opi₂-*B 'to grow, get bigger'

OJ *puru-* B 'to be old' → *puri-* ?B 'to get old'

---

[27] The derived verbs discussed in Section 6.4.1 suggest that the roots *kana- and *kata- were originally verbal adjectives. The bound property word OJ *kata(-)* may represent a verbal adjective, whereas unbound attestations may reflect switched nominal encoding.

Deverbal

Causative from intransitives

    OJ *ak-* A 'to open (intr.)' → *ake₂-* A 'to open (tr.)'

    OJ *mi₁t-* B 'to get full' → *mi₁te-* B 'to fill (tr.)'

    OJ *tat-* B 'to stand, be built (intr.)' → *tate-* B 'to erect (tr.)'

    OJ *uk-* A 'to float (intr.)' → *uke₂-* A 'to float, let float (tr.)'

    OJ *yam-* A 'to stop, cease (intr.)'→ *yame₂-* A 'to stop, quit (tr.)'

Causative from transitives

    OJ *ayabum-* A 'to feel anxiety over, fear (tr.)' → *ayabume-* A 'to put in danger, endanger, compromise (tr.)'

    OJ *ap-* B 'to meet, fit, agree (tr.)' → *ape₂-* B 'to join, to dress (vegetables with condiments) (tr.)'

    OJ *pak-* ?A 'to slip (sth.) on, wear (tr.)'→ *pake₂-* A 'to have/let (sb.) wear (tr.)'

Anticausative from transitives

    OJ *ok-* A 'to put (tr.)' → *oki₂-* B 'to arise (intr.)'[21]

    OJ *sak-* ?B 'to rip, split (tr.)' → *sake₂-* ?B 'to get ripped, split (intr.)'

    OJ *to₂k-* B 'to untie, solve, melt (tr.)' → *toke₂-* B 'to come untied, be solved, get melted (intr.)'

    OJ *yak-* A 'to burn, roast (tr.)' → *yake₂-* A 'to get burned, get roasted (intr.)'

    OJ *war-* A 'to split, break, halve (tr.)' → *ware-* A 'split in two, be broken in two (intr.)'

Anticausative from intransitives

    OJ *ar-* B 'to be, exist' → *are-* B 'to appear, be born'

    pJ *wo-* in OJ *wor-* A 'to sit, be at' → OJ *wi-* A 'to be'[28]

Whereas I follow Unger and Martin in reconstructing a causative-anticausative suffix *-(C)i-* as the source of the bigrade conjugation, e.g. *puka-* 'to be deep' + *-(C)i-* (consonant deletion) > *pukay-* (contraction) > *puke₂-* 'to deepen', Whitman (2008: 159–173) proposes that the source of the bigrade conjugation is the verb $e_{(2)}$- 'to get, obtain, be able to', e.g. *puka-* 'be deep' + $e_{(2)}$- (vowel raising) > *pukay-* (contraction) > *puke₂-* 'to deepen'. Thus, in Whitman's scenario **e-* was first used to

---

28 On the basis of aspectual differences, Kinsui 2006 argues that OJ *wi-* is the nonstative counterpart of OJ *wor-*.

derive an intransitive change of state from verbal adjectives extended to deriving anticausatives from transitive verbs and finally developed a causative function.

Whitman (2008: 164) points to four problems with Unger's reconstruction: (1) the different transitivity patterns of lower and upper bigrade stems, (2) the low type frequency of the upper bigrade stems as compared to the upper bigrade stems, (3) the cognacy with the Korean causative-passive pK *-ki- and, (4) the assumed grammaticalization pathway from causative to anticausative. I would like to propose an explanation for each of these points.

First, the majority of verbs in the lower bigrade class are transitives (e.g. OJ ake_2- 'to open (tr.)'), whereas the majority of verbs in the upper bigrade class are intransitives (e.g. OJ $nobi_2$- 'to extend (intr.)'). This can be explained by the assumption that the majority of underlying quadrigade stems originally had *a*-vocalism and that most other stem-final vowels such as *i- and *u- developed later by way of assimilation. In the case of OJ $nobi_2$- 'to extend (intr.)', the attestation of the equipollent causative OJ *nobas*- 'to extend (tr.)' and the lower bigrade alternant OJ $nobe_2$- 'to extend (tr.)' suggests an original *a*-vocalic ambitransitive root pJ *$nənpa$-'to extend (tr. / intr.)' which assimilated its stem final vowel to pJ *$nənpi$- 'to extend (tr. / intr.)'. Since the *-(C)i- gradually developed anticausative meaning, the earlier derivations built on a-vocalic stems tend to be intransitive, while later derivations built on stems with assimilated vowels tend to be intransitive.

This explanation can also account for the second problem: upper bigrade stems like OJ $nobi_2$- 'to extend (intr.)' are less frequent than lower bigrade stems because they are based upon sporadic vowel assimilations.

Third, unlike the proposed Korean cognate pK *-ki- causative-passive, the formant deriving Japanese bigrade intransitives has anticausative, not passive meaning. According to Whitman, this observation stands in the way of the comparison between pK *-ki- and pJ *-(C)i-. However, since one of the four possible pathways of grammaticalization of passive morphology worldwide according to Haspelmath (1990: 46–49, 54) is the development from causative to anticausative to passive, it is clear that Korean must have passed the "anticausative" stage in the course of its development. Note that the unidirectionality of grammaticalization does not imply that every process will reach complete execution (Croft 1991: 24). For pJ *-(C)i- the grammaticalization from causative to passive is not taken beyond the anticausative stage.

Whitman's (2008: 165) fourth objection is his assumption that "Typological parallels become relevant here: while passives derived from inchoatives and *causatives derived from passives are robustly attested across languages* inchoatives derived from passives or causatives are not" [emphasis added]. This is contradicted by Haspelmath's (1990: 49) study of the development of passive morphology across the world: "And note that there is again unidirectionality: a causative can become a passive, but to my knowledge *there is no evidence for a case of a passive becoming a causative*" [emphasis added]. Therefore, the reconstruction of a causative suffix *-(C)i- that gradually grammaticalized into an anticausative marker remains the best way to account for the development of the bigrade verb class.

Since there are no strings of two subsequent vowels in Old Japanese (Martin 1987: 64–65), pJ *-(C)i- must go back to a consonant initial suffix, but what is the most plausible candidate for the bracketed consonant? Velar elision before a high front vowel is sporadically attested in the history of Japanese, both word-internally, such as for instance in OJ *tukitati* > *tuitati* 'first day of the month, new moon' that is derivable from OJ *tuki₂* 'moon' and a deverbal noun from OJ *tat-* 'stand', as on suffix boundaries, such as in the adjective attributive OJ -*ki* that developed into contemporary -*i* (e.g. adnominal OJ *taka-ki* for J *taka-i* 'high'). Due to a phenomenon known as Sapirian drift, similar sound changes may recur at chronologically separated times in a single language or in related languages, such as for instance the loss of initial [h] before a resonant in the German and the English branch of West Germanic, as in OE *hlūd* > NE *loud*, OHG *hlūt* > NHG *Laut* (Joseph 2013). Given the external evidence for an initial velar, I do not exclude that velar elision before a high front vowel had occurred earlier in the prehistory of Japanese as well. Therefore pJ *-ki- is the most plausible reconstruction for the causative-anticausative suffix.[29]

The period in which this suffix was productive as a causative and anticausative must predate the split of Mainland Japanese and Ryukyuan because pJ *-(C)i- has lexicalized in all its functions in cognate Ryukyuan verb stems such as Shuri *qatir-* A 'to hit, strike, guess, succeed (tr.)', *qakir-* A 'to open (tr.); to get bright, dawn (intr.)', *qarir-* A 'to rage, run wild, get devastated (intr.)', *qatir-* B 'to use as a side dish (to go with rice)', *yukkwir-* A 'to end (of the day)', *nagir-* B 'to throw (away), abandon (tr.)', *qwiir-* 'to grow, get bigger', *micir-* B 'to fill (tr.)', *tatir-* B 'to erect (tr.)', *yamir-* A 'to stop, quit (tr.)', *qeer-* B 'to join, dress (tr.)', *hakir-* A 'to have/let (sb.) wear (tr.)', *qukir-* B 'to arise (intr.)', *sakir-* B 'to get ripped, split (intr.)', *tukir-* B 'to come untied, be solved, get melted (intr.)' and *yakir-* A 'to get burned, get roasted (intr.)'.

---

29 Note that for reasons explained in Robbeets (2005: 53–55) I do not reconstruct voice distinction in proto-Japanese.

6.7.2 pK *-ki-

In (Middle) Korean, we find the causative-passive suffixes K -ki-, -hi-, -i- MK -·ki-, -·Gi-, -·hi-, -·i- that can be derived through velar lenition as allomorphs from pK *-ki- (Ramstedt 1939: 133–137, Lewin 1970: 14, Martin 1992: 221–225, 623, Yeon 2003: 142–146). As illustrated below, the suffix derives verbs from verbal adjectives, adding the causative meaning 'to create the property expressed by the base' and, from other verbs, adding causative or passive meaning. Causatives are derived from transitive and intransitive verbs, while passives are derived only from transitive verbs.

Deadjectival

    MK *molk-* 'to be clear' → *mol·ki-* 'to clear up (tr.)'

    MK *nuk-* 'to be soft, wet' → *nu·ki-* 'to soften (tr.)'

    MK *cec-* 'to be wet' → *ce·ci-* 'to moisten (tr.)'

    MK *nep-* 'to be wide' → MK *ne·phi-* 'to widen (tr.)'

    MK *kot-* 'to be straight' → MK *ko·thi-* 'to correct (tr.)'

Deverbal
Causative from intransitives

    K *nem-* 'to exceed, pass beyond (intr.)' → K *nemki-* 'to pass, exceed, make go over (tr.)'

    K *olm-*, MK ¨*wolm-* 'to move (intr.)' → K *olmki-*, MK *wolm·ki-* 'to move (tr.)'

    K *swum-*, MK ·*swum-* 'to lie hidden (intr.)' → K *swumki-*, MK *swum·ki-* 'to conceal (tr.)'

    K *nal-*, MK *nol-* 'to fly (intr.)' → K *nalli-*, MK *nol·Gi-* 'to cause to fly (tr.)'

    K *sal-*, MK ¨*sal-* 'to live' → MK *sal·Gi-* 'to cause to live (tr.)'

Causative from transitives

    K *cwuk-*, MK *cwuk-* 'to die' → K *cwuki-*, MK *cwu·ki-* 'kill'

    K *ip-*, MK *nip-* 'to wear' → K *iphi-*, MK *nip·hi-* 'to cause to wear'

    K *mek-*, MK *mek-* 'to eat' → K *meki-*, MK *me·ki-* 'to feed'

    K *pes-*, MK *pes-* 'to remove, strip off (tr.)' → K *peski-*, MK *pes·ki-* 'to unclothe (tr.)'

    K *tuT-*, MK *tuT-* 'to hear (tr.)' → K *tulli-* 'to get heard (intr.)' ~ K *tulli-*, MK *tul·Gi-* 'cause to hear (tr.)'

Passive from transitives

K *a:n-* 'to embrace (tr.)' → K *a:nki-* 'to embrace (tr.), get embraced (intr.)'
K *ccic-* 'to tear (tr.)' → K *ccicki-* 'to be torn (intr.)'
K *elk-*, MK *elk-* 'to tie (tr.)' → K *elkhi-*, MK *el·khi-* 'to get tied (intr.)'
K *sim-* 'to plant (tr.)' → K *simki-* 'cause to plant (tr.); get planted (intr.)'
K *ttut-* 'to bite, graze (tr.)' → K *ttutki-* 'to cause to graze (tr.), get bitten (intr.)'

6.7.3 pTg *-gi:-

The suffix pTg *-gi:- derives verbs from nouns and adjectives, adding the meaning 'to create the concept or property expressed by the base' and from transitive or intransitive verbs, adding causative meaning. There are no clear examples of anticausative use.

Benzing (1955a: 1065) advanced evidence for the reconstruction of a denominal suffix pTg *-gi- 'to do, make', while he treated the deverbal causative suffix pTg *-gi- as a distinct marker (1955a: 1070). Due to phonological fusion with the root ("wegen kombinatorischen Lautwandels meist schwer zu erkennen"), the reflexes of these suffixes are difficult to recognize; they include Even -(A)g- ~ -gi:- ~ -ngi:- ~ -i:-; Evk. -gi:- ~ -ng- ~ -ngi:- ~ -ki:-; Ud. -ngi-, -gi- and Na. -gi-. The derivations below suggest that in the Northern Tungusic languages, pTg *-gi:- devoices to -ki:- after voiceless stops and assimilates to -ngi:- after the dental nasal -n-. In the southern Tungusic languages and in Manchu, the reflexes are less consistent due to sporadic velar lenition and incorporation in a suffix chain. The original Tungusic verb pTg *xür- 'to ripen, become ripe', reflected in Ma. *ure-*, Evk. *ir-*, Even *ir-*, Neg. *iy-*, Olcha *xuru-*, Orok *xuri-* and Na. *xuru-*, for instance, was derived as pTg *xürgi- 'to make ripe, feed, raise'. The contemporary reflexes of the causative verb are Ma. *uji-*, Evk. *irgi:-*, Even *irgi-*, Neg. *iggi-* 'id.', Solon *iggi-* ~ *irgi-*, Oroch *iggi-*, Ud. *igisi-* and Na. *xuygie-* (Cincius 1975: 325–326), which indicate that pTg *-gi:- was reflected as a liquid cluster on the morpheme boundary in Manchu (*rg > j) and incorporated in the Nanai and Udehe suffix chain.

Given that the grammaticalization of verbs meaning 'to make' into causative suffixes is well attested cross-linguistically (Moreno 1993), it is plausible that the homophonous denominal and deverbal suffixes go back to a single origin.

Although the suffix pTg *-gi:- was productive in proto-Tungusic, it seems to have been highly lexicalized in most contemporary languages. Hence, some languages reflect derived verbs, although they have lost the corresponding base : the base corresponding to Neg. *kesegi:-* 'to punish (tr.)', for instance, is reflected in Evk. *kese:-* 'to suffer (intr.)', but not in Negidal (Cincius 1975: 454–455). The base corresponding to Neg. *samŋi:-*, Na. *samŋici-* and Evenki *samŋi:-* 'to fumigate (tr.)' is preserved in a derived noun Evk. *saŋñan* 'smoke' and in Even *ha:n-* 'to be smoky', but not in Negidal or Nanai (Cincius 1977: 60).

6.7.3.1 Manchu
Although clear reflexes of pTg *-gi-* are absent in Manchu, the suffix may be incorporated in Ma. *-nggi-* 'to send sb. to do sth.', which stands in a causative relation to Ma. *-na- / -ne- / -no-* 'to go to do sth.' (Gorelova 2002: 239–240, 250), e.g *alana-* 'to go to report' → *alanggi-* 'to send to report' and *tuwana-* 'to go to examine' → *tuwanggi-* 'to send to examine'.

6.7.3.2 Even
The Even suffix *-(A)g-*, *-gi:-*, *-ngi:-*, *-i:-* derives verbs from nouns and adjectives, adding the meaning 'make, create the concept or property expressed by the base' (Benzing 1955b: 34) and from intransitive verbs, adding causative meaning (Benzing 1955b: 43). The allomorph *-gi-* appears after consonant stems, while the allomorph *-g-* appears after vowel stems. The vowel in *-Ag-* is the result of reanalysis of originally vocalic stems that have dropped their stem-final vowel. The velar nasal in *-ngi-* is the result of assimilation to a stem-final nasal *-n-*. There are some lexicalizations in which the suffix has further lenited to *-i-*.

Denominal 'to create the concept expressed by the base'
> Even *hotoran* 'road, way' → *hotarag-* 'to pave a way, make a road (tr.)'
> Even *awun* 'hat' → *awug-* 'to sew a hat (tr.)'
> Even *kam* 'yukola (fish)' → *kamgi:-* 'to prepare yukola (tr.)'
> Even *ęlarda:* 'three pips in a play → *ęlarda:g-* 'to triple (tr.)'
> Even *hanga:r* 'hole, gap, opening' → *hanga:rag-* 'to cut through, to cut in (tr.)'

Deadjectival 'to create the property expressed by the base'
> Even *emer* 'pointed, spiky' → *emereg-* 'to sharpen (tr.)'
> Even *ha:n-* (~ *ha:ń-*) 'to be smoky' → *ha:mngi:-* 'to fumigate, smoke (fish, meat) (tr.)'

Deverbal causative from intransitives
> Even *da:w-* 'to get infected, be transmitted (of disease) (intr.)' → *da:wgi:-* 'to infect, transmit (disease) (tr.)'
> Even *mün-* 'to become sour, bad (intr.)' → *münngi:-* 'to ensile, to ferment (tr.)'
> Even *ńamal-* 'to grow warm, to heat (intr.)' → *ńamalgi:-* 'to heat, to protect against the cold (tr.)'

Even *ńen-* 'to dissolve (in water) (intr.)' → *ńenngi:-* 'to dissolve (in liquid) (tr.)'
Even *hi:l-* 'to suffer, worry (intr.)' → *hi:lgi:-* 'to harm, bother, plague (tr.)'
Even *hi:w-* 'to extinguish, go out (of fire) (intr.) → *hi:wi:-* 'to extinguish (fire) (tr.)'

6.7.3.3 Evenki

The Evenki suffix *-gi:-* ~ *-ng-* ~ *-ngi:-* ~ *-ki:-* derives verbs from nouns and adjectives, adding the meaning 'to create the concept or property expressed by the base' (Konstantinova 1964: 198, Nedjalkov 1997: 301, 303–304) and from transitive and intransitive verbs, adding causative meaning (Vasilevič 1940: 93, Nedjalkov 1997: 230). The suffix *-gi:-* is the regular form, while *-ki:-* appears in voiceless clusters. The velar nasal in the allomorph *-ngi-* is the result of assimilation to a stem-final nasal *-n-*. In longer sequences the suffix vowel of *-ngi-* can be omitted, yielding *-ng-*, a form which has probably spread by analogy in the denominal and deadjectival derivation.

Denominal 'to create the concept expressed by the base'
  Evk. *gule* 'house' → *guleng-* 'to build a house'
  Evk. *kolobo* 'bread' → *kolobong-* 'to bake bread'
  Evk. *sirba* 'soup' → *sirbang-* 'to cook soup'

Deadjectival 'to create the property expressed by the base'
  Evk. *a:cin* 'nonexistent, absent' → *a:cinngi:-* 'to liquidate (tr.)'
  Evk. *aya* 'good' → *ayang-* 'to improve'
  Evk. *kete* 'many, much' → *keteng-* 'to increase'

Deverbal causative from intransitives
  Evk. *aru-* 'to regain consciousness (intr.)' → *arugi:-* 'to revive (tr.)'
  Evk. *jalup-* 'to get filled (intr.)' → *jalupki:-* 'to fill (tr.)'
  Evk. *kese:-* 'to suffer (intr.)' → *kese:gi:-* 'to torture (tr.)'
  Evk. *ńure:-* 'to neal, glow (of metal) (intr.)' → *ńure:gi:-* 'to temper, make red-hot (tr.)'
  Evk. *ulap-* 'to get wet (intr.)' → *ulapki:-* 'to make wet (tr.)'

Deverbal causative from transitives
  Evk. *ini-* 'to carry on one's back (tr.)' → *inigi:-* 'to fix a pack to a (persons or an animals) back (tr.)'
  Evk. *sekte-* 'make the bed with branches (tr.)' → *sektegi:-* 'to order sb. to make the bed with branches'

6.7.3.4 Udehe

The Udehe suffix *-ngi-* derives verbs from nouns, adding the meaning 'to create the concept or expressed by the base' (Nikolaeva 1999: 171). The absence of clear examples of deverbal derivation may be due to phonological attrition, given that Ud. *-g-*, the reflex of pTg **-g-*, frequently lenits to *-w-*, *-y-* and Ø in intervocalic position. The velar nasal allomorph *-ngi-* seems to have generalized in denominal derivation, perhaps under the influence of the original stem-final nasal in many proto-Tungusic nouns, such as pTg **poktaran* 'road' or **abun* 'hat' underlying Ud. *xokto* and *au*, respectively.[30]

Denominal

    Ud. *xokto* 'road' → *xoktongi-* 'to make a road'
    Ud. *au* 'cap' → *aungi-* 'to make a cap'
    Ud. *anga* 'night shelter' → *angangi-* 'to make a night shelter'
    Ud. *ogdö* 'coffin' → *ogdöngi-* 'to make a coffin'
    Ud. *momugu* 'firewood' → *momugungi-* 'to collect firewood'

6.7.3.5 Nanai

The Nanai suffix *-gi-* has sporadically lexicalized, as the in verb pairs below.

Deverbal causative

    Na. *sa:n-* 'stretch oneself, spread, lengthen out (intr.)' → *sa:ngi-* 'to stretch, strain (tr.)'

    Na. *u:n-* 'to melt, thaw (intr.)' → *u:ngi-* 'to melt, thaw (tr.)'

    Na. *xuru-* 'to become ripe (intr.)' → Na. *xuygie-* 'to nurse, feed, raise (tr.)'

6.8 The historical development of valence and voice in Transeurasian

The Transeurasian languages preserve evidence supporting the reconstruction of five suffixes of valence and voice: a causative pTEA **-ti-*, a reflexive-anticausative pTEA **-pU-*, a fientive pTEA **-dA-*, an anticausative pTEA **-rA-* and a causative pTEA **-gi-*. This is illustrated in Table 2.

---

[30] Note that some verbs preserve traces of other allomorphs, e.g. Ud. *ileugi-* 'to do something for the third time' is the verb corresponding to Even *ęlarda:g-* 'to triple (tr.)'.

Table 2. Reflexes of suffixes of valence and voice in the Transeurasian languages

pTEA	pJ	pK	pTg	pMo	pTk
*-ti- causative	*-ta- causative intensive resultative passive	*-ti- causative	*-ti- causative intensive resultative passive	*-ti- causative	*-tI- causative intensive resultative passive
deverbal	deverbal	deverbal	deverbal	deverbal	deverbal
*-pU- reflexive anticausative	*-pa- reflexive anticausative	*-pO- reflexive anticausative	*-p- reflexive anticausative	*-βU- reflexive anticausative	*-U- reflexive anticausative
de-adjectival deverbal	de-adjectival deverbal	de-adjectival deverbal	deverbal	deverbal	de-adjectival deverbal
*-dA- fientive	*-ya- fientive passive		*dA:- fientive	*-dA- fientive passive	*-(A)d- fientive anticausative
denominal de-adjectival	denominal de-adjectival deverbal		denominal de-adjectival	denominal de-adjectival deverbal	denominal de-adjectival deverbal
*-rA- anticausative	*-ra- anticausative	*-(u)l- anticausative	*-rA- anticausative	*-rA- anticausative	*-rA- anticausative
de-adjectival deverbal	de-adjectival deverbal	de-adjectival deverbal	de-adjectival deverbal	de-adjectival deverbal	de-adjectival deverbal
*-gi- creative causative	*-(k)i- creative-fientive causative anticausative	*-ki- creative causative passive	-gi:- creative causative		
denominal de-adjectival deverbal	denominal de-adjectival deverbal	de-adjectival deverbal	denominal de-adjectival deverbal		

a) *Formal assessment*

The consonants involved in the comparisons in Table 2 correspond regularly according to the correspondences 3. (*-t-), 1. (*-p-), 4. (*-d-), 11. (*-r-) and 6. (*-g-) in Section 3.3.1. The velar stop in the Japonic causative *-(k)i- is bracketed because its reconstruction relies in part on external evidence, even if the internal evidence suggests that a velar stop is a plausible candidate for the elided consonant. The lack of an initial -p- in the Old Turkic anticausative suffix -U- may be due to the sporadic elision of a labial stop in front of a labial vowel.

The vowels involved in the comparisons correspond regularly according to the correspondences 12. (*-a-), 13. (*-e-) and 20. (*-i-) in Section 3.3.2. According to the correspondences 12. (*-a-) and 13. (*-e-), the vowel harmony between pTEA *-a- and *-e- regularly merges into pJ *-a-. Due to this merger, all Japanese suffixes reflecting -a- ~ -e- harmony display a-vocalism. The irregular low central vowel in the Japonic causative-anticausative suffix *-ta- with respect to correspondence 20. (*-i-) may be the result of eidemic resonance, the wide-spread a-vocalism in the diathetic paradigm having probably triggered the replacement of *-ti- by *-ta- (see Section 3.2.2.1).[31]

The vowel correspondence of the reflexive-anticausative resembles the one appearing under influence of conditioning factor 19b (*PʊRʊ-). Even though the suffix is monosyllabic, it can be noted that, as a reflexive, it is frequently followed by the anticausative suffix *-rA-, e.g. in OJ *itapar-* 'to fall ill', OJ *mazipar-* B 'to mingle'; WMo. *jilbura- ~ jilγura-* 'to fall out (of hair) (intr.)', *julburang* 'short-haired fur coat' and OTk. *alaŋur-* 'to become weak (intr.)' above. The addition of *-rA- yields the environment that conditions the observed vowel development.

b) *Functional assessment*

Many morphemes share a specific polysemy, such as causative-passive, reflexive-anticausative, fientive-passive, etc. whereby one function is less grammaticalized than the other.[32] Moreover, there is a correlation between the parts of speech to which the base may belong, which enables us to reconstruct the basic parts of speech in the ancestral language.

c) *Combinational assessment*

As far as combinational correlations are concerned, the ordering of the particular morphemes in the valence and voice chain display a general overlap. The leftmost positions are occupied by the causative pTEA *-ti- and the reflexive-anticausative pTEA *-pU-. The suffixes underlying pTEA *-ti- and pTEA *-pU- all

---

31 Note that Janhunen (1982: 33) reconstructs proto-Uralic *-tå- / -tä- as a denominal factitive and a deverbal causative suffix. In spite of the aberrant vowel and the absence of grammaticalization into passive, the correspondence might not be entirely coincidental.

32 Note that Collinder (1965: 121) reconstructs a deverbal element *-w- yielding intransitives, reflexives, anticausatives and passives in Uralic with a form and function similar to the reflexive-anticausative pTEA *-pU-.

seem to occupy the first position in the chain of valence and voice markers, since they are never preceded by these markers. The only apparent exception is the Mongolic equipollent causative WMo. -či-, which occupies a position more to the right in the suffix chain, similar to the one occupied by its anticausative counterpart WMo. -rA-. The following position is occupied by the fientive pTEA *-dA- since it is usually not found preceding markers of voice and valence, except perhaps for Japanese.[33] If Martin (1987: 741) is correct in analyzing OJ omop- 'think, feel' as a compound of omo-, maybe reflecting the quality verb omo- 'be heavy', and the anticausative suffix pJ *-pa-, the suffix pJ *-ya- follows the anticausative in OJ omopoye- 'remember, learn, know'.

The anticausative pTEA *-rA- can be positioned to the right of the suffix chain because it can follow the reflexive pTEA *-pU- and of the fientive pTEA *-dA-, as reflected in most languages, see for instance the examples of compounding with the reflexes of the reflexive pTEA *-pU- in Japonic, Mongolic and Tungusic above. The rightmost position is occupied by the causative pTEA *-gi-: any of the discussed valence and voice suffixes can be followed by this suffix, e.g. OJ mazipe- 'to mix, cross, exchange (tr.)' (< *-pa-Ci-), OJ usure- A 'to get thin, pale, abate (intr.)' (< *-ra-Ci-); K (k)kwupuli- 'to bend, curve (tr.)' (< *-l-(k)i-) and Evk. ulapki:- 'to make wet (tr.)' (< *-p-gi-).

The observation that suffixes to the left in the suffix chain tend to be less frequently attested, while those to the right are more frequent indicates that there is a correlation between the position in the chain and the relative time-depth at which the suffix was productive. Older suffixes started to lexicalize at an earlier period and are thus positioned nearer to the root and underwent more attrition, while the opposite is true for younger suffixes.

d) *Typological assessment*

The synchronic co-occurence of different valence and voice functions on most suffixes above seems to be the result of cross-linguistically well-established processes of grammaticalization whereby the direction of the change is unidirectional.

The reflexes of the causative suffix pTEA *-ti- in all languages, except Mongolic, share a development from causative over non-valence changing meanings such as intensive, iterative and progressive to resultative to passive. The development of non-valence changing meanings on causative markers is widespread across the languages of the world and its semantic mechanism is well

---

33 Note for instance that its Khitan reflex *-d- seems to precede the causative *-ha- in *kė-d-ha-ai (bury-PASS-CAUS-CONV) 'having been buried'.

understood (Aikhenvald 2011b). The manipulative effort implied by causatives from intransitive verbs can be transferred to mark intensive action, which can subsequently grammaticalize over iterative to progressive action. Since verbs of position and location such as 'to sit', 'to stand' are commonly lexicalized as punctual change of state verbs in the Transeurasian languages, progressives may easily be interpreted as resultatives here and the development may gradually be transferred to other verbs (Shirai 1998). The final development of resultative into passive meaning has been observed by Nedjalkov & Jaxontov (1988: 61), Bybee et al. (1994: 67), Haspelmath (1990: 54). The reflexive suffix pTEA *-pU- was probably already on its way to grammaticalization in the ancestral language, a development that resulted in the reflexive-anticausative polysemy in the individual languages. The grammaticalization of reflexive to anticausative meaning is well known from the Indo-European languages, where anticausative verbs are formed with the reflexive pronoun pIE *sue (German *sich*, French *se*, Russian *-sja* etc.). The transition from reflexive to anticausative is an instance of semantic bleaching, whereby the agency restriction on reflexives is dropped (Haspelmath 1990: 42–47). The expression *I hurt myself*, for instance, is reflexive if I willfully did so, but anticausative if this was not the case.

The reflexes of the fientive suffix pTEA *-dA-, which derive a process of becoming from nouns and adjectives, have developed to deverbal anticausative or passive suffixes in all branches, except for the Tungusic languages. This development resembles the grammaticalization of passive auxiliaries from verbs 'to become', which is well known from Indo-European languages (Haspelmath 1990: 38–40).

The creative suffix pTEA *-gi-, which adds the meaning 'to create' the basic noun or adjective, was probably already on its way to grammaticalization into a deverbal causative in the ancestral language. This development has resulted in the creative-causative polysemy of the Japanic, Koreanic and Tungusic reflexes. The grammaticalization from causative to anticausative then was restricted to the common ancestor of Japanic and Koreanic, whereas the passive meaning developed only in Korean. This development resembles the grammaticalization of causative auxiliaries from verbs 'to do, make' (Moreno 1993). The development from causative to anticausative, then, is a common stage on the unidirectional pathway leading to passive meaning (Haspelmath 1990: 46–49, 54).

In Section 2.5.3.1, globally shared grammaticalization is advanced as a strong indication of common ancestorship. This does not necessarily imply that the grammaticalization processes were already accomplished in proto-Transeurasian and inherited as polysemy in the daughter languages. Cases in which the grammaticalization process is not fully accomplished in all branches, such as the causative-passive development under pTEA *-ti-, the fientive-passive development under pTEA *-dA- and the causative- passive development under pTEA *-gi-, indicate that the grammaticalization took place independently in the daughter languages, a phenomenon known a "Sapirian drift". Cases in which the grammaticalization process is shared between all branches, such as the reflexive-anticausative development under pTEA *-pU- or the creative to causative development under pTEA *-gi-, suggest that the development was already on its way in the ancestral language and inherited as polysemy in the daughter languages.

7 Nominalization and the development of finite temporal distinctions

7.1 Direct insubordination and its diachronic relevance

One of the driving forces of morphosyntactic change in the Transeurasian languages is a recurrent tendency to grammaticalize non-finite suffixes to finite suffixes. Crosslinguistically, finite forms can be defined through their morphological marking: they typically carry the maximum marking for such categories as tense and agreement permitted in the language, and, through their syntactic function: they prototypically function as the only predicate of an independent clause (Trask 1993: 103–104, Nedjalkov 1995: 97, Givón 2001: 25–26, Bisang 2001, Malchukov 2006b, Nikolaeva 2008: 1–7). In contrast, participles, converbs and verbal nouns are non-finite verb forms whose prototypical function is to mark adnominal, adverbial and argument subordination, respectively (Haspelmath 1995).

The languages of the world use a variety of mechanisms for developing finite function on formerly non-finite forms, a process that will be referred to as "finitization". One common strategy is when the matrix predicate is reduced to an affix or a particle on the erstwhile dependent verb. In example (1), for instance, the matrix verb *bimbata* 'it is audible' in Ket is reduced to a present suffix *-bɛta ~ -bata* on verbs expressing sound production, whereas the past verb *bil'ata* 'it was heard' has evolved into the past suffix *-bilɛta ~ bil'ata* (Malchukov 2013: 196–197). Similarly, Evenki in (2a) represents the original proto-Tungusic pattern whereby a preposed negative verb carries all finite marking and a lexical verb assumes a non-finite form, whereas in Nanai in (2b), the finite negative verb is reduced to a suffix on the erstwhile dependent lexical verb (see Section 4.3.3).

(1) reduction of finite verb to affix in Ket
    a.   *tam bis'ɛŋ in'ŋɛj bi-mbata*
           PT   what sound be.audible-PRS
           'a certain sound is audible' (Werner 1997: 170)
    b.   *p-kutəl'ej-bɛta*
           1SG.POSS-whistle-PRS
           'I whistle' (Werner 1997: 187)

(2) reduction of finite verb to affix in Tungusic

    a. Evk. *nungan nekun-mi   e-ce-n*
             he   younger.brother-POSS.REFL NEG-PST-3SG
           suru-v-re.
           go.away-CAUS-ADN
           'He did not lead his younger brother away.'

    b. Na. *xola:-ci-si*
           read.NEG-PST-2SG
           'You didn't read.'

Alternatively, a construction consisting of a nominal predicate plus finite copula can be reanalyzed as a verbal predicate, whereby the copula may be subsequently lost. A classical example is given in (3a/b), whereby in Old Russian a nominal construction plus copula 'the land is the one that came about' becomes reanalyzed as a verbal predicate 'the land came about' and then, later in Russian, the copula is dropped. The loss of the copula may go over an intermediate stage whereby the erstwhile copula grammaticalizes to a sentence-final particle, as is often seen in the Tibeto-Burman languages (DeLancey 2011). The Sizang (Northern China) finite clause in (4b), for instance, can be derived from a nominalized construction because the clitic used for verb agreement is a possessive proclitic, also used with nouns as in example (4a). The equational copula *hi* of the original construction has left a trace in the homophonous final particle.

(3) verbalization of nominal predicates plus finite copula in Russian

    a. OR   *rusk-aja   zemlja   sta-l-a   es-tĭ*
               Russian-F.SG land   come.about-PERF.PCP-F.SG be-3SG
            'The Russian land has come to exist'
            (Tale of bygone years , The Laurentian codex, 1377)

    b. Rus. *ty spa-l-a*
            you sleep-PST-F.SG
            'You slept'

(4) verbalization of nominal predicates plus finite copula in Sizang

    a. *kâ   mei*
       1POSS tail
       'my tail' (DeLancey 2011: 350)

    b. *ká   pài: hî:*
       1POSS go   PT
       'I go / went' (DeLancey 2011: 350)

A third strategy involves the entire omission of the matrix predicate and the maintenance of the complement, which then takes on the function of the missing matrix as in example (5) from Japanese where the dependent conditional clause 'if you would give it a try' takes on the propositional meaning of the matrix predicate. This is the type, to which Evans (2007: 367) applies the term "insubordination", defining it as "the conventionalized main clause use of what, on prima facie grounds, appear to be formally subordinate clauses".

(5) omission of verbal predicate in Japanese
    a.   yatte   mi-tara   dou   desu-ka
        do-CONV see-COND how be-Q
    b.   yatte   mi-tara?
        do-CONV see-COND
        'Why don't you give it a try?'

Finally, a non-finite predicate may be directly reanalyzed as a finite one, without the omission of a specific matrix predicate, as in example (6) from Barbareño Chumash (Mithun (forthcoming)) or in example (7) from Dyirbal (Dixon 1972: 104, Evans 2007: 408–409). More examples of direct reanalysis can be found in Kayardild (Evans 2007: 408–409), Navajo and Central Alaskan Yup'ik (Mithun 2008).

(6) direct reanalysis of non-finite verb form in Barbareño Chumash
    a.   K-e-ča'min   ʔal-asnes-waš
        1-NEG-know   NML-do-PST
        'I don't know how he did it'
    b.   No'no   ʔal-ʔitaxmayšis   hi=heʔ=l=maliwana.
        very   NML-be.wonderful DEP=PROX=ART=marijuana
        'Marijuana is really wonderful.'

(7) direct reanalysis of non-finite verb form in Dyirbal
    a.   D baŋgu   yugu-ŋgu   [gunba-**ŋu**-ru baŋgul   yaṟa-ŋgu]
           DEM.ERG.IV tree-ERG   cut-**REL**-ERG DEM.ERG.IV man-ERG
           ŋayguna biriḍu balga-n
           1SG.ACC   nearly hit-PRS/PST
           'The tree which the man cut nearly fell on me'
    b.   D ŋaḍa   babil-ŋa-**ŋu**   ba-gu-m   miraɲ-gu
           1SG.NOM scrape-ANTIPASS-**REL** DEM-DAT-III black.bean-DAT
           'I've scraped the beans'

Evans's (2007: 384) requirement that "the resultant construction draws its material from only the old subordinate clause" explicitly excludes the examples in (1) to (4) as instances of "insubordination" because predicate material from the independent clause is retained here. In (1b) the original Ket matrix verb 'be audible' is preserved as a present marker in a reduced form, in (2b) the original finite negative verb leaves a trace in the lengthening of the Nanai verb stem and in (4b) the original copula is preserved as a final particle in Sizang. Although the copula is entirely lost in the contemporary Russian example in (3b) the ending *-l-a* reflects predicate material from the independent clause because the erstwhile nominal predicate was reanalyzed as a periphrastic perfect verbal predicate before the copula was dropped.

Malchukov (2013) proposes distinguishing between instances like (5), which he subsumes under the term "insubordination proper" and (3) to (4), which he refers to as "verbalization", but contrary to Evans' and my approach, he does not include (6) to (7) as a possible insubordination scenario. Similarly, Bisang (forthcoming: 31) objects to subsuming the development of nominalized forms to finite forms under "insubordination", arguing that "they should at least be separated as a special subpart of insubordination if they are not completely dissociated from that term". In the present approach, however, a distinction is made between nominalized forms that are directly reanalyzed as a finite forms as in (6) to (7) and nominalized forms that are reanalyzed as verbal predicates through the use of a copula as in (3) to (4). The former are separated as a special subpart of insubordination, i.e. "direct insubordination", whereas the latter are kept completely dissociated from that term. This distinction is highly relevant for the present discussion because it is exactly the mechanism of direct reanalysis illustrated in (6) to (7) that is one of the driving forces of morphosyntactic change in the Transeurasian languages.

In view of numerous examples of the opposite development, whereby main predicates are reanalyzed as subordinate predicates, the development whereby non-finite morphemes take up finite function seems to contradict the general direction of syntactic change (Lehmann 1985: 16–20; Heine & Reh 1984: 15; Campbell 1991; Hopper & Traugott 1993: 176, 190; Harris & Campbell 1995: 25–27; Traugott & Heine 1991: 6–7). A standard example is complementation with *that* in English, which can be traced back to two independent sentences with a cataphoric *that* (e.g. *He says that. It rains.* > *He says [that it rains.]*) In contrast, insubordination reverses the syntactic pathway: an erstwhile subordinate clause containing a non-finite morpheme upgrades its status to a main clause. However, from a morphological viewpoint, the development whereby the non-finite morpheme takes up finite function without retention of main clause material can be considered a standard process of grammaticalization.

From classical definitions of grammaticalization such as Kurylowicz (1965: 52): "the increase of the range of a morpheme advancing from a lexical to a grammatical, or from a less grammatical to a more grammatical status" or Heine & Reh (1984: 15): "an evolution whereby linguistic units lose in semantic complexity, pragmatic significance, syntactic freedom and phonetic substance", it becomes clear that grammaticalization consists in an increase of grammatical status and a loss of semantic content, phonetic substance, categorial properties and syntactic freedom, aspects all of which can be found in insubordination.

First, insubordination involves an increase of grammatical status. Finite suffixes are typically inflectional: they are fully productive, generally applicable and do not change the word-class of the base. Non-finite suffixes are more towards the derivational end of the morphological scale (see Section 6.1) because they change the word-class of the base. Suffixes for the derivation of deverbal nouns are relatively derivational because they do not apply productively to all bases, while suffixes for the derivation of participles and converbs are on the interface between derivation and inflection: they are category-changing but also generally applicable and productive. In view of factors such as paradigmatic organization, productivity, syntactic relevance etc., inflectional morphemes reflect a higher grammatical status than derivational morphemes. Therefore, the gradual transition from derivation to inflection reflects an increase of grammatical status, whereby the cline is from deverbal noun affixes over participial affixes to finite affixes.

Second, semantic content is gradually lost as one moves on the insubordination cline. Contrary to finite markers, non-finite suffixes may change the meaning of the base. The German deverbal noun *Kratz-er*, for instance, can have various concrete meanings such as 'scratch' and 'scraper', but the finite inflection *er kratz-t* always means 'he scratches'.

Third, insubordination obviously involves loss of phonetic substance when the entire verbal predicate gets lost as in (i). In instances of (ii), the finite affixes may be phonologically reduced vis-à-vis their non-finite sources; see for instance the assumed vowel loss in pJ *-ra* and pTk *-(A)rV* below.

Fourth, insubordination involves loss of categorial properties because it can be viewed as a gradual process of denominalization. As Malchukov (2004: 88–93) explains, the loss of nominal properties is gradual and follows a cline, starting with the loss of case markers, to the loss of possessive marking to the loss of number marking.

Finally, syntactic freedom is lost because the use of the suffixes becomes more and more obligatory in the process of insubordination. Whereas the use of a deverbal noun or participle is optional in a sentence, the use of finite markers is obligatory.

Insubordination may be interrelated with a range of other grammaticalization processes, such as the development of modal or temporal distinctions. Globally shared grammaticalization *per se* is already taken as a strong indication of genealogical relatedness (see Section 2.5.3.1), but when shared insubordination can be supplemented by other processes such as temporal development, the evidence will become increasingly convincing. Besides, under the assumption that direct insubordination is cross-linguistically less common than insubordination proper, and within the East Asian area less common than the verbalization of copula constructions, its concentration in the Transeurasian languages may serve as additional support in favor of common ancestorship.

7.2 Previous research

This chapter will be concerned with the reconstruction of five suffixes reflecting the development of (ad)nominalizers into finite tense markers: three aspectually unmarked nominalizers pTEA *-rA, *-mA and *-n and two resultative nominalizers pTEA *-xA and *-sA.

Poppe (1955b, 1964: 12–13) payed specific attention to the prototypical structural feature, whereby nominalizers tend to develop into finite forms in the Turkic, Mongolic and Tungusic languages, but he did not compare the specific forms of any nominalizers for reconstructional purposes. This had been done to a certain extent by Ramstedt (1952: 86–89, 94–100, 104–107), who touched upon some of the Turkic, Mongolic, Tungusic and Korean reflexes of the nominalizers under discussion in this chapter. Martin (1968: 406) hinted at possible Ryukyuan connections of the Korean (ad)nominalizers pK *-l, *-m and *-n reconstructed in Ramsey's study. Given that the paper in question appeared in the form of a brief three-page report to a conference proceedings, Martin (1968: 405) promised the reader to elaborate his proposal elsewhere, but this enterprise was postponed to the end of his career and reduced to a brief summary in Martin (1991a: 285–286, 2002: 378). Lee (1977: 23–24) recapitulated Ramstedt's etymologies for pK *-l, *-m and *-n, leaving out the Ryukyuan cognates proposed by Martin and he was in turn cited by Menges (1984: 258, 261). Although Lee (1977: 214) considered the use of pK *-l and *-n as a deverbal noun suffix "eigentümlich (idiosyncratic)", this chapter will show that there is nothing peculiar about this behavior, when it is put in the perspective of insubordination across the Transeurasian languages. In part this has been worked out in my previous research (Robbeets 2009a) in which I explored the details of the triple correlations including Japanese and Ryukyuan cognates and explained the developments in the light of Evans's (2007: 367) concept of "insubordination". In Lee and Ramsey's view (2011: 22–23) "the correspondence of this Korean triad with three almost identical Altaic morphemes constitutes the most serious evidence brought forward so far in making the case for a genetic relationship between the languages."

Possible reflexes of the nominalizer pTEA *-rA have also been studied in isolation, without determining systemic correlations with reflexes of pTEA *-mA and *-n. Miller (1980: 91–92) compared the Tungusic adnominalizers pTg *-rA- and *-ri:- with a variety of different – and probably originally distinct – Japanese suffixes such as the deverbal noun suffix in OJ *sakura* 'blossom' from OJ *sak-* 'to bloom', the conclusive suffix in OJ *ari* 'to exist' and the anticausativizer in OJ *ar-* < pJ **a-ra-* 'to exist'. Baskakov (1981: 73), however, followed Ramstedt's (1952: 86–89) proposal to relate pTg *-rA- and *-ri: to the Turkic and Mongolic deverbal noun suffixes proposed in this chapter. His proposal is in turn followed by Vovin 1998, who added the Korean cognates proposed earlier by Martin and proposed the Old Japanese adnominal form in *-uru* as a cognate. Vovin's proposal, then, is repeated in Starostin et al. (2003: 227). In Vovin (2001: 189–190), however, the Turkic and Mongolic members are silently eliminated from the etymology. Recently, Vovin (2008a: 82–83) has rejected the entire etymology because, in his view, the analysis of the OJ adnominal form in *-uru* as a grammaticalized auxiliary contradicts the external comparison. In this chapter, however, I will argue that Vovin's internal analysis is correct, but can be used as an argument in favor of the etymology. Finally, Choi (2002: 32–33) proposed to relate pK *-l to the deverbal noun suffixes OTk -(X)l in OTk. *ïd-* 'to send' → *ïdïl* 'foray, expedition' (Erdal 1991: 330–332) and WMo. -l in WMo. *ükü-* 'to die' → *ükül* 'death' (Poppe 1954: 47) and to a deverbal adjective suffix *-li petrified in Even forms such as *bungñuli* 'round' for which – contrary to Choi's claim – no bases are attested and which derives from pTg *-li:n (Benzing 1955a: 1038) rather than from pTg *-l as proposed by Choi. The Turkic and Mongolic cognates are functionally less equivalent than the proposals made in this chapter because they do not undergo insubordination as in the case of the Korean suffix.

Previously, studies of the reflexes of the nominalizer pTEA *-mA have also been made outside the context of triad correlations with pTEA *-rA and *-n. Poppe (1955a: 262) mentioned the alternation between pTEA *-m and *-mA reflected in Turkic, Mongolic and Tungusic. Street and Miller (1975: 137) note the correspondence of *-mA, deriving color adjectives in Turkic and Mongolic. Baskakov (1981: 73), followed Ramstedt's (1952: 104–107) proposal to relate the Turkic, Mongolic and Korean deverbal noun suffixes, but eliminated the Tungusic member proposed by Ramstedt, contrary to Choi (2002: 33–34), who recapitualted Ramstedt's entire etymology.

I am unaware of any proposals adding the Old Japanese conclusive form in *-u* to this etymology, as I did in this chapter. Other proposals including the Japanese conclusive exist, however: Boller (1857: 229) was the first to suggest that OJ -*u* was related to a copula inherited from pA **bi, *bu* 'to be' and reflected in the final predication markers Ma. -*bi* and WMo. *bui* 'it is', an etymology also provided by Murayama (1978: 259) and mentioned by Miller (1985: 47–49). Miller (1985: 47–49) also considered different connections for this suffix, such as the Even nomen actoris in -*gu:*. Seemingly independently of previous work, Vovin (2001: 190) ventured a similar interpretation for the Japanese conclusive, relating it to the final predication markers Old Korean OK -*ta-Wi* and Ma. -*bi*, an assumption which he does not reject in Vovin (2008a). He regarded the nominalizer pJ **-m*, reconstructed on the basis of the accent class 2.5 as a different etymon, which he compared to the Korean nominalizer in Vovin (2001: 187), but then again rejected his former idea in Vovin (2008a: 78), explaining it as an early borrowing from Korean into Japanese.

Isolated discussions of reflexes of the nominalizer pTEA **-n*, independent of the connections with pTEA **-rA* and **-mA* are limited to Poppe's (1955: 262–263) comparison of the Mongolic, Turkic and Korean cognates proposed by Ramstedt (1952: 94–100). Later, Poppe (1972b: 45–46) further adds the Tungusic cognate proposed by Ramstedt. I am unaware of any etymologies including the Japanese conclusive form proposed in this chapter.

As far as the reflexes of pTEA **-xA* are concerned, Ramstedt (1952: 89–92) reconstructed an original optative future pA **-gai*, which he saw reflected in some of Turkic, Mongolic, Tungusic and Korean cognates discussed in this chapter. However, Poppe (1955: 273) proposed to relate the so-called "nomen imperfecti" WMo. -*ya(i)* ~ -*ge(i)* in Ramstedt's etymology to pA **a* with *y/g* as "Hiatustilger". Contrary to my approach, Poppe (1972b: 45–46) kept this suffix separate from the deverbal noun suffix WMo. -*ya* ~ -*ge* in e.g. *uda*- 'to last, be tardy' → *udaya* 'occasion, instance, time', which he compared with the deverbal noun suffix OTk. -*gA* and with a suffix -*gA* which sporadically occurs in Evenki, e.g. in *jew*- 'to eat' → *jewge:* 'food'.

Ramstedt's proposal was followed by Menges (1984: 261), by Baskakov (1981: 72–73), who left out the Korean member and by Choi (2002: 29), who eliminated the Tungusic member. Vovin (1998) cited the comparison proposed by Baskakov, adding the Korean perfective suffix MK -*ke*-/-*ka*- and the Japanese past finite OJ -ki_1 and reconstructing a perfective pA **-k'e*. Vovin's proposal, then, is repeated in Starostin et al. (2003: 227). In Vovin (2001: 189–190), however, the Turkic and Mongolic members are silently eliminated from the etymology and the remaining part of the proposal is ultimately rejected in Vovin (2008: 84–85) on suspicion of borrowing. In this chapter, I propose an alternative Japanese cognate to OJ -ki_1, but I leave the possibility open that the finite past form is a secondary derivation from the cognate that I propose.

As far as the reflexes of pTEA *-sA are concerned, Sanžeev (1962: 280–282) and Bese (1974: 7), segmented the Mongolic negative WMo. *ese* along the same line as the nominalized form of the negative verb pTg **e-se*, proposing a cognate element *-sA. Bese (1971: 220–221) further proposed to consider this element a part of the deverbal perfective nominalizer WMo. *-ysan ~ -gsen / -qsan ~ -ksen*, Earlier, Ramstedt (1952: 130–132) had proposed that the the Chuvash perfective converb on *-sA* was related with the perfective nominalizers WMo. *-ysan ~ -gsen / -qsan ~ -ksen* and pTg **-ksa*, but, contrary to my approach, he considered the Old Turkic conditional *-sA(r)* as a distinct etymon. His analysis was supported by Poppe (1974: 146). I am unaware of any other proposals suggesting that the nominalizers OJ *-sa* and Old Ryukyuan *-sa* which derive resultative adnominal forms from verbal adjectives are to be related, a proposal made in this chapter. Whitman (1985: 230) proposes to relate OJ *-sa* to the Korean bound noun MK *so* 'act, state, fact'. However, I reject this proposal because, unlike the Japanese suffix, this form is nominal in origin and occurs after the adnominal form of verbs. Under the present analysis, I leave the possibility open that the adnominal suffix OJ *-si*, which attaches to verbal adjectives is a secondary derivation from OJ *-sa*. In this light, Miller's (1985: 71) comparison of OJ *-si* with the Tungusic (ad)nominalizer pTg **-si:* gains credibility, but Whitman's (1985: 165) proposal to compare OJ *-si* with the denominal adjectivizer MK *ci-* 'is, is characterized by' is unlikely.

As compared to previous studies, the present approach intends to be innovative in the following ways. First, it reviews earlier proposals in a critical way by eliminating improbable elements and by adding new cognates, with special attention to Japanese. The Japonic cognates proposed here, for instance, under pTEA *-mA, pTEA *-n, pTEA *-xA and pTEA *-sA have not yet been proposed elsewhere. Second, the reconstruction of some phonological aspects of the suffixes under consideration, such as for instance the velar fricative in pTEA *-xA is a novelty. Third, the reconstruction of the suffixes on the basis of derivational word pairs or productive morphemes is carried out in more detail, relying on recent descriptive studies of individual contemporary languages and historical varieties. Fourth, the comparisons go beyond the traditional form-function analysis by integrating diachronic typology into the argumentation, such as Evan's concept of "insubordination" and recent work on the grammaticalization of temporal from aspectual distinctions. And finally, the individual etymologies are given a certain paradigmatic coherence, whereby aspectually neutral nominalizers develop into finite non-past forms while resultative nominalizers develop into finite past forms.

7.3 pTEA *-rA aspectually neutral (ad)nominalizer

7.3.1 pJ *-ra (~ *-rə)

The deverbal noun suffix pJ *-ra derived nominal and adnominal forms from verbal adjectives such as in OJ aka- 'to be red' → akara 'red' (e.g. in akara tatibana 'red mandarin-oranges (MYS XVIII: 4060)), usu- 'to be fine' → usura 'fine', uma- 'to be tasty' → umara 'tasty', yo_2- 'to be good' → $yo_2 ra$ 'good', sakasi- 'to be wise' → sakasira 'wisdom', kanasi- 'to be sad' → kanasira 'sadness', EMJ be- necessitive → bera nar- necessitive etc. (Antonov 2007: 102, 111, 128–132, 153, 160, 196, Vovin 2009a: 436–440). Some word pairs such as OJ $woso_2$ 'precocious, early ripening' → OJ $woso_2 ro_2$ 'precocious, early ripening' suggest that the suffix vowel assimilated to the root vowel (Antonov 2007: 174, 178, 198). Unless OJ tatara 3.4 'foot-bellows' can be derived from OJ tat- B 'stand' (< *tata-) and this suffix, there are no indications of deverbal derivation.

Clausal (ad)nominalization makes use of a suffix pJ *-oro reflected as -uru/ -ru / -u in Old Japanese and as *-uru / -ru in the Ryukyuan languages. In literature, we find different analyses of the Japonic adnominal form. While some linguists derive it from a morphologically complex form (Yamaguchi 1978: 52, Unger 1977: 63–65, 2000, 664: < pJ *-u conclusive + *-ra nominalizer + -u adnominal; Serafim 2005, Russell 2006: 198: < pJ *-ur- stative extension + *ə attributive; Whitman 1990: 539, Frellesvig 2008: 190, 2010: 100–101: *-u conclusive + *-ru adnominal), others reconstruct a simplex adnominalizer (Hayata 2000: pJ *-rua; Vovin 2005c: 51, 2009a: 632: pre-OJ *-uro; Whitman 2012: 34: pJ *-or). Taking these different proposals into account, I propose to derive the (ad)nominalizer as a complex form, which grammaticalized from a periphrastic construction based on the auxiliary pJ *wo- 'to be' and the (ad)nominalizer pJ *-ra. This seems to be the best way to reconcile the internal, dialectal, comparative Ryukyuan and external Transeurasian data, discussed below.

Although the standard use of this suffix is adnominal, it can be used as a finite form marking independent sentences in both Old Japanese and the Ryukyuan languages. In such cases, the insubordinated form signals the evaluative nature of the proposition and it may be accompanied with focus particles specifying the exact nature of the speakers reaction such as question, exclamation, confirmation, explanation etc., a phenomenon known as kakari-musubi in Japanese.

The examples below suggest that pJ *-ra began as a lexical nominalizer applied to verbal adjective stems to create noun stems: 'be sad' → 'sadness'.[1] In

---

[1] Nominalization in essence is a process for forming nouns. In this chapter, I will make a distinction between lexical nominalization and clausal nominalization (Comrie & Thomp-

Old Japanese – as in most Transeurasian languages – noun stems could be juxtaposed to other nominals to add supplementary information, thus functioning as property nouns, i.e. nominally encoded adjectives: 'be red' → 'red (oranges)'. Whereas lexical nominalizations were derived by adding the suffix *-ra directly to verbal stems, clausal nominalizations incorporated the copula pJ *wo- 'to sit, be'. The nominalized auxiliary pJ *wo-ra fused into a suffix and became the clausal (ad)nominalizer OJ -uru, pR *-uru, which marked complement clauses and relative clauses. The relative clauses developed one step further to mark syntactically independent sentences which added supplementary information in discourse. The synchronic co-occurence of the different functions nominalizer/ adnominalizer/ finite in Old Japanese and Ryukyuan thus seems to be the result of an insubordination process, whereby the direction of the grammaticalization was from non-finite to finite marker. It is plausible that the grammaticalization process was already accomplished in Japonic and that it was inherited as polysemy in the daughter branches.

In the past, a number of objections have been raised to deriving the adnominal form from a nominalized auxiliary pJ *wo-ra, which fused with the preceding verb. Vovin (2009a: 632) objects to "tracing back the attributive form not only in Ryukyuan, but in Japonic in general to the attributive wor-u of the verb wor- 'to exist'" because "[f]irst, medial -w- is not lost in Old Japanese in intervocalic position" and "[s]econd, [...] under this explanation it appears that only wor- could have an independent attributive form -u < *-wo , while all other verbs could not add the attributive directly to their stems." However, under the present analysis, w- is lost in word-initial position, at a time when the formant was still an unbound auxiliary. Sporadic elision of initial pJ *w- is reflected in pairs such as OJ a ~ OJ wa 'I', OJ akat – 'to divide, distribute, spread about' / OJ akare – 'to get divided, get spread' ~ OJ wakat – 'to divide, distribute, spread about' / OJ wakare- 'get divided, get spread' etc.. Second, the reason why, unlike other verbs, the copula could take the deadjectival nominalizer *-ra is that copula take an ambivalent position between verb and verbal adjective (see Section 3.4).

Russell's (2006: 196–197) objections are following: "First, [...] why would a nominalizer be part of a verbal morpheme that does not function as a noun?". "Second, there is no evidence for the vowel /a/ in this form" and "finally, ... if -Ci is an evidential marker why would [it] be suffixed to a noun to create a verbal form?". Her first question can be answered in reference to the assumed

---

son 1985). Lexical nominalization is the derivation of nouns from lexical verbs and adjectives, whereby the resulting noun can function as the head of a noun phrase and has the same morpho-syntactic characteristics as non-derived nouns. On the contrary, clausal nominalization is the nominalization of a whole clause.

process of insubordination, whereby non-finite nominalizers develop to finite forms. Second, although pJ *wo-ra is believed to have assimilated to pJ *woro, traces of the original vowel /a/ can be found: the adjective (ad)nominalizer pJ *-ra reflects original a-vocalism and the exclamatory ("izenkei", "evidential", "subjunctive") form OJ -ure can be derived from the adnominal form as pJ *wo-ra i, in which i is a substantivizer following adjectival nouns (e.g. OJ taka 'high' → take₂ 'peak'; OJ awo 'blue' → awi 'indigo plant'; OJ aka 'red' → ake₂ 'red object, red cloth'), cognate with the bound noun OJ i 'fact (that); that (which)' (Whitman 1985: 44, 246; Martin 1987: 64–65, 420). Since pre-OJ did not tolerate sequences of vowels, there were two different ways of resolving them: synchronically, in the course of speech production, one of the vowels on a morpheme boundary could drop according to Unger's (1977: 41; 2000: 662–664) vowel deletion rules, e.g. OJ me₂si-age₂- (summon-give) > me₂sage₂- 'to confiscate, seize by authority'; diachronically, in the course of language change, the vowels coming together in a single morpheme contracted through consonant loss or through univerbation due to the loss of constituent transparency, e.g. OJ -ki₁ am- (PST TENT) > OJ -ke₁m- tentative (see Section 5.6.1). The vowel contraction assumed to yielded OJ -ure belongs to the latter type, whereby the loss of constituent transparency of the substantivizer i in the process of grammaticalization resulted in the contraction of the vowels.

This analysis is also related to Russell's third question: the exclamatory form is derived from a substantivizer 'fact (that)' juxtaposed to an adnominal form of the verb. Driven by information structure, the dependency gradually came to reach beyond the sentence, resulting in a finite exlamatory verb form.

Finally, Frellesvig questions the derivation of monosyllabic bigrade verbs, but in Section 7.3.1.2 it will be shown that these can be regularly derived, if one assumes that *-Ci- was the original shape of the causative-anticausative marker.

7.3.1.1 Ryukyuan

The Ryukyuan languages provide particularly valuable insights into the reconstruction of three (ad)nominalizers pJ *-ra, pJ *-m and pJ *-n. In Shodon, a northern Ryukyuan language spoken on Kakeroma Island, one of the Amami islands southwest of Amami Ōshima, non-finite and finite markers of imperfective aspect go back to periphrastic constructions with the proto-Japanese auxiliary *wo- 'to be' plus one of these endings.

As illustrated in Table 1, Shodon -r is incorporated as an (ad)nominalizer in imperfective constructions on -ur and perfective constructions on -ar. It can be noted that r changes automatically to s before s, for instance before sa 'because'. Whereas the (ad)nominalizer -ur attaches to the converb of the imperfective base of the verb, -*ar* attaches to the converb of the perfective base. The attachment of the (ad)nominalizer to converbial forms supports the derivation of the composite elements -*u*- and -*a*- from the copula auxiliaries **wo*- 'to sit, be' and **a*- 'to be, exist', respectively (see Section 3.4.1).[2] The following morphological analysis may account for the -*ur* derivation of verbs: Shodon *yubyúr* < pJ **yonp*- 'to call' + **-i* CONV + **wo*- 'to be' + **-ra* NML.

The Shodon suffix -*ur* corresponds to -*uru* in other Ryukyuan languages, such as Yamatoma, a northern Ryukyuan language spoken on the Amami islands and Shuri, a central Ryukyuan language spoken in Okinawa. Hirara, a southern Ryukyuan language spoken on the Miyako Islands has -*ï* (< **ïrï* < **-uru*) (Russell 2005: 641–644, Vovin 2009a: 633).[3] These forms suggest that the nominalized auxiliary pJ **wo-ra* assimilated to pJ **[w]oro* and lost its initial labial. As -*oro* started fusing with the converbial form of the verb, it regularly raised to pR **-uru*.

Note that in most contemporary Ryukyuan languages the suffix -*uru* follows both consonant and vowel verbs, but the allomorph -*ru* appears as an alternative form after vowel verbs. In Shuri, for instance, the verb *ni*- 'to boil' has two possible attributive forms, i.e. *ni-y-uru* and *ni-i-ru*. The allomorphy for vowel stems indicates that pR **-uru* was the original suffix, but that the suffix-initial -*u*- occasionally dropped following vowels. Therefore, it is plausible that pR **-uru* also underlies in the derived Shuri form *ya-ru* from the copula *ya*- 'to be'.

The Shodon perfective constructions on -*ar* correspond to the complex suffixes Shuri -*a-ru* and Hirara -*a-ï*, which have grammaticalized from the auxiliary pR **a*- underlying Shuri *a*- 'to exist' and Hirara *ar*- 'to exist' (Russell 2005: 527, 571) plus the (ad)nominalizer pR **-(u)ru*, with the suffix initial -*u*- dropping following the vowel of the auxiliary. From this perspective, the following morphological analysis may account for the -*ar* derivation of Shodon verbs: *yudár* < pJ **yonp*- 'call' + **-i* CONV + **-ta*- PERF + **-i* CONV + **a*- 'to exist' + **-[w]oro* NML. Thus, the grammaticalization of the Shodon perfective constructions on -*ar* has taken place in Ryukyuan, whereas the grammaticalization of the imperfective constructions on -*ur* can be traced back to the Japonic stage.

---

2 This inference is in line with Vovin (2009a: 632) "... historically the [Ryukyuan] attributive suffix -*uru* is likely to be an auxiliary that followed the infinitive form -*i*."

3 Contary to Vovin's (2009a: 633) analysis of the Ryukyuan attributive as -*uru* (< pR **-uru*), Russell (2005: 480, 485, 530, 535, 571, 575) considers the form of the suffix to be Yamatoma attributive -*ru*, Shuri -*ru* and Hirara -*ï* (< pR **-ru*), while she analyzes the preceding element Yamatoma -*yu*-, Shuri -*u* and Hirara -*u*- as non-past stative auxiliary. I agree with Vovin that shape of the suffix was **-uru* in proto-Ryukyuan, but in line with Russel's suggestion, it had probably grammaticalized from an auxiliary construction. In my opinion this grammaticalization had already been accomplished in proto-Japanese.

Table 1. The use of the Shodon imperfective and perfective constructions incorporating -r (Martin 1970: 128–131)

	imperfective	perfective
adnominal	yuby-**ús** sa ... call.CONV-**ADN** because 'Because I will call ...'	yud-**ás** sa ... call.PFV.CONV-**ADN** because 'Because I called...'
finite	Yúp na! Yuby-**úr**! call PROH call.CONV-**FIN** 'Don't call! I WILL call!'	Yud-**ár** call.PFV.CONV-**FIN** 'He called'

As shown in Table 1, the Shodon imperfective -*ur* and perfective -*ar* constructions can function as non-finite as well as finite predicates (Martin 1970: 128–131). The imperfective finite use is restricted to cases where there is either an interrogative word within the sentence, where a prohibition is being defied or in emphatic sentences marked with particles such as *do(o)* 'indeed' and *yaa* 'confirmative'. Similarly, the Yamatoma and Shuri adnominalizers -*uru* can function as a finite suffix in emphatic sentences marked with the particle *du* or in questions (Russell 2005: 485, 535–536). In Hirara, the adnominalizer -*ï* is often described as the "shūshikei" (Hirayama 1983) because it is used as the default finite marker, beyond emphatic or interrogative contexts. Example (8) illustrates how this suffix is used for argument subordination, nominal modification and main clause marking.

(8) The use of the Hirara (ad)nominalizer -*ï*

    a. nominal
       *kak-**ï**   yuïsa yum   du   masï*
       write-**NML** COMP read.ADN thing better
       'Reading is better than writing' (Hirayama 1983: 187, Russell 2005: 577)

    b. adnominal
       *a-ïta-**ï**   mun:-ba   bassi-tt   o:*
       say-PERF-**ADN** thing-ACC forget-PERF EMPH
       '[He] forgot the things that were said'
       (Hirayama 1983: 187, Russell 2005: 577)

    c. finite
       *tabaku: fuk-**ï**   padïmi-**ï***
       tobacco smoke-**NML** begin-**FIN**
       '[I] began smoking' (Hirayama 1983: 187, Russell 2005: 577)

7.3.1.2 Mainland Japanese

The Western Old Japanese (ad)nominalizer ("rentaikei") has three allomorphs, namely WOJ *-uru* / *-ru* / *-u*. The main allomorph *-uru* follows bigrade verbs (e.g. OJ *ake₂-* 'to open (tr.)' → *ak-uru*; OJ *oki₂-* 'arise (intr.)' → *ok-uru*) and irregular verbs (e.g. OJ *ko₂-* to come' → *k-uru*; OJ *se-* 'to do' → *s-uru*), except *r*-irregulars. The allomorph *-ru* follows a small class of about 7 upper monograde verbs, which are monosyllabic bases of the shape $Ci_{(1)}$- (e.g. OJ mi_1- 'to see' → mi-ru). The allomorph *-u* follows quadrigrade and r-irregular verbs (e.g. OJ *ak-* 'to open (intr.)' → *ak-u*; OJ *ar-* 'to exist' → *ar-u*; OJ *wor-* 'to be, exist' → *wor-u*).

Before the separation of Ryukyuan and Mainland Japanese, the nominalized auxiliary pJ **wo-ra* probably assimilated to pJ **[w]oro*, dropping its initial labial. Contrary to the Ryukyuan case, where the auxiliary fused with the converbial form of the verb, it is attached directly to the verb stem in Old Japanese. Since the converbial form of the verb was identical to the verb root in bigrade and monograde verbs (e.g. OJ *ake₂-* 'to open (tr.)' → *ake₂* CONV), there was a strong basis for substituting the converb by the bare root in the quadrigrade and irregular verbs.

Unger's (1977: 41; 2000: 662–664) rule of vowel deletion (VD), Whitman's (1985: 190–201, 1990) rule of medial **r* loss (rL) and Frellesvig and Whitman's (2008) rule of mid vowel raising (MVR) can account for the different allomorphs. In line with Unger's rule, vowel deletion will occur where vowels come together on a morpheme boundary. When a monosyllabic vowel final root meets a polysyllabic vowel initial suffix, the second vowel is expected to drop. Thus, for the upper monograde the phonological rules sequence as following: *mi_1-oro* (VD) > *mi_1-ro* (MVR) > OJ mi_1-*ru* (see.ADN). In monosyllabic irregular verbs the suffix initial vowel drops, while the stem-final vowel assimilates to the vowel of the suffix: **kə-oro* (VD) > **kəro* (ASS) > **koro* (MVR) > *kuru* (come.ADN); **sə-oro* (VD) > *səro* (ASS) > *soro* (MVR) > *suru* (do.ADN). Since the verb root was monosyllabic and therefore automatically long, Whitman's rule of mediale **r* loss did not apply here. Note that in Section 3.3.4 (47), OJ *in-* 'to go, leave, depart' along with the other verbs belonging to the n-irregular verb paradigm are derived from a single monosyllabic verb root pJ **na-* 'to go', which explains their adnominal form *-uru*.

Still in line with Unger's rule, the first vowel is expected to drop, when a polysyllabic vowel final root meets a polysyllabic vowel initial suffix. Thus, for the quadrigrades, the development is as following: **aka-oro* (VD) > **ak-oro* (rL) > **ak-o* (MVR) > *aku* (open.ADN). Here, Whitman's rule, suggesting that **r* was lost in pre-OJ if the preceding vowel was short, but retained if the preceding vowel was long, applies. If the causative-anticausative suffix **-Ci-* indeed was the source of the bigrade conjugation, as suggested in Section 6.7.1, it follows that all bigrades are originally polysyllabic in origin. Therefore, we expect that the stem-final vowel will drop. However, since this vowel is a diphthong and since it is the only means to distinguish the causativity of the root, it will leave a trace in the length of the following suffix: *aka-Ci-oro > *akay-oro (VD) > *ak-o:ro (MVR) > OJ akuru; *iki-Ci-oro > *ikiy-oro > ik-o:ro (MVR) > ok-uru (raise.CAUS. ADN). Because monosyllabic bigrade verbs can be derived from originally disyllabic stems, Unger's rule that the first vowel will be deleted, applies here as well. The adnominal form of OJ pi_2- 'to dry (intr.)' and OJ pe_2- 'to pass, elapse (intr.)', for instance, derives as OJ *pu-Ci-oro > *pui-oro (VD) > p-o:ro (MVR) > OJ puru (dry. ANTICAUS.ADN) and *pa-Ci-oro > *pay-oro (VD) > *p-o:ro (MVR) > OJ puru (pass. ANTICAUS.ADN), respectively.

The standard use of WOJ -uru / -ru / -u is adnominal, but there are cases when this suffix is used as a nominal or a finite form. Well-known examples of finite use are cases of the *kakari-musubi* phenomenon, a kind of agreement in which certain focus particles are believed to trigger the use of the suffix as a finite form in the main clause. Wrona (2008: 205), however, argues that "Diachronically, however, *kakari-musubi* involves two interdependent morpho-syntactic elements, the particle and the predicate form. No triggering was originally involved." Indeed, in cases of so-called *kakari-musubi*, the insubordinated form signals the evaluative nature of the proposition, whereas the focus particles specify the exact nature of the speakers reaction such as question, exclamation, confirmation, explanation etc.[4] This viewpoint can be further supported by advancing cases, such as the example of finite use in (9c), where the adnominalizer is insubordinated, even though *kakari-musubi* particles are absent. Example (9) illustrates the non-finite and finite use of the WOJ (ad)nominalizer -uru / -ru / -u.

(9) The use of the Western Old Japanese (ad)nominalizer -u / -uru / -ru

    a. clausal nominalization
          $punapi_1to_2$-wo mi_1-**ru**-ga to_2mo_2si-sa
          boat.people-ACC see-**NML**-GEN enviable-NML
          'How enviable it is to see the boat-people!'
          (MYS 15: 3658; Wrona 2008: 206)

    b. clausal adnominalization
          op-i_1-k-**uru** mo_2no_2
          pursue-CONV-come-**ADN** thing
          'the things that pursue [us]' (MYS 5: 804; Vovin 2009a: 613)

---

[4] Note that in instances of replacement of finite forms by verbal nouns cross-linguistically, these forms often express the speakers reaction to the proposition, for instance, in independent exclamative clauses in a number of Daghestanian languages (Kalinina and Sumbatova 2007: 210, 224–225) or in Barbareño Chumash, Navajo and Central Alaskan Yup'ik (Mithun 2008, (forthcoming)).

c. finite
ide ika-ni kokodaku ko₁p-**uru**
Oh why so.much love-**FIN**
'Oh, why do I love her this much?' (MYS 12: 2889; Wrona 2008: 206)

According to Vovin's (2009a: 627) description of the Eastern Old Japanese (ad) nominalizer, "the functions are the same as in WOJ", that is both non-finite (ad) nominal and finite use are attested. The suffix has three allomorphs EOJ *-uru* / *-ru* / *-u*, which have the same distribution as in Western Old Japanese. Besides, Eastern Old Japanese has a special adnominal form $-o_1$ that can be used alternatively instead of *-u* following quadrigrade and r-irregular verbs (e.g. OJ *ar-* 'to exist' → *ar-u* ~ *ar-o₁*). EOJ $-o_1$ can also follow the *-n-* perfective, which belongs to the n-irregular verb class and thus has an alternative attributive on *-uru* (e.g. ki_1-*n-uru* ~ ki_1-*n-wo* come-CONV-PERF-ADN). In line with Frellesvig & Whitman (2008: 22–24) and Frellesvig (2008: 190), the *-u* ~ o_1 allomorphy can probably be seen as an instance of partial mid vowel raising in final position, whereby EOJ did not completely accomplish the raising of pJ *o > o_1 (*wo*) > *u*, as reflected for instance in WOJ *sugu-s-* ~ EOJ $sugo_1$-*s-* 'to pass (tr.)'. Thus, for quadrigrades and *r*-irregular verbs in certain varieties of EOJ, the final vowel of the adnominalizer has only partially raised, e.g. in the adnominal form of OJ *ak-* 'to open (intr.)': **aka-oro* (VD) > **ak-oro* (rL) > **ak-o* (partial MVR) > EOJ *ak-o₁*. Given that the adnominal $-o_1$ occurs much less than the allomorph *-u*, it can be seen as a relic of a phonological change that was under way in Eastern Old Japanese.

This morphological analysis of the allomorph EOJ $-o_1$ leaves room for Russell's (2006: 641–644) reconstruction of pJ *-ə as a more archaic (ad)nominalizer that became replaced by pJ *(w)oro. The suffix pJ *-ə is reflected in the adnominal form WOJ n-o_2 of the defective copula WOJ *n-*, in some exceptional adnominal forms such as EOJ *map-am-o₂* (dance-TENT-ADN) '[she] is going to dance' (FK 7), in the adnominal forms on *-o* in the dialects of Hachijo /Aogashima, Tosima and Akiyama (Pellard 2008: 139–141)[5] and in the adnominal and emphatic finite suffix pR *-o* (Thorpe 1983: 182–183, Pellard 2008: 141–143). Note that Ryukyuan *o* provides no basis for distinguishing between pJ *ə (> OJ o_2) and pJ *o (> OJ o_1), but the Old Japanese forms support the reconstruction of pJ *-ə as the earlier (ad) nominalizer.

---

5 Tosima has also insubordinated the suffix to a finite *-o*.

7.3.2 pK *-l

Korean provides evidence for the reconstruction of a clausal (ad)nominalizer pK *-l, with imperfective or perfective interpretation according to the telicity of the verb base. The contemporary Korean adnominalizer K -(u)l is usually called "prospective" because reference to the future is the most common meaning today. In Middle Korean, however, MK -(·u/o)l is the default imperfective adnominalizer, in essence time neutral (Martin 2002: 376).[6] This is seen in the explanation of the meanings of Chinese characters, such as MK nwo·phol KWO 'KWO meaning to be tall.' Moreover, the postadnominal cek 'time (when)' in (10b), which is a general statement, calls for the adnominalizer regardless of the time. It is interesting to note that the adnominalizer is reflected in some time expressions like K onul, MK wo·nol 'today' and K wolhay, MK wol ·hoy 'this year', which contain an adnominal form of the verb K o-, MK wo- 'to come', deriving from *wo-[l] ·nal (come-ADN day) and *wo-l ·hoy (come-ADN year), respectively.[7] Since 'today' and 'this year' are not equivalent to 'the coming day' and 'the coming year', but rather should be interpreted as 'the day that has (just) come' and 'the year that has (just) come', these lexicalized expressions suggest a (recent) perfective interpretation following telic verbs. Compare the use of MK ·wo-no-n ·hoy (come-PROC-ADN year) for 'next year', i.e. 'the year that is coming' and MK ·ni-·ke-n ·hoy (depart-RES-ADN year) for 'last year', i.e. 'the year that has departed'.

The modulator MK -·wᵘ/o- sometimes appears before MK -(·u/o)l. In case the modified noun is semantically the object of the adnominalized verb, as in example (10c), the modulator is always added; otherwise, the modulator is not obligatory. There are only few examples left of lexical nominalization reflecting pK *-l such as MK kuch- 'to stop' → ku·chul 'cessation' in MK ku·ch-ul-s ·sus (stop-NML-GEN time) 'a period of cessation' (1459 Wel 7: 58b; Martin 1992: 873); MK hhoyng ho- 'to travel' → hhoyng hol 'traveler' in MK HHOYNG ho-·l-oy ·PPYEN-NGUY (travel do-NML-GEN comfort) 'the comfort of the traveler' (1463/4 Yeng 2: 31a) or K cis-, MK ciž- 'to make, buid, compose, manifacture' → K ci:l, MK ·cil 'procedure' (< *cižul).

However, it is not unlikely that originally lexical nouns were derived with pK *-l, while sentential nominalization needed the incorporation of the copula pK *wo-, which would be in line with the behavior of the nominalizer pK *-m in Section 7.4.2. If the modulator indeed goes back to an original copular verb pK

---

[6] After a consonant-final stem an epenthetic vowel is inserted. The choice of the Middle Korean allomorphs -·ul or -·ol is determined by vowel harmony with the vowel of the preceding syllable.

[7] MK /l/ drops before /n/ and the other apicals /s/, /c/ and /t/.

wo- (see Section 3.4.2), then the construction pK *wo-l* (be-NML) parallels the derivation of the Japanese adnominal form pJ *wo-ra* (exist-NML) in Section 7.3.1.

While the standard function of MK *-(·u/o)l* is nominal modification, it may also be used for complementation, preceding case suffixes, such as the Middle Korean genitive marker *s* in (10a). As a finite marker the suffix precedes the interrogative marker MK *·kwo* expressing rhetorical, exclamatory or quoted questions (Martin 1992: 667) and is incorporated in the ending of explicit statement K *-uli*, MK *-(·u/o)·l i* (Martin 1992: 856–857) and in the subjunctive attentive ending K *-(u)la*, MK *-(·u/o)·la* (Martin 1992: 851, 2002: 378–379), as illustrated in (10d). The subjunctive attentive is morphologically segmentable into the imperfective adnominalizer and the vocative particle *a*, which follows nouns (e.g. K *palk-un tal-a* (shine-ADN moon-VOC) 'Oh shining moon!') and occurs in finite assumptive constructions with the nominalizer K *-(u)m* (e.g. K *Kitali-m-a* (wait-NML-VOC) 'I'll be expecting you.'). The explicit ending derives from the adnominalizer and a bound noun MK *i* 'fact (that); that (which)', which is parallel to the derivation of the Old Japanese exclamatory *-ure* in Section 7.3.1.

(10) The use of the Middle Korean (ad)nominalizer *-(·u/o)l*
    a. clausal nominalization
       "se ·twoy tu· li-l-s HHWA-PPYENG-·ul nwo-·khwo
       three measure contain-**NML**-GEN vase-ACC place-CONV
       'Placing a vase with a capacity of three cupfuls'
       (1459 Wel 10: 119 a; Martin 1992: 873)

    b. clausal adnominalization
       wo-l ce·k-uy ·kilh-i "ki-two-·ta
       come-**ADN** time-DAT way-NOM be.long-EMO-FIN
       'The way is long when coming [here]'
       (1481 Twusi 17: 17a; Martin 2002: 376)

    c. modulated clausal adnominalization
       ccywung-soyng-oy nip-wu-l wos
       common.people-NOM wear-MOD-**ADN** clothing
       'clothes that the common people wear'
       (1459 Wel 8: 65; Ramsey & Lee 2011: 206)

    d. finite
       ·QILQ-SIM-·u·lwo kwoyGwoy ho-·la
       wholehearted-ADV silence do-**SUBJ**
       'Be utterly quiet!' (1464 Kumkang 12a; Martin 1992: 851)

The examples above suggest that pK *-l began as a derivational nominalizer applied to verb stems to create nouns: 'to stop' → 'cessation'. Noun stems expressing properties could be juxtaposed to other nominals to add supplementary information. Whereas lexical nouns were derived by adding the suffix *-l directly to verbal stems, clausal nominalizations incorporated the copula *wo- 'to be'. The relative clauses marked with pK *-(wo)-l developed one step further to mark syntactically independent sentences which added supplementary information in discourse such as question, exclamation, confirmation and explanation. As such, the deverbal (ad)nominalizer pK *-l does not only correspond to pJ *-ra in form and function, but the correlations also involve the incorporation of a cognate copula *wo- 'to be' in clausal (ad)nominalization and the further development to finite use in particular discourse contexts.

7.3.3 pTg *-rA

The deverbal noun suffix pTg *-rA can be reconstructed as a suffix that derived nominal and adnominal forms from verb stems on the basis of a few lexicalized relics, mainly in Even and Evenki. The suffix is better preserved as a marker of clausal (ad)nominalization in the Tungusic languages. In most Tungusic languages, the adnominalizer -rA occurs on the lexical verb in negative constructions in which the negative verb e- acts as a finite form (see Section 4.3.3). Only in Manchu the suffix is still productive as a marker of argument subordination and nominal modification. In the other Tungusic languages, more recent deverbal noun suffixes of the shape pTg *-ri: have replaced the old ones on *-rA in the adnominal and nominal functions. In the Southern Tungusic languages, the reflex of pTg *-ri: is also gradually replacing the older finite forms in *-rA.

Similar to the Old Japanese exclamatory -ure and the Middle Korean explicit ending -(·u/o)·l i (see Sections 7.3.1. and 7.3.2), the Tungusic formant pTg *-ri: can be derived from the (ad)nominalizer *-ra and a bound noun pTg i: 'fact, thing'. Benzing (1955a: 1072, 1076) proposes to derive pTg *-ri: from the adnominalizer *-ra and a nominalizer *-gi:, but this is unlikely because the Northern Tungusic languages preserve no trace of a velar. In line with Benzing (1955a: 978), intervocalic *-g- is expected to be preserved in the Northern Tungusic languages, while it would drop in Manchuric and Southern Tungusic (e.g. pTg *tege- 'to sit, sit down' > Evk./Sol. tege-, Even teg-, Neg. teVet-, Ma te-, Orok/Oroch./Ud. te:-, Na. te:si-). It is more plausible to derive pTg *-ri: from *-rA-i, a derivation also considered by Menges (1968: 205) and Street (1978: 174).[8]

---

[8] Sunik (1962: 227) reconstructed pTg *ray as the ancestor of both nominalizers -rA and -ri:.

The forms reflecting pTg *-rA are maintained, however, in the finite paradigms throughout the Tungusic languages. Except for Manchu, the Tungusic languages display conjugational classes, in which an adnominal form of the verb – most frequently derived with *-rA – is followed by personal predicative suffixes. In the Southern Tungusic languages, the reflexes of pTg *-ri: with original present progressive-habitual meaning are gradually replacing the reflexes of pTg *-rA with original present meaning.

It is interesting to see that in some Northern Tungusic languages, such as Even and Evenki, the finite temporal interpretation depends on actional semantics of the verb: derived from telic verbs, -rA refers to the recent past, whereas derived from atelic verbs, it refers to the present. This suggests that the proto-Tungusic clausal adnominalizer pTg *-rA displayed imperfective or perfective interpretation according to the telicity of the verb base and recalls the etymology of Korean 'today' and 'this year' (Section 7.3.2).

The examples below suggest that pTg *-ra began as a derivational nominalizer applied to verb stems to create nouns: 'to snow' → 'snow'. In Tungusic – as in most Transeurasian languages – noun stems expressing properties could be juxtaposed to other nominals: 'to snow' → 'snow (man)'. The (ad)nominalizers were then extended to the clause level to mark clausal (ad)nominalization in complement and relative clauses. The relative clauses developed one step further to mark syntactically independent sentences. Initially, these constructions may have added supplementary information, but gradually they generalized as the default indicative ending.

7.3.3.1 Manchu -rA

In Manchu, the imperfective (ad)nominalizer -ra ~ -re ~ -ro is productive in adnominal, nominal and finite function, as illustrated in example (11). Manchu has no conjugational paradigm reflecting finite forms because unlike the other Tungusic languages it has no grammatical category of person.

(11) The use of the Manchu (ad)nominalizer -rA

    a.   clausal nominalization
           *mama-de   ala-**ra**-de,   mama   hendu-me...*
           old.woman-DAT tell-**NML**-DAT old.woman say-CONV
           'When [he] tells [it] to the old woman, the old woman says: "..."'
           (Gorelova 2002: 257)

    b.   clausal adnominalization
           *bargiyata-**ra**   niyalma*
           protect-**ADN**   people
           'people who protect [him]' (Gorelova 2002: 485)

c. finite
si   nene-me   isinji-ci   uthai   sin-de   bu-re
you   be.first-CONV come-CONV at.once you-DAT   give-FIN
'If you come first, I shall give [it] to you straight away'
(Gorelova 2002: 256)

7.3.3.2 Even

In Even, *-ra ~ -re* is reflected in some lexicalized nouns and nominal adjectives, which derive from verbs, such as Even *da:l-* 'to be sweet, pleasant, light' → *dalra* 'sweet, tasty', Even *eden-* 'to be windy, to blow (of wind)' → *edenre* 'windy', Even *eman-* 'to snow, fall (of snow)' → *emanra* 'snow, snow-', e.g. *eman-ra beike:n* (snow-ADN doll) 'a snowman'. In finite function, *-rA* is productive on the vast majority of verbs as a conjugational basis to which person endings are added. Table 2 illustrates the common division into conjugational classes in Even (Benzing 1955a: 1079–1080, Benzing 1955b: 90, Malchukov 1995: 16, Menges 1968: 122–123). Most Even verbs take a *-rA* base, following the pattern of *ma:-* 'to kill' (< pTg **wa:-*) or *ngen*$_{(2)}$*-* 'to go' (< pTg **ŋene-*). A few verbs, however, follow the pattern of *gu:n*$_{(1)}$*-* 'to say', *bi-* 'to be' or *ga-* 'to take', taking different bases on *-nA*, *-sA* or *-dA*, which can be derived from aspectually distinctly marked (ad)nominalizers. The temporal interpretation of the finite form depends on the actional semantics of the preceding verb. Derived from telic verbs, *-rA* refers to the recent past, e.g. Even *em-re-n* (come-FIN-3SG) '(he) has just come', whereas derived from atelic verbs, it refers to the present, e.g. Even *hong-ra-n* (weep-FIN-3SG) 'he weeps' (Malchukov 2000: 443).

Table 2. Conjugational classes in Even

	ma:- 'kill'	< pTg **wa:-*	*ngen*$_{(2)}$*-* 'go'	*gu:n*$_{(1)}$*-* 'say'	*bi-* 'be'	*ga-* 'take'
1SG	ma:-ra-m	*wa:-rA-n(A)-bi	ngen-re-m	gu:-ne-m	bi-se-m	ga-da-m
2SG	ma:-nri	*wa:-rA-n(A)-si	ngene-nri	gu:-ne-nri	bi-se-nri	ga-da-nri
3SG	ma:-n	*wa:-rA-ni	ngen-re-n	gu:-n-ni	bi-s-ni	ga-d-ni
1PL	ma:-ra-p	*wa:-rA-pti	ngen-re-p	gu:-ne-p	bi-se-p	ga-da-p
1EX	ma:-r-u:	*wa:-rA-bu	ngen-r-u	gu:-n-u	bi-s-u	ga-d-u
2PL	ma:-s	*wa:-rA-su	ngene-s	gu:-ne-s	bi-se-s	ga-da-s
3PL	ma:-r	*wa:-rA	ngen-re	gu:-n	bi-s	ga-d

7.3.3.3 Evenki

Except for a few lexicalized deverbal adjectives such as Evk. *langa-* 'to break a tooth' → *langara* 'toothless' (Nedjalkov 1997: 305), Evenki *-ra ~ -re* is maintained in the finite verb paradigm. Table 3 illustrates the common division into conjugational classes in Even (Benzing 1955a: 1079, Menges 1968: 84, Nedjalkov 1997: 259, Bulatova & Grenoble 1999: 35).

Table 3. Conjugational classes in Evenki

	wa:- 'kill'	< pTg *wa:-*	*ngene-* 'go'	*gu:n-* 'say'	*bi-* 'be'	*ga-* 'take'
1SG	wa:-m	*wa:-rA-n(A)-bi	ngene-m	gu:-ne-m	bi-si-m	ga-m
2SG	wa:-nni	*wa:-rA-n(A)-si	ngene-nni	gu:-ne-nni	bi-si-nni	ga-nni
3SG	wa:-re-n	*wa:-rA-ni	ngene-re-n	gu:-ne-n	bi-si-n	ga-da-n
1PL	wa:-re-p	*wa:-rA-pti	ngene-re-p	gu:-ne-p	bi-si-p	ga-da-p
1EX	wa:-re-w(un)	*wa:-rA-bu	ngene-re-w	gu:-ne-w	bi-si-w	ga-da-w
2PL	wa:-re-s(un)	*wa:-rA-su	ngene-re-s	gu:-ne-s	bi-si-s	ga-da-s
3PL	wa:-re	*wa:-rA	ngene-re	gu:-ne	bi-si	ga-da

The temporal interpretation of Evk. *-rA* depends on the actional semantics of the preceding verb (Nedjalkov 1997: 237–237). Derived from telic verbs, i.e. verbs of achievement, accomplishment and from activity verbs in which a temporal boundary is arbitrary but implied, *-rA* refers to the recent past, as illustrated in (12a) and (12b). Derived from atelic verbs, such as verbs derived with the habitual aspect marker *-ngnA* and verbs of state, *-rA* refers to the present, as illustrated in (12c) and (12d).

(12) The use of the Evenki finite *-rA*

    a. *Ami-m eme-**re**-n.*
       father-1SG.POSS come-**FIN**-3SG
       'My father has come' (Nedjalkov 1997: 237)

    b. *Nungartïn amin-du-ver bele-**re**.*
       they father-DAT-REFL.POSS help-**FIN**
       'They helped their father' (Nedjalkov 1997: 237)

    c. *Nungartïn amin-du-ver bele-ngne-**re***
       they father-DAT-REFL.POSS help-HAB-**FIN**
       solo-s-toki-n.
       boat.upstream-SMLF-CONV-3SG.POSS
       'They always help their father when he goes upstream in a boat'
       (Nedjalkov 1997: 238)

d. *Sa:-**re**-n*
   know-**FIN**-3SG
   'He knows' (Nedjalkov 1997: 237)

7.3.3.4 Udehe

Due to *-r-* loss, the reflexes of the (ad)nominalizer pTg *-rA* in Udehe are not readily identifiable. In the finite paradigm, the suffix has completely fused with preceding vowel stems like Ud. *wa:-* 'kill' and *ŋene-* 'go'. The consonant stems belonging to the class of Ud. *gun-* 'say', however, include stems ending in a consonant different than *-n-*, notably in *-p-, -g-, -m-* such as Ud. *bap-* 'to understand', *nag-* 'to get in, reach' and *cam-* 'to break (intr.)'. The finite bases of these verbs are *bapta-, nagda-,* and *camna-*, respectively, reflecting assimilations of pTg *-ra-* to the stem-final consonant. Table 4 illustrates the conjugational classes in Udehe (Benzing 1955a: 1078; Nikolaeva 1999: 120–125, 141, Menges 1968: 161–162).

Table 4. Conjugational classes in Udehe

	wa:- 'kill'	< pTg *wa:-	*ngene-* 'go'	*gun-* 'say'	*bi-* 'be'	*ga-* 'take'
1SG	*wa:-mi*	**wa:-ra-n(A)-bi*	*ngene-mi*	*gu-ne-mi*	*bi-mi*	*ga-da-mi*
2SG	*wa:-(h)i*	**wa:-ra-n(A)-si*	*ngene-(h)i*	*gu-ne-(h)i*	*bi:*	*ga-da-(h)i*
3SG	*wa:-i-ni*	**wa:-ra-i:-ni*	*ngene-i-ni*	*gu-ne-i-ni*	*bi:-ni*	*ga-da-i-ni*
1PL	*wa:-fi*	**wa:-ra-pti*	*ngene-fi*	*gu-ne-fi*	*bi-fi*	*ga-da-fi*
1EX	*wa:-u*	**wa-ra-bu*	*ngene-u*	*gu-ne-u*	*bi-u*	*ga-da-u*
2PL	*wa:-(h)u*	**wa:-ra-su*	*ngene-(h)u*	*gu-ne-(h)u*	*bi-(h)u*	*ga-da-(h)u*
3PL	*wa:-i-ti*	**wa:-ra-i:-ti*	*ngene-i-ti*	*gu-ne-i-ti*	*bi:-ti*	*ga-da-i-ti*

As illustrated in (13), the originally composite suffix Ud. *-i* (< pTg *-ri:* < *-ra-i:*) has replaced the reflex of pTg *-ra* in the third person finite, similar to the renewal in argument subordination and nominal modification. The temporal interpretation of the finite suffix is restricted to the present, it mainly expresses progressive or habitual meaning.

(13) The use of the Udehe (ad)nominalizer *-i*
   a. clausal nominalization
      Bi   sa:-mi   Iwana eme-gi:-we-ni
      I   know.PST-1SG   Ivan come-REP.**NML**-ACC-3SG
      'I knew that Ivan is coming.' (Nikolaeva 1999: 161)

b. clausal adnominalization
   *ni:-we   wa:-**i**   amba*
   man-ACC kill-**ADN** spirit
   'the spirit who kills people' (Nikolaeva 1999: 160)

c. finite
   *Wasia   mäusa-wa   zawa-**i**-ni*
   Vasya   gun-ACC   take-**FIN**-3SG
   'Vasya is taking the gun' (Nikolaeva 1999: 146)

7.3.3.5 Nanai

In Nanai, the reflexes of the (ad)nominalizer pTg *-rA* are still visible in the finite paradigm, following verb stems ending in a long vowel, such as Na. *wa:-* 'to kill'. In short vowel stems, such as Na. *ene-* 'go', the *-r-* of the suffix dropped and the vowel fused with the stem. The conjugational class of Na. *un-* 'to say' includes a few consonant verbs ending in a consonant different than *-n-*, notably in *-l-* and *-p-*, such as Na. *jep-* 'to eat' and *mal-* 'to destroy'. The finite bases of these verbs are *jep-ta-* / *jep-ci-* and *mal-ji-*, respectively, reflecting assimilations of pTg of *-ra-*/*-ra-i-* to the stem-final consonant. Table 5 illustrates the conjugational classes in Nanai (Benzing 1955a: 1078, Menges 1968: 223–225, Avrorin 1961: 102, Sunik 1962: 51).

Table 5. Conjugational classes in Nanai

	wa:- 'kill'	< pTg *wa:-	*ene-* 'go'	*un-* 'say'	*bi-* 'be'	*ga-* 'take'
1SG	wa:-ra-m-bi	*wa:-ra-n(A)-bi	ene-:-m-bi	un-de-m-bi	bi-e-m-bi	ga-da-m-bi
2SG	wa:-ra-ci	*wa:-ra-n(A)-si	ene-:-ci	un-de-ci	bi-e-ci	ga-da-ci
3SG	wa:-ra	*wa:-ra	ene-re	un-de	bi-e	ga-da
1PL	wa:-ra-pu	*wa:-ra-puti	ene-:-pu	un-de-pu	bi-e-pu	ga-da-pu
2PL	wa:-ra-su	*wa:-ra-su	ene-:-su	un-de-su	bi-e-su	ga-da-u
3PL	wa:-ra-l	*wa:-ra-l	ene-re-l	un-de-l	bi-e-l	ga-da-l

As illustrated in (14), the originally composite suffix Na. *-i* (< pTg *-ri:* < *-ra-i:*) has completely replaced the Nanai reflex of pTg *-ra* in nominal and adnominal use. In finite function, both markers are still in use, whereby the Nanai reflex of pTg *-ra* expresses the present tense and Na. *-i* the present progressive (Menges 1968: 225).

(14) The use of the Nanai (ad)nominalizers

a. clausal nominalization
Alosimji mi daiji xola-i-wa   makta-xa-ni.
teacher I loud read-**NML**-ACC praise-PST-3SG
'The teacher praised my reading aloud.' (Avrorin 1961: 82)

b. clausal adnominalization
mi xola-i daŋsa
me read-**ADN** book
'the book that I read' (Benzing 1955a: 1078)

c. finite
xola:-mbi.   *xola-i:.*
read.**FIN**-1SG   read-**FIN**.1SG
'I read' (Benzing 1955a: 1078)   'I am reading'

7.3.4 pMo *-r

The deverbal noun suffix pMo *-r can be reconstructed as a suffix that derived verb stems from nouns in Mongolic. As illustrated in (15a), the suffix -r, with the epenthetic vowel -u- / -ü- if the stem ends in a consonant, commonly derives deverbal nouns in Mongolic (Poppe 1954: 49; Street 1957: 58).

In Written Mongolian, there are relics of clausal nominalization in the converb of goal in -rA (see (15b)), which can be derived from *-r marking a complement clause plus the dative suffix in *-A and in the preparative converb in -run, which is a compound of *-r and the genitive suffix in *-un (Ramstedt 1952: 87; Poppe 1954: 59, 98, 180; Baskakov 1981: 73).[9]

Lexical adnominalization is reflected in adjectives and in lexicalized adnominal constructions, such as the ones given in (15c), which commonly combine a nominal and adnominal use. Derivations from transitive verbs may represent either subject nouns (e.g. WMo. *irüger* 'prayer', *sibar* 'mud', *üyer* 'flood') or object nouns (e.g. WMo. *belčiger* 'grass on a pasture', *čilger* 'slender', *öndür* 'high, height', *qayir* 'gravel'), which suggests that the suffix *-r could express either imperfective or perfective aspect. Although the examples in (15) do not suggest a clear-cut relation between the aspect distinction and the semantics of

---

9 As for the converb of goal in WMo. -rA, Vovin (1998) contends that "there is no internal Mongolic evidence for this segmentation, as -Vr does not occur by itself or with other case markers besides alleged dative-locative -a/-e." but the existence of the preparative converb in WMo. -run and the attestation of the forms in (15a) contradict his claim.

the preceding verb, telicity seems to correlate with past tense in Khitan, a sister language of proto-Mongolic. Examples of finite use in Mongolic are lacking, but it is remarkable that among the markers of past tense in Khitan, we find the suffix -*r*, which is only preserved in telic expressions, such as 'become', 'become appointed', 'become awarded', 'compose an edict', 'write this text' (Kane 2009: 145–146), see example (15d).

(15) The use of the Written/Middle Mongolian (ad)nominalizer -*(U)r* and the Khitan past -*r*

   a. lexical nominalization

   MMo. *andaqa-* 'swear an oath of friendship' → *andaqar* 'oath of friendship'

   WMo. *belčige-* 'to pasture, graze (tr.)' → *belčiger* 'pasture, grazing grounds, grass on a pasture'

   WMo. *čayi-* 'to become white, turn pale, turn grey (of hair); dawn, grow light (intr.)' -> *čayir* 'zinc, tin'

   WMo. *irüge-* 'bless, pray, wish well (tr. /intr.)' → *irüger* 'prayer, blessing'

   WMo. *üyi-* 'to put meat, vegetables or other ingredients into boiling water or soup (tr.)' → *üyer* 'inundation, flood'

   b. clausal nominalization

   WMo. eke-yügen   eri-**re**   od-bai
        mother-ACC   search-**CONV**   go-PST
   'He went to find her mother' (Sárközi 2004: 47)

   c. lexical adnominalization

   MMo. / WMo. *amu-* 'to rest, relax; be relieved (intr.)' → *amur* 'peace, quiet, calm, rest; easy; peacefully, quietly', e.g. *amur azil* 'easy work'

   WMo. *čilege-* 'to tire, exhaust, render weak (tr.) ' → *čilger* 'slender, well-proportioned (of body)'

   WMo. *siba-* 'to plaster, apply mud, cover or gather thickly on something (as insects) (tr. /intr.)' → *sibar* 'mud, slush, clay, plaster; covered with mud', e.g. *sibar bayising* 'adobe house'

   WMo. *öndüyi-* 'to raise one's hand, raise oneself, rise slightly (intr.)' → *öndür* 'high, tall; height'

   WMo. *qayi-* 'to hew, square; cut, chop (tr.)' → *qayir* 'gravel, coarse sand, pebbles', e.g. *qayir cilayu* 'coarse gravel'

   WMo. *qusu-* 'to scrape, shave (tr.)' → *qusur* 'pointed', e.g. *qusur sumun* 'arrow without a whistling head'

d. finite

    Khitan *puu giuuŋ shï po-**or***
               fu   gong shi become-**PST.FIN**
    'He was appointed a fu gong shi' (Kane 2009: 146)

The examples above suggest that pMo *-r began as a derivational nominalizer applied to verb stems to create nouns: 'to pray' → 'prayer', whereby noun stems expressing properties could be juxtaposed to other nominals: 'to relax' → 'easy (work)'. The (ad)nominalizers were then extended to the clause level to mark clausal (ad)nominalization. There is no evidence that these dependent clauses developed one step further to mark syntactically independent sentences in Mongolic proper, but they probably did in the para-Mongolic language of the Khitan.

7.3.5 pTk *-rV

7.3.5.1 Old Turkic

The deverbal noun suffix pTk *-rV is reflected as a suffix that derived nouns from verb stems in Old Turkic such as in a number of derivational pairs given in (16a). Derivations from transitive verbs may represent either subject nouns (e.g. Tk. *keser* 'adze', OTk *tiler* 'the praying mantis') or object nouns (e.g. OTk. *üŋür* 'cave, cavity'), which suggests that the suffix pTk *-rV could express either imperfective or perfective aspect.

In Old Turkic, the clausal adnominalizer *-(A)r*, which is known under the label "aorist", is still productive in its adnominal use as in (16b), but it is used more often as a finite predicate as in (16c) (Erdal 2004: 282, 284). It is formed with *-Ar* after most simple consonant stems, *-Ur* or *-Ir* after diathetic consonants stems and *-yUr* or *-r* after vowel stems. In Runic Old Turkic we find a number of monosyllabic verb stems that exceptionally form their adnominal form on *-Ur* or *-Ir*, such as *kel-* 'come' → *kelir* and *bar-* 'go' → *barïr*. In section 3.4.1 it has been argued that the allomorphs *-yUr* /*-Ur* and *-Ar* derive from suffix strings in which pTk *-rV follows the copular verbs *u- 'to become' and *a- 'to be', respectively, while the allomorph *-Ir* would reflect a stem-final *-i*.

(16) The use of the Old Turkic adnominalizer *-(A)r*

    a.   lexical nominalization

          OTk *kes-* 'to cut (tr.)' → Tk. *keser* 'adze' (Poppe 1964: 12–13)

          OTk. *kïs-* 'to compress, squeeze, pinch (tr.)' → *kïsïr* 'having the sexual organs constricted, sterile, barren (of woman, animal)'

OTk. *tam-* 'to drip (intr.)' → OTk. *tamar* 'vein, artery'

OTk *teg-* 'to reach, be worth (intr.)' → *tegir* 'share, value, price'

OTk *tile-* 'to seek, desire, pray for (tr.)' → *tiler* 'the praying mantis, name of some kind of insect'

OTk. *tug-* 'to be born, to rise (of sun) (intr.)' → *tugar* 'sunrise, east'

OTk *u-* 'to be able, capable (intr.)' → *uyur / uyar* 'ability; capable, powerful'

OTk. *üŋ-* 'to dig a hole in, to hollow out (tr.)' → *üŋür* 'cave, cavity, something hollowed out'

OTk. *yat-* 'to lie down (intr.)' → *yatar / yatur* '(something) lying down, invalid'

b. clausal adnominalization

ak-ïp   kel-ir   sogïk suv
flow-CONV come-**ADN** cold water
'cold water flowing forth (or coming up)' (TT I 104; Erdal 2004: 284–285)

c. finite

Ölüm-tä   oz-upan   ögir-ä   savin-ü   yorï-r.
death-ABL escape-CONV rejoice-CONV be.happy-CONV go.on-**FIN**
'Having been saved from death it happily goes on with its life.'
(Erdal 2004: 325)

The examples above suggest that pTk *-rA* began as a derivational nominalizer applied to verb stems to create nouns: 'to rise' → 'sunrise', whereby noun stems expressing properties could be juxtaposed to other nominals: 'to lie down' → '(thing) lying down'. The (ad)nominalizers were then extended to the clause level to mark clausal (ad)nominalization. Relative clauses developed one step further to mark syntactically independent sentences with a present continuous meaning.

The final vowel in the reconstruction of pTk *-rV* is supported by the negative adnominalizer OTk. *-mA-z*, in which *-z* follows the negative suffix, where the positive adnominalizer has *-r* after vowels. The assumption that in coda position, pTk *-r* became *-z* in Eastern Old Turkic, but was preserved as *-r* in Western Old Turkic and its modern representative Chuvash, could very well apply to the development of OTk. *-mA-z*, if we assume that the suffix originally had an additional vowel (Erdal 2004: 84–85).[10] This vowel would have dropped in the

---

[10] This hypothesis, known as "zetacism", is supported by internal doublets such as OTk. *köküz* 'breast' vs. *kökr-äk* 'breast(-DIM)' and by the correspondence with *-r(-)* in Chuvash and

negative adnominalizer earlier than in the positive, as stress was on the syllable preceding -mA- in the first case but on the suffix in the second.[11] When the vowel in the negative adnominalizer pTk *-ma-r[V] dropped, "zetacism" was still operative and yielded OTk -ma-z. For reason of stress, however, the vowel was retained longer in the positive adnominalizer *-rV and when it dropped, "zetacism" was no longer operative, which led to r- retention in OTk. -(A)r.

7.3.5.2 Chuvash

Johanson (1975) proposed that the Turkic aorist has been preserved in Chuvash, surviving as a so-called finite "future" in -Ă. However, his proposal will not be considered here for the following reasons. First, the phonology of this derivation is complex, requiring the determination of a possible environment for -r loss and the development of the final lax vowel -Ă.[12] Second, although the habitual and generic use of this suffix may be compatible with the meaning of the Turkic aorist, its futuritive function expressing modal connotations such as wish, necessity, expectation and intention is not. Third, Chuvash -Ă has an alternative internal etymology, proposed by Pritsak (1960: 148–153), relating it to the deverbal noun suffix -Ă, which is phonologically and semantically less problematic and has a convincing external parallel (see Section 8.4.5.2).

---

in the Transeurasian languages, e.g. OTk *yüz* 'face', Chuvash *śăvar* 'mouth', WMo. *düri* 'form, appearance, expression of the face, look', Neg. *dujun / dujin*, Evk. *durun*, Olcha. *duru(n)*, Orok *duru(n)* 'pattern, design', Ma. *durugan* 'picture' and OJ *tura* 2.3. 'cheeks, face' (Robbeets 2005: 77–79, 342–343). Opponents of "zetacism" would argue that this development is unseen cross-linguistically, while the opposite development, known as "rhotacism" is very frequent across the languages of the world. However, in Gedaged (Oceanic), there is evidence of a regular sound change of *r > z (e.g. GED *pizi* 'to weave' < POc **piri* and GED *zez* 'to be afraid' < POc **rere*) and Straka (1979) discusses /r/ > [z] in the history of French (Juliette Blevins pc.).

11 Erdal (2004: 98) assumes that in Old Turkic, the verbal negation suffix -mA- was pre-stressed as it is in contemporary Turkic languages.

12 Note that the development of -Ă may be due to the addition of final lax vowel in Chuvash to words originally ending in a consonant, illustrated in Section 7.5.5.2. The addition of the lax vowel to the suffix *-(A)r may have yielded an additional syllable in the adnominal form which triggered the deletion of the binding vowel. When the resulting consonant clusters involved *t, m, n*, they may have provided an environment for r-loss because Chuvash verbs with stem-final -r, drop -r when they cluster with *t-, m-* or *n-* initial suffixes (e.g. *tăr-* 'stand' → *tă-tă-m* (stand-PST-1SG), *tă-nă* (stand-PFV.PCP), *tă-ma* (stand-NML)). This development may be schematized as following: pTk *yėt-ere > *yėt-er (overtake-ADN) > pWOT * śit-er (reach-ADN) > (lax vowel addition) *śit-erĕ > (binding vowel deletion) *śit-rĕ > (cluster -r-loss) śit-ĕ. However, this explanation cannot account for the r-loss in stems ending in consonants other than *t, m* and *n*.

A more plausible cognate may be Chu. -r, with the allomorph -t following stems ending in l, n, r. The suffix occurs in the derivational pair in (17a), which is cognate with OTk. kïs- → kïsïr above (Fedotov 1996: 330). The high vowel of the ending reflects an original stem-final *ï, i.e. pTk *kïsï- → kïsïr. This suggests that the derivation already took place in proto-Turkic and was then inherited as a lexical item in the western and eastern branches of Turkic. As illustrated in (17b), Chu. -r further marks perfective relative clauses. Finally, the suffix -r is used to express a finite past tense, which Krüger (1961: 145) describes as expressing "a clearly past action, not relative to any other past, being more like a perfect tense: I have seen, have written."; see example (17c). He adds that "[s]ome persons speculate that these formations like the preterite arose from an original noun, in this case, in -r, to which reduced personal pronouns were added, ...". The negative marker mar 'no, not' that occurs before verbs and as a postposition in the negative imperative and voluntative may preserve a trace of the allomorph -r with non-past function (see Sections 4.3.5.2 and 4.4).

(17) Reflexes of the deverbal noun suffix pTk *-rV in Chuvash

    a. lexical nominalization

        Chu. xĕs- 'to compress, squeeze, pinch (tr.)' → xĕsĕr 'sterile, barren'

    b. clausal adnominalization

        xura   vărman   vitĕr   tux-**r**-ăm   čux-ne
        black   forest   through   go.out-**PFV.NML**-POSS.1SG   time-DAT
        'When I went out through the black forest' (Benzing 1959: 742)

    c. finite

        văl   sirĕ   palla-**r**-ĕ
        he   you.OBL   recognize-**PST.FIN**-POSS.3SG
        'He recognized you' (Krüger 1961: 146)

7.3.5.3 Yakut

Yakut has two imperfect paradigms. The first paradigm is composed of the so-called "analytic" imperfect, e.g. *Min bar-ar ä-ti-m* (I go-NML be-PST-POSS.1SG) 'I was going away'. The second paradigm, illustrated in Table 6, is composed of the so-called "synthetic" imperfect, e.g. *Min bar-ar-ïm* (I go-NML-POSS.1SG)'I was going away' (Stachowski 2006; Johanson 2014), in which the cognate Yakut aorist -Ar- expresses the imperfect. Stachowski (2006: 138) and Johanson (2014: 239–241) find that the past use of this marker is highly remarkable for a Turkic language and consider the possibility that it has been copied from the Even past paradigm in -ri. Alternatively, under the present analysis, the preterite use may represent an inherently Turkic feature.

Table 6. The "synthetic" imperfect paradigm in Yakut based on the verb *bar-* 'to go' (Johanson 2014: 236)

	SG	PL
1	Bar-ar-ïm	Bar-ar-bït
2	Bar-ar-ïŋ	Bar-ar-bït
3	Bar-ar-a	Bar-al-lar-a

In the common ancestor of Old Turkic, Yakut and Chuvash, the finite temporal interpretation of the adnominalizer may have depended on the actional semantics of the verb base, as it did in other Transeurasian languages: derived from telic verbs it may have derived perfective forms, whereas derived from atelic verbs such as the negative existential verb, it may have derived imperfective forms. In finite position, perfective adnominals developed to past tense, while imperfective adnominals developed continuous present meaning. In Chuvash, the original functional distinction disappeared in favor of perfective and past meaning, with the exception of the negative existential, in which the present meaning has petrified. In Yakut, the original functional distinction disappeared in favor of perfective and past meaning. In Old Turkic, the original distinction disappeared in favor of imperfective and continuous present meaning.

7.4 pTEA *-mA

7.4.1 pJ *-m

The deverbal noun suffix pJ *-m can be reconstructed as a suffix that derived nominal forms from verbal adjectives. The evidence comes from the accent class 2.5 of disyllabic nouns with a unique low-falling pitch, which is limited to the Kansai dialects. Polivanov (1924: 126) was the first to link the origins of this accent class with the loss of a final consonant pJ *-m. Vovin (1994: 250; 2008b: 142–150) identifies the lost consonant as the nominalizer pre-pJ *-m in verbal adjectives denoting colors, such as in OJ *awo-* B 'to be blue/green' and derived *awo* 2.5 'blue/green (n.)' (< *awo-* 'be blue/green' + *-m NML). It is possible that lexical nouns were generally derived by adding the suffix directly to verb stems, while sentential nominalizations incorporated the copula *wo-. This would have yielded alternations between derived nouns in *-m and *-wo-m. The vowel alternation in some adjectives such as OJ *kura-* 'to be dark' ~ OJ *kuro$_1$* 'black'; OJ *sira-* ~ OJ *siro$_1$* 'white'; OJ *kusa-* 'to be ill-smelling'~ OJ *kuso$_1$* 'dung' suggests that the latter may be derived from the former as, respectively, **kura-wo-m* (thick-COP-NML), **sira-wo-m* (thick-COP-NML) and **kusa-wo-m* (stinky-COP-NML); see also Section 3.2.7 (7), (13).

Although its standard use is finite, the suffix pJ **-om* reflected as *-u* in Old Japanese and as **-um* in the Ryukyuan languages, can be used for clausal (ad)nominalization.

Whereas some analyses of the Japonic conclusive form reconstruct it as a simplex ending **-yu* (Russell 2006: 654) or **-u* (Miller 1985: 47–49; Whitman 1985: 48; Unger 2000: 664, Frellesvig 2008: 190, 2010: 100–101), which is added to the verb stem, others derive it from an auxiliary **-um* that followed a converb in *-i* (Hattori 1972 [1968]; Martin 1968: 406; Vovin 2009a: 609). In line with the latter analysis, I propose to trace the conclusive back to a clausal (ad)nominalizer, deriving it from a periphrastic construction based on the auxiliary pJ **wo-* 'to sit, be' and the (ad)nominalizer pJ **-m*. This seems to be the best way to reconcile the internal Japanese, comparative Ryukyuan and external Transeurasian data, discussed below.

The examples below suggest that before pJ **-ra* started to grammaticalize, an earlier cycle of parallel grammaticalization had already taken place in Japanese, involving the derivational nominalizer pJ **-m*. Similarly, lexical nouns were derived by adding the suffix **-m* directly to verbal stems, whereas clausal (ad)nominalizations incorporated the copula **wo-* 'to sit, be'. These clausal (ad) nominalization ultimately developed to mark syntactically independent sentences. It is plausible that the insubordination process was already accomplished in Japonic and that it was inherited as a polysemy nominalizer/ adnominalizer/ finite in the daughter branches.

Vovin (2009a: 611) objects to connecting the conclusive **-um* with the copular verb OJ *wor-* 'to exist', as proposed here in agreement with Hattori and Martin. His objections are similar to the ones raised for the adnominal form in Section 7.3.1, notably that – first – to avoid circularity, Ryukyuan finite forms of the copula such as Shuri *wuN* 'it exists' would, in contrast to all other verbs, have to be derived from direct suffixation of **-m* to the copular stem and that – second – medial *-w-* is not lost in Old Japanese in intervocalic position.

Due to its ambivalent position between verb and verbal adjective (see Section 3.4), however, the copular verb pJ **wo-* could take the deadjectival nominalizer pJ **-m*, unlike other verbs. Still at the proto-Japonic stage, the nominalizer and the copula fused together to produce the deverbal (ad)nominalizer **wo-m* > **-um*. The attested reflexes of this suffix in Ryukyuan and Mainland Japanese can productively apply to all verb bases, including copular verbs (compare English *I am* *going to go*). In this process, *w-* was lost in word-initial position, at a time when the formant was still an unbound auxiliary, see Section 7.3.1 for examples of sporadic elision of initial pJ **w-* elsewhere in Old Japanese.

7.4.1.1 Ryukyuan

As illustrated in Table 7, Shodon *-m* is incorporated as an (ad)nominalizer in imperfective constructions on *-um* and perfective constructions on *-am*. In adnominal use, imperfective *-um* can precede the two postadnominal nouns *hatí / hát* 'expectation' and *timooryi / timor* 'intention', whereby *timor* changes to *timod* before *dya* 'it is'. Imperfective *-um* and perfect *-am* are further used preceding a number of particles and particle sequences such as *bam* 'but', *mun* 'although', *tyi* 'I hear that; they say that; indeed', *tyi yo* or *tyo* 'indeed', *tyi ba* or *tyis ka* or *tyin na* 'I hear that' and *tyid do* 'they do say indeed that'. In finite use, the endings *-um ~ -un ~ -ur* and *-am ~ -an ~ -ar* are in free variation, but the endings that incorporate *-m* are preferred.

Table 7. The use of the Shodon imperfective and perfective constructions incorporating *-m* (Martin 1970: 128–131)

	imperfective	perfective
adnominal	*yuby-úm timod dya* call.CONV-**ADN** intention be 'I intend to call'	
finite	*Yuby-úm* call.CONV-**FIN** 'He calls / He will call'	*Yud-ám* call.PFV.CONV-ADN 'He called'

Similar to Shodon *-ur* and *-ar* in Section 7.3.1.1, the (ad)nominalizer *-um* attaches to the converb of the imperfective verb base, while *-am* attaches to the converb of the perfective base. This supports the derivation of the composite elements *-u-* and *-a-* from the copula auxiliaries **wo-* 'to sit, be' and **a-* 'to be, exist', respectively. The following morphological analyses may account for the *-um* and *-am* derivation of verbs: Shodon *yubyúm* < pJ **yonp-* 'to call' + **-i* CONV + **wo-* 'to be' + **-m* NML; Shodon *yudám* < pJ **yonp-* 'to call' + **-i* CONV + **-ta-* PERF + **-i* CONV+ **a-* 'to exist' + **-[w]om* NML.

The Shodon suffix *-um* corresponds to nasal-final suffixes with similar function in other Ryukyuan languages, such as Shuri *-uŋ*, Koniya *-um*, Hirara *-ïm*, Hateruma *-uŋ*, Yonaguni *-uŋ*, etc., which also attach to convervial forms of the verb, e.g. Shuri *kac-uŋ* 'I write', Koniya *'iky-um* 'I go' (Hagers 2000: 14–16; Russell 2005: 541, 578, 654; Bentley 2008: 75–83, 147–152, 188–192; Vovin 2009a: 609–

611). These forms suggest that the final consonant of the suffix is a labial nasal. The Shuri suffix *-uŋ*, for instance, alternates with an interrogative form *-um-i (e.g.* Shuri *kac-um-i* (go-FIN-Q) 'Will you write?'), in which the underlying **-um* surfaces. The attachment of the suffix to converbial forms of the verb further indicates that **-um* grammaticalized from an auxiliary verb. Hence, it is plausible to reconstruct a nominalized auxiliary pJ **wo-m*, which lost its initial labial and then fused with the converbial form of the verb, raising from pJ **-om* to pJ **-um*.

7.4.1.2 Mainland Japanese

Except for r-irregular verbs and upper monogrades that mark final predication with an allomorph *-i* (see Section 8.3.1), the Western Old Japanese conclusive form ("shūshikei") is *-u*. In Middle Japanese, upper monograde verbs replace their old conclusive forms of the shape OJ mi_1 by attributive forms of the shape MJ *mi-ru* to mark main-clause-hood (Vovin 2009a: 595–596).

In line with Vovin (2009a: 609), the conclusive OJ *-u* from can be derived from an original auxiliary pJ **-um* that was added to a converbial form of the verb. In my view, pJ **-um* derives from an original periphrastic construction with an existential auxiliary **wo-* and an adnominalizer pJ **-m* , as illustrated in (18).

(18)

pJ **kak-i [w]o-m* (write-CONV exist-NML) > pJ **kak-i-um* (write-CONV-FIN) ⟨ WOJ *kak-u* (write-FIN) / Shodon *khaky-um* (write.CONV-FIN)

Note that Whitman (1985: 130–131; Frellesvig & Whitman 2008: 20) reconstructs nouns with final *r* and *m* in proto-Japonic, with the final consonant being lost before the subject marker **-i*. The apophonic noun OJ mi_2 'body' ~ *mu-* (in e.g. *muzane* 'the real person'), for instance is derived as pJ **muy < *mu-i < *mum-i* (body-NOM).

In line with Unger's vowel delition rule, the first vowel is expected to drop, when a polysyllabic or a monosyllabic vowel final root meets a monosyllabic vowel initial suffix. From the perspective of vowel deletion (VD), mid vowel raising (MVR) and word-final *m*-loss (mL) we expect the following developments: for monosyllabic irregular verbs, including pJ **na-* 'to go': **kə-om* (VD) > **kom* (MVR) > *kum* (mL) > *ku* (come.FIN); for quadrigrades : **aka-om* (VD) > **ak-om* (MVR) > **ak-um* (mL) > *aku* (open.FIN) and for all bigrades **akay-om* (VD) > **ak-om* (MVR) > **akum* (mL) > OJ *aku*.

Although the standard use of WOJ *-u* is finite as in (19d), we find a few relic examples of nonfinite use. Nominal use is preserved following the negative suffix OJ *-(a)z-* in constructions where the negative nominalizer *-(a)zu* marks the argument of the converbs *ni* or *site* of the defective copula *n-* or the verb *se-* 'to do', respectively; see (19a) (Vovin 2009a: 760–763). As illustrated in (19b), the negative nominalizer -(a)zu has also developed converbial use, a grammaticalization pathway that is frequently observed in the Transeurasian languages (see Section 8.1). Vovin considers the nominalizer OJ -u, the converb OJ -u and the finite OJ -u as three unrelated, homophoneous suffixes. Except for the assumed insubordination and converb development, which can explain the polysemy as the result of grammaticalization, we find an indication of the common origin of these suffixes in their unique combination with the negative allomorph OJ -(a)z-: only the converb, nominalizer and finite -u can combine with OJ -(a)z-, whereas all other verb suffixes chose OJ -(a)n-.

Adnominal use of -u is contested but it may surface in some lexicalizations, such as J izumi '(well-)spring', which derives from *id-u mi_1 (emerge-ADN water) and OJ yo_2s-u-ka (stop-ADN-place) 'a place to hold' (MYS VII: 1382; BS 18; Martin 1987: 807). There are also instances where vowel-stem verbs, such as OJ mi_1te- 'to fill (tr.)' in (21c), take an adnominal form on -u instead of the standard -uru.

(19) The use of Western Old Japanese -u

    a. clausal nominalization

        ki_1mi_1 imas-az-**u**   s-i-te
        lord   come(HON)-NEG-**NML** do-INF-CONV
        '[my] lord does not come, and..' (MYS V: 878; Vovin 2009a: 761)

    b. converbial

        i-ki_1r-az-**u** so_2 k-uru
        ACT-cut-NEG-**CONV** PT come-FIN
        '[I] return without cutting [them] there' (KK 51; Vovin 2009a: 717)

    c. clausal adnominalization

        so_1ra $mi1t$-u Yamato-no kuni-ni
        sky   fill-ADN Yamato-GEN land-LOC
        'in the land of sky-filling Yamato' (K 722; Martin 1987: 809)

    d. finite

        aki_1-no_2 no_1-ni   sawosika nak-i_1-t-**u**.
        autumn-GEN field-LOC male.deer cry-CONV-PERF-**FIN**
        'Male deer cried in the autumn field.' (MYS 25: 3678; Vovin 2009a: 602)

In Eastern Old Japanese -u occurs in the same functions as in Western Old Japanese (Vovin 2009a: 607), including two occurrences of the negative nominalizer -(a)zu in front of the converb site (Vovin 2009a: 762) and three examples of the necessitive -ube_2- (Vovin 2009a: 879).

7.4.2 pK *-*m*

The deverbal noun suffix MK -(·*u/o*)*m*, K -(*u*)*m* underlies the reconstruction of the nominalizer pK *-*m*. As in Contemporary Korean, the Middle Korean suffix was used to derive lexical nouns and to nominalize sentences, but in Middle Korean, the morphology of these two uses was different (Ramsey & Lee 2011: 176–177). Lexical nouns were generally derived by adding the suffix directly to verb stems, while sentential nominalizations incorporated the modulator MK -·*w*ᵘ/*o*-; for both uses, see (20a). However, the distinction showed already instability in the fifteenth century and fell into disuse in the sixteenth century, yielding many exceptions to this rule such as (20b). Note that the modulator has been derived from an original copular verb pK **wo*- in Section 3.4.2. The construction pK **wo-m* (be-NML) yields a nice parallel with the derivation of the Japanese conclusive in Section 7.4.1.

Except for some expressions such as K *wul-um swori* (cry-NML voice) 'a tearful voice', where the nominal modification can be interpreted as an unmarked genitive case, the suffix is not used as an adnominalizer. However, it can appear as a marker of finiteness. As illustrated in (20c), the Middle Korean finite -(·*u/o*)*m* is always followed by the vocative particle *a*, which is also incorporated in the subjunctive attentive MK -(·*u/o*)·*la*, discussed in Section 7.3.2. However, in the documentary style of written contemporary Korean K -(*u*)*m* appears in main clauses without the vocative, often expressing an impersonal proposition as in (20d).

(20) The use of MK -(·*u/o*)*m*, K -(*u*)*m*

    a.   lexical vs. clausal nominalization in MK

        tywoh-on   *yel-**um***   *yel-**wu-m**-i*
        be.good-ADN   bear.fruit-**NML**   bear.fruit-**MOD-NML**-NOM
        'the bearing of good fruit' (1459 Wel 1: 12; Ramsey & Lee 2011: 177)

    b.   unmodulated clausal nominalization in MK

        … *kes-ul*   *meki-**m**-i*   *mastang* *thi*   *ani*   *ho-n-i*
        thing-ACC feed-**NML**-NOM proper   do.SUSP NEG do-ADN-NML
        'It is unsuitable to feed them things [such as watermelon or pear or orange]' (1608 Twu-cip 2: 4b; Martin 1992: 887)

    c.   finite in MK

        ·*na-y*   *ne*   *to·ly·e*   *nil·G-wo-·**m**-a*
        I-NOM you accompany-CONV say-MOD-**FIN**-VOC
        'I will tell you.' (1517 Pak 1: 32b; Martin 1992: 932)

d. finite in K

*onul-un   swuep-i   eps-**um**.*
today-TOP   class-NOM   not.exist-**FIN**
'No class today.'

The examples above suggest that lexical nouns were derived by adding the suffix pK *-m directly to verbal stems, whereas clausal (ad)nominalizations incorporated the copula pK *wo- 'to be' and ultimately they developed to mark syntactically independent sentences in particular discourse contexts. As such, the deverbal noun suffix pK *-m does not only correspond to pJ *-m in form and function, but the correlations also involve the incorporation of a cognate copula *wo- 'to be' in clausal (ad)nominalization, the stages in the development to finite use and the cyclicity of the development.

7.4.3 pTg *-mA

The deverbal noun suffix pTg *-mA can be reconstructed as a suffix that derived nominal and adnominal forms from verb stems, such as in the Even, Evenki and Udehe lexicalizations below. It is particularly frequent in the derivation of colour nouns and adjectives, which recalls the color derivations in Japanese in Section 7.4.1. In Sibe the corresponding suffix -m is still productive as the citation form of verbs and it is used for deriving infinitives as well as for marking independent clauses. Historically, infinitives often derive from deverbal nouns and therefore could be claimed to involve an increase of verbal properties on the part of deverbal noun that is integrated into the verbal paradigm (Haspelmath 1989; Malchukov 2004: 120).

The deverbal noun suffix has developed into an infinitive marker into a clausal nominalizer and, finally, into a converb suffix, with imperfective or perfective interpretation according to the telicity of the verb base. The converb suffix is used in adverbial clauses in which the subject is always co-referential with the matrix clause subject. In most Tungusic languages, the converb has distinct singular and plural forms, e.g. Evk. *-mi / -mil*, Nanai *-mi / -mari / -meri*, Ud. *-mi / -mei*, Olč *-mi / -mari / -meri*, Oroč *-mi / -mai*. This number distinction reflects contraction of an original nominal form pTg *-mA with the possessive-reflexive suffixes pTg *-wi singular and pTg * -wari plural, respectively (Benzing 1955 a: 1090; Menges 1968: 212). The presence of the possessive-reflexive marker gives the converb an inherently co-referential function, which means that it can only be used in same-subject constructions. The use of the *-mi (< *-mA-wi) converb as a nominalizer in complement clauses is – unlike most other converb suffixes – characteristic of all Tungusic languages, an observation that also supports the proposed origin of the suffix.

In some cases where the suffix is incorporated in finite markers, such as in Udehe and Manchu, it preserves traces of a copula construction, but comparative evidence suggests that these copula represent later additions. In Sibe, for instance, the finitization involves direct reanalysis of the non-finite predicate as a finite one, without copula loss.

Perfect and perfective interpretations in Manchu, Sibe and in some Northern Tungusic languages indicate that the aspectual interpretation of pTg *-mA depended on the semantics of the preceding verb: derived from telic verbs, pTg *-mA obtained a perfective connotation, whereas derived from atelic verbs, it obtained imperfective meaning.

In sum, the examples below suggest that the deverbal noun suffix pTg *-mA was extended to the clause level, leaving a trace in clausal adverbialization, which can be derived from original nominalization. Although in most Tungusic languages, the suffix does not display insubordination, Sibe leaves a trace of the use of the suffix in independent clauses.

7.4.3.1 Manchu

The Manchu converb of simultaneity -*me* in (21b), which can also be used to embed complement clauses as in (21a), indicates that pTg *-mA was originally used as a nominalizer (Gorelova 2002: 267–273, 315–316). The observation that Ma. -*me* does not alter according to vowel harmony indicates that the original distinction between pTg *-ma and *-me was neutralized through the addition of a possessive-reflexive suffix pTg *-wi, which yielded *-mai and *-mei, respectively. Both alternants contracted to -*me* in Manchu, but Jurchen, the immediate ancestor of Manchu, preserved the distinction between *-mai and *mei (Menges 1968: 212).

(21) The use of Manchu -*me*

    a. clausal nominalization

        *usin tari-**me**   boo   ara-**me**   deribu-he*
        field cultivate-**CONV** house build-**CONV** begin-PST.FIN
        '[He] began to cultivate a field and to build a house'
        (Pashkov 1950 (1): 91; Gorelova 2002: 270)

    b. converb

        *muse   sibiya makta-**me** dasame dende-ki*
        we.INCL lot   throw-**CONV** again   divide-OPT
        'Casting lots, we shall divide [it] again' (ZAKH 191; Gorelova 2002: 268)

The nominalizer pTg *-ma is further incorporated in the finite ending Ma. -mbi, (Gorelova 2002: 232, 286–288, 441–443). As illustrated in (22a), Ma. -mbi can mark habitual, generic and progressive present as well as future tense, but there are also instances such as (22b), where it seems to mark recent past.

Although controversy marks the literature about the exact derivation of this suffix, most authors agree that it derives from a nonfinite form followed by the predicative copula Ma. bi (Benzing 1955a: 1077; Menges 1943: 242 : < *-n (ADN) bi; Zakharov 1879: 173, Avrorin 1949, Sinor 1968, Gorelova 2002: 289: < *-me (CONV) bi; Gorelova 1996: 156: < *-mA (ADN) bi). The most plausible account seems to Gorelova's proposal that Ma. -mbi is formed by the (ad)nominalizer *-mA and the predicative copula Ma. bi. This is supported by the observation, first, that Ma. bi is an obligatory component of the predicate in the nominal type of predication and, second, that the imperfective in -mbi has a parallel in the past in -hAbi which is derivable from the perfective adnominalizer Ma. -hA and bi (see Section 7.6.3.1).

(22) The use of Manchu finite -mbi

 a. imperfective

   indahu:n dobori tuwahiya-**mbi**, coko   erde
   dog   night   guard-**FIN**   chicken early.in.the.morning
   hu:la-**mbi**.
   sing-**FIN**
   'A dog keeps guard at night, a rooster crows early in the morning.'
   (Orlov 1873: 193; Gorelova 2002: 287)

 b. perfect

   šun dekde-re ergi uce-be   tuci-**mbi**.
   sun rise-ADN side door-ACC appear-**FIN**
   'A rising sun has appeared in the doorway.' (NSB: 70–1; Gorelova 2002: 288)

 c. imperfective past

   bi kwmuni   ere-be   niyalma-de   ere-**mbi-he**
   I   constantly this-ACC people-DAT   hope-**FIN-PST**
   'I constantly inspired people with this hope' (Orlov 1873: 194; Gorelova 2002: 445)

Comparative evidence, notably the parallel with Ma. -hAbi constructions and the presence of a finite marker -m without copula intervention in Sibe, suggests that the Manchu copula -*bi* in -*mbi* represents a secondary addition.[13] It is not unlikely that the copula constructions in Manchu, a highly siniticized language, developed under Chinese influence. The addition of the copula enables the speaker to mark the insubordinated form with the maximum of inflectional categories, such as the addition of tense marking in (22c).

Sibe, a contemporary descendant of Manchu, has a suffix -*m*, which is the citation form of verbs and is used for deriving infinitives as in (23a) as well as for marking main-clause-hood as in (23b). Since the form -*m* can also be used as a nonfinite marker and since there is no phonological trace of *bi, it is unlikely that the predicative element *-*bi* was involved in the insubordination process. Therefore, it is safe to assume that Sibe -*m* is a reflex of the simplex (ad)nominalizer pTg *-*mA* and that it underwent direct insubordination without copula loss.

(23) The use of Sibe -*m*

a. nominal

*tumaqe   da   er   sahenzi-ni   da   songu-**m**   songu-me*
and.then PT   this daughter-POSS PT   cry-**NML**   cry-CONV
'And then this daughter cried and..' (Jang & Payne 2012: 234)

b. finite

*age-ni   sas   du-makeng-ni   gisere-**m**.*
older.brother-DEF   foolish   younger.brother-COM-DEF   say-IPFV.**FIN**
'Older brother speaks with foolish younger brother.'
(Clever Foolish 220; Jang, Jang & Payne (in preparation))

The Sibe converb of simultaneity -*me* can, like its Manchu equivalent, be derived from pTg *-*mA-wi*. It can be used to embed complement clauses as in (24a) and it can also obtain a perfective converbial interpretation following some telic verbs as in (24c). It is found in finite imperfective use by Norman (1974: 169) as in (24d), but Jang, Jang & Payne (in preparation) do not find examples of finite -*me* in their corpus.[14]

---

13 In Section 7.5.3.1, it will be argued that the Manchu alternant in -*hA* reflects the original construction, which developed through direct insubordination from the perfective adnominalizer because in Northern Tungusic languages such as Even and Southern Tungusic languages such as Nanai and Udehe the corresponding finite perfect suffix is not accompanied by a copula.

14 Norman (1974: 169) further finds instances of a finite suffix -*mi*, which is used by elder people in narrating stories. He assumes that this form may be a borrowing of literary Manchu -*mbi*.

(24) The use of Sibe *-me*

    a. clausal nominalization

        *bii sivee gisun gisure-**me** bahene-me*
        I Sibe language speak-**NML** know-FIN
        'I know how to speak Sibe and ...' (Norman 1974: 169)

    b. imperfective converb

        *fase-**me** bucě-hi*
        hang-**CONV** die-PERF.FIN
        'He died by hanging' (Norman 1974: 170)

    c. perfective converb

        *yave-m tang alkan gene-**me***
        walk-INF 100 step go-**CONV**
        da ter baobei sere-f ba-he-i.
        PT that treasure spring-ACC find-PERF-FIN
        'Going 100 steps, (she) found the precious spring.'
        (Blind Daughter 053; Jang, Jang & Payne (in preparation))

    d. finite

        *bii sivee gisun gisure-me bahene-**me**.*
        I Sibe language speak-NML know-**FIN**
        'I know how to speak Sibe' (Norman 1974: 169).

7.4.3.2 Even

The Even converb *-mi* can be used to embed complement clauses and to derive adverbial clauses with temporal, conditional or causal meaning (Benzing 1955b: 104; Malchukov 1995: 17–18). Within a temporal clause it denotes an event which is either simultaneous as in (25b), or immediately anterior to the primary event as in (25c), depending on the telicity of the base verb.

(27) The use of the Even *-mi*

    a. clausal nominalization

        uliki-w ulmi-mi boloni-du ewse ke:ŋeli biwe:t-ten
        squirel-ACC hunt-NML autumn-DAT very bad be.usual-INCL
        'Hunting squirrels usually tends to be very bad in autumn.' (Benzing 1955b: 104)

b. imperfective converb
taŋ-mi,   bi   hok-na-m
read-CONV I   rejoice-FIN-1SG
'When I read, I enjoy myself' (Benzing 1955b: 104)

c. perfective converb
em-mi   gu:n-ji-m
come-CONV say-FUT-1SG
'When [I] come, I shall tell [it]' (Malchukov 1995: 18)

7.4.3.3 Evenki

In Evenki, the deverbal noun suffix *-ma ~ -me ~ -mo* is reflected in some lexicalized nouns and nominal adjectives, which derive from verbs, such as *girku-* 'to walk' → *girkuma* 'pedestrian', *omngo-* 'forget' → *omngomo* 'forgetful, absent-minded', *tuksa-* 'run' → *tuksama* 'running', *muru-* 'to walk round, return' → *murume* 'round' (Vasilevič 1948: 769, Poppe 1955: 262, Menges 1968: 67, Nedjalkov 1997: 305). It is particularly frequent in the derivation of colour nouns and adjectives, such as *bagda-* 'to become white, freeze' → *bagdama* 'white (adj. and n.)', *koŋno-* 'to be black' → *koŋnomo* 'black (adj. and n.)' and pTg **pula-* 'to be red' (in Evk. *hularin* 'red', Even *hulal-* 'to become red', *hulaña-* 'red') → *hulama* 'red (adj. and n.)', which recalls the color derivations in Japanese (Section 7.4.1).

The deverbal noun suffix is incorporated in the clausal complementizer and temporal-conditional converb suffix *-mi (*Nedjalkov 1995: 455–457). The converb may take the plural marker in *-l*, which signals its origin as a nominalizer. Similar to the Even converb, the interpretation of either anteriority or simultaneity of situations expressed by the converb, correlates with the actional semantics of the base verb: a telic verb yields a perfective converb, whereas an atelic verb yields an imperfective converb; see (26).

(26) The use of Evenki *-mi*

a. clausal nominalization
Bejetken alba-ra-n   bira-va   elbesce-mi
boy   can.not-FIN-3SG river-ACC swim-NML
'The boy could not swim across the river' (Nedjalkov 1995: 457)

b. imperfective converb
Bejetke-r evi-mi   ike-mi   bejukte-je-ce-tin
boy-PL   play-CONV sing-CONV   hunt-IPFV-PST-3PL
'The boys were hunting, singing and playing at the same time.' (Nedjalkov 1995: 456)

c. perfective converb

Sama-sel   eme-mi   asi-va-n   ice-re
shaman-PL   come-CONV   wife-ACC-3SG   see-FIN.3SG
'Having come, the shamans saw his wife.' (Nedjalkov 1995: 456)

7.4.3.4 Udehe
In Udehe, the deverbal noun suffix *-ma* ~ *-me* is reflected in some lexicalized nouns and nominal adjectives, which derive from verbs, such as *sigili-* 'stir' → *sigilime* 'thick soup', *kua-* 'cut, make a frame-work' → *kuaima* 'log', *xui-* 'boil' → *xuili-me* 'boiling', *zegde-* 'burn' → *zegdelime* 'burning' (Nikolaeva 1999: 113).

The deverbal noun suffix is incorporated in the clausal complementizer and converb suffix *-mi*, which has a a distinct plural form *-mei* (Nikolaeva 1999: 164). The converb expresses simultaneous temporal, causal and concessive meaning and is co-referential with the matrix verb; see (27b). In combination with the copula *bi-* 'to be' it forms a finite predicate, denoting progressive aspect. In the present the copula is usually, but not always, omitted; see (27c).

(29) The use of Udehe *-mi*

a. clausal nominalization

min-du   o-du   te:-mi   aya.
me-DAT   here-DAT   sit-NML   good.
'It is nice for me to sit here' (Nikolaeva 1999: 164)

b. converb

nuani   ŋele-mi   susa-gi-e-ni.
He   get.frightened.CONV escape-REP-PST-3SG
'Being frightened, he escaped.' (Nikolaeva 1999: 164)

c. finite

wakca-mi   [bi:-ni].
hunt-CONV   [be-3SG]
'He is hunting.'

7.4.3.5 Nanai
In Nanai, the (ad)nominalizer is incorporated in clausal nominalization and in converbs in *-mi* with simultaneous temporal, causal and concessive meaning (Avrorin 1961: 142; Menges 1968: 208, 212–213). As illustrated in (28), it has a distinct plural form *-mari* ~ *meri*, in which the plural reflexive-possessive pTg *-wari* can be recognized.

(28) The use of Nanai *-mi*

    a.   clausal nominalization

        Kolxozńika-sal   givanaidoańi   jobo-mari   deru:-ri-ci
        Kolkhoz-farmer-PL early.in.the.morning work-NML.PL begin-FIN-3PL
        'The Kolkhoz-farmers begin to work early in the morning'
        (Menges 1968: 213)

    b.   converb

        naisal   giam-ba   duere-meri,   jari-xa-ci.
        people road-ACC walk-CONV.PL sing-PST-3SG
        'People were singing as they were walking along the road.'
        (Avrorin 1961: 142)

7.4.4 pMo *-m(A)

The deverbal noun suffix pMo *-mA* alternates with *-m* and can be reconstructed as a suffix that derived nominal and adnominal forms from verb stems, as shown by the derivational pairs in (29a) to (29d) (Poppe 1954: 47–48, 1955: 261–262, 262; Street 1957: 58). There are doublets, such as *degerem ~ degerme* 'robbery, robber' and *toyum ~ toyuma* 'sensibleness; good behavior' that indicate that the (ad)nominalizers *-ma* and *-m* share a common origin. The observation that nominalizations with *-m* outnumber those with *-mA* suggests that *-mA* is the more archaic alternant, which probably lost its final vowel in the course of grammaticalization.

Janhunen (2012b: 166–167) notes that the marker of the preconditional converb *-mAA/n* in the Central Mongolic languages, e.g. *sour-maa/n* (study-CONV) 'only if you study', can be derived from the deverbal noun suffix *-m* and the reflexive possessive marker *-AA/n*. This identification is confirmed by the fact that the final /n follows the pattern of the possessive-reflexive marker, being present in some dialects (as in Chakhar) and absent in others (as in Khalkha). Similar to the Tungusic converb in Section 7.4.3, the possessive-reflexive marker gives the converb an inherently co-referential function. As such, clausal adverbialization can be derived from clausal nominalization.

In Middle Mongolian texts of the thirteenth and fourteenth century, *-m* is the common ending for the imperfective present (Poppe 1955: 261; Weiers 1966: 143–150); see (29e). This suffix is less used in Written Mongolian, where it has been replaced by *-mUi* or *-mU*. Poppe (1955a: 262) assumes that the final *ui* is due to analogy with finite forms such as *ajisui* 'he approaches', *odui* 'he goes away', *bui* 'he is', etc. According to Weiers (1966: 143, 153–161) *-Ui* and *-U* are finite predicative endings.

The most common meaning of the finite MMo. *-m* is imperfective present, but it can also be used to express past meaning; see (29f). Taken together with the observation that the deverbal noun suffix may derive subject nouns (e.g. MMo. *daqama* 'menses', WMo. *degerme* 'robber', WMo. *barim* 'width of fist', WMo. *toqom* 'saddle cloth') as well as object nouns (e.g. Mgr. *gurma* 'plaited hair', WMo. *jirum* 'line', WMo. *jisüm* 'slice', WMo. *naɣadum* 'play') from transitive verbs, this indicates that the aspectual interpretation of the suffix was originally dependent on the semantics of the base verb.

In sum, the examples below suggest that the deverbal noun suffix pMo *-mA > *-m* was extended to the clause level, the original clausal nominalization leaving a trace in converbial sentences in the Central Mongolic languages. Ultimately, the suffix developed into a finite present marker in independent clauses.

(29) The use of the Written/Middle Mongolian (ad)nominalizers *-mA* and *-m*

    a. lexical nominalization in *-mA*

        MMo. *daqa-* 'to follow (tr.)' → *daqama* 'menses' (Poppe 1955: 262)

        pMo *degere-* 'to lift (tr.)' in *degerede-* 'to be lifted' → *degerem ~ degerme* 'robbery, violence; bandit, robber'

        Mgr. *guru-* 'to plait' → *gurma* 'plaited hair'

        WMo. *jaɣura-* 'to jam, be locked, be arrested in motion; to close tightly (tr. / intr.)' → *jaɣurma* 'interrupted, incomplete; that which has not reached its end; on the way (n./adj./adv.)'

        WMo. *toɣu-* 'to esteem, value' → *toɣum ~ toɣuma* 'sensibleness; good behavior'

    b. lexical nominalization in *-m*

        WMo. *bari-* 'to seize, hold, grasp (tr.)' → *barim* 'grip, width of fist'

        WMo. *jiru-* 'to draw (line, picture), to strike (match), to scratch (tr.)' → *jirum* 'line, line of action, norm'

        WMo. *jisü-* 'to cut lengthwise, cut into strips, slice (tr.)' → *jisüm* 'something cut off lengthwise, strip, slice'

        WMo. *naɣadu-* 'to play, enjoy oneself (tr./intr.)' → *naɣadum* 'play, game, entertainment'

        MMo. *quri-* 'to come together (intr.)' → *qurim* 'feast'

        WMo. *toqo-* 'to saddle (tr.)' → *toqom* 'saddle cloth'

c.   lexical adnominalization in -mA

WMo. *bayi-* 'to be, exist, reside (intr.)' → *bayima* 'such (place) where there can be something'

WMo *yayiqa-* 'to wonder, marvel, be astonished (int.)' → *yayiqama* 'wonderful, astonishing'

WMo *ulayi-* 'to get red-hot, become red (intr.)' → *ulayima* 'red, red-hot'

WMo. *jayilu-* 'rinse, wash out (tr.)' → *jayiluma usu* 'brook [lit. water where one rinses]'

d.   lexical adnominalization in -m

WMo. *čoqu-* 'to agree, confirm, make a resolution (intr.)' → *čoqum* 'real, correct, exact; reality; indeed, as a matter of fact (n. / adj. / adv.)'

WMo. *toyuri-* 'to go about, circle, surround (tr.)' → WMo. *toyurim* 'approximate, about, around; environment (n./adj)'

e.   finite imperfective in -m

MMo. udurit-basu   ber   ulu   busire-m.
        guide-COND   PT   NEG   believe-IPFV.FIN
'Even if you guide them, they don't believe' (HY; Weiers 1966: 144)

f.   finite perfect in -mU

MMo. ulus   ba   joba-'a-mu
       state   PT   suffer-CAUS-PST.FIN
'He bedeviled even the state' (SH 152; Weiers 1966: 143)

7.4.5 pTk *-m(A)

On the basis of reflexes in Old Turkic and Chuvash, the deverbal noun suffix pTk *-mA* alternating with *-m*, can be reconstructed as a suffix that derived nominal and adnominal forms from verb stems. It derives action nouns, subject nouns from intransitive verbs, and either subject nouns or object nouns from transitive verbs. The perfective (i.e. in object nominals) or imperfective interpretation (i.e. in subject nominals) of the suffix probably depended on the semantics of the preceding verb base. Whereas the derivation of object and subject nominals is well-reflected in in Old Turkic, it is restricted to only a few lexicalizations in Chuvash, where the role of the suffix in the derivation of action nouns has led to its development as a productive infinitive suffix. The suffix pTk *-(X)m*, which was similarly to pTk *-mA* used for the derivation of action nouns, subject and object nominals, probably represents an instance of final-vowel loss. Since lexicalized derivations with *-m outnumber those with *-mA in Old Turkic as well as in Chuvash, pTk *-m can be regarded as a younger, phonologically eroded variant of *-mA.

7.4.5.1 Old Turkic

The Old Turkic deverbal noun suffixes -mA and -(X)m are reflected in nouns, such as in the examples in (30a/b), as well as in adjectives, such as in the examples in (30c/d) (Erdal 1991: 290–300, 316–320). Since -mA and -(X)m have similar functions and produce near doublets such as OTk. örüm 'something knitted' ~ örma 'plaited', they probably go back to a single origin. The observations that derivations with *-m outnumber those with *-mA (Erdal 2002: 151), suggests that *-m is a younger, phonologically eroded variant of *-mA. The suffixes -mA and -(X)m derive a few action nouns (e.g. ölüm 'death'), but usually they derive subject nominals from intransitive verbs and either subject nominals (e.g. OTk. erksinme 'dominant', tutma 'chest', tutum 'handful', yarma 'crack', yilim 'glue') or object nominals (e.g. OTk. ičim 'drink', örüm 'something knitted', örme 'plaited', yarïm 'half') from transitive verbs. This indicates that -mA and -(X)m have either imperfective or perfective meaning, dependent on the aspectual semantics of the verb base. Similar to the Mongolic suffixes in Section 7.4.4, there are only few examples where -(X)m is used for nominal modification; see (30d).

(30) The use of the Old Turkic (ad)nominalizers -mA and -(X)m

    a. -mA nominal

        OTk. eg- 'to rise, climb (intr.)' → egme arch (in a house)'
        OTk. tüg- 'to bind a knot' → tügme 'button'
        OTk. tut- 'to hold, grasp, seize (tr.)' → tutma 'chest, coffer'
        OTk. yel- 'to trot, amble (intr.)' → yelme 'reconnoitring patrol'
        OTk. yar- 'to split (open) (tr.)' → yarma 'crack'

    b. -(X)m nominal

        OTk ič- 'to drink (tr.)' → ičim 'drink'
        OTk kör- 'to see (tr.)' → körüm 'view, omen'
        OTk. öl- 'to die (intr.)' → ölüm 'death'
        OTk. ör- 'to plait (tr.)' → örüm 'something knitted'
        OTk. tut- 'to hold, grasp, seize (tr.)' → tutum 'handful'
        OTk. yar- 'to split (open) (tr.)' → yarïm 'half'
        OTk. yil- 'to catch on to something, to hang, to fasten (tr.)' → yilim 'glue'

c. *mA* adnominal

OTk. *erksin-* 'to have power or authority over (tr.)' → *erksinme* 'dominant'

OTk. *ïd-* 'send, allow to go, release (tr.)' → *ïdma yïlkï* 'animal which is allowed to go free'

OTk. *kutur-* 'be excessive, exceed, overhang (intr.)' → *kuturma börk* 'a cap which has two flaps, in front and behind'

OTk. *ör-* 'to plait' → *örme sač* 'plaited hair'

d. *-(X)m* adnominal

OTk. *ïsïr-* 'to bite (tr.)' → *ïsrïm kiši* 'a man who clenches his teeth and scowls'

OTk. *yil-* 'to catch on to something, to hang, to fasten (tr.)' → *yilim yï* 'creeper plant'

7.4.5.2 Chuvash

The Chuvash deverbal noun suffixes *-mA* and *-(X)m* are reflected in nouns, such as in the examples in (31a/b/c), as well as in adjectives, such as in the examples in (31d). The suffix *-mA* is lexicalized in action nouns and leaves a trace of deriving object nouns from transitive verbs in, for instance, Chu. *eśme* 'drink, beverage' and *vïrma* 'stubble, stubble-field' (Levickaya 1974: 160; Fedotov 1996: 336). However, it has specialized in the derivation of action nouns and as such, it became productive as the standard infinitive marker in contemporary Chuvash in (31b) (Krüger 1961: 156–157). The Chuvash (ad)nominalizer, *-(Ă)m* derives action nouns (e.g. *vulĕm* 'death'), subject nouns from intransitive verbs (e.g. *śiśĕm* 'lightning') and either object or subject nouns from transitive verbs (e.g. *turam* 'slice') (Benzing 1959: 719; Levickaya 1974: 157–158; Fedotov 1996: 335). The observation that lexicalized derivations with *-(X)m* outnumber similar lexicalizations with *-mA* suggests that the underlying pTk **-mA* is of relatively older age.

(31) The use of the Chuvash (ad)nominalizers *-mA* and *-(Ă)m*

a. lexical nominalization in *-mA*

Chu. *eś-* 'to drink (tr.)' → *eśme* 'drink, beverage, drinking'

Chu. *lar-* 'to sit (down), seat oneself (intr.)' → *larma* '(young people's) gathering, sojourning as a guest'

Chu. *śiter-* 'to feed, cause to eat (tr.)' → *śiterme* 'pasturage of cattle during the day'

Chu. *vïr-* 'to reap (tr.)' → *vïrma* 'stubble, stubble-field'

b. infinitive in -*mA*

   mana   tup-ma   xuša-t.
   I.DAT   find-INF   order-3SG
   'He orders me to find [them].' (Krüger 1961: 157)

c. lexical nominalization in *-(X)m*

   Chu. *šĕkle-* 'to load (tr.)' → *šĕklem* 'load'
   Chu. *śiś-* 'to light up, flash (intr.)' → *śiśĕm* 'lightning, flash'
   Chu. *tux-* 'to go out, come out, rise (of sun) (intr.)' → *tuxăm* 'departure, leave'
   Chu. *tura-* 'to reduce, chop (tr.)' → *turam* 'cut piece, slice'
   Chu. *vul-* 'to die' → *vulĕm* 'death'

d. lexical adnominalization in *-(X)m*

   Chu. *pĕr-* 'to turn round, twist (tr.)' → *pĕrĕm* 'spiral, helical, screw (adj./ n)'
   Chu. *pĕt-* 'to end, finish, become complete (intr.)' → *pĕtĕm* 'all, entire, whole'
   Chu. *put-* 'to sink (intr.)' → *putam* 'swampy, marshy; a place where you can drown'
   Chu. *ujĕr-* 'to divide (tr.)' → *ujrĕm* 'separate, detached, independent'

7.5 pTEA *-*n* aspectually neutral (ad)nominalizer

7.5.1 pJ *-*n*

Incorporations in examples of sequential voicing in adjective-noun compounds as well as in the conditional converb in Ryukyuan and Mainland Japanese suggest that the deverbal noun suffix pJ *-*n* can be reconstructed as a suffix that derived adnominal forms from verbs and verbal adjectives. It is not unlikely that lexical nouns were generally derived by adding the suffix directly to verb stems, while sentential nominalizations incorporated the copula *wo-*. This would have yielded alternations between derived nouns in *-*n* and *-*wo-n*. Some Ryukyuan languages use an adnominalizer suffix *-un*, which like the reflexes of pR *-*um* and *-*uru*, can be derived from *-*wo-n*. This suffix is used for argument subordination, nominal modification and finite marking, suggesting an insubordination process, whereby the direction of the grammaticalization was from non-finite to finite marker. A reflex of the adnominalizer pJ *-*wo-n* may be present in the Eastern Old Japanese tentative suffix *-unam-*.

7.5.1.1 Ryukyuan

In free variation with the adnominalizers Shodon -*r* and -*m* discussed above, Shodon -*n* is the standard adnominal marker, incorporated in imperfective constructions in -*un* and perfective constructions in -*an*. As nominal modifiers, Shodon -*un* and -*an* occur before most nouns, including the occurrence of -*an* before *hatí* / *hát* 'expectation' and *timooryi* / *timor* 'intention'. Imperfective -*un* also precedes the particles and particle sequences *n(y)a* 'question', *yo* 'indeed', *khara n* 'because', *ga nyi n* or *ga tu n* 'so as to', whereas -*an* also occurs before the particle *yo* 'indeed' and the sequence *khara n* 'because'. As illustrated in Table 8, both endings -*un* and -*an* are used as markers of finiteness.

Table 8. The use of the Shodon imperfective and perfective constructions incorporating -*m* (Martin 1970: 128–131)

	imperfective		perfective	
adnominal	*yuby-ún* call.CONV-**ADN**	*tyu* person	*yud-án* call.PFV.CONV-**ADN**	*tyu* person
	'the person who does / will call'		'the person who called'	
finite	*Yuby-ún.* call.CONV-**ADN**		*Yud-án.* call.PFV.CONV-**ADN**	
	'He calls, he will call.'		'He called'	

As has been shown for Shodon -*ur*/ -*ar* and -*um*/-*am* in Sections 7.3.1.1 and 7.4.1.1, the (ad)nominalizer -*un* also attaches to the converb of the imperfective verb base, while -*an* attaches to the converb of the perfective base. This supports the derivation of the composite elements -*u*- and -*a*- from the copula auxiliaries **wo*- 'to sit, be' and **a*- 'to be, exist', respectively. The following morphological analysis may account for the -*un* and -*an* derivation of verbs: Shodon *yubyún* < pJ **yonp*- 'to call' + **-i* CONV + **wo*- 'to be' + **-n* NML; Shodon *yudám* < pJ **yonp*- 'to call' + **-i* CONV + **-ta*- PERF + **-i* CONV+ **a*- 'to exist' + **-[w]on* NML.

Similar to Shodon -*un*, Ura, a northern Amami language spoken on Amami Ōshima, uses an adnominalizer -*uN* for argument subordination, nominal modification and main clause marking, as illustrated in (32).

(32) The use of the Ura (ad)nominalizer -*uN* (Shibatani 2011)

    a.   clausal nominalization

        ʔama-zyi   *taccy-**uN**-ga*   *wakya-N*   *ʔkwa-kkwa*
        there-LOC   stand.CONV-**NML**-NOM   we-GEN   DIM-child
        'The one standing there is our child'

b. clausal adnominalization

*ʔama-zyi taccy-**uN** ʔkwa-kkwa*
there-LOC stand.CONV-**ADN** DIM-child
'the child who is standing there'

c. finite

*ʔkwaa-ga ʔama-zyi taccy-**uN***
child there-LOC stand.CONV-**FIN**
'A child is standing there'

The alternation between *-ur*, *-um* and *-un* in Shodon, corresponds to similar alternations in a few other Ryukyuan languages, such as in Yamatoma where the adnominal and finite marker *-un* alternates with *-ï* (< pR *-um*) and *-uru* (< pR *-uru*). Russell (2005: 485) proposes to regard *-un* as a phonological development of *-uru* because one source for final *-n* in Yamatoma is a voiced consonant plus a high vowel, thus *-ru* > *n*. However, from this perspective it remains to be explained why not all instances of Yamatoma finite *-uru* have developed in *-un* and why other Ryukyuan languages like Shodon reflect triplets of the type *-ur*, *-um* and *-un* as well. Therefore, it is plausible to reconstruct a nominalized auxiliary pJ *wo-n*, which lost its initial labial and then fused with the converbial form of the preceding verb, raising from pJ *-on* to pJ *-un*.

7.5.1.2 Old Japanese

There is no cognate for the incorporated Ryukyuan adnominalizer *-un* available in Western Old Japanese, which may suggest that the form is very archaic and therefore, practically worn-out in Mainland Japanese. A reflex of the adnominalizer pJ *-wo-n* may be present, however, in the Eastern Old Japanese tentative suffix *-unam-*, illustrated in (33).

(33) The use of the EOJ tentative *-unam-*

wanu-ni kwop-unam-o$_1$
I-DAT long.for-TENT-FIN
'[You] will probably long for me.' (MYS XIV: 3476; Vovin 2009a: 819)

Vovin (2009a: 818–819) notices that

> It is widely believed that an EOJ cognate of WOJ *-uram-* ~ *-ram-* is *-unam-*. This seems plausible at first glance, but there is one problem: the correspondence of EOJ *-n-* to WOJ *-r-* is attested only for this cognate [...]. I think this might mean that EOJ *-unam-* and WOJ *-uram-* are in all likelihood only partially related (in their *-am-* part), but the initial parts of these two morphemes probably have different origins.

The reconstruction of the (ad)nominalizers pJ *-n and *-ra supports the composite nature of the tentative suffixes: WOJ -uram- < pJ *wo-ra am- (be-ADN TENT) and EOJ -unam- < pJ *wo-n am- (be-ADN TENT). This derivation is consistent with the proposal in Sections 3.4. and 5.6.1 to derive the tentative suffix -am- from the copular verb *a- and the inclinational suffix *-m-. Such an analytic origin would explain the original requirement of an invariant, adnominal form of the verb before the tentative auxiliary.

Moreover, the copula construction pJ *wo-n (be-ADN) may be incorporated in the Old Japanese necessitive suffix -ube_2- and the adjective ube_2- 'to be proper, to be indeed'. Unger (2013) argues that the OJ -ube_2- is the product of grammaticalization of a double affirmative necessitive contruction of the type 'only if V, it is suitable', consisting of a "conclusive" verb form in -u followed by a conditional pJ *pa and the adjective pJ *(y)i- 'to be good'. The conditional pJ *pa can be traced back to pJ *pa 'place', reflected in OJ ba 'place' and cognate with MK ·pa 'place' (Martin 1997: 11, 24; Robbeets 2005: 403). Thus, OJ yuk-ube_2- 'to be necessary to go' can ultimately be derived from *yuk-[w]o-n pa yi- (go-be-ADN place be.good). The reconstruction of a final nasal in the (ad)nominalizer is necessary to account for the voicing of the labial stop in OJ -ube_2-. In line with this derivation, the independent adjective OJ ube_2- 'to be proper, to be indeed' can be traced back to *wo-n pa yi- (be-ADN place be.good).[15]

The adnominalizer pJ *-n may further be incorporated in the conditional converb OJ -(a)ba, thus deriving OJ yukaba 'if one goes' < *yuka-n-pa (go-ADN place). A similar grammaticalization is assumed to have resulted into Middle Korean ··(u/o)n ·pa 'the situation that', which has subsequently developed into a conditional, temporal and causal converb 'if, when, since' (Martin 1990: 494, 1991a: 285, 1992: 906–907). The past finite OJ -ki_1, the past adnominal OJ -si and the subjective OJ -(a)masi yield conditionals -ke_1ba, -seba and -(a)maseba, respectively, suggesting that they have resulted from contraction with an analytic construction aba, which can be derived from pJ *a-n-pa (be-ADN-situation).

Another trace of the deverbal noun suffix pJ *-n, deriving (ad)nominal forms of the verb without intervening auxiliary *wo-, may be present in sequential voicing in compounds between adjectives and nouns, a phenomenon known to Japanologists as "rendaku" or "compound nigori". In compounds between nouns, sequential voicing has been traced back to the insertion of a nasal genitive n[o], compare OJ yamakawa 'mountains and streams' vs. yamagawa 'mountain stream' < *yama-n[o]-kawa. There are also instances of secondary voicing

---

15 The proposed derivation of OJ ube_2- 'to be proper, to be indeed' contradicts Vovin's (2009: 871) claim that OJ -ube_2- "is certainly a grammaticalized form of the adjective OJ ube_2- 'to be proper, to be indeed'".

between a seemingly zero-marked verbal adjective and a noun, such as OJ *akadama* 'red jewel, coral', MJ *wakagimi* 'young nobleman', J *aozora* 'blue sky', J *akaguro* 'reddish black', etc., in which the insertion of a nasal genitive would not be expected. In such compounds, the voicing may go back to an original adnominalizer pJ *-*n* rather than to a genitive, thus deriving MJ *wakagimi* from pJ *waka-n kimi (be.young-ADN nobleman). Examples of sequential voicing in adjective-noun compounds are relatively frequent in the Ryukyuan languages, e.g. Shodon *thúú gunyi(i)* 'a far country' from *kunyi(i)* 'country'.

7.5.2 pK *-*n*

The (ad)nominalizer pK *-*n* can be reconstructed on the basis of the adnominalizer K -(*u*)*n*, MK -(·*u/o*)*n* (Martin 1992: 719, 722, 924, 2002: 380; Lee & Ramsey 2011: 214). When attached to verbal adjectives, copula and the processive MK -(·)*no*-, it signals imperfective aspect as in MK ῭*wu*-·*nu*-*n swo*·*li* (cry-PROC-ADN sound) 'the sound of crying' (1447 Sek 19: 14b; Martin 1992: 722). When attached to other verbs, it marks perfective aspect as in MK *anc-on ce*·*k*-*uy* (sit.down-ADN time-DAT) 'when seated' (1463 Pep 5: 193b; Martin 2002: 380). However, MK -(·*u/o*)*n* was in essence aspect-neutral: it combined with aspectual morphemes such as MK (·)*no*- processive, MK ··*te* retrospective, MK ··*ke*- perfective to form the corresponding modifiers MK -*non*, ··*ten* and ··*ken*. Before the sixteenth century, lexical adnominalization was generally derived by adding the suffix directly to verb stems as in MK ῭*wu*-·*nu*-*n swo*·*li*, while some clausal adnominalizations incorporated the modulator MK ··*w*ᵘ/*o*- as in (34b). Basically, the modulator was added in case the modified noun was semantically the object of the adnominalized verb, but the distinction soon disappeared. Again, the reconstruction pK *wo-n (be-NML) yields a parallel with the derivation of the Ryukyuan (ad)nominalizer in Section 7.5.1.1.

In the fifteenth century, MK -(·*u/o*)*n* also served as a nominalizer. Although rare, textual examples of clausal nominalization like (34a) can be found, where the suffix is used to nominalize sentences before case suffixes like the instrumental suffix -(*u/o*)*lwo*. And, as best we can tell from the extant data, it had this very function in Old Korean, the earliest documented stage of the language (Ramsey, pc.). MK -(·*u/o*)*n* further leaves a trace in lexical nominalization, e.g. MK ·*ppyeng ho-* 'to be ill' → ·*ppyeng hon* 'ill person' in MK ·*ppyeng ho*-·*n*-*oy neks* 'The spirit of the ill' (1447 Sek 9: 31b; Martin 1992: 924) and in the noun *elGwun* 'adult', which was formed as a deverbal noun.

As a marker of finiteness, MK -(·*u/o*)*n* should always be followed by the clitic noun MK ·*i* 'fact', as illustrated in (34c). However, Contemporary Korean has examples of finite use of the suffix in the logophoric domain, such as in (34d), in which the speech of an individual distinct from the speaker is reported on.

In sum, pK *-n began as a derivational nominalizer applied to verb stems to create nouns like 'adult'. Noun stems expressing properties could be juxtaposed to other nominals to add supplementary information. Whereas lexical nouns were derived by adding the suffix *-n directly to verbal stems, clausal nominalizations incorporated the copula *wo- 'to be'. The relative clauses marked with pK *-(wo)-n developed one step further to mark syntactically independent sentences which added supplementary information in discourse.

(34) The use of the adnominalizer K -(u)n and MK -(·u/o)n

    a. clausal nominalization in MK

        *QWUY-HWA CIN-LYE ho-si-**n**-olwo*
        Wihwa   victorious.return make-HON-**NML**-INSTR
        YE-MANG-i   ta mwot-coW-ona
        public.support-NOM all gather-HUM-CONV
        'By making a victorius return from Wihwa, all public support came together [for him], but...' (1445 Yong; Lee & Ramsey 2011: 214)

    b. clausal adnominalization in MK

        *tut-n-**wo-n**   swoli*
        hear-PROC-**MOD-ADN** sound
        'the sound that one hears' (1459 Wel 2: 53a; Lee & Ramsey 2011: 206)

    c. finite in MK

        MK ··*manh-i   tut-·tolwok ··etwuk ·sin-thi   a·ni*
            be.many-ADV hear-extent more believe-NML NEG
        ·*ho-no-·**n**-i.*
        do-PROC-**ADN**-fact
        'The more I hear, the less I believe.'
        (1482 Nam 1: 36 b; ; Martin 1992: 719)

    d. finite in K

        *to:n-i   iss-nu**n**?*
        money-NOM be.present-PROC.**ADN**
        'He has money [you said]?' (Martin 1992: 722)

7.5.3 pTg *-n(A)

The deverbal noun suffix pTg *-n can be reconstructed as a suffix that derived nominal and adnominal forms from verb stems in most Tungusic languages. This suffix probably is a phonologically reduced from of an original deverbal noun suffix pTg *-nA, the final vowel being lost when the suffix is incorporated in lexicalizations or petrified suffix strings, but preserved when the suffix is still productive as a nominalizer, converb or finite verb form.

As a deverbal noun suffix and clausal nominalizer, pTg *-nA is reflected in the Evenki "nomen perfecti". Complex converb markers incorporating this suffix such as Even -ni-ke:n and Evk. -dyAnmA further testify to its origin as a nominalizer. In most Tungusic languages, except Manchu, however, the nominalizer pTg *-nA has evolved into a converb marker (Benzing 1955a: 1091). From Evenki and Udehe it becomes clear that the interpretation of either simultaneity or immediate anteriority of situations expressed by the converb originally correlated with the telicity of the preceding verb: the converb had imperfective meaning following atelic verbs, while it expressed perfective meaning following telic verbs. In Nanai the reflexes of the converb are restricted to a few relic adverbial expressions.

In most Tungusic languages, except Manchu, the finite use of pTg *-nA is reflected in the person endings of the first and second person singular as well as in the class of verbs, which forms its conjugational base on -nA-. The element -n- found in the endings of the first and second person singular is assumed to be a relic of an older (ad)nominal form (Menges 1943: 239, 241–43; 1968: 80, Benzing 1955a: 1080). The person endings have developed from the personal pronouns in the nominative in pTg *bi 1SG, *si 2SG, *ni 3SG, *büe 1PL EX, *miti 1PL IN, *süe 2PL and *ti 3PL, but in the first and second person singular, however, we find an additional element pTg *-n-. Ikegami (1995: 9–10) objects to assuming an intermixture of two originally different paradigms in the present indicative endings. Such a selective incorporation, however, can be compared to what happened in the case of the Latin inceptive suffix -sc-, which leaves a trace in the first singular in Italian fini-sco 'I finish', but not in the first plural fini-amo 'we finish' and in the first plural in French (nous) fini-ss-ons 'we finish', but not in the first singular (je) fini-s 'I finish' (Greenberg 1991: 311).

In Even, Evenki and Udehe, pTg *-nA also appears as a finite marker in verbs such as pTg *gu:n- 'to say', which form a conjugational base *gu:-nA- from an originally vocalic verb stem *gu:-. The vocalic stem is present in a number of deverbal derivations which are logically incompatible with a nominalized base.

In sum, comparative Tungusic evidence suggests that the deverbal noun suffix pTg *-n(A) was extended to the clause level, first, as a nominalizer, later, developing into a converb marker. The nominalizer also developed into a finite present marker in independent clauses.

7.5.3.1 Manchu

A shown in (35), Ma. *-n* is the most common suffix to derive nouns from verbs, but it is less frequently used for adnominal modification (Gorelova 2002: 194–195). The nominalizations include action nouns (e.g. *acan* 'meeting'), subject nouns from intransitive verbs (e.g. *edun* 'wind') and object (e.g. *efin* 'game') or subject nouns (e.g. *gu:nin* 'mind') from transitive verbs.

Except from some relics in exceptional verb derivations such as Ma. *bi-si-re* (be-si-ADN) 'being' and *o-jo-ro* (become-jo-ADN) 'becoming', the Tungusic division into 4 different verb classes has been reduced to only one class of *-rA* inflection in Manchu. Moreover, unlike the other Tungusic languages, Manchu has no grammatical category of person. The predicate correlates to its agent analytically, through the use of a subject. Therefore, traces of finite use of pTg *-n* have been completely erased.

(35) The use of the Manchu (ad)nominalizer *-n*

    a. lexical nominalization

        aca- 'to meet, combine, be in harmony (intr.)' → *acan* 'meeting, harmony, union'

        edu- 'to blow (of wind) (intr.)' → *edun* 'wind'

        efi- 'to play (tr.)' → *efin* 'game, play'

        gu:ni- 'to think, consider, intend (tr.)' → *gu:nin* 'mind, spirit, thought, opinion'

    b. lexical adnominalization

        necihiye- 'to console, calm down, pacify' → *necihiyen* 'pacification, peaceful, tranquil, serene'

7.5.3.2 Even

In Even, the deverbal noun suffix *-(A)n* derives nouns and adjectives from verbs, such as those illustrated in (36), including action nouns (e.g. *cidakan* 'peeping'), subject nouns from intransitive verbs (e.g *tangun* 'number') and object nouns from transitive verbs (e.g. *bu:n* 'gift'). Reminiscent of the derivation of the *-mi* nominalizer and converb in Section 7.4.3, the deverbal noun suffix is also incorporated in the suffix string pTg *-nA-wi* (ADN-REFL-POSS) reflected in Even *bi-*

'to be' → *bini* 'life, way of life' (Benzing 1955b: 39). As a clausal nominalizer, it is incorporated in the converb *-ni-ke:n*, which is derived from *-ni* and the diminutive *-ke:n* (Benzing 1955b: 105).[16] The western Even dialects use a converb in *-n*, e.g. *begi:-n* 'freezing, while it is freezing', which can be traced back to the nominalizer and converb pTg *-nA* (Benzing 1955a: 1091).

(36) The use of the Even deverbal noun suffix *-(A)n*

a. lexical nominalization

Even *aya:w-* 'to love, adore, wish, want (tr.)' → *aya:wan* 'disposition, wish'

Even *bi-* 'to be' → *bin* 'stay, residence'

Even *bu:-* 'to give, deliver (tr.)' → *bu:n* 'gift, present, delivery'

Even *cidak-* 'to peep, whistle (of squirrel)' → *cidakan* 'peeping, whistling'

Even *nalda-* 'to flow together, converge, fuse (intr.)' → *naldan* 'confluence, junction'

Even *tangu-* 'to be counted (intr.)' → *tangun* 'number, figure, quantity, numeration'

b. lexical adnominalization

Even *del-* 'to become silent' → *delen* 'secret, confidential'

Even *delmi:-* 'to free, to release' → *delmi:n* 'free, independent, unhampered; freedom, release'

Even *dolda-* 'to hear (clearly), to perceive, to sense (tr.)' → *doldan* 'obedient, perceptive, sensitive; obedience, message'

Even *ereng-* 'to care for, to exert oneself (intr.)' → *erengen* 'careful, diligent; care, diligence'

The finite use of pTg *-nA* is reflected in the person endings of the first and second person singular as well as in the class of verbs, which forms its conjugational base on *-nA-*.

As illustrated in Table 2 above, Even verbs incorporate an additional element *-n-* in the endings of the first and second person singular. The forms *ma:-ra-m* (kill-FIN-1SG), *ma:-nri* (kill.FIN-2SG) can be derived from pTg **wa:-rA n(A)-bi* (kill-ADN n-1SG), **wa:-rA n(A)-si* (kill-ADN n-2SG), respectively.

Although most Even verbs take a *-rA* base, a few verbs, however, follow the pattern of *gu:n$_{(1)}$-* 'to say', *bi-* 'to be' or *ga-* 'to take', taking different bases on

---

16 Negidal uses a converb *-na-xan*, which is also derived by the diminutive pTg *-kA:n* (Benzing 1955a: 1091).

-nA, -sA or -dA; see Table 2. The bases on -sA and -dA are not of interest for the present argument, but -$n_{(1)}$ final verbs like gu:$n_{(1)}$- 'to say' deserve our attention because they form a base in -nA, in contrast with -$n_{(2)}$ final verbs like ngen$_{(2)}$- 'to go', which form a standard base in -rA. This may be taken as an indication that -$n_{(1)}$ in gu:$n_{(1)}$- 'say' is originally not part of the verb stem, but incorporates an older adnominalizer pTg *-nA. Additional internal support for the morphological origin of stem final -$n_{(1)}$ comes from the fact that -$n_{(1)}$ is dropped before the majority of aspectual, diathetical and actional suffixes, whereas -$n_{(2)}$ is maintained as a part of the stem in this position, e.g. with -ke:c- intensive: gu:ke:c- 'to repeat over and over again', with -(e)m- optative: gu:m- 'to want to say', with -(e)l inchoative: gu:l- 'to start to speak', with -me:c- reciprocal: gu:me:c- 'to speak to eachother', etc.. The lack of -$n_{(1)}$ when deverbal suffixes are added to the verb base is consistent with its origin as an adnominalizer. Moreover, following verb suffixes that have an origin as case markers or bound nouns, -$n_{(1)}$ is retained, which is in line with its (ad)nominal origin. This is for instance the case before the supinum -dA:i (Benzing 1955b: 97–98), which originates from a dative-locative marker -dA (Benzing 1955b: 32–33) and a possessive-reflexive -i, and before the debtitive marker -so:- 'to have to willy-nilly', which derives from a bound noun -s 'fact' and the verb o- 'to become', e.g. gun-so-n (say-DEB-3SG) 'willy-nilly one must say' (Benzing 1955b: 46–47).

7.5.3.3 Evenki

In Evenki, the deverbal noun suffix -n is reflected in action nouns and object nouns (Nejalkov 1997: 298), such as those illustrated in (37). As a clausal nominalizer, Evenki -n is also incorporated in the converb of simultaneity -dyAnmA, which can be derived from the imperfective -dyA-, the nominalizer -n and the accusative -mA (Nedjalkov 1995: 451).

(37) The use of the Evenki deverbal noun suffix -n

Evk. ala- 'to cross (a mountain)' → alan 'mountain pass'
Evk. kusi- 'to fight' → kusin 'fight'
Evk. davdï- 'to win' → davdïn 'victory'
Evk. gogo- / govo- 'bark' → govon / gogon 'barking'
Evk. ngene- 'to go' → ngenen 'motion, moving ahead, walk'

The Evenki suffix -na ~ -ne ~ -no is used as a so-called "nomen perfecti" or a resultative deverbal noun suffix as illustrated in (38a) (Menges 1968: 81, 82). It is extended to mark clausal nominalization, preceding the ablative case marker -duk or the equative case marker -gAcin 'like, equal to' in (38b). The adverbial insubordination expressed by the Evenki converb -nA probably developed from the nominalizing function. The interpretation of either simultaneity or immediate anteriority of situations expressed by the converb correlates with the telicity of the preceding verb: the converb has imperfective meaning following atelic verbs, while it expresses perfective meaning following telic verbs (Menges 1968: 81–82; Nedjalkov 1995: 453–454, 1997: 270); see (40c/d).

(38) The use of Evenki -nA

    a. lexical nominalization

        *duku:-**na**-w*
        write-**NML**-1SG.POSS
        'That what I wrote' (Menges 1968: 82)

    b. clausal nominalization

        dyu   dagadun mo: baldï-dyara-n
        house near   tree grow-PRS-3SG
        *ekun-mal tegevken-**ne**-gecin-in*
        who-PT   plant-**NML**-EQT-3SG.POSS
        'The tree grows near the house, as if someone planted it.'

    c. imperfective converb

        *nungan alagumni bi-**ne**   ayat   haval-ja-ca-n*
        he   teacher   be-**CONV** good work-IPFV-PST-3SG
        'He worked well as a teacher.' (Nedjalkov 1995: 454)

    d. perfective converb

        *timani-tekin   erde tege-**ne**   beyukte-wki   bi-ce-n*
        morning-every early get.up-**CONV** hunt-HAB.ADN be-PST-3SG
        'Getting up early every morning, he usually immediately went hunting.' (Nedjalkov 1995: 453)

The finite use of pTg *-nA is reflected in the person endings of the first and second person singular as well as in the class of verbs, which forms its conjugational base on -nA-.

As illustrated in Table 3 above, Evenki verbs incorporate an additional element -n- in the endings of the first and second person singular, which can be reconstructed as a trace of the adnominalizer pTg *-nA. The forms *wa:-m* (kill.FIN-1SG), *wa:-nni* (kill.FIN-2SG) can be derived from pTg *wa:-rA n(A)-bi (kill-ADN n-1SG), *wa:-rA n(A)-si (kill-ADN n-2SG), respectively.

As a finite marker, pTg *-nA also appears in verbs such as *gu:n-* 'to say', which form a conjugational base in *-nA-* from an originally vocalic verb stem. The alternating vocalic stem *gu:-* 'to speak' is present in a number of deverbal derivations (Menges 1968: 57, 79).

7.5.3.3 Udehe

There are only a few lexicalizations in Udehe suggesting deverbal derivation with pTg *-n, e.g., pTg *caba- 'to grip' reflected in Evenki *cawari:-*, Negidal *cawa-*, Na. *cawaci-* 'to grip (with claws)', *cawa-kta* 'claw', Orok *cawa-kta* 'claw' is derived in Udehe as *caban* 'claw'.

As illustrated in (39), the Udehe suffix *-na ~ -ne* functions as a perfective converb following a closed class of telic verbs, such as *zawa-* 'to take', *xebu-* 'to bring', *gazi-* 'to take' and *wende-* 'to leave'.

(39) The use of the perfective converb Ud. *-nA*

Bi   abuga-i   bi   in'ei-we-i   xebu-ne: ŋene:-ni
me   father-1SG   me   dog-ACC-1SG   bring-CONV   go.PST-3SG
'My father left, having taken my dog' (Nikolaeva 1999: 139)

The finite use of pTg *-nA is reflected in the Udehe person endings of the first person singular as well as in the class of verbs, which forms its conjugational base on *-nA-*. As illustrated in Table 4 above, Udehe verbs incorporate an additional element *-n-* in the ending of the first person singular, which can be reconstructed as a trace of the adnominalizer pTg *-n(A)*: the form *wa:-mi* (kill.FIN-1SG), for instance, can be derived from pTg *wa:-rA n(A)-bi* (kill-ADN n-1SG).

As a finite marker, pTg *-nA also appears in verbs such as *gun-* 'say', which form a conjugational base *gu-ne-*, but occasionally drop the suffix *-nA* before some verb suffixes, such as the nominalizer *-mi*, e.g. *kepte-we-ne-* (lie-CAUS-FIN-) vs. *kepte-we-mi* (lie-CAUS-NML) 'making somebody lie'; the converb of goal *-lAgA*, e.g. *diga-na-* (talk-FIN-) vs. *diga-laga* (talk-CONV) and the deverbal noun *-nA'A*, e.g. *diga-na-* (talk-FIN-) vs. *diga-na'a* (talk-NML) (Nikolaeva 1999: 140; Menges 1968: 159–160). Considering the probable nominal origin of the finite suffix *-nA*, it would indeed be expected to be logically exclusive with nominalizers and converbs.

7.5.3.4 Nanai

Traces of the deverbal noun suffix pTg *-n are faint in Nanai because an original final nasal is reflected as nasality on the preceding vowel, occasionally completely eroding. However, a few lexicalizations suggest deverbal derivation with pTg *-n, e.g., pTg *tama- 'to pay' is reflected in Evk. tama-, Even tam-, Neg. tama-, Olch. tama-, Orok tama-, Sol. tama-, Oroch tama- and derived in Nanai as tamã 'price'; pTg *jura- 'to draw (a line)' is reflected in Oroch jura-ra 'striped', Olcha jura-n 'scratch, line', Ud. ju:nda- 'to draw', Solon juri:- 'to draw', Neg. joya-n 'scratch, line', Evk. juru:- 'to draw' and derived in Nanai as jorã 'scratch, line'.

The Nanai suffix -na ~ -ne has lexicalized as an adverbializer in a few temporal expressions such as balana 'long ago, earlier', wasoana 'not long ago', tutuene 'in the next year', cimana 'tomorrow'. Although attestations of the underlying verbal bases are lacking, derivations with the deverbal adjective suffix -pci such as bala-pci 'old, ancient, bygone, longstanding' and tutue-pci 'which will take place in the next year' lead to the reconstruction of verbs such as *bala- 'to go by (of time)' and *tutue- 'to follow (in time)'.[17]

The finite use of pTg *-nA is reflected in the Nanai person endings of the first and second person singular. As illustrated in Table 5 above, Nanai verbs incorporate an additional element -n- in verb forms such as wa:-ra-m-bi (kill.FIN-1SG) and wa:-ra-ci (kill.FIN-2SG), which can be derived from pTg *wa:-rA n(A)-bi (kill-ADN n-1SG) and *wa:-ra-n(A)-si (kill-ADN n-1SG), respectively. In contrast to the other Tungusic languages, the conjugational class represented by the verb un- 'say' does not preserve any trace of the suffix since the finite form has merged with the ending -dA- in irregular verbs.

7.5.4 pMo *-n

The deverbal noun suffix pMo *-n, with the epenthetic vowel -u- / -ü- if the stem ended in a consonant, can be reconstructed as a suffix that derived nominal and adnominal forms from verb stems, as shown by the Written Mongolian and Middle Mongolian derivational pairs in (40a/b) (Poppe 1954: 49; 1955: 262; 1972: 45–46; Street 1957: 26). The derivations represent action nouns e.g. MMo. ayun 'fear') as well as subject nouns from intransitive verbs (e.g. WMo. orcin 'surroundings' and object nouns from transitive verbs (e.g. WMo. nayadun 'play, game').

A relic of clausal nominalization is found in the endings of the imperfective present WMo./MMo. -nam, -nAi, -nA which are commonly derived from the *-n nominalizer and a present form of the copula a- 'be' (Poppe 1955: 262–263; Weiers 1966: 151); see Section 7.4.4 for finite present -m and Section 8.3.4 for finite -i and example (40c) for an illustration of the use of MMo. -nam. These suf-

---

17 The suffix Na. -pci derives adjectives from verbs such as Na. amda- 'to imitate' → amdapci 'contagious, provocative, causing the desire of imitation', yada- 'to be(come) tired (of)' → yadapci 'tiresome, tiring' (Avrorin 1961: 203).

fixes indicate that a clause nominalized by pMo *-*n* was originally embedded by the copula **a-*.

According to Poppe (1954: 96; 1955: 276), the nominalizer in *-*n* developed into a converb of manner at a very early date in Mongolic. The nominal origin of the converb can be observed from the fact that it builds a plural form, replacing the ending -*n* by WMo. -*d* and MMo. -*t*. Moreover, in archaic folkloric texts in Khalkha, the -*n* converb can be extended by a diminutive suffix in -*xAn* (Janhunen 2012b: 165), reminiscent of the diminutives incorporated in the converbs in Negidal and Even (see Section 7.5.3.2). This seems to be the only case in which a converb marker takes a nominal derivative suffix in Mongolic.

As illustrated in (40e), the -*t* plural of the deverbal noun suffix in -*n* is used as a finite form in Middle Mongolian (Poppe 1955: 262–264; Weiers 1966: 151–153). Mogol preserves traces of the finite use of *-*n* in its conjugational paradigm, e.g., *irambi* < **ire-* 'come' + *-*n* FIN **bi* 1SG 'I come', *irantši* < **ire-* 'come' + *-*n* FIN + **ci* 2SG 'you come', etc.

In sum, the examples in (40) suggest that the deverbal noun suffix pMo *-*n* was extended to the clause level, the original clausal nominalization leaving a trace in converbial use. Ultimately, the suffix developed into a finite present marker in independent clauses.

(40) The use of the (ad)nominalizer WMo. / MMo. -*(U)n*

    a. lexical nominalization

        MMo. *ayu-* 'to be afraid' → *ayun* 'fear'

        MMo. *hice-* 'to be ashamed'→ *hicen* 'shame'

        MMo. *kökö-* 'to suck, nurse' → *kökön* 'breast'

        WMo. *naγad-* 'to play' → *naγadun* 'play, game'

        WMo. *orci-* 'to turn around, revolve, rotate, transmigrate (intr.)' → *orcin* 'around, in the neighborhood, near, about; neighborhood, surroundings (adv. / postp.)'

        WMo. *talki-* 'to use a scraping stick or beating stick in tanning leather, to beat someone very hard, beat to exhaustion (tr.)' → *talkin* 'scraper or beating stick used in in tanning leather; yoke, burden; an instrument used for torture'

    b. lexical adnominalization

        WMo. *büri-* 'to cover, envelop, upholster (tr.)' → *bürin* 'all, everything, complete; wholly, completely, fully (adj. / adv.)'

        WMo. *ece-* 'to become lean, thin, exhausted, tired (intr.)' → *ecen* 'emaciated, meager, thin (adj.)'

WMo. *gene-* 'to commit mistakes through carelessness, to be negligent'
→ *genen* 'silly, careless, negligent, naïve (adj.)'

WMo. *ilbi-* 'to smooth with the hand, stroke, caress, appease (tr.)' → *ilbin* 'bent, curved, twisted; sly, artful (adj.)'

WMo. *singge-* 'to be absorbed, to dissolve (in liquid), to be saturated (intr.)' → *singgen* 'fluid, thin (in density or consistency), sparse (of vegetation, hair) (adj.)'

c. clausal nominalization in MMo.

*adu'u ire-ge kerey bayi-**nam***
horse come-NML legal.case be-**FIN**
'The horse must be delivered' (Weiers 1966: 152)

d. converb in WMo.

Molon Toyin nis-ün ire-bei
Molon Toyin fly-CONV come-PST
'Molon Toyin arrived flying' (Sárközi 2004: 46)

e. finite in MMo.

ba ulus irgen ulu temece-t
we land people NEG strive.for-FIN.PL
'we do not strive for land and people' (SH 64; Weiers 1966: 151)

7.5.5 pTk *-*n*

The deverbal noun suffix pTk *-*n* can be reconstructed as a suffix that derived nominal and adnominal forms from verb stems on the basis of reflexes in Old Turkic and Chuvash. The suffix derived action nouns, such as the ones reflected in Chuvash and subject or object nouns, such as the ones reflected in Old Turkic.

It was gradually extended to the clausal level, deriving complement clauses, relics of which are still reflected in Old Turkic and Chuvash and relative clauses, which are restricted to Chuvash. The perfective or imperfective interpretation of the original suffix probably depended on the telicity of the preceding verb base. Although the original distinction was lost, the imperfective reading left a trace in the Chuvash negative marker. Only in Chuvash, the perfective adnominalizer grammaticalized into a perfect finite marker.

7.5.5.1 Old Turkic

The Old Turkic deverbal noun suffix -(*X*)*n* that derives nominal and adnominal forms from verb stems is illustrated in the derivational pairs in (41a/b) (Poppe

1972: 45–46; Ramstedt 1952: 94; Erdal 1991: 301–307). The suffix derives subject nominals from intransitive verbs (e.g. *yašïn* 'lightning') and object nominals from intransitive verbs (e.g. *san* 'number, set of things counted'). Deverbal nouns in *-(X)n* are commonly derived with the denominal verbalizer *-A-*, and most rarely with the verbalizer *-lA-*. Since *-lA-* became more common than *-A-* with time, Erdal (2002: 301) takes this as an indication that "*-Xn* may have been more active in early pre-Turkic stages than in later ones." The observation that deverbal nouns in *-(X)n* all go back to underived verb roots further supports their archaic nature.

The unique association of the deverbal noun suffix *-Xn* with the verbalizer in *-A-* suggests that the origin of *-A-* may be a copula pTk **a-* 'to be' (see Section 3.4.1). This hypothesis is supported by the parallel with the incorporation of the Mongolian copula *a-* 'to be' in the present marker WMo. *-nam* (see Section 7.5.4). If this analysis is correct, the example in (41c) can be regarded as a trace of the use of pTk **-n* in clausal nominalization, whereby the complement clause is embedded by the copula pTk **a-* 'to be'.

(41) The use of the (ad)nominalizer OTk. *-(X)n*

    a.   lexical nominalization

           OTk. *ek-* 'to sow (tr.)' → *ekin* 'sown land, the crop growing on it'
           OTk. *sa-* 'to count (tr.)' → *san* 'number, set of things counted'
           OTk. *tüg-* 'to bind a knot (tr.)' → *tügün* 'knot'
           OTk. *yaro-* 'to be(come) bright (intr.)' → *yarïn* 'dawn, the morrow'
           OTk. *yašï-* 'to flash (intr.)' → *yašïn* 'lightning'
           OTk. *yal-* 'to flame (intr.)' → *yalïn* 'flame'

    b.   lexical adnominalization

           OTk. *adïr-* 'to separate' → *adïn* 'other, different'
           OTk. *büt-* 'to become complete (intr.)' → *bütün* 'complete, entire, whole'
           OTk. *irk-* 'to collect, assemble' → *irkin* 'collected together in one place'
           OTk. *kalï-* 'to rise in the air (intr.)' → *kalïn* 'thick, massive, dense'
           OTk. *yak-* 'to be near, to approach (intr.)' → *yakïn* 'near'
           OTk. *yïg-* 'to heap up (tr.)' → *yïgïn* 'heaped up'

    c.   clausal nominalization

           kök-in   *yašï-**n**-a-yur*   *köl*   *suv-lar-ï*
           blue-POSS flash-**NML**-VBL-FIN lake water-PL-POSS
           'the lake's waters are flashing with the blue of ...' (Erdal 1991: 427)

7.5.5.2 Chuvash

In Chuvash, the so-called "nomen perfecti" *-nă ~ -nĕ* functions mainly as a perfective adnominalizer and a perfect finite form, but contracting with the possessive third singular on *-i* to *-ni*, it can derive deverbal nouns (Krüger 1961: 154–155), as illustrated in (42a). Taking arguments as in (42b), *-ni* can be used as a clausal nominalizer.

(42) The use of the nominalizer Chu. *-ni*

    a. lexical nominalization

        vula- 'to read' → *vulani* 'reading , the act of reading'

        tărăš- 'to try, strive, busy oneself, be diligent' → *tărăšni* 'striving, endeavor'

    b. clausal nominalization

        kĕneke vula-ni usăllă
        book   read-NML useful
        'Reading books is useful' (Krüger 1961: 154)

The simplex ending *-nă ~ -nĕ* is used to form complement clauses or relative clauses as in (43a/b). As a finite marker, the suffix is used to express perfect tense, as illustrated in (43c).

(43) The use of the (ad)nominalizer Chu. *-nĂ*

    a. clausal nominalization

        Kaχal kay-nă-ne kur-sassăn
        Lazybones come-NML-ACC see-PFV.CONV
        'When they saw Lazybones coming' (Krüger 1961: 154)

    b. clausal adnominalization

        esĕ kur-nă etem
        you see-ADN person
        'the man whom you saw' (Krüger 1961: 153)

    c. finite

        śïn kur-nă
        person see-FIN
        'The person saw' (Krüger 1961: 153)

The development of the suffix final *-Ă* is probably due to the addition of final lax vowel in Chuvash to words originally ending in a consonant, such as in Chu. *külĕ* 'lake' (cf. OTk *köl* 'large body of water, pool, lake'), Chu. *ută* 'straw' (cf. OTk *ot* 'grass, vegetation'), Chu. *yĭtă* 'dog' (cf. OTk *it* 'dog'), etc. There is no final vowel added in the corresponding negative form *-mA-n*; see (44). This can be explained by the fact that default stress is word-final in Turkic languages, while the negative is prestressed. Lack of stress on the negative suffix, probably blocked the addition of the final lax vowel.

(44) The use of the negative (ad)nominalizer Chu. *-mAn*

a. nominalization

pĕl-men-ten   an   ıyt.
know-NEG.NML-ABL NEG ask.IMP
'Don't ask a man who doesn't know.'

b. adnominalization

pĕl-men   sămax
know-NEG.ADN   word
'an unknown word; a word one didn't know' (Krüger 1961: 154)

c. finite

śemyi-sem pĕri te sis-men.
family-PL one PT notice-NEG.FIN
'Not one of the family members noticed' (Krüger 1961: 154)

The negative adnominalizer *-mAn* can have either an imperfective or perfective reading, as illustrated in (45b). I do not exclude that the imperfective or perfective connotation of the adnominalizer originally depended on the telicity of the verb base, but that the imperfective connotation was gradually lost, leaving a trace in the negative only.

7.6 pTEA *-xA ~ *-kA

7.6.1 pJ *-ka

The resultative adnominalizer pJ *-ka*, which derives resultative adnominal forms from verbal adjectives and verb stems can be reconstructed on the basis of Ryukyuan and Old Japanese data. In Ryukyuan, the derivations are restricted to verbal adjective stems. Whereas Shodon testifies to the original use of this suffix without the intervention of a copula, the periphrastic constructions found in Old Ryukyuan, the Miyako dialects and in Yonaguni are probably secondary. In Mainland Japanese, the derivations with *-ka* seem to involve original verb stems as well as verbal adjectives. The finite use of the suffix, observed in some Kyushu dialects and in Shodon, may have developed over clausal adnominalization, as suggested by one Old Japanese adjective etymology.

7.6.1.1 Ryukyuan

The common pattern in Ryukyuan verbal adjective inflection is to contract forms of a structure that consists of the nominalizing *-sa (see Section 7.6.1.1) plus the auxiliary a(r)- 'to be'. However, in certain Southern Ryukyuan languages, such as in the Miyako and Yonaguni dialects and in some Northern Ryukyuan languages, such as in Shodon, adjective inflection is built upon a nominalizing *-ka. In the Miyako dialects and in Yonaguni, this construction involves an auxiliary a(r)- 'to be', but in Shodon, it appears without copula. As illustrated in example (45a), Shodon has three competing possibilities for adnominal modification: the bare adjective base in its nominal encoding without verbal ending; the adnominal form in -kha or; most commonly, the contracted construction consisting of nominalizing -sa plus the adnominal form of the copula a-n (for Shodon adnominal -n see Section 7.5.1.1). In finite position, -kha is used more frequently than the periphrastic construction consisting of -sa plus the present form of the copula a-m (for Shodon finite -m see Section 7.4.1.1). However, further inflections for tense, aspect, mood etc. build on the periphrastic construction, e.g. Qaháá-sa-ta-m (red-NML-COP.PERF-FIN) 'it was red'.

(45) The use of the Shodon adnominalizer -kha as compared to other adnominalizing constructions (Martin 1970: 134)

    a. adnominal

        Qaháá   *mun*
        red   thing
        Qaháá-kha   *mun*
        red-ADN   thing
        Qaháá-sa-n   *mun*
        red-NML-COP.ADN thing
        'a red thing'

    b. finite

        Qaháá-kha
        red-FIN
        Qaháá-sa-m
        red-NML-COP.FIN
        'it is red'

It is commonly suggested that the Shodon ending -*kha* is a reduction from the converb -*ku* and the copula *a*- 'to be' (Martin 1970: 133; Vovin 2009a: 460–461), but this derivation has two problems: first, it cannot account for the aspiration in the Shodon suffix and, second, it fails to explain why -*kha*, in contrast to -*sa*, is not followed by inflected forms of the contracted copula. In Shodon, voiceless stops were aspirated before mid and low vowels, i.e. /k/ became /kh/ before /e, o, a/ but unaspirated before high vowels, i.e. k remained unchanged before /i, u/. By consequence, pR *-*ka* is expected to yield Shodon -*kha*, while pR *-*ku* will yield Shodon *-*ku*. Besides, the forms in -*kha* do not bear traces of copula inflection such as -*m*, -*n*, -*tam*, etc. in the -*sa* constructions. Therefore, I derive Shodon -*kha* from the adnominalizer pR -*ka* < pJ *-*ka* without copula intervention.

Even if the Miyako adjective inflections in -*k-ar*- and the zero affixed Yonaguni cognates are combined with the auxiliary *ar*- 'to exist' (Bentley 2008: 238–239, 243–301), there is no evidence that they should be derived from *-*k[u] ar*- rather than from *-*k[a] ar*-, the latter being phonologically somewhat more plausible because of the juxtaposed low vowels. Although in Old Ryukyuan the construction -*sa ar*- was predominantly used, Vovin (2009a: 460–461) provides some relic examples such as *yo-k-ar-u* (good-NML-exist-ADN) and *kiya-k-ar-u* (bright-NML-exist-ADN) testifying to the gradual replacement of an older competing periphrastic construction *-*ka ar*-.

7.6.1.2 Mainland Japanese

Old Japanese preserves evidence for the lexicalization of a resultative adnominalizer pJ *-*ka*, which derives adnominal forms from verbal adjectives and verb stems, as illustrated in (46a).[18] Apart from OJ *nipaka* 'sudden', OJ *ogosoka* 'solemn, majestic', OJ *paruka* 'far, distant, remote' and OJ *sayaka* 'clear, bright' below, deverbal derivation is also frequently seen in verb stems derived with the fientive verbalizer *-*ya*- (see Section 6.5.1): OJ *awoyaka* 'blue' (< OJ *awo* 'blue'), OJ *ko₁mayaka* 'densely (growing)' (< pJ *koma*- 'to be small, fine'); OJ *matoyaka* 'round' (< OJ *mato* 'round'); OJ *mame₂yaka* 'serious' (< OJ *mame₂* 'sincere'); OJ *nagoyaka* 'soft'(< pJ *nanko*- 'to calm down' in OJ *nag*- 'to mow (tr.), become

---

18 As mentioned in Section 3.2.1, there are also some instances in which nominal bases are derived with pJ *-*ka*, such as pJ *ak-i-ra* (open-NML-NML) 'open, clear' → OJ *aki₁raka* (4.11) 'evident, unmistakable, clear, pure' ; OJ *kasu* (2.4) 'dregs' → MJ *kasuka* (3.7b) 'faint (sound or color), dim'; OJ *madara* (3.1) 'spots' → OJ *madaraka* (4.11) 'striped, mottled' ; OJ *pada* (2.4) 'skin, flesh' → OJ *padaka* (3.6) 'naked'; OJ *pono* (?2.3) 'faint, slight' → OJ *ponoka* (3.7b) 'subtle'; OJ *sidu* (?2.5) 'poor, miserable' → OJ *siduka* (3.7b) 'quiet'; OJ *tap₁ira* (3.5a) 'flat' → OJ *tap₁iraka* (4.11) 'flat'; OJ *tas*- A 'add' + OJ -*i* NML in OJ *tasi ni* 'adequately' → OJ *tasika* (3.7 b) 'certain, sure' and OJ *tuyu* (2.5) 'dew' → OJ *tuyuka* (3.7 b) 'dewy, tearful'.

calm (intr.)', OJ *nagi*₂- 'to become calm', OJ *nago*₁*m*- 'to calm down'); OJ *nikoyaka* 'gentle' (< OJ *niko*₁(-) 'soft'); OJ *panayaka* 'gorgeous, graceful' (< OJ *pana* 'flower'); OJ *sumiyaka* 'swift, clear' (< OJ *sum*- 'to become clear' + OJ -*i* NML); etc. Since pJ **-ya*- derives fientive meaning in the sense of 'to become like the property of the base', it requires a resultative suffix pJ **-ka* to derive a stative adjectival noun 'being the property'. The resultative meaning of the adnominal suffix is also evidenced by the observation that it derives object nominals from transitive verbs, e.g. OJ *paruka* 'far, distant, remote' expresses the meaning 'what is removed' rather than 'removing'.

Since the suffix is lexicalized in only a few adjectival nouns and thus no longer productive in Old Japanese, there is no evidence left of its original syntactic behavior. Nevertheless, the etymological analysis of OJ *me*₂*duraka* 'strange, rare, precious' in (46b) suggests, that the adnominal verb forms originally could take arguments such as OJ *me*₂ 'eye' in the dative, much like a relative clause. Finite forms ending in -*ka* such as *yo-ka* 'it is good', *na-ka* 'it is not' are found in parts of Kyushu (Martin 1987: 803; 1988: 373); see (46c).

Note that in contrast to both Middle and Contemporary Japanese, Old Japanese -*ka* adjectives can directly modify head nouns without intervening copula. From Middle Japanese onwards nominal modification needs the intervention of the adnominal form *naru* of the copula *nari* 'to be', which is abbreviated to *na* from Late Middle Japanese onwards (e.g. J *tasika na hito* 'trustworthy person').

(46) Reflexes of the use of pJ **-ka* in Mainland Japanese

    a. lexical adnominalization

        pJ **ata*- ~ *atu*- 'to be warm' in place name Atami (< **ata-umi* 'warm sea'), OJ *atu*- B 'to be warm' → OJ *atataka* (4.11) 'warm'

        pJ **isasa*- 'to be little, few' in Kikai *qisaa*- B 'to be little, few' → OJ *isasaka* (4.x) 'a little, somewhat, slight'

        pJ **koma*- 'to be small, fine' in Shuri *guma*- 'small', Yo. *kuma*- B 'fine', OJ *ko*₁*mayaka* 'densely (growing)' → MJ *komaka* (3.7b) 'fine, small, detailed'

        pJ **nipa*- 'to appear suddenly' in OJ *nipasi*- 'sudden', OJ *nipi*₁ 'new' (OJ -*i* NML, see Section 8.3.1) → OJ *nipaka* (3.7b) 'sudden'

        pJ **ənkə-sə*- (be.majestic-CAUS-) 'make majestic (tr.)' in OJ *ogo*₂*r*- A 'to be extravagant, get proud, be arrogant' → OJ *ogosoka* (4.11) 'solemn, majestic' pJ *paru- 'to clear, remove (tr.)' in OJ par- B 'to open ground, clear land (cultivation)' → OJ paruka (3.7b) 'far, distant, remote'[19]

pJ *saya- 'to become clear, pure' in OJ saye- ?B 'to get clear, bright; get cold', OJ sayame$_2$- ?B 'to clean, purify (tr.)' → OJ sayaka (3.7b) 'clear, bright'

OJ tura- A 'to be tough' → OJ me$_2$duraka (4.11) 'strange, rare, precious'

b. clausal adnominalization

OJ   me$_2$duraka pi$_1$to$_2$
pre-OJ *me$_2$-n(i) tura-ka   pi$_1$to$_2$
       eye-DAT be.tough-ADN person
       'strange person'

c. finite

Kyushu dialects   yo-ka
                      good-FIN
                      'It's good; OK.'

7.6.2 pK *-kAi

Although Vovin (2001: 192) proposes to include the Korean perfective marker MK -·ke-/-·ka-/-·Ge-/-·Ga- / -·e- / -·a- in the present etymology, his proposal yields too many problems involving external comparison and internal analysis and should therefore be rejected. As far as external comparison is concerned, the Middle Korean suffix is restricted to the marking of aspect, unlike the other cognates proposed here; it lacks nominal, adnominal or finite function. In order to express these functions, a specific suffix must be attached to MK -·kA-, such as for instance the adnominalizer -n in example (47).

(47) The use of the perfective MK -·kA-

¨ti·na-**ke**-n   ¨nyey ¨nwuy
pass.by-**PFV**-ADN   old   world
'a long past ancient world'

As far as internal analysis is concerned, the perfective MK -·kA- is commonly explained as a grammaticalization of the verb MK ·ka- 'to go' (Martin 1992: 263,

---

[19] See Section 3.3.4 (50) for other stems reflecting pJ *paru- 'to clear, remove (tr.)'

601; 2002: 374) because it can not mark perfective aspect on other motion verbs such as MK ·wo- 'to come', MK ·na- 'to emerge' and MK ·ka- 'to go'. The perfective stem of MK ·wo- 'to come' is exceptionally derived with MK ·na- 'to emerge', substituting for the stem MK ·ka- 'go', which would have been incompatible with 'come'. The verb MK ·na·ka- is taken as 'go out' rather than as the perfective of 'to emerge'. The combination *·ka·ka- is impossible in Korean, suggesting an unwanted iteration. The fact that monosyllabic high-accent stems that end in a vowel retain their accent before -·kA-, but lose it before most other verb morphemes, also indicates that the perfective goes back to a bound verb stem. On the basis of these observations, the perfective marker MK -·kA- will not be considered in the reconstruction of the Transeurasian resultative nominalizer.

However, Korean reflects a deverbal resultative and instrumental noun suffix K -kay / -key, -ay/ -ey , MK -·kay / -·key, -·Gay/ -·Gey (Martin 1992: 429, 600). As illustrated in (48), the suffix derives object nouns from transitive verbs (e.g. kkalkay 'cushion') as well as subject nouns from intransitive verbs (e.g. kalikay 'a twofold screen').

(48) The use of the deverbal noun suffix K -kAy ~ -Ay, MK -·KAy

K cci- 'to steam (tr.)' → ccikey 'thin stew'

K elk- 'to weave, make (tr.)' → elkay 'structure'

K kkal- 'to spread out (e.g. a bed, a mat), lay out, sit on (tr.)' → kkalkay 'cushion'

K kali- 'to hide, shield (tr.)' → kalikay 'a twofold screen'

K kalu- 'to split, cut, divide (tr.)' → kallay 'division'

MK kuž- 'draw a line (around), delimit, cut off' → ˙˙kužGay 'scissors'

K kkwumi- 'to decorate, ornament (tr.)' → kkwumikay 'ornament'

K nal-, MK nol- 'to fly (intr.)' → K nalkay, MK ·nolkay 'wing'

K nol- 'to play, enjoy oneself (intr.)', nolli- 'to let/ make someone play' → nolikay 'a plaything, a toy; a pendent trinket worn by ladies at their waist'

MK pyey- 'to pillow' → MK ·pyekay 'pillow'

K teph- 'to cover with, put on (e.g. bedclothes) (tr.)' → tephkay 'bedding, bed clothes, quilt, (bed) covers'

The deverbal noun suffix MK -·KAy has gradually developed into an adverbializer in the history of Korean, e.g. K ki:l- 'to be long' → killay '(for) long'; K molu- 'not to know' → mo:llay 'secretly'. Rhee (1996: 111) notes that it was rarely used in this function prior to the 20th century. Middle Korean reflects a transitional stage between deverbal noun suffix and adverbializer, in which the suffix assumes an infinitive-like function in verb compounding, such as in causative constructions with the auxiliary MK *ho-* 'to do' or in prohibitive constructions with MK *¨ma(l)-*'to refrain from'.

Given that the contemporary monophthongs *ay* and *ey* go back to Middle Korean diphthongs, in which the *y* offglide commonly derives from contraction of a syllable with a high front vowel (e.g K *ka:y* < MK *ka·hi* 'dog'), it is not unlikely that MK -·*kAy* ultimately derives from pK *-*kA-i*, in which *-*kA* would be a resultative adnominalizer and *-*i* the bound noun 'fact (that); that (which)' reflected in MK *i*. This reconstruction gains credibility in the light of the analysis of the Korean explicit ending in Section 7.3.2 and of the comparative evidence.

7.6.3 pTg *-xA: ~ *-kA:

The Tungusic languages provide evidence for the reconstruction of two allomorphs of one resultative deverbal noun suffix: pTg *-*xA:* and pTg *-*kA:*. The allomorphs show signs of being variants of the same suffix in two different phonological positions in Manchu and Udehe. In the Northern Tungusic languages, where as illustrated in (49), the reflexes of pTg *-*k-* and *-*x-* have merged into Evk. -*k-* and Even -*k-*, it is not possible to distinguish between both allomorphs (Benzing 1955a: 976–977; Starostin et al. 2003: 158, 160). Note that Benzing's (1955a: 989) reconstruction of pTg **x-* was limited to word-initial position. The reconstruction of intervocalic pTg *-*x-* has been proposed by Dybo (1990) and has been followed in Starostin et al. (2003: 158).

(49) Sound correspondences reflecting pTg *-k- and *-x-

pTg	Ma.	Na.	Olč.	Orok	Oroč.	Ud.	Sol.	Neg.	Evk.	Even
*-k-	k~h	k	k	k	k~x	k~x~g~'	k~g~x	k~x	k	k
*-x-	k~h	x~ø	x~ø	x~ø	k~x~ø	k~x~g~'	k~g~x~ø	k~x	k	k

The Manchu and Udehe reflexes of pTg *-*xA:* ~ *-*kA:* show variation in a similar environment: in Manchu most verb stems are thematic and take -*hA*, whereas verbs originally ending in *n or *b (? < *β) take -*kA*; in Udehe most thematic verbs stems take -*gA*, whereas verb stems ending in an original continuant *n, *m, *y or *β take -*kA*, but there is a limited set of high-frequency verbs, which has preserved -*xA*. This suggests that the de-fricativization of *-*xA* in continuant environment was already accomplished in proto-Tungusic. Tracing the allomorphy back to the proto-Tungusic level is further supported by the observation that -*kA*- can even follow verb stems with a stem-final vowel in Manchu and elsewhere in Manchuric, that must be reconstructed with a stem-final continuant in proto-Tungusic.

Lexicalizations in Even and Evenki suggest that pTg *-xA: ~ *-kA: originally functioned as a resultative deverbal noun suffix, deriving subjects of intransitive verbs and objects of transitive verbs. Juxtaposed to other nouns, some deverbal nouns developed into nominal adjectives. The use of the Manchu suffix in complement and relative clauses indicates that the resultative nominalizer was extended to the clause level. This observation is confirmed by the analysis of converbial forms in Udehe and Nanai reflecting pTg *-xA-pi ~ *-kA-pi as compounds of the resultative nominalizer and the accusative suffix in the reflexive (pTg *-pi < *-pA-i ACC-REFL; Benzing 1955b: 1091). The perfective adnominalizer probably underwent insubordination, resulting in the finite use preserved in Manchu, Even, Nanai and Udehe. The insubordination process triggered the development of temporal from aspectual distinctions, i.e. a grammaticalization from resultative nominal to perfective adnominal to perfect finite marking.

7.6.3.1 Manchu

The resultative nominalizer in Manchu is *-ha ~ -he ~ -ho* with a voiceless velar fricative, while about 185 verbs take the allomorph *-ka ~ -ke ~ -ko* with a voiceless velar stop and some 14 verbs take the allomorph *-ngka ~ -ngke ~ -ngko* (Gorelova 2002: 240–41, 255–256). Vovin (1997: 271–274) proposes that Manchu intervocalic *-k-* goes back to proto-Manchu *-nk-*. In many cases, the *-kA-* allomorph is indeed attached to verbs, which had an original stem final nasal, e.g. Ma. *dosi-* 'to enter' → *dosi-ka*, whereby the causative Ma. *dosim-bu* still preserves a trace of the original stem-final nasal. However, it seems that the allomorphy goes back to the proto-Tungusic level and that *-kA-* appears following verb stems with stem-final *-b-* (? < *-β-*) as well, e.g. Ma. *je-* 'eat' → *je-ke*, whereby the Northern and Southern Tungusic languages (Evk. / Even *jep- ~ jeb-*, Neg. *jep-*, Solon *jeb-*, Na. *jeb- ~ jep-*, Ud. *jepte-*, Orok *deptu-*) reflect a stem-final *b* in pTg *jeb-* 'to eat', which was already lost in proto-Manchuric (Sibe *je-*, Ma. *je-*, Jurchen *je-fu* 'to eat').[20] Moreover, in Section 6.4.3.1 a large number of anticausative verbs such as *akša-* 'to become spoiled', *arsu-* 'to sprout' and *badara-* 'to become wide, expand', which take the irregular allomorph *-kA* have been argued to incorporate an original anticausative suffix *-p-*.

---

20 Proto-Tungusic velar clusters, consisting of a sonorant or labial stop *p* plus a velar stop *k*, yielded the reflex *-k-* in Manchu, e.g., pTg *purke:-* 'to be bored, angry' in Evk. *hurke:-*, Even *hörken-* 'to be bored' yielded Ma. *fuke-* 'to be angry' or pTg *japkun* 'eight' in Evk. *japkun*, Na. *jakpõ*, Ud. *jakpun*, etc. yielded Ma. *jakun*.

When Manchu *-hA* meets a stem-final nasal, which developed later in the course of Manchu history, the suffix undergoes defricativation, while the nasal undergoes velarization, resulting in the allomorph *-ngkA*. In most instances, the allomorph Ma. *-ngkA* reflects the contraction of the processive suffix in *-nA* (See Section 5.4.3.1) plus the resultative nominalizer in *-hA* (Ma. *-ngkA* < *-nkA* < *-nhA* < *-nA-hA*). The verbs Ma. *ba-* 'to be lazy, tired, gnaw a hole', *jo-* 'to bring to mind, recall, mention', *we-* 'to melt' all form resultatives in *-ngkA*, i.e. *bangka, jongko, wengke*, but these verbs have corresponding lexicalized derivations with the processive suffix, i.e. *bana-* 'to be(come) lazy', *jono-* 'to recall', *wene-* 'to melt' on which their resultative form seems to be built.[21] In such cases, contrary to Vovin's proposal, Ma. *-k-* does not go back to proto-Manchu *-nk-*. It therefore appears that following *-n-* and *-b-* stems, the reflex of pTg *-xA* underwent defricativation to pTg *-kA* and was reflected in Ma. *-kA*, whereas following other stems the original voiceless velar fricative was retained and reflected in Ma. *-hA*.

Example (50a) illustrates the use of the resultative nominalizer followed by the dative suffix, a construction which denotes an action after which another action starts. The converb in *-hAi ~ -kAi* denoting durative, frequentative and intensive action is thought to have originated from the nominalizer followed by the marker of the genitive case *-i* (Gorelova 2002: 281). As illustrated in (50b), *-hA / -kA* is also used as a perfective adnominalizer of relative clauses. In (50c), it appears as a finite past marker. There is an alternative past form in *-hAbi*, which can be derived from the form of the resultative nominalizer and the copula *bi*. Since a corresponding form *-kAbi* is lacking, it can be argued that the construction with the copula is a relatively new formation.

(50) Reflexes of the resultative deverbal noun suffix pTg *-kA*: in Manchu

a. clausal nominalization

*muse ere wakšam-be geli wa-**ha**-de*
we this frog-ACC also kill-**NML**-DAT
muke iningdari lakcaraku: eye-mbi
water every.day uninterruptedly flow-FIN
'After we kill these frogs water will flow uninterruptedly'
(SK 68; Gorelova 2002: 257–258)

b. clausal adnominalization

*ere abala-me gene-**he** gucu-sa*
this hunt-CONV go-**ADN** companion-PL

---

21 The processive suffix Ma. *-nA-* also surfaces in the imperfective (ad)nominal forms Ma. *bandara, jondoro* and *wendere* (Gorelova 2002: 255).

>   ji-ci   ai   seme   ala-mbi
>   come-CONV what   reason   tell-FIN
>   'What will (our) companions, who have gone hunting, tell (us) when they return?' (SK 64; Gorelova 2002: 257)

c. finite

>   ahu:n   ji-he   turgun-de,   deo   gene-**he**
>   elder.brother come-ADN   reason-DAT,   younger.brother go-**FIN**
>   'Since the elder brother came, the younger brother went away' (Gorelova 2002: 488)

7.6.3.2 Even

Although Benzing (1955b: 38) labels Even *-ka: ~ -ke:* as an instrumental deverbal noun suffix, the derivational pairs in (51a) suggest that the suffix can also derive action nouns (e.g. *hi:lka* 'suffering'), subject nouns (e.g. *etka* 'power, government, regime) and object nouns (e.g. *ewi:ke:* 'game, toy') as well as adjectives (e.g. *no:dika*: 'beautiful, appealing'). The derivation of object nouns from transitive verbs suggests that the original meaning of the suffix is resultative.

As a finite suffix, Even *-kA* is used to express warnings in the sense of 'Watch out or you will … !' (Benzing 1955a: 1089; 1955b: 99, 101–102); see (51b). These expressions are probably derived from an original perfective meaning, comparable to the use of English 'you are dead' in the meaning of 'Watch out or you will die!". The future suffix *-ji- ~ -ci-* can optionally precede the ending, without observable change in meaning, e.g. *Ma:-k* (kill-FIN) and *Ma-ji-k* (kill-FUT-FIN) both mean '(Watch out or) he will kill you!'

(51) Reflexes of the resultative deverbal noun suffix pTg *-kA:* in Even

a. lexical (ad)nominalization

>   *el-* 'to rise, elevate (intr.)' → *elke:-* 'appearance, exhibition' in *elke: o:-* 'to appear, exhibit'
>
>   *et-* 'to conquer, master, get the upper hand (intr.)' → *etka* 'power, government, regime, law; legal, lawful, lawgiving'
>
>   *ewi:-* 'to play (game, instrument) (tr.); to enjoy oneself, to pass the time (intr.)' → *ewi:ke:* 'game, toy'
>
>   *hi:l-* 'to suffer, be needy, agonize (intr.)' → *hi:lka* 'suffering, agony, need; miserable, needy, poor'
>
>   *hi:ral-* 'to become angry' → *hi:raŋka* 'angry, furious'

no:diw- 'to gloat over the sight of something, observe something with joy, enjoy; to appeal to' → *no:dika*: 'beautiful, appealing'

te:w- 'to put (into), to insert; to load, to fill (tr.)' → *tepke* 'cover, bag, casing, husk, container'

b. finite

mu-le: *tik-ci-**ke**-riw*
water-DAT fall-FUT-**FIN**-1SG
'[Watch out or] I will fall into the water!' (Benzing 1955b: 102)

7.6.3.3 Evenki

In Evenki, the resultative deverbal noun suffix has been preserved in a few derivational pairs, such as those in (52) deriving nouns and adjectives from verb stems (Doerfer 1978: 8; Nedjalkov 1997: 306).

(52) Reflexes of the resultative deverbal noun suffix pTg *-kA:* in Evenki

culbin- 'to grow thin' → *culbika* 'thin, meagre'
kalta- 'to split in halves' → *kaltaka* 'half, one of a pair'
upcu- 'to argue, dispute' → *upcuke* 'disputable'
sukca- 'to ruin' → *sukcaka:* 'ruin'

7.6.3.4 Udehe

In Udehe, the resultative nominalizer pTg *-kA:* is reflected in the finite perfect paradigm, which refers to perfective events in the past (Nikolaeva 1999: 147, 147; Benzing 1955a: 1089: "Präteritum II"). As opposed to the past tense, it implies perfective meaning in the sense of relevance for the current situation, adding the semantic element 'already'. The suffix *-ga-/ -'a- ~ -ge-/ -'e-* is added after most vowel stems as in (53b), while *-ka- ~ -ke-* follows consonant stems, e.g. Ud. *diang-ka-i* 'I have (already) said it'. However in the small class of irregular verbs that conjugates like Ud. *ga-* 'to take' and further includes Ud. *o-* 'to become', *bu-* 'to die', *ne-* 'to insert' and *nag-* 'to meet', the perfect appears as *-xa*, e.g. Ud. *ga-xa-mi* 'I have (already) taken'. This seems to indicate an original velar fricative suffix pTg *-xA*, which was preserved as such in a limited set of high-frequency – and therefore irregular – verbs, but devoiced to * *-γA-* between vowels (*..u-xa > *..uγa > ..uga, *..i-xa > *..iγa > ..iga, *..a-xa > *a-γa > ..'a, *..e-xe > *..e-γe > ..'e), while it underwent de-fricativization following sonorants and fricatives (*..n-xa > *..n-ka > ..ngka, *..y-xa > *..y-ka > ..gka, *..ß-xa > *..ß-ka > ..kpa, *..m-xa > *..m-ka > ..ngka). Note that Menges (1968: 138) and Simonov (1988: 55) postulate a voiced fricative /y/ in opposition to the voiced stop /g/ for some Udehe dialects, but the phonological contrast seems to have merged in the southern varieties of Udehe, described by Nikolaeva (1999: 29).

As illustrated in (53a), the Udehe converb suffix for same-subject forms -*si* is added to the perfect verb stem, e.g. *diang-ka-si* 'having said', *eme-ge-si* 'having come' (Nikolaeva 1999: 147, 147). Diachronically, this seemingly unusual derivation can be explained by tracing -*si* back to pTg *-pA-i*, the accusative suffix in its reflexive form. In this way the converbial clause goes back to an original complement clause.

(53) Reflexes of the resultative deverbal noun suffix pTg *-kA:* in Udehe

a. clausal nominalization

Uta   xegise-li   kongko   dieli:-ni,   xegise-li   eme-ge-si.
that   above-PROL   croak.croak   fly.FIN-3SG   above-PROL   come-NML-CONV
'That [raven] croak, croak, flies down from above, having come from above.' (Nikolaeva 1999: 507)

b. finite

Bi   emegi-ge-i
I   come-FIN-1SG
'I have (already) come back' (Nikolaeva 1999: 148)

It can further be noted that in the Udehe past tense, the suffix -*hA* is added after most vowel stems, e.g. Ud. *wa:-ha-mi* 'I killed', while -*ki* is added to consonant stems, e.g. *diang-ki-mi* 'I said' and -*xi* is added to the small class of irregular verbs that conjugates like Ud. *ga-* 'to take', e.g. Ud. *ga-xi-mi* 'I took' (Benzing 1955a: 1088). It is not unlikely that the suffixes -*ki* and -*hi* are innovations deriving from a complex suffix consisting of the perfective adnominalizer *-xA* and a bound noun *-i* 'fact, being'. This replacement recalls the substitution of the (ad) nominalizers *-rA* and *-sA* by pTg *-ri:* < *rA-i* and *-si* < *sA-i* described in Sections 7.3.3 and 7.7.3 respectively.

7.6.3.5 Nanai

The Nanai reflexes -*ka* ~ -*ke* of the resultative nominalizer pTg *-xA* ~ *-kA:* occur in the finite perfect paradigm; see example (54b) (Benzing 1955: 1089; Menges 1968: 225–226; Malchukov 2000: 450). As illustrated in (54a), the Nanai perfective converb, cognate with the -*ka-si* construction in Udehe is -*ka-p* (Menges 1968: 207). The second element is the converb -*p*, which is also only used in case of coreferential subjects and derived from an original accusative-reflexive construction.

(54) Reflexes of the resultative deverbal noun suffix pTg *-kA: in Nanai

a. clausal nominalization

Ule:n jorici-ka-p miocala-xam-bi
good aim-NML-CONV shoot-PST-1SG
'I aimed well and shot immediately' (Menges 1968: 207)

b. finite

Ge, mi hay ung-ke-i?
Well I what say-FIN-1SG
'Well, what did I say ?' (Menges 1968: 226)

7.6.4 pMo *-xA ~ *-kA

Derivational pairs in Written Mongolian, such as those in (55a) enable the reconstruction of pMo *-xA as a resultative deverbal noun suffix. Since the suffix derives object nouns from transitive verbs (e.g. *idege* 'food') and stative property nouns from punctual change of state verbs (e.g. *edüge* 'contemporary'), it can be reconstructed as an original resultative marker. The most widespread reflex of pMo *-xA is WMo. *-ya ~ -ge* , MMo. *-'a ~ -'e*, whereby WMo. [γ] is the allophone of /g/ before back vowels *a, o, u* in the same way as [q] is the allophone of /k/ in that position. However, there are at least two derivational pairs that reflect a voiceless allomorph WMo. *-qa ~ -ke* following *-r-* and *-b-* (< intervocalic [β]), i.e. WMo. *cubu-* 'move one after another in single file; to fall in drops or single grains' → *cubqa* 'leaves of a tree' in *čubqa julγura-* 'leaves are falling of' and WMo. *toγuri-* 'to go about, circle, surround (tr.) → *toγurqa* 'the encirclement of the tent'. From a phonological point of view, it is difficult to motivate the devoicing of a voiceless velar stop in a voiced environment. Assuming that the resultative nominalizer had a fricative onset, i.e. pMo *-xA, can explain the devoicing: given that in intervocalic position pMo *b became a bilabial voiced fricative *β (Poppe 1955: 99), vowel syncope would have led to the juxtaposition of two original continuants *rx and *βx. Being articulatory inconvenient, these clusters would have been avoided by dropping the feature [+ continuant] from the second consonant, i.e. pMo *-xA became WMo. -kA. In the majority of cases, however, pMo *-xA would have been attached to a thematic vowel stem, where it became realized as a voiced fricative -yA and, velar fricatives merging with velar stops, it is now transcribed as WMo. -gA; see the phonological development proposed in Sections 7.6.3 and 7.6.5.

The suffix also appears as a perfective marker in complement or relative clauses, often modifying temporal expressions derived from a noun in the dative case, such as *inaqsi(-da)* (this.side-DAT) 'as long as not' in (55c) and *udu'ui(-e)* (still.lack-DAT) or *edügüi* (still.lack) 'before, not yet' in (55b).[22] Note that the suffix occasionally alternates with a voiceless alternant *-kA*, such as MMo. *-qa* in (55c). This allomorphy probably goes back to the allophony between pMo *-xA* and *-kA*, conditioned by certain continuants. If the perfective converb WMo. *-yad* ~ *-ged*, MMo. *-yat* ~ *-get* (Weiers 1966: 214–216; Poppe 1954: 97) can be derived from the resultative nominalizer in the dative case WMo. / MMo. *-dA* ~ *-tA*, it also reflects the use of the suffix as a nominalizer embedding complement clauses.

In literature, the suffix is known as the "nomen imperfecti" (Poppe 1954: 94, Weiers 1966: 197, Sárközi 2004: 44) or as the "imperfective past participle" (Orlovskaya 1999: 101), implying an action that started in the past but continues into the present. In reality, the suffix has perfective aspectual meaning in its nonfinite use, while it has developed imperfect temporal meaning in its finite use. The use of MMo. -'*a* ~ -'*e* in independent sentences is illustrated in (55d).

(55) Reflexes of the resultative deverbal noun suffix pMo *-gA* in Mongolic

    a.   lexical (ad)nominalization in WMo.

        bos- 'to rise, stand up (intr.)' → *bosuya* 'doorsill, threshold (n.), vertical, upright, erect (adj.)'

        edü- 'to begin, start, commence (tr.)' → *edüge* 'now, at present, contemporary (adj. and adv.)'

        ide- 'to eat, consume (tr.)' → *idege* 'food'

        ir- 'to fill up, to heap up, to be folded (as a hem) (intr.)' → *iraya* 'ripples on the surface of water'

        jalya- 'to connect (tr. / intr.)' → *jalyaya* 'connection (n.); connected (adj.)'

        kebte- 'to lie down, recline (intr.)' → *kebtege* 'lying down, horizontal (adj. and adv.)'

        mede- 'to know, understand, perceive, find out (tr. / intr.)' → *medege* 'information, message, intelligence (n.)'

        melje- 'to make a bet (tr.)' → *meljege* 'bet, argument (n.)'

        qolbu- 'to unite, connect, link (tr.)' → *qolbuya* 'tie, link, double, pair (n. / adj)'

        sana- 'to think, reflect (tr. / intr.)' → *sanaya* 'thought, idea, reflection'

        tüle- 'to set on a fire, burn (tr.)' → *tülege* 'firewood, kindling'

---

[22] The negative particle MMo. *udu'ui*, *edügüi*, WMo *edüi* 'not yet, before' is commonly derived from *edüge* 'now' and *ügei* 'absence, lack'.

b. clausal (ad)nominalization in MMo.

*basa   ber   nasun-dur   kürü-**ge**   edügüi   a-mu*
besides PT   long.time-DAT reach-**NML** still.lacking be-FIN
'And besides you didn't reach the full age yet' (TD 33.19; Orlovskaya 1999: 102)

c. clausal (ad)nominalization in MMo.

Bi   ber   Manjusiri-yin   sayin-tur   bayasqulang   oron-i
I   PT   Manjusiri-GEN   goodness-DAT   peace   place-ACC
*olu-**qa**   inaqsi   ger-tecegen   qar-qu   minu*
find-**NML** this.side   house-ABL   go.out-NML   my
bütü-kü   bol-tuqai
carry.out-CONV become-IMP.3SG
'As long as I haven't found the place of peace through the goodness of the Manjusiri, my leaving the house [as a monk] should be carried out' (Weiers 1966: 200)

d. finite in MMo.

*Sigi Qutuqu   ese   abu-**'a***
Sigi Qutuqu   NEG   take-**FIN**
'Sigi Qutuqu has not taken' (SH 252; Weiers 1966: 198)

For reasons explained in Section 5.7.4. deverbal nouns on WMo. -*yai* ~ *gei* (< pMo *-gA-i* INCH-NML) can be distinguished from deverbal nouns in WMo. -*ya* ~ *ge* (< pMo *-gA* RES.NML). However, the suffix WMo. -*yai* ~ *gei*, MMo. -*'ai* ~ -*'ei*, which alternates with WMo. -*ya* ~ *ge*, MMo. -*'a* ~ -*'e* in clausal (ad)nominalization and finite function (Poppe 1954: 94; Weiers 1966: 197–206) is probably a derivation of the adnominalizer plus a reflex of the original bound noun pTEA *i* 'fact, thing, this (one)'. Note that in Middle Mongolian the finite use of MMo. . -*'a* ~ -*'e* is never embedded by a copula, while the finite use of the secondary suffix MMo. -*'ai* ~ -*'ei* can optionally be followed by a copula. This suggests that copula represent a later addition, an assumption that is corroborated by the observation that the corresponding so-called "nomen imperfect" -*gAA* in the contemporary Central Mongolic languages may be optionally followed by a copula (Janhunen 2012b: 161–162).

The Khitan suffix -*hu* ~ -*ho* ~ -*gi*, which derives deverbal nouns and adnominal forms from verbs is probably cognate with WMo. -*ya* ~ *ge* (Kane 2009: 155–156). The examples provided by Kane all involve perfective relative clauses of the kind of example (56a).While the allomorph -*gi* follows front-vocalic stems, the allomorphs -*hu* ~ -*ho* follow back-vocalic stems, whereby -*ho* follows stems with back rounded vowels. As illustrated in (56b), the suffix is also found as a marker of past tense.

(56) Reflexes of the resultative deverbal noun suffix pMo *-xA in Khitan

    a. clausal adnominalization

        oju-hu   DAY
        close-ADN day
        'the day [the coffin] was closed' (Kane 2009: 155)

    b. finite

        qihu ai   bas [...] *juung śiúling o-ho*
        that year then   zhongshuling become-FIN
        'That year, he was then appointed secretariat director' (Kane 2009: 83, 121)

7.6.5 pTk *-xA ~ *-kA

The deverbal noun suffix pTk *-xA can be reconstructed as a resultative suffix that derived nominal and adnominal forms from verb stems; it derived subject nouns from intransitive verbs, object nouns from transitive verbs and stative property nouns from change of state verbs. It was gradually extended to the clausal level, deriving perfective non-past relative clauses, relics of which are still reflected in Old Turkic. Since Chuvash and Old Turkic share the perfective future connotation in their finite reflexes of this suffix, the insubordination was probably already accomplished in proto-Turkic.

    The suffix pTk *-xA used an allomorph *-kA which arose through de-fricativation following the continuants *r and *β. Both Old Turkic and Chuvash preserve some lexicalizations that are suggestive of this original conditioning factor. Since the large majority of proto-Turkic verb stems was thematic, the initial fricative phoneme of pTk *-xA was most frequently rendered by a voiced allophone *-γA. The allomorph *-γA spread into Chuvash as -A and into Old Turkic as -γA, where it became transcribed as -gA due to the merger of OTk /γ/ and /g/.

7.6.5.1 Old Turkic

The Old Turkic deverbal noun suffix -gA derives nominal and adnominal forms from verb stems, as illustrated in the derivational pairs in (57a) (Erdal 1991: 376–382). Since the suffix mainly derives action nouns and subject nouns from intransitive verbs (e.g. OTk. *kükrege* 'thundering'; *öpke* 'lung'), object nouns from transitive verbs (e.g. OTk. *tilge* 'strip') and stative property nouns from change of state verbs (e.g. *kïsga* 'short'), it can be characterized as a resultative nominalizer. Similar to the alleged "dissimilation" of other suffixes after /r, l, n/ such as the causative suffix OTk. *-Xz-*, in which /z/ seems to devoice to /s/ (Erdal 1991: 704, 757–760), the deverbal noun suffixes *-gXn* (Erdal 1991: 327–329; 2002: 120), *-gAn* (Erdal 1991: 382), *-gOk/ -gUk* (Erdal 1991: 359–362), *-gI* (Erdal 1991: 320–323) and the inchoative causative OTk. *-gAr-* (see Section 5.7.5), there are some instances in which the suffix OTk *-gA* seems to devoice to *-kA* following /r, p/, e.g. in *ötürke, tarka, öpke* and perhaps in pre-OTk **yupka* 'thin, slender, unsubstantial' reflected in OTk. *yuyka*, Kharakh. *yupka*, Turkish *yufka*, Uzbek *yupqa* etc. if this adjective can be derived from an obsolete verb **yup-* 'to become thin'.

(57) Reflexes of the resultative deverbal noun suffix pTk **-xA* in Old Turkic

    a.   lexical (ad)nominalization

        OTk. *bil-* 'to know (tr.)' → *bilge* 'wise; a wise person, counsellor'
        OTk. *köli-* 'to be shady, shaded; to shade, give shade to (tr./intr.)' → OTk. *kölige* 'shadow, deep shade'
        OTk. *köši-* 'to obstruct light (intr.)' → *köšige* 'light shadow'
        OTk *kïs-* 'to pinch, squeeze, reduce (tr.)' → *kïsga* 'short'
        OTk. *kükre-* 'to thunder (intr.)' → *kükrege* 'thundering'
        OTk. *öp-* 'to kiss, sip or suck in the air or a liquid' → *öpke* 'generated in the lung; lung, anger'
        OTk *ötür-* 'to cause or force to pass through' → *ötürke* 'purgative'
        OTk. *sal-* 'move, put in motion, agitate' → *salga* 'restive'
        OTk. *tar-* 'disperse, send away (tr.)' → *tarka* 'alone, lonely'
        OTk. *til-* 'to cut into strips (tr.)' → *tilge* 'strip'
        OTk. *tut-* 'to hold, catch (tr.)' → *tutga* 'handle'

    b.   clausal adnominalization

        *nirvan-ka   bar-**ga**-sok-ta*
        nirvana-DAT   go-**ADN**-one.time-LOC
        'When one goes to Nirvana' (Erdal 1991: 159)

    c.   finite

        *čeviš   ay-u   bẹr-**ge**   men*
        method   explain-CONV   give-**FIN**   1SG
        'I will explain the method for you' (KP 75, 2)

It is important, however, to realize that the rendering of the distinction between /g/ and /k/ in Old Turkic sources is imprecise. In traditional Turcological transcription (a.o. Erdal 2004: 78), the Old Turkic sources are thought to represent a system whereby voiced /g/ and voiceless /k/ are distinguished before back vowels, but not before front vowels. The back-harmonic variant of /g/ is thought to have been a fricative [ɣ], whereas the front variant is thought to have been a voiced stop [ġ]. Traditionally, the East Old Turkic runiform sign «k¹», the Ancient Uighur «ḥeth» sign and the Karakhanid Arabic «qaːf» are thus interpreted as the back voiceless stop [ḳ], whereas the East Old Turkic runiform sign «k²», the Ancient Uighur «keph» sign and the Karakhanid Arabic "kaːf" sign are interpreted as either a front voiceless stop [ḵ] or a front voiced stop [ġ]. The East Old Turkic runiform sign «γ¹», the double dots in Ancient Uighur and the Karakhanid Arabic «ghain» sign are taken as the back vocalic alternant of /g/ which is pronounced as a [ẏ] and stands in opposition to the back vocalic alternant of /k/. Hence, the notations OTk. *kïsga* 'short', OTk. *yuyka* 'thin', OTk. *kölige* 'shadow' and OTk. *öpke* 'lung' transcribe what is commonly believed to be rendered in the sources as [kïsẏa], [yuyḳa], [köliḵe ~ köliġe] and [öpḵe ~ öpġe], respectively. The determination of a voiced velar stop in the notation of OTk. *kölige* 'shadow', but a voiceless velar in OTk. *öpke* 'lung' is dependent upon the reflexes in the contemporary Turkic languages, which display a voiced velar in the former case, but a voiceless in the latter; e.g., for 'shadow': Tk. *gölge*, Gag. *gölge*, Az. *kölgä*, Tkm. *kölge*, Tat. *külεgε*, Bash. *külεgε*, Uig. *kölige*, Tuva *xölege*, Tof. *xölege*, etc.; for 'lung': Tk. *öfke* 'anger', *öyken* 'lung', Gag. *üfke*, Az. *öxbä*, Tkm. *öyken*, Tat. *üpkä*, Kir. *öpkö*, Bash. *üpkä*, Sal. *öhhen*, Uz. *ǫpka*, Uig. *öpkä*, SUig. *ökpe*, Shor *ökpe*, Tuva *ökpe*, Tof. *öʻkpe*, etc.

Johanson (1979, 2012, pc.), however, proposes a different interpretation of the Old Turkic signs for velars. In his view, the East Old Turkic runiform sign «k¹», the Ancient Uighur «ḥeth» sign and the Karakhanid Arabic «qaːf» cannot only stand for a back voiceless stop [ḳ], but also for a back voiced stop [ġ], while the East Old Turkic runiform sign «k²», the Ancient Uighur «keph» sign and the Karakhanid Arabic "kaːf" sign stand for either a front voiceless stop [ḵ] or a front voiced stop [ġ]. Since the East Old Turkic runiform sign «γ¹» which stands for a back fricative [ẏ] has a front counterpart «γ²», he interprets γ² as a front fricative [ẏ], rather than as front voiced stop [ġ] in traditional transcription. As such East Old Turkic mirrors a separate fricative phoneme /ɣ/, which is not the mere back-vocalic allophone of /g/ as commonly assumed. In the following stages of Ancient Uighur and Karakhanid, the front fricative [ẏ] is no longer entitled to a separate sign, merging with the front stops rendered by the Ancient Uighur «keph» and the Karakhanid Arabic "kaːf", whereas the back fricative /ɣ/ continues to be marked by the double dots in Ancient Uighur and by the «ghain» sign in Karakhanid. Hence, the notations OTk. *kïsga* 'short', OTk. *yuyka* 'thin',

OTk. *kölige* 'shadow' and OTk. *öpke* 'lung' transcribe what Johanson believes to be rendered in the sources as [*kïsẏa ~ kïsẋa*], [*yuyḳa ~ yuyġa*], [*kölike̊ ~ kölig̊e ~ köliẏe ~ köliẋe*] and [*öpḳe ~ öpġe ~ öpẏe ~ öpẋe*], respectively. Contemporary languages, especially Oghuz Turkic, allow us to determine the Old Turkic voicing, but not the place of articulation (stop or fricative). As for OTk. *kïsga* 'short', the sources mark it as a fricative and the contemporary languages indicate that it was voiced, i.e. [*kïsẏa*]: Tk. *kısa*, Az. *ġısa*, Tkm. *ġısġa*, Dolg. *kıhalga* / Yak. *kıhalga* 'straits, sorrow'. OTk. *yuyka* 'thin' is marked in the sources as a stop and the contemporary languages indicate that it was voiceless, i.e. [*yuyḳa*]: Tk. *yufka*, Gag. *jufqa*, Az. *yuxa*, Tkm. *yu:qa*, Tat. *yuqa*, Kirg. *župqa*, Kaz. *žuqa*, Bash. *yoqa*, Karaim *yuwγa ~ yufqa*, Uz. *yupka*, Uig *yupqa*, SUig. *yuqa*, Sal. *yoχba*, etc. OTk. *kölige* 'shadow' is marked in the sources as either stop or fricative and the contemporary languages mentioned above indicate that it was voiced, i.e. [*kölig̊e ~ köliẏe*]. Finally, OTk. *öpke* 'lung' is marked in the sources as either stop or fricative and the contemporary languages mentioned above indicate that it was voiceless, i.e. [*öpḳe ~ öpẋe*].

Thus, if /γ/ really had a phonemic status in early Old Turkic and before, the allomorphs of our resultative nominalizer are -*ga* (< pre-OTk *-*γa*), -*ka* (< pre-OTk *-*ka*), -*ge* (< pre-OTk *-*γe* or *-*ge*), -*ke* (< pre-OTk *-*ke* or *-*xe*). The principle of Occam's razor then leads us to reconstruct a voiced fricative suffix pre-OTk *-*γA* and a voiceless stop allomorph *-*kA* in sonorant and labial obstruent environment. It cannot be excluded that the original velar fricative had no phonological voice distinction and that is was realized as [γ] in vocalic environment, but as [x] in consonantal positions. In other words pTk *-*xa* was pronounced [-xa ~ -xe] following consonants, but [-γa ~ -γe] in intervocalic position, which was in the majority of cases, given that most original verb bases ended in a vowel.

Assuming that the resultative nominalizer had a fricative onset can explain the voiceless stop allomorph, while the assumption that it had a voiced stop onset cannot. From a phonological point of view, it is difficult to motivate the devoicing of a voiceless velar stop in a sonorant environment. However, defricativization is commonly seen in this environment, for instance in Spanish and Icelandic (Johanson 1979: 30).[23] The high sonority of the sonorants *r, l, n, m* makes the articulation of a following consonant possible without an intermediate vowel. Therefore, vowels are expected to drop more easily following sonorants. Vowel syncope leads to the juxtaposition of two continuants, which is articulatory inconvenient and will be avoided by dropping the incomplete oral closure from the second consonant: the fricative will become a stop. Note that the glide

---

[23] Spanish /d/ is realized as a fricative [ð] in most environments (e.g. *nada* [naða] 'nothing'), except in word-initial position, following nasals and [l] where it is realised as a stop [d].

in OTk. *yuyka*, the labiodental fricative reflexes in Tk. *yufka*, Gag. *jufqa*, Karaim *yuwya ~ yufqa* and the voiced bilabial stop in Sal. *yoχba* may suggest an earlier bilabial fricative in pre-OTk. **yußka* 'thin' and likewise the continuants in Tk. *öfke* 'anger', *öyken* 'lung', Az. *öxbä* 'lung', Gag. *üfke*, Tkm. *öyken*, Sal. *öhhen* may point to pre-OTk. **ößke*. The continuant *ß* would then provide an environment for the de-fricativation of the original suffix pTk **-xA*. Johanson (1979: 79) finds that vowel syncope following [r] occurred later in pre-Old Turkic than vowel delition following [l] and [n]. This seems to suggest a higher sonority of [l] and [n], which probably yielded the voiced allophone in a following pre-OTk **-yA* similar to vocalic positions, whereas following [r] de-fricativation took place similar to other continuant positions. Since Johanson's assumption of an original fricative phoneme offers a phonological motivation for the observed allomorphy, I am inclined to reconstruct pTk **-xA ~ *-kA* as the resultative nominalizer.

Although clausal (ad)nominalization of OTk *-gA* is not overtly attested, there are some indications of such use reflected in the compounding of the suffix with OTk *-sOk*, which is a denominal suffix that seems to indicate 'one (element/place/time) out of several options', e.g. *sïngar* 'one of two/more sides' → *sïngar-sok* 'hindquarters of a horse, i.e. the place where a second rider sits' (Erdal 1991: 157–158). When added to the resultative deverbal noun suffix OTk *-gA* it designates one specific time out of several future options and it is often used in a context of 'the time of future death, the time when one will have died', as illustrated in (57b). In these constructions OTk *-gA* can be interpreted as a perfective future adnominalizer.

OTk *-gA* has further developed into a marker of finiteness, denoting future meaning such as in example (57c) (Erdal 1991: 382, 2004: 242). The development from resultative into a finite future can be explained over a perfective with non-past reference, as in German "Morgen bin ich schon abgefahren". Comrie (1976: 66) gives examples of this development from ancient Greek and Russian. Interestingly, OTk. *-gA* alternates with OTk. *-gAy* in the derivation of seemingly adnominal forms in the OTk *-gA-sOk* construction (Erdal 1991: 157–158) and of future finite forms (Räsänen 1957: 124–125, von Gabain 1959: 115, Erdal 2004: 242). The inability of *-gAy* to derive deverbal nominal forms seems to suggest that it represents a later formation consisting of OTk. *-gA* in its adnominal use plus the nominalizer OTk *-I* (see Section 8.3.5), which gradually replaced the original suffix in *-gA*, at a time when the lexicalizations of the deverbal nouns in *-gA* were already accomplished. The hypothesis that *-gAy* is derived from *-gA* is proposed by Erdal (1979c: 89, 2004: 243), but he identifies the final element *-y* as the nominative form of the archaic demonstrative pronoun **-I*, postposed for subject reference. Ultimately this pronoun and the nominalizer **-I* may go back to a single form.

7.6.5.2 Chuvash

Chuvash ø being the regular correspondence of OTk. -*g*- (Benzing 1959: 712; Starostin et al. 2003: 143–144)[24], the corresponding Chuvash suffix is -*a* ~ -*e*, a suffix which derives nominal and adnominal forms from verb stems, as illustrated in the derivational pairs in (58a) (Levickaya 1974: 152–153; Fedotov 1997: 327–328). Since the suffix mainly derives subject nouns from intransitive verbs (e.g. *makra* 'cry-baby'), object nouns from transitive verbs (e.g. *śïra* 'line') and stative property nouns from change of state verbs (e.g. *śavra* 'round'), it can be characterized as a resultative nominalizer. The Chuvash cognates of OTk. *öpke* 'generated in the lung; lung, anger' and OTk. *yuyka* 'thin, slender, unsubstantial' are Chu. *öpke*, *üpke* 'lung' and Chu. *śüxe* 'thin, narrow', whereby OTk. -*k*- regulary corresponds to Chuvash -*k*- or -*x*- and goes back to pTk *-k- (see Section 5.7.5). Given that the voiceless velar stop allomorph has lexicalized in Eastern Old Turkic, as well as in Chuvash, which belongs to the Western Turkic branch, the derivation and de-fricativization must have taken place already in proto-Turkic, the common ancestor of both branches.

The optative mood in Chuvash in e.g., *vulam* 'I would like to read' (< *vula-a-m* read-OPT.NML-POSS.1SG) and *vular* 'We would like to read' (< *vula-a-r* read-OPT.NML-POSS.PL) has been compared to the finite future OTk -*gA* (Räsänen 1957: 125). Since the imperative plural *vulăr* 'read!' includes the second plural possessive suffix -*ăr* (e.g. *ača* 'child' → *ač-ăr* 'your (PL) child'), it probably derives from an optative nominalization **vula-a-ăr* (read-OPT.NML-POSS.2PL) as well. It is not unlikely that the optative, illustrated in (58b) reflects the finite use of the Chuvash resultative nominalizer -*A*, going over a perfective future reading.

(58) Reflexes of the resultative deverbal noun suffix pTk *-*xA* in Chuvash

    a.   lexical nominalization

        makăr- 'to cry' → *makra* 'cry-baby'

        śavăr- 'to turn, whirl, go round' → *śavra* 'round'

        śarat- 'to expose, bare, strip (tr.)' → *śarata* 'glade, clearing, open space surrounded by woods'

        śïr- 'to draw, write (tr.)' → *śïra* 'line'

        vit- 'to cover (tr.)' → *vite* 'cow-house, cattle-shed'

    b.   finite

        leš   těnče-ne   an-sa   kur-**ar**

        other   world-ACC   descend   see-**OPT.1PL**

        'Let's go down and see the other world' (Krüger 1961: 159)

---

[24] The sound correspondence is reflected in, for instance, OTk. *buzagu* and Chu. *păru* 'calf' and in OTk. *boyuz* and Chu. *pïr* 'throat'.

7.7 pTEA *-sA

7.7.1 pJ *-sa

The resultative nominalizer pJ *-sa, which derives resultative adnominal forms from verbal adjectives and copula can be reconstructed on the basis of Ryukyuan and Old Japanese data.

Whereas Classical Ryukyuan testifies to the original use of this suffix without the intervention of a copula, the periphrastic constructions with *a(r)-* 'to be' found in the contemporary Ryukyuan languages are secondary innovations. Similarly, the copula constructions found in later stages of Japanese are secondary developments. The Old Japanese deverbal nominalizer *-usa-* can be derived from an original copula pJ **wo-* 'to be' and the de-adjectival nominalizer *-sa*, consistent with the assumed insertion of a copula in other deverbal suffixes such as the negative imperative OJ *-una*, the adnominal OJ *-uru/ -ru / -u* and the finite OJ *-u*. The lack of examples of clausal (ad)nominalization and the use of arguments in the genitive case only suggests that the finite use of the suffix, observed in Ryukyuan and Old Japanese, has probably developed straight from the lexical nominalization, without intermediate stage of complement or relative clauses.

7.7.1.1 Ryukyuan

As illustrated in the Shodon example in (59a), the most common pattern in Ryukyuan verbal adjective inflection is to contract forms of a structure that consists of the de-adjectival nominalizing *-sa* plus the auxiliary *a(r)-* 'to be'. However, from Classical Ryukyuan it becomes clear that the copula constructions are innovations since the Classical use of *-sa* is nearly identical with Old Japanese (Vovin 2009a: 484); see (58b). In Ryukyuan there are no instances of deverbal derivation, corresponding to the use of the Old Japanese suffix *-usa*.

(59) Reflexes of the resultative deverbal noun suffix pJ *-sa* in Ryukyuan

    a. Lexical nominalization in Shodon

        *Qaháá-**sa**-m*
        red-**NML**-COP.FIN
        'it is red'

    b. Finite in Old Ryukyuan

        mi-kutu   *ma-faya-**sa***
        HON-word INT-fast-**NML**
        'The august words [are] really fast' (OS III: 88; Vovin 2009a: 484, Wrona 2011: 429)

7.7.1.2 Mainland Japanese

Old Japanese uses a lexical nominalizer -*sa*, which productively derives nouns from verbal adjectives, as illustrated in (60a). There is also a lexical nominalizer OJ -*u-sa*, which derives nouns from verbs, as illustrated in (60b), but usually this marker is considered as a dinstinct suffix (Vovin 2009a: 482; Wrona 2011: 427). Although this analysis may hold synchronically at the Old Japanese level, it is likely that diachronically, the de-adjectival and deverbal nominalizer -*sa* go back to the same origin because they correspond formally and functionally.

From a formal perspective, the traditional Japanese analysis (Omodaka et al. 1967: 317) is to segment the deverbal nominalizer into an ending of the verb -*u* and the nominalizer -*sa*. Since OJ ko_2- 'to come' derives as *k-u-sa*, this analysis implies that -*sa* follows the so-called "shūshikei" or finite form OJ *k-u*, rather than the so-called "rentaikei" or adnominal OJ *k-uru*. On the basis of the incompatibility of a nominalizer with a finite verb form, Vovin (2009a: 776) deduces that the vowel -*u*- should be regarded as part of the suffix itself. However, a more plausible explanation may be to analyze -*usa*- as a compound suffix consisting of an original copula pJ **wo*- 'to be' and the de-adjectival nominalizer -*sa*. This analysis is consistent with that of the negative imperative OJ -*una*, the adnominal OJ -*uru*/ -*ru* / -*u* and the finite OJ -*u* in Sections 4.2.1.2, 7.3.1 and 7.4.1 respectively.

From a functional perspective, it is relevant that in Old Japanese de-adjectival -*sa* and deverbal -*usa* both appear in lexical nominalization and finite use, but lack the function of clausal nominalization. Therefore, it is likely that both suffixes go back to a single suffix pJ **-sa* which derived deverbal nouns from verbal adjectives and copula. Original deverbal derivation may be reflected in a handful of lexicalized word pairs such as OJ *tob*-, dial. J *tub*- 'to fly' → *tubasa* '(bird's) wing' and pJ **kira*- 'to cut' in OJ *kir*- 'to cut' → pJ **kinsa* ~ *kisa* 'a cut, cut material' in OJ *kiza* 'a cut; a notch' and OJ ki_1sa- 'shaving, scraping' in OJ ki_1sage_2- 'to shave metal or stone'. The resultative meaning of pJ **-sa* is evidenced by the observation that OJ -*usa*- is often used in temporal expressions with a perfective connotation; in (60b), for instance', the nominalizer derives a stative result 'a time when one has forgotten' from the punctual change of state verb 'forget'. If OJ ki_1sa- 'shaving, scraping' indeed reflects a derivation with pJ **-sa*, it is the object noun of a transitive verb 'to cut', which would support the resultative meaning of the suffix.

In particular discourse contexts, the nominalizer OJ -*sa* / -*usa* is used as a finite form, signaling the evaluative nature of the proposition. As opposed to other instances of insubordination in Japanese discussed above, the insubordinated form, e.g. to_2mo_2si-*sa* in (60c) takes arguments in the genitive case (*ga*) only. This seems to confirm the assumption that the insubordination did not go through an intermediate stage of clausal nominalization.

Vovin's (2009: 482) observation that OJ -sa can occur with the final predicate of a given sentence, but never occurs in the last line of a given text is an indication of the fact that the development of finiteness in these examples is primarily driven by information structure and has gone through an intermediate stage of dependency beyond the sentence in longer stretches of discourse (Mithun 2008). Note that contrary to later stages of Japanese, there are no examples of -sa clauses embedded under a copula in Old Japanese (Wrona 2011: 428). This suggest that the copula constructions are secondary developments.

(60) Reflexes of the resultative deverbal noun suffix pJ *-sa in Old Japanese

    a. Lexical nominalization from verbal adjectives

        $ko_2yo_2pi_1$-no_2 naga-**sa**   ipo-yo_1 $tugi_1$-ko_1so_1
        tonight-GEN be.long-**NML** five.hundred-night continue.NML-PT
        'Please continue the length of tonight for five hundred nights'
        (MYS IV: 985; Wrona 2011: 428)

    b. Lexical nominalization from verbs

        omo_2 kata-no_2 wasur-**usa**   ar-anpa
        face   shape-GEN   forget-**NML** exist-COND
        'If there is a time that I forget your face' (MYS XI: 2580; Vovin 2009a: 778)

    c. Finite from verbal adjectives

        $punapi_1to_2$-wo mi_1-ru-ga to_2mo_2si-**sa**
        boat.people-ACC see-NML-GEN be.enviable-**FIN**
        'How enviable it is to see the boat-people!' (MYS 15: 3658; Wrona 2008: 206)

    d. Finite from verbs

        wa-ga se-ko_1-ga ko_1p-uru to_2 ip-u ko_2to_2 pa
        I-GEN beloved-DIM-GEN long.for-ADN DV say-ADN matter TOP
        ko_2to_2 n-o_2 nag-**usa** so_2
        word DV-ADN be.consoled-**NML** PT
        'By the fact that my beloved tells me that [he] longs [for me], I am [only] verbally consoled.' (MYS IV: 656; Vovin 2009a: 777–778)

It has been suggested that the adnominal form WOJ -ki_1 and the finite form WOJ -si, which are attached to verbal adjective bases should be related to the nominalizers discussed here. In Eastern Old Japanese the corresponding suffixes are EOJ -ki_1 and EOJ -si, but there are also some instances of adnominal forms in EOJ -$ke_{1/2}$ (spelled variously as -ke_1 or -ke_2), that are, however, less frequent and restricted to a particular region. Martin (1987: 806) finds three examples of de-adjectival -ki_1 and two examples of -si in Ryukyuan, but it is generally believed that these are borrowed from Mainland Japanese (Vovin 2009a: 466, 473).

Martin (1967: 260–261; 1987: 806–808, 812; 1995: 148; 1997: 5) proposed to derive OJ -ki_1 and OJ -si from a contraction of the converb -ku plus the finite form of the copula *ari* 'to be' and the nominalizer -*sa* plus the same copula form, respectively. He suggested that the differentiation of function between adnominal OJ -ki_1 and finite OJ -si must have set in well after the time of the contraction because Old Japanese preserves evidence that OJ -ki_1 and OJ -si were used in both functions; see examples (61b/c) and (62b/c).

(61) The use of the de-adjectival adnominal form OJ -ki_1

    a. nominal

        ap-ube₁-ki_1   *yo₂si-no₂*   *na-ki_1-ga*   *sabusi-sa*
        meet-DEB-**ADN**   chance-GEN   not.be-**NML**-GEN   sad-NML
        'sadness of the absence of a chance to be able to meet'
        (MYS XV: 3734; Vovin 2009a: 471)

    b. adnominal

        opo₂-ki_1   *to₁-yo₁ri*
        big-**ADN**   door-ABL
        'from the big door' (NK 18; Vovin 2009a: 467)

    c. finite

        ki_1mi_1   *pa*   *ya*   *na-ki_1*
        lord   TOP   PT   not.be-**FIN**
        'Do not [you] have a lord?' (NK 104; Vovin 2009a: 469)

(62) The use of the de-adjectival finite form OJ -si

    a. nominal

        yo₂-k-e₁ku   *pa*   *na-si-ni*
        good-ADN-NML   TOP   not.be-**NML**-LOC
        'As there was no improvement, …' (MYS V: 904; Vovin 2009a: 465)

    b. adnominal

        pasi-ki_1   *yo₂-si*   *wa-g-i_1pe_1*
        lovely-ADN   good-**ADN**   I-GEN-house
        'my lovely and good house' (NK 21; Vovin 2009a: 464)

c. finite

*ko₁ko₁ro₁ sa mane-**si***
thought   so many-**FIN**
'thoughts are so many' (MYS I: 82; Vovin 2009a: 463)

From the functional perspective, Martin's analysis is convincing, but as Pellard (2008: 151) points out, there are two formal problems, first, because the adnominal form of the copula is OJ *aru*, not *ari* and second, because the construction OJ *-ku ar-* is expected to contract to *-kar-*. However, considering the derivation of the "izenkei" OJ *-ure* from an adnominalizer plus substantivizer pJ **wo-ra-i* in Section 7.3.1 and the derivation elsewhere in Transeurasian of compound nominalizers on the basis of an adnominal suffix **-rA*, *-xA* or *-sA* plus a substantivizer **-i*, it is inviting to derive OJ *-ki₁* from pJ **-ka-i* and OJ *-si* from pJ **-sa-i* in which *-i* is a substantivizer following adjectival nouns. This would solve Pellard's objections because insubordination would explain the development from nominal to adnominal to finite use and because pJ **-ka-i* and **sa-i* would regularly contract to OJ *-ki₁* and *-si* according to Unger's vowel deletion rules. The EOJ alternative form *-ke₂* could be interpreted as a competing way of resolving the vowel sequence through univerbation due to the loss of constituent transparency, comparable to the analysis of OJ *-ure* above.

There is no consensus as to whether the two deverbal perfect forms, i.e. finite OJ *-ki₁* and adnominal OJ *-si* in (63b) – which are complementary in their syntactic distribution with de-adjectival adnominal OJ *-ki₁* and finite OJ *-si* – are to be identified with the adjective endings.[25] As illustrated in example (63a), there are contractions of the shape *-ke₁ku* with the nominalizer *aku*, in which OJ *-ki₁* can also function as a perfective adnominal form and (63c) shows that OJ *-si* can sporadically occur as a finite perfect form. If the perfect endings are indeed identified with the adjective endings, as proposed by Whitman (1985: 228–229) and Martin (1987: 127, 808), the largely opposite distribution of function may result from an earlier competition by each form for both functions. As such the (re-)nominalized resultative constructions pJ **-ka-i* and **-sa-i* may have derived a stative interpretation from verbal adjectives, which originally meant 'to be(come) a property', whereas they derived a perfective interpretation from verbs. Insubordination may then have led to the development of present

---

25 Note that for most verbs the perfect finite OJ *-ki₁* and perfective adnominal OJ *-si* follow the converb form rather than the stem. With the irregular verbs OJ *ko₂-* to come' and OJ *se-* 'to do', however, the perfect suffixes follow the stem, e.g. *ko₂-si*, *se-si*. Since the converb forms of vowel verbs coincide with their stems, it is not unlikely that the perfect suffixes originally attached to the stem, but were reanalyzed as attaching to converb forms following consonant verbs.

meaning following adjectives and past meaning following verbs in independent sentences.

Except for one example of the perfective adnominal -*si* in Old Ryukyuan, which is believed to be borrowed form Middle Japanese, there are no examples of the perfect suffixes in Ryukyuan (Vovin 2009a: 85, 935). This observation indicates that the secondary constructions pJ *-ka-i and *-sa-i were formed after the separation of the Ryukyuan languages from Mainland Japanese.

(63) The use of the deverbal perfect suffixes OJ -ki_1 and OJ -*si*

a. adnominal OJ -ki_1

*nunapa kur-i-pape$_2$-**k**-e$_1$ku sir-an-i*
water.shield pull.in-CONV-stretch.CONV-**ADN**-NML know-NEG-CONV
'Not knowing that you pulled in the watershield' (KK 44; Vovin 2009a: 922)

b. adnominal OJ -*si* and finite OJ -ki_1

mi_1-*tat-as-i s-er-i-**si** isi tare mi_1-**ki_1***
HON-stand-HON-NML do-PROG-CONV-**ADN** stone who see-**FIN**
'Who saw the stone on which [she] took [her] stand?' (MYS V: 869; Vovin 2009a: 922)

c. finite OJ -*si*

*pyito$_2$-mo$_2$to$_2$ n-o$_2$ nadesiko$_1$ uwe-**si***
one-CL be-ADN carnation plant-**FIN**
'I planted one carnation' (MYS XVIII: 4070; Vovin 2009a: 928)

7.7.2 pK *-s

In previous work (Robbeets 2012: 436, 2013: 158), I have suggested to include the Korean instrumental and resultative deverbal noun suffix in K -*(u)s*, which derives nominal adjectives and adverbs, often with an expressive connotation, in this etymology.[26] However, there is no trace of a final vowel in Korean, the suffix does not extend to the clausal or independent sentence level and there

---

[26] Reflexes of the resultative deverbal noun suffix pK *-s in Korean are K *cilki-* 'to be tough, be durable, be lasting, be persisting' → *cilkis* 'firm, unyielding', *cilkis ha-* 'to be tough, stiff, stubborn'; K *cop-* 'to be narrow' → *copus ha-* 'to be a bit narrow'; K *kwuki-* 'to crumple, wrinkle, rumple (tr.)' → *kwukis* 'wrinkled, crumpled, full of wrinkles'; K *kulu-* 'to be wrong' → *kulus* 'by mistake, mistaking it'; K *(nwun-ul) hulki-* 'to leer (with one's eyes), to glare (tr.)' → *hulkis hulkis* 'glaring, leering'; K *mi:-* 'to be(come) bald, grow bald' → *mis mis* 'long and smooth' ; K *mulu-* 'to become soft, tender, to ripen' → *mulus ha-* 'to be rather soft, tender' and K *phulu-* 'to be blue' → *phulus phulus* 'to be spotted with blue'.

is a corresponding suffix *-s in Tungusic and Mongolic, which is formally and functionally distinct from the resultative nominalizer discussed here. Therefore, I have chosen to insert K -(u)s as an etymon into a separate etymology.

7.7.3 pTg *-sA

The Tungusic languages provide evidence for the reconstruction of a deverbal resultative (ad)nominalizer pTg *-sA, which was eventually replaced by a composite nominalizer pTg *-si: < *-sA-i, incorporating a bound noun *i: 'fact, thing'. This replacement recalls the substitution of the imperfective (ad)nominalizer *-rA by pTg *-ri: < *rA-i, described in Section 6.3.3. Whereas the complex forms in pTg *-si: < *-sA-i are well reflected across the Tungusic languages, the simplex forms in *-sA are only marginally preserved in the Udehe adnominal and final form of the copula and in the finite forms of the Even -sA conjugation.

The examples below suggest that pTg *-sA began as a resultative nominalizer applied to telic verb stems to create stative nouns and adjectives: 'to become cold' → 'cold(ness)', 'to sit down' → 'sitting'. The (ad)nominalizers were then extended to the clause level to mark clausal (ad)nominalization in complement and relative clauses. The relative clauses developed one step further to mark syntactically independent sentences. Since the original nominalizer pTg *-sA derived stative nouns 'being a property, being in a position' from telic verb bases 'to become a property, to reach a position', *-sA developed into a marker of present tense in finite position. As such, finite forms in *-sA existed along other present verb forms based on the imperfective adnominalizer *-rA, but they were restricted to a limited set of originally telic verbs. This restriction ultimately led to the distinction of conjugational classes in *-rA and *-sA, which developed already at the proto-Tungusic stage. The complex constructions in pTg *-sA-i evolved cyclically, along the same pathway, replacing the original forms in *-sA.

Tables 2 to 5 above illustrate the common division into conjugational classes in the Tungusic languages. Benzing (1955a: 1071–1076) argued for the reconstruction of three different verb classes taking bases on *-rA, *-sA or *-dA, suffixes which can be derived from aspectually distinct (ad)nominalizers. As proposed in Section 7.5.3, it is possible to add a fourth conjugational class, formed on the basis of the (ad)nominalizer *-nA. As such, the large majority of Tungusic verbs took a *-rA base, following the pattern of pTg *wa:- 'to kill' and pTg *ŋene- 'to go', whereas some other verbs took *-nA following pTg *gu:- 'to say' or *-dA following *ga- 'to take'. The existential and negative auxiliaries *bi- 'to be, exist' and *e- 'not to be, not to exist' as well a limited set of stative verbs took the adnominalizer *-sA as their conjugational base.

Note that the resultative nominalizer pTg *-sA may be incorporated in the perfective nominalizer pTg *-xsAn, reflected in the Northern Tungusic perfective converbs Even -s(A) Benzing (1955b: 250) and Evenki -ksA (Nedjalkov 1995: 447) as well as in the Southern Tungusic finite perfect forms Na. -xAn, Olč -xAⁿ, Oroč -xA, Ud. -hA(n) (Benzing 1955a: 1088–1089; Menges 1968: 163; Avrorin 1961: 67, 79; Nikolaeva 1999: 121). In agreement with Benzing (1955: 1088), the consonant correspondence should yield the reconstruction of an original consonant cluster in this suffix. However, the reconstructed cluster cannot be pTg *ks, because this would cause us to expect the reflexes given below according to Benzing (1955a: 989).

pTg	Ma.	Na.	Olč.	Orok	Oroč.	Ud.	Sol.	Neg.	Evk.	Even
*-ks-	ks	ks	ks	ks	ks	h'~k'	ks	ks	ks	s

Since the Northern Tungusic languages reflect *x* instead of *ks*, it is more plausible to reconstruct a fricative cluster in pTg *-xsAn which underwent de-fricativation in Northern Tungusic and loss of the second fricative in Southern Tungusic.

7.7.3.1 Manchu

There is only one irregular verb form in Manchu, which bears a trace of the proto-Tungusic *-sa conjugation: the adnominal form Ma. *bisire* is derived from the existential verb Ma. *bi-* 'to be, to exist', which in this case is used in the irregular form *bisi-* (Gorelova 2002: 255). The stem *bisi-* reflects the ancient (ad)nominalizer pTg *-si < *sa-i. There are also a few adjectives such as Ma. *jušuhun* 'sour' and *gosihon* 'bitter' and a verb stem *debsi-* 'to unfold one's wings' in which the deverbal resultative pTg *-si:* may be petrified.

7.7.3.2 Even

In Even, the class of verbs that takes -sA as a conjugational base includes the existential and negative auxiliaries *bi-* 'to be, exist' and *e-* 'not to be, not to exist' as well as a limited set of stative verbs such as Even *asa-* 'to be(come) angry, erupt, rage, to be in a rage', *da:l-* 'to be sweet, pleasant, light', *eb-* 'to drip, seep, leak', *en-* 'to hurt, be painful (intr.)', *gabar-* 'to burn in the eyes, to prick', *gel-* 'to be cold', *ha:ṅ-* 'to be smoky', *ha:nún-* 'to choke, be choking, be hot and humid (intr.)', *hata-* 'to be dark', *huy-* 'to cook (intr.)', *huk-* 'to be warm, hot, steam (intr.)', *i-* 'to be audible, to sound, to reach (of tones)', *ngal-* 'to hold in the hand(s)', *tuk-* 'to carry in the hands', *untun-* 'to have scabies' (Benzing 1955a: 1072–1074, 1955b: 88). The stative verb Even **juyir-* 'to be sour' is not attested as such but it has a defective -sA inflection in the third person singular, i.e. *juyis-sa-n* 'it is sour' and it is also encoded as a nominal adjective in *juyir* 'sour'. Two other verbs taking -sA conjugation can either have a telic interpretation as a punctual change of state verb or an atelic interpretation as an activity verb, i.e. *deg-* 'to rise, to ascend, to go up, to fly away, to fly' and *hul-* 'to go away, to set oneself in motion, to leave, to wander, move around'. The optative suffix *-(A)m-* 'to want to V, to be in a V-ing mood' and the suffix *-(A)ng-* expressing a durative situation with an endpoint follow the -sA conjugation as well (Benzing 1955b: 43, 47).[27] However, the suffix *-(A)ng-* can take a -rA base in cases in which the endpoint is not yet reached at the reference time; see example (64).

(64) The conjugation of the suffix *-(A)ng-* in Even

    a.   -sA conjugation

        bi   alac-ing-si-w
        I   wait-DUR-PST.FIN-POSS.1SG
        '[Back then,] I waited for a while' (Benzing 1955b: 43)

    b.   -rA conjugation

        turaki: urelde-ng-re-n
        raven   be.happy-DUR-FIN-3SG
        'The raven is happy for a while' (Benzing 1955b: 43)

As illustrated in (65a), most of the verbs conjugating with -sA form deverbal nouns and adjectives on *-si:*.[28] Therefore, it is plausible to derive *-si:* from pTg **-sa-i* (ADN-fact), similar to the derivation of Even *-ri* from the (ad)nominalizer pTg **-ra* and a bound noun **i:* 'fact, thing' in Section 7.3.3. Given that the verbs express an unchanging state when they are derived with -sA, the original aspectual meaning of -sA was probably resultative, while the original inherent aspect of the underlying verbs was probably telic, in the sense of 'to become a property'. This is supported by the observation that a few verbs with telic meaning that conjugate on the basis of -rA can derive a resultative noun on *-si:* as well, e.g. *ha:tar-* 'to become dark' (*ha:tar-ra-n*) → *ha:tarsi:* 'darkness'. Note also that durative situations with a perfective endpoint as in example (64a) always conjugate with -sA, whereas situations with an imperfective endpoint as in example

---

[27] Note that Even *-rA*, *-dA*, *-sA* and *-nA* conjugational bases form a past on *-ri*, *-di*, *-si* and *-ni*, respectively and are followed by the possessive suffixes (Benzing 1955b: 94).

[28] The conjugated form in the third person singular is given between brackets, thus *da:l-sa-n* (be.sweet-FIN-3SG) 'it is sweet'.

(64b) may take a -rA base. Moreover, given the original telic meaning 'go up' reconstructed for pTg *deg- (see Section 3.2.7 (8)), it would seem that pTg *deg-sa originally denoted the resultative 'having gone up, flying', which would explain the coinciding telic and atelic meaning in Even. In the same way, pTg *puli- can be reconstructed as 'to go away', while *puli-sa meant 'having gone, wandering', which would explain the combined meaning of Even hul- 'to go away, to wander' as well as the Nanai reflexes puli-lu- 'to start going away' and pulsi- 'to walk, wander'. On the basis of these observations pTg *-sA can be reconstructed as an original resultative nominalizer.

The originally complex nominalizer -si (< pTg *-sA-i) is also used in complement and relative clauses, as illustrated in (65b). The suffix pTg *-sA in its simplex form is only preserved in the finite conjugation as in example (65c).

(65) Reflexes of the resultative deverbal noun suffix pTg *-sA in Even

    a.   lexical (ad)nominalization

        Even bi- 'to be, exist' (bi-s-ni) → bisi: 'being; life, way of life, condition, inhabitant, reality, fact'

        Even da:l- 'to be sweet, pleasant, light' (da:l-sa-n) → dalsi: 'flavorful, sweet, appetizing'

        Even deg- 'to rise, to ascend, to go up, to fly away, to fly' (deg-se-n) → degsi: 'flying; flight'

        Even en- 'to hurt, be painful (intr.)' (en-se-n) → ensi: 'ill, suffering; sick person, patient'

        Even gẹl- 'to be cold' (gẹl-sa-n) → gelsi: 'cold'

        Even ha:ń- 'to be smoky' (ha:ń-sa-n) → ha:ńsi: 'smoky, full of smoke'

        Even hata- 'to be dark' (hata-s-ni) → hatasi: 'darkness'

        Even huy- 'to cook (intr.)' (huy-se-n) → huysi: 'boiling, hot; boiling water'

        Even huk- 'to be warm, hot, steam (intr.)' (huk-se-n) → huksi: 'warm, hot; heat, glow'

    b.   clausal nominalization

        bi nongma:n ho ai gurge:wcimnge bi-si:-w-en
        I he very good worker be-NML-ACC-POSS.3SG
        ha:-ra-m
        know-FIN-SG
        'I know that he is a very good worker' (Doerfer et al. 1980: 94)

c. finite

> *bi hupkucimnge bi-se-m*
> I   teacher   be-FIN-1SG
> 'I am a teacher' (Doerfer et al. 1980: 86)

7.7.3.3 Evenki

In Evenki, the class of verbs that takes *-si* (< pTg *-sa-i*) as a conjugational base is restricted to the existential and negative auxiliaries *bi-* (*bi-si-n*) 'to be, exist' and *e-* (*e-si-n*) 'not to be, not to exist'. All verbs corresponding to the Even stative verbs above have been moved to the *-rA* conjugational class, e.g Evk. *i:-* (*i-re-n*) 'to sound', *huyu-* (*huyu-re-n*) 'to cook (intr.)', etc..

There are examples in which *-si* is used to derive lexical (ad)nominalizations as in Evk. *bisi* 'being, life', but it is also extended to the clausal level as in the relative clause in (66a) and to finite position as in (66b).

(66) Reflexes of the resultative deverbal noun suffix pTg *-sA* in Evenki

a. clausal adnominalization

> *Beje e-si-duk-iv   nungan-man alat-te   darigida-duk*
> man   not.be-ADN-ABL-1SG   he-ACC   wait-ADN   side-ABL
> *iche-vu-l-le-n*
> see-PASS-INCH-NFUT-3SG
> 'The man came in sight from the side from which I hadn't expected him' (Nedjalkov 1997: 101)

b. finite

> *beyetke:n-du: kniga bi-si-n*
> boy-DAT   book be-FIN-3SG
> 'The boy has a book'

7.7.3.4 Udehe

In Udehe, the *-sA* conjugation leaves a trace in the existential and negative auxiliaries *bi-* (*bie ~ bi-hi-ni*) 'to be, exist' and *e-* (*e-hi-ni*) 'not to be, not to exist' as well as in a number of stative verbs, such as Ud. *aha-, a:-* (*aha-hi-ni, a:-hi-ni*) 'chase, pursue', Ud. *do:-* (*do:-hi-ni*) 'to sit, be sitting', Ud. *egdenge-* (*egdenge-hi-ni*) 'to be amazed', Ud. *ili-* (*ili-hi-ni*) 'to stand, be standing', Ud. *sebjengke-* (*sebjengke-hi-ni*) 'to be interested' Ud. *te:-* (*te:-hi-ni*) 'to sit, be sitting', Ud. *to:-* (*to:-hi-ni*) 'to lie, be lying (of animals)', Ud. *xui-* (*xui-hi-ni*) 'to cook (intr.)' and in one telic verb *ngene-* (*ngene-hi-ni*) 'to penetrate (through clothing)' (Benzing 1955a:

1072–1074). Note that intervocalic pTg *-s- yields -s- in all Tungusic languages, including Even, except in Udehe where its reflex is -h- or ø and in Oroch where pTg *-si- yields -hi- (Benzing 1955a: 991; Starostin et al. 2003: 157); e.g. pTg *po:sikta 'star' is reflected as Evk. o:si:kta, Even o:si:kat, Ma. usixa, Na. xosakta, Orok wasikta and Ud. wahikta, waikta. Due to the ongoing lenition of Ud. -h- to ø, the suffix -hi- < pTg *-si- is only marked as length on the preceding stem by some scholars; Nikolaeva (1999), for instance, notes Ud. bi:-ni (be.FIN-3SG) '[it] is' for what appears as bi-hi-ni in Schneider (1936), Benzing (1955a), Menges (1968) and Kormušin (1998).

As illustrated in (67a), some verbs conjugating with -sA in Ewen relate to deverbal adjectives in -hi in Udehe. Although the verbal base is no longer attested as such in Udehe, it is reflected elsewhere in Tungusic and can thus be reconstructed for proto-Tungusic.

Examples (67b/c) illustrate extension of the nominalizer to the clausal level. In alternation with bi-hi-ni > bi:-ni '[it] is', the existential auxiliary and copula bi- 'to be, exist' derives a special impersonal form bie 'there is, there are', which is used both in adnominal (see (67b)) and finite (see (67d)) position. This form can be derived from the simplex resultative nominalizer pTg *-sA, whereas bi-hi-ni reflects the replacement of pTg *-sA by *sA-i.

The original resultative meaning of Ud. -hi (< pTg *sa-i) is supported by the observation that five verbs, i.e. Ud. do:-, Ud. ili-, Ud. te:-, Ud. to:- Ud. xui-, switch between *-rA and *-sA conjugation according to the telicity of their meaning: do:-i-ni '[it] sits down' vs. do:-hi-ni '[it] is sitting'; ili:-ni '[he] stands up' vs. ili-hi-ni '[he] is standing'; te:-i-ni '[he] sits down' vs. te:-hi-ni '[he] is sitting'; to:-i-ni '[it] lies down' vs. to:-hi-ni '[it] is lying' and xui:-ni '[it] comes to boil' vs. xui-hi-ni '[it] is boiling'. This observation indicates that pTg *-rA and *-sA originally had a different aspectual connotation, i.e. imperfective vs. resultative, but they had a similar (ad)nominal status, which underwent insubordination in both cases. Finite use of the Udehe reflexes of pTg *-sA and *-sA-i is illustrated in (67d) and (67e).

(67) Reflexes of the resultative deverbal noun suffix pTg *-sA in Udehe

   a. lexical adnominalization

   pTg *xingü:- 'to be(come) cold, freeze' in Evk. inginipcu, Even ingeńsi: 'frost, coldness; frosty, cold', Orok siŋgu:-, Na. si:ŋgu- 'to freeze' → Ud. inginihi 'cold'

   pTg *gil- 'to be(come) cold' in Even gęl- (gęl-sa-n) 'to be cold', gelsi: 'cold', Evk. gildi, Neg. giligdi, Oroch gicisi, Na. gicisi 'cold' → Ud. gilihi 'cold' pTg *goti- 'to be(come) bitter' in Ma. *gosihon* 'bitter', Even *gotac* 'bitter', *gotan* 'bitterness', Evk. *goci*, Neg. *gotigdi*, Na. *gocesi*, Olcha *gotuli* 'bitter' → Ud. *guacihi* 'bitter'

pTg *juyor-* 'to be(come) sour' in Ma. *jušuhun* 'sour', Even *juyis-sa-n* 'it is sour', *juyir* 'sour', Sol. *jišil-* 'to turn sour', Neg. *joyayigdi*, Olcha *juyursi*, Na. *joyorsi* 'sour'→ Ud. *ju:hi* 'sour'

pTg *peku- 'to be(come) hot' → Even *huk- (huk-se-n)* 'to be warm, hot, steam (intr.)', *huksi:* 'warm, hot; heat, glow', Evk. *heku* 'hot', Neg. *xekugdi*, Na. *peku*, Oroch. *xeku, xekusi*, Sol. *exu:gdi* → Ud. *xekuhi* 'hot'

pTg *pakti- 'to be(come) dark' in Even *hata- (hata-s-ni)* 'to be dark', *hatasi:* 'darkness', Evk. *haktïrasi:* 'dark, darkness' → Ud. *xaktihi* 'dark'

b. clausal adnominalization of Ud. *bie*

Aya-da   tongdo-do   bie   daumi-we   zoko:-ni
good-FOC   straight-FOC   be.ADN   bridge-ACC   put.PST-3SG
'He made a bridge that is good and straight' (Nikolaeva 1999: 400)

c. clausal adnominalization of Ud. *bi-hi-*

Bi ise:-mi   ei   sungta   bi:-we-ni   singe-we
I see.PST-1SG   NEG   deep   be.ADN-ACC-3SG   well-ACC
'I saw a well that is not deep' (Nikolaeva 1999: 400)

d. finite Ud. *bie*

Uti   a:nta   gar-gar   bie
this   woman   vivid   be.FIN
'This woman is (usually) vivid' (Nikolaeva 1999: 356)

e. finite Ud. *bi-hi-*

Uti   a:nta   gar-gar   bi:-ni
this   woman   vivid   be.FIN-3SG
'This woman is vivid' (Nikolaeva 1999: 356)

7.7.3.5 Nanai

In Nanai, verbs that originally conjugated on the basis of *-sA have all been moved to the *-rA conjugation, including the existential auxiliary and copula *bi-* (*bi-ni*) 'to be, to exist'. However, the resultative adnominalizer pTg *sA-i: > *-si: has petrified in verb stems, where it expresses resultative aspect. As illustrated in (68b), the verb pairs reflecting the resultative suffix Na. -si- correspond to verbs belonging to the *-sA conjugation in Even and/or Udehe (Benzing 1955a: 1074, Avrorin 1961: 19). In Nanai these verbs all fall into the *-rA conjugation.

Like in Udehe, Na. -*si* has also petrified in deverbal adjectives, which derive from a verbal base that is not always attested as such in Nanai. However, the base can be reconstructed in proto-Tungusic on the basis of contemporary Tungusic reflexes, some of which can be traced back to the *-sA* conjugation; see (68a).

A trace of clausal adnominalization is preserved in the negative adnominal suffix -*esi*, in which the negative auxiliary *e-* 'not to be, not to exist' is reduced to a suffix on the lexical verb (Section 4.3.3.4). The example in (68b) is thus a contraction of **jobo-ra e-si: nay* (work-ADN not.exist-ADN person).

(68) Reflexes of the resultative deverbal noun suffix pTg *-sA* in Nanai

    a.   lexical nominalization

        pTg **amta-* 'to perceive a physical sensation (tr.)' in Even/ Evk. /Neg. *amta-* 'to taste, smell, sense (tr.)' → Na. *amtasi* 'sweet'

        Na. *gekci-* 'to be cold, freeze' → Na. *gekcisi* 'cold'

        pTg **gil-* 'to be(come) cold' in Even *gęl-* (*gęl-sa-n*) 'to be cold', *gelsi:* 'cold', Evk. *gildi*, Neg. *giligdi*, Oroch *gicisi*, Ud. *gilihi* 'cold'→ Na. *gicisi* 'cold'

        pTg **goti-* 'to be(come) bitter' in Ma. *gosihon* 'bitter', Even *gotac* 'bitter', *gotan* 'bitterness', Evk. *goci*, Neg. *gotigdi*, Ud. *guacihi*, Olcha *gotuli* 'bitter' → Na. *gocesi* 'bitter'

        pTg *juyor-* 'to be(come) sour' in Ma. *jušuhun* 'sour', Even *juyis-sa-n* 'it is sour', *juyir* 'sour', Sol. *jišil-* 'to turn sour', Neg. *joyayigdi*, Olcha *juyursi*, Ud. *ju:hi* 'sour' → Na. *joyorsi* 'sour'

    b.   clausal adnominalization

        jobo-a-si   nay
        work-ADN.NEG-ADN person
        'a man who does not work'

    c.   resultative aspect

        Na. *enulu-* 'to fall ill' (Na. -*lu-* inchoative; Menges 1968: 199) → *enusi-* 'to hurt, be painful (intr.)'

        Na. *pulilu-* 'to start going' (Na. -*lu-* inchoative) → *pulsi-* 'to walk, wander'

        Na. *puyu-* 'to cook, bring to boil (tr.)' → *puysi-* 'to cook, be boiling (intr.)'

        Na. *te:-* 'to sit down' → *te:si-* 'to sit, be sitting'

7.7.4 pMo *-sA

The deverbal resultative nominalizer pMo *-sA is only preserved in WMo *ese* 'not', *ese-* 'not to be, not to exist', which is derived from to the negative verb and auxiliary pMo *e- 'not to be(come), be(come) non-existent, come to lack' in Section 4.3.4. As shown there, the suffix *-sA can be used to derive either an adverbial or a finite form from the negative verb, which recalls negative constructions of the type pTg *e-se and *e-si: < *e-se-i in Tungusic. The segmentation of WMo *ese*(-) along these lines has been proposed earlier, among others by Bese (1974: 7) and Sanžeev (1962: 280–282). Bese (1971: 220–221) further proposed to consider the deverbal perfective nominalizer WMo. and MMo. -ysan ~ -gsen / -qsan ~ -ksen as a composite suffix consisting of this element, an idea also supported by Poppe (1974: 146). Note that the alternation of voiced and voiceless velars in this suffix suggest a velar fricative in the reconstruction pMo *-Xsan.

Even if occurrence of the nominalizer and finite form *-se may be very restricted, the Mongolic languages reflect a functionally similar suffix *-si, which derives resultative deverbal nouns as in (69a). As illustrated in (69b), WMo. -si is particularly frequent in negative expressions with *ügei*, where it occasionally alternates with the resultative nominalizer WMo. -ya ~ ge (see Section 7.6.4). Given the external parallels, it is not unlikely that pMo *-si ultimately derives from *-sA-i.

(69) Reflexes of the resultative deverbal noun suffix pMo *-si in Written Mongolian

a. lexical nominalization

WMo. *ide-* 'to eat, consume (tr.)' → *idesi* 'food, nourishment, edibility'

WMo. *üde-* 'to see off, send off, bid farewell, accompany to the point of parting (tr.)' → *üdesi* 'evening, in the evening'

WMo. *tata-* 'to chop, grind (as meat) (tr. / intr.) → *tatasi* 'chopped, minced or ground meat; soup made of minced meat'

WMo. *tegege-* 'to load, convey, transport (tr.)' → *tegegesi* 'load, fright, loading capacity'

WMo. *tege-* 'to do so, to do that way (tr.)' → *tegesi* 'that way, thither'

b. negative constructions

WMo. *bara-* 'to finish, end (tr. / intr.), to destroy (tr.)' → *barasi ügei* 'imperishable, indestructable, inexhaustible'

WMo. *bari-* 'to hold, grasp, seize, to build, establish (tr.)' → *barisi ügei* 'which cannot be caught, intangible, elusive'

WMo. *moqu-* 'to get tired, weaken, exhaust one's strength (intr.)' → *moqusi ügei* 'inexhaustible'

WMo. *urba-* 'to turn around, to break away from (intr.)' → *urbasi ügei ~ urbaya ügei* 'remaining steadfast, firm or unchangeable, irreversible'

Example (70) illustrates the Khitan use of a perfective converb *-sii*, translated as 'after, as a result' (Kane 2009: 150–151), which is likely to be cognate with the resultative nominalizer WMo. *-si*. The subject of the dependent clause is different of that of the main clause. The juxtaposition of two high front vowels in this form supports the reconstruction of proto-Khitan-Mongolic *-sii* < *-sA-i*.

(70) The use of the perfective converb Khitan *-sii*

sin oŋ-on   tuur-sii,   SOUTH WEST
Qin   prince-GEN die-PFV.CONV   south west
jau tau   poju-l-er
bandit.suppression.commissioner   be.in.a.position-CAUS-PST
'after the death of the Prince of Qin, he was appointed the bandit suppression commissioner of the south west' (Kane 2009: 150)

7.7.5 pTk *-sA

The Turkic languages provide evidence for the reconstruction of a perfective nominalizer pTk *-sA*. In Old Turkic as well as in Chuvash, this suffix is reflected as *-sA*, but in Old Turkic, a new complex suffix *-sAr* deriving from a copula construction, gradually replaced the original suffix. The suffix is petrified as a nominalizer, marking complement and relative clauses, in some complex converb suffixes in Chuvash. The nominalizer pTk *-sA* then grammaticalized into a converb suffix along the pathway discussed in Section 8.1, resulting in a perfective converb *-sA* in Old Turkic and Chuvash, which later developed conditional / concessive and imperfective use, respectively. The reflex of pTk *-sA* in independent sentences in some Chuvash dialects suggests direct insubordination from clausal nominalizer into a perfective past marker, probably not passing over the converbial use of the suffix.

7.7.5.1 Old Turkic

The Old Turkic converb *-sA ~ -sAr* has a temporal, conditional and concessive function (Erdal 2004: 480–481; 320–322). An example of perfective temporal use with the subject of the dependent clause being different of that of the main clause is given in (71a). This function occurs less frequently than the conditional use, illustrated in (71b). In Old Uighur the alomorph *-sAr* is more frequent than *-sA*, but Karakhanide uses *-sA* consistently (Erdal 2004: 320). In Old Uighur, the conditional converb *-sAr*, can take the suffix *-lAr* to show that the subject is in the plural.

(71) The use of the Old Turkic converb *-sA ~ -sAr*

    a. perfective

        *yïlkï-ka   yütür-**ser**   yïlkï   kötürü   u-ma-tï*
        horse-DAT load-**CONV** horse lift.up-CONV be.able-NEG-PST
        'When they loaded it on a horse, the horse couldn't carry it.' (U I 8; Erdal 2004: 480)

    b. conditional

        *ol   altun   tag-ka   teg-**ser**   siz,*
        that golden mountain-DAT reach-**CONV** you
        kök   lenxwa   kör-gäy   siz
        blue lotus see-FIN you
        'If you reach that golden mountain, you will see blue lotuses'
        (KP 38: 1; Erdal 2004: 494)

The converb OTk *-sAr* has been thought to derive from the adnominal form in *-(A)r* of the verb pTk **sa:-* 'to reckon (as), count (on), desire' reflected in Karakhanide *sa-* 'to count, reckon (as)' and perhaps cognate with the Old Turkic desiderative suffix *-sA-* (Bang 1923: 116–119; Gabain 1950: 153; Räsänen 1957: 214; Johanson 1995: 336, Janhunen 2012c: 46). However, there are a number of objections against this proposal: First, given the widespread development of temporal connectives into conditionals (Hopper & Traugott 1993: 179; Heine & Kuteva 2002: 293), it is safe to assume that the original meaning of OTk. *-sAr* was perfective converb. This is supported by the observation that in the sources, examples of the converb reflecting perfective use are less frequent than those reflecting conditional use. The original perfective meaning, however, is hard to reconcile with the meaning 'to count, reckon (as)' of OTk. *sa-*.

Second, as Erdal (2004: 320) notes, if OTk. *-sAr* derives from a lexical verb, it should have been added to the vowel converb of the preceding verb, but there is no actual trace of a putative converb vowel before *-sAr* within any attested example.

Third, the negative counterpart of this suffix has the shape *-mAsA(r)*. In case OTk. *-sAr* really had a lexical origin, one would expect the negation to follow the main verb and take the negative counterpart OTk. *-mAz* of adnominal *-(A)r*, i.e.

**-*sAmAz*. Parallel to the derivation of OTk -*mAz* from pTk *-*mA-rA* involving an imperfective (ad)nominalizer (see Section 7.3.5.1), the negative -*mAsA(r)* thus seems to derive from pTk *-*mA-sA* involving a perfective (ad)nominalizer.

Given the relative infrequency of -*sA* converbs vis-à-vis -*sAr* allomorphs, I assume that the forms in -*sA* represent the primary stage, reflecting converbial use of an original perfective nominalizer (see Section 8.1). The forms in -*sAr* probably go back to periphrastic copula constructions of the shape *-*sA a-r* (NML COP-NML) and may have replaced the original synthetic forms in -*sA*. In support of this analysis, it can be observed that in none of the examples of the perfective converbs in -*sAr*, which reflect the primary temporal meaning, there is an analytical phrase consisting of a verb form together with OTk. *är-sär* (COP-CONV) (Erdal 2004: 481). The reluctance of the copula to enter such periphrastic constructions may be explained by the very origin of -*sAr* as an analytical copula construction. The optional plural agreement of -*sAr* supports its grammaticalization from an original appositive adnominal construction, as discussed in Section 8.1.

7.7.5.2 Chuvash

The corresponding Chuvash converb -*sa* ~ -*se* is restricted to temporal meaning, both imperfective as in (72a), expressing that the actions expressed by the converb and the main verb occur simultaneously and perfective as in (72b), expressing that the action expressed by the converb occurs before the main action (Benzing 1959: 744; Krüger 1961: 163–164).

In some Chuvash dialects, this form may function as a finite perfective past form, expressing states that were already completed in the past; see example (72e).

Composite suffixes indicate that -*sA* originated as a nominalizer of complement or relative clauses, preceding case suffixes or modifying nouns. The perfective converb -*sAn* 'after V-ing', illustrated in (72a), for instance, can be derived as an instrumental case in -*(Ă)n* from a nominal form in -*sA* underlying the converb (Poppe 1974: 146). This analysis is supported by the observation that -*san* is often followed by the emphatic particle -*Ah* 'even, just, yet', which is frequently added to adverbial expressions (e.g. *tap-ah* instantly-PT in (72a)) , some of which are derived with the instrumental -*(Ă)n*.

The perfective converb -*sAssĂn* 'after V-ing', illustrated in (72b), then, is a compound of an adnominal form in -*sA* underlying the converb plus a bound noun -*ssĂn* 'end', which is cognate with OTk. *soŋ*, MTk. *soŋ*, Tk./Az. *son*, Tkm. *soŋ*, Tat. *sŭŋ*, Kirg *soŋ*, Uigh. *soŋ*, Tuva *soŋ*, Shor *so:n*, etc. 'end, back, after' (Benzing 1959: 744).

(72) Reflexes of the perfective nominalizer pTk *-sA in Chuvash

a. clausal nominalizer

śuna šïni-sem čul-a perĕn-**sen**-eh,
sleigh tire-PL stone-DAT hit-**CONV**-PT
laša-sem tap-ah tăr-aśśĕ
horse-PL instantly-PT stand-DUR.PRS.3PL
'As soon as the sleigh tires hit on a stone, the horses stand instantly still.'
(Benzing 1959: 744)

b. clausal adnominalizer

Kaxal kay-nă-ne kur-sassăn, ...
Lazybones go-NML-ACC see-CONV
'When they saw Lazybones coming, they ...'

c. imperfective converb

šïv-a vïrt-**sa** păx-nă
water-ACC lie-**CONV** watch-PST
'He lay and watched the water' (Krüger 1961: 163)

d. perfective converb

un pat-n-e pïr-**sa** kala-nă
he.GEN side-INSTR-DAT go-**CONV** say-PST
'He went up to him and said' (Benzing 1959: 743; Krüger 1961: 163)

e. finite

ep un-a ača-n-ah kur-**sa**.
I he-ACC child-INSTR-PT see-**FIN**
'I have known him already as a child' (Benzing 1959: 744)

As for the negative counterpart of this suffix, the shape -mA-sA, which corresponds to the Old Turkic negative form, is preserved in only a few incorporations, such as in the negative pluperfect -mA-sA-ttĂ- vs. affirmative -sA-ttĂ- (< *-sA-är-tĂ- (-CONV-COP-PST)) and in the negative perfective converbs -mA-sA-n and -mA-sA-ssĂn. In the majority of cases, however, the negative employs the suffix -masĂr, which is commonly derived from the verbal noun in -mA plus the privative morpheme -sĂr 'without', cognate with OTk. -sïz, e.g. vaska-masăr 'without hurrying, the fact of not hurrying' (Benzing 1959: 744; Krüger 1961: 163).

7.8 The historical development of finite suffixes in Transeurasian

The Transeurasian languages preserve evidence supporting the reconstruction of five suffixes reflecting the development of aspectually marked (ad)nominalizers into finite tense markers : three aspectually unmarked nominalizers *-rA, *-mA and *-n and two resultative nominalizers *-xA and *-sA. The relevant reconstructions in the individual proto-languages are compared in Table 9.

Table 9. Form-function comparison of insubordination in the Transeurasian languages

pTEA	pJ	pK	pTg	pMo/ pKMo	pTk
*-rA	*-ra	*-l	*-rA	*-r	*-rV
lexical NML	lexical NML	lexical NML	lexical NML	lexical NML	lexical NML
	*-wo-ra	*-wo-l			
	clausal NML	clausal NML	clausal NML	clausal NML	—
	clausal ADN	clausal ADN	clausal ADN	—	clausal ADN
	FIN	FIN	FIN	FIN	FIN
*-mA	*-m	*-m	*-mA	*-mA ~ *-m	*-mA ~ *-m
lexical NML	lexical NML	lexical NML	lexical NML	lexical NML	lexical NML
	*-wo-m	*-wo-m			
	clausal NML	clausal NML	—	clausal NML	
	clausal ADN	—	—	—	
	FIN	FIN	FIN	FIN	
*-n	*-n	*-n	*-nA ~ *-n	*-n	*-n
lexical NML	lexical NML	lexical NML	lexical NML	lexical NML	lexical NML
	*-wo-n	*-wo-n			
	clausal NML	clausal NML	clausal NML	clausal NML	clausal NML
	clausal ADN	clausal ADN	—	—	clausal ADN
	FIN	FIN	FIN	FIN	FIN
*-xA ~ *-kA	*-ka	*-ka(-)i	*-xA: ~ *-kA:	*-xA ~ *-kA	*-xA ~ *-kA
lexical RES.NML	lexical RES.ADN	lexical RES.NML	lexical RES.NML	lexical RES.NML	lexical RES.NML
	—		clausal PFV.NML	clausal PFV.NML	clausal PFV.FUT.ADN
	clausal RES.ADN		clausal PFV.ADN	clausal PFV.ADN	
	RES.FIN		PST.FIN	PST.FIN	FUT.FIN
*-sA	*-sa		*-sA ~ *-si: < *sA-i:	*-sA ~ *-si: < *sA-i:	*-sA
lexical RES.NML	lexical RES.ADN		lexical RES.NML	lexical RES.NML	
	—		clausal RES.NML	clausal RES.NML	clausal PFV.NML
	—		clausal RES.ADN		
	RES.FIN		RES.FIN	RES.FIN	PFV.PST.FIN

The comparative evidence, summarized in Table 9, indicates that the markers under comparison originated as deverbal noun suffixes, marking a derivational process at the lexical level, were then extended to function as (ad)nominalizers in dependent clauses at the syntactic level, and were eventually – through a pragmatic role in discourse – extended still further to mark finite forms in independent clauses. The sharing of this insubordination process does not necessarily imply that the insubordination of the suffixes was already completed in proto-Transeurasian and inherited as finite / nonfinite polysemy in the daughter languages. Rather, the following observations suggests that some of the developments took place on cognate suffixes independently and at different times after separation from proto-Transeurasian. First, the reflexes of the deverbal noun suffixes pTEA *-rA, *-mA and *-n underwent an innovation in the proto-Japanese-Korean branch in the sense that clausal nominalization required a copula construction involving pJK *wo- 'to be' plus the deverbal noun suffix. Finite meanining was subsequently developed on the basis of these secondary copula constructions. Second, finite use seems to have still been in development in some historically attested stages, for instance, MK -(·u/o)l, -(·u/o)m, MK -(·u/o)n still required the addition of a vocative particle or a clitic noun in finite position, whereas contemporary K -(u)n and -(u)m do not. Third, the Turkic reflex of pTEA *-mA functions only as a deverbal noun suffix. In this context, a scenario in which Turkic has lost its functions as a clausal nominalizer and a finite form is more complicated than simply assuming that these functions never developed in Turkic, while they did elsewhere in Transeurasian. Fourth, the Turkic reflex of the perfective (ad)nominalizer pTEA *-xA specializes as a perfective future adnominalizer and further develops future finite meaning, whereas the future connotation is absent from the other Transeurasian languages. And finally, fifth, in contrast to the continental "Altaic" languages, the Japanese reflex of the resultative deverbal noun suffix pTEA *-sA develops directly into finite use, without intermediate clausal stages, a development which is confirmed by the observation that the insubordinated form takes arguments in the genitive case only. These observations suggest that in these cases clausal (ad)nominalization and/or finite use have developed independently on cognate nominalizers in the different branches.

a) *Formal assessment*

According to the correspondences 12. (*-a-), 13. (*-ə-) in Section 3.3.2., the vowel harmony between pTEA *-a- and *-ə- regularly merges into pJ *-a-. Given the absence of the vowel in the proto-Koreo-Japanese reflex, and the alternating vowel loss in Mongolic and Turkic, the final vowel in pTEA *-mA may already have been sporadically dropped at the proto-Transeurasian level. In contrast, the final vowel in the Korean and Mongolic reflexes of pTEA *-rA has probably been dropped in the course of their individual histories. Vowel erosion in word-final suffixes is to be expected in a process of grammaticalization, especially following sonorants such as /m/ and /r/, because their high sonority makes the articulation possible without final vowel. This may also explain why the vowels are retained in the reflexes of pTEA *-sA and *-xA ~ *-kA.

With the exception of the velar fricative reconstructed in pTEA *-xA, the consonants correspond regularly according to the correspondences 11. (*-r-), 8. (*-m-), 9. (*(-)n-) and 7. (*-s-) in Section 3.3.1.

In this chapter, I have followed Dybo (1990) and Starostin et al. (2003: 158) in their proposal that the medial velar fricative *-x- can be reconstructed as a separate phoneme in Tungusic. Since the number of Tungusic words reflecting pTg *-x- is relatively low to begin with, very few of them have an acceptable Japanese cognate. Establishing sound correspondences in Chapter 3 and in Robbeets (2005), I have only taken etymologies with a Japanese member into account. This approach has the advantage of reducing the probability of borrowing, but the drawback of overlooking sound correspondences that are not sufficiently reflected in Japanese. The reconstruction of the velar fricative pTEA *-x- probably represents such a case.

As shown in Table 10, verbs reflecting pTg *-x- correspond to proto-Mongolic and proto-Turkic verb stems reflecting an alternation between voiced *-g- and voiceless *-k-. The underlying etymologies are given in footnote 29.

---

29 (1) pTEA *daxa- 'to come near'

Neg. daxaw-, Sibe dahə-, Ma. daha-, Jur. tai-xa, Olč. daxau̯-, Orok daxu̯rị-, Na. daxa- Oroč daxu- 'to follow, obey', Ud. dahala- 'to agree', pTg *daxa- 'to follow'
WMo. daɣa-, MMo. daqa-, Khal. daga-, Bur. daxa-, Kalm. daxə-, Ordos daGa-, Dong. daGa-, Bao. daGa-, Dag. daga-, SYug. таʁa-, Mgr. daGa:- 'to follow' , pMo *daka- ~ *daga- 'to follow'
OTk. yak- ~ yagu- '1 to approach, be(come) near to' , yakïn ~ yagru ~ yaguk ' 2 near', yakïš- ~ yaguš- '3 to draw near to each other', Karakh. yaxšï '4 good', MTk. yavu- 1, yakïn ~ yavuk 2, yaxšï 4, Tk. yakïn ~ yavuk 2, yakïš- 3, yakšï 4, Az. yavï- 1, yaxïn ~ yowuG 2, yaxšï 4, Tkm. yak- ~ yovu- 1, yowuq 2, yaGšï 4, Tat. yakïn ~ yawuk 2, yaxšï 4, Kirg. žū- 1, žakïn ~ žu:q 2, žakšï 4, Kaz. žuw- 1, žakïn ~ žuwïk 2, žaksï 4, Nog. yuwï- 1, yakïn 2, yaxšï 4, KKalp. žuw- 1, žakïn ~ žuwïk 2, žaksï 4, Uz. yakin ~ jɔvuq 2, jaxši 4, Uigh. yak- 1, yekin 2, yakši 4, Chu. śïvăx 2, pTk *yak- ~ yagu- 'to become near'

(2) pTEA *toxu- 'to turn around'

Ma. tohoro '1 wheel, hoop', Evk. tokor- '2 to go round, turn round', tokčika '3 curved, bent', Neg. toxoy- 2, tokčoka 3, Orok to:rolị- 'to grind', Na. toxoriɣō 'pulley, a wheel used to transmit power', pTg toxo- 'to turn round'
WMo. toɣuri- '1 to go about, circle, surround, tour, roll (tr.)', toɣurig 'orbit, circumference', toɣurigu 'roundabout (adv. /ad.)', toɣuna/ toɣunu 'smoke-hole in the top of a yurt', WMo. tokir, takir 'bent, crippled', takiyar 'crooked, crippled', takirla- 'to be bent, crippled', MMo. to'ori- 'to turn around (in combat)', to'oriqa- 'to encircle, orbit', togorigai, togarik '2 round' , Khal. tögrög, dugarig 2, toxir '3 curved, bent', Bur. tüxerig, toxir 3,

Table 10. Verbal etymologies reflecting pTEA *-x-

TEA	Japonic	Koreanic	Tungusic	Mongolic	Turkic
*-x-	*-k-	*-k-	*-x-	*-g- ~ *-k-	*-g- ~ *-k-
(1) pTEA *daxa- 'to come near'			Na. daxa- 'follow' pTg *daxa-	WMo. daya- MMo. daqa- 'follow' pMo *daga- ~ *daka-	OTk. yak- OTk. yagu- 'become near' pTk *yagu- ~ *yak-
(2) pTEA *toxu- 'to turn around'			Evk. tokor- 'turn round' pTg *toxo-	WMo. toyuri- 'surround' WMo. tokir 'bent' pMo *togu- ~ *toki-	Balk. tögerek 'round' Balk. toxun 'wheel' pTk *togu- ~ *toku-
(3) pTEA *moxu- 'to become ruined'			Na. moxo- 'become exhausted' pTg *moxo-	WMo. moqu- 'become exhausted' WMo. moyutur 'blunt' pMo *mogu- ~ *moku-	

Kalm. *tögərəg*, *duyərγə* 2, *tokṛ* 'crippled, mutilated, dislocated', Ordos *tögörök* 2, Dag. *tukurin* 2, pMo *togu- ~ *toki- 'to turn round'

OTk. *tegirmi* '1 round', Karakh. *tegirme* 1, Az. *däjirmi* 1, Tk. *degirmi* 'circle', Tkm. *tegelek*, toGalaq, Uz. *tugarak* 1, *toyin* '2 wheel, hoop', Uigh. *düglăk* 1, Tat. *tügerek* 1, *tuyïm* 2, Karaim *togerek*, Kaz. *toyïn* 2, Nog. *tögerek* 1, *toyïn* 2, Bash. *tüŋäräk* 1, *tuyïn* 2, Balk. *tögerek* 1, *toxun* 2, KKalp. *döŋgelek* 1, *toyïn* 2, Khak. *toyïlax* 1, Shor *toyalaq* 1, Oirat *toyoloq* 1, SUigh. *doGïr* 1, Yak. *tier-* '3 to turn round', Dolg. *tier-* 3 Chu. *toğăn* 2, pTk *togu ~ toku-* 'to turn around'

(3) pTEA **moxu-* 'to become exhausted'

Ma. *moho-* '1 to lose powers, be(come) exhausted', Olč. *moxo-* 1, Na. *moxo-* 1, Even *mukay* 'need, poverty, distress, hardship', *mukay-* 'to live in poverty', Evk. *mukčere:-* 'to die', pTg **moxo-* 'to become exhausted'

WMo. *moqu-* 'to get tired, weaken, exhaust one's strength, be blunt (intr.)', WMo. *moyulcar*, *moyutur* 'blunt, without point, hornless', WMo. *mökü-* '1 to become extinct, die out, collapse, perish', Khal. *möxö-*1, Bur. *müxe-* 1, Bao. *mεgə-* 1, Dag. *muku-* 1, Kalm. *mökr-* 'be unable', Ordos *möxö-* 'to get into misery', pMo **mogu- ~ *moku-* 'to become exhausted'

Note that Korean has K *muk-*, MK *muk-* 'to get old, outdated, outworn, stale', pK **muk-* 'to become old, stale', but the vowel does not correspond regularly.

This alternation in lexemes cannot be ascribed to a particular phonological environment, but it recalls the allomorphy between the Mongolic and Turkic reflexes of the resultative nominalizer *-xA, in which a voiced velar suffix *-gA alternates with a voiceless allomorphs *-kA in certain continuant environments. The most plausible explanation for this peculiar alternation is to reconstruct pMo *-xA and pTk *-xA as the original morpheme. The evidence suggests that pTg *-kA: arose through de-fricativation of pTg *-xA: following *n, *m, *y or *ß, while pMo *-xA and pTk *-xA underwent defricativization following *r and *ß.

In non-continuant environment, the main allomorph pTg *-xA: was retained as a fricative in Ma. -hA and in some high-frequency verbs in Udehe as Ud. -xA or, alternatively in Udehe, it voiced to * -γA- and – through merger of /γ/ an /g/ – yielded Ud. -gA- following vowels The reflex of pTg *-x- being -k- in the Northern Tungusic languages, however, pTg *-xA: following non-continuants there merged with its allomorph *-kA following continuants, yielding only -kA(:) in Even and Evenki. Environments other than stem-final *r and *ß in Mongolic and Turkic were in the majority of cases represented by vowel-final verbs. There, pMo *-xA and pTk *-xA became realized as a voiced fricative -γA and, velar fricatives merging with velar stops, the suffix became transcribed as WMo. -gA and OTk. -gA. By analogy these forms spread to verbs ending in a consonant other than *r and *ß.

The shared allomorphy between the resultative nominalizers pTg *-xA: ~ *-kA:, pMo *-xA ~ *-kA and pTk *-xA ~ *-kA is a strong argument in favor of genealogical relatedness because (i) the allomorphs appear in a similar, but peculiar phonological environment, (ii) the allomorphy is a sporadic, seemingly irregular phenomenon in the individual Turkic, Mongolic and Tungusic branches, but it can be traced back to regular phonological behavior on the Altaic level and (iii) as explained in Section 2.5.3.4, sharing unreduced allomorphy is an indication against borrowing. Assuming that just like the feature of voice distinction in general, the fricativation of pTEA *-xA became neutralized in proto-Koreo-Japanic, we can thus reconstruct the allomorphy between pTEA *-xA and *-kA following the continuants *n, *m, *r, *x and *ß.

b) *Functional assessment*

The five etymologies discussed here can all be traced back to original deverbal noun suffixes: pTEA *-rA, *-mA and *-n had aspectually unmarked meaning, whereas pTEA *-xA and *-sA had resultative meaning. In the majority of cases, the reflexes of the deverbal noun suffixes pTEA *-rA, *-mA and *-n were aspectually unmarked in the sense that they derived either action nouns (e.g. *to write* → *writing*) or subject nouns (e.g. *to write* → *writer*) from transitive and intransitive verbs. There are also some relics frequently following telic verbs, however, in which reflexes of pTEA *-rA, *-mA and *-n expressed resultative meaning in the sense that they derived object nouns (e.g. *to write → written (material)*) from transitive verbs. In the process of insubordination, then, the aspectually unmarked reflexes of pTEA *-rA, *-mA and *-n developed imperfective adnominal and finite non-past use, whereas the resultative alternants developed perfective adnominal and (perfective) past use.

For pTEA *-rA, there are derivations of object nouns from transitive verbs in Northern Tungusic, Mongolic, Old Turkic and Chuvash. Korean, Northern Tungusic and Chuvash display perfective adnominal use following telic verbs. Indications of finite past use are found in Khitan and Chuvash.

For pTEA *-mA, there are derivations of object nouns from transitive verbs in Tungusic, Mongolic and Turkic and examples displaying perfective clausal nominalization following telic verbs in Tungusic. Note that resultative meaning is also implied in the common derivation of color nouns and adjectives from original change of state verbs in Tungusic: 'to become a color' → 'color (n./adj.)', a function that is also frequently observed for the lexical (ad)nominalizer pJ *-m in Japanese.

For pTEA *-n, there are derivations of object nouns from transitive verbs in Tungusic, Mongolic and Old Turkic. Korean and Tungusic display perfective adnominal use with exception of atelic verbs, while Chuvash generalized perfective use to all verbs with exception of the negative existential. Chuvash also reflects finite past use.

The observation that the development of resultative meaning on aspectually neutral nominalizers usually seems to be dependent on the telicity of the base verb can be explained by Bybee's (1985: 147) observation that "Languages do not show one aspect as clearly unmarked and the other marked because for some verbs (in particular, activity verbs and stative verbs), imperfective is the conceptually unmarked member, while for other verbs (in particular, telic or event verbs), perfective is the conceptually unmarked member." Different conceptualizations may even occur on the same base verb. Some verbs can be conceptualized as atelic when unaccompanied by an object (e.g. *He writes*) and telic when an object is present (e.g. *He writes a novel*). The deverbal noun of the verb 'write' can then be interpreted in both the imperfective sense 'my writing' or in the perfective sense 'my written thing'. As such, a specific deverbal noun suffix may specialize for either imperfective adnominal/ non-past finite (e.g. *writing / I write*) or for perfective adnominal/ past finite meaning (e.g. *written / I wrote*) in the course of its insubordination process. Alternatively, the deverbal noun suffix may develop both meanings, either dependent on the telicity of the verb as in Korean and Tungusic, or not as in Chuvash.

In contrast to the aspectually neutral deverbal noun suffixes, the reflexes of the deverbal noun suffixes pTEA *-xA and *-sA can be characterized as resultative because they derived object nouns from any transitive verb or stative nouns and adjectives from change of state verbs. Whereas pTEA *-xA may have had both functions, pTEA *-sA was probably restricted to the derivation of stative nouns and adjectives from change of state verbs. In the process of insubordination, then, these suffixes developed stative adnominal and non-past meaning when attached to change of state verbs, including verbal adjectives, while they developed perfective adnominal and perfective (non-)past meaning following other verbs.

As far as the reflexes of pTEA *-xA are concerned, there are derivations of object nouns from transitive verbs in combination with stative nouns and adjectives from change of state verbs in Japanese, Tungusic, Mongolic and Turkic and following Japanese verbs originally meaning 'to become a property' we find indications of stative adnominal or non-past finite use, whereas other verbs may have been derived as perfective adnominal or past finite forms. The Tungusic and Mongolic languages share the development into perfective adnominal and past finite forms, whereas the Turkic languages develop perfective non-past adnominal and finite use.

The hypothesized path of diachronic evolution from a resultative deverbal noun into a perfective adnominal into a past finite marker is well-attested cross-linguistically (Comrie 1976: 99–101; Bybee 1985: 196; Bybee et al. 1994: 86; Johanson 2000b; Malchukov 2000: 447). The development from a resultative into a perfective future adnominal into a finite future in Turkic, can be explained over a perfect with non-past reference, as in German "Morgen bin ich schon abgefahren" Comrie (1976: 66) gives examples of this development from ancient Greek and Russian.

The use of pTEA *-sA may have been originally restricted to change of property verbs 'to be(come) a property' and copular verbs 'to be(come)', negative 'not to be(come)', which would explain the limited distribution of the Japonic and Tungusic deverbal noun suffixes and the restriction to only one negative verb in Mongolic. The suffixes developed stative adnominal and non-past finite meaning in attachment to this limited class of verbs, but in Japanese, pre-OJ *-si < *sa-i became added to non-property verbs as well, deriving perfective adnominal and past meaning, probably to restore paradigmatic equivalence with pre-OJ *-ki < *ka-i. The Turkic languages attached their reflex of the suffix to any verb, irrespective the meaning of the verb base, leaving traces of perfective clausal nominalization and perfective past finite use.

c) *Combinational assessment*

It appears that the Transeurasian languages have a number of compounds based on the above cognate (ad)nominalizers in common. The evidence suggests, however, that these strings were formed at different stages in the individual histories of the languages under discussion. Table 11 presents the possible suffix strings along with the language stages in which the compounding presumedly took place.

Table 11. Shared suffix strings based on cognate adnominalizers across the Transeurasian languages

pTEA	+ *i 'fact, thing, this (one)'	*wo- + 'to be'	+ pKJ *pa 'place'	*-xA-+ +-n INCH- -SG	+ *-kAn diminutive	+ REFL-POSS
*-rA	pre-OJ, MK, pTg	pJ, pK				
*-mA		pJ, pK				pTg, CMo.
*-n	MK, pTg	pJ, pK	pJ, pK		pTg, Khal.	
*-xA	pre-OJ, pK, pTg, pMo, pre-OTk					
*-sA	pre-OJ, pTg, pKMo			pTg, pMo		

The suffix that appears to be most commonly attached to the (ad)nominalizers is pTEA *i, which can be reconstructed as a bound noun meaning 'fact, thing, this (one)'. It is reflected in Old Japanese as a bound noun *i* 'fact (that); that (which)' (Whitman 1985: 44, 246; Martin 1987: 64–65, 420, 1991a: 283, 286), for instance in the expression OJ *aruiwa* 'perhaps, or' < pJ *ar-u i pa* (be-ADN fact TOP), and it is probably related to the demonstrative pronoun pJ *i* 'this' reflected in OJ *ima* 'now' (< pJ *i-ma* this-interval). Middle Korean has a bound noun ·*i* 'thing, one, person' (Martin 1992: 548), which is probably related to the nominal and adnominal demonstrative pronoun MK ·*i* 'this one, this person, this thing; this'. The Tungusic languages share a suffix *-i: that derives ordinal from cardinal numbers, e.g. Evk. *ïlan* 'three' → *ïli:* 'the third one, third' (< pTg *ila-i:* three-thing) (Benzing 1955a: 1051), which might be related to the third person pronoun Manchu *i*. The Turkic demonstrative pronoun *I, which was postposed for subject reference may ultimately go back to this form as well (Erdal 1979: 89, 2004: 207, 243). The demonstrative *I / In- 'that (one)' has lexicalized in expressions such as OTk. *ïn-ča ~ in-ča* 'the following, in the following way' vs. *an-ča* 'the previous, in the previous way', OTk. *ïn-tïn* '(the one) on the other side' vs. *mun-tïn* 'the one on this side', OTk. *ïnaru ~ iŋaru* 'forward; from … on', the demonstrative interjection *ïna* etc.

It is probably relevant that a reflex of pTEA *i can be added to any (ad)nominalizer under discussion, except for the reflexes of the nominalizer pTEA *-mA. As opposed to the other (ad)nominalizers, the reflexes of pTEA *-mA are the only suffixes for which adnominal use is generally lacking. This distribution suggests that the reflex of pTEA *i is a postadnominal bound noun. It was added to the suffixes after they had developed adnominal use, the resulting string tended to replace the earlier simplex form of the nominalizer and in its turn underwent insubordination. This tendency for postadnominal compounding and replacement of the corresponding simplex nominalizers is recurrent and repetitive on all reflexes of pTEA *i, independent of chronology. Thus, the development may occur at different chronological stages, for instance in pre-Old Japanese, Middle Korean, proto-Tungusic, proto-Mongolic, proto-Khitan-Mongolic and pre-Old Turkic after separation of the daughter languages, a phenomenon which can be regarded as "parallelism in drift" (see Section 2.2.3.2).

In contrast with the independent compounding of reflexes of pTEA *i, the combining of aspectually neutral nominalizers with a reflex of the copular verb pTEA *bɔ:l- 'to sit, be(come)' (see Section 3.4.2), seems to have been a common innovation in proto-Koreo-Japanic. Thus, the insertion of a copula pKJ *wo- 'to sit, be(come)' in the formation of clausal (ad)nominalization may have already been underway in the common ancestor of Koreanic and Japanic.

The noun pKJ *pa 'place' has been reconstructed in Robbeets (2005: 172, 403, 481). OJ ba 'place' can be derived from pJ *(-)n-pa ((-)GEN-place), the prenazalized voiced stop in the Old Japanese word being a trace of a petrified genitive in analogy with the genitive in frequent compounds such as J *tatiba* 'standpoint', J *hiroba* 'market place' etc. Traces of the voiceless alternant pJ *pa 'place' may be preserved in OJ pi_1dipa 'bank, shore' (< OJ pi_1di 'mud, durt' + *pa 'place'), OJ *nipa* 'garden' (< OJ *ni* 'earth' + *pa 'place') and – according to Martin (1990; 494; 1991a: 285) – also in the topic marker OJ *pa*. The Korean cognate for this word is K, MK *pa* 'place'. The common word for 'place' entered compounds with the adnominalizers pK *-n and pJ *-n to result in constructions 'the situation that' and then developed into conditional markers. In Japanese, pJ *pa 'place' is incorporated in the conditional converb OJ -(a)ba, thus deriving OJ *yukaba* 'if one goes' from pJ *yuka-n-pa (go-ADN place) and probably also in the necessitive suffix OJ -ube_2- (e.g. OJ yuk-ube_2- 'to be necessary to go' < *yuk-[w]o-n pa yi- (go-be-ADN place be.good)) and the adjective OJ ube_2- 'to be proper, to be indeed' (< *wo-n pa yi- (be-ADN place be.good)). In Korean, the grammaticalization has resulted into the construction MK ··(u/o)n ·pa 'the situation that', which has subsequently developed into a conditional, temporal and causal converb 'if, when, since' (Martin 1990: 494, 1991a: 285, 1992: 906–907). It is likely that the construction pKJ *-n pa 'the situation that' had already grammaticalized in the common ancestor, while the conditional meaning 'if, when, since' developed independently in both families.

The Tungusic and Mongolic languages share a perfective nominalizer pTgMo*-*xsAn* which is reflected in the Mongolic perfective nominalizer *-*XsAn* yielding WMo. and MMo. -*ysan* ~ -*gsen* / -*qsan* ~ -*ksen* and in the Tungusic perfective nominalizer *-*xsAn* yielding the perfective converbs Even -*s(A)* and Evenki -*ksA* and the finite perfect forms Na. -*xAn*, Olč -*xA^n*, Oroč -*xA*, Ud. -*hA(n)*.

Although the nominalizer and diminutive suffix may ultimately be cognate, the sharing of the compound converbs between the Northern Tungusic languages Even -*ni-ke:n*, Neg. -*na-xan* (CONV-DIM) and Khalkha -*n-xAn* (CONV-DIM) may be a case of selective combinational copying, enhanced by the formal equivalence of the elements. Borrowing is a likely explanation because the distribution of the compound converbs is restricted to Northern Tungusic and Khalkha Mongolic. Since this seems to be the only case in which a converb marker takes a nominal derivative suffix in Mongolic, the combinational borrowing probably went from Tungusic into Mongolic.

Combinational borrowing probably also explains the sharing of a converb construction consisting of reflex of the nominalizer pTEA *-*mA* plus a reflexive possessive marker, giving the converb its typical co-referential function. Since the Central Mongolic reflexive possessive -*maa(n)* is formally different from the Tungusic reflexive possessive pTg *-*wi* and since the compound converb is restricted to the contemporary central Mongolic languages, it probably concerns an instance of combinational borrowing from Tungusic into Mongolic, possibly enhanced by the formal equivalence of the first element.

d) *Typological assessment*

The five etymologies summarized in Table 9 all share a diachronic feature whereby a nominalizer began as a derivational marker at the lexical level, was then extended to mark dependent clauses at the syntactic level, and eventually developed into a marker of independent clauses. This is a grammaticalization process to which Evans' (2008: 367) term "insubordination" can be applied because formally dependent clauses become conventionalized as independent clauses, which draw their morphological marking only from the former dependent clause.

Since the examples given in this chapter do not involve the ellipsis of a matrix verb, they can be subsumed under "direct insubordination": the nominalized forms are directly reanalyzed as finite forms rather than being part of an original copula construction which became verbalized and then lost its copula. This can be deduced from the observation that the examples show virtually no trace of an eroding copula such as the final particle in (4b). An apparent exception to this general tendency is the finite imperfective -*mbi* and the finite past -*hAbi* in Manchu, which can be derived from a reflex of the Tungusic nominalizers *-*mA* and *-*xA* plus the Manchu predicative copula Ma. *bi*. In Section 7.4.3.1, however, it has been argued that the copula represents a later addition perhaps under influence of Sinitic, allowing for maximum inflectional marking on the insubordinated nominalized form. A periphrastic construction with a copula seems to be a way out when the subordinate origin of the finite marker does not allow the verb to be marked with several categories at once.

Similarly, there are instances in Mongolic, in which historical evidence suggests that copula are secondarily added to nominalized forms, only after these forms have developed into markers of finiteness. In section 7.6.4, it has been argued that the optional use of a copula *yum* in finite constructions consisting of a so-called "nomen imperfect" -*gAA* in the contemporary Central Mongolic languages is probably secondary, given the observation that the finite use of the ancestral form MMo. -*'a* ~ -*'e* is never embedded by a copula. Having made a rough count, Rybatzki (p.c.) finds that in Middle Mongolian, nominalizers indicating finite forms occur more frequently without intervention of a copula than in the contemporary Mongolic languages.

Note that the assumption of secondary addition of copula in Mongolic solves Mithun's (2008: 102) puzzle that – contrary to other nonfinite forms in Khalka, which have directly extended to markers of finiteness – the use of the temporal-aspectual nominalizers as finite forms "does not appear to be the result of direct extension, however. They appear in compound tense formations, as complements of a finite verb 'be' or 'become'". The observation that these copula constructions may be secondary further contradicts Bisang's (forthcoming: 11, 30) viewpoint that the use of the copula *yum* in finite nominalized constructions in Khalkha can be seen as an indication of original clefting, whereby subsequent copula loss would lead to the development of finite future function on the nominalizer. It does not alter Bisang's basic argumentation, however, that the development of finiteness in these examples is primarily driven by information structure.

In line with Yap, Matthews & Horie (2004), Yap & Matthews (2008: 6–9), Horie (2008: 176–177), Bisang (forthcoming: 28) has also argued that the use of nominalizers as finite forms in Japanese derives from finite copula constructions, in which the copula has been lost. Wrona (2011), however, provides historical evidence from Japanese, showing that some finite nominalizations such as the ones marked by -*sa*, discussed in Section 7.7.1.2 have never been embedded by a copula throughout the history of the Japanese language, whereas for others such as nominalizations with *no* and *koto* the so-called "stand-alone" type of nominalization is attested before the copula type. There are, for instance, no examples of a finite copula following ko_2to_2 in Old Japanese; only examples of the type illustrated in (73b) are found. Copula constructions as in the contemporary Japanese example in (73c) emerged later in Japanese history, perhaps under Chinese influence.

(73) Development of the nominalizer OJ ko_2to_2

    a.   Clausal nominalization in Old Japanese

           ip-umasizi-ki_1 ko_2to_2 mo_2 ip-i_1-n-u
           say-NEG.POT-ADN thing PT say-CONV-PERF-FIN
           '[He] also said things that [he] should not have said.' (SM 27)

    b.   Finite in Old Japanese

           karakuni-wo   ika-ni   ip-u ko_2to_2 so_2
           land.of.Kara-VOC why-DAT say-ADN NML   PT
           'Oh, the land of Kara! Why is it called so?'

    c.   Finite copula construction in Japanese

           Nani-yori daiji-na   koto-wa   hanasiai-de kaiketsu suru
           what-ABL important-ADN thing-TOP talk-INST   solution make
           koto   da.
           NML   be
           'The most important thing is to find a solution through talks' (Kaiser et al. 2001: 223)

In sum, direct insubordination is a typological diachronic feature characteristic for the Transeurasian languages. Given its ubiquity and its central role in the development of inflection from derivation, it can be regarded as one of the driving forces of morphosyntactic change in these languages. The majority of insubordinated nominalizations discussed in this chapter has never been embedded by a copula and in the rare cases where such copula constructions appear, historical and comparative evidence suggests that the copula represents a secondary addition.

In the etymologies under discussion, the insubordination process is intertwined with yet another grammaticalization process, i.e. the development of temporal from aspectual distinctions. The grammaticalization from deverbal noun suffix to adnominalizer to finite suffix involves a change in the part-of-speech status from noun to adjective to verb. The etymologies of pTEA *-rA, *-mA and *-n lead to the reconstruction of aspectually unmarked meaning, while those for pTEA *-xA and *-sA reflect resultative meaning. When these forms are verbalized, an actional interpretation is forced on an originally adnominal and therefore more stative form. This leads to the development of tense distinctions from original aspect distinctions, a cross-linguistically well-attested process, the details of which are assessed from a functional perspective in Section b).

The Uralic languages also display a recurrent tendency of direct insubordination. Deverbal noun suffixes such as pUr *-k, *-pÄ, *-mə and *-śÄ are thought to have developed into finite markers for present (*-k, *-pÄ) and past (*-mə, *-śÄ) tense, either in proto-Uralic or after the separation of the daughter languages (Collinder 1965: 110–115; Janhunen 1982: 36–37). From a formal and functional perspective, the action and completed action noun suffix pUr *-mə and the action, actor and completed action noun suffix pUr *-śÄ seems to represent a match with the Transeurasian suffixes *-mA and *-sA. In view of other correlations (see Sections 4.4, 5.4, 6.3, 6.4 and 8.5), these correspondences are suggestive of a historical connection – perhaps even a remote genealogical connection – between the two language families concerned.

8 Converbs

8.1 Converbs and their diachronic relevance

From a typological perspective, the Transeurasian languages are known as converb-prominent languages because they are characterized by an extensive use of converbs rather than by the use of adverbial subordinators like many European languages or by mere verbal juxtaposition like in Chinese (Bisang 1995, 1998; Johanson 1995; Nedjalkov 1995; Alpatov & Podlesskaya 1995; Malchukov 2012). Originally coined by Ramstedt (1903: 55), the very term 'converb' was adopted in general linguistics from Transeurasian linguistics to denote a cross-linguistic category. Converbs, also known as gerunds or adverbial participles, can be defined as nonfinite verb forms whose main function is to mark adverbial subordination (Haspelmath 1995: 3).

In the light of the continuum approach, which views inflection and derivation as opposite poles on a morphological scale (see Section 6.1), converbs can be seen as transitional. They can be considered inflectional because they are characterized by obligatoriness, unlimited applicability, non-recursivity, the possibility of cumulative expression and unchanging base semantics. However, they change the word class of the base from verb into adverb, and in this sense they can be regarded as derivational. Haspelmath (1996) introduces the notion of word-class-changing inflection: at the level of internal syntax inside the clause, converbs preserve the word-class of the base, governing a subject or object and taking adverbial modification; at the level of external syntax outside the clause, on the other hand, they reflect the word-class of the word-form, functioning as adverbs modifying the main predicate.

As far as the diachronic origins of converbs are concerned, Haspelmath (1995: 17) finds two basic sources for the development of converbs across the languages of the world, i.e. case-marked deverbal nouns and appositive participles. The first and most common source consists of adpositional or case forms of deverbal nouns which have become independent from their original paradigm. Here, it seems possible to further distinguish between (a) converbs which developed from deverbal nouns in peripheral cases on the one hand and (b) converbs which developed from deverbal nouns in core cases, on the other. Whereas peripheral cases, such as locative, dative, instrumental, terminative, adessive, abessive, etc. express various concrete semantic roles, core cases such as nominative and accusative express more abstract syntactic relations, such as subject and object.

In many Uralic languages, new converbial forms seem to be constantly developing from action nominals in peripheral cases (Ylikoski 2003: 202–205), e.g. the

Komi converb *-ömön* derives from an action nominal in *-öm* in the instrumental case *-ön*; the Komi terminative converb *-tödz* 'until' consists of an earlier deverbal noun in *-t followed by the terminative case suffix *-ödz*; the Finnish adessive and abessive converbs *-malla* 'by' and *-matta* 'without' consist of the deverbal noun suffix *-mA* followed by nominal adessive and abessive case endings; etc.

This grammaticalization pattern is also commonly observed in western varieties of the Transeurasian languages, but less frequently in the eastern varieties. In Old Turkic, for instance, the converb suffix OTk. *-(X)pAn* derives from a nominal form in pTk *-bA* in the instrumental case in *-In*; OTk. *-čA* consists of the vowel converb *-A, -I, -U* and *-yU* with the equative suffix *-čA*; the negative converb suffix *-mAtIn* derives from the negative *-mA- in a nominal form in *-tI followed by the instrumental case in *-In*; OTk. *-GInčA* 'as long as, until', derives from a deverbal noun in *-(X)g* with the third person possessive suffix and the equative case ending and; the deverbal noun suffix in *-dOk* combines with the instrumental *-In*, the dative *-KA* and the locative *-DA* to form various converb forms (Johanson 1988, 1995: 316–317). Peripheral cases of deverbal nouns are also productive in Mongolic converb formation (Poppe 1954: 180–181), for instance, in the final and preparative converbs WMo. *-rA* and *-run*, which derive from a deverbal noun suffix in *-r* followed, respectively, by the dative case in *-A* or genitive in *-un* (see Section 7.3.4); in the perfective converb MMo. *-GAt*, derived from the resultative nominalizer in the dative case MMo. *-tA* (see Section 7.6.4); in the terminative converb WMo. *-tAlA* 'until' consisting of a deverbal noun suffix in *-tAl* and the dative in *-A*; in the abtemporal converb *-GsAGAr*, derived from the perfective nominalizer WMo. *-GsAn* and the ancient instrumental case in *-GAr* and; in the contemporal converb *-mAGčA* 'scarcely had one done something, when ...' derived from the deverbal noun suffix *-mAG* in the equative case *-čA*. To a certain extent, the tendency for converbs to develop from deverbal nouns in peripheral cases is also present in the Tungusic languages (Benzing 1955a: 1085, 1090–1092; Nedjalkov 1995: 446–458): in Evenki, for instance, the anterior converb Evk. *-cala* can be derived from the perfective noun in *-ca* and the allative case in *-la*; the temporal-conditional converb in Evk. *-raki* goes back to the deverbal noun suffix in pTg *-rA* in an ancient locative case in pTg *-ki*. Furthermore, the Even converb of goal *-dA:i* originates from a dative-locative marker *-dA* and a possessive-reflexive *-i*, added after a stem-final remnant of a deverbal noun suffix *-n*$_{(1)}$ (Section 7.5.3.2) and the Manchu converb in *-hAi ~ -kAi* derives from the perfective nominalizer in the genitive case *-i* (Section 7.6.3.1).

However, the Tungusic languages also contain many examples of converbs developing from deverbal nouns in core cases, especially marked in the accusative. In Evenki, for instance, the anterior converb Evk. *-ktAvA* derives from the deverbal noun in *-ktA* and the accusative in *-vA* and; the simultaneous converb

Evk. *-dyAnmA* derives from the deverbal noun suffix in *-n*, the imperfective aspect in *-dyA-*, and the accusative allomorph *-mA* (see Section 7.5.3.3). Similarly, the perfective converbs Ud. *KA-si* and Na. *-kA-p* derive from an original accusative-reflexive construction pTg *xA-pA-i (PFV.NML-ACC-REFL) (Section 7.6.3).

The second source from which converbs can be developed is participles, gradually losing their adjectival inflection when used in non-attributive adverbial or so-called "appositive" or "copredicative" function. This type is well known from some European languages such as, for instance, in the Latin example in (1). Here, the participle *mittentes*, which is normally used attributively in constructions such as *milites mittentes sortem* 'soldiers who cast lots' takes on a converb-like function, while maintaining its original gender, number and case agreement.

(1) Latin

(Milit-es)   *divis-erunt*   *vestiment-a* *eju*s,
Soldier.M-NOM.PL   divide.PERF-3PL   garment-PL   his
mitte-nt-es   *sort-em*   *super* *e-is*
cast-PCP-NOM.PL.M   lot-ACC   upon   they-ABL
'(The soldiers) parted his garments, casting lots upon them, ...'
(Mark 15: 24; Haspelmath 1995: 18)

Whereas the Uralic languages make exclusive use of the first strategy, the Transeurasian languages employ a number of converb suffixes, which are regarded as "primary" (Johanson 1995: 316) or "genuine" (Poppe 1954: 95) in the sense of being morphologically unanalyzable as a case-marked deverbal noun. In some cases, these converb suffixes still leave a hint of their adnominal origin as they coexist with homophoneous deverbal (ad)nominal suffixes, e.g. the negative (ad)nominalizer and converb OJ *-(a)zu* (Section 7.4.1.2); the Korean deverbal noun suffix and adverbializer K *-kAy* (Section 7.6.2) and the Chuvash petrified (ad)nominalizer and converb *-sA* (Section 7.7.5.2). In other cases, these converbs have preserved a certain tendency for agreement in the incorporation of plural or reflexive suffixes, which is a strong indication of their appositive participial origin. This is the case, for instance, for some converbial suffixes discussed in Chapter 7, e.g., the reflexive singular vs. plural formation pTg *-*mA-wi* (-NML-POSS.REFL.SG) ~ * *mA-wari* (-NML-POSS.REFL.SG) reflected in the converbs Evk. *-mi / -mil*, Nanai *-mi / -mari / -meri* , Ud. *-mi / -mei*, Olč *-mi / -mari / -meri*, Oroč *-mi / -mai*; the reflexive possessive marker *-AA/n* in the preconditional converb *-mAA/n* in the Central Mongolic languages (Section 7.4.4); the reflexive possessive and diminutive incorporated in the Even converb *-ni-ke:n* (Section 7.5.3.2); the number agreement in the converb MMo. *-n* (SG) vs. *-t* (PL) (Section

7.5.4) and the optional plural marking with -*lAr* on the Old Uighur conditional converb -*sAr* (Section 7.7.5.1).

Note that there are also instances in which case-unmarked deverbal noun affixes seem to have developed directly into converb affixes, without passing through an appositive participial stage. This is the case, for instance, for the English -*ing* converb, whose immediate ancestor is a deverbal action noun rather than an appositive participle. In Old English, the ending of the present participle -*ende* was distinct from the suffix -*ung*/-*ing* of the deverbal noun. The merger of both endings as -*ing* is only a feature of some Middle English dialects. As it happens, the earliest developments of converbs in -*ing* occurred in the north of England, where the two endings remained distinct. Therefore, it is argued that the converb suffix developed directly from the deverbal noun suffix, quite independently of the present particle (Fanego 2004: 12). As such, the origin of the English -*ing* converbs seems to conform to the first source, i.e. adpositional forms of deverbal nouns in peripheral cases (e.g. I answer by writing > I answer by writing a letter) as well as case-unmarked deverbal nouns in the nominative (His writing frightens you > Writing, he frightens you.) Through the ambiguity of certain involved constituents that could readily occur in both noun phrase and verb phrase structures, a noun phrase became reanalyzed as a verb phrase. Thus, reinterpretation at the syntactic level seems to have triggered the grammaticalization of the deverbal noun suffix -*ing* into a converb suffix at the morphological level.

The development of converbs along these lines can be viewed as a grammaticalization process because it involves a gradual increase in grammatical status from less inflectional deverbal nouns and participial suffixes to relatively more inflectional converb suffixes. Second, semantic content is gradually lost, as deverbal nouns may show some ideosyncracies, while converbs can be essentially attached to any main verb, without changing the meaning of the base. Third, the development may involve a loss of phonetic substance, as composite constructions contract. Finally, it involves a loss of categorial properties because it can be viewed as a gradual process of denominalization.

Since the suffixes below reflect a shared process of grammaticalization from deverbal noun suffixes to converb suffixes in addition to sharing formal and functional correspondences, they can be taken as a strong indication of genealogical relatedness (see Section 2.5.3.1). Furthermore, it is interesting to note that the development of converbial markers from core-case marked deverbal nouns and from appositive participial forms is a developmental characteristic that delimits the Transeurasian languages from the neighboring Uralic languages.

8.2 Previous research

This chapter will be concerned with the reconstruction of two suffixes reflecting the development of deverbal noun suffixes to converb suffixes: pTEA *-i ~ ø and pTEA *-xU ~ *-kU.

Ramstedt (1945) was the first to compare the deverbal noun in -i between Korean and the Turkic, Mongolic and Tungusic languages, including a number of derivations in Nanai such as *alosi* 'education, educating' and *deduli* 'respect', which do not occur in the dictionaries. This proposal was repeated in Ramstedt's 1952 (103–104) monograph and supported by Poppe (1955a: 264, 1960: 13). Street (1978: 173–175) added the Japanese deverbal noun suffix in -i to the etymology. Disregarding the Altaic cognates, Martin (1968: 406) proposed that the so-called Japanese "infinitive" ending -i should be related to the Korean deverbal noun suffix, but later (1987: 265, 667; 1990: 483, 488, 500) he reconstructed the Japanese form as pJ *-Ci with an unspecified consonant, which made the comparison with Korean problematic. Whitman (1985: 44, 246) challenged Martin's reconstruction, maintaining pJ *-i as the original infinitive form, cognate to the Korean deverbal noun suffix. Martin (1995: 142), accepting Whitman's argumentation, finally suggested that the Korean adverbializer -i should be added to the comparison. Recently, Whitman (2012: 34) summarized the etymology, including both the deverbal nominal use and adverbial/infinitive use in Japanese and Korean.

As opposed to Martin and Whitman's approach, Vovin (1998, 2001: 190, 195–196) regarded the Japanese nominalizer and infinitive as two distinct morphemes, with two different etymologies. On the one hand, he derived the Japanese nominalizer from pJ *-Ci, connecting it with the nominalizer K, MK -ki and with the unproductive nominalizer OTk. -i/-i , which he speculatively derived from pTk *-gi. On the other hand, he compared the Japanese infinitive pJ *-i with the Korean -e/ -a infinitive and the Turkic -A converb. In the 2001 version of the paper, the Turkic participants were left out, and the Japanese nominalizer became reconstructed as pJ *-i, while its Korean cognate was substituted by the Korean bound noun *i* 'fact, thing'. Finally, the etymology for the infinitive was entirely rejected (Vovin 2008a: 83–84; 2009: 716), while the common nominalizer was attributed to borrowing (Vovin 2008a: 87–88). Starostin et al. (2003: 227) accepted the comparison of the Japanese infinitive proposed by Vovin (1998a) and added the Mongolic deverbal resultative suffix WMo. -ya ~ -ge (see Section 7.6.4) to the etymology. Their proposal was followed by Kortlandt (2010: 160), who changed the underlying reconstructions (pTk *-(y)a, pMo *ya and pK *-a/e) of the nominalizers to pTk *-ya, pMo *-ya and pK *-ya.

As far as my reconstruction pTEA *-xU ~ *-kU is concerned, Ramstedt (1952: 92–94) first proposed that the so-called "nomen futuri" -yu ~ -gü in Turkic could be compared to -qU(i) ~ -gU(i) in Mongolic. In spite of the problematic vocalism, he added the Southern Tungusic imperative -gi ~ -ki and the Korean nominalizer -ki to his comparison. In a review of Ramstedt's monograph, Poppe (1953) supported the comparison of the nomen futuri, reconstructing it as pA *-ku. He further suggested that the Mongolic voiced allomorph might represent a deverbal adjective formant pMo *-gU:, which he considered an internal Mongolic specialization of the original nomen futuri. Street (1978: 209–210, 217–219), however, considered it necessary to reconstruct two different morphemes in proto-Altaic: one was the nomen futuri pA *-ku, the other the deverbal adjective formant pA *-gu:. He regarded the Old Japanese adjectival "infinitive" -ku as a reflex of the latter form. Miller (1985: 65–68) elaborated on the Old Japanese cognate and added the Korean converb -ko, MK ··kwo as well as the Tungusic instrumental nominalizer reflected in Ma. -ku: and Na. -ko ~ -ku to the etymology. The comparison between the Japanese and Korean members, proposed in the same year and recently recapitulated by Whitman (1985: 222; 2012: 34), was also supported by Martin (1991a: 286; 1995: 148). Vovin (1998; 2001: 196–197) proposed a new Tungusic parallel consisting of different converb forms such as the Nanai gerund of goal -gU and the Orok subordinative gerund -gAtci. Recently, however, he rejected his former proposal (Vovin 2008a: 88, 2009a: 461).

Another converb that has been etymologized in the literature is Old Turkic -(X)p. Ramstedt (1952: 132–134) argued this form should be related to the Mongolian past tense in -bA and to the Tungusic converb pTg *pa-wi: singular / *pa-wari plural reflected in Ma. -fi ~ -pi, Na. -pi/ -pAri and Ud. -si. Starostin et al. (2003: 227) added the conditional converb OJ -(a)ba to this etymology. However, the external etymology is overruled by the internal analysis of some of its members. As suggested by the parallel with the conditional construction Middle Korean ··(u/o)n ·pa 'the situation that', OJ -(a)ba < pJ *(...a)-n-pa can be analyzed as an adnominal form plus the noun 'place' (see Section 7.5.1.2). The Tungusic converb may be derived from a denominal verb suffix *-n plus the accusative in -pA plus the reflexive suffix pTg *-wi: (SG)~ *-wari (PL) (Benzing 1955a: 1091). Therefore, this etymology will not be included here.

In this chapter, I intend to study the correspondences between the converb suffixes pTEA *-i ~ ø and pTEA *-xU ~ *-kU in greater detail than has previously been done. Unlike earlier studies, my analysis will pay attention to the combination of deverbal nominal and converbial function recurring on most of the markers involved. As far as the nominalizing use is concerned, distinguishing between specific types of nominalization will allow us to describe the parallels in terms of instrumental, resultative and actional/stative characteristics. The comparisons will go beyond the traditional form-function analysis by integrating diachronic typology and grammaticalization theory into the argumentation, including recent theories about the development of action nouns to infinitives to converbs. Another novelty is the reconstruction of shared allomorphy between *-i ~ ø and *-xU ~ *-kU. Especially in the latter case, which reflects a rather unusual conditioning factor, the common allomorphy may be telling for the distinction between borrowing and inheritance.

8.3 pTEA *-i ~ ø deverbal noun suffix

8.3.1 pJ *-i ~ ø

The deverbal noun suffix pJ *-i ~ ø, which derived action/state nouns, resultative and instrumental nouns from verbs, developed into a converb suffix used in adverbial subordination and verb compounding. The assumption that the deverbal noun and the converb go back to the same source is compatible with the higher degree of lexicalization of deverbal nouns as compared to converb forms; it is also supported by the morphophonological similarity in the distribution of the allomorphs pJ *-i ~ ø. The zero allomorph pJ *ø was originally restricted to stems with stem-final -i, as a consequence of the reduction of two subsequent high front vowels. Since infinitives often derive from deverbal nouns and involve an increase in verbal properties on the part of deverbal noun, the infinitive-like function in verb compounding seems to represent a transitional stage between the deverbal noun and the converb.

8.3.1.1 Mainland Japanese
The deverbal noun suffix pJ *-i ~ ø is reflected in numerous West and East Old Japanese nouns, such as those illustrated in (2). The suffix, which nominalizes the preceding verb rather than the whole clause, frequently derives action/state nouns, but there are also examples of resultative (e.g. mi_1-ke_1si 'garment') and instrumental nominalization (e.g. $mayo_1$-$gaki$ 'eyebrow liner'). Derived nouns in OJ -$i_{(1)}$ ~ ø do not take plural or diminutive suffixes. There are no examples of attributive use, modifying a nominal head. Apparent exceptions in lexicalizations such as OJ $saki_2de$ 'skin-cracked hands', OJ mo_1mi_1tiba 'maple leaves' and OJ $sakaribi_1to_2$ 'blooming people, people in their prime' all display voicing of the initial consonant of the second member, which indicates the insertion of an original nasal genitive (< *sak-i-n-tai (split-NML-GEN-hand); *momit-i-n-pa (redden-NML-GEN-leaf) and *sakar-i-n-pitə (bloom-NML-GEN-person)).

(2) The Old Japanese deverbal noun suffix -$i_{(1)}$ ~ ø

OJ ko_1pi_2- 'to love' → ko_1pi_2 'love'
OJ *kak-* 'to write, draw; scratch, stroke' → $mayo_1$-*gaki* 'eyebrow liner'
OJ *kazas-* 'to put into the hair as adornment, adorn' → *kazasi* 'adornment'
OJ ke_1s- 'to wear' → mi_1-ke_1si (HON-garment) 'garment'
OJ *mom-* 'to rub (with both hands), massage' → *momi* 'cloth rub-dyed solid red'
OJ mo_1mi_1t- 'to turn red (of leaves)' → OJ mo_1mi_1ti 'autumn colors, red leaves'
OJ oko_2nap- 'act, do, perform' → oko_2napi_1 'performance'
OJ $omo_{(1)}p$- 'to think, feel' → $omo_{(1)}pi_1$ 'thought'
OJ to_2mar- 'to stop, anchor, lodge' → to_2mari 'stopping place, lodging'

The deverbal nouns show clear indications of lexicalization given that some verbs lack a nominal form, that some meanings have specialized (e.g. *momi* 'cloth rub-dyed solid red'), and that the accent has neutralized. According to (Martin 1987: 211; 1995: 149), the -*i* converb leads to a change of pitch in the verb at the point where the ending is added, e.g. OJ *kum-* 'to assemble' (B = initial L) → *kumi* 'assemble and' (LH) and OJ *kob-* 'to flatter' (A = initial H) → *kobi* (HL) 'flatter', while the deverbal noun suffix simply erases that change: the forms are atonicized, e.g. OJ *kumi* 'set' (LL) and *kobi* 'flattery' (HH). The use of the converb suffix for adverbial insubordination is illustrated in (3a). In this example, as well as in some other rare cases, the converb and the main verb have a different subject. Example (3b) shows that the converb is also used for building verbal compounds, whereby the main verb often takes the function of an auxiliary expressing actionality or politeness.[1]

(3) The use of the Old Japanese converb suffix -$i_{(1)}$ ~ ø

    a.   adverbial insubordination

        ip-u ko_2to_2 *yam-i_1* ino_2ti *taye-n-ure*
        say-ADN thing stop-**CONV** life cease-PERF-SUBJ
        '[he] stopped speaking and [his] life ended' (MYS V: 904; Vovin 2009a: 704)

    b.   verb compounding

        mi_1-$ko_2ko_2ro_2$-wo *$sizume_2$-tamap-u*
        HON-heart-ACC calm.down.CONV-grant-FIN
        '[she] deigned to calm down [her] august hart'
        (MYS V: 813; Vovin 2009a: 1005)

---

[1] Linguists writing on Japanese in English usually follow Samuel Martin in using the term infinitive rather than converb for this suffix because it is also used to form verbal compounds.

In spite of Vovin's (2009: 753–754) insistence that "[t]he nominalizer -[y]i must be distinguished from the infinitive -[y]i: although they might look similar, they have different accent patterns, not to mention their completely different syntactic functions," and a similar remark by Russell (2006: 204), it is likely that the converb developed from the deverbal noun suffix, a viewpoint also held by Martin (1995: 149; 1997: 10) and Whitman (2012: 34). Answering to Vovin and Russel's objection, the different syntactic functions could be accounted for as the source and the target of a cross-linguistically common grammaticalization process discussed in Section 8.1, while the accentual difference between the deverbal noun and converb suffix could be explained by the lexicalization of the alleged source of grammaticalization as opposed to the productivity of the target.[2]

Moreover, the distribution of the allomorphs OJ -$i_{(1)}$ vs. ø shows a peculiar morphophonological similarity between both suffixes: like the converb, the deverbal noun suffix takes the allomorph -$i_{(1)}$ following consonantal stems, i.e. in quadrigrade (e.g. OJ ak- 'to open (intr.)' → ak-i_1) and r-/ n-irregular verbs (e.g. OJ ar- 'to exist' → ar-i; OJ in- 'to go' → in-i)). For both suffixes, the zero allomorph follows vowel stems, i.e. in bigrade (e.g. OJ ake₂- 'to open (tr.)' → ake₂; OJ oki₂- 'arise (intr.)' → oki₂) and monograde verbs (e.g. OJ mi₁- 'to see' → mi₁). And, finally, the allomorph -$i_{(1)}$ surpresses the final vowel of the stem in irregular verbs (e.g. OJ ko₂- to come' → k-i_1; OJ se- 'to do' → s-i). Historically, Unger's (1977: 41; 2000: 662–664) rule of vowel deletion can account for most allomorphs: when a monosyllabic suffix meets a stem-final vowel, the stem-final vowel is expected to drop. As such, the expected developments are, for consonant stems, pJ *aka-i (VD) > ak-i_1; for monogrades, pJ *mi-i / *mV-i > m-i_1 and; for irregulars pJ *kə-i > k-i_1. The observation that the bigrades yield ake₂ and oki₂ rather than **aki_1 and **oki_1 does not contradict Unger's rule, if one assumes that the causative-anticausative suffix *-Ci- was indeed the source of the bigrade conjugation and that the pJ *-i was suffixed to the root plus causative-anticausative before monophthongization occurred, i.e. pJ *aka-Ci-i > *akaCi > *akay > ake₂. Thus, the zero allomorph was originally restricted to stems with stem-final -i, as a consequence of the reduction of two subsequent high front vowels. Note that the monophthongization of pJ *aka-Ci- in the verbal paradigm must have been blocked due to the ambiguity that this would create between causatives such as **aki_1 'one opens it and' and anticausatives such as aki_1 'it opens and'.

---

[2] Martin (1995: 149; 1997: 10) does not regard the accentual difference as an obstacle to derive -i nominalizer and converb from the same original morpheme, but – contrary to my suggestion – he claims that the converbs underlie derived nouns, which goes against the cross-linguistic directionality discussed in Section 8.1.

8.3.1.2 Ryukyuan

As illustrated in (4), the deverbal noun suffix *-i ~ ø* is also widely attested in the Ryukyuan languages, where it derives action/state nouns and resultative nouns (Russell 2006: 489–490, 542, 582; Vovin 2009a: 760). In contrast to Mainland Japanese, there are examples of attributive use such as (5), in which the derived form modifies a nominal head.

(4) The Ryukyuan deverbal noun suffix *-i ~ ø*

Yamatoma *ʔakk-* 'to walk' → *ʔakki* 'walk'
Yamatoma *hanas-* 'to talk' → *hanasi* 'story'
Yamatoma *ʔomo'-* 'to think' → *ʔome* 'thought'
Shuri *fanas-* 'to talk' → *ʔu-fanasi* (HON-story) 'story'
Shuri *hwizu-* 'to be cold' → *hwizui* 'coldness'
Shuri *ashib-* 'to play' → *ashibi* 'playing, play'
Hirara *nar-* 'to sing, sound' → *nari* 'song, sound'

(5) Adnominal use of Shuri *-i ~ ø*

kure: tu:-i   miči   ya-n
this.TOP   pass-ADN   street be-FIN
'This is the passage' (Russell 2006: 582)

The Ryukyuan languages make use of a homophoneous converb suffix *-i ~ ø* for adverbial insubordination and verb compounding, as illustrated in the Old Ryukyuan example in (6) (Martin 1970: 131–132; Russell 2006: 473–474, 519–520, 567; Bentley 2008: 77, 189–194; Vovin 2009a: 714–715). As is the case in Mainland Japanese, the allomorphs *-i* vs. *ø* are similarly distributed over the deverbal noun suffix and the converb suffix, whereby the zero allomorph appears following vowel-final verb stems.

(6) The use of the Yonaguni suffix *-i ~ ø*

a. adverbial insubordination

kubasima-ni   *tsuta-ik-**i***   *miyarabi-ba*
Kuba Island-DAT   transmit.CONV-go-**CONV**   maiden-PT
*mikag-i-your-**i***
wed-CONV-HON-**CONV**
'I travel across Kuba Island and wed there a fair maiden and..'
(Hokama 1979: 457; Bentley 2008: 190)

b. verb compounding

nisi-ma-zima   *watar-**i**-mir*-i
north-space-island   cross-**CONV**-see-CONV
'I try to cross over the Island of the north and..'
(Hokama 1979: 457; Bentley 2008: 190)

8.3.2 pK *-i ~ ø

The deverbal noun suffix K *-i ~ ø*, MK *··i ~ ø* is incorporated in some Korean and Middle Korean nouns such as those illustrated in (7), where it derives action/state nouns (e.g. MK *hali* 'slandering'), resultative nouns (e.g. MK *·stuy* 'belt', MK *nwo·phoy* 'height') and instrumental nouns (e.g. MK *·toy* 'measure') from verbs and verbal adjectives (Martin 1992: 553; Lee & Ramsey 2011: 176–177). There are no examples of attributive use, in which the derived form modifies a nominal head. The zero allomorph attaches itself to verbs in stem-final *-i* or *-y*, as a consequence of the merger of two subsequent high front vowels into one. The suffix was productive in Middle Korean, but by the 17th century it had already lost productivity in favor of the nominalizer MK *··ki*.

(7) The Middle Korean deverbal noun suffix *··i ~ ø*

MK *ciz-* 'to compose' → MK *kul-cizi* (letter-composition) 'literary composition'
MK *hal-* 'to slander' → MK *hali* 'slandering'
MK *ke/a·li-* 'to branch off, be forked (intr.)' → MK *ke/a·li* 'branch, fork'
MK *khu-* 'to be big' → MK *khuy*, K *khi* 'stature'
MK *kil-* 'to be long' → MK *kiluy* 'length'
MK *kiph-* 'to be deep' → MK *ki·phu/oy*, K *kiphi* 'depth'
MK *nep-* 'to be wide' → MK *nepuy* 'width'
MK *nwoph-* 'to be high' → MK *nwo·phoy*, K *nophi* 'height'
MK *nwu(·)pi-* 'to quilt' → MK *nwu·pi* 'quilting'
MK *stuy-* 'to wear on the waist' → MK *·stuy*, K *tti* 'belt'
MK *·toy-* 'to measure' → MK *·toy* 'measure'

The deverbal noun suffix developed into a deverbal adverbializer, which derives adverbs from verbs and verbal adjectives, as in the examples in (8) (Martin 1992: 553; Lee & Ramsey 2011: 182–183). Whereas the adverbializer *··i ~ ø* was remarkably productive in Middle Korean, occurrences of *-i* are now confined to a fixed set of lexical items such as K *kath-* 'to be similar' → *kathi* 'similarly' and K *kakkap-* 'to be near' → *kakkai* 'near, nearby (adv.)'.

(8) The Middle Korean deverbal adverbializer -·i ~ ø

MK ·ha- 'to be numerous, big' → MK ¨hay 'numerously'
MK kotok ho- 'to be full' → MK kotok hi, K katuk hi 'filled completely'
MK khu- 'to be big' → MK ·khi 'greatly'
MK ¨kil- 'to be long' → MK kili, K kili 'lengthily'
MK kiph- 'to be deep' → MK ki·phi, K kiphi 'deeply'
MK nep- 'to be wide' → MK ne·pi 'widely'
MK nik- 'to ripen' → MK ni·ki 'thoroughly, ripely'
MK nilu- 'to lead to, arrive' → MK ni·luli 'so as to lead to'
MK nwoph- 'to be high' → MK now·phi, K nophi 'highly'
MK nowoy- 'to repeat' → MK nowoy 'repeatedly'

Because not every verb stem can derive an adverbial form in -·i, the suffix is regarded as a derivational suffix rather than as a part of the inflectional paradigm. From a historical viewpoint, however, there are indications of earlier inflectional behavior of this suffix. A residue of adverbial insubordinate clause structure is left in the ability of some -i adverbs, such as eps-i 'not existing' in (9a), to take a subject in the nominative case as well as in their ability to be negated by a sentential negator. While in contemporary Korean the negator is the inflected auxiliary anh-, e.g. K cek-ci an-h-i (be.small-NML NEG-be-ADV) 'in no small measure', in Middle Korean adverbialized forms could be directly negated by the negative adverb an, as illustrated in (9b).

(9) Residue of adverbial insubordination in the use of K -i, MK -·i

a. Korean

Ku   yeca-ka   eps-i   sa-l   su-ka
that woman-NOM not.exist-ADV live-ADN possibility-NOM
eps-ta.
not.exist.FIN
'I cannot live without that woman'

b. Middle Korean

ani   sulph-i   neki-l   i   ep-te-ni
NEG be.sad-ADV regard-ADN person not.exist-RETR-CONV
'as there was nobody who did not regard [it] as not sad.'
(Seongha Rhee pc; Samkang 1431, 26)

The deverbal nouns in pK *-i can be argued to have been productively derived at an earlier stage than the converbs in pK *-i, because verbs that lost a stem-final thematic vowel still reflect this vowel in the lexicalized deverbal nouns, but not in Middle Korean adverbs. The verb MK *nwoph-* 'to be high', for instance, goes back to an original thematic stem pK **nopkʌ-*, with the vowel reflected in MK *nwo·phoy* 'height', but not in MK *now·phi* 'highly', which suggests that the adverb was derived at a time when the stem-final vowel had already been dropped.

8.3.3 pTg *-i: ~ ø

The deverbal noun suffix pTg *-i: ~ ø* is reflected in the Northern Tungusic languages, where it mainly derives instrumental, resultative and state nouns from verbs. A petrified reflex may also be present in Manchu. The zero allomorph attaches itself to verbs in stem-final *-i*, as a consequence of the merger of two subsequent high front vowels into one. There are some examples of derived adnominal forms, but adverbial or converbial use of this suffix is not attested.

8.3.3.1 Ma. -i ~ ø
Manchu has preserved a relic of the suffix in the predicative copula Ma. *bi*, which is probably a derived state noun from the existential verb Ma. *bi-* 'to be, to exist' and the zero allomorph of the deverbal noun suffix.

8.3.3.2 Even
Benzing (1955 b: 38) describes Even *-i: ~ ø* as an instrumental deverbal noun suffix (e.g. *teti:* 'garment'), but the derivations in (10) seem to include some resultative (e.g. *geltali:* 'white, light') and agentive nouns (e.g. *degi:* 'bird') as well. There are some examples of derived adnominal forms (e.g. *joki:* 'affirmative, positive').

(10) The Even deverbal noun suffix *-i: ~ ø*

Even *das-* 'to cover, mantle (tr.)' → *dasi:* 'cover, coverage'
Even *deg-* 'to fly' → *degi:* 'bird'
Even *dur-* 'to burn, be on fire, catch fire' → *duri:* 'fire, blaze, forest fire'
Even *geltal-* 'to become light, white, to lighten' → *geltali:* 'white, light'
Even *jok-* 'to agree (on sth.), come to an agreement' → *joki:* 'affirmative, positive; agreement'
Even *ju:pti:-* 'to double (tr.)' → *jupti:* 'double, twofold'
Even *mang-* 'to become solid, hard' → *mangi:* 'hard, rigid'
Even *tet-* 'to dress oneself' → *teti:* 'garment, uniform'
Even *toli:-* 'to even out, level' → *toli:* 'full (to the brim)'

8.3.3.3 Evenki

As illustrated in (11), Evenki *-i: ~ ø* is incorporated in a few deverbal instrumental nouns (e.g. *usi:* 'rope, belt'), resultative nouns (e.g. *suli* 'sharpened') and agentive nouns (e.g. *degi* 'bird'). There are examples of derived adnominal forms (e.g. *suli* 'sharpened').

(11) The Evenki deverbal noun suffix *-i ~ ø*

Evk. *co:li:-* 'to gossip, prattle, babble' → *co:li:* 'tongue'
Evk. *congki:-* 'to peck' → *congki:* 'beak'
Evk. *deg-* 'to fly' → *degi* 'bird'
Evk. *sul-* 'to sharpen (pencil)' → *suli* 'sharpened, sharp, pointed'
Evk. *ug-* 'to mount' → *ugi:* 'up, above'
Evk. *usi:-* 'to bind' → *usi:* 'rope, belt'

8.3.4 pMo *-i ~ ø*

The deverbal noun suffix pMo *-i* is incorporated in a few Written and Middle Mongolian nouns, such as those illustrated in (12), where it derives action/state nouns (e.g. WMo. *büi* 'existence, existing') and resultative nouns (e.g. WMo. *elei* 'confused). If WMo. *büci* 'tie, ribbon, band, lace' represents a true derivate, the suffix may also have had instrumental use. The Mongolic voluntative in WMo. *-yA* is usually analyzed as a dative in *-A* of an original action noun in *-i*, e.g. WMo. *yabu-ya* 'let us go' < **yabu-i-a* (go-NML-DAT) 'towards the going' (Ramstedt 1945: 6; Poppe 1955: 264; Street 1978: 174). Note that insubordination has led to finite use of the suffix, with *-i* added immediately to consonant stems in Middle Mongolian (e.g. MMo. *ayis-i* (approach-NML) 'he comes'), whereas a binding vowel was inserted in Written Mongolian (e.g. WMo. *ayis-u-i* 'he comes') (Weiers 1964: 153–162). The forms WMo. *büci* 'tie, ribbon, band, lace' and WMo. *qari* 'separation, leave' in the expression *qari bol-* 'to separate from, leave' may illustrate the use of the zero allomorph following a verb stem ending in a high front vowel.

(12) The Written and Middle Mongolian deverbal noun suffix *-i*

MMo. *bol-* 'to be, become' → *boli* 'good, enough'
WMo. *bü-* 'to be, exist' → *büi* 'existence, existing'
WMo. *büci-* 'to surround, gather around (tr./ intr.)' → *büci* 'tie, ribbon, band, lace'
WMo. *ele-* 'to wear out (as by attrition) (tr.)' → *elei* 'confused, dim (of the mind)'

WMo. *bayura-* 'to decline, diminish, weaken' → *baɣurai* 'feeble, powerless, small, narrow'

WMo. *muru-* 'to go astray, act contrarily' → *murui* 'curve, crookedness; slanting, bending'

WMo. *sönü-* 'to be extinguished, go out (of fire), cease to be' → *söni* 'night, at night'

WMo. *qari-* 'to return, go back, to subside (as flood, swelling, etc.)' → *qari* 'separation, leave' in WMo. *qari bol-* 'to separate from, leave'

The deverbal noun suffix developed into a form used for verbal adverbialization, preserved in WMo. *söni* 'at night' and in a few deverbal adverbs such as those given in (13).

(13) The Written Mongolian adverbializer -*i*

WMo. *ɣar-* 'to go out, pass over, exceed (intr.)' → *ɣarui* 'more than, beyond, over (adv.)'

WMo. *daru-* 'to press, follow, be near' → *darui* 'immediately, at once, thereafter (adv.)'

It is not unlikely that the adverbs in -*i* represent lexicalizations of an earlier converbial form in pMo *-*i*. In Mongolic proper, the suffix is no longer productive as a converb marker, but Kane (2009: 149–150) lists the Khitan converb in vowel plus -*i*, which is used for adverbial subordination, expressing the meaning 'then, after that'; see example (14). The various notations used for the converb marker are <ai>, <ui>, <oi>, <ei>, <ii> and <i>, whereby the final vowel of the preceding stem is often repeated, e.g. in Khitan *kė-dha-ai* (bury-PASS-CONV) 'having been buried' or Khitan *dem-lege-ei* (grant-PASS-CONV) 'having been granted (a title)' (Kane 2009: 149–150). Whereas the common converbial element is -*i*, the repetition of the stem-final vowel may be a result of the Khitan orthographical system, which is based on Chinese characters.

(14) The Khitan converb in vowel plus -*i*

*tai zï śiauu sh dem-lege-**ei***
taizi shaoshi grant-PASS-CONV
*dieên sieên du dêm gieêm poju-**ii** syiên xuŋ a-ar*
palace command chief inspector establish-CONV zianggün be-PST
'he was given the title of *taizi shaoshi*, was appointed chief inspector of the palace command and had [the position of] court ceremonial.' (Kane 2009: 152)

8.3.5 pTk *-I ~ ø

The deverbal noun suffix pTk *-I ~ ø is reflected in Old Turkic nouns such as those illustrated in (15) (Erdal 1991: 340–341). It derives resultative (e.g. OTk. *tögi* 'crushed cereal'; OTk. *köni* 'straight') and instrumental nouns (e.g. OTk. *yapï* 'horse-blanket') from transitive and intransitive verbs. Some derivates can be used attributively (e.g OTk. *köni buryuk* 'an upright minister').

(15) The Old Turkic deverbal noun suffix *-i*

OTk *adïr-* 'to separate (tr.)' → *adrï* 'fork, forked'

OTk *egir-* 'to surround, encircle; spin something around (tr.)' → *egri* 'hunch-backed form of camels; bent, crooked'

OTk. *kal-* 'to remain (intr.)' → **kalï* 'remainder' in *kalï-sïz* 'without remainder'

OTk. *kön-* 'to be(come) straight (intr.)' → *köni* 'straight, upright'

OTk. (Karakh.) *siŋ-* 'to be absorbed or digested, penetrate' → *siŋi* 'easily digestible'

OTk. *tög-* 'to pound, crush (tr.)' → *tögi* 'cleaned and/or crushed cereal'

OTk. *yap-* 'to cover (tr.)' → *yapï* 'horse-blanket'

Moreover, Old Turkic makes use of a converb of the shape *-I* after the *-(X)t-* causative suffix and in some exceptional converbial forms such as OTk. *alï, barï, kalï, keli, siŋi* and *tegi* derived respectively from OTk. *al-* 'to take', *bar-* 'to go to', *kal-* 'to remain', *kel-* 'to come', *siŋ-* 'to penetrate' and *teg-* 'to reach'. The variants *-A*, *-U* and *-yU* alternate as in the adnominal or "aorist" form, (see Section 7.3.5.1) i.e. *-A* after most simple consonant stems, *-U* after most derived consonant stems and *-yU* after vowel stems. Given the limited attachment to high frequency verbs and the phonologically unconditioned distribution of the *-I* converb as opposed to the other vowel converbs, *-I* probably represents the earlier converb suffix, which became replaced by new converb formations based upon nominal forms of copular verbs (i.e. *-A* < **a* 'being' and *-U* < **u* 'becoming') or on a construction consisting of a converb and a copular verb (i.e *-yU* < **-i u*); see Section 3.4.1. In verbs that derive both their adnominal form on *-Ir* and their converb on *-I*, such as OTk. *kal-* 'to remain', OTk. *bar-* 'to go to' and the *-(X)t-* causatives, the high vowel is probably part of the original verb stem, thus pTk **keli-* 'to remain', pTk **barï-* 'to go to' and pTk **-ti-* causative (as reconstructed in Section 6.3.5). The converb was then derived by adding the zero allomorph to verb-stems ending in a high front vowel, resulting in the converbs OTk. *keli, barï* and *-tI*, while the adnominal form was derived by adding pTk **-r*, resulting in OTk. *kelir, barïr* and

-tIr. In verbs in which the converb vowel *-I* is different from the vowel of the adnominal form, such as OTk *siŋ-* 'to be absorbed, to penetrate', the converb was derived by adding the default *i*-allomorph, resulting in OTk. *siŋi*, whereas the adnominal form was based upon the post-consonantal allomorph *-Ar*, resulting in OTk. *siŋär*.

The use of the converb suffix for adverbial subordination is illustrated in (16a). The subjects are mainly coreferential, but in some rare cases, for instance involving temporal expressions such as OTk. *taŋ ata käli* (dawn break-CONV come-CONV) 'at sunrise, ...', the converb and of the main verb have a different subject. In verb compounding, the main verb often takes the function of an auxiliary expressing actionality or politeness, as is the case in (16b).

(16) The use of the Old Turkic converb suffix *-I*

    a. adverbial subordination

        toruk at sämrit-i [...] *yügür-ü bar-mïš*
        lean horse make.fatt-CONV run-CONV go-INFR
        'After a lean horse fattened itself, it went running' (VATEC Irk 16: 17(r): 02–05)

    b. verb compounding

        aviš tamu-ka bar-ï yarlïka-dï
        Avi:ci: hell-DAT go-CONV deign.PST
        '[he] deigned to go in the Avi:ci: Hell' (VATEC MaitrGeng0090 v05)

Finally, petrified converbs, such as those given in (17) have lexicalized in deverbal adverbs.

(17) The Old Turkic adverbializer *-i*

    OTk *bar-* 'to go to' → *barï* 'as much as there is'

    OTk. *karïš-* 'to disagree with one another, to be opposite to one another' → *karšï* 'a place opposite, the opposite, opposition (n.); opposed, opposite (adj.); against, with opposition (adv.)'

    OTk. *körüš-* 'to see eachother' → *körši* 'with a view on, in view of'

    OTk. *tak-* 'to attach' → *takï* 'more, yet, and, too, also'

Erdal (1991: 340) argued that the deverbal noun suffix and the converb suffix in *-I* have a distinct origin for the following reasons:

> Firstly, the verbs which are here found expanded with [the deverbal noun suffix] *-I* form their converbs with other vowels ... Secondly, *-I* lexemes are used nominally or adjectivally, whereas converbs consistently have adverbial function. Thirdly, lexemes formed

with *-I* denote the object of transitive bases or the subject if their bases happen to be intransitive and thus show ergative behaviour.

However, his argumentation can be challenged, first, by the expectation that derivational markers, such as deverbal noun suffixes, tend to survive inflectional markers, such as converb suffixes, because the latter will not lexicalize in a language after being replaced. The verb OTk. *yap-* 'to cover (tr.)', for instance, has petrified *-I* in the deverbal noun *yapï* 'horse-blanket' but has replaced it by a newer formant *-A* in the converb *yap-a*, whereas OTk. *kal-* 'to remain (intr.)' has preserved *-I* in both the deverbal noun and the converb. Secondly, the different syntactic functions can be accounted for as the source and the target of a cross-linguistically common grammaticalization process discussed in Section 8.1. Thirdly, deverbal noun suffixes that denote the object of transitive bases as well as the subject of intransitive bases are typically known as "resultative" or "objective" nouns (Comrie & Thompson 2007: 340–342); hence, there is no need to account for them in terms of ergativity.

8.4 pTEA *-xU ~ *-kU deverbal noun suffix

8.4.1 pJ *-ku

The deverbal noun suffix pJ *-ku*, which derived state nouns from static verbs such as verbal adjectives and copulae developed into a suffix deriving converbial and adverbial forms. Since the deverbal nominalizing function is only preserved in a number of archaic constructions in Mainland Japanese and since it has completely disappeared from the Ryukyuan languages, it probably represents the older source function. Gradually, the deverbal noun suffix assumed an infinitive-like function in verb compounding, which is preserved in both Mainland Japanese and Ryukyuan. A further increase in verbal properties led to the use of the suffix as an adverbial insubordinator in both branches. Since verbal adjectives and copulae only take a subject as their argument, converbial use of the suffix yielded simple adverbs in the majority of cases. On the basis of the Old Japanese data, we might expect that OJ *-ku* derives from pJ *-ko*, with raising of pJ *o > u*, typical for Western Old Japanese, but this is not the case, as the Ryukyuan forms clearly support the reconstruction of the mid vowel in pJ *-ku*.

8.4.1.1 Mainland Japanese

As a deverbal noun suffix, pJ *-ku* is mainly attached to verbal adjectives in West and East Old Japanese. In this function, it is preserved before the defective verb *n-* 'to be' and before the genitive case marker no_2, as illustrated in (18a). As such, it can also be found in OJ *-ku ar-* (-NML exist-) constructions, which may further include focus particles, e.g. *-ku mo_2 ar-* (-NML PT exist-) and *-ku si ar-* (-NML PT exist-) or a topic particle, e.g. *-ku pa ar-* (NML TOP exist-); see (18b).

(18) The use of the West Old Japanese deverbal noun suffix *-ku*

    a. ko_1pi_2si-**ku**-no_2 opo-k-ar-u   ware pa
        be.longing-**NML**-GEN   big-NML-exist-ADN   I   TOP
        mi_1-tutu $sino_1p$-am-u
        see(CONV)-COOR   yearn-TENT-FIN
        'I, who has great longing, will be looking and yearning'
        (MYS XX: 4475; Vovin 2009a: 448)

    b.   kanasi-**ku**   pa   ar-e-do_2
        be.sad-**NML**   TOP   exist-SUBJ-CONC
        'Although [I] am sad, [I will go to serve]'
        (MYS XX: 4398; Vovin 2009a: 453)

The deverbal noun suffix pJ **-ku* is also incorporated in the nominalizer OJ *-aku*, which has been derived as a reinforced periphrastic construction consisting of the copula pJ **a-* 'to be' plus pJ **-ku* (Martin 1987: 805; Section 3.4.1). Since this suffix follows the adnominal form of verbs (e.g. OJ mi_1-*r-aku* (see-ADN-NML) 'seeing' < **mi-ru aku*) and verbal adjectives (e.g. OJ *tura-ke_1ku* (hard-ADN-NML) 'what is trying' < **tura-ki aku*), it is likely to go back to a bound noun. In contrast to OJ *-i* and OJ *-ku*, which are only used to nominalize the preceding verb or verbal adjective, OJ *-aku* nominalizes the entire clause, as illustrated in (19). This behavior supports the derivation of OJ *-aku* as a more recent periphrastic formation with the copula.

(19) The use of the West Old Japanese clausal nominalizer *-aku*

    ume_2-no_2 pana   tir-aku   pa   iduku
    plum-GEN   flower   fall-NML   TOP   where
    'Where [will] the falling of the plum blossoms [be]?'
    (MYS V: 823; Vovin 2009a: 766)

As illustrated in (20), the deverbal noun suffix further developed into a converb suffix following verbal adjectives in West and East Old Japanese. The converbial use includes verb compounding in constructions of the type OJ *-ku nar-*, adverbial insubordination and the formation of adverbs.

(20) The use of the West Old Japanese converb suffix -ku

    a.   verb compounding

        ke_2 naga-ku   nar-i-n-u
        day   be.long-CONV   become-CONV-PERF-FIN
        'the days became long' (KK 88, Vovin 2009a: 449)

    b.   adverbial insubordination

        tutum-u ko_2to_2 na-ku   paya $kape_1$r-i-mas-e
        have.difficulty-ADN   fact   not.be-CONV   fast   return-CONV-deign-IMP
        'Return quickly, without having difficulties'
        (MYS XV: 3582; Vovin 2009a: 445)

    c.   adverb

        opo ki_1mi_1-ni   kata-ku $tukape_2$-matur-am-u
        great   lord-DAT   strong-CONV   serve(CONV)-present-TENT-FIN
        '(I) intend to serve faithfully to the emperor' (NK 78, Vovin 2009a: 446)

8.4.1.2 Ryukyuan

The Ryukyuan languages do not leave a trace of pJ *-ku in the function of deverbal noun suffix following verbal adjectives or incorporated in the nominalizer. However, as illustrated in the Shuri example in (21a), they reflect a transitional infinitive-like stage between the nominalizer and the converb. Adverbial insubordination and the formation of adverbs, as in the examples in (21b/c), mark the final stage of the grammaticalization process.

(21) The use of the Shuri converb suffix -ku

    a.   verb compounding

        nuku-ku   na-ti   kee-t-ee
        warm-CONV   become-CONV   change-PERF-PROG
        '[Now it] is changing and becoming warmer' (Russell 2006: 527)

    b.   adverbial insubordination

        tatanoo   mii-ku   tuzee   huru-ku
        tatami.TOP   be.new-CONV   wife.TOP   be.old-CONV
        'The tatami is new and the wife is old ...' (Vovin 2009a: 459)

    c.   adverb

        munoo   maa-ku   kam-ee
        thing.TOP   be.delicious-CONV   eat-IMP
        'Eat food with gusto!' (Vovin 2009a: 459)

8.4.2 pK *-ku ~ *-k(ʌ)

A few deverbal derivations in Korean, such as those listed in example (22), suggest the reconstruction of an original deverbal suffix pK *-k, deriving action/state nouns and adverbs.

(22) The use of the Korean non-finite suffix -(u)k

    a. deverbal noun

        K *ilwu-* 'to achieve' → *ilwuk ha-* 'to undertake, build';

        MK *kuž-* 'to draw a line (around), delimit, cut off' → K *kuuk*, MK *kužuk* 'secluded, secret, private (adj. noun)'

    b. adverb

        K *cis-*, MK *ciž-* 'to make, buid, compose, manufacture' → *-(c)cik* suffix that derives adjectival nouns and adverbs [3]

        pK **santi-* in K *santule ci-* 'to be lively, vivacious, gay', *santul* 'light', *santul santul* 'gently, softly, in cool ripples', *santtus* 'clean, fresh, light' → *san(t) tuk* 'with a sudden chill, with chills running up and down ones spine'

Example (23) illustrates the use of an uncommon adverbializer MK *··koy ~ ··Goy*, which is also used for adverbial subordination. This suffix may represent a reinforcement of pK *-kʌ with a bound noun *-i the 'fact (that); that (which)' (see Section 7.3.2; 7.6.2). The minimal low back vowel in this suffix may have dropped word-finally, yielding pK *-k.

(23) The use of the Middle Korean adverbializer MK *··koy ~ ··Goy*

    MK ·wo·s-i   como··koy   "wu·l-usi··kwo   nilu··sya
          clothes-NOM settle-CONV cry-HON-CONV say-HON.CONV
    'letting his clothes settle, he said in tears: ...'
    (1459 Wel 8: 101a; Martin 1992: 649).

In most cases, pK *-k seems to combine with the converbial form of the verb K *-e/a*, MK *··e/a* to derive deverbal nouns and adverbs in K, MK *-Ak*, as illustrated

---

[3] The suffix K *-(c)cik* 'in the way of the base' occurs, for instance, in K *ilu-* 'to be early' → *ilccik* 'early' and K *kiph-* 'to be deep' → *kiphcik* 'rather deep'. The semantic opposition between this suffix, K *cil* 'process' and K *ci:s* 'an act, a gesture' is clearly adverbial vs. imperfective vs. resultative and therefore supports the deverbal derivation from MK *ciž-* 'to make, buid, compose, manifacture' plus imperfective nominalizer *-l (see Section 7.3.2), perfective nominalizer *-s and adverbializer *-k (Martin 1992: 343).

in the examples in (24a/b). Given that the converbial form was derived from the copula *a- 'to be' in Section 3.4.1, the suffix K, MK -Ak seems to have grammaticalized as a reinforced construction using similar elements (pK *a-k be-NML) as the nominalizer OJ -aku in Section 8.4.1.1.

(24) The use of the Korean non-finite suffix -Ak
    a.   deverbal noun
        K *ka:m-* 'to be black' → *(k)kamak* 'black, dark, ignorant (adjectival noun)'
        K *kwu:l-* 'to act, behave (toward a person), treat (a person)' → *kwulek ha-* 'the do the act (of)'
        K *pu:s-* 'to swell up' → *pusek pusek ha-* 'to be somewhat swollen'
    b.   adverb
        K *pa:s-* 'to break' → *pa:sak* 'with a crunch/ rustle'
        pK **il-e* (be.like.this-CONV) / **tyel-e* (be.like.that-CONV) in K *ile cele* 'somehow or other' → *ilek celek* 'somehow or other'
        pK **kɨl-e* (be.like.that-CONV) in *kule cele* 'such and such' → *kulek celek* 'such and such'
        K *nuli-*, MK *nuluy-* 'to be slow, sluggish' → *nulek nulek* 'sluggishly'

Martin (1992: 592) suggests that the converb suffix K *-kwu ~ -ko*, MK *-·kwu ~ -·kwo* should be related to the deverbal noun and adverb suffix in K *-(u)k*. This suffix, which attaches itself to verbs as well as to verbal adjectives, is used in verb compounds such as in (25a) as well as for adverbial subordination as in (25b), marking two events or states as separate in the sense of 'and then; and also'.

(25) The use of the Middle Korean converb suffix -·*kwu* ~ -·*kwo*
    a.   verb compounding
        tyoh-on   *chapan* *mek-**kwo*** *is-ywotoy*
        be.good-ADN food   eat-**CONV** exist-CONC
        'Although you eat delicious food, ...' (Sek 1449 24: 28; Rhee 1996: 100)
    b.   adverbial insubordination
        sywoping *sa-**kwo***   *kwoki* *pwosk-a*   *mek-**kwo***
        bread   buy-**CONV** meat   roast-CONV eat-**CONV**
        tina   *ka-cye*
        pass.CONV go-HORT
        'Let's buy bread, roast and eat meat, and then continue on our way' (No 1517; Rhee 1996: 99)

While the suffix MK -·*kwu* appears as a rare allomorph of the more widespread suffix MK -·*kwo*, the alternation is random. The suffixes do not form a vowel harmonic set: MK -·*kwo* can follow stems of any shape without its vowel changing, e.g. *kuchikwo* 'stopping', *cwukwo* 'giving', etc. The converb suffix MK -·*kwo* was gradually used more frequently over the course of Korean history (Rhee 1996: 98). Therefore, I reconstruct pK *-*ku* underlying MK -·*kwu* as the original morpheme and I assume that MK -·*kwo* began to replace -·*kwu* later in the history of Korean.

MK -·*kwu* (< pK *-*ku*) may have originated as a variant of the deverbal noun suffix and adverbializer -*k* (< pK *-*kʌ*). As indicated by the gradual increase in frequency, the converbial use of these suffixes may have developed from deverbal nominal use. The observation that in Middle Korean, -·*kwu* ~ -·*kwo* was often followed by focus markers, such as the topic particle -*(o/u)n*, the emphatic -*k*, or the intensifier -*m*, supports its origin as a deverbal noun suffix. As such, the use of MK -·*kwu* ~ -·*kwo* in verb compounding reflects a transitional stage between the deverbal nominalization and adverbial insubordination.

8.4.3 pTg *-*xu:* ~ *-*ku:*

The deverbal noun suffix pTg *-*xu:* ~ *-*ku:* is reflected throughout the Tungusic languages, deriving instrumental nouns from verbs and state nouns from verbal adjectives and copulae. In Even, the suffix can also derive action nouns from verbs. There are indications that the suffix developed to a converb marker in the Southern Tungusic languages. Manchu, Even and Udehe further reflect adverbial use of the suffix.

The data below represent the proposed reconstruction of an original velar fricative suffix *-*xu:*, with a de-fricativized allomorph *-*ku:* following certain verb stems ending in a continuant such as *n* or *b* (? < *β). This allomorphy is reminiscent of the phonological variants of the resultative deverbal noun suffix pTg *-*xA:* ~ *-*kA:* (Section 7.6.3) in similar environments. The reconstruction of a velar fricative in this suffix is supported by the alternation between Ud. -*gu* and -*ku*, whereby Ud. -*ku* seems to follow verb stems that originally ended in *n* or *b* (? < *β). In Manchu, the negative noun Ma. *aku:*, which incorporates this suffix, can be derived from a negative verb with stem-final nasal. Moreover, Jurchen cognates of some nouns derived in Manchu, such as Jur. *etuxun* for Ma. *etuku* 'clothing, garment' point to a fricative for this suffix. The observation that Even and Evenki exclusively reflect this suffix with a voiceless stop can be explained by the merger of pTg *-*k*- and *-*x*- as -*k*- in these languages. Since none of the Tungusic languages, except Nanai, reflect vowel harmony for this suffix, the suffix is reconstructed as pTg *-*xu:* without vowel-harmonic allomorph.

8.4.3.1 Manchu

As illustrated in (26a), the Manchu suffix *-ku* / *-ku:* derives instrumental nouns from verbs, including instruments, utensils and professional helpers (Gorelova 2002: 196). There are also a few instances, such as the examples in (26b), in which it derives state nouns from static verbs such a verbal adjectives and copulae.

(26) The Manchu deverbal noun suffix *-ku* / *-ku:*

    a.   instrumental noun

        Ma. *ali-* 'to receive; support, hold up' → *aliku:* 'tray used for weighing on a scale'

        Ma. *ana-* 'to push' → *anaku:* 'key'

        Ma. *etu-* 'to put on clothing, wear' → *etuku* 'clothing, garment'

        Ma. *elbe-* 'to cover' → *elbeku* 'cover'

        Ma. *hafumbu-* 'to translate, interprete' → *hafumbuku:* 'translator, interpreter'

        Ma. *taci-* 'to learn, study' → *taciku:* 'school'

        Ma. *te-* 'to sit' → *teku* 'chair'

    b.   state noun

        pTg **an(a)-* 'not to exist' (see Section 4.3.3.1) → Ma. *aku:* 'absence; not existing; there is not'

        Ma. *nemśe-* 'to be desirous' → *nemśeku* 'desirous'

The Manchu suffix is restricted to deverbal nominal use, except in the case of the negative noun Ma. *aku:*, which also exhibits adverbial use, as illustrated in (27); (27b) is repeated from (15d) in Section 4.3.3.1.

(27) The use of the Manchu negative noun *aku:*

    a.   deverbal noun

        min-i sargan akū-be   dahame
        I-GEN wife   absence-ACC since
        'Since I have no wife...' (SK 98; Gorelova 2002: 273)

    b.   adverb

        muke inengdari lakca-ra-ku: eye-mbi
        water every.day break.off-ADN-NEG flow-FIN
        'Water will flow uninterruptedly every day.' (SK; Gorelova 2002: 263)

8.4.3.2 Even

As illustrated in (28), the Even suffix *-(A)k* derives instrumental nouns from verbs as well as action/state nouns from verbs/verbal adjectives (Benzing 1955b: 40). There are also a few relics of adverbial forms, such as those in (28b).

(28) The Even deverbal noun suffix *-(A:)k*

    a. instrumental noun

        Even *aw-* 'wash (oneself)' → *awa:k* 'towel'
        Even *elbe-* 'to cover (a tent)' → Even *elbek* '(tent) cover'
        Even *hupkuc-* 'to learn' → *hupkuce:k* 'education, class, school'
        Even *tawac-* 'to forge' → *tawaca:k* 'blacksmith'
        Even *tuges-* 'to overwinter, hibernate' → *tugese:k* 'hibernation, wintering grounds, furred winter clothing'
        Even *uc-* 'to turn, to get going' → *u:cak* 'reindeer for riding, leading reindeer'

    b. action/state noun

        Even *bali:-* 'to become blind' → *bali:k* 'blind'
        Even *cakab-* 'to unite' → *cakaba:k* 'assembly'
        Even *en-* 'to be painful' → *enek* 'disease'
        Even *gaj-* 'to accrete, to take upon oneself' → *gaja:k* 'intake'
        Even *te:mac-* 'to swim, bath' → *te:maca:k* 'bathing'
        Even *urli-* 'to be jealous' → *urlik* 'jealous'

    c. adverb

        Even *erel-* 'to surround, encompass' → *erelek ~ erele:k* 'around, in an encircling way'

8.4.3.3 Udehe

Udehe preserves evidence of a suffix that derives instrumental nouns from verbs and state nouns from verbal adjectives. As illustrated in (29), the suffix has two different forms *-ku* and *-gu*, which at first sight seem to be randomly distributed. Few nouns are derived with *-ku* (Nikolaeva 1999: 95) but, interestingly, there are indications that their basic verbs had a stem final continuant **n* or **ß* in proto-Tungusic. Ud. *tekpu* 'sheath, sack', for instance, derives from Ud. *teu-* 'to put, insert, fill, gather', which goes back to pTg **teb-* (? < **teß-*), whose stem-final consonant is visible in other Tungusic languages such as in Even *te:w-*, Evk. *tew-*, Neg. *tew(u)-*, Ma. *tebu*, Na. *teu-*, Oroch *tewu-/ teu-*. Among other instrumental derivations from this verb, we find Ma. *tebku* 'uterus' and Orok *tepku* and *tekpu* 'sheath, sack,' an alternation which explains the Udehe *kp* cluster. Ud. *nimangku* 'fairy-tale' is derived from an original verb pTg **nimnga:n-* 'to shamanize', which is reflected in Evk. *nimnga:n-*, Olcha *ṅiŋman-* and Orok *niŋman-*. The Udehe instrumental noun *akpuŋku* 'fan, broom' probably derives from the deverbal processive *akpu-n(o)-* of the verb 'to sweep' (see Section 5.4.3.4).

Other nouns are derived with *-gu* (Nikolaeva 1999: 92). In most cases the derivation seems to go back to the proto-Tungusic stage. The state noun *unugu* 'disease', for instance, is derived from pTg **enu:-* 'be sick, be painful', which is reflected in Even *en-*, Evk. *enu:t-*, Orok *enu:-*, Na. *enusi-* and Solon *enu:n-*. A similar derivation is found in Solon *enexu:* 'disease'. The state noun Ud. *kaŋdugu* 'half' is derived from pTg **kongdo-* 'to break in two (tr.)', which is reflected in Oroch *kondo* 'half', Evk. *kongdor*, Even *kongdos* 'crosswise' and Even *kongdok-*, Evk. *kongdorgo-* 'to break, snap, be broken (intr.)'. The instrumental noun Ud. *cugu* 'ax' is derived from pTg **cok-* 'to dig, delve, stick into', which is reflected in Evk. *cok-*, Even *cuk-* 'to dig, delve', Neg. *cok-* 'to gauge', Ma. *coki-* 'to stick into' and Na. *coki-* 'to peck'. Nikolaeva (1999: 92) notes that some derivations in *-gu* are preceded by an unclear semantic element *-mu-* ~ *-bu-*, e.g. *kiso-bu-gu* 'quiver' and *sangńa-mu-gu* 'flue for smoke'.

(29) The Udehe deverbal noun suffix *-ku* ~ *-gu*

    a. instrumental

        Ud. *akpu-* 'to sweep' → *akpungku* 'fan, broom'
        pTg **cok-* 'to dig, delve, stick into' → Ud. *cugu* 'ax'
        pTg **nimnga:n-* 'to shamanize' → Ud. *nimangku* 'fairy-tale'
        Ud. **safu-* in *safulingku* 'box for chopsticks' → *safugu* 'chopsticks'
        Ud. *sou-* 'to pick on' → *souku* 'tease, teaser'
        pTg **teb-* in Ud. *teu-* 'to put, place, fill, gather' → *tekpu* 'sheath, sack'
        Ud. *zomi-* 'to steal' → *zomugu* 'thief'

    b. state noun

        pTg **enu:-* 'to be sick, be painful' in Ud. *uni-* 'be sick' → *unugu* 'disease'
        pTg **kongdo-* 'to break in two (tr.)' → Ud. *kaŋdugu* 'half'

Finally, Udehe preserves a number of adverbial expressions such as *bokcogu* 'rolled up' and *kicogu:* 'sticking out', which are formed with an element *-gu(:)*. This is illustrated in example (30). Since *au* 'cap' is not marked with a possessive third person suffix, the construction with *-gu* does not function as a nominal modifier to the omitted third person. Rather, it seems to be a residue of a converbial construction whereby *au* represents the subject of the subordinated clause, different from the third person subject in the main clause.

(30) The Udehe adverbial suffix *-gu(:)*

joxo   ca-la-ni   digene:-ni   au   kicogu:-da.
kettle   behind-LOC-3SG   hide.PST-3SG   cap   sticking.out-FOC
'He hid behind the kettle with his cap sticking out' (Tolskaya 2012: 104)

8.4.3.4 Nanai

As illustrated in (31), the Nanai suffix *-ku ~ -ko* derives instrumental nouns from verbs (Avrorin 1959: 117).

(31) The Nanai instrumental deverbal noun suffix *-ku ~ -ko*

Na. *jara-* 'to catch with a floating net' → *jarako* 'floating net'
Na. *kedere-* 'to rake up, shovel up' → *kedereku* 'rake, horse-rake'
Na. *ńiru-* 'to write' → *ńiruku* 'writing utensil'
Na. *sekpen-* 'to grab with the teeth' → *sekpenku* 'mouth piece of a bridle'
Na. *xado-* 'to mow' → *xadoko* 'scythe'

Interestingly, these verbal nouns may take an attribute in the accusative rather than in the genitive, e.g. *use-we tari-ko* (seed-ACC sow-NML) 'sowing machine' (Menges 1978: 395). This indicates an increase in verbal properties on the part of the deverbal noun, which is gradually losing its original noun-like syntax.

Nanai further uses a converb of goal *-gu ~ -go*, illustrated in (32) (Avrorin 1961: 169–170, Menges 1968: 216–217). In same-subject constructions, the converb is combined with possessive-reflexive suffixes, while it takes possessive suffixes in different-subject constructions. This agreement indicates that the suffix must have developed from a nominalizer.

(32) The Nanai converb of goal *-gu ~ -go*

mi   epem-be   sia-go-i   japa-hambi
I   pancake-ACC   eat-CONV-POSS.1SG   take-PST
'I took a pancake to eat' (Avrorin 1961: 170)

Since the expected reflex of pTg **-x-* is Na. *x~ø*, while the reflex of pTg **-g-* is Ø in vocalic environment, the Na. *-gu ~ -go* may reflect a velar in consonantal, non-continuant environments (? < **C-xU-*). In the conjugational class represented by Na. *un-* 'to say' and in the irregular class represented by *ga-* 'take' an unclear semantic element *-pu- ~ -po-* can optionally be added between the verb stem and the converb suffix, e.g. *ung-gu-i-we* (speak-CONV-POSS.1SG-OBL) in alternation with *um-pu-gu-i-we* (speak-*pu*-CONV-POSS.1SG-OBL) 'in order that I speak' (Menges 1968: 216). This element, which may be cognate with the anticausative pTg *-p- (see Section 6.4.3) recalls the Udehe element -mu- ~ -bu- mentioned in Section 8.4.3.3 and indicates that the Udehe instrumental deverbal noun suffix and the Nanai converb suffix have a common origin.

8.4.4 pMo *-gU ~ *-kU < ? *-xU ~ *-kU

In spite of its name, the so-called "nomen futuri" (Poppe 1954: 94, 1955: 83, 269–74; Weiers 1966: 181–190) or "futuritive participle" (Rybatzki 2003a: 76–77; Janhunen 2012b: 160) WMo. and MMo. -qu / -kü ~ -yu / -gü often lacks a specific temporal reference. As a deverbal noun suffix, it can derive purpose nouns as in example (33a) or action/state nouns as in example (33b). As illustrated in (33a), the suffix can denote the subject of the passive verb 'to be cried upon' as well as the object of the transitive verb 'to embrace', but the common denominator here is 'target/purpose of the action expressed by the base verb'. Although purpose nouns may have a future connotation (e.g. WMo. *yabu-qu* 'the one who will go'), action/state nouns do not (e.g. WMo. *yabu-qu* 'the act of going'). For this reason, the action noun is also widely used as the "dictionary form" of verbs. The suffix can also be used as an adnominal form, possibly expressing a modal connotation of willingness, expectation, purpose or intention. It has further developed into a finite marker, expressing the future tense, as in (33b/d). The suffix can also take part in verb compounding, preceding finite forms of copular verbs such as *bol-* 'to become', *bui* 'is' and *bule'e* 'was', as illustrated in (33c). The Khalka reflex of the deverbal noun suffix of purpose *-(e)x* can also combine with the quotative auxiliary *ge-* 'to say, call' to form intentional constructions, e.g. *yab-ex ge-sen youm* (go-NML say-PFV.NML COP) 'I intend to go' (Janhunen 2012b: 285). Moreover, there are some examples, such as the one in (33d), in which the suffix seems to have developed converbial use as a marker of adverbial insubordination.

(33) The use of the Middle Mongolian deverbal noun suffix *-KU ~ -GU*

    a. purpose noun

        *uila-da-**qu**   činọ   usu-t   olon   ketul-ba*
        cry-PASS-NML your water-PL many cross-PST
        'Your beweeped has crossed many waters'

        *teberi-**gu**   činọ   daba'a-t   olon   daba-ba*
        embrace-NML your mountain-PL many cross-PST
        'Your embraced has crossed many mountains'

        (SH 56; Weiers 1966: 182)

b. action/state noun

*ot-**qu**-yi   ino   ulu   toduge-gu*
go-**NML**-ACC his NEG hinder-FIN
'One should not hinder his going' (HI a23; Weiers 1966: 183)

c. verb compounding

*e'uri   jirqa-**qu**   bol-tuqai*
there enjoy.oneself-**CONV** become-IMP.3SG
'Let him enjoy himself over there!'
(big Chü-yung-kuan inscription 9; Weiers 1966: 184)

d. adverbial insubordination

*alda-**qu**   üku-gu*
offend.the.law-**CONV** die-FIN
'If he offends the law, he will die'
(Minusinsk P'ai-tzu b2; Weiers 1966: 184)

Khitan uses a marker *te.gu* to introduce a quotation, the semantic equivalent of which is 'said' (Kane 2009: 112). Similar to the other Transeurasian languages, the Mongolic languages tend to develop quotation markers from a converbial form of a verb 'to say'. The quotation markers WMo. *keme-n* and Khalkha *ge-j*, for instance, are derived, respectively, as a modal converb in WMo. -*n* or as an imperfective converb in Khal. -*j* from a verb 'to say, call' (Poppe 1954: 183–184; Janhunen 2012b: 283). In view of this tendency as well as of the existence of the verb OTk *te*- 'to say', the Khitan quotation marker is likely to have been derived as a converb in **-gu* from **te*- 'to say'. Hence, it may be possible to trace the converbial use of **-ku ~ -*-gu* back to the proto-Khitan-Mongolic stage.

Among the compound suffixes derived from WMo. and MMo. -*KU ~ -GU*, we find -*KUi ~ -GUi* and -*KUn ~ -GUn*. The suffix -*KUn ~ -GUn*, which incorporates the plural suffix WMo. / MMo. -*n* (Poppe 1954: 72), originally functioned as a marked plural form. The suffix -*KUi ~ -GUi* may have been used as a specifically feminine form, but it also leaves traces of being used as a substantive noun, while the adnominal noun was marked with -*KU ~ -GU*. The latter observation suggests that -*KUi ~ -GUi* incorporates the substantivizer pMo **i*, a reflex of the original bound noun pTEA **i* 'fact, thing, this (one)', which is also an element of the resultative nominalizer WMo. -*yai ~ gei*, MMo. -*'ai ~ -'ei* (See Section 7.6.4).

The alternation between voiceless allomorphs of the shape -*KU* and voiced allomorphs of the shape -*GU* seems to be completely random. In the Secret History, for instance, we find *ire-gü(i)* next to *ire-küi* (come-NML). It is not unlikely that it goes back to **-xu ~ *-ku* allomorphy in proto-Mongolic and that the original conditioning factors according to the environments described in Section 7.6.4 became obsolete.

8.4.5 pTk *-xU ~ *-kU

The deverbal noun suffix pTk *-xU derived instrumental nouns and action/state nouns from verbs. In Old Turkic, it gradually developed into an infinitive marker in verb compounding, preceding certain auxiliaries.

The suffix pTk *-xU used an allomorph *-kU which arose through de-fricativation following the continuants *n, *r, *č and *ß. This allomorph is reflected as OTk -kU and Chu. -Ă. Both Old Turkic and Chuvash preserve some lexicalizations that are suggestive of this original conditioning factor. Since the large majority of proto-Turkic verb stems was thematic, the initial fricative phoneme of pTk *-xU was most frequently rendered by a voiced allophone *-γU. The allomorph *-γU spread into Chuvash as -Ă and into Old Turkic as -γA, where it was eventually transcribed as -gA due to the merger of OTk /γ/ and /g/.

8.4.5.1 Old Turkic

The Old Turkic deverbal noun suffix -gu ~ -gü has been given various labels, such as "nomen futuri" (Ramstedt 1952: 92), "participium necessitatis" (Pritsak 1960: 144), "verbal nominal of purpose" (Erdal 1991: 359) and "projection participle" (Erdal 2004: 301). It can productively derive purpose nouns, as in example (34b), or action/state nouns as in example (34c). The suffix has petrified in a number of instrumental nouns, such as those listed under (345a), a function which has probably given rise to its use as a verbal nominal of purpose. Among the lexicalisations of derived action nouns are OTk. kül- 'to laugh' → külgü 'laughter', OTk. ič- 'to drink' → ičkü ~ ičgü 'drinking, drink' and OTk. udï- 'to sleep' → Uig. uduqu 'sleeping, sleep'.[4] OTk -gU can also take part in verb compounding, preceding auxiliaries such as ol- 'to become' in the construction in (34d), which expresses obligation or advice. The observation that -gU in this function is negated by -mA-, e.g. kör-ma-gü ol 'one should not divine', indicates that it has developed into a converbial form, being more inflectional than the deverbal noun suffix.

---

[4] In some sources in Manichaean script, in which voiced g and voiceless k are represented by distinct letters, OTk. ičgü appears as ičkü (Erdal 2004: 115).

(34) The use of the Old Turkic deverbal noun suffix *-gU*

    a. instrumental noun

        OTk. *bil-* 'to know' → *belgü* 'sign, mark'[5]
        OTk. *bič-* 'to cut' → *bičgu* 'saw or other cutting instrument'
        OTk. *yüli-* 'to shave' → *yüligü* 'razor'
        OTk. *yėlpi-* 'to fan, winnow' → *yėlpigü* 'fan'

    b. purpose noun

        adïn   *bėr-gü-m*   *yok*   *üčün*
        different give-NML-POSS.1SG be.non-existent because
        'because I have nothing else to give'
        (Sa 2,2 in Samml. Uig. Kontr. 2; Erdal 2004: 303)

    c. action/state noun

        küre-gü-ŋ-in   *üčün...*
        desert-NML-POSS.2SG-GEN because
        'because of your unruliness...' (KT: E23 and BQ: E19; Erdal 2004: 301)

    d. verb compounding

        munï   *sözle-gü*   *ol*
        this(ACC) pronounce-CONV become.3SG
        'One should pronounce the following' (Zweispr. Fr. r 2; Erdal 2004: 526)

Erdal (1991: 357–359) derived the instrumental deverbal noun suffix OTk. *-gUč* as a diminutive in -(X)č of the instrumental *-gU*. This would explain why instrumental nouns, such as OTk. *bičgu* 'saw or other cutting instrument', *yüligü* 'razor' and *yėlpigü* 'fan', correspond to *-gUč* derivates such as OTk. *bičguč* 'scissors', Cumanian *yülügüč* 'razor' and MTk. *yėlpigüč* 'fan'. Pointing to derived doublets such as OTk. *ör-* 'to plait' → *örKüč ~ örčüK* 'woman's braid or tuft', Erdal further argued that OTk. *-gUč* underwent methatesis to *-čUg*. However, after the continuants /r/ and /n/ the metathetical variant was *-čUk*, e.g. OTk. *ban-* 'to fasten' → *mančuk* 'any bag that is hung on a saddle' and OTk. *olor-* 'to sit' → *olorčuk* 'seat'. The complementary distribution between pre-OTk. *-gU-č* and *-kU-č* suggests the reconstruction of pTk *-xU* as the original instrumental suffix, alternating with a defricativized allomorph pTk *-kU following continuants such as /r/ and /n/. This recalls the phonological reconstruction of the resultative deverbal noun suffix pTk *-xA ~ *-kA in Section 7.6.5.

---

[5] Note that Tatar and Bashkir have *bel-* 'to know'.

8.4.5.2 Chuvash

Chuvash ø being the regular correspondence of OTk. -g- (see Section 7.6.5.2) and Chuvash -Ă- corresponding to OTk. -U- (Benzing 1959: 706), the cognate of the Old Turkic instrumental -gu ~ -gü is Chuvash -ă ~ -ĕ. This suffix derives instrumental nouns such as those listed under (35a) and action/ state nouns such as those under (35b) (Benzing 1959: 740; Pritsak 1960: 145; Levickaya 1974: 154). Interestingly, the suffix alternates with Chu. -kă ~ -kĕ, which has a similar function (Benzing 1943: 53; Levickaya 1974: 155; Fedotov 1997: 332) and corresponds regularly to the Old Turkic voiceless allomorph -ku ~ -kü. Note that the Chuvash deverbal nouns correspond to parallel formations in Old Turkic, such as OTk. ačguc 'key' (from ač- 'to open') , OTk. belgü 'sign, mark', OTk. bïčgu 'saw', OTk. ičkü ~ ičgü 'drinking, drink' and OTk. külgü 'laughter', which suggests that the derivation may already have taken place at the proto-Turkic level.

(35) The use of the Chuvash deverbal noun suffix -Ă ~ -kĂ

    a. instrumental noun

        Chu. avăt- 'to dig out' → avtă 'concave, semicircular instrument used for digging'
        Chu. cïś- 'to punch' → cïśkă 'punch'
        Chu. kar- 'to stretch out' → kară 'stretching frame'
        Chu. păč- 'to cut' → păčkă 'knife'
        Chu. palla- 'to know, recognize' → pallă 'sign, characteristic'
        Chu. śup- 'to hit' → śupkă 'slap in the face'
        Chu. uś- 'to open' → uśă 'key'

    b. action/state noun

        Chu. ĕś- 'to drink' → ĕśkĕ 'drinking, drink'
        Chu. kul- 'to laugh'→ kulă 'laughter'
        Chu. tïtăn- 'to stick to, adhere' → tïtănkă 'steadfastness, pertinacity'
        Chu. śi- 'to eat' → śikĕ 'eating, food'
        Chu. xĕrĕn- 'to become red-hot, warm up' → xĕrĕnkĕ 'blushing'

The derived instrumental suffix pTk *-gU-č and *-kU-č is also reflected in Chuvash. The reflex of pTk *-kU-č is Chu. -kĂč / -kĂś, e.g. in Chu. uś- 'to open' > uśkăč 'key', Chu. kar- 'to stretch out' → karkăč 'stretching frame' and Chu. xïr- 'to shave, scrape, clean' → xïrkăč 'grater, scraper' (Levickaya 1974: 156–157; Fedotov 1997: 334). The reflex of pTk *-gU-č is -Ăś, but suffixation of this form has led to contractions, such as in Chu. śĕśĕ 'knife'. This form has contracted from *śĕl-ĕś, the verb base of which is Chu. śŏl- 'to rip, tear, pluck, mow'. A cognate formation is OTk. *yüli-* 'to shave' and the derived nouns OTk. *yüligü* and Cumanian *yülügüč* 'razor' (Pritsak 1960: 145; Levickaya 1974: 157).

The voiceless allomorphs *-kĂ* (< pTk *-kU*) an *-kĂč / -kĂś* (< pTk *-kU-č*) mainly seem to occur following verb stems ending in *n, r, p, č* and *ś*. Since /p/ may go back to a bilabial fricative *ß* and /ś/ goes back to pTk *č*, it appears that the distribution was originally conditioned by the presence of certain continuants such as **n*, **r*, **č* and **ß*. Taken together with the alternation in Old Turkic, the Chuvash allomorphy therefore reflects an original variation between pTk *-xU* and *-kU*. Note that the attestation of OTk. *ičkü* as a cognate of *éśkĕ* 'drinking, drink' seems to support original de-fricativation following pTk *č*.

Benzing (1959: 740) and Pritsak (1960: 148–153) proposed that the so-called Chuvash finite "future" in *-Ă*, illustrated in (36), developed from the deverbal noun suffix. In spite of its label, this suffix often lacks a specific temporal reference and expresses modal connotations such as wish, necessity, expectation or intention. It is also used in habitual and generic expressions.

(36) The use of the Chuvash future in *-Ă*

    ülemren   *kur-ay-mă-n*
    in.the.future see-POT-NEG.FIN-2SG
    'You will not be able to see him in the future.' (Krüger 1961: 143)

Although Johanson (1975) has proposed that this suffix may be related to the so-called Turkic "aorist" (see Section 7.3.5.2), the earlier proposal gains credibility in the light of the parallel development for the Mongolic cognate discussed in Section 7.4.4.

Benzing (1959: 740) further proposed that the Chuvash potential nominalizer in *-i*, illustrated in (37) could be derived as a compound of the instrumental in *-Ă* and the third person possessive in *-i*. However, Pritsak (1960: 152) has pointed out that this derivation is problematic because the third person of the Chuvash future is *ĕ* and not **i*, as would be expected on the basis of this derivation. It would be more plausible to derive the potential in *-i* from an earlier compound of pTk *-xU* plus *-i*, in which *-i* would be the Turkic reflex of the bound noun pTEA **i* 'fact, thing, this (one)' (see Section 7.8).

(37) The use of the Chuvash potential nominalizer in *-i*

    *kur-**i***   *kuś-a*   *kur-**mi***   *tu*
    see-POT.**NML** eye-ACC see-**NEG.POT.NML** make(IMP)
    'Make the seeing eye blind.' (Johanson 1975: 125)

8.5 The historical development of converb suffixes in Transeurasian

The Transeurasian languages preserve evidence supporting the reconstruction of two suffixes that reflect the development of deverbal noun suffixes into converb markers: pTEA *-i and pTEA *-xU ~ *-kU. The relevant reconstructions in the individual proto-languages are compared in Table 1.

Table 1. Form-function comparison of converbialization in the Transeurasian languages

pTEA	pJ	pK	pTg	pMo/ pKMo	pTk
*-i ~ ø	*-i ~ ø	*-i ~ ø	*-i: ~ ø	*-i ~ ø	*-i ~ ø
instrumental n.	instrumental n.	instrumental n.	instrumental n.	instrumental n.	instrumental n.
resultative n.	resultative n.	resultative n.	resultative n.	resultative n.	resultative n.
action/state n.	action/state n.	action/state n.	action/state n.	action/state n.	—
	infinitive	—		—	infinitive
	converb	converb	converb	converb	converb
		adverb	adverb	adverb	adverb
*-xU ~ *-kU	*-ku	*-k(ʌ) / *-ku	*-xu: ~ -ku:	*-xU ~ -kU	*-xU ~ -kU
instrumental n.			instrumental n.	purpose n.	instrum. / purpose n.
action/state n.	state noun	action/state n.	action/state n.	action/state n.	action/state n.
infinitive	infinitive	infinitive	—	infinitive	infinitive
	converb	converb	converb	converb	
	adverb	adverb	adverb		

a) *Formal assessment*

The vowels involved in these comparisons correspond regularly according to the correspondences 18. (*-u-), 19. (*-ʊ-) and 20. (*-i-) in Section 3.3.2. The vowel harmony archphoneme pTEA *U represents the alternation between attracted *u and retracted *ʊ within a system of tongue root harmony. The merger of the original vowel harmonic alternants into a single marker in Japonic and Tungusic is in line with the merger of pTEA *-u- and *-ʊ- as pJ *-u- and pTg *-u- in lexical cognates. In Korean, the suffix *-ku is the regular reflex of pTEA *-xu, whereas a separate suffix with similar function pK *-k(ʌ) is the expected reflex of pTEA *-xʊ. Hence, the Korean suffixes do not represent vowel-harmonic allomorphs in Korean, but they can be traced back to original vowel harmonic alternants at the Transeurasian level.

The reconstructed allomorphy between the velar fricative suffix pTEA *-xU and its de-fricativized allomorph *-kU recalls the allomorphy reconstructed for pTEA *-xA ~ *-kA in Section 7.8. In line with the environment for de-fricativization determined there, the evidence suggests that pTg *-ku: arose from pTg *-xu: following *n or *β while pTk *-xU underwent defricativization following *n, *r, *č and *β. The Mongolic allomorphy seems to be completely random, but it may originally go back to de-fricativization in fricative environment, similar to the case of pMo *-xA ~ *-kA in Section 7.6.4.

b) *Functional assessment*

Not only can both etymologies discussed here be traced back to original deverbal noun suffixes, but the correlations also hold for the specific type of nominalization concerned, i.e. instrumental, resultative and action/state nominalization. In the case of pTEA *-xU, the instrumental meaning was preserved in the Altaic branch of Transeurasian, but it was lost in the Koreo-Japanic branch. Japanese subsequently lost the function of action noun, which is why the suffix only attached itself to verbal adjectives and copulae. As the development to converbial marker took place after the separation from the common ancestor, the converbial function developed independently in the individual daughter languages. As a result, the Japonic converb pJ *-ku was restricted to verbal adjectives and some branches did not develop converbial function on certain nominalizers, as in the case of pTg *-i and pTk *-xU.

c) *Combinational assessment*

Similar to the suffixes discussed in Section 7.8, the reflexes of the nominalizer *-xU tend to be replaced in the Transeurasian languages by reinforced constructions consisting of this very suffix plus an additional cognate element. Table 2 presents such innovative suffix strings along with the language stages in which the compounding presumably took place. For the reconstruction of the bound noun pTEA *i 'fact, thing, this (one)', I refer to the Sections 7.8 and 3.4.1, respectively.

Table 2. Reinforced constructions consisting of the nominalizer in question and an additional element

pTEA	+ *i 'fact, thing, this (one)'	*a:- + 'to be'
*-xU	pK *-kʌ-i, pMo *-xU-i, pTk *xU-i	pre-OJ *a-ku, pK *a-k

d) *Typological assessment*

In both etymologies summarized in Table 1, the deverbal noun suffix originally derived the instrument by which the action expressed by the verb was carried out. Passing through a stage of ambiguous cases, such as 'laughter', which can be interpreted both as an instrument and as an action, the instrumental nominalizer developed into a marker, which derived the name of the activity or state designated by the verb or verbal adjective. Action nominals typically have some of the syntactic characteristics of both sentences and non-derived noun phrases, i.e. they occupy an intermediate position between verbs and nouns (Malchukov 2004; Comrie & Thompson 2007: 343–376). An action nominal construction such as 'His rapid crossing of the river', for instance, looks like an ordinary noun phrase in that it takes genitive attributes and is modified by an adjective, but it parallels a sentence in that it expresses the subject, object and manner of the action. In the Transeurasian languages, action/state nouns in a core case governed by a main verb (e.g. He tried the rapid crossing of the river; Its length came into being) can easily be reinterpreted as an infinitive-like element (e.g. He tried to cross the river rapidly; It became long) because core cases often remain unmarked and pronouns may be omitted when they are pragmatically inferable. As such, the internal structure becomes almost completely verbal: the genitive attributes lose their marking and the adnominal modifier is reinterpreted as an adverb. Infinitives are typically intermediate between action nouns and converbs in that they occur both in complement clauses and adverbial clauses of purpose (Haspelmath 1989; Ylikoski 2003: 200). The verbalization of the form is complete when the complement clause becomes reanalyzed as an adverbial clause (e.g. His crossing the river rapidly frightens you > Crossing the river rapidly, he frightens you), giving rise to a converbial construction. The converbial reflexes of pTEA *-i and *-xU thus originate in instrumental and action nouns losing their original noun-like syntax, i.e., the nominalization of a verb is denominalized. The traces left by the suffix in adverbs across the Transeurasian languages are considered to be lexicalizations of earlier converbial froms.

It can be noted that Janhunen (1982: 34) reconstructs proto-Uralic *-j and *-k as two deverbal noun suffix deriving agentive, resultative and action nouns and imperfective action nouns, respectively. Although these are monophonemic markers, they seem to reflect a historical connection – perhaps even a remote genealogical connection – between the two language families concerned, especially when taken together with other correlations (see Sections 4.6; 6.8 and 7.8).

9 Evaluation

9.1 The correlations

In addition to the correspondences in form and function between the verb roots discussed in Chapter 3, I find 19 corresponding sets of verb morphemes. An overview is given in Table 1.

Table 1. Overview of verb morphology shared between the Transeurasian languages

	pTEA	pJ	pK	pTg	pMo	pTk
1	*ana- negation	*ana- negation	*an- negation	*ana- negation		[*an-] negation
2	*ə- negation			*e- negation	*e-se- negation	*e- negation
3	*-lA- manipulative	*-ra- manipulative		*-lA:- manipulative	*-lA- manipulative	*-lA- manipulative
4	*-nA- processive	*-na- processive	*-nO- processive	*-nA- processive	*-nA- processive	*-(X)n- processive
5	*(-)ki- 'do, make' iconic	*-ka- iconic	*-ki- iconic	*-ki- iconic	*(-)ki- 'do, make' iconic	*ki(-)l- /-kI- 'do, make' iconic
6	*-mA- inclination	*-ma- inclination	*-mO- inclination	*-mA- inclination	*-mA- inclination	
7	*-gA- inchoative	*-ka- inchoative	*-k(O)- inchoative	*-gA- inchoative	*-gA- inchoative	*-(X)k-~-(X)g- inchoative
8	*-ti- causative	*-ta- causative passive	*-ti- causative passive	*-ti- causative passive	*-ti- causative	*-tI- causative passive
9	*-pU- reflexive anticausative	*-pa- reflexive anticausative	*-pO- anticausative	*-p- reflexive anticausative	*-βU- reflexive anticausative	*-U- reflexive anticausative
10	*-dA- fientive	*-ya- fientive passive		*dA:- fientive	*-dA- fientive passive	*-(A)d- fientive anticausative
11	*-rA- anticausative	*-ra- anticausative	*-(u)l- anticausative	*-rA- anticausative	*-rA- anticausative	*-rA- anticausative
12	*-gi- creative causative	*-(k)i- creative-fientive causative anticausative	*-ki- creative causative passive	-gi:- creative causative		

Table 1. (continued)

	pTEA	pJ	pK	pTg	pMo	pTk
13	*-rA lexical NML	*-ra lexical NML *-wo-ra clausal NML relativizer finite	*-l lexical NML *-wo-l clausal NML relativizer finite	*-rA lexical NML — clausal NML relativizer finite	*-r lexical NML — clausal NML — finite	*-rV lexical NML — — relativizer finite
14	*-mA lexical NML	*-m lexical NML *-wo-m clausal NML relativizer finite	*-m lexical NML *-wo-m clausal NML — finite	*-mA lexical NML — clausal NML — finite	*-mA ~ *-m lexical NML — clausal NML — finite	*-mA ~ *-m lexical NML
15	*-n lexical NML	*-n lexical NML *-wo-n clausal NML relativizer finite	*-n lexical NML *-wo-n clausal NML relativizer finite	*-nA ~ *-n lexical NML — clausal NML — finite	*-n lexical NML — clausal NML — finite	*-n lexical NML — clausal NML relativizer finite
16	*-xA ~ *-kA resultative lexical NML	*-ka resultative lexical NML — relativizer finite	*-ka(-)i resultative lexical NML	*-xA: ~ *-kA: resultative lexical NML clausal NML relativizer past finite	*-xA ~ *-kA resultative lexical NML clausal NML relativizer past finite	*-xA ~ *-kA resultative lexical NML — PFV.FUT relativ. future finite
17	*-sA resultative lexical NML	*-sa resultative lexical NML — — finite		*-sA ~ *-si: < *sA-i: resultative lexical NML clausal NML relativizer finite	*-sA ~ *-si: < *sA-i: resultative lexical NML clausal NML — finite	*-sA perfective — clausal NML — past finite
18	*-i ~ ø nominalizer	*-i ~ ø nominalizer infinitive converb	*-i ~ ø nominalizer converb adverb	*-i: ~ ø nominalizer	*-i ~ ø nominalizer converb adverb	*-I ~ ø nominalizer infinitive converb adverb
19	*-xU ~ *-kU nominalizer infinitive	*-ku nominalizer infinitive converb adverb	*-k(ʌ) / *-ku nominalizer infinitive converb adverb	*-xu: ~ -ku: nominalizer converb adverb	*-xU ~ -kU nominalizer infinitive converb	*-xU ~ -kU nominalizer infinitive

9.1.1 Formal correlations

The consonants involved in the comparisons correspond regularly according to the correspondences given in Section 3.3.1. An exception is the particular behavior of two velar suffixes (i.e. resultative nominalizer and nominalizer/infinitive) in a phonological environment that often involves continuants. Since the velar involved becomes a voiceless obstruent in this environment, I have suggested that it arose through de-fricativation. This assumption has led to the reconstruction of pTEA *x in Chapter 7, in addition to the consonant inventory reconstructed in Robbeets (2005: 373) and summarized in Section 3.3.1.

The vowels involved in the comparisons correspond regularly according to the correspondences given in Section 3.3.2. According to these correspondences, the vowel harmony between pTEA *-a- and *-ə- regularly merges into pJ *-a-, while the harmony between pTEA *-u- and -ʊ- regularly merges into pJ *-u-. Given this merger and the widespread *A-vocalism in the proto-Transeurasian suffixes, the large majority of Japanese suffixes display a-vocalism. The irregular low central vowel in the Japonic iconic suffix *-ka- and causative-anticausative suffix *-ta- may be the result of resonance with the other suffixes in the verbal paradigm.

The consistently reduced vowel reflexes (*-i- / -ʌ-) in the Korean suffixes are probably due to vowel reduction in unstressed position, reminiscent of the frequent weakening of the final vowel involved in lexical items. Morphological items, especially suffixes, tend to be unstressed and are therefore liable to undergo irregular reductive developments such as the loss of word-final vowels in some reflexes of the lexical nominalizers pTEA *-rA and *-mA. Vowel erosion in word-final suffixes is to be expected especially following sonorants such as /m/ and /r/, because their high sonority allows them to be articulated without final vowel. This may explain why the vowels are retained in the reflexes of other word-final suffixes such as pTEA *-sA and *-xA ~ *-kA.

The vowel harmony archphonemes in Table 1 represent the following alternations: pK *O = *i ~ ʌ ; pTg *A = *a ~ e [RTR *a ~ ə]; pMo *A = *a ~ e [RTR *a ~ ə]; pMo *U = *ü ~ u [RTR *u ~ ʊ]; pTk *A = *a ~ e, pTk *U = ü ~ u, pTk *I = ï ~ i and pTk *X = ï ~ i ~ u ~ ü. The reinterpretation of the quality of the Koreanic, Tungusic and Mongolic vowels in the light of Ko's (2012) RTR interpretation leads to the reconstruction of RTR harmony in the original Transeurasian suffixes with archphonemes pTEA *A = *a ~ ə and pTEA *U = *u ~ ʊ. As proposed in Chapter 3, it is plausible that Turkic shifted to a palatal harmony system and that the RTR system became distorted in Japanese, due to areal influences at the periphery of the Transeurasian family. A number of Japonic verb suffixes in Table 1 have left traces of a vowel harmonic-like alternation, notably pJ *-ra- ~ -rə- denominal verbalizer, pJ *-na- ~ *-nə- processive, pJ *-ma- ~ *-mə- inclination, pJ *-pa- ~ -pə- reflexive-anticausative and pJ *-ra ~ *-rə nominalizer (Section 7.3.1). This opposition may imply an original RTR based contrast.

9.1.2 Functional correlations

The functional correspondences go beyond general tags such as denominal verbalizer or deverbal noun suffix since they also hold for the specific type of verbalization or nominalization concerned, i.e. manipulative, iconic, processive, inclinational and inchoative verbalization or instrumental, resultative and action/state nominalization. Moreover, there are correlations between the concrete submeanings that make up these functional specializations. The manipulative meaning of the denominal verbalizer, for instance, falls apart in several submeanings, such as 'to achieve, overcome or execute a difficult action with success on the base noun', 'to make use of the base noun' and 'to sound or feel like the base onomatopoea', all of which correlate across the individual branches. Moreover, many morphemes share a specific polysemy, such as causative-passive, reflexive-anticausative, fientive-passive, nominalizer-relativizer-finite or nominalizer-infinitive-converb, whereby one function is less grammaticalized than the other.

9.1.3 Combinational correlations

Similarities in the combination of morphemes manifest themselves in the parallel order of morphemes in the affix chain, in the sharing of suffix strings, in common restrictions on the part of speech of the derivational base, in the shared ability to combine with copied or onomatopoetic bases and in the common atypically preposed position of certain markers.

The categories in the suffix chain tend to follow the order actionality-diatheses-negation-tense-mood-person-number across the Transeurasian languages, whereby negation is usually sandwiched between derivation and inflection. While this broad ordering of different categories is universally predictable (see Section 2.2.2.3), it is perhaps more telling that the order of individual morphemes within derivational categories such as actionality and diathesis is also similar. In the actionality chain, for instance, the manipulative, occupies the leftmost position in all languages, followed by the processive, while the inclinational and the inchoative tend towards the rightmost positions in most languages. In the diathetical chain, the leftmost positions are generally occupied by the causative and the reflexive, followed by the fientive, the anticausative and the passive.

It further appears that the Transeurasian languages have a number of compound suffixes in common, the morphological complexity of which is shared by all languages.[1] The nominalizers, for instance, join in parallel suffix strings with reflexes of pTEA *wo- 'to be', *a- 'to be', *i 'fact thing', *pa 'place' *xa-..-n (INCH-...-SG) and *-kAn diminutive.

There are also common restrictions on the part of speech or other characteristics of the derivational base. The reflexes of the manipulative, for instance, derive from nominal bases only, whereas reflexes of the processive and the inchoative can also be derived from adjectival and verbal bases in most branches. Only one denominal verbalizer, notably the manipulative, can be used to derive verbs from copied bases, whereas the other denominal verbalizers cannot be used in this way. The manipulative and the iconic are further able to derive from onomatopoetic adverbs, whereas the other verbalizers do not share this ability.

Moreover, the observation that the Transeurasian languages share an aberrant original verb initial word order and an atypically preposed position of markers in negative constructions can also serve as comparative evidence.

9.1.4 Typological correlations

When typological correlations involve matches between mere structural features of the language system at different levels such as phonology, morphology, or syntax, they are often too indeterminate to be advanced as a genealogical arguments. Nevertheless, some structural phenomena that are relatively infrequent and randomly spread across the world's languages but frequent and geographically concentrated in a specific group of languages may still be significant. In Robbeets (forthcoming a), I have provided a typological profile of the Transeurasian languages with special attention to distinguishing the effects of code-copying from those of inheritance.

The present study, however, has only been concerned with structural similarities insofar as the sharing of a typological feature or process coincides with the sharing of morphological form and function. The typological correlations involve either an abstract trait of a certain morpheme, or, alternatively, a process of grammaticalization according to which the morpheme developed. Instances in which an abstract feature coincides with form-function matches include mixed adjective typology (Chapter 3), RTR harmony (Chapter 3), main clause status and preposed position of negative verbs of the shape *ana-, *ə- and *ma- (Chapter 4) and the non-verbal strategy of verbal borrowing employing a verbal-

---

[1] Note that unilateral morphological complexity would be an indication of code-copying (see Section 2.4.2.2), whereas shared complexity is not.

izer of the common shape *-lA- (Chapter 5). Instances in which the morphemes share a process of grammaticalization in addition to form and function include the development of suffixes or preposed particles from negative verbs of the common shape *ana-, *ə- and *ma- (Chapter 4), the development of a loan verb marker from a denominal verbalizer (Chapter 5), the transference of actional markers from nominal to adjectival to verbal bases (Chapter 5), the causative to passive development involving suffixes of the common shape *-tA- and *-ki- (Chapter 6), the transition from reflexive to anticausative involving suffixes of the common shape *-pU- (Chapter 6), the development of fientive to anticausative or passive involving suffixes of the common shape *-dA- (Chapter 6), the grammaticalization of causatives from creative verbs of the common shape *-gi- (Chapter 6), direct insubordination involving suffixes of the common shape *-rA-, *-mA, *-n, *-xA ~ *-kA and *-sA (Chapter 7), the interrelated development of tense from aspectual distinctions on these suffixes (Chapter 7) and converbialization of instrumental and action nouns of the common shape *-i and *-xU (Chapter 8).

9.1.5 Paradigmatic correlations

Paradigms are characterized as "organized set[s] of derivationally or inflectionally related items that derive a particular semantic or morphosyntactic category from a common base or root" (see Section 2.2.2.5). The morphemes in Table 1 can be divided into organized sets of derivationally related items such as an actional subsystem (3 to 7) and a diathetical subsystem (8 to 12) as well as into sets of inflectionally related items such as aspect/tense (13 to 17), converbs (18 and 19) and negation (1 and 2). Taken together, the reconstructed subsystems build up an ancestral grammatical system. Paradigmatic correlations are understood as internal cohesion between the ordered slots of a set of forms, shared idiosyncrasies in specific parts of the system and external relationships of grammatical patterning among different subsystems. The correlations in Table 1 can be regarded as "paradigmatic" in the following way.

9.1.5.1 Ordered sets
Contrary to what is the case for the Indo-European languages, the subsystems do not form a closed set of form slots with positions defined by intersections of the dimensions person and number agreement.[2] This is due to the typological

---

[2] The basic inflected forms of Japanese grammar are *mizenkei* (pseudostem), *rentaikei* (adnominal), *renyōkei* (converb), *shūshikei* (indicative), *izenkei* (subjunctive) and *meireikei* (im-

characteristic that Transeurasian languages to the north and west (Turkic, Mongolic, Tungusic) have recently grammaticalized person-number agreement from subject pronouns, whereas those to the south and east (Manchu, Korean, Japanese) lack person-number agreement on the verb altogether. Nevertheless, even if the sets are not closed, they can be regarded as relatively ordered because some cognates display correlations in grammatical patterning, which are suggestive of multidimensional paradigmaticity. As illustrated in Table 2, the reflexes of the pTEA nominalizers *-rA and *-n, for instance, suggest correlations in grammatical patterning defined by the intersections of the dimensions telicity of the verb base and finiteness. Following atelic verb bases, the suffixes tend to function as imperfective relativizers and non-past finite forms, whereas following telic verb bases they tend to function as perfective relativizers and past finite forms.

Table 2. Multidimensional paradigmaticity shared by the reflexes of pTEA *-rA and *-n

	non-finite	finite
atelic verb base	IPF	non-PST
telic verb base	PF	PST

9.1.5.2 Quirks

Apart from the paradigmatic characteristics outlined above, the morphologies of the individual languages have their little quirks: they display some peculiar traits or idiosyncrasies that are difficult to explain on the basis of internal linguistic analysis alone. Phonological oddities include (i) the irregular voiceless velar allomorphs of the Mongolic and Turkic resultative suffixes in certain continuant environments as well as the irregular Manchu allomorph -kA of the perfective adnominal -hA; (ii) the numerous vowel alternations in the so-called Turkic "aorist" and the unusual characteristic that so many Japanese verb suffixes should begin with the vowel /a/ and; (iii) the derivation of verbs from verbal and nominal bases through strikingly homophonous suffixes with similar semantic content throughout the Transeurasian languages.

---

perative). They form an inherently closed set of inflectionally related items from which the entire Japanese inflectional verb paradigm can be deduced. As shown in Robbeets (2014), every single cell in the Japanese paradigm can be matched with a materially corresponding form in the same functional domain. Thus, it is possible to trace a closed set of forms back to its Transeurasian origins, even if the cognates do not necessarily make up an inherently closed set in the other Transeurasian languages.

The first oddity can be explained by reconstructing an original resultative pTEA *-xA, which defricativized to *-kA in continuant environment (see Chapter 7). The second one can be attributed to the inherent Transeurasian tendency to replace nominalizers by a reinforced periphrastic constructions consisting of a copula and the same nominalizer (see Chapter 3 and 7). The third peculiarity then can be accounted for by the recurrent transference of actional markers from nominal to verbal bases, which is facilitated by mixed adjective typology (Chapter 3 and 5).

There are also a number of semantic oddities, such as a derivational peculiarity in time expressions such as K *onul* 'today' and K *wolhay* 'this year', in which he imperfective element *-ul* gets perfective interpretation and the frequency of color terms in the Japanese accent class 2.5. The peculiar perfective interpretation can be explained in reference to the ancestral Transeurasian stage in which the aspectual interpretation of the relativizer depended on the telicity of the verb base (Chapter 7). The second oddity seems to go back to a common Transeurasian semantic peculiarity, whereby the lexical nominalizer pTEA *-mA was frequently used in the derivation of colour nouns from descriptive verbs meaning 'to be(come) the colour' (Chapter 7).

Syntactic oddities, finally include (i) the unusual negative constructions in the Chuvash prohibitive paradigm based on preposed negative particle *an* and a postposed *mar;* (ii) the highly remarkable preterite use of the Yakut aorist in *-Ar*; (iii) the exceptional use of the Old Japanese *rentaikei* (adnominal) as a finite form, while the *shūshikei* (indicative) can be used in nonfinite function and; (iv) the insertion of the Middle Korean modulator in relative constructions in case the modified noun is semantically the object of the adnominalized verb. The unusual prohibitive paradigm can be explained in reference to the origination of negative markers from preposed negative auxiliaries (Chapter 4). The second oddity can be explained by referring to the common Transeurasian stage in which the aspectual interpretation of a nonfinite form depended on the telicity of the verb base (Chapter 7). The third irregularity can be attributed to direct insubordination in the Transeurasian languages (Chapter 7). Finally, the insertion of the modulator in relative clauses when the modified noun is semantically the object of the adnominalized verb can be explained by deriving the modulator from an original copula pK *(w)o-*, cognate with the Japanese copula *wo-* (Chapter 3 and 7). In sum, irregularities in the morphologies of the individual languages can be derived from regularity in the ancestral paradigm.

9.1.5.3 Extended paradigmaticity

Paradigmatic coherence also consists in an external correlation of grammatical patterning between different paradigms. As such, the paradigm of denominal verbalizers is connected with the paradigm of deverbal actional suffixes; the paradigm of lexical nominalizers correlates with that of clausal nominalizers, relativizers and finite forms and there is also a connection between the paradigms of lexical nominalizers and those of infinitives and converbs. In other words, there are external connections between separate paradigms, which are caused by shared tendencies of grammaticalization.

In sum, the evidence in Table 1 is paradigmatic in that the cognates reflect an internally ordered organization, share certain idiosyncrasies and display external relations of grammatical patterning.

9.2 How likely is coincidence?

Although any one of the morphological correspondence sets summarized in Table 1 would not be sufficient to establish a historical relationship between the Transeurasian languages, the cumulative force of the etymologies suggests that they should be treated as such. Out of the low average number of verb morphemes – say 80 – in a language, there are 19 sets of corresponding morphemes. Out of these, 12 correspondence sets stretch over all 5 branches, while 5 sets stretch over 4 branches. The probability of the observed correspondences being due to chance is comparable to making 80 attempts of rolling 5 black dice and getting 5 sixes in a row for 12 tosses and 4 sixes in a row for 5 tosses. Needless to say that the probability of such a success is very low to begin with. However, our findings are less likely to be coincidental than tossing dice in this successful manner. This is because in as many as 16 etymologies the number of matched segments is higher than one, whereby a match is verifiable on the basis of sound correspondences in the lexicon. The observed similarities resemble a situation in which you add 5 blue dice to your game and get 5 additional blue sixes in addition to the black row for 12 tosses and 4 additional blue sixes in addition to the black row for 5 tosses. Furthermore, our cognate sets display shared polysemy, shared irregularity and paradigmatic correlations, which further decrease the likelihood that the observed similarities are to be explained by coincidence. Therefore, it is fair to say that the correlations in Table 5 most probably are not coincidental but deserve a historical explanation, be it borrowing or inheritance.

9.3 How likely is borrowing?

9.3.1 Guidelines

Comparing copying patterns with genealogical patterns in a cross-linguistic sample of languages, I have developed 14 guidelines for distinguishing between the effects of contact and inheritance in shared morphology in Section 2.4. These guidelines are summarized in Table 3. In what follows, I will apply these criteria to the verb morphology shared by the Transeurasian languages. The outcome of this analysis will contribute to the distinction between areal and genealogical explanations of common Transeurasian verb morphology.

Table 3. Indications of code-copying and inheritance

	Indications of code-copying		Indications of inheritance
1	Productivity restricted to shared roots	1	Globally shared grammaticalization
2	Unilateral morphological complexity	2	Categorial opacity
3	Mismatch of morpheme boundaries	3	Shared cumulation
4	Multiple marking of a single inflectional category	4	Unreduced allomorphy
5	Functional mismatch	5	Multiple comparative setting
6	Phonological mismatch	6	Missing intermediaries
7	Distribution limited to contact zones		
8	Specific morphosyntactic subsystems affected		

9.3.2 Indications against code-copying

For the etymological evidence summarized in the Table 1, none of the indications of codecopying (1 to 8) are present.

1. *Productivity restricted to shared roots*

The productivity of the Transeurasian verb affixes is not restricted to etymologically equivalent roots. In examples of the manipulative verbalizer, e.g., OJ *wata* 'sea' → *watar-* 'to cross over, span, get transferred (tr./ intr.)', Even *mu:* 'water' → *mu:le:-* 'to gather water, go to get water', WMo. *usun* 'water' → *usula-* 'to water (animals/plants), irrigate (tr.)' and OTk. *adut* 'palm of one's hand' → *adutla-* 'to scoop up with the palm of one's hand (tr.)', it is clear that the verbs are derived from native roots. It is further noticeable that the verbalizers derive comparable meaning from bases that are semantically very similar but etymologically clearly distinct. This is remarkable, for instance, in the case of manipulative derivations such as OJ *ipo* 'hut' → *ipor-* 'to lodge in a hut', Ud. *anga* 'night shelter' → *angala-* 'to make a night shelter', WMo. *ger* 'yurt, house' → *gerle-* 'to found a house of his own, marry' and OTk. *ev* 'house' → *evle-* 'to furnish (sb.) with dwellings, marry (sb.) off', or in the case of inchoative derivations such as OJ $mi_1 du$ 'water' → $mi_1 duk$- 'to get soaked (in water)', MK *·mul* 'water' → *mulk-* 'to be watery, thin' and *čï* 'moist' → OTk. *čïk-* 'to get moist.

One could object that some bases, such as Ma. *ejen* 'ruler' in *ejele-* 'to rule, establish control over', Even *gïd* 'spear' in *gïdla:-* 'to pierce with a lance', WMo. *ang* 'game' in *angla-* 'to hunt, catch (game) (tr.)' and MMo. *čag* 'time' in *čagla-* 'to spend time, deliberate (intr.)' are clearly borrowings from WMo. *ejen* 'ruler', WMo. *jida* 'spear', OTk. *ang* 'game' and OTk *cag* 'time', respectively. While this may be true, it is not relevant to the present analysis. The criterion proposed here is *restriction* of productivity to shared bases only. When a verbalizer is highly productive in a language as is the case for the manipulative in the Tungusic, Mongolic and Turkic languages, it is of course assumed to derive both from native and foreign stems.

2. Unilateral morphological complexity

The majority of the morphemes compared in Table 1 are either monophonemic or monosyllabic and as such there is no internal evidence to suggest that they are further segmentable into compound morphemes. It can be noted that *multilateral* morphological complexity cannot be taken as an indication of borrowing. Shared suffix strings that are morphologically segmentable in each and every language under comparison may well be inherited. The nominalizers (13 to 19) in Table 1, for instance, take part in parallel suffix strings with reflexes of pTEA **wo-* 'to be', **a-* 'to be', **i* 'fact thing', **pa* 'place' **xa-...-n* (INCH-...-SG) and **-kAn* diminutive. Another example is the compounding of the iconic suffixes OTk. *-kIr-* and WMo. *-kirA-* which may have taken place in Altaic, i.e. the most recent common ancestor of Turkic and Mongolic (see Section 5.5.4).

3. Mismatch of morpheme boundaries

For the majority of comparanda in Table 1, the morpheme boundaries overlap in such a way that they delimit an initial consonant and a final vowel. Among the exceptions are the Turkic processive, inchoative and fientive verbalizers in Table 1 (4, 7 and 10). In these cases, there is a mismatch with respect to the vowel *-A-* or the reduced vowel *-X-* following consonant-final stems as well as in the lack of a suffix-final vowel. For example, the processive OTk. *–(X)n* in e.g., OTk. *ar-* 'to be tired, weak' → *arïn-* 'to tire (intr.)' mismatches the processive suffixes in e.g., OJ *ama-* 'to be sweet' → *amanap-* 'to be nice to (intr.)', MK ·*hoy-* 'to be white, light' → ·*hoyno-* 'to become light, dawn', Ud. *ede* 'weak' → *edene-* 'to become weak' and WMo. *bülteger* 'bulging (of eyes); pop-eyed person' → *bültegene-* 'to open one's eyes wide, to stare (intr.)'. However, the insertion of reduced vowels and the deletion of suffix-final vowels is also found elsewhere in the history of Turkic. The mismatch of morpheme boundaries may thus be due to an early internal development in the ancestral Turkic language.

4. Multiple marking of a single inflectional category

Inflectional markers such as the finite forms (13 to 17) and the converbs (18 and 19) in Table 1 do not occur repeatedly on a single verb stem in any of the languages under comparison. This criterion obviously does not hold for derivational categories, such as valence markers. The double causative constructions that have been reconstructed in Chapter 6, for instance, reflect a cross-linguistic tendency to use two causative markers in expressing double causation or intensivation of the first causative.

5. Functional mismatch

There are no functional mismatches of the type "infinitive vs. verbalizer" that may suggest reinterpretation of a common verb ending in the model language as a verbalizer in the recipient language. Except for the manipulative, the denominal verbalizers are not attested as loan verb markers and, as such, do not reflect the primary stage in the standard borrowing process of denominal verbalizers.

Moreover, the functional correspondences of the comparanda are not restricted to a meaning that is demonstrably secondary to one of the participating morphemes. Whenever a secondary meaning, such as passive or converb, is shared, the morphemes share at least the primary meaning, such as causative or nominalizer.

6. Phonological mismatch

As explained in Section 9.1, the consonants and vowels involved in the comparisons generally confirm the sound correspondences established on the basis of lexical comparison.

7. Distribution limited to contact zones

The reconstruction of the verb affixes in the individual branches is based upon well-distributed morphemes that are not restricted to a certain contact zone. For Proto-Turkic, I take at least Chuvash and Old Turkic into account; for Mongolic, Written Mongolian, Middle Mongolian and Khitan Mongolic when attestations are preserved; for Tungusic, Northern Tungusic, Southeastern Tungusic and

Southwestern Tungusic; for Korean, Middle Korean and contemporary Korean and; for Japanese, Old Japanese and Ryukyuan languages. Moreover, language families such as Turkic and Japonic clearly stand in a low-contact relationship to each other.

8. Specific morphosyntactic subsystems affected

Finally, the comparanda in the list are not restricted to specific morphosyntactic subsystems. The comparisons of derivational morphemes in Table 1 (3 to 12) do not outnumber the inflectional evidence in the etymologies (1 and 2, 13 to 19). Both finite and non-finite morphology are compared. Various categories such as actionality, diathesis, negation, aspect and tense are represented. Therefore, it appears that there are no observable imbalances across morphosyntactic subsystems.

9.3.3 Indications in support of inheritance

Besides the indications against code-copying presented in Table 3, the evidence also reveals a number of characteristics suggesting that the languages under inspection are genealogically related.

1. Globally shared grammaticalization

All but one etymology in Table 1 share the source and the target of a grammaticalization process in addition to sharing complete formal correspondence. The grammaticalization processes involved are the development of negative particles and affixes from formerly independent verbs (1 and 2), the development of a loan verb marker from a denominal verbalizer (3), the transference of actional markers from nominal to adjectival to verbal bases (4 to 7), grammaticalizations of valence and voice such as causative to passive (8 and 12), reflexive to anticausative (9) or fientive to passive (10), direct insubordination along with the development of temporal from aspectual distinctions (13 to 17) and converbialization (18 and 19). Arguably, these instances of globally shared grammaticalization provide strong support for inheritance.

A number of additional criteria reduce the likelihood of the similarities observed being due to universal factors or contact, thus strengthening the case for genealogical relatedness:

(i) Most globally shared grammaticalizations involve a cross-linguistically infrequent and randomly spread development. The proto-typically Transeurasian grammaticalization of negation occurs in less than 17 % of languages worldwide (Section 4.1). In Wohlgemuth's (2009: 157) sample, 24 % of languages worldwide use indirect insertion by way of verbalizers to accommodate for verbal borrowing. I am unaware of the cross-linguistic frequency of the transfer of verbalizers from nominal to adjectival and verbal bases, but I have argued in Section 5.8 that the phenomenon is enhanced by mixed and switched adjective typology. Worldwide, 27 % of languages have mixed encoding, while the proportion of languages exhibiting mixed and switched encoding has been estimated at 10 % (Section 3.2.6). Haspelmath (1990: 37–52) lists five different diachronic sources for the evolution of passive markers, whereby the development of passives from causatives appears to be less frequent than other strategies. Therefore, an educated guess would be that it occurs in less than 20 % of languages worldwide. The development of reflexive to anticausative and fientive to passive, however, is well-spread. In Section 6.1, I have mentioned four different strategies for developing finite function on formerly non-finite forms. Since the strategy of "direct insubordination" seems to be relatively less common than the other strategies, it is likely to be a predominant strategy in less than 25 % of the languages world-wide. Not only are there relatively few converb-prominent languages worldwide, but development of converbs from case-unmarked deverbal nouns is relatively infrequent (see Section 8.1). If we define infrequent grammaticalization processes as developments that occur in less than a third (33 %) of languages worldwide, it appears that 16 etymologies in Table 1 involve infrequent grammaticalizations.

(ii) There are multiple instances of globally shared grammaticalization across the Transeurasian languages, namely at least 18 instances in verb morphology alone.

(iii) Globally shared grammaticalization mainly involves the development from a less grammaticalized to a more grammaticalized bound morpheme. Except for the negative markers (1 and 2) and the possible verbal origin 'do, make' of the iconic suffix (5), the shared source of grammaticalization is a bound morpheme in all relevant etymologies.

(iv) Globally shared grammaticalization has spread over more than two proto-languages in all cases. There are 7 instances (i.e. 3, 6, 8, 9, 16, 17 and 18), in which the grammaticalization is globally shared across four branches. There are also 7 instances (i.e. 4, 5, 7, 13, 14, 15, 19), in which it occurs in all five branches.

(v) The specific grammaticalization pathway recurs in more than one cognate set. The specific negative grammaticalization is reflected in at least two sets (1 and 2); the transference of actional markers from denominal towards deverbal occurs in four sets (4 to 7); direct insubordination in five sets (13 to 17) and converbialization in two sets (18 and 19).

Therefore, based on the criteria relating to globally shared grammaticalization developed in Section 2.4.3.1, it is unlikely that universals or contact can account for the shared properties It follows that the case for genealogical relatedness is very strong.

2. *Categorial opacity*

Sixteen etymologies have members that are categorially opaque. In the etymologies 4 to 7 the suffix lacks morphosemantic transparency because it can derive from either nouns, adjectives or verbs. In etymologies 8 and 12, the morpheme can be interpreted as a causative or a passive marker, depending on the morphosyntactic environment in which it occurs In etymologies 13 to 17, the function of the morpheme as a nominalizer, relativizer or finite verb form can be understood only by its broader morphosyntactic context. In etymologies 18 and 19, the interpretation of the suffix as an infinitive or a converb depends on the sentence in which it occurs. This lack of categorial clarity is a strong indication of inheritance.

3. *Shared cumulation*

Nine etymologies share cumulative exponence because the morphemes under comparison simultaneously blend distinct functions together. The denominal verbalizers (3 to 7) do so in the sense that they not only derive verbs from nouns but also modify the meaning of the preceding base as manipulative, processive, inclinational and inchoative. The shared modification of meaning even affects common submeanings. The manipulative verbalizer in 3, for instance, shares distinct meanings such as 'to achieve, overcome or execute a difficult action with success on the base noun', 'to make use of the base noun' and 'to sound or feel like the base onomatopoea', all of which correlate across the individual branches. Etymologies 16 and 17 combine the derivation of a nominalizer or relativizer with resultative or perfective aspect, respectively. Etymologies 18 and 19 combine the derivation of deverbal nouns with specific modifications such as instrumental, resultative or action/state noun. Since cumulation of function is shared across the languages under comparison, the probability of inheritance further increases.

4. *Unreduced allomorphy*

Three etymologies share a particular allomorphy that is phonologically conditioned. Two etymologies (i.e. 16 and 19) involve a velar fricative segment *x that becomes a voiceless obstruent *k in continuant environment. In one etymology (18), the high front vowel *i is replaced by a zero allomorph in stems with stem-final -i. Given the tendency towards reduction of allomorphy in contact situations, this shared allomorphy is indicative of inheritance. However, the common vowel harmonic alternants of the affixes in all individual languages, except

Japanese, do not necessarily imply genealogical relatedness. We cannot exclude the possibility that vowel harmony may be a structural feature that diffused across the Transeurasian languages. Therefore, unreduced vowel harmonic allomorphy does not allow us to distinguish between borrowing and inheritance in this case.

5. *Multiple comparative setting*

Twelve etymologies (i.e. 4 to 9, 11, 13 to 16, 18 and 19), have members in each of the five individual branches of the Transeurasian family. In a contact scenario, the morphemes would have needed to cross four linguistic boundaries. Not only is the likelihood of a single verb morpheme progressing from one contact language into the other, repeatedly for four times, very low but the probability of as many as fourteen verb morphemes following the same pathway is close to zero. The observation that the corresponding morphemes are simultaneously attested in five branches strongly favors an internal explanation of the similarities observed.

6. *Missing intermediaries*

The absence of comparable morphemes in certain branches may be relevant for the distinction between inheritance and borrowing. Three etymologies (i.e 3, 10 and 17) lack a Korean member in spite of the presence of a Japanese member. Given the geographical and historical isolation of Japan, it is difficult to explain, for instance, how Tungusic and Japanese managed to transfer the manipulative verbalizer *-lA without a Korean intermediary. The distribution of the gaps in the etymologies can thus be taken as an indication of genealogical relatedness. Moreover, the gap for the Turkic inclinational verbalizer (6) may be relevant as well. Verbalizers are usually borrowed over loan verbs hosting the particular morpheme. Within a borrowing scenario, we would thus need to explain why certain derived verbs, such as inchoatives and processives would have been so extensively borrowed between Turkic and Mongolic (and the other Transeurasian languages), while verbs derived with inclinational suffixes remained totally immune from borrowing.

In sum, for the common verb morphemes of the Transeurasian languages, none of the indications of code-copying are present, whereas the data exhibit a number of characteristics suggesting that the languages under inspection are genealogically related. It is therefore safer to identify the shared verb morphemes listed in Table 1 as cognates than to consider them as copies.

9.4 Why is the evidence not consistent with the Indo-European model?

9.4.1 Inconsistency

Applying the same historical comparative method that led to the establishment of the Indo-European family to the Transeurasian languages, we find lexical, phonological and morphological evidence in support of inheritance. Nevertheless, we must admit that the evidence in support of the relatedness of the Transeurasian languages is not as overwhelming as the Indo-European evidence. Both Indo-European and Transeurasian languages have basic vocabulary in common (Chapter 3, Robbeets 2004a), but in Indo-European there are simply more items. Both Indo-European and Transeurasian languages display regular correspondences for consonants and vowels whereby the overall inventories are symmetrical and natural (Chapter 3, Robbeets 2005). However, the correspondences in Indo-European are more rigourous. Both Indo-European and Transeurasian languages have paradigmatic verb morphology in common in that the cognates reflect an internally ordered organization, share certain idiosyncrasies and display external relations of grammatical patterning (see Section 9.1.5). However, contrary to what is the case for the Indo-European languages, the morphosyntactic subsystems corresponding between the Transeurasian languages do not form a closed set of form slots with positions defined by intersections of category dimensions, that can be defined independently from the forms filling them. Moreover, the Transeurasian languages have a smaller proportion of inflectional morphology in common, share far fewer idiosyncrasies and display less multidimensional paradigmaticity than is the case for Indo-European. Understandably, this situation leads critics such as Janhunen (2014: 3) to reject the affiliation hypothesis of the Transeurasian languages: "In any case, to prove the relatedness of languages we would need clearcut inflectional paradigms in the core parts of nominal and verbal morphology, like those used in the classic Indo-European comparisons (Bopp 1816)." However, the nature and the characteristics of the Indo-European languages provide a very specific set of circumstances, different from languages outside Europe. The different nature of the evidence cannot be used as an argument against genealogical affiliation because it is a consequence of the typological and chronological differences between both language families.

9.4.2 Typological differences

As far as relevant typological differences are concerned, the Transeurasian languages differ from the Indo-European languages in that (i) they lack or "recycle" person-number agreement on the verb, (ii) display a strong tendency of direct insubordination and (iii) belong to the agglutinative type.

(i) Many Transeurasian languages tend to "recycle" person-number agreement on the verb: they display cycles of grammaticalization, whereby subject pronouns can be postposed for discourse-pragmatic reasons and then develop into agreement suffixes on the verb, eventually replacing earlier sets of agreement markers. This recycling is especially visible in languages to the north, west and center of the Transeurasian region, such as in most Turkic, Mongolic and Tungusic languages. In the Mongolic languages, the grammaticalization of pronouns is relatively recent, as is shown by the absence of verb agreement in Middle Mongolian in contrast to contemporary Mongolic languages. Languages to the south and the east, such as Manchu, Japanese and Korean, which are intensively influenced by Chinese, lack person-number agreement on the verb. The absence of this category can be explained by the fact that – due to frequential copying from Chinese – these languages are pro-drop in the sense that subject pronouns may be omitted when they are pragmatically inferable. The lack of obligatory expression of subject pronouns prevents the expected grammaticalization from pronouns to person-number markers (Bisang 2004: 133–134; 2008: 33; 2014). In contrast, due to obligatory marking of person-number on the verb and the fusional nature of morphology, the Indo-European paradigms are shaped in a different way: they form closed systems with positions defined by intersections of the person-number agreement category and other categories. As a result of the secondary development or lack of person-number agreement on the verb, the Transeurasian languages cannot be expected to reflect such a closed system with person-number and category intersections.

(ii) The observation that verb agreement markers have developed from person pronouns, projects the nature of matching person-number endings back to the lexical level. Similarly, finite inflectional forms can be derived from nonfinite derivational forms by way of a grammaticalization process labeled "direct insubordination" in Chapter 7. Contrary to the Indo-European languages, where the phenomenon is much weaker, the Transeurasian languages display a strong tendency for direct insubordination. This tendency projects the nature of finite inflectional evidence back to the derivational level. It follows that the paradigmatic evidence in the Transeurasian languages will have a strong derivational character, as compared to the mainly inflectional nature of the Indo-European evidence.

(iii) The Transeurasian languages are of the agglutinative type, while Indo-European languages tend to be more fusional. Morphological elements, especially suffixes, tend to be unstressed and are therefore liable to undergo phonological reduction, which eventually leads to complete loss. As a result of the fusion of form, phonemes that have been subject to loss are more likely to leave a trace in the preceding segment in Indo-European, while they tend to disappear completely in Transeurasian. In this sense, morphological attrition is often more drastic in the Transeurasian languages than in more fusional languages like Indo-European, where lost morphemes are often recoverable in word stems. The Proto-Germanic causative *-j-, which was added to the ablaut stem (e.g. *sat- from *sit- 'sit') of strong verbs, for instance, eroded phonologically, but left a trace in the umlaut of verb stems such as German *setzen* 'put'. By contrast, the phonology of suffixes is not expected to influence the shape of the preceding verb root in the Transeurasian languages. Indeed, the phenomenon of vowel harmony in the Transeurasian languages typically operates in the other direction, i.e. the quality of the suffix vowel is determined by the vocalism of the root. Due to the agglutinative character and the direction of vowel harmony, a morpheme that gets lost is no longer traceable, fused with preceding elements. Therefore, we expect to find fewer shared formational irregularities in the forms filling the Transeurasian verb paradigm.

Moreover, as a result of the fusion of form and function in the Indo-European languages, many morphemes are cumulative in the sense of having an unanalyzable form that simultaneously blends several distinct morphosyntactic functions. Even if internal reconstruction seems to suggest that the first person present indicative ending pIE *-mi in *$h_1$es-mi 'I am' should be anayzed as a going back to a first person singular *-m and a present tense *-i (Joseph 2004: 1665), the ancestral suffix *-mi simultaneously expressed present, indicative, first person and singular meaning. By contrast, in the Transeurasian languages, there is a one-to-one relationship between the morpheme and its meaning whereby the morphemes are attached linearly. Complex meanings are thus expressed by suffix strings rather than by single suffixes. Given the extractability of compound morphemes, the grammatical patterning between related paradigms such as between indicative present and indicative past or between indicative, subjunctive and imperative is transparent in the Transeurasian languages, whereas multidimensional paradigmaticity is more rigorous in Indo-European due to use of portmanteau suffixes.

9.4.3 Chronological differences

Whereas the unity of Indo-European is usually estimated at a time-depth of ca. 4000 BC (Gimbutas 1985, Mallory 1996), the unity of Transeurasian has been correlated with the appearance of Neolithic culture in prehistoric Manchuria between 5000 and 6000 BC (see Section 1.2.3). In addition, whereas the estimated time depth is at least one millennium earlier, the written sources for the Transeurasian languages are roughly more than one millennium younger than those for Indo-

European: The written records go back to ca. 1000 B.C. for Sanskrit, ca. 800 B.C. for Homeric Greek, ca. 500 B.C. for Latin, ca. 400 A.D. for Gothic and ca. 800 A.D. for Old Church Slavonic, but the first unambiguous and fully accessible attestations for Japanese go back to ca. 700 A.D., for Korean to ca. 1400 A.D., for Tungusic to ca. 1600 A.D., for Mongolic to ca. 1200 A.D. and for Turkic to ca. 700 A.D.

Given this time gap of at least two millennia, we would expect more cognate attrition in the lexicon, less rigorous sound correspondences and less basic vocabulary, which is indeed the case for Transeurasian reconstruction. Another consequence of this time gap is the diachronic behavior of verb morphology. Bybee (1985) finds that verb affixes with high semantic content and relevance, such as actional and diathetical suffixes, are expected to lexicalize easily, while inflectional categories, such as tense, mood and agreement are not. When sufficient time has lapsed, replacement will lead to the complete loss of inflectional markers, while lexicalized derivation remains unaffected (see Section 5.1). In this sense, derivation is more resistant to replacement and loss, which might explain why derivational morphology is genealogically more stable than inflectional morphology when reconstructing at profound time depths.

In the passage from Latin to the Romance languages, the Latin future marker in Lat. *canta-bimus* 'we will sing', for instance, was lost and replaced by a new periphrastic expression Lat. *cantare habemus* (> *cantarabémus* > *cantarémus*) 'we have to sing', which developed into the French future marker Fr. *chanterons* 'we will sing'. After being replaced, the old future marker did not leave a single trace in the contemporary languages. The Latin inchoative suffix *-esc-* / *-isc-* used in *alb-us* 'white' → *alb-esc-o* 'to become white', however, also lost its productivity as Latin developed into the modern Romance languages, but having fossilized in some stems of certain Romance verbs, such as in Italian *fini-sc-o* 'I finnish' and in French *nous fini-ss-ons* 'we finish' (Greenberg 1991: 311), it can still be recovered from contemporary Romance. At profound time depths, derivation is thus expected to yield better evidence than inflection, simply because these forms remain petrified in the language for a longer period of time. This expectation is in accordance with the categories reconstructed for the Transeurasian languages.

In sum, even if there is a certain inconsistency between Indo-European and Transeurasian verb paradigms and their evidentiary value, in both families common morphology is patterned in such a way that the entirety is more telling than the sum of the individual items. The particular circumstances encountered within Indo-European are often taken as standards of historical comparative research, but shifting our attention to the agglutinating languages of Transeurasia, we should adjust our expectations concerning the nature of the correlations. Nevertheless, the present study has shown that in spite of typological and chronological differences, it remains possible to assess the Transeurasian evidence in terms of formal, functional, combinational, typological and paradigmatic behaviour.

9.5 Conclusion: a family picture through morphology

Although the genealogical relationship between Japanese and the Transeurasian languages has been a source of contention for nearly two centuries, scholars seem to agree that paradigmatic morphology could substantially help to prove relatedness. Starting from this consensus and given the relative stability of verb morphology in particular, I have investigated the presence of common verb morphology in the Transeurasian languages. In addition to examining whether the Transeurasian languages indeed have morphological items in common, I have evaluated whether the correlations can be characterized as "paradigmatic" and whether they could have resulted from non-genealogical determinants such as chance, universals or borrowing. For this purpose, I have used the traditional comparative method as a basic tool. However, I have supplemented classical form-function comparisons by integrating combinational properties and diachronic typology, including grammaticalization theory, into the argumentation. In this way, I have identified 19 verb suffixes, displaying formal, functional, combinational, typological and paradigmatic correlations. Given the number and the nature of the similarities, I was able to rule out chance and universal principles in linguistic structuring rather easily. The crux of the matter, however, is whether all shared forms are generated by borrowing, or are whether some of them are residues of inheritance. To this end, I have developed 14 guidelines for distinguishing between the effects of contact and inheritance in shared morphology. I have found that especially for agglutinative languages, grammaticalization theory may provide a powerful tool to distinguish between copies and cognates in bound morphology. Applying these criteria to the verb morphology shared by the Transeurasian languages, I have argued that the common morphology can best be accounted for by inheritance from a common ancestor. Certainly, the morphological evidence in the agglutinative Transeurasian languages does not have the same degree of conclusiveness as in fusional languages such as Indo-European languages, where common inflectional paradigms and shared ideosyncrasies afford particularly fruitful comparisons. Nevertheless, in consideration of the time-depth and typological nature of the Transeurasian family and in combination with previously established lexical evidence, the evidence from verb morphology is sufficient to conclude that the Transeurasian languages are indeed genealogically related.

As illustrated in Figure 1, the branching of the family proposed on the basis of shared innovations in phonology and vocabulary (Section 1.2.3) appears to be corroborated by shared innovations in verb morphology. The first split between Koreo-Japanic on the one hand and Altaic on the other is confirmed by shared innovations in the Altaic branch, such as the replacement of the original negative pTEA *ana- by an innovative negative auxiliary pA *ə- (etymology 1 in Table 1). Moreover, it is supported by common innovations in Koreo-Japanic, such as the common development of the causative pKJ *-ki- towards the passive end of the grammaticalization cline (12), the reduction of *-xA ~ *-kA allomorphy of the resultative nominalizer to a single voiceless stop allomorph (16) and the shared grammaticalization with copula pKJ *wo- in clausal (ad)nominalizations (13 to 15) or with the copula pKJ *a- in the converb construction pKJ *a-ku (19).

The second split between Turkic on the one hand and Tunguso-Mongolic on the other is supported by shared innovations in Tunguso-Mongolic, such as the common specialization of the nominalizer pTgMo*-mA for converbial and finite use (14). Moreover, it is supported by innovations in Turkic, such as the shared innovation of the perfective adnominal pTEA *-xA to perfective non-past (16) and the development of palatal vowel harmony in the common ancestor of Chuvash and Old Turkic.

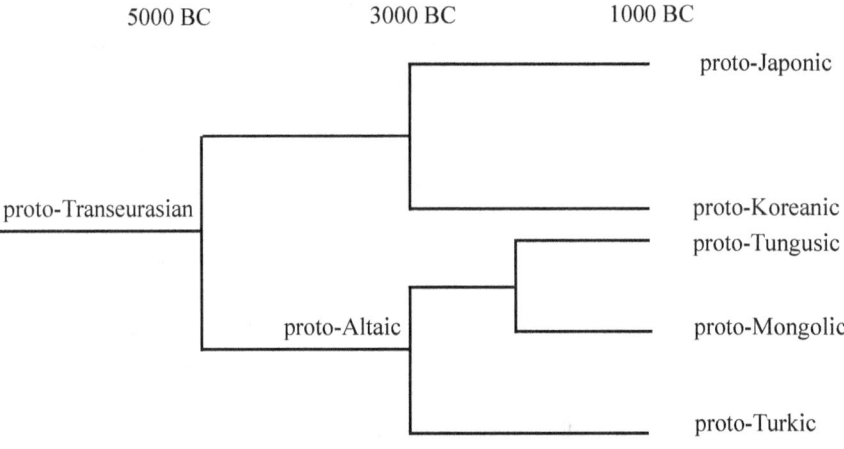

Figure 1. Confirmation of the classification of the Transeurasian family proposed in Chapter 1

Hence, Japanese indeed shares verb morphology that can be characterized as paradigmatic with the Transeurasian languages. It is linguistically more reasonable to attribute these commonalities to inheritance than to other factors such as chance, universals or borrowing.

Abbreviations

a) Linguistic forms

ABL	ablative	INCH	inchoative
ACC	accusative	INDEF	indefinite
ACT	active	INDEP	independent
adj.	adjective	INST	instrumental
ADN	adnominal	INT	intensive
adv.	adverb	intr.	intransitive
ADV	adverbializer	INF	infinitive
AL	alienable possession	INFR	inferential
ANTICAUS	anticausative	IPFV	imperfective
ANTIPASS	antipassive	ITER	iterative
CAUS	causative	LAT	lative
CL	classifier	LOC	locative
CLT	clitic	MOD	modulator
COND	conditional	n.	noun
CONV	converb	N	noun phrase
COOR	coordinative	NEG	negative
COM	comitative	NML	nominalizer
CONC	concessive	NOM	nominative
COP	copula	NFUT	nonfuture
DAT	dative	OBL	oblique
DEB	debitive	OPT	optative
DEF	definite	PASS	passive
DEM	demonstrative	PCP	participle
DEP	dependent	PERF	perfect
DIM	diminutive	PERM	permissive
DIR	directive	PERS	person agreement
DUR	durative	PFV	perfective
DV	defective verb	PL	plural
EMO	emotive	PLUPERF	pluperfect
ENCL	enclitic	POSS	possessive
EQT	equative	POST	postposition
ERG	ergative	POT	potentialis
EX	exclusive	PREF	prefix
FIN	finite	PREP	preposition
FOC	focus	PRES	presumptive
GEN	genitive	PROC	processive
HAB	habitual	PROG	progressive
HON	honorific	PROH	prohibitive
HORT	hortative	PROJ	projective
HUM	humble	PROL	prolative
IMP	imperative	PROP	proprietive
IN	inclusive	PRS	present
INCL	inclination	PST	past

PT	particle	SMLF	semelfactive
Q	question marker	SUBJ	subjunctive
REL	relative	SUF	suffix
REFL	reflexive	SUSP	suspective
REP	repetitive	TENT	tentative
RES	resultative	TOP	topic
RETR	retrospective	tr.	transitive
RTR	retracted tongue root	VBL	verbalizer
SG	singular	VOC	vocative

b) Symbols

**	grammatically incorrect	>	develops into
*	reconstruction	>>	is borrowed as
†	historically attested but interpretation remains insecure	→	is derived as
		~	alternates with

c) Languages

A	Ainu	Hi.	Hirara
Alt.	Altai Turkic	Hung.	Hungarian
Av.	Avestan	J	(contemporary, standard
Az.	Azerbaijanian		Tokyo) Japanese
Balk.	Balkar	Jur.	Jurchen
Bao.	Bao'an	K	(contemporary, standard
Bash.	Bashkir		Seoul) Korean
Bur.	Buriat	Kag.	Kagoshima
Ch.	Chinese	Kalm.	Kalmuk
Chag.	Chaghatai	Kang.	Kangwŏndo
Che.	Chejudo	Karakh.	Karakhanide (Old Turkic)
Chŏng.	Chŏngsangdo	Kas.	Kazan (Idil)
Chu.	Chuvash	Kaz.	Kazakh
CIA	Copper Island Aleut	KBalk.	Karachay-Balkar
CMo.	Central Mongolic	Khal.	Khalkha
Cum.	Cuman	Khak.	Khakas
Dag.	Dagur	Kirg.	Kirghiz
Dolg.	Dolgan	KKalp.	Kara-Kalpak
Dong.	Dongxiang (Santa)	Kog.	Koguryŏ
D	Dyirbal	Krm.	Karaim
Eng.	English	Ksang.	Kyŏngsangdo
EOJ	Eastern Old Japanese	Kum.	Kumyk
Evk.	Evenki (Tungus)	Kyo.	Kyoto
Gag.	Gagauz	Lat.	Latin
Gil.	Gilyak (Nivhk)	LMG	Late Middle German
Ham.	Hamgyŏngdo	Ma.	Manchu
Hat.	Hateruma	Mi.	Miyako

MCh.	Middle Chinese	pKMo	proto-Khitano-Mongolic
MJ	Middle Japanese	pMo	proto-Mongolic
MK	Middle Korean	pN	proto-Nostratic
MMo.	Middle Mongolian	pNC	proto-Niger-Congo
Mgr.	Monguor	pNS	proto-Nilo-Saharan
MHG	Middle High German	pOgh	proto-Oghuric
Mo.	Mongolian	pR	proto-Ryukyuan
Mod. J	Modern Japanese	pSam	proto-Samoyedic
Mogh.	Moghol	pTEA	proto-Transeurasian
MTk.	Middle Turkic	pTg	proto-Tungusic
Na.	Nanai (Goldi, Hezhe)	pTgMo	proto-Tunguso-Mongolic
Neg.	Negidal	pTk	proto-Turkic
NHG	New High German	pUr	proto-Uralic
Nog.	Noghay	R	Ryukyuan
OCh.	Old Chinese	Rus.	Russian
OCS	Old Church Slavonic	Sal.	Salar (Uighur)
Oir.	Oirat	Sd.	Shodon
OE	Old English	SJ	Sino-Japanese
OHG	Old High German	SK	Sino-Korean
OJ	Old Japanese	Skt.	Sanskrit
Olch.	Olcha (Ulcha, Ulchi, Olchi)	Sol.	Solon
OR	Old Russian	Sr.	Shuri
Ordos	Ordos	SUig.	Sary-Uighur
Oroch	Oroch	SYug.	Shira-Yughur
Orok	Orok (Uilta, J Uiruta)	Tat.	(Volga) Tatar
Osm.	Osmanli	TEA	Transeurasian
OTk.	Old Turkic	Tk.	Turkish
OUigh.	Old Uighur	Tkm.	Turkmenian
Oyr.	Oyrot (Mountain Altai Turkic)	Tof.	Tofalar
pA	proto-Altaic	Ud.	Udehe (Ude, Udege)
pC	proto-Chadic	Uig.	Uighur
pD	proto-Dravidian	Uzb.	Uzbek
pGerm	proto-Germanic	WMo.	Written Mongolian
pIE	proto-Indo-European	WOJ	Western Old Japanese
pJ	proto-Japonic	WOT	Western Old Turkic
pJap	proto-Japanic	Ya.	Yaeyama
pK	proto-Koreanic	Yak.	Yakut
pKart.	proto-Kartvelian	Yo.	Yonaguni
pKJ	proto-Koreo-Japanic		

c) Languages

Chinese
HHS	Houhanshu (Fan 1965)
SKC	San-kuo chih (Ch'en 1959)

Japanese
BS	753 Bussoku seki no uta
FK	ca. 737 Fudoki kayō
K	712 Kojiki
MYS	ca. 759 Man'yōshū
NK	720 Nihonshoki kayō

Korean

Kok	1449 Welin chenkang ci kok
Kumkang	1464 Kumkang panya phalamil kyeng enhay
Nam	1482 Nammyeng-chen kyeysong enhay
No	1517 Nokeltay
Pak	1517 Pak thongsa enhay
Pep	1463 Pephwa = Myopep yenhwa-kyeng enhay 1–7
Samkang	1481 Samkang hayngsil-to
Sek	1447 Sekpo sangcel
Sohak	1586 Sohak enhay
Twu-cip	1608 Twuchang cipyo enhay
Twusi	1481 Twusi enhay
Twusi-cwung	1632 Twusi enhay cwung kan
Wel	1459 Welin sekpo
Yong	1445 Yongpi echen ka

Manchu

NSB	Nisan samani bithe [The Tale of the Nisan Shamaness] (Volkova 1961)
QW	Qing we n qi me ng [Principles of Manchu Reading and Writing] (Zakharov 1879)
SK	Sidi Kur [The Bewitched Corpse] (Lebedeva & Gorelova 1994)

Mongolic

Altan tobči	ca. 1600 Altan tobči [Golden Summary] (Vietze & Lubsang 1992)
HY	1389 Hua-Yi Yiyu (Lewicki 1949)
IM	Ibnü-Mühenna lûgati (Battal 1934)
Muq.	Muqaddimat al-Adab Mongolian version (Poppe 1938)
SH	1241 Mongyol-un niyuca tobčiyan [The Secret History of the Mongols] (Pelliot 1949)

Turkic

DLT	Dīvān Luġāti 't-Turk [Compendium of the Turkic Dialects] by Mahmūd al-Kāšyarī (Dankoff & Kelly 1982–1985)
KP	Kalyānamkara ve Papāmkara (Hamilton et al. 1998)
TT I-VI	Various editions of Buddhist Uighur texts specified in Erdal (1991: 12)
VATEC	Vorislamische Alttürkische Texte: Elektronisches Corpus (Nevskaya et al. 2004)

References

Ahn, Sung-Mo. 2010. The emergence of rice agriculture in Korea: Archaeobotanical perspectives. *Archaeological and Anthropological Sciences* 2: 89–98.
Aikhenvald, Alexandra Y. 2007 [1985]. Typological distinctions in word-formation. In Timothy Shopen (ed.), *Language Typology and Syntactic Description (Grammatical Categories and the Lexicon 3)*, 1–65. Cambridge: Cambridge University Press.
Aikhenvald, Alexandra Y. 2002. *Language Contact in Amazonia*. Oxford: Oxford University Press.
Aikhenvald, Alexandra Y. 2007. Grammars in contact: A cross-linguistic perspective. In Alexandra Y. Aikhenvald & Robert M. W. Dixon (eds.), *Grammars in Contact: A Cross-Linguistic Typology* (Explorations in Linguistic Typology 4), 1–66. Oxford: Oxford University Press.
Aikhenvald, Alexandra Y. 2011a. Word-class changing derivations in a typological perspective. In Alexandra Y. Aikhenvald & Robert M. W. Dixon (eds.), *Language at Large: Essays on Syntax and Semantics*, 221–289. Leiden: Brill.
Aikhenvald, Alexandra Y. 2011b. Causatives which do not cause: On non-valency-increasing effects of valency-increasing derivations. In Alexandra Aikhenvald & Bob Dixon (eds.), *Language at Large: Essays on Syntax and Semantics*, 86–142. Leiden: Brill.
Aikhenvald, Alexandra Y. & Robert. M. W. Dixon (eds.) 2001. *Areal Diffusion and Genetic Inheritance: Problems in Comparative Linguistics*. Oxford: Oxford University Press.
Alpatov, Vladimir M. & Vera I. Podlesskaya. 1995. Converbs in Japanese. In Martin Haspelmath & Ekkehard König (eds.), *Converbs in Cross-Linguistic Perspective: Structure and Meaning of Adverbial Verb Forms – Adverbial Participles, Gerunds* (Empirical Approaches to Language Typology 13), 465–485. Berlin & New York: Mouton de Gruyter.
Ameka, Felix K. 2007. Grammars in contact in the Volta Basin (West Africa): On contact-induced grammatical change in Likpe. In Alexandra Y. Aikhenvald & Robert M. W. Dixon (eds.), *Grammars in Contact: A Cross-Linguistic Typology* (Explorations in Linguistic Typology 4), 114–142. Oxford: Oxford University Press.
Andersen, Stephen R. 1992. *A-Morphous Morphology*. Cambridge: Cambridge University Press.
Andreev, I. A. & I. P. Pavlov. 1957. *Morphologija* [Morphology] (Materialy po grammatike čuvašskogo jazyka 1). Čeboksary: Čuvašskoe gosudarstvennoe izdatel'stvo.
Antonov, Anton. 2007. *Le rôle des suffixes nominaux en /+rV/ dans l'expression du lieu et de la direction en japonais et l'hypothèse de leur origine "altaïque"*. Paris: Institut National des Langues et Civilisations Orientales PhD dissertation.
Anttila, Raimo. 1989. *Historical and Comparative Linguistics*. Amsterdam: Benjamins.
Aronoff, Mark. 1994. *Morphology by Itself: Stems and Inflectional Classes*. Cambridge: MIT Press.
Asato, Susumu & Naomi Doi. 1999. *Okinawajin wa doko kara kita ka: Ryūkyū=Okinawajin no kigen to seiritsu* [Where did the Okinawans come from? The origins and formation of the Ryukyuans = Okinawans]. Naha: Bōdaa Inku.
Auwera, Johan van der. 2009. The Jespersen cycles. In Elly van Gelderen (ed.), *Cyclical Change* (Linguistics today 146), 35–71. Amsterdam: John Benjamins.
Auwera, Johan van der. 2010. On the diachrony of negation. In Laurence R. Horn (ed.), *The Expression of Negation*, 73–101. Berlin & New York: Mouton de Gruyter.
Avrorin, Valentin Aleksandrovič. 1959. *Grammatika Nanajskogo jazyka. Fonetičeskoe vvedenie i morfologija imennych častej reči* [Grammar of Nanai. Phonetics and Nominal Morphology]. Moscow: Nauk.

Avrorin, Valentin Aleksandrovič. 1961. *Grammatika Nanajskogo jazyka. Morfologija glagol'nych i narečnych častej reči, meždometij, služevnych slov i castišč* [Grammar of Nanai. Verbal Morphology]. Moscow: Nauk.
Avrorin, Valentin Aleksandrovič. 1963. *O klassifikacii tunguso-man'čžurskih jazykov* [On the Classification of the Manchu-Tungusic Languages]. Moscow: Nauka.
Backhouse, Anthony E. 1984. Have all the adjectives gone? *Lingua* 62: 169–186.
Baerman, Matthew & Greville G. Corbett. 2010. Introduction. Defectiveness: Typology and diachrony. In Matthew Baerman, Greville G. Corbett & Dunstan Brown (eds.), *Defective Paradigms: Missing Forms and What They Tell Us*, 1–18. Oxford: Oxford University Press.
Bakker, Dik & Ewald Hekking. 2012. Constraints on morphological borrowing: Evidence from Latin America. In Lars Johanson & Martine Robbeets (eds.), *Copies Versus Cognates in Bound Morphology* (Brill's Studies in Language, Cognition and Culture 2), 187–219. Leiden: Brill.
Bakker, Peter. 1997. *A language of our own: The Genesis of Michif, the Mixed Cree-French Language of the Canadian Métis*. New York: Oxford University Press.
Bakker, Peter & Yaron Matras (eds.). 2003. *The Mixed Language Debate: Theoretical and Empirical Advances*. Berlin & New York: Mouton de Gruyter.
Bang, Willy. 1923. Das negative Verbum der Türksprachen. *Sitzungsberichte der Preussischen Akademie der Wissenschaften* 17: 114–131.
Barnes, Gina Lee. 1993. *The Rise of Civilization in East Asia: The Archaeology of China, Korea and Japan*. London: Thames and Hudson.
Baskakov, Nikolaj A. 1970. Areal'naja konsolidacija drevnejših narečij I genetičeskoe rodstvo altajskich jazykov [Areal consolidation of old dialects and genealogical affiliation of Altaic languages]. *Voprosy jazykoznanija* 4. 43–53.
Baskakov, Nikolaj A. 1974. On the common origin of the categories of person and personal possession in the Altaic Languages. In Ligeti, Louis (ed.), *Researches in Altaic Languages: Papers Read at the 14th Meeting of the Permanent International Altaistic Conference held in Szeged, August 22–28, 1971*, 7–13. Budapest: Kiadó.
Baskakov, Nikolaj A. 1981. *Altaiskaja sem'ja jazykov i ee izučenie*. Moscow: Nauk.
Battal, Aptullah. 1934. *Ibnü-Mühenna lûgati. Istanbul nüshasının türkçe bölüğünün endeksidir*. Istanbul: Türk Dili Tetkik Cemiyeti.
Bauer, Laurie. 1997. Evaluative morphology: A search for universals. *Studies in Language* 21: 533–575.
Baxter, William &, Laurent Sagart. (n.d.). Baxter-Sagart Old Chinese reconstruction (Version 1.00). http://crlao.ehess.fr/document.php?id=1217 (accessed 10 December 2011).
Beckwith, Christopher. 2004. *Koguryo: The Language of Japan's Continental Relatives*. Leiden: Brill.
Beekes, Robert S. P. 1995. *Comparative Indo-European Linguistics: An Introduction*. Amsterdam: John Benjamins.
Bellwood, Peter. 2005a. *First Farmers: The Origins of Agricultural Societies*. Malden: Blackwell.
Bellwood, Peter. 2005b. Examining the farming language dispersal hypothesis in the East Asian context. In Laurent Sagart, Roger Blench & Alicia Sanches-Mazas (eds.), *The Peopling of East Asia: Putting Together Archaeology, Linguistics and Genetics*, 17–30. Oxford: Routledge Curzon.
Bellwood, Peter. 2011. *First Migrants: Ancient Migration in Global Perspective*. Malden: Blackwell.

Bellwood, Peter & Collin Renfrew (eds.). 2002. *Examining the Farming/Language Dispersal Hypothesis*. Cambridge: McDonald Institute for Archaeological Research.
Bentley, John. 1998. A new look at Paekche and Korean: Data from *Nihon Shoki*. In Park, Byung-Soo & James Hye Sook Yoon (eds.), *Selected Papers from the 11th International Conference on Korean Linguistics*, 318–325. Seoul: International Circle of Korean Linguistics.
Bentley, John R. 2001. *A Descriptive Grammar of Early Old Japanese Prose* (Brill's Japanese Studies Library 15). Leiden: Brill.
Bentley, John. 2008. *A Linguistic History of the Forgotten Islands: A Reconstruction of the Proto-Language of the Southern Ryūkyūs* (Languages of Asia 7). Folkestone: Global Oriental.
Benzing, Johannes. 1943. *Kleine Einführung in die Tschuwaschische Sprache*. Berlin: Verlagsanstalt Otto Stollberg.
Benzing, Johannes. 1955a. Die tungusischen Sprachen: Versuch einer vergleichenden Grammatik. *Abhandlungen der geistes- und sozialwissenschaftlichen Klasse* 11. 949–1099.
Benzing, Johannes. 1955b. *Lamutische Grammatik mit Bibliographie, Sprachproben und Glossar*. Wiesbaden: Otto Harrassowitz.
Benzing, Johannes. 1959. Das Tschuwaschische. In Jean Deny, Kaare Grönbech, Helmuth Scheel & Zeki Velidi Togan (eds.), *Philologiae Turcicae Fundamenta. Tomus Primus*, 695–751. Wiesbaden: Steiner.
Bese, Lajos. 1974. On the etymology of prohibition and negation in Mongolian. *Central Asiatic Journal* 18: 5–8.
Bickel, Balthasar & Johanna Nichols. 2007. Inflectional morphology. In Timothy Shopen (ed.), *Language typology and syntactic description (Grammatical Categories and the Lexicon 3)*, 169–240. Cambridge: Cambridge University Press.
Binnick, Robert. 1987. On the Classification of the Mongolian Languages. *Central Asiatic Journal* 31: 178–195.
Bisang, Walter. 1995. Verb serialization and converbs: Differences and similarities. In Haspelmath, Martin & Ekkehard König (eds.), *Converbs in Cross-Linguistic Perspective: Structure and Meaning of Adverbial Verb Forms – Adverbial Participles, Gerunds* (Empirical Approaches to Language Typology 13), 137–88. Berlin & New York: Mouton de Gruyter.
Bisang, Walter. 1996. Areal typology and grammaticalization: Processes of grammaticalization based on nouns and verbs in East and Mainland South East Asian languages. *Studies in Language* 20 (3): 519–597.
Bisang, Walter. 1998. Structural similarities of clause combining in Turkic, Mongolian, Manchu-Tungusic and Japanese: A typological alternative to the hypothesis of a genetic relationship. In Lars Johanson (ed.), *The Mainz Meeting: Proceedings of the Seventh International Conference on Turkish Linguistics*, 199–223. Wiesbaden: Harrasowitz.
Bisang, Walter. 2001. Finite vs. non finite languages. In Martin Haspelmath, Ekkehard König, Wulf Oesterreicher & Wolfgang Raible (eds.), *Language Typology and Language Universals*, (Handbücher zur Sprach- und Kommunikationswissenschaft 2), 1400–1413. Berlin & New York: Mouton de Gruyter.
Bisang, Walter. 2004. Grammaticalization without coevolution of form and meaning: The case of tense-aspect-modality in East and Mainland Southeast Asia. In Walter Bisang, Nikolaus Himmelmann & Björn Wiemer (eds.), *What Makes Grammaticalization? A Look from Its Fringes and Its Components*, 109–138. Berlin & New York: Mouton de Gruyter.
Bisang, Walter. 2006. Contact-induced convergence: Typology and areality. In Keith Brown (ed.), *Encyclopedia of Language and Linguistics*, vol. 3, 88–101. Oxford: Elsevier.

Bisang, Walter. 2008. Grammaticalization and the areal factor: The perspective of East and mainland Southeast Asian languages. In Maria Jose Lopez-Couso & Elena Seoane (eds.), *Proceedings of New Reflections on Grammaticalization 3*, 15–35. Amsterdam & Philadelphia: John Benjamins.

Bisang, Walter. 2014. On the strength of morphological paradigms: A historical account of radical pro-drop. In Martine Robbeets & Walter Bisang (eds.), *Paradigm Change: In the Transeurasian Languages and Beyond* (Studies in Language Companion Series 161), 23–60. Amsterdam: Benjamins.

Bisang, Walter. Forthcoming. Finiteness, nominalization and information structure: Convergence and divergence.

Blažek, Václav. 2009. Koguryo and Altaic: On the role of Koguryo and other Old Korean idioms in the Altaic etymology. *Journal of Philology* 31. *Ural-Altaic Studies* 1: 13–25.

Blench, Roger. 2008. Stratification in the peopling of China: How far does the linguistic evidence match genetics and archaeology? In Alicia Sanchez-Mazas, Roger Blench, Malcolm D. Ross & Marie Lin (eds.), *Past Human Migrations in East Asia: Matching Archaeology, Linguistics and Genetics* (Routledge Studies in the Early History of Languages 5), 105–132. London: Routledge.

Boas, Franz. 1917. Introductory. *International Journal of American Linguistics* 1 (1): 1–8.

Boas, Franz. 1938. *General Anthropology*. Madison: United States Armed Forces Institute.

Boer, Elisabeth de. 2005. *The Historical Development of Japanese Pitch Accent*. Leiden: Leiden University Ph.D. dissertation.

Boer, Elisabeth de. 2010. *The Historical Development of Japanese Tone: I. From Proto-Japanese to the Modern Dialects, II. The Introduction and Adaptation of the Middle Chinese Tones in Japan* (Veröffentlichungen des Ostasien-Instituts der Ruhr-Universität Bochum 59). Wiesbaden: Harrassowitz.

Boller, Anton. 1857. Nachweis, daß das Japanische zum ural-altaischen Stämme gehört. *Sitzungsberichte der philosophisch-historischen Classe der Kaiserlichen Akademie der Wissenschaften* 33: 393–481.

Booij, Geert. 1997. Autonomous morphology and paradigmatic relations. In Geert Booij & Jaap van Marle (eds.), *Yearbook of Morphology 1996,* 35–53. Dordrecht: Kluwer Academic Publishers.

Bopp, Franz. 1816. *Über das Conjugationssystem der Sanskrit-Sprache, in Vergleichung mit jenem der griechischen, lateinischen, persischen und germanischen Sprache, Herausgegeben und mit Vorerinnerungen begleitet von Dr. K. J. Windischmann*. Frankfurt am Main: Andreäische Buchhandlung.

Borg, Alexander. 1994. Some evolutionary parallels and divergencies in Cypriot Arabic and Maltese. *Mediterranean Language Review* 8: 41–67.

Brace, Charles Loring & Masafumi Nagai. 1982. Japanese tooth size: Past and present. *American Journal of Physical Anthropology* 59: 399–411.

Bulatova, Nadežda J. & Leonore A. Grenoble. 1999. *Evenki* (Languages of the World 141). Munich: Lincom.

Bybee, Joan L. 1985. *Morphology: A Study of the Relation Between Meaning and Form*. (Typological Studies in Language 9). Amsterdam: Benjamins.

Bybee, Joan L., Revere Perkins & William Pagliuca. 1994. *The Evolution of Grammar: Tense, Aspect and Modality in the Languages of the World*. Chicago: University of Chicago Press.

Byington, Mark. 2004. A study of cultural and political relations between Puyŏ and Koguryŏ. *Journal of Inner and East Asian studies* 2 (1): 65–78.

Campbell, Lyle. 1988. Review of Joseph H. Greenberg, 1987, *Language in the Americas*. Stanford: Stanford University Press. *Language* 64: 591–615.
Campbell, Lyle. 1991. Some grammaticalization changes in Estonian and their implications. In Elizabeth Traugott & Bernd Heine (eds.), *Approaches to grammaticalization, vol. 1*, 285–299. Amsterdam: Benjamins.
Campbell, Lyle. 1998. *Historical Linguistics: An Introduction*. Edinburgh: University Press.
Campbell, Lyle. 2003. How to show languages are related: Methods for distant genetic relationship. In Brian D. Joseph & Richard D. Janda (eds.), *The Handbook of Historical Linguistics*, 262–282. Oxford: Blackwell.
Campbell, Lyle & Alice C. Harris. 2002. Syntactic reconstruction and demythologizing "Myths and the prehistory of grammars". *Journal of Linguistics* 38: 599–618.
Campbell, Lyle & William J. Poser. 2008. *Language Classification: History and Method*. Cambridge: Cambridge University Press.
Capidan, Theodor. 1925. *Meglenoromânii* [Meglenoromanian], *vol. 1*. Bucharest: Academia Română.
Choi, Han-Woo. 2002. A comparative morphology of Altaic languages: Deverbal noun suffixes. *International Journal of Central Asian Studies* 7: 23–40.
Choi, Han-Woo. 2005. Evidences of the affinity of Korean and Turkic. *International Journal of Central Asian Studies* 10: 29–52.
Ch'en, Shou. 1959. *San-kuo chih* [*Book of the Three States*]. Peking: Chung-hua shu-chü.
Cincius, Vera Ivanovna. 1949. *Sravnitel'naja fonetika tunguso-man'čžurskich jazykov* [Comparative phonetics of Manchu-Tungusic languages]. Leningrad: Učpedgiz.
Cincius, Vera Ivanovna (ed.). 1975–1977. *Sravnitel'nyj slovar' tunguso-man'čžurskich jazykov* [Comparative dictionary of Manchu-Tungusic languages], *vols. 1–2*. Moscow: Nauk.
Clark, Larry. 1980. Turkic Loanwords in Mongol, I: The treatment of non-initial s, z, š, č. *Central Asiatic Journal* 24: 36–59.
Clauson, Gerard. 1972. *An Etymological Dictionary of Pre-thirteenth-Century Turkish*. Oxford: Clarendon Press.
Collinder, Björn. 1965. *An Introduction to the Uralic Languages*. Berkeley: University of California Press.
Comrie, Bernard. 1976. *Aspect: An Introduction to the Study of Verbal Aspect and Related Problems*. Cambridge: Cambridge University Press.
Comrie, Bernard. 1981. Negation and other verb categories in the Uralic languages. In Osmo Ikola (ed.), *Congressus quintis internationalis Fenno-Ugristarum, vol. 6*, 350–355. Turku: Suomen Kielen Seura.
Comrie, Bernard. 2008. Inflectional morphology and language contact, with special reference to mixed languages. In Peter Siemund & Noemi Kintana (eds.), *Language Contact and Contact Languages* (Hamburg studies on multilingualism 7), 15–32. Amsterdam: Benjamins.
Comrie, Bernard. 2010. The role of verbal morphology in establishing genealogical relations among languages. In Lars Johanson & Martine Robbeets (eds.), *Transeurasian Verbal Morphology in a Comparative Perspective: Genealogy, Contact, Chance* (Turcologica 78), 21–31. Wiesbaden: Harrassowitz.
Comrie, Bernard & Sandra Thompson. 1985. Lexical nominalization. In Timothy Shopen (ed.), *Language Typology and Syntactic Description: Grammatical Categories and the Lexicon, vol. 3*, 349–398. Cambridge: Cambridge University Press.

Crawford, Gary W. & Gyoung-Ah Lee. 2003. Agricultural origins in the Korean Peninsula. *Antiquity* 77: 87–95.

Crawford, Gary W. & Chen Shen. 1998. The origins of rice agriculture: Recent progress in East Asia. *Antiquity* 72: 858–66.

Croft, William. 1990. *Typology and Universals*. Cambridge: Cambridge University Press.

Croft, William. 1991. The evolution of negation. *Journal of Linguistics* 27: 1–27.

Csató, Éva Ágnes. 2002. Karaim: A high-copying language. In Mari C. Jones & Edith Esch (eds.), *Language Change: The Interplay of Internal, External and Extra-Linguistic Factors*. (Contributions to the sociology of language 86), 315–327. Berlin & New York: Mouton de Gruyter.

Dahl, Östen. 1979. Typology of sentence negation. *Linguistics* 17: 79–106.

Dahmen, Wolfgang. 1989. Rumänisch: Areallinguistik IV: Istrorumänisch. In Günter Holtus, Michael Metzeltin & Christian Schmitt (eds.), *Lexikon der Romanistischen Linguistik*, vol. 3, 448–460. Tübingen: Niemeyer.

Dale, Peter N. 1985. *The Myth of Japanese Uniqueness*. London: Routledge.

Dankoff, Robert & James Kelly. 1982, 1984, 1985. *Compendium of the Turkic Dialects by Maḥmūd al-Kāšyarī, 3 vols*. (Sources of Oriental Languages & Literatures 7, Turkish Sources VII). Duxbury: Harvard University Printing Office.

Darnell, Regna & Joel Sherzer. 1971. Areal linguistics in North America: A historical perspective. *International Journal of American Linguistics* 37: 20–28.

DeLancey, Scott. 2011. Finite structures from clausal nominalization in Tibeto-Burman. In Foong Ha Yap, Karen Grunow-Harsta & Janick Wrona (eds.), *Nominalization in Asian Languages* (Typological Studies in Language 96), 343–359. Amsterdam: John Benjamins.

De Smedt, A. & Antoine Mostaert. 1964. *Le dialecte monguor, II: grammaire*. (Uralic and Altaic Series 30). The Hague: Mouton.

Denoon, Donald, Mark Hudson, Gavan McCormack & Tessa Morris-Suzuki (eds.). 1996. *Multicultural Japan: Palaeolithic to Postmodern*. Cambridge: Cambridge University Press.

Diamond, Jared & Peter Bellwood. 2003. Farmers and their languages: The first expansions. *Science* 300. 597–603.

Dixon, Robert M. W. 1972. *The Dyirbal Language of North Queensland*. Cambridge: Cambridge University Press.

Dixon, Robert M. W. 1977. Where have all the adjectives gone? *Studies in Language* 1: 19–80.

Dixon, Robert M. W. 1982. Where have all the adjectives gone? In Robert Dixon (ed.), *Where Have All the Adjectives Gone?*, 1–62. Amsterdam: Mouton.

Doerfer, Gerhard. 1963–1975. *Türkische und Mongolische Elemente im Neupersischen, unter besonderer Berücksichtigung älterer neupersischer Geschichtsquellen, vor allem der Mongolen- und Timuridenzeit, vols. 1–4*. Wiesbaden: Franz Steiner.

Doerfer, Gerhard. 1964. Klassifikation und Verbreitung der Mongolischen Sprachen. In Bertold Spuler (ed.), *Mongolistik*. (Handbuch der Orientalistik 5, 2). 35–50. Leiden: Brill.

Doerfer, Gerhard. 1966. Zur Verwandtschaft der altaischen Sprachen. *Indogermanische Forschungen* 71: 81–123.

Doerfer, Gerhard. 1973. Zur Sprache der Hunnen. *Central Asiatic Journal* 17: 1–50.

Doerfer, Gerhard. 1974. Ist das Japanische mit den altaischen Sprachen verwandt? *Zeitschrift der Deutschen Morgenlandische Gesellschaft* 124: 103–142.

Doerfer, Gerhard. 1978. Classification problems of Tungus. In Gerhard Doerfer & Michael Weiers (eds.), *Tungusica, vol. 1*, 1–26. Wiesbaden: Harrassowitz.

Doerfer, Gerhard. 1981. The conditions for proving the genetic relationship of languages. *Bulletin of the International Institute for Linguistic Sciences Kyoto Sangyo University* 2: 39–38.

Doerfer, Gerhard. 1982. Nomenverba in Türkischen. In Aldo Gallotta & Ugo Marazzi (eds.), *Studia turcologica memoriae Alexii Bombaci dicata*, 101–114. Naples: Istituto Universitario Orientale.
Doerfer, Gerhard. 1985. *Mongolo-Tungusica*. Wiesbaden: Steiner.
Doerfer, Gerhard. 1993. The older Mongolian layer in Ancient Turkic. *Türk Dilleri Araştırmalari* 1993: 79–86.
Doerfer, Gerhard, Wolfram Hesche & Hartwig Scheinhardt. 1980. *Lamutisches Wörterbuch*. Wiesbaden: Harrassowitz.
Dressler, Wolfgang U. 1989. Prototypical differences between inflection and derivation. *Zeitschrift für Phonetik, Sprachwissenschaft und Kommunikationsforschung* 42: 3–10.
Driem, George van. 2012. The ethnolinguistic identity of the domesticators of Asian rice. *Comptes Rendus Palevol* 11 (2): 117–132.
Dryer, Matthew S. 1992. The Greenbergian word order correlations. *Language* 68: 81–134.
Dryer, Matthew S. 2005. Negative morphemes. In Martin Haspelmath, Matthew S. Dryer, David Gil & Bernard Comrie (eds.), *The World Atlas of Language Structures*, 454–457. Oxford: Oxford University Press.
Dulik, Matthew C. et al. 2012. Mitochondrial DNA and Y chromosome variation provides evidence for a recent common ancestry between Native Americans and Indigenous Altaians. *The American Journal of Human Genetics* 90. 1–18.
Dybo, Anna. 1990. Inlautnye guttural'nye v Tunguso-Man'čžurskom i pra Altajskom [Medial gutturals in Manchu-Tungusic and Altaic]. In *Sravitelno-istorieskoe yazykoznanie na sovremennom ètage* [Historical Comparative Linguistics on a Contemporary Level]. Moscow: Nauk.
Dybo, Anna & George Starostin. 2008. In defense of the comparative method, or the end of the Vovin controversy. *Aspects of Comparative Linguistics* 3: 119–258.
Elšík, Viktor & Yaron Matras. 2008. Modality in Romani. In Hansen, Björn & Ferdinand de Haan (eds.), *Modals in European Languages*. Berlin & New York: Mouton de Gruyter.
Erdal, Marcel. 1979a. The chronological classification of Old Turkish texts. *Central Asiatic Journal* 23: 151–175.
Erdal, Marcel 1979b. Die Konverb- und Aoristendungen im Alttürkischen. *Ural-Altaische Jahrbücher* 51: 104–126.
Erdal, Marcel 1979c. Die Morphemfuge im Alttürkischen. *Wiener Zeitschrift für die Kunde des Morgenlandes* 71: 83–114.
Erdal, Marcel 1991. *Old Turkic Word Formation: A Functional Approach to the Lexicon* (Turcologica 7). Wiesbaden: Harrassowitz.
Erdal, Marcel 2004. *A Grammar of Old Turkic*. Leiden: Brill.
Evans, Nicholas 2007. Insubordination and its uses. In Irina Nikolaeva (ed.), *Finiteness: Theoretical and Empirical Foundations*, 366–431. Oxford: Oxford University Press.
Fan, Ye. 1965. *Hòuhànshū* [Book of the later Han]. Peking: Zhonghua Shuju.
Fedotov, M. R. 1996. *Čuvašskij yazyk: Istoki otnossënie k Altajskim i Finno-Ugorskim Jazykam istoričeskaya grammatika* [The Chuvash Language: Historical Grammar with Connections to the Altaic and Finno-Ugric Languages]. Čeboksary: Izdatel'stvo Čuvašskogo Universiteta.
Finch, Roger. 1985. Particles used with the 'absolutive case' in the Altaic Languages. *Journal of Turkish Studies* 9: 27–36.
Finch, Roger. 1987. Verb classes in the Altaic languages. *Sophia Linguistica* 26: 41–61.
Finch, Roger. 1999. The case system of the Altaic Languages. *Surugadai University Studies* 18: 87–112.

Fischer, Wolfdietrich. 1961. Die Sprache der arabischen Sprachinsel in Uzbekistan. *Der Islam* 36: 232–263.
Fiskesjö, Magnus & Yue-ie Caroline Hsing. 2011. Preface: Rice and language across Asia. *Rice* 4 (3): 75–77.
Fleischman, Suzanne. 1982. *The Future in Thought and Language: Diachronic Evidence from Romance* (Cambridge Studies in Linguistics 36). Cambridge: Cambridge University Press.
Fox, Anthony. 1995. *Linguistic Reconstruction: An Introduction to Theory and Method.* Oxford: Oxford University Press.
Frellesvig, Bjarke. 2001. A common Korean and Japanese copula. *Journal of East Asian Linguistics* 10: 1–35.
Frellesvig, Bjarke. 2008. On reconstruction of proto-Japanese and pre-Old Japanese verb inflection. In Bjarke Frellesvig & John Whitman (eds.), *Proto-Japanese: Issues and Prospects* (Current Issues in Linguistic Theory 294), 175–192. Amsterdam: Benjamins.
Frellesvig, Bjarke. 2010. *A History of the Japanese Language.* Cambridge: Cambridge University Press.
Frellesvig, Bjarke & John Whitman. 2008. Evidence for seven vowels in proto-Japanese. In Bjarke Frellesvig & John Whitman (eds.), *Proto-Japanese: Issues and Prospects* (Current Issues in Linguistic Theory 249), 15–41. Amsterdam: Benjamins.
Friedman, Victor. 2003. Evidentiality in the Balkans with special attention to Macedonian and Albanian. In Alexandra Y. Aikhenvald &, Robert M. W. Dixon (eds.), *Studies in Evidentiality* (Typological Studies in Language 54), 189–218. Amsterdam: John Benjamins.
Friedman, Victor. 2006. Turkish in Romani outside of Turkey: Balkan perspectives. Key note lecture presented at the thirteenth International Conference on Turkish linguistics, University of Uppsala 16–20 August.
Friedman, Victor. 2009. Turkish presents in Romani dialects. In Éva Csató, Gunvald Ims, Joakim Parslow Finn Thiesen & Emel Türker (eds.), *Turcological Letters to Bernt Brendemoen* (Festschrift), 109–121. Oslo: Novus.
Friedman, Victor. 2012. Copying and cognates in the Balkan Sprachbund. In Lars Johanson & Martine Robbeets (eds.), *Copies Versus Cognates in Bound Morphology* (Brill's Studies in Language, Cognition and Culture 2), 323–336. Leiden: Brill.
Gabain, Annemarie von. 1950. *Alttürkische Grammatik.* Leipzig: Harrassowitz.
Gabelentz, Hans von der. 1861. Über das Passivum: Eine sprachvergleichende Abhandlung. *Abhandlungen der Königlich-Sächsischen Gesellschaft der Wissenschaften* 8. 450–546.
Gardani, Francesco. 2008. *Borrowing of Inflectional Morphemes in Language Contact.* (Europäische Hochschulschriften 21: Linguistik, Band 320). Vienna: Peter Lang.
Gardani, Francesco, Nino Amiridze & Peter Arkadiev (eds.). 2014. *Borrowed morphology.* (Language Contact and Bilingualism 8). Berlin & Boston: De Gruyter Mouton.
Gast, Volker & Johan van der Auwera. 2010. *What is 'contact-induced grammaticalization'? evidence from Mayan and Mixe-Zoquean languages.* Ms.
Gelderen, Elly van. 2008. Negative cycles. *Linguistic Typology* 12: 195–243.
Georg, Stefan. 2003. Japanese, the Altaic theory and the limits of language classification. In Osada, Tosiki & Alexander Vovin (eds.), *Perspectives on the Origins of the Japanese Language*, 429–448. Kyoto: International Research Center for Japanese Studies.
Georg, Stefan. 2005. *Chips from an Anti-Altaic Workshop: Turkic *z ("*r²") and Korean *r in the Newest Version of the Altaic Hypothesis.* Paper presented at the international conference on the language(s) of Koguryo and the reconstruction of Old Korean and neighboring languages, Universität Hamburg, 23–24 September.

Georg, Stefan. 2007. Review of Martine Robbeets, 2005, *Is Japanese related to Korean, Tungusic, Mongolic and Turkic?* Wiesbaden: Harrassowitz. *Korean Studies* 31: 247–278.
Georg, Stefan, Peter A. Michalove, Alexis Manaster Ramer, Alexis & Paul J. Sidwell. 1998. Telling general linguists about Altaic. *Journal of Linguistics* 35: 65–98.
Gil, David. 2005. Adjectives without nouns. In Martin Haspelmath, Matthew S. Dryer, David Gil & Bernard Comrie (eds.), *The World Atlas of Language Structures*, 250–253. Oxford: Oxford University Press.
Gimbutas, Maria. 1985. Primary and secondary homeland of the Indo-Europeans: Comments on the Gamkrelidze-Ivanov articles. *Journal of Indo-European Studies* 13: 185–202.
Givón, Talmy 1979. *On Understanding Grammar*. London: Academic Press.
Givón, Talmy. 2001. *Syntax: An Introduction, vol. 1.* Amsterdam: Benjamins.
Gokcumen, Omer et al. 2008. Genetic variation in the enigmatic Altaian Kazakhs of South-Central Russia: Insights into Turkic population history. *American Journal of Physical Anthropology* 136: 278–293.
Gorelova, Liliya M. 1996. Manchu as compared with the other Tungus-Manchu languages within the paradigm of syntheticism / analytism. In Giovanni Stary (ed.) *Proceedings of the 38th Permanent International Altaistic Conference (PIAC)*, 153–158. Wiesbaden: Harrassowitz.
Gorelova, Liliya M. 2002. *Manchu Grammar*. Leiden: Brill.
Greenberg, Joseph H. 1966. Some universals of grammar with particular reference to the order of meaningful elements. In Joseph Greenberg (ed.), *Universals of Language*, 73–113. Cambridge: MIT Press.
Greenberg, Joseph H. 1991. The last stages of grammatical elements: Contractive and expansive desemanticization. In Elizabeth Traugott & Bernd Heine (eds.), *Approaches to Grammaticalization, Vol. 1: Focus on Theoretical and Methodological Issues*, 301–314. Amsterdam: Benjamins.
Greenberg, Joseph H. 2000. *Indo-European and Its Closest Relatives: The Eurasiatic Language Family, vol. 1: Grammar*. Stanford: Stanford University Press.
Greenberg, Joseph H. 2002. *Indo-European and Its Closest Relatives: The Eurasiatic Language Family, vol. 2: Lexicon*. Stanford: Stanford University Press.
Grönbech, Karl. 1936. *Der Türkische Sprachbau*. Kopenhagen: Levin & Munksgaard.
Gruntov, Il'ja Aleksandrovič. 2002. *Rekonstrukcija padežnoj sistemy praaltajskogo jazyka. Padežnye sistemy altajskich jazykov: Opyt diachroničeskoj interpretacii* [A reconstruction of the case system of Proto-Altaic. Case systems of Altaic languages: a diachronic interpretation]. Moscow: Russian State University for Humanities Ph.D. Dissertation.
Grunzel, J. 1894. *Entwurf einer vergleichenden Grammatik der altaischen Sprachen*. Leipzig.
Gruzdeva, Ekaterina. 1998. *Nivkh* (Languages of the World Materials 111). Munich: Lincom.
Gugán, Katalin. 2012. Zigzagging in language history: Negation and negative concord in Hungarian. *Languages and Linguistics* 1: 89–97.
Gutiérrez-Morales, Salomé. 2012. Morphological borrowing in Sierra Popoluca. In Lars Johanson & Martine Robbeets (eds.), *Copies vs. Cognates in Bound Morphology* (Brill's Studies in Language, Cognition and Culture 3), 221–232. Leiden: Brill.
Haase, Martin & Nau, Nicole (eds.). 1996. Einleitung: Sprachkontakt und Grammatikalisierung. *Sprachtypologie und Universalienforschung* 49 (1). Bremen: Akademie Verlag.
Habu, Junko. 2004. *Ancient Jomon of Japan*. Cambridge: Cambridge University Press.
Haenisch, Erich. 1939. *Wörterbuch zu Manghol un Niuca Tobca'an*. Leipzig: Harrassowitz.

Hagers, Steven. 2000. The attributive and conclusive forms of modern Japanese and Ryukyuan dialects in a historical perspective. *Studia Etymologia Cracoviensia* 5: 13–42.
Hamilton, James, Ece Korkut & İsmet Birkan. 1998. *Budacı İyi ve Kötü Kalpli Prens Masalının Uygurcası: Kalyānamkara ve Papāmkara* (Türk Dilleri Araştırmaları Dizisi 11). Ankara: Simurg.
Hammer, Michael F. et al. 2006. Dual origins of the Japanese: Common ground for hunter-gatherer and farmer Y chromosomes. *Journal of Human Genetics* 51: 47–58.
Hamp, Eric P. 1970. On the Altaic numerals. In Roman Jakobson & Shigeo Kawamoto (eds.), *Studies in General and Oriental Linguistics Presented to Shirō Hattori on the Occasion of His Sixtieth Birthday*, 188–197. Tokyo: TEC.
Han, Kangxin & Takahiro Nakahashi. 1996. A comparative study of ritual tooth ablation in Ancient China and Japan. *Anthropological Sciences* 104 (1): 43–64.
Hanihara, Kazuro 1991. Dual structure model for the population history of the Japanese. *Japan Review* 2: 1–33.
Harris, Alice & Lyle Campbell. 1995. *Historical syntax in cross-linguistic perspective*. Cambridge: Cambridge University Press.
Harrison, Sheldon P. 2003. On the Limits of the Comparative Method. In Brian D. Joseph & Richard D. Janda (eds.), *The Handbook of Historical Linguistics*, 213–243. Oxford: Blackwell.
Harunari, Hideji. 1990. *Yayoi jidai no hajimari* [The beginning of the Yayoi period]. Tokyo: University Press.
Harunari, Hideji & Mineo Imamura. 2004. *Yayoi jidai no jitsu nendai* [The actual duration of the Yayoi period]. Tokyo: Gakuseisha.
Haspelmath, Martin. 1989. From purposive to infinitive: A universal path of grammaticization. *Folia Linguistica Historica* 10: 287–310.
Haspelmath, Martin. 1990. The grammaticization of passive morphology. *Studies in Language* 14 (1): 25–71.
Haspelmath, Martin. 1993. More on the typology of inchoative/causative verb alternations. In Bernard Comrie & Maria Polinsky (eds.), *Causatives and Transitivity*, 87–120. Amsterdam: Benjamins.
Haspelmath, Martin. 1995. The converb as a cross-linguistically valid category. In Haspelmath, Martin & Ekkehard König (eds.), *Converbs in Cross-linguistic Perspective: Structure and Meaning of Adverbial Verb Forms – Adverbial Participles, Gerunds* (Empirical Approaches to Language Typology 13), 1–55. Berlin & New York: Mouton de Gruyter.
Haspelmath, Martin. 1996. Word-class-changing inflection and morphological theory. In Geert Booij & Jaap van Marle (eds.), *Yearbook of Morphology 1995*, 43–66. Dordrecht: Kluwer Academic Publishers.
Haspelmath, Martin. 2002. *Understanding Morphology*. London: Hodder Education.
Hattori, Shirō. 1972 [1968]. Nihongo no Ryūkyū hōgen ni tsuite [On the Japanese dialect of the Ryukyu Islands]. In Dhuzen Hokama (ed.), *Okinawa bunka ronsō 5: Gengo-hen* [Discussions about Okinawan culture 5: Language], 46–64. Tokyo: Heibonsha.
Hattori, Shirō. 1976. Ryūkyū hōgen to hondo hōgen [The dialects of the Japanese main islands and the Ryukyuan dialects]. In Ifa Fuyū Seitan Hyakunen Kinenkai (ed.), *Okinawagaku no reimei* [The dawn of Okinawan studies], 7–55. Tokyo: Okinawa Bunka Kyokai.
Heath, Jeffrey. 1978. *Linguistic Diffusion in Arnhem Land* (Australian Aboriginal Studies: Research and Regional Studies 13). Canberra: Australian Institute of Aboriginal Studies.

Heggarty, Paul & Beresford-Jones, David. 2014. Farming-language dispersals: A worldwide survey. In Claire Smith (ed.), *Encyclopedia of global archaeology*, 1–9. New York: Springer.
Heine, Bernd. 1994. Areal influence on grammaticalization. In Martin Pütz (ed.), *Language Contact and Language Conflict,* 56–68. Amsterdam: John Benjamins.
Heine, Bernd, Ulrike Claudi & Friederike Hünnemeyer. 1991. *Grammaticalization: A Conceptual Framework*. Chicago: The University of Chicago Press.
Heine, Bernd & Tania Kuteva. 2002. *World Lexicon of Grammaticalization*. Cambridge: Cambridge University Press.
Heine, Bernd & Tania Kuteva. 2005. *Language Contact and Grammatical Change*. Cambridge: Cambridge University Press.
Heine, Bernd & Tania Kuteva. 2006. *The Changing Languages of Europe*. Oxford: Oxford University Press.
Heine, Bernd & Mechthild Reh. 1984. *Grammaticalization and Reanalysis in African Languages*. Hamburg: Helmut Buske.
Heinrich, Patrick. 2008. Casting light on the past: Lessons on the origin and formation of Japanese-Ryukyuan. In Ölschleger, Hans Dieter (ed.), *Theories and Methods in Japanese Studies: Current State and Future Developments*, 185–204. Bonn: Bonn University Press.
Heinrich, Patrick. 2012. *The Making of Monolingual Japan. Language Ideology and Japanese Modernity*. Toronto: Multilingual matters.
Hirayama, Teruo. 1983. *Ryūkyū Miyako shotō hōgen kiso goi no sōgōteki kenkyū* [Integral research on the basic vocabulary of the dialects of the Miyako Ryukyu islands]. Tokyo: Ōfūsha.
Hock, Hans Heinrich. 1991. *Principles of Historical Linguistics*. Berlin & New York: Mouton de Gruyter.
Hodge, Carleton T. 1970. The linguistic cycle. *Language Sciences* 13: 1–7.
Hong, Wontack. 2010. *East Asian history: A Tripolar Approach*. Seoul: Kudara International.
Hopper, Paul. 1990. Where do words come from? In William Croft, Kessler Denning & Suzanne Kemmer (eds.), *Studies in Typology and Diachrony: Papers Presented to Joseph H. Greenberg on his 75th Birthday* (Typological studies in language 20), 151–160. Amsterdam: John Benjamins.
Hopper, Paul & Elizabeth Traugott. 1993. *Grammaticalization, 2nd edn*. Cambridge: Cambridge University Press.
Horie, Kaoru. 2008. The grammaticalization of nominalizers in Japanese and Korean. In Mariá José López-Couso & Elena Seoane (eds.), *Rethinking Grammaticalization: New Perspectives*, 169–187. Amsterdam: John Benjamins.
Howe, Stephen. 1996. *The Personal Pronouns in the Germanic Languages: A Study of Personal Pronoun Morphology and Change in the Germanic Languages from the First Records to the Present Day* (Studia Linguistica Germanica 43). Berlin & New York: Mouton de Gruyter.
Hudson, Mark. 1999. *Ruins of Identity: Ethnogenesis in the Japanese Islands*. Honolulu: University of Hawai'i Press.
Hudson, Mark. 2002. Agriculture and language change in the Japanese Islands. In Peter Bellwood & Colin Renfrew (eds.), *Examining the Farming/Language Dispersal Hypothesis*, 311–318. Cambridge: McDonald Institute for Archaeological Research.
Hyman, Larry M. 2007. Niger-Congo verb extensions: Overview and discussion. In Payn, Doris L. & Jaime Peña (eds.), *Selected Proceedings of the 37th Annual Conference on African Linguistics*, 149–163. Somerville: Cascadilla.

Hyman, Larry M. 2014. Reconstructing the Niger-Congo verb extension paradigm: What's cognate, copied or renewed? In Martine Robbeets & Walter Bisang (eds.), *Paradigm Change: In the Transeurasian Languages and Beyond* (Studies in Language Companion Series 161), 103–127. Amsterdam: Benjamins.

Igla, Birgit. 1996. *Das Romani von Ajia Varvara. Deskriptive und historisch-vergleichende Darstellung eines Zigeunerdialekts*. Wiesbaden: Harrassowitz.

Ikegami, Jiro. 1974. Versuch einer Klassifikation der Tungusischen Sprachen. Gyorgi Hazai (ed.), *Sprache, Geschichte und Kultur der Altaischen Volker*, 271–272. Berlin: Akademie Verlag.

Ikier, Steven. 2006. *On the Attributive and Final Predicate Forms in Eastern Old Japanese*. Honululu: University of Hawai'i M.A. Thesis.

Itabashi, Yoshizō. 1988. A comparative study of the Old Japanese accusative case suffix *wo* with the altaic accusative case suffixes. *Central Asiatic Journal* 32: 193–231.

Itabashi, Yoshizō. 1989. The origin of the Old Japanese prosecutive case suffix *yuri*. *Central Asiatic Journal* 33: 47–66.

Itabashi, Yoshizō. 1990. The origin of the Old Japanese accusative case suffix *i*. *Ural-Altaische Jahrbücher Neue Folge* 9: 152–173.

Itabashi, Yoshizō. 1991. The origin of the Old Japanese genitive case suffixes **n/nö/na/Nga* and the Old Korean genitive case suffix **i* in comparison with Manchu-Tungus, Mongolian, and Old Turkic. *Central Asiatic Journal* 35: 231–278.

Jakobson, Roman. 1944. Franz Boas' approach to language. *International Journal of American Linguistics* 10: 188–195.

Jang, Taeho & Thomas E. Payne 2012. Dependency and clause combining in Xibe. In Andrej L. Malchukov & Lindsay J. Whaley (eds.), *Recent Advances in Tungusic Linguistics* (Turcologica 89), 229–254. Wiesbaden: Harrassowitz.

Jang, Taeho, Kyungsook Lim Jang & Thomas E. Payne. Forthcoming. *A grammar of modern spoken Xibe*.

Janhunen, Juha. 1981. Korean vowel system in North Asian perspective. *Hangeul* 172: 129–146.

Janhunen, Juha. 1982. On the structure of proto-Uralic. *Finnisch-ugrische Forschungen* 44: 23–42.

Janhunen, Juha. 1996a. *Manchuria: An Ethnic History* (Mémoires de la Société Finno-Ougrienne 222). Helsinki: Suomalais-Ugrilainen Seura.

Janhunen, Juha. 1996b. Prolegomena to a comparative analysis of Mongolic and Tungusic. In Giovanni Stary (ed.), *Proceedings of the 38th Permanent International Altaistic Conference in Kawasaki, Japan, 7–12 August 1995*, 209–218. Wiesbaden: Harrassowitz.

Janhunen, Juha. 1998. Ethnicity and language in prehistoric Northeast Asia. *Archaeology and Language* 2: 195–208.

Janhunen, Juha. 1999. A contextual approach to the convergence and divergence of Korean and Japanese. *Central Asiatic Journal* 43: 1–23.

Janhunen, Juha. 2001. Indo-Uralic and Ural-Altaic: On the diachronic implications of areal typology. In Carpelan, Christian, Asko Parpola & Petteri Koskikallio (eds.), *Early Contacts Between Uralic and Indo-European: Linguistic and Archaeological Considerations*, 207–220. Helsinki: Suomalais-Ugrilainen Seura.

Janhunen, Juha. 2003a. Proto-Mongolic. In Juha Janhunen (ed.), *The Mongolic Languages*, 1–29. London: Routledge.

Janhunen, Juha. 2003b. Para-Mongolic. In Juha Janhunen (ed.), *The Mongolic Languages*, 390–402. London: Routledge.

Janhunen, Juha. 2005a. Tungusic: An endangered language family in Northeast Asia. *International Journal of the Sociology of Language* 173: 37–54.

Janhunen, Juha. 2005b. The lost languages of Koguryo. *Journal of Inner and East Asian Studies* 2: 66–86.
Janhunen, Juha. 2005c. *Khamnigan Mongol*. München: LINCOM.
Janhunen, Juha. 2010. Correctness and controversies in Asian historiography. *Studia Orientalia* 109: 127–145.
Janhunen, Juha. 2012a. The expansion of Tungusic as an ethnic and linguistic process. In Andrej Malchukov & Lindsay Whaley (eds.), *Recent Advances in Tungusic Linguistics*, 5–16. Wiesbaden: Harrassowitz.
Janhunen, Juha. 2012b. *Mongolian* (London Oriental and African Language Library 19). Amsterdam: John Benjamins.
Janhunen, Juha. 2012c. Non-borrowed non-cognate parallels in bound morphology: Aspects of the phenomenon of shared drift with Eurasian examples. In Lars Johanson & Martine Robbeets (eds.), *Copies vs. Cognates in Bound Morphology* (Brill's Studies in Language, Cognition and Culture 3), 23–46. Leiden: Brill.
Janhunen, Juha. 2014. Ural-Altaic: The polygenetic origins of nominal morphology in the Transeurasian zone. In Robbeets, Martine & Walter Bisang (eds.), *Paradigm Change: In the Transeurasian Languages and Beyond* (Studies in Language Companion Series 161), 311–333. Amsterdam: Benjamins.
Jasanoff, Jay. 2003. *Hittite and the Indo-European Verb*. Oxford: Oxford University Press.
Jendraschek, Gerd. 2007. Basque in contact with Romance languages. In Alexandra Y. Aikhenvald & Robert M. W. Dixon (eds.), *Grammars in Contact: A Cross-Linguistic Typology* (Explorations in Linguistic Typology 4), 143–162. Oxford: Oxford University Press.
Jespersen, Otto. 1917. *Negation in English and Other Languages* (Konelige Danske Videnskabernes Selskab. Historisk-filologiske Meddelelser I, 5) Copenhagen: A. F. Høst & Søn.
Jinam, Timothy, et al. 2012. The history of human populations in the Japanese Archipelago inferred from genome-wide SNP data with a special reference to the Ainu and the Ryukyuan populations. *Journal of Human Genetics* 57: 787–795.
Johanson, Lars. 1974. Zur Syntax der alttürkischen Kausativa. In Wolfgang Voigt (ed.), *XVIII. Deutscher Orientalistentag vom 1. bis 5. Oktober 1972 in Lübeck. Vorträge.* (Zeitschrift der Deutschen Morgenlandische Gesellschaft, Supplement 2), 529–540. Wiesbaden: Harrassowitz.
Johanson, Lars. 1975. Das tschuwaschische Aoristthema. *Orientalia Suenica* 24: 106–158.
Johanson, Lars. 1979. *Alttürkisch as 'dissimilierende Sprache'* (Abhandlungen der Akademie der Wissenschaften und der Literatur, Mainz, Geistes-und sozial-wissenschaftliche Klasse 3). Wiesbaden: Steiner.
Johanson, Lars. 1988. On the renewal and reinterpretation of 'instrumental' gerunds in Turkic. *Oriens* 31: 136–153.
Johanson, Lars. 1992. *Strukturelle Faktoren in türkischen Sprachkontakten* (Sitzungsberichte der Wissenschaftlichen Gesellschaft an der J. W. Goethe-Universität Frankfurt am Main 29, 5). Stuttgart: Steiner.
Johanson, Lars. 1995. On Turkic converb clauses. In Martin Haspelmath & Ekkehard König (eds.), *Converbs in Cross-Linguistic Perspective: Structure and Meaning of Adverbial Verb Forms – Adverbial Participles, Gerunds* (Empirical Approaches to Language Typology 13), 313–347 Berlin & New York: Mouton de Gruyter.
Johanson, Lars. 1996. On Bulgarian and Turkic indirectives. In Norbert Boretzky, Werner Enninger & Thomas Stolz (eds.), *Areale, Kontakte, Dialekte: Sprache und ihre Dynamik in mehrsprachigen Situationen* (Bochum-Essener Beiträge zur Sprachwandelforschung 24), 84–94. Bochum: Brockmeyer.

Johanson, Lars. 1998. The history of Turkic. In Lars Johanson & Éva Á. Csató (eds.), *The Turkic Languages*, 81–125. New York: Routledge.
Johanson, Lars. 1999. Cognates and copies in Altaic verb derivation. In Karl Heinrich Menges & Nelly Neumann (eds.), *Language and Literature: Japanese and the Other Altaic Languages* (Studies in Honour of Roy Andrew Miller on His 75th Birthday), 1–14 Wiesbaden: Harrassowitz.
Johanson, Lars. 2000a. Traces of a Turkic copula verb. *Turkic Languages* 4: 235–238.
Johanson, Lars. 2000b. Viewpoint operators in European languages. In Östen Dahl (ed.), *Tense and Aspect in the Languages of Europe*, 27–187. Berlin & New York: Mouton de Gruyter.
Johanson, Lars. 2001. *Vom Alttürkischen zu den modernen Türksprachen*. In Martin Haspelmath, Ekkehard König, Wulf Oesterreicher & Wolfgang Raible (eds.), *Language typology and language universals*, 1719–1742. Berlin & New York: Mouton de Gruyter.
Johanson, Lars. 2002a. *Structural Factors in Turkic Language Contacts*. Richmond: Curzon.
Johanson, Lars. 2002b. Contact-induced change in a code-copying framework. In Mari C. Jones & Edith Esch (eds.), *Language Change: The Interplay of Internal, External and Extra-Linguistic Factors* (Contributions to the sociology of language 86), 285–313. Berlin & New York: Mouton de Gruyter.
Johanson, Lars. 2005. Participles in Caucasus Turkic. In Dag Haug & Eirik Welo (eds.), *Haptačahaptāitiš: Festschrift for Fridrik Thordarson* (The Institute for Comparative Research in Human Culture, Serie B: Skrifter 116), 151–156. Oslo: Novus forlag.
Johanson, Lars. 2006. Adjectives and nouns in South Siberian. In Marcel Erdal & Irina Nevskaya (eds.), *Exploring the Eastern Frontiers of Turkic in South Sibera*. (Turcologica 60), 57–78 Wiesbaden: Harrassowitz.
Johanson, Lars. 2008. Remodeling grammar: Copying, conventionalization, grammaticalization. In Peter Siemund & Noemi Kintana (eds.), *Language Contact and Contact Languages* (Hamburg studies on multilingualism), 61–80. Amsterdam: Benjamins.
Johanson, Lars. 2012. *From the Intimate Life of Turkic Sonorants*. Paper presented at the Workshop "West Old Turkic: Turkic loanwords in Hungarian" dedicated to Professor András Róna-Tas on the occasion of his 80th birthday. The Szeged Committee of the Hungarian Academy of Sciences, 11 March.
Johanson, Lars. 2014. A Yakut copy of a Tungusic viewpoint aspect paradigm. In Martine Robbeets & Walter Bisang (eds.), *Paradigm Change: In the Transeurasian Languages and beyond* (Studies in Language Companion Series 161), 235–242. Amsterdam: Benjamins.
Johanson, Lars & Martine Robbeets. 2010. Introduction. In Lars Johanson & Martine Robbeets (eds.), *Transeurasian Verbal Morphology in a Comparative Perspective: Genealogy, Contact, Chance* (Turcologica 78), 1–5. Wiesbaden: Harrassowitz.
Johanson, Lars & Martine Robbeets (eds.). 2012. *Copies vs. Cognates in Bound Morphology* (Brill's Studies in Language, Cognition and Culture 3). Leiden: Brill.
Joseph, Brian D. 2004. Morphological reconstruction. In Geert Booij, Christian Lehmann & Joachim Mugdan (eds.), *Morphologie: Ein internationales Handbuch zur Flexion und Wortbildung*, 1661–1667. Berlin & New York: Mouton de Gruyter.
Joseph, Brian D. 2006. On projecting variation back into a proto-language, with particular attention to Germanic evidence and some thoughts on 'Drift'. In Thomas D. Cravens (ed.), *Variation and Reconstruction*, 103–118. Amsterdam: John Benjamins.
Joseph, Brian D. 2012. A variationist solution to apparent copying across related languages. In Lars Johanson & Martine Robbeets (eds.), *Copies vs. Cognates in Bound Morphology* (Brill's Studies in Language, Cognition and Culture 3), 151–166. Leiden: Brill.

Joseph, Brian D. 2013. Demystifying 'drift': A variationist account. In Martine Robbeets & Hubert Cuyckens (eds.), *Shared Grammaticalization With Special Focus on the Transeurasian Languages* (Studies in Language Companion Series 132), 43–65. Amsterdam: John Benjamins.
Joseph, Brian D. 2014. On arguing from diachrony for paradigms. In Martine Robbeets & Walter Bisang (eds.), *Paradigm Change: In the Transeurasian Languages and Beyond*. (Studies in Language Companion Series 161), 89–102. Amsterdam: Benjamins.
Josephson, Judith. 2012. The historical background of the transfer of a Kurdish bound morpheme to Neo-Aramaic. In Lars Johanson & Martine Robbeets (eds.), *Copies vs. Cognates in Bound Morphology* (Brill's Studies in Language, Cognition and Culture 3), 355–370. Leiden: Brill.
Kaiser, Mark & Vitaly Shevoroshkin. 1988. Nostratic. *Annual Review of Anthropology* 17: 309–329.
Kaiser, Stefan, Yasuko Ichikawa, Noriko Kobayashi & Hirofumi Yamamoto. 2001. *Japanese: A Comprehensive Grammar*. London: Routledge.
Kane, Daniel. 2009. *The Kitan Language and Script*. Leiden: Brill.
Kara, György. 1987. On the Khitan writing systems. *Mongolian Studies* 10: 19–24.
Kara, György. 1997. Nomina-verba mongolica. *Acta Orientalia Academiae Scientiarum Hungaricae* 50: 155–162.
Kara, György. 2007. Review of Martine Robbeets, 2005, *Is Japanese Related to Korean, Tungusic, Mongolic and Turkic?* Wiesbaden: Harrassowitz. *Anthropological Linguistics* 49: 95–98.
Kazama, Shinjiro. 2012. Designative case in Tungusic languages. In Andrej Malchukov & Lindsay Whaley (eds.), *Recent Advances in Tungusic Linguistics*. Wiesbaden: Harrassowitz.
Kempf, Béla. 2008. Review of Sergej Starostin, Anna Dybo & Oleg Mudrak, 2003, *Etymological dictionary of the Altaic languages*, Leiden: Brill. *Acta Orientalia Hungarica* 61: 403–408.
Khabtagaeva, Bayarma. 2009. *Mongolic elements in Tuvan* (Turcologica 81). Wiesbaden: Harrassowitz.
Kiessling, Roland. 2004. Kausation, Wille und Wiederholung in der verbalen Derivation der westlichen Ring-Sprachen (Weh, Isu). In Raimund Kastenholz & Anne Storch (eds.), *Sprache und Wissen in Afrika*, 159–181. Köln: Rüdiger Köppe Verlag.
Kincses Nagy, Éva. 2006. *Verbal Borrowings in Turkic Languages*. Paper presented at the 13th International Conference on Turkish Linguistics, University of Uppsala, 16–20 August.
King, Ruth. 1999. *The Lexical Basis of Grammatical Borrowing: A Prince Edward Island French Case Study*. Amsterdam: John Benjamins.
Kinsui, Satoshi. 2006. *Nihongo sonzai hyōgen no rekishi*. [The history of Japanese existential expressions] Tokyo: Hitsuji Shobō.
Kim, Stephen S. 2003. Santa. In Juha Janhunen (ed.), *The Mongolic Languages*, 347–363. London: Routledge.
Kivisild, Toomas et al. 2002. The emerging limbs and twigs of the East Asian mtDNA tree. *Molecular Biology and Evolution* 19: 1737–1751.
Kiyose, Gisaburō. 2002. The relationship among the languages of the Korean Three Kingdoms, Proto-Japanese, and Tungusic, based on historical sources. *Transactions of the International Conference of Eastern Studies* 47: 121–122.
Klausenburger, Jürgen. 2000. *Grammaticalization: Studies in Latin and Romance Morphosyntax* (Amsterdam studies in the theory and history of linguistic science 193). Amsterdam: John Benjamins.

Knüppel, Michael. 2006. Ein Beitrag zur Japanisch-Koreanisch-Altaischen Hypothese. *Wiener Zeitschrift für die Kunde des Morgenlandes* 98: 353–364.

Ko, Yengkun. 1987. *Phyocwun cwungsey kwuke munpeplon* [A Grammar of Middle Korean]. Seoul: Cipmuntang.

Ko, Seongyeon. 2012. *Tongue Root Harmony and Vowel Contrast in Northeast Asian Languages.* New York: Cornell University Ph.D. dissertation.

Ko, Seongyeon, John Whitman & Andrew Joseph. 2014. Comparative consequences of the tongue root harmony analysis for proto-Tungusic, proto-Mongolic, and proto-Korean. In Martine Robbeets & Walter Bisang (eds.), *Paradigm Change: In the Transeurasian Languages and Beyond* (Studies in Language Companion Series 161), 141–176. Amsterdam: Benjamins.

Koch, Harold. 1996. Reconstruction in morphology. In Mark Durie & Malcolm Ross (eds.), *The Comparative Method Reviewed: Regularity and Irregularity in Language Change*, 218–263. Cambridge: University Press.

Koch, Harold. 2003. Morphological reconstruction as an etymological method. In Barry J. Blake & Kate Burridge (eds.), *Historical Linguistics 2001: Selected Papers from the 15th International Conference on Historical Linguistics, 13–17 August 2001*. Amsterdam: John Benjamins, 271–291.

Kōno, Rokurō. 1987. The bilingualism of the Paekche language. *Memoirs of the Research Department of the Toyo Bunko* 45: 75–86.

Konstantinova, Olga A. 1964. *Evenkijskij jazyk: Fonetika i morfologija* [Evenki: Phonology and Grammar]. Moscow: Nauka.

Korkina, Evdokija I. 1982. *Grammatika sovremennogo jakutskogo literaturnogo jazyka* [Grammar of Contemporary Yakut Literary Language]. Moscow: Nauka.

Kormušin, Igor Valentinovič. 1976. O passivnom značenii kauzativnych glagolov [About the passive interpretation of causative verbs]. In S.G. Kljaštornyj et al. (eds.), *Turkologica: K semidesjatiletiju akademika A. H. Kononov* [Turcology: in Honour of A. H. Kononov], 89–93. Leningrad: Nauka.

Kormušin, Igor Valentinovič. 1984. *Sistemy vremen glagola v altajskich jazykach* [Verbal Tense Systems in the Altaic Languages]. Moscow: Nauka.

Kormušin, Igor Valentinovič. 1998. *Udyhejskij jazyk* [The Udehe Language]. Moscow: Nauka.

Kortlandt, Frederik. 1993. The origin of the Japanese and Korean accent systems. *Acta Linguistica Hafniensia* 26: 57–65.

Kortlandt, Frederik. 1997. Japanese *aru, iru, oru* 'to be'. *Studia Etymologica Cracoviensia* 2: 167–170.

Kortlandt, Frederik. 2010. Indo-Uralic and Altaic revisited. In Lars Johanson & Martine Robbeets (eds.), *Transeurasian Verbal Morphology in a Comparative Perspective: Genealogy, Contact, Chance* (Turcologica 78), 153–164. Wiesbaden: Harrassowitz.

Kossmann, Martin. 2010. Parallel system borrowing: Parallel morphological systems due to the borrowing of paradigms. *Diachronica* 27: 459–487.

Krishnamurti, Bhadriraju. 2003. *The Dravidian Languages.* Cambridge: Cambridge University Press.

Krüger, John. 1961. *Chuvash Manual: Introduction, Grammar, Reader and Vocabulary* (Uralic and Altaic series 7). The Hague: Mouton.

Kulikov, Leonid I. 1993. The "second causative": A typological sketch. In Bernard Comrie & Maria Polinsky (eds.), *Causatives and Transitivity*, 121–154. Amsterdam: Benjamins.

Kurylowicz, Jerzy. 1965. Zur Vorgeschichte des germanischen Verbalsystems. In *Beiträge zur Sprachwissenschaft, Volkskunde und Literaturforschung: Wolfgang Steinitz zum 60. Geburtstag*, 242–247. Berlin: Akademie-Verlag.
Kuteva, Tania. 2000. Areal grammaticalization: The case of the Bantu-Nilotic borderland. *Folia Linguistica* 34 (3–4): 267–283.
LaPolla, Randy J. 1994. Parallel grammaticalizations in Tibeto-Birman languages: Evidence of Sapir's "drift". *Linguistics of the Tibeto-Burman Area* 17: 61–80.
Larrivée, Pierre. 2011. Is there a Jespersen cycle? In Larrivée, Pierre & Richard P. Ingham (eds.), *The Evolution of Negation: Beyond the Jespersen Cycle* (Trends in Linguistics, Studies and Monographs 235), 1–22. Berlin & New York: Mouton de Gruyter.
Lebedeva, E. R. & Liliya M. Gorelova. 1994. *Sidi Kur: A Sibe-Manchu Version of the "Bewitched Corpse" Cycle Transcribed by V. V. Radlov* (Aetas Manjurica 4). Wiesbaden: Harrassowitz.
Lee, Ki-Mun. 1977. *Geschichte der Koreanischen Sprache*. Wiesbaden: Dr. Ludwig Reichert Verlag.
Lee, Ki-Mun & Robert Ramsey. 2011. *A History of the Korean Language*. Cambridge: Cambridge University Press.
Lee, Sean & Toshikazu Hasegawa. 2011. Bayesian phylogenetic analysis supports an agricultural origin of Japonic languages. *Proceedings of the Royal Society* B 278: 3662–3669.
Lee-Smith, Mei W. 1996. The Ejnu language. In Stephen A. Wurm, Peter Mühlhäusler & Darrell T. Tryon (eds.), *Atlas of Languages of Intercultural Communication in the Pacific, Asia, and the Americas*, vol. 2.2, 851–863. Berlin & New York: Mouton de Gruyter.
Lehmann, Christian. 1985. *Thoughts on Grammaticalization*. München: Lincom.
Levickaya, L. S. 1976. *Istoričeskaja morfologija čuvašskogo jazyka* [Historical Morphology of Chuvash]. Moscow: Nauka.
Lewicki, Marian. 1949. *La langue mongole des transcriptions chinoises du XIVe siècle. Le Houa-yi yi-yu de 1389.* [The Mongolian language of the Chinese transcriptions of the 14th century. The Houa-yi yi-yu of 1389] (Travaux de la Société des Sciences et des lettres de Wroclaw, Seria A, Nr. 29). Wroclaw.
Lewin, Bruno. 1970. *Morphologie des koreanischen Verbs* (Veröffentlichungen des Ostasien-Instituts der Ruhr-Universität Bochum). Wiesbaden: Harrassowitz.
Li, Fengxiang & Lindsay J. Whaley. 2000. Emphatic reduplication in Oroqen and its Altaic context. *Linguistics* 38 (2). 355–372.
Li, Fengxiang & Lindsay J. Whaley. 2011. The grammaticalization cycle of causatives in Oroqen dialects. In Andrej Malchukov & Lindsay Whaley (eds.), *Recent Advances in Tungusic Linguistics*, 165–180. Wiesbaden: Harrassowitz.
Ligeti, Louis. 1970. Mots de civilization de Haute Asie en transcription chinoise. *Acta Orientalia Hungarica* 1: 141–188.
Lubotsky, Alexander. 2001. Reflexes of Proto-Indo-European *sk in Indo-Iranian. *Incontri linguistici* 24: 25–57.
Malchukov, Andrej. 1995. *Even* (Languages of the world. Materials 12). München: LINCOM.
Malchukov, Andrej. 2000. Perfect, evidentiality and related categories in Tungusic languages. In Lars Johanson & Bo Utas (eds.), *Evidentials: Turkic, Iranian and Neighbouring Languages*, 441–469. Berlin & New York: Mouton de Gruyter.
Malchukov, Andrej. 2003. Russian interference in Tungusic languages in an areal-typological perspective. In Sture Ureland (ed.), *Convergence and divergence of European languages* (Studies in Eurolinguistics 1), 235–251. Berlin: Logos.

Malchukov, Andrej. 2004. *Nominalization/Verbalization: Constraining a Typology of Transcategorial Operations*. München: LINCOM.
Malchukov, Andrej. 2006a. Yakut interference in North-Tungusic languages. In Hendrik Boeschoten & Lars Johanson (eds.), *Turkic Languages in Contact* (Turcologica 61), 122–138. Wiesbaden: Harrassowitz.
Malchukov, Andrej. 2006b. Constraining nominalization: Function/form competition. *Linguistics* 44: 973–1009.
Malchukov, Andrej. 2013. Verbalization and insubordination in Siberian languages. In Martine Robbeets & Hubert Cuyckens (eds.), *Shared Grammaticalization with Special Focus on the Transeurasian Languages* (Studies in Language Companion Series 132), 177–208. Amsterdam: John Benjamins.
Malchukov, Andrej & Igor Nedjalkov. 2010. Ditransitive constructions in Tungusic languages. In Andrej Malchukov, Martin Haspelmath & Bernard Comrie (eds.), *Studies in Ditransitive Constructions*, 316–352. Berlin & New York: Mouton de Gruyter.
Mallory, James Patrick. 1996. The Indo-European homeland problem: A matter of time. In Karlene Jones-Bley & Martin E. Huld (eds.), *The Indo-Europeanization of Northern Europe*, 1–22. Washington: Institute for the study of man.
Martin, Samuel Elmo. 1966. Lexical evidence relating Korean to Japanese. *Language* 42: 185–251.
Martin, Samuel Elmo. 1968. Grammatical elements relating Korean to Japanese. *Proceedings of the Eighth International Congress of Anthropological and Ethnological Sciences* 2. 405–407.
Martin, Samuel Elmo. 1970. Shodon: A dialect of the northern Ryukyus. *Journal of the American Oriental Society* 90 (1): 97–139.
Martin, Samuel Elmo. 1987. *The Japanese Language Through Time*. New Haven: Yale University Press.
Martin, Samuel Elmo. 1990. Morphological clues to the relationships of Japanese and Korean. In Philip Baldi (ed.), *Linguistic Change and Reconstruction Methodology* (Trends in Linguistics. Studies and Monographs 45), 483–509 Berlin & New York: Mouton de Gruyter.
Martin, Samuel Elmo. 1991a. Recent research on the relationships of Japanese and Korean. In Sydney M. Lamb & Douglas E. Mitchell (eds.), *Sprung from Some Common Source: Investigations Into the Prehistory of Languages*, 269–292. Stanford: Stanford University Press.
Martin, Samuel Elmo. 1991b. *A Reference Grammar of Japanese*. Tokyo: Tuttle.
Martin, Samuel Elmo. 1992. *A Reference Grammar of Korean*. Tokyo: Tuttle.
Martin, Samuel Elmo. 1995. On the prehistory of the Korean grammar: Verb forms. *Korean Studies* 19: 139–150.
Martin, Samuel Elmo. 1996. *Consonant lenition in Korean and the Macro-Altaic question*. Honolulu: University of Hawai'i Press.
Martin, Samuel Elmo. 1997. Un-Altaic Features of the Korean Verb. *Japanese/Korean Linguistics* 6: 3–40.
Martin, Samuel Elmo. 2002. Coming and going: Deictic verbs in Korean and Japanese. In Sang-Oak Lee & Gregory K. Iverson (eds.), *Pathways Into Korean Language and Culture: Essays in Honor of Young-Key Kim-Renaud*. Seoul, 373–381: Pagijong Press.
Martin, Samuel Elmo. 2006. What do Japanese and Korean have in common: The history of certain grammaticalizations. *Korean linguistics* 13: 219–234.
Maslova, Elena. 2003. *A Grammar of Kolyma Yukaghir* (Mouton Grammar Library 27). Berlin & New York: Mouton de Gruyter.

Matras, Yaron. 1998. Utterance modifiers and universals of grammatical borrowing. Linguistics 36: 281–331.
Matras, Yaron. 2009. *Language Contact*. Cambridge: Cambridge University Press.
Matras, Yaron & Jeanette Sakel (eds.). 2007. *Grammatical Borrowing in Cross-Linguistic Perspective*. Berlin & New York: Mouton de Gruyter.
McConvell, Patrick & Felicity Meakins. 2005. Gurindji Kriol: A mixed language emerges from Code-switching. *Australian Journal of Linguistics* 25 (1): 9–30.
Meillet, Antoine. 1921 [1912]. *Linguistique historique et linguistique générale*. Paris: Honoré Champion.
Meillet, Antoine. 1925. *La méthode comparative en linguistique historique*. Paris: Honoré Champion.
Mel'čuk, Igor. 1993. The inflectional category of voice: Towards a more rigorous definition. In Bernard Comrie & Maria Polinsky (eds.), *Causatives and Transitivity*, 1–46. Amsterdam: Benjamins.
Menges, Karl Heinrich. 1943. The function and origin of the Tungusic tense in *-ra*, and some related questions of Tungus grammar. *Language* 19: 237–251.
Menges, Karl Heinrich. 1960. *Morphologische Probleme I: Zum Genitiv und Accusativ*. Wiesbaden: Harrassowitz.
Menges, Karl Heinrich. 1968a. *Die Tungusischen Sprachen* (Handbuch der Orientalistik 1: Der Nahe und der Mittlere Osten 5, Altaistik 3: Tungusologie). Leiden: Brill.
Menges, Karl Heinrich. 1968b. *The Turkic Languages and Peoples: An Introduction to Turkic Studies*. Wiesbaden: Otto Harrassowitz.
Menges, Karl Heinrich. 1975. *Altajische Studien II: Japanisch und Altajisch* (Abhandlungen für die Kunde des Morgenlandes 41, 3). Wiesbaden: Steiner.
Menges, Karl Heinrich. 1977. Dravidian and Altaic. *Anthropos* 72: 129–179.
Menges, Karl Heinrich. 1978. Problems of Tungus linguistics. *Anthropos* 73: 382–400.
Menges, Karl Heinrich. 1984. Korean and Altaic. A Preliminary Sketch. *Central Asiatic Journal* 28: 234–295.
Miestamo, Matti. 2005. *Standard negation: The Negation of Declarative Verbal Main Clauses in a Typological Perspective* (Empirical Approaches to Language Typology 31). Berlin & New York: Mouton de Gruyter.
Miller, Roy Andrew. 1971. *Japanese and the Other Altaic Languages*. Chicago: The University of Chicago Press.
Miller, Roy Andrew. 1979. Old Korean and Altaic. *Ural-Altaische Jahrbücher* 51: 1–54.
Miller, Roy Andrew. 1980. *Origins of the Japanese Language*. Seattle: University of Washington Press.
Miller, Roy Andrew. 1981. Altaic origins of the Japanese verb classes. In Yoël L. Arbeitman (ed.), *Bono Homini Donum: Essays in Historical Linguistics in Memory of J. Alexander Kerns*, 815–880. Amsterdam: Benjamins.
Miller, Roy Andrew. 1982a. Japanese evidence for some Altaic denominal verb-stem derivational suffixes. *Acta Orientalia Academiae Scientarum Hungaricae* 36: 391–403.
Miller, Roy Andrew. 1982b. *Japan's Modern Myth: The Language and Beyond*. New York: Weatherhill.
Miller, Roy Andrew. 1985. Altaic connections of the Old Japanese negatives. *Central Asiatic Journal* 31: 35–84.
Miller, Roy Andrew. 1987. Proto Altaic *x-. *Central Asiatic Journal* 31: 19–63.

Miller, Roy Andrew. 1990. Archaeological light on Japanese linguistic origins. *Asian and Pacific Quarterly* 22: 1–26.
Miller, Roy Andrew. 1991a. Anti-Altaists *contra* Altaists. *Ural-Altaische Jahrbücher* 63: 5–62.
Miller, Roy Andrew. 1991b. Genetic connections among the Altaic languages. In Sydney M. Lamb & Douglas E. Mitchell (eds.), *Sprung from some Common Source: Investigations Into the Prehistory of Languages*, 293–327. Stanford: Stanford University Press.
Miller, Roy Andrew. 1993. On some petrified case formations in the Altaic Languages. *Acta Orientalia Academiae Scientarum Hungaricae* 46: 288–310.
Miller, Roy Andrew. 1994. The original geographic distribution of the Tungus languages. In Howard I. Aronson (ed.), *Non-Slavic Languages of the USSR*, 272–297. Columbus: Slavica Publishers.
Miller, Roy Andrew. 2008. Comparing Japanese and Korean. In Alicia Sanchez-Mazas, Roger Blench Malcolm Ross, Il'ja Peiros & Marie Lin (eds.), *Past Human Migrations in East Asia: Matching Archaeology, Linguistics and Genetics* (Routledge studies in the early history of languages 5), 263–286. London: Routledge.
Mithun, Marianne. 2008. The extension of dependency beyond the sentence. *Language* 84 (1): 69–119.
Mithun, Marianne. Forthcoming. Shifting finiteness in nominalization: From definitization to refinitization. Finiteness and Nominalization. In Claudine Chamoreau (ed.). Amsterdam: John Benjamins.
Miyake, Marc Hideo. 1997. Pre-Sino-Korean and Pre-Sino-Japanese: Reexamining an old problem from a modern perspective. *Japanese/Korean Linguistics* 6: 179–211.
Miyake, Marc Hideo. 1999. *The Phonology of Eighth Century Japanese Revisited: Another Reconstruction Based Upon Written Records*. Honolulu: University of Hawai'i at Manoa Ph.D. Dissertation.
Miyamoto, Kazuo. 2009. *Nōkō no kigen o saguru: Ine no kita michi* [Searching for the origins of agriculture: The way through which rice arrived]. Tokyo: Yoshikawa kōbunkan.
Moravcsik, Edith A. 1975. Borrowed verbs. *Wiener Linguistische Gazette* 8: 3–30.
Moravcsik, Edith A. 1978. Universals of language contact. In Joseph Greenberg (ed.), *Universals of Human Language*, 93–122. Stanford: Stanford University Press.
Moreno, Juan C. 1993. "Make" and the semantic origins of causativity: A typological study. In Bernard Comrie & Maria Polinsky (eds.), *Causatives and Transitivity*, 155–164. Amsterdam: John Benjamins.
Mostaert, Antoine. 1941–1944. *Dictionnaire ordos* [Ordos Dictionary], vols. 1–3 (Monumenta Serica, Monograph Series 5). Peking: The Catholic University.
Murayama Shichirō. 1957. Vergleichende Betrachtung der Kasus-Suffixe im Altjapanischen. In Pritsak, Omeljan (ed.), *Studia Altaica: Festschrift für Nikolaus Poppe zum 60. Geburtstag am 8 August 1957*, 126–131. Wiesbaden: Otto Harrassowitz.
Murayama Shichirō. 1978. *Nihongo keitō no tankyū* [Investigations into the Ancestry of Japanese]. Tokyo: Kōbun-dō.
Mureeva, Anna N. 1964. Očerk govora učurskich èvenkov [A study of the Učur Evenki dialect]. In Agnija V. Romanova & Anna N. Mureeva (eds.), *Očerki učurskogo, majskogo i tottinskogo govorov* [Studies on the Učur, Mayic and Tottinic Dialects], 6–74. Moscow: Nauk.
Muysken, Pieter. 2000. *Bilingual Speech: A Typology of Code-Mixing*. Cambridge: Cambridge University Press.
Nasilov, D. M. 1978. Formy vyraženija sposobov glagol'nogo dejstvija v altajskich jazykov (v svjazi s problemoj glagol'nogo vida). In Orest Petrovič Sunik (ed.), *Problema obščnosti altajskich jazykov*, 77–88. Leningrad: Nauka.

Nau, Nicole. 1995. *Möglichkeiten und Mechanismen kontaktbewegten Sprachwandels unter besonderer Berücksichtigung des Finnischen* (Edition Linguistik 08). Munich: Lincom.
Nedjalkov, Igor V. 1993. Causative-passive polysemy of the Manchu-Tungusic *-bu/-v(u)*. *Linguistica Antverpiensa* 27: 193–202.
Nedjalkov, Igor V. 1994. Negation in Evenki. In Peter Kahrel & René van den Berg (eds.), *Typological Studies in Negation*, 1–34. Amsterdam: John Benjamins.
Nedjalkov, Igor V. 1995. Converbs in Evenki. In Martin Haspelmath & Ekkehard König (eds.), *Converbs in Cross-Linguistic Perspective: Structure and Meaning of Adverbial Verb Forms – Adverbial Participles, Gerunds* (Empirical Approaches to Language Typology 13), 97–136. Berlin & New York: Mouton de Gruyter.
Nedjalkov, Igor V. 1997. *Evenki (Descriptive Grammars)*. London: Routledge.
Nedjalkov, Vladimir P. & Sergej Je. Jaxontov. 1988. The typology of resultative constructions. In Vladimir P. Nedjalkov & Bernard Comrie (eds.), *Typology of Resultative Constructions*, 3–62. Philadelphia: John Benjamins.
Nelson, Sarah M. 1993. *The Archaeology of Korea* (Cambridge World Archaeology). Cambridge: Cambridge University Press.
Nelson, Sarah M. 1995. Conclusion. In Sarah M. Nelson (ed.), *The Archaeology of Northeast China: Beyond the Great Wall*, 251–254. London: Routledge.
Nevskaya, Irina, Marcel Erdal, Jost Gippert, Klaus Röhrborn & Peter Zieme. 2004. Vorislamische Alttürkische Texte: Elektronisches Corpus; http://vatec2.fkidg1.uni-frankfurt.de/index.htm#Texte
Nichols, Johanna & Tandy Warnow. 2008. Tutorial on computational linguistic phylogeny. *Language and Linguistics Compass* 2 (5): 760–820.
Nichols, Johanna. 1992. *Linguistic Diversity in Space and Time*. Chicago: University of Chicago Press.
Nichols, Johanna. 1996. The comparative method as heuristic. In Mark Durie & Malcolm Ross (eds.), *The Comparative Method Reviewed: Regularity and Irregularity in Language Change*, 39–71. Oxford: Oxford University Press.
Nichols, Johanna. 2003. Diversity and stability in language. In Brian D. Joseph & Richard D. Janda (eds.), *The Handbook of Historical Linguistics*, 283–310. Oxford: Blackwell.
Nichols, Johanna. 2010. Proof of Dene–Yeniseian relatedness. In James Kari & Ben A. Potter (eds.), *The Dene-Yeiseian Connection* (Anthropological papers of the University of Alaska, New Series 5), 266–278. Fairbanks: Alaska Native Language Center.
Nichols, Johanna. 2014. Derivational paradigms in diachrony and comparison. In Martine Robbeets & Walter Bisang (eds.), *Paradigm Change: In the Transeurasian Languages and Beyond* (Studies in Language Companion Series 161), 61–88 Amsterdam: Benjamins.
Nikolaeva, Irina Alekseevna. 1999. *A Grammar of Udehe*. Leiden: Leiden University Ph.D. dissertation.
Nikolaeva, Irina Alekseevna. 2008. Introduction. In Irina Nikolaeva (ed.), *Finiteness: Theoretical and Empirical Foundations*, 1–19. Oxford: Oxford University Press.
Nikolaeva, Irina Alekseevna & Maria Tolskaya. 2003. *A Grammar of Udihe*. Berlin & New York: Mouton de Gruyter.
Norman, Jerry. 1974. A sketch of Sibe morphology. *Central Asiatic Journal* 28: 157–174.
Nugteren, Hans. 1997. On the classification of the "peripheral" Mongolic languages. In Árpád Berta (ed.), *Historical and Linguistic Interaction Between Inner-Asia and Europe* (Studia uralo-altaica 39), 207–216. Amsterdam: Benjamins.
Nugteren, Hans. 2003. Shira Yughur. In Juha Janhunen (ed.), *The Mongolic Languages*, 265–285. London: Routledge.

Nugteren, Hans. 2011. Mongolic phonology and the Qinghai-Gansu languages. Utrecht: LOT. Leiden University Ph.D. Dissertation.
Omodaka, Hisakata, Tetsu Asami, Teizō Ikegami, Itaru Ide, Hiroshi Itō Yoshiaki Kawabata, Masatoshi Kinoshita, Noriyuki Kojima, Atsuyoshi Sakakura, Akihiro Satake, Kazutami Nishimiya, Shirō Hashimoto (eds.). 1967. *Jidaibetsu kokugo daijiten: Jōdaihen* [Japanese dictionary per historical period: Old Japanese]. Tokyo: Sanseidō.
Omoto, Keiichi & Naruya Saitou. 1997. Genetic origins of the Japanese: A partial support for the 'dual structure hypothesis'. *American Journal of Physical Anthropology* 102: 437–446.
Ōno, Susumu. 1953. Nihongo no dōshi no katsuyōkei no kigen ni tsuite [On the origins of Japanese verb inflection]. *Kokugo to kokubungaku* [Japanese Language and Literature] 350. 47–56.
Orlov, A. M. 1873. *Grammatika man'čžurskogo jazyka* [Manchu Grammar]. Saint Petersburg.
Orlovskaya, M. N. 1999. *Yazyk mongolskich textov XIII-XIV* [The Language of the Mongolian Texts of the 13th and 14th Century]. Moscow: Nauka.
Pakendorf, Brigitte. 2009. Intensive contact and the copying of paradigms: An Even dialect in contact with Sakha (Yakut). *Journal of Language Contact* 2: 85–110.
Pashkov, B.K. 1950. *Sintaksis man'čžurskogo prostogo predloženija, vol 1 & 2* [Syntax of the simple sentence in the Manchu Language]. Moscow: PhD dissertation.
Payne, John R. 1985. Negation. In Timothy Shopen (ed.), *Language Typology and Syntactic Description, vol. 1: Clause Structure*, 197–242. Cambridge: Cambridge University Press.
Pedersen, Holger. 1938. *Hittitisch und die anderen indoeuropäischen Sprachen*. Copenhagen: Levin & Munksgaard.
Pellard, Thomas. 2008. Proto-Japonic *e and *o in Eastern Old Japanese. *Cahiers de linguistique – Asie Orientale* 37 (2): 133–158.
Pellard, Thomas. 2009. *Ōgami: Éléments de description d'un parler du Sud des Ryūkyū*. Paris: École des hautes études en sciences sociales.
Pellard, Thomas. 2011. Ryukyuan perspectives on the Proto-Japonic vowel system. *Japanese/Korean Linguistics* 20: 1–15.
Pelliot, Paul. 1949. *Histoire secrète des Mongols. Restitution du texte mongol et traduction française des chapitres I à VI*. [The Secret History of the Mongols. Restitution of Mongolian text and French translation of chapters I to VI.] Paris.
Pevnov, Alexander M. 2011. The problem of the localization of the Manchu-Tungusic Homeland. In Andrej Malchukov & Lindsay Whaley (eds.), *Recent Advances in Tungusic Linguistics*, 17–40. Wiesbaden: Harrassowitz.
Pinkster, Harm. 1987. The strategy and chronology of the development of future and perfect tense auxiliaries in Latin. In Martin Harris & Paolo Ramat (eds.), *Historical Development of Auxiliaries*, 193–223. Berlin & New York: Mouton de Gruyter.
Plank, Frans. 1994. Inflection and derivation. In R. E. Asher (ed.) 1994. *The Encyclopedia of Language and Linguistics, vol. 3*, 1671–1678. Oxford: Pergamon Press.
Plank, Frans. 1998. The covariation of phonology with morphology and syntax: A hopeful history. *Linguistic typology* 2: 195–230.
Polivanov, Evgenij Dmitrvič. 1924. K rabote o muzykal'noj akcentuacii v japonskom jazyke (v svjazi s malajskim) [Work on the musical accent in Japanese (with reference to Malaysian)]. *Bjulleten' 1-go Sredne-Aziatskogo gosudarstvennogo universiteta* 4: 101–108.
Poppe, Nicholas. 1938. *Mongol'skij slovar' Mukaddimat al-Adab* [Mongolian Dictionary Mukaddimat al-Adab]. Moscow: Izdatel'stvo Akademii nauk SSSR.

Poppe, Nicholas. 1953. Bemerkungen zu Ramstedts Einführung in die altaische Sprachwissenschaft. *Studia Orientalia* 19: 5–13.
Poppe, Nicholas. 1954. *Grammar of Written Mongolian*. Wiesbaden: Otto Harrassowitz.
Poppe, Nicholas. 1955a. *Introduction to Mongolian Comparative Studies* (Mémoires de la société Finno-Ougrienne 110). Helsinki: Suomalais-Ugrilainen Seura.
Poppe, Nicholas. 1955b. Tempus und Aspekt in den Altaischen Sprachen. *Studium Generale* 9: 556–561.
Poppe, Nicholas. 1960. *Vergleichende Grammatik der altaischen Sprachen, Teil 1: Vergleichende Lautlehre* (Porta Linguarum Orientalium, Neue Serie 4). Wiesbaden: Otto Harrassowitz.
Poppe, Nicholas. 1964. Der altaische Sprachtyp. In Bertold Spuler, Hartwig Altenmüller, Nicholas Poppe (eds.), *Mongolistik* (Handbuch der Orientalistik 5, 2), 1–16 Leiden: Brill.
Poppe, Nicholas. 1972a. Über einige Verbalstammbildungssuffixe in den altaischen Sprachen. *Orientalia Suecana* 21: 119–141.
Poppe, Nicholas. 1972b. A new symposium on the Altaic Theory. *Central Asiatic Journal* 16: 37–58.
Poppe, Nicholas. 1974. Zur Stellung des Tschuwaschischen. *Central Asiatic Journal* 18 (2): 135–147.
Poppe, Nicholas. 1976. Ancient Mongolian. In Walter Heissig (ed.), *Tractata Altaica: Denis Sinor sexagenario optime de rebus altaicis merito dedicata*, 463–478. Wiesbaden: Otto Harrassowitz.
Poppe, Nicholas. 1977a. On some Altaic case forms. *Central Asiatic Journal* 21: 55–74.
Poppe, Nicholas. 1977b. The problem of Uralic and Altaic affinity. *Mémoires de la Société Finno-Ougrienne* 58: 221–225.
Ramsey, Samuel Robert. 1975. Middle Korean *w-*, *z-*, and *t/l-* verb stems. *Ŏhak yŏngu* 11: 59–67.
Ramsey, Samuel Robert. 1977. S-clusters and reinforced Consonants. In Chin-W. Kim (ed.), *Papers in Korean Linguistics*, 59–66. Columbia: Hornbeam Press.
Ramsey, Samuel Robert. 1978. *Accent and Morphology in Korean dialects: A Descriptive and Historical Study*. Seoul: Tower Press.
Ramsey, Samuel Robert. 1979. The old Kyoto dialect and the historical development of Japanese accent. *Harvard Journal of Japanese Studies* 39: 157–175.
Ramsey, Samuel Robert. 1982. Language change in Japan and the odyssey of a *teisetsu*. *Journal of Japanese Studies* 8: 97–131.
Ramsey, Samuel Robert. 1986. The inflecting stems of Proto-Korean. *Language Research* 22: 183–194.
Ramsey, Samuel Robert. 1991. Proto-Korean and the origin of Korean accent. In William G. Boltz & Michael C. Shapiro (eds.), *Studies in the Historical Phonology of Asian Languages* (Current Issues in Linguistic Theory 77), 215–238. Philadelphia: Benjamins.
Ramsey, Samuel Robert. 1993. Some remarks on reconstructing earlier Korean. *Language Research* 29: 433–441.
Ramsey, Samuel Robert. 1997. The invention of the Korean alphabet and the history of the Korean language. In Young-Key Kim-Renaud (ed.), *The Korean Alphabet: Its History and Structure*, 131–143. Honolulu: University of Hawai'i Press.
Ramstedt, Gustaf John. 1903 [1969]. *Über die Konjugation des Khalkha-Mongolischen* (Mémoires de la Société Finno-Ougrienne 19). Osnabrück: Otto Zeller.
Ramstedt, Gustaf John. 1912. Zur Verbalstammbildungslehre der mongolisch-türkischen Sprachen. *Journal de la Société finno-ougrienne* 28: 1–86.

Ramstedt, Gustaf John. 1924a. A comparison of the Altaic languages with Japanese. *Transactions of the Asiatic Society of Japan* 2 (1): 41–54.
Ramstedt, Gustaf John. 1924b. Die Verneinung in den altaischen Sprachen: Eine semasiologische studie. *Mémoires de la Société Finno-Ougrienne* 52: 196–215.
Ramstedt, Gustaf John. 1935. *Kalmückisches Wörterbuch*. Helsinki: Suomalais-Ugrilainen Seura.
Ramstedt, Gustaf John. 1939. *Studies in Korean Etymology* (Mémoires de la Société finno-ougrienne 95). Helsinki: Suomalai-Ugrilainen Seura.
Ramstedt, Gustaf John. 1945. Das deverbal Nomen auf -*i* in den Altaischen Sprachen. *Studia Orientalia* 11 (6): 1–8.
Ramstedt, Gustaf John. 1952. *Einführung in die altaische Sprachwissenschaft II: Formenlehre*. (Mémoires de la Société finno-ougrienne 104, 2). Helsinki: Suomalais-Ugrilainen Seura.
Ramstedt, Gustaf John. 1957. *Einführung in die altaische Sprachwissenschaft I: Lautlehre* (Mémoires de la Société finno-ougrienne 104, 1). Helsinki: Suomalais-Ugrilainen Seura.
Räsänen, Martti. 1957. *Materialien zur Morphologie der türkischen Sprachen* (Studia Orientalia 21). Helsinki: Suomalais-Ugrilainen Seura.
Reckel, Johannes. 1995. *Bohai, Geschichte und Kultur eines mandschurisch-koreanischen Königsreiches der Tang-Zeit* (Aetas Manjurica 5). Wiesbaden: Harrassowitz.
Rhee, Seongha. 1996. *Semantics of Verbs and Grammaticalization: The Development in Korean from a Cross-Linguistic Perspective*. Austin: University of Texas Ph.D. dissertation.
Rickmeyer, Jens. 1989. Japanisch und der altaische Sprachtyp: Eine Synopsis struktureller Entsprechungen. *Bochumer Jahrbuch zur Ostasienforschung* 12: 313–323.
Robbeets, Martine. 2004a. Swadesh 100 on Japanese, Korean and Altaic. *Tokyo University Linguistic Papers* 23: 99–118.
Robbeets, Martine. 2004b. Does Doerfer's Zufall mean 'cognate'? The case of the initial velar correspondence in Altaic. *Turkic Languages* 8: 146–178.
Robbeets, Martine. 2005. *Is Japanese Related to Korean, Tungusic, Mongolic and Turkic?* (Turcologica 64). Wiesbaden: Harrassowitz.
Robbeets, Martine. 2007a. How the actional suffix chain connects Japanese to Altaic. *Turkic Languages* 11 (1): 3–58.
Robbeets, Martine. 2007b. The causative-passive in the Trans-Eurasian languages. *Turkic Languages* 11 (2): 235–278.
Robbeets, Martine. 2007c. Koguryo as a Missing Link. In Remco Breuker (ed.), *Korea in the Middle. Festschrift for Boudewijn Walraven*, 118–141. Leiden: CNWS.
Robbeets, Martine. 2008. If Japanese is Altaic, how can it be so simple? In Alexander Lubotsky, Jos Schaeken & Jeroen Wiedenhof (eds.), *Evidence and Counter-Evidence: Essays in Honour of Frederik Kortlandt, vol. 2: General Linguistics* (Studies in Slavic and General Linguistics 33), 337–367. Amsterdam: Rodopi.
Robbeets, Martine. 2009a. Insubordination in Altaic. *Journal of Philology* 31. Ural-Altaic Studies 1: 61–79.
Robbeets, Martine. 2009b. Review of John Whitman & Bjarke Frellesvig (eds.), 2008, *Proto-Japanese: Issues and prospects* (Current Issues in Linguistic Theory 294), New York: Benjamins. *Journal of language relationship* 2: 144–150.
Robbeets, Martine. 2010. Transeurasian: Can verbal morphology end the controversy? In Lars Johanson & Martine Robbeets (eds.), *Transeurasian Verbal Morphology in a Comparative Perspective: Genealogy, Contact, Chance* (Turcologica 78), 81–114. Wiesbaden: Harrassowitz.

Robbeets, Martine. 2012. Shared verb morphology in the Transeurasian languages: Copy or cognate? In Lars Johanson & Martine Robbeets (eds.), *Copies Versus Cognates in Bound Morphology* (Brill's Studies in Language, Cognition and Culture 3), 427–446. Leiden: Brill.
Robbeets, Martine. 2013. Genealogically motivated grammaticalization. In Martine Robbeets & Hubert Cuyckens (eds.), *Shared Grammaticalization: With Special Focus on the Transeurasian Languages* (Studies in Language Companion Series 132), 147–175. Amsterdam: Benjamins.
Robbeets, Martine. 2014. The Japanese inflectional paradigm in a Transeurasian perspective. In Martine Robbeets & Walter Bisang (eds.), *Paradigm Change: In the Transeurasian Languages and Beyond* (Studies in Language Companion Series 161), 197–232. Amsterdam: John Benjamins.
Robbeets, Martine. Forthcoming. Japanese, Korean and the Transeurasian languages. In Raymond Hickey (ed.), *The Cambridge Handbook of Areal Linguistics* (Cambridge Handbooks in Language and Linguistics). Cambridge: Cambridge University Press.
Robbeets, Martine & Hubert Cuyckens. 2013. Towards a typology of shared grammaticalization. In Martine Robbeets & Hubert Cuyckens (eds.), *Shared Grammaticalization: With Special Focus on the Transeurasian Languages* (Studies in Language Companion Series 132), 1–20. Amsterdam: Benjamins.
Robbeets, Martine & Walter Bisang (eds.). 2014. *Paradigm Change: In the Transeurasian Languages and Beyond* (Studies in Language Companion Series 161). Amsterdam: Benjamins.
Robbeets, Martine & Walter Bisang. 2014. When paradigms change. In Martine Robbeets & Walter Bisang (eds.), *Paradigm Change: In the Transeurasian Languages and Beyond*. (Studies in Language Companion Series 161), 1–19. Amsterdam: Benjamins.
Róna-Tas, András. 1982. The periodization and sources of Chuvash linguistic history. In András Róna-Tas (ed.), *Chuvash Studies*, 113–169. Budapest: Akadémiai Kiadó.
Róna-Tas, András. 1998. The reconstruction of Proto-Turkic and the genetic question. In Lars Johanson & Éva Ágnes Csató (eds.), *The Turkic Languages*, 67–80. New York: Routledge.
Róna-Tas, András. 1999. *Hungarians and Europe in the Early Middle Ages: An Introduction to Early Hungarian History*. Budapest: Akadémiai Nyomda.
Siiri Rootsi et al. 2007. A counter-clockwise northern route of the Y-chromosome haplogroup N from Southeast Asia towards Europe. *European Journal of Human Genetics* 15: 204–211.
Rozycki, William, 1994. *Mongol elements in Manchu* (Uralic and Altaic Series 157). Indiana: Bloomington.
Rozycki, William. 2006. Review of Martine Robbeets, 2005, *Is Japanese Related to Korean, Tungusic, Mongolic and Turkic?* Wiesbaden: Harrassowitz. *Mongolian Studies* 28: 114–115.
Röhrborn, Klaus. 1972. Kausativ und Passiv im Uigurischen. *Central Asiatic Journal* 16: 70–77.
Russell, Kerri L. 2006. *A Reconstruction and Morphophonemic Analysis of Proto-Japonic Verbal Morphology*. Honolulu: University of Hawai'i Ph.D. Dissertation.
Rybatzki, Volker. 2003a. Middle Mongol. In Juha Janhunen (ed.), *The Mongolic Languages*, 57–82. London: Routledge.
Rybatzki, Volker. 2003b. Intra-Mongolic taxonomy. In Juha Janhunen (ed.), *The Mongolic Languages*, 364–390. London: Routledge.
Sagart, Laurent 2008. The expansion of Setaria farmers in East Asia: A linguistic and archaeological model. In Alicia Sanchez-Mazas, Roger Blench, Malcolm D. Ross, Ilia Peiros, Marie Lin. (eds.) 2008. *Past Human Migrations in East Asia: Matching Archaeology, Linguistics and Genetics* (Routledge studies in the early history of languages 5), 133–158. London: Routledge.

Sagart, Laurent. 2011. How many independent rice vocabularies in East Asia? *Rice* 4 (3): 121–133.
Sakakura, Atsuyoshi. 1966. *Gokōsei no kenkyū* [Investigations in word compounding]. Tokyo: Kadokawa shoten.
Sanžeev, G. D. 1962. K voprosu ob otricanii v mongol'skich jazykach [On negation in the Mongolian language]. *Acta Orientalia Hungarica* 15. 273–282.
Sanžeev, G. D. 1964. *Sravnitel'naja grammatika mongol'skich jazykov* [Comparative grammar of Mongolic languages]. Moscow: Nauka.
Sapir, Edward. 1921. *Language*. New York: Harcourt, Brace & World.
Sapir, Edward. 1929. A study of phonetic symbolism. *Journal of Experimental Phonology* 12: 225–239.
Sárközi, Alice. 2004. *Classical Mongolian*. München: LINCOM.
Schachter, Paul. 1985. Parts-of-speech systems. In Timothy Shopen (ed.), *Language Typology and Syntactic Description, Vol. 1: Clause Structure*, 3–61. Cambridge: Cambridge University Press.
Schneider, E. 1936. *Kratkij udegejsko-russkij slovar'* [A concise Udehe-Russian dictionnary]. Leningrad: Učpedgiz.
Schönig, Claus. 2003. Turko-Mongolic relations. In Juha Janhunen (ed.), *The Mongolic Languages*, 403–419. London: Routledge.
Schönig, Claus. 2008. Review of Lars Johanson, 2002, *Structural Factors in Turkic Language Contacts*, Richmond: Curzon. *Zeitschrift der Deutschen Morgenlandische Gesellschaft* 158: 197–200.
Seifart, Frank. 2012. The principle of morphosyntactic subsystem integrity in language contact: Evidence from morphological borrowing in Resígaro (Arawakan). *Diachronica* 29: 471–504.
Sekerina, Irina A. 1994. Copper Island (Mednyj) Aleut (CIA): A mixed language. *Languages of the World* 8: 14–31.
Serafim, Leon A. 1985. *Shodon: The Prehistory of a Northern Ryukyuan Dialect of Japanese*. Tokyo: Hompo Shoseki.
Serafim, Leon A. 2003. When and where did the Japonic language enter the Ryukyus? A critical comparison of language, archeology and history. In Toshiki Osada & Alexander Vovin (eds.), *Perspectives on the Origins of the Japanese Language*, 463–476. Kyoto: International Research Center for Japanese Studies.
Serafim, Leon A. 2008. The uses of Ryukyuan in understanding Japonic language history. In Bjarke Frellesvig & John Whitman (eds.), *Proto-Japanese: Issues and Prospects* (Current issues in linguistic theory 249), 79–99. Amsterdam: Benjamins.
Shimoji, Michinori. 2010. Ryukyuan languages: An introduction. In Michinori Shimoji & Thomas Pellard (eds.), *An Introduction to Ryukyuan Languages*, 1–13. Tokyo: ILCAA.
Shirai Yasuhiro. 1998. Where the progressive and the resultative meet. *Studies in Language* 22 (3): 661–692.
Simensen, Erik 2002. The Old Nordic lexicon. In Oskar Bandle, Kurt Braunmüller, Ernst Håkon Jahr, Allan Karker, Hans-Peter Naumann & Ulf Teleman (eds.), *The Nordic Languages: An International Handbook of the History of the North Germanic Languages* (Handbücher zur Sprach- und Kommunikationswissenschaft 22, 1), 951–963. Berlin & New York: Mouton de Gruyter.
Simonov, Michail. 1988. Fonologičeskaya sistema Udegejskogo Yazyka. In Michail Simonov & Aleksandr Anikin (eds.), *Istoriko-tipologičeskie issledovaniya po Tungusi-Tunguso-Man'čžurskim yazykam*, 44–88. Novosibirsk: Nauk.

Sinor, Dennis. 1963. Observations on a new comparative Altaic phonology. *Bulletin of the School of Oriental and African Studies* 26: 133–144.
Sinor, Denis. 1968. *La langue mandjoue* (Handbuch der Orientalistik I, V, Altaiistik 3). Leiden: Brill.
Sinor, Dennis. 1988. The problem of the Ural-Altaic relationship. In Dennis Sinor (ed.), *The Uralic Languages: Description, History and Foreign Influences*, 706–741. Leiden: Brill.
Slater, Keith W. 2003. *A Grammar of Mangghuer: A Mongolic Language of China's Qinghai-Gansu Sprachbund*. London: Routledge Curzon.
Sohn, Ho-min. 1994. *Korean*. London: Routledge.
Stachowski, Marek. 2006. Der Ursprung des synthetischen Imperfekts im Jakutischen. *Studia Etymologica Cracoviensia* 11: 135–139.
Starostin, Sergej A. 1991. *Altajskaja problema i proisxoždenie japanskogo jazyka* [The Altaic problem and the origins of Japanese]. Moscow: Nauk.
Starostin, Sergej A. 2008. Altaic loans in old Chinese. In Alicia Sanchez-Mazas, Roger Blench, Malcolm D. Ross, Ilia Peiros & Marie Lin (eds.), *Past Human Migrations in East Asia: Matching Archaeology, Linguistics and Genetics* (Routledge Studies in the Early History of Languages 5), 254–262. London: Routledge.
Starostin, Sergej A., Anna Dybo & Oleg Mudrak. 2003. *Etymological Dictionary of the Altaic Languages*. Leiden: Brill.
Stassen, Leon. 1997. *Intransitive Predication*. Oxford: Clarendon Press.
Stassen, Leon. 2005. Predicative adjectives. In Martin Haspelmath, Matthew S. Dryer, David Gil & Bernard Comrie (eds.), *The World Atlas of Language Structures*, 478–481. Oxford: Oxford University Press.
Straka, Georges. 1979. Contribution à l'histoire de la consonne *R* en français. In Georges Straka (ed.), *Les sons et les mots*, 465–499. Paris: Librairie C. Klincksieck.
Street, John. 1957. *The Language of the Secret History of the Mongols*. New Haven: American Oriental Society.
Street, John. 1978. *Altaic Elements in Old Japanese, Part 2*. Madison: Manuscript.
Street, John. 1985. Japanese reflexes of the Proto-Altaic lateral. *Journal of the American Oriental Society* 105: 637–651.
Street, John & Roy Andrew Miller. 1975. *Altaic Elements in Old Japanese, Part 1*. Madison: The Authors.
Stump, Gregory T. 2001. *Inflectional Morphology: A Theory of Paradigm Structure* (Cambridge Studies in Linguistics 93). Cambridge: Cambridge University Press.
Sunik, Orest Petrovič. 1959. *Tunguso-man'čžurskije jazyki* (Mladopi'mennyje jazyki narodov SSSR) [The Manchu-Tungusic languages (Languages of the Soviet Union)]. Moscow: Nauka.
Sunik, Orest Petrovič. 1962. *Glagol v tunguso-man'čžurskich jazykach* [The verb in the Manchu-Tungusic languages]. Moscow: Nauk.
Swadesh, Morris. 1951. Diffusional cumulation and archaic residue as historical explanations. *Southwestern Journal of Anthropology* 7: 1–21.
Swadesh, Morris. 1955. Towards greater accuracy in lexicostatistic dating. *International Journal of American Linguistics* 21: 121–137.
Tadmor, Uri, Martin Haspelmath & Bradley Taylor. 2010. Borrowability and the notion of basic vocabulary. *Diachronica* 27 (2): 226–246.
Takeuchi, Lone. 1999. *The structure and history of Japanese*. New York: Longman.
Tanaka, Masashi et al. 2004. Mitochondrial genome variation in eastern Asia and the peopling of Japan. *Genome Research* 14: 1832–1850.

Tekin, Talât. 1982. On the structure of Altaic echoic verbs in {-KIrA}. *Acta Orientalia Academiae Scientarum Hungaricae* 36: 503–513.
Tekin, Talât. 1990. A new classification of the Turkic languages. *Türk Dilleri Araştïrmalari* 1990: 5–18.
Thomason, Sarah Grey. 1983. Genetic relationship and the case of Ma'a (Mbugu). *Studies in African linguistics* 14 (2): 195–231.
Thomason, Sarah Grey. 1997. Mednyi Aleut. In Sarah Grey Thomason (ed.), *Contact Languages: A Wider Perspective*, 449–468. Amsterdam: Benjamins.
Thomason, Sarah Grey. 2001. *Language Contact: An Introduction*. Washington: Georgetown University.
Thomason, Sarah Grey & Terrence Kaufman. 1988. *Language Contact, Creolization, and Genetic Linguistics*. Berkeley: University of California Press.
Thorpe, Maner Lawton. 1983. *Ryukyuan Language History*. Los Angeles: University of Southern California Ph.D. dissertation.
Toh, Soo-hee 2005. About early Paekche language mistaken as being Koguryo language. *Journal of Inner and East Asian Studies* 2: 10–31.
Trask, Robert Lawrence. 1993. *A Dictionary of Grammatical Terms in Linguistics*. London: Routledge.
Trask, Robert Lawrence. 1996. *Historical Linguistics*. London: Arnold.
Traugott, Elizabeth & Bernd Heine. 1991. Introduction. In Elizabeth Traugott & Bernd Heine (eds.), *Approaches to Grammaticalization I*, 1–14. Amsterdam: Benjamins.
Uemura, Yukio. 2003. *The Ryukyuan Language*. Kyoto: Endangered Languages of the Pacific Rim.
Unger, James Marshall. 1977. *Studies in Early Japanese Morphophonemics*. Indiana: University Linguistics Club, Yale University Ph.D. dissertation.
Unger, Jim Marshall. 2000a. Reconciling comparative and internal reconstruction: The case of Old Japanese /ti, ri, ni/. *Language* 76: 655–681.
Unger, Jim Marshall. 2000b. Rendaku and Proto-Japanese accent classes. *Japanese-Korean Linguistics* 9: 17–30.
Unger, James Marshall. 2005. When was Korean first spoken in Southeastern Korea? *Journal of Inner and East Asian Studies* 2: 87–105.
Unger, James Marshall. 2009. *The role of contact in the origins of the Japanese and Korean languages*. Honolulu: University of Hawai'i Press.
Unger, James Marshall. 2012. The likelihood of morphological borrowing: The case of Korean and Japanese. In Lars Johanson & Martine Robbeets (eds.), *Copies Versus Cognates in Bound Morphology* (Brill's Studies in Language, Cognition and Culture 2), 411–426. Leiden: Brill.
Ureland, Sture. 1984. The influence of American English on American Swedish: A case study on the nature of interference. In Sture P. Ureland & Iain Clarkson (eds.), *Scandinavian Language Contacts*, 281–324. Cambridge: Cambridge University Press.
Vanhove, Martine, Thomas Stolz, Aina S. Urdze & Hitomi Otsuka (eds.). 2012. *Morphologies in Contact* (Studia Typologica 10). Berlin: Akademie Verlag.
Vasilevič, Glafira M. 1948. *Očerki dialektov evenkijskogo jazyka* [Study on Evenki dialects]. Leningrad: Nauka.
Vasilevič, Glafira M. 1960. *K voprosu o klassifikacii tunguso-man'čžurskix jazykov* (Voprosy jazykoznanija 1960, 2) [On the classification of the Manchu-Tungusic languages (Issues in linguistics 1960, 2)]. Moscow: Nauka.

Vietze, Hans-Peter & Gendeng Lubsang. 1992. *Altan Tobči. Eine mongolische Chronik des XVII. Jahrhunderts von Blo bzaṅ bstan 'jin*. Tokyo: Institute for the Study of Languages and Cultures of Asia and Africa.
Volkova, M. P. 1961. *Nisan samani bithe. Predanije o nišanskoi šamanke* [The Tale of the Nisan Shamaness]. Moscow: Nauk.
Vovin, Alexander. 1993. Towards a new classification of the Tungusic languages. *Ural-Altaische Jahrbücher* 65: 99–113.
Vovin, Alexander. 1994. Genetic affiliation of Japanese and methodology of linguistic comparison. *Journal de la Société finno-ougrienne* 85: 241–256.
Vovin, Alexander. 1995. The origin of register in Japanese and the Altaic theory. *Japanese/Korean Linguistics* 6: 113–133.
Vovin, Alexander. 1997a. On the syntactic typology of Old Japanese. *Journal of East Asian Linguistics* 6: 237–290.
Vovin, Alexander. 1997b. Voiceless velars in Manchu. *Journal de la Société Finno-Ougrienne* 87: 263–280.
Vovin, Alexander. 1998. Altaic, so far. *Migracijske Teme* 15: 155–213.
Vovin, Alexander. 2001. Japanese, Korean and Tungusic. Evidence for genetic relationship from verbal morphology. In David B. Honey & David C. Wright (eds.), *Altaic Affinities* (Proceedings of the 40th meeting of the PIAC, Provo, Utah 1997), 183–202 Indiana University: Research Institute for Inner Asian Studies.
Vovin, Alexander. 2003. *A reference grammar of Classical Japanese prose*. London: Routledge-Curzon.
Vovin, Alexander. 2005a. The end of the Altaic controversy. *Central Asiatic Journal* 49: 71–132.
Vovin, Alexander. 2005b. Koguryŏ and Paekche: Different languages or dialects of Old Korean? *Journal of Inner and East Asian Studies* 2: 108–140.
Vovin, Alexander. 2005c. *A Descriptive and Comparative Grammar of Western Old Japanese, Part 1: Sources, Script and Phonology, Lexicon, Nominals* (Languages of Asia 3). Folkestone: Global Oriental.
Vovin, Alexander. 2008a. *Koreo-Japonica: A Re-Evaluation of a Common Genetic Origin* (Center for Korean Studies Monograph). Honolulu: University of Hawai'i Press.
Vovin, Alexander. 2008b. Proto-Japanese beyond the accent system. In Bjarke Frellesvig & John Whitman (eds.), *Proto-Japanese: Issues and Prospects* (Current Issues in Linguistic Theory 294), 141–156 Amsterdam: Benjamins.
Vovin, Alexander. 2009a. *A Descriptive and Comparative Grammar of Western Old Japanese, Part 2: Adjectives, Verbs, Adverbs, Conjunctions, Particles, Postpositions* (Languages of Asia 8). Folkestone: Global Oriental.
Vovin, Alexander. 2009b. Review of Martine Robbeets, 2005, *Is Japanese Related to Korean, Tungusic, Mongolic and Turkic?* Wiesbaden: Harrassowitz. *Central Asiatic Journal* 53, 105–147.
Vovin, Alexander. 2011. Why Japonic is not demonstrably related to 'Altaic' or Korean. In *Historical Linguistics in the Asia-Pacific Region and the Position of Japanese, Handouts*, 17–25. Osaka: National Museum of Ethnology.
Wang, Penglin. 1993. *Description of Dagur Verb Morphology*. Honolulu: University of Hawai'i at Manoa Ph.D. Dissertation.
Weiers, Michael. 1966. *Untersuchungen zu einer historischen Grammatik des präklassischen Schriftmongolisch*. Bonn: Rheinischen Friedrich-Wilhelms-Universität Ph.D dissertation.

Weinreich, Uriel. 1953. *Languages in Contact: Findings and Problems*. New York: Publications of the Linguistic Circle of New York.
Werner, Heinrich. 1997. *Die ketische Sprache*. Wiesbaden: Harrassowitz.
Whaley, Lindsay J., Lenore A. Grenoble & Fengxiang Li.1999. Revisiting Tungusic classification from the bottom up: A comparison of Evenki and Oroqen. *Language* 75: 286–321.
Whitman, John Bradford. 1985. *The Phonological Basis for the Comparison of Japanese and Korean*. Cambrige: Harvard University Ph.D. dissertation.
Whitman, John Bradford. 1999. *Primary Root Shape in Japanese and Korean*. Paper presented at the workshop on Japanese and Korean comparative linguistics at the international conference on historical linguistics, Vancouver, 9–13 August.
Whitman, John Bradford. 2002. Review of Mark Hudson,1999, *Ruins of Identity: Ethnogenesis in the Japanese Islands,* Honolulu: University of Hawai'i Press. *Harvard Journal of Asiatic Studies* 62: 256–265.
Whitman, John Bradford. 2008. The source of the bigrade conjugation and stem shape in pre-Old Japanese. In Bjarke Frellesvig & John Whitman Bradford (eds.), *Proto-Japanese: Issues and Prospects* (Current Issues in Linguistic Theory 294), 159–173 Amsterdam: Benjamins.
Whitman, John Bradford. 2011. Northeast Asian linguistic ecology and the advent of rice agriculture in Korea and Japan. *Rice* 4: 149–158.
Whitman, John Bradford. 2012. The relationship between Japanese and Korean. In Nicolas Tranter (ed.), *The Languages of Japan and Korea* (Routledge Language Family Series), 24–38 London: Routledge.
Wichmann, Søren & Jan Wohlgemuth. 2008. Loan verbs in a typological perspective. In Thomas Stolz, Dik Bakker & Rosa Salas Palomo (eds.), *Aspects of Language Contact: New Theoretical, Methodological and Empirical Findings with Special Focus on Romancisation Processes*, 89–121. Berlin & New York: Mouton de Gruyter.
Wilkins, David P. 1996. Morphology. In Hans Goebl, Peter H. Nelde, Zdeněk Starý & Wolfgang Wölck (eds.), *Contact Linguistics: An International Handbook of Contemporary Research*, 109–117. Berlin & New York: Mouton de Gruyter.
Willis, David, Christopher Lucas & Anne Breitbarth. 2013. Comparing diachronies of negation. In David Willis, Christopher Lucas & Anne Breitbarth (eds.), *The History of Negation in the Languages of Europe and the Mediterranean, Vol. 1: Case Studies*. (Oxford Studies in diachronic and historic linguistics), 1–50. Oxford: Oxford University Press.
Wohlgemuth, Jan. 2009. *A Typology of Verbal Borrowings* (Trends in Linguistics. Studies and Monographs 211). Berlin & New York: Mouton de Gruyter.
Wrona, Janick 2008. The nominal and adnominal forms in Old Japanese: Consequences for a reconstruction of pre-Old Japanese syntax. In Bjarke Frellesvig & John Whitman (eds.), *Proto-Japanese: Issues and prospects* (Current Issues in Linguistic Theory 294), 193–215. Amsterdam: Benjamins.
Wrona, Janick. 2011. A case of non-derived stand-alone nominalization: Evidence from Japanese. In Foong Ha Yap, Karen Grunow-Harsta & Janick Wrona (eds.), *Nominalization in Asian Languages* (Typological Studies in Language 96), 423–443. Amsterdam: John Benjamins.
Wu, Yingzhe & Juha Janhunen. 2010. *New Materials on the Khitan Small Script* (Languages of Asia 9). Leiden: Brill.
Yanagida, Yuko & John Whitman. 2009. Alignment and word order in Old Japanese. *Journal of East Asian Linguistics* 18: 101–144.

Yap, Foong Ha & Stephen Matthews. 2008. The development of nominalizers in East Asian and Tibeto-Burman languages. In María José López-Couso & Elena Seoane (eds.), *Rethinking Grammaticalization: New Perspectives* (Typological Studies in Linguistics 76), 309–341. Amsterdam: John Benjamins.

Yap, Foong Ha, Stephen Matthews & Kaoru Horie. 2004. From pronominalizer to pragmatic marker: Implications for unidirectionality from a crosslinguistic perspective. In Olga Fischer, Muriel Norde & Harry Perridon (eds.), *Up and Down the Cline: The Nature of Grammaticalization* (Typological Studies in Language 59), 137–168. Amsterdam: John Benjamins.

Yeon, Jaehoon. 2003. *Korean Grammatical Constructions. Their Form and Meaning*. London: Saffron.

Ylikoski, Jussi. 2003. Defining non-finites: Action nominals, converbs and infinitives. *SKY Journal of Linguistics* 16: 185–237.

Zakharov, Ivan Il'ič. 1879. *Grammatika man'čžurskogo jazyka* [Grammar of Manchu] (Languages of Asia Classic Texts 1). Leiden: Brill.

Language index

Acadian French, 70
Afro-Asiatic languages, 58
Afshar, 10
Agia Varvara Romani, 65, 66
Akiyama, 346
Albanian, 48, 50, 52, 66, 70, 77, 78, 514
Aleut, 71, 72, 78, 532, 534
Amami, 29, 30, 341, 342, 380
Ancient Greek, 54
Ancient Uighur, 413
Aogashima, 346
Arabic languages, 9, 65, 78, 413, 510
Arghu, 8
Arli Romani, 65
Arman, 19
Armenian, 50, 224
Austroasiatic languages, 32, 172
Austronesian languages, 29, 32, 81
Avar, 7
Aynallu, 10

Balkar, 109, 158
Bantu languages, 72
Bao'an, 15, 66, 77
Barbareño Chumash, 332, 345
Bashkir, 10, 479
Bora (Witotoan), 71
Bulgarian, 8, 52, 68, 69, 519
Bulghar, 7, 8
Buriat, 14, 15, 109, 143, 167, 169, 222

Caucasus Turkic languages, 154, 520
Central Alaskan Yup'ik, 332, 345
Central Mongolic languages, 374, 375, 410, 445, 446, 451
Chakhar, 374
Chinese, 7, 9, 12–16, 19, 21, 22, 25, 33, 35, 40, 73, 75, 126, 140, 171, 172, 216, 224, 281, 347, 370, 447, 449, 463, 502, 508, 510, 523, 533
Chinhan, 21
Classical Persian, 78
Classical Ryukyuan, 417

Common Turkic, 7, 34, 85
Copper Island Aleut, 71, 72, 78
Cree (Algonquian), 72
Crimean Tatar, 10
Cumanian, 479, 481
Cushitic languages, 72

Daco-Romanian, 68, 69
Daghestanian languages, 345
Dagur, 14, 26, 147, 157, 535
Danube Bulghar, 8
Dolgan, 10, 145, 245
Dongxian (Santa), 15, 508, 525, 542
Dravidian, 58, 59, 81, 522, 525
Dyirbal, 332, 512

Early Chaghatay, 9
Early Middle Korean, 22, 35
Eastern Miwokan, 60
Eastern Old Japanese, 27, 28, 35, 37, 84, 138, 156, 160, 179, 180, 182, 183, 346, 365, 379, 381, 419, 518, 528
Eastern Old Turkic, 239, 358, 416
Eastern Turkic languages, 8–10, 203, 225, 239
Eastern Yughur, 15, 167, 222
Eastern Yugur, 146
East Old Turkic, 9, 413
English, 47, 49, 64–66, 70, 74, 77, 167, 172, 209, 216, 224, 249, 269, 281, 319, 333, 362, 405, 452, 456, 519, 534
Eskimo, 207
Estonian, 175, 176, 199, 511
Eynu, 167, 224

Finnish, 64, 79, 172, 175, 176, 450
Finno-Permic languages, 175
Finno-Ugric languages, 8, 79–81, 200, 513
Formosan languages, 29
Frasheriote Aromanian, 66, 71, 77
French, 47, 49, 56, 64, 66, 69, 70, 72–74, 77, 79, 172, 174, 204, 268, 328, 359, 385, 504, 521, 528

Gagauz, 10
German, 48–50, 66, 69, 73, 75, 79, 172, 209, 217, 273, 319, 328, 334, 415, 442, 503
Germanic languages, 6, 47, 50, 66, 70, 84, 273, 319, 517, 520, 532
Gilyak, 24
Gothic, 48, 54, 84, 85, 153, 504
Greek, 8, 36, 48, 52, 54, 64, 65, 68, 69, 78, 85, 153, 172, 415, 442, 504
Guarani, 65, 225
Gurindji, 71, 72, 525
Gurindji Kriol, 71, 72, 525

Hachijō, 28, 346
Han languages, 21, 22, 85
Hateruma, 35, 363
Hindi-Urdu, 288
Hirara, 29, 35, 342, 343, 363, 458
Hitite, 48, 50
Hmong, 73
Hmong-Mien, 87, 172
Homeric Greek, 85, 153, 504
Hungarian, 8, 67, 114, 172, 176, 207, 515, 520, 531
Huzhu Monguor, 162

Indo-European languages, 2, 4, 44, 45, 48, 49, 52–54, 58, 60, 61, 77, 79–81, 83, 88, 153, 154, 164, 175, 176, 207, 269, 273, 328, 490, 501–505, 508, 515, 518, 519, 524
Iranian, 48, 50, 523
Iraqi Arabic, 78
Ishigaki, 29
Italian, 47, 64, 65, 73, 74, 385, 504

Japanese-Koguryoic, 109
Jurchen, 13, 17–19, 24, 34, 178, 196, 368, 403, 471

Kalmuck, 15
Kamnigan, 15
Kamnigan Mongol, 15
Kangjia, 146
Kansai dialects, 361
Karachay, 158

Karachay-Balkar, 10
Karaim, 10, 101, 109, 111, 138, 143–145, 167, 245, 257, 414, 415, 439, 512
Karakalpak, 11, 111, 154, 167, 245
Karakhanide, 9, 34, 148, 178, 200, 202, 245, 257, 269, 413, 433
Kartvelian, 58, 207
Kaya languages, 21
Kayardild, 332
Kazakh, 11, 26, 146, 167, 169, 224, 245
Ket, 330, 333
Khakas, 10, 158
Khaladj, 37
Khalaj, 8, 9, 34, 101, 106, 111, 112, 140, 143, 145, 154, 158, 160, 162
Khalkha, 14, 15, 26, 42, 85, 374, 392, 445, 446, 477
Khanty, 176
Khazar, 7, 114
Khitan, 12–14, 34, 36, 83, 85, 154, 157, 160, 162, 199, 221, 225, 226, 305, 327, 356, 357, 410, 411, 432, 441, 463, 477, 496, 521, 536
Khitanic languages, 13, 34, 85
Khorasani Turkic, 10
Kili, 19, 20
Kipchak, 8–10, 12, 158
Kipchak Turkic languages, 9, 10
Kirgiz, 9, 11
Koguryo, 16, 21, 24, 25, 35–37, 113, 508, 510, 514, 519, 530, 534
Komi, 450
Koniya, 363
Kriol, 71, 72, 525
Kumyk, 10, 12, 111, 158, 245
Kurdish, 78, 521
Kyushu dialects, 27–29, 397, 399, 400

Lamunkhin Even, 66–68, 71, 78
Late Common Indo-European, 45
Latin, 36, 47, 48, 50, 54, 56, 66, 69, 70, 74, 79, 85, 153, 174, 204, 209, 385, 451, 504, 508, 521, 528
Lithuanian, 70, 71
Livonian, 175, 176

Ma'a, 71, 72, 534
Macedonian, 52, 514
Mahan, 21, 25
Maltese, 64, 510
Manchuric languages, 16–19, 220, 349, 403
Mandarin (see Chinese)
Mangghuer, 98, 162, 169, 222, 533
Mansi, 176
Mari (Cheremis), 8, 200
Meadow Mari, 8
Megleno Romanian, 68, 69
Michif, 71, 72, 508
Middle Chinese, 171, 510
Middle German, 79
Middle High German, 69
Middle Japanese, 29, 84, 85, 92, 112, 132, 144, 181, 183, 249, 364, 399, 422
Middle Kipchak, 9
Middle Low German, 79
Middle Mongolian, 13, 14, 33, 34, 36, 38, 84, 85, 99, 157, 198, 199, 305, 356, 374, 375, 391, 392, 410, 446, 462, 476, 496, 502
Middle Turkic, 9, 111, 162, 245
Miyako dialects, 29, 214, 342, 396–398, 517
Modern Greek, 78
Modern Kirgiz, 11
Modern Uighur, 12
Modern Uzbek, 12
Moghol, 14, 15, 98
Mongol, 9, 12–15, 511, 519, 531
Monguor, 15, 26, 106, 107, 162, 167, 222
Mon-Khmer languages, 87
Mordovic languages, 80
Mordvinian, 8

Nahuatl, 67, 78
Ñantoq Baoan, 167
Navajo, 332, 345
Negidal, 17, 19, 191, 321, 322, 387, 390, 392
Neo-Aramaic languages, 78, 521
New Persian, 78
Ngandi, 76, 77
Niger-Congo, 58, 517, 518
Nilo-Saharan, 58
Nogai, 12, 158

Northern Tungusic languages, 19, 35, 69, 70, 303, 321, 349, 350, 368, 370, 402, 424, 440, 441, 445, 461, 496
Nu, 76

Ob-Ugric languages, 176
Oghur, 225
Oghuric languages, 7, 34, 85
Oghuz Turkic languages, 9, 10, 162, 200, 414
Ogur, 7
Oirat, 15, 439
Okchŏ, 25
Okinawa, 29, 30, 342, 516
Olcha, 17, 19, 20, 97, 151, 191, 196, 242, 260–262, 297, 321, 359, 391, 429, 430, 474
Old Anatolian, 10
Old Chinese, 73, 172, 508
Old Church Slavonic, 8, 48, 50, 78, 85, 504
Old English, 47, 49, 269, 452
Old French, 64, 66, 69, 77, 79
Old Greek, 48
Old High German, 48–50
Old Kirgiz, 9
Old Nordic, 79, 532
Old Paekche, 35
Old Russian, 331
Old Uighur, 9, 34, 114, 245, 433, 452
Ordos, 14, 15, 99, 106, 109, 111, 112, 115, 137–139, 141, 143, 144, 146–148, 152, 160, 167, 169, 244, 438, 439, 526
Orkhon Turkic languages, 9
Oroch, 17–20, 89, 90, 110, 114, 136, 137, 140–142, 145, 149, 151, 191, 196, 204, 242, 259, 260, 286, 289, 296, 321, 349, 367, 391, 402, 424, 428–430, 438, 445, 451, 473, 474
Orok, 17–20, 89, 90, 97, 109, 112, 136, 137, 139–142, 145, 149, 151, 152, 161, 190, 191, 196, 197, 204, 242, 260, 261, 286, 289, 296, 297, 321, 349, 359, 390, 391, 402, 403, 424, 428, 438, 454, 473, 474
Oroqen, 19, 26, 296, 523, 536
Otomi, 65, 225
Oyrat, 111

Paekche Old Korean, 21, 24, 35, 36, 83, 84, 140, 509, 522, 534, 535
Pajapan Nahuatl, 67
Pare, 72
Persian, 9, 78, 167, 224
Portuguese, 73, 74
proto-Austronesian, 23
proto-Chadic, 58, 59
proto-Dravidian, 58, 59
proto-Eastern Miwok, 45
proto-Germanic, 49, 273
proto-Japano-Koreanic, 2, 3, 25, 44, 163, 278, 437, 483, 506
proto-Japonic, 33, 35
proto-Khitanic, 13, 34
proto-Khitan-Mongolic, 85, 157, 221, 225, 305, 432, 444, 477
proto-Mongolo-Tungusic, 32
proto-Niger-Congo, 58, 59
proto-Nilo-Saharan, 58, 59
proto-Nostratic, 58
proto-Ryukyuan, 28, 29, 342
proto-Samhan-Wa, 23
proto-Samoyedic, 7
proto-Uralic, 58, 59, 175, 208, 268, 326, 448, 484, 518
Puyo, 16, 25, 26
Puyo-Koguryoic languages, 21
Puyo-Paekche, 25
Pyonhan languages, 21, 24

Qashqay, 10
Quechua, 65, 225

Resígaro (Arawakan), 71, 532
Ritharngu, 76, 77
Romance languages, 47, 66, 68, 70, 73, 74, 504, 514, 519, 521
Romani, 65–67, 69, 513, 514, 518
Romanian, 52, 68, 71, 78
Russian, 8, 10, 12, 16, 19, 37, 70–72, 78, 167, 169, 202, 209, 220, 222, 224, 260, 328, 331, 333, 415, 442, 515, 523

Saamic, 80
Sakishima languages, 29, 30

Salar, 162
Samoyedic, 79, 175, 225
Sanskrit, 36, 48, 50, 54, 79, 85, 153, 504
Semenderé, 68, 77
Semitic languages, 6, 65, 207
Serbo-Croatian, 52
Shira-Yughur, 15, 204
Shodon, 30, 35, 37, 154, 156, 159, 160, 301, 341–343, 363, 380, 381, 383, 396–398, 417, 524, 532
Shor, 8–10, 12, 107, 109, 111, 143, 148, 160, 245, 413, 434, 439
Shuri, 30, 35, 107, 108, 110–112, 114, 116, 117, 132, 138–143, 145, 147, 148, 151, 154, 159, 160, 214, 228, 240, 246, 255, 276, 293, 294, 301, 309, 319, 342, 343, 362–364, 399, 458, 468
Sibe, 17–19, 96, 114, 142, 161, 296, 367–371, 403, 438, 527
Siberian Turkic languages, 9, 10
Sierra-Populuca, 67
Silla Old Korean, 21, 22, 24, 25, 35, 134, 135, 157
Sino-Tibetan languages, 32, 81
Sizang, 331, 333
Slavic languages, 8, 50, 65, 68, 70, 71, 530
Solon, 14, 17, 19, 140, 142, 147, 161, 242, 260–262, 296, 297, 321, 391, 403, 474
Sorbian, 73, 75
Southeast Asian languages, 73, 510
Southern Tungusic languages, 35, 259, 349, 350, 370, 403, 424, 454, 471
Spanish, 65, 67, 73, 74, 78, 225, 414
Swedish, 79, 534

Tabgach, 12, 13, 85
Tai-Kadai languages, 87, 172
Tatar, 10, 110, 167, 479
Telengit, 10
Teleut, 10
Thai, 73
Tibetan, 167, 222, 224
Tibeto-Burman languages, 87, 331, 512, 523, 537
Tofa, 10, 167, 169

Tofalar, 111, 148
Tosima dialect, 346
Turkish, 7, 10, 65, 66, 68, 69, 77, 167, 169, 224, 290, 412, 509, 511–514, 521
Turkmen, 10, 37
Tuva, 10, 101, 106, 107, 111, 112, 139, 142, 143, 145, 146, 148, 160, 162, 167, 169, 245, 257, 413, 434, 521

Uchur Evenki, 66–68, 71, 78
Ugric languages, 176
Uighur Turkic languages, 9, 10, 12
Uralic languages, 59, 60, 73, 80, 81, 83, 126, 168, 175–179, 183, 207, 208, 326, 448, 449, 451, 452, 511, 512, 518, 522, 529, 531, 533
Uzbek, 12, 167, 412

Vietnamese, 73, 75
Volga Bulghar, 8
Volga Kipchak, 8
Votic languages, 176, 181, 200
Votyak, 8

Western Mari, 201
Western Old Turkic, 225, 239, 358
Western Turkic languages, 203, 224, 238, 239, 308, 416
Western Yughur, 167, 169, 224
Wutun, 66, 77

Yaeyama, 29
Yakut, 10, 37, 66–70, 78, 144, 162, 167, 169, 220, 224, 245, 252, 360, 361, 492, 520, 522, 524, 528
Yamatoma, 342, 343, 381, 458
Ye-Maek, 25
Yonaguni, 29, 30, 106, 116, 363, 396–398, 458
Yuulngu languages, 77

Subject index

achievement verbs, 281
actionality, 4, 43, 51, 193, 197, 209, 210, 230, 231, 266, 268, 272, 456, 465, 488, 497
action noun, 376–378, 386, 388, 391, 393, 405, 411, 440, 448, 452, 455, 462, 471, 476, 478, 483, 484, 490
active verb, 44, 50, 61, 117, 150, 209, 210, 237, 239, 249, 271, 309, 315, 394, 507, 508, 519
adjectivizer, 149, 338
agglutination 48, 77, 88, 502–505
Aktionsart (see actionality)
ambitransitive verb, 276, 318
analytic expression, 87, 174, 182, 203, 310, 360, 382, 386, 434
appositive participle, 434, 449, 451, 452
Arisaka's law, 125, 151
asymmetric negation, 174
attrition, 83, 84, 164, 165, 172, 199, 210, 273, 274, 324, 327, 462, 503, 504

backwards diffusion, 64
basic vocabulary, 2, 62, 88, 164–166, 172, 501, 504, 521, 537
Boas-Sapir controversy, 62
borrowability (see copiability)

categorial
  clarity, 76, 499
  opacity, 76, 494, 499
clausal
  ~ adnominalization, 345, 348, 350, 354, 355, 358, 360, 365, 381, 383, 384, 395, 397, 400, 404, 411, 412, 427, 429, 430
  ~ adverbialization, 368, 374
  ~ complementizer, 372, 373
  ~ negation, 174
  ~ nominalization, 339, 340, 345, 348–350, 353, 355, 356, 365, 366, 368, 371–375, 380, 383, 384, 388, 389, 391–395, 404, 407, 408, 418, 426, 437, 441, 442

code-copying, 2–4, 45, 46, 61–64, 68, 70–72, 75, 77, 79, 107, 171, 210, 273, 274, 489, 494, 497, 500, 524
color noun, 60, 441
combinational copy, 445
comparative method, 1, 3, 45, 46, 55, 80–82, 85, 86, 501, 505, 517, 520, 526, 531
complementation, 333, 348
Comrie's hierarchy, 197
conditional converb (see converb)
conjugational class, 78, 232, 350–354, 391, 423, 427, 475
consonant cluster, 242, 256, 257, 291, 299, 359, 424
contact
  chain, 171, 172
  zone, 70, 71, 227, 494, 496
contact-induced grammaticalization (see grammaticalization)
continuum approach, 271, 272, 449
converbialization, 57, 482, 490, 497, 498
converb
  conditional ~, 198, 372, 374, 379, 382, 433, 444, 450–452, 454
  ~ of simultaneity, 368, 370, 388
  imperfective ~, 371, 372, 389, 435, 477
  perfective ~, 338, 370–373, 389, 390, 407, 409, 424, 432–435, 445, 450, 451, 477
  prominent ~, 449, 498
  temporal-conditional ~, 372, 450
copiability, 61–64, 164, 210, 273, 537
core case, 449, 450, 484
creolization, 3, 538
cumulative exponence, 76, 77, 83, 227, 272, 449, 493, 499, 503, 537
cyclic grammaticalization (see grammaticalization)

Dawenkou culture, 23, 24, 32, 33
decausative, 147, 259, 261–263, 275, 298, 311
demorphologization, 47
diagrammatic equivalence, 47, 273

diatheses, 43, 210, 272, 488
direct insertion, 166–170, 172, 216, 220, 224, 498
direct insubordination, 57, 330, 333, 335, 370, 432, 445, 447, 448, 490, 492, 497, 498, 502
directionality (*see also* unidirectional), 55, 276, 318, 319, 457, 541
discourse, 51, 209, 236, 340, 349, 367, 384, 418, 419, 437, 502
distributive, 135, 231, 243, 263, 281, 285, 286
Donghu, 12, 16
drift, 56, 57, 114, 206, 299, 319, 329, 444, 523–525, 527

economy, 55, 56
eidemic resonance, 49, 326
emphatic reduplication, 91, 96, 98, 100, 527
extended paradigmaticity, 54, 493

Farming/Language Dispersal Hypothesis, 32, 512, 513, 521
fientive verb, 59, 60, 115, 154, 268, 271, 274, 275, 293, 301, 303, 305–308, 324–328, 398, 399, 485, 488, 490, 495, 497, 498
finitization, 187, 190, 191, 330, 368, 530
forward diffusion, 64
frequential copy, 502

global copy, 61, 76, 79
grammaticalization
~ cline, 282, 506
contact-induced ~, 72, 73, 75, 207, 518
cyclic ~, 43, 47, 52, 56, 151, 179, 197, 199, 202, 206, 502, 527
family-inherent ~, 56, 57
globally shared ~, 72–75, 270, 212, 328, 335, 494, 497, 498, 506, 525, 528, 535

habitual, 50, 154, 158, 209, 285, 350, 352, 353, 359, 369, 481, 507
heteroganic cluster, 147–149
homeland, 6, 15, 16, 31–33, 519, 528, 532
homoganic cluster, 147, 148

iconic verb, 49, 165, 211, 215, 235, 239–246, 266, 268–270, 485, 487–489, 495, 498
imperfective converb (*see* converb)
inclinational verb, 155, 211, 212, 239, 246, 249, 250, 252, 253, 266–268, 382, 488, 499, 500
indefinite accusative, 187, 188
indirect insertion, 166–170, 216, 224, 498
instrumental noun, 401, 455, 459, 462, 464, 471–475, 478–480
isostructuralism, 53
iterative suffix, 106, 109, 110, 135, 136, 146, 153, 179, 199, 234, 253, 293

Jespersen's cycle, 174, 176, 204
Jomon culture, 26, 519

kakari-musubi, 339, 345

language mixing, 3, 63
Leipzig-Jakarta list, 164
light verb, 166–169, 216, 224

manipulative verb, 125, 213, 217, 221, 223, 266, 268, 269, 281, 328, 485, 488, 489, 494–496, 499, 500
mixed adjective typology, 91, 94, 96, 101, 102, 104, 105, 163, 164, 270, 489, 492
modulator, 128, 154, 159, 161, 166, 310, 347, 348, 366, 383, 492, 507
morpheme
~ boundary, 67, 68, 321, 341, 344, 494–496
~ distance, 272
morphological
~ attrition, 503
~ borrowing, 62, 63, 64, 75, 78, 211, 512, 519, 536, 538
~ comparison, 58, 87
~ complexity, 66, 155, 170, 489, 494, 495
~ correspondence, 51, 88, 493
~ paradigm, 62, 65, 514
~ reconstruction, 44, 48, 53, 55, 524, 526
~ regularity, 49
~ scale, 271, 334, 449

Subject index — **549**

morphosyntactic subsystem, 57, 71, 72, 494, 497, 501, 536
multidimensional paradigmaticity, 54, 491, 501, 503
multilateral comparison, 4
multiple comparison, 59, 86, 78, 87, 172, 494, 500

necessitive, 293, 339, 365, 382, 444
negative
 ~ adjective, 183, 184
 ~ auxiliary, 175, 176, 178–185, 191, 193–199, 201–206, 208, 430, 506
 ~ cycle, 179, 207, 518
 ~ existential, 178, 183, 192, 196, 199, 202, 206, 361, 441
 ~ imperative, 180–182, 184, 196, 197, 200–202, 360, 417, 418
 ~ interjection, 200, 202
 ~ nominalizer, 364, 365
 ~ noun, 174, 177, 178, 186–191, 196, 197, 199, 285, 471, 472
 ~ particle, 76, 174–176, 185, 187, 188, 195, 197, 198, 200, 203, 409, 492, 497
 proprietive, 187
noun-verb distinction, 90

object noun, 355, 357, 375, 376, 378, 386, 388, 391, 393, 401, 405, 408, 411, 416, 418, 441, 442
obligatoriness, 271, 449
observational selection, 82, 83
Occam's razor, 55, 104, 414
onomatopoea, 51, 213, 215, 216, 221–224, 235–237, 239–244, 246, 247, 250, 251, 269, 488, 489
optative, 54, 200, 203, 337, 388, 416, 425, 507

paradigm
 derivational ~, 531
 inflectional ~, 62, 63, 460, 501, 505, 535
 morphological ~, 62, 65, 514
paradigmatic equivalence, 442

paradigmaticity, 53, 54, 72, 491, 493, 501, 503
parallel drift (*see also* Sapirian drift), 56, 57
partitive accusative, 187
perfective converb (*see* converb)
peripheral case, 449, 450, 452
personal pronoun, 2, 54, 360, 385, 521
phonological
 ~ attrition, 324
 ~ correspondence, 2, 4, 48, 88, 118, 163, 171
 ~ reconstruction, 48, 55, 479
 ~ regularity, 49
pitch, 2, 29, 39, 111, 153, 215, 243, 256, 257, 361, 456, 514
polysemy, 56, 58, 60, 157, 159, 161, 163, 185, 206, 259, 295, 326, 328, 329, 340, 362, 365, 437, 488, 493, 531
portmanteau, 76, 77, 503
progressive, 162, 199, 229, 281–283, 285–287, 290, 292, 327, 328, 350, 353, 354, 369, 373, 507, 536
prohibitive, 178, 200, 201, 402, 492, 507
proto-language, 33, 55–57, 75, 84, 85, 124, 132, 157, 159, 161, 436, 482, 498, 513, 524
proto-morpheme, 47, 48, 55
punctual change of state verb, 281, 288, 328, 408, 418, 425
purpose noun, 476, 478, 479
Puyo, 16, 21, 25, 26, 547

quirk (*see also* shared irregularity), 491

reciprocal, 50, 135, 169, 202, 230, 236, 237, 271, 314, 388
recursivity, 271, 272, 449
register, 93, 132, 133, 140, 141, 150, 213, 224, 227, 229, 246, 255, 297, 539
relatability, 81, 82
replication, 45, 61, 72
rhotacism, 359

Sapirian drift (*see also* parallel drift), 56, 114, 206, 319, 329

secondary semantics, 69, 170, 226
selective copy, 61
semantic
~ content, 210, 269, 272, 334, 452, 491, 504
~ copy, 72
~ relevance, 51, 209, 268, 269, 272
~ transparency, 76, 272, 499
sequential voicing, 379, 382, 383
shared irregularity (*see also* quirk), 48, 54, 57, 58, 60, 493
split morphology, 271
stability, 52, 61, 62, 163–165, 172, 210, 269, 272, 273, 366, 505, 531
state noun, 455, 458, 459, 461, 462, 466, 469, 471–474, 476–480, 482, 484, 499
strata of loanwords, 171
subject noun, 355, 357, 375, 376, 378, 386, 391, 401, 405, 411, 416, 440
Sushen, 12, 16
Swadesh list, 164
synthetic expression, 88, 151, 174, 197, 310, 360, 361, 434, 519

telicity, 60, 209, 347, 350–352, 356, 361, 367, 368, 370–372, 385, 389, 390, 393, 396, 423, 425–428, 440, 441, 491, 492

temporal-conditional converb (*see* converb)
transitivity flipper, 315

unidirectional (*see also* directionality), 79, 171, 276, 295, 316, 318, 319, 327, 328, 541
universal principles, 45, 51, 52, 163, 177, 224, 268, 505

vocative, 348, 366, 391, 437, 508
voluntative, 200, 360, 462
vowel deletion rule, 364
vowel harmony, 37–40, 125, 126, 151, 213, 227, 230, 242, 246, 267, 293, 326, 347, 368, 437, 471, 482, 487, 500, 503, 506

Xinglongwa culture, 31, 32
Xiongnu, 7, 12, 25

Yangshao culture, 31–33
Yayoi culture, 23, 26–28, 520

zero
~ affix, 398
~ allomorph, 455, 457–459, 461, 462, 464, 499
~ derivation, 89, 250
zetacism, 358, 359